RICHARD PETERSON

LOOKING AT PAINTING IN FLORENCE

13TH-16TH CENTURIES

A LEARNER'S HANDBOOK

EDIZIONI POLISTAMPA

Cover: Fra Bartolomeo, *Mystic Marriage of Saint Catherine*,
Galleria Palatina, 1512 (see p. 192).
© Studio Fotografico Quattrone, Florence.

Design
Francesco Bertini

Editing
Paolo Piazzesi

I^st^ edition: February 2014
I^st^ reprint: July 2015

www.polistampa.com

Via Livorno, 8/32 - 50142 Firenze
Tel. 055 737871 (15 linee)
info@polistampa.com - www.leonardolibri.com

ISBN 978-88-596-1327-5

Table of Contents

Foreword

Some fifty years ago Kenneth Clark – of *Civilization* fame – wrote a slim volume called *Looking at Pictures*. It was dedicated to the memory of the art critic Roger Fry who, wrote Clark, "taught my generation how to look". Clark's book was to be my own teenaged epiphany – in which that sheer breathless joy experienced in the presence of great art was later to be balanced – but happily not tempered – by an art historical training.

In Richard Peterson's *Looking at Painting in Florence* we have that essential equilibrium of rigorous research carried out over many years on site, in the library, and in discussions with experts, together with palpable evidence of his enduring passion for the paintings he has examined at first hand. Peterson is not a trained art historian and this fact puts him – and the reader – at a clear advantage for a book aimed at the student or the discerning traveller to Florence. He has avoided at once the superficiality of some guidebooks and the often impenetrable language of art historical texts (of which he has absorbed and synthesized a prodigious amount).

Richard Peterson wears his heart on his sleeve and it is easy to spot his favourites – Giotto and Pontormo are tops, the late Mannerists not really his cup of tea. It is precisely these particulars, together with the structure of the book, which engage and instruct the reader. Skilfully organized around fourteen of the most significant Florentine sites – churches, museums, monasteries and palaces – and interspersed with passages of historical background, the incomparable panoply of Florentine painting over more than four centuries is unfurled and the nature of the leading masters described. The extensive Addenda section addresses many of Peterson's main interests – the conquest of pictorial space through linear perspective, volume, light, and, above all, colour.

To read this book is akin to being taken by the hand by a close friend who quietly and undidactically observes, describes, and interprets: "... note the creepy Judas...", "... the long reptilian slope of his body...", "... see how on the left figure the yellow sleeve shifts to green...". His clear descriptions and observations have sent me back to renew acquaintance with frescoes and altarpieces which I thought I knew intimately over some forty years.

Susan Madocks Lister
Head of Art History
The British Institute of Florence

Preface

When my wife and I went to Europe for the first time in the summer of 1987, we armed ourselves with a slew of guidebooks and, with the naïve determination of first-time travelers, set out to explore the paintings of the Renaissance. It was in the great museums and churches of Florence where we found ourselves fascinated, stunned, and often unsettled. When we returned to Berkeley, I was struck by the realization that I had understood little of what I had seen.

As I began to plunge deeper into Florentine painting, I found myself persistently vexed by the fundamental question: "Why is this painting important?"

Despite the enormous number of books published about Florence, I could not find a single one devoted exclusively to the entire course of Florentine painting. Guides and museum catalogs are necessarily limited in scope, and the best writing on the art in churches is wildly scattered in scholarly texts and specialty journals. Thus, the gap in knowledge between the academic world and the public world is wide and growing. I have written *Looking at Painting in Florence* in the hope of breaching that void.

Organized around the critical churches, cloisters, museums, and palaces that house the city's vast collections of painting, the book teaches the skills and insights that I set out to master over the many years since that initial visit to Florence. It tells a story of origins, tracing the abrupt decline of the naturalism that defined ancient Roman art, the rise of a thousand years of Byzantine art, and the role the rediscovery of early Christian murals played in influencing Giotto, the first artist in a thousand years to capture the visible world. Woven throughout the text are descriptions of the plagues, blood feuds, and the intellectual and commercial triumphs that helped shape the art and the intrigues of the papacy and Medici that in the end did much to decimate it.

It is also a handbook about learning, whether the student is a newcomer or a veteran of the arts. To that end, I have placed heavy emphasis on the techniques employed in painting. Lines and outlines, silhouettes and relief, light and shadow, brushstrokes and pigments—in short, an artist's signature—all play a pivotal part in unraveling the differences among paintings. Color, rarely discussed in detail even in academic works, occupies a central role at every stage in this book.

But most important, the book puts a premium on ensuring that what is written on the page corresponds to what can be seen in the painting.

Because paintings have historically been open to a wide range of interpretation, I have drawn on two sources: my research on the opinions advanced by the leading authorities in the field and my own experience in living with these paintings over the past twenty-five years, often on-site for months at a time. This experience has allowed me to synthesize the frequently difficult and arcane prose of the art historian and to put it into a language accessible to a lay audience.

To sharpen the book's concepts, throughout the past five years I have turned to Eve Borsook, senior research fellow at Harvard's campus for Renaissance studies in Florence, and to Susan Madocks Lister, past dean of Florence University of the Arts and now chair of art history at the British Institute where her elegant lectures have shaped the education of so many students. I owe a great debt to Loren Partridge, professor of Art History at the University of California at Berkeley, who, for the past twenty-five years, has generously mentored me through his lectures and made invaluable suggestions on a first draft. And to Robert Hass, professor of English at the University of California at Berkeley, whose first appraisal of an early draft was critical to my continuing on; to Kathrine Wayne, Fine Art Librarian, University of California, for her support these many years.

I would like to thank my editor, Sharon Silva, whose love of the written word has been a constant source of inspiration. To Paami Disston for her unerring sense of design. To Mauro Pagliai, publisher of Polistampa, for having the vision to publish this book, and to the staff at Polistampa, including Barbara Niccoli, Paolo Piazzesi, and Francesco Bertini, for their expertise. To the staff at the British Institute for providing a warm atmosphere for studying in their remarkable library. To Alan Millen, whose early acquaintance in Florence inspired me to look at painting in fresh ways.

I am most grateful to my dear family and friends. It was the shared experience of looking at painting together over so many decades that made the task of writing such a pleasure. In particular: to my brother Jim, who devoted much time in teaching me how to write a sentence and to find its place in a paragraph, and to my brother Rob who has read so many of these pieces over the years. To Malcolm McLorg, lifelong friend, for his keen eye for art, and for his endless enthusiasm for whatever painting I was currently working on. To Sheri Clyde for being the first friend to edit a portion of the book. To my friends Leeds Disston and Bruce Flushman for their generous advice early on. To my son Richard, who has helped me every step of the way and, to my great delight, has learned much about Florentine painting in the process.

Last and foremost, this book is dedicated to my wife Susan who shared that moment nearly thirty years ago when we first gazed upon a painting in Florence. It was her idea that I write the book and without her continuing support, this book would never have seen the light of day.

Introduction
How to Approach the Art

Here you will learn the importance of each site, what it contains, and how it fits in relation to the other sites in the city. Ideally, see the sites in chronological order, that is, according to the period of the majority of their collections. Chronology is not suggested in guidebooks, which favor seeing the city by neighborhood. But by happenstance and circumstance over the centuries the city's patrons have made this task fairly easy, because they tended to decorate their churches and palaces at different times. And because the most important works have not been dispersed to the museums of the world, Florence can be seen as one complete and glorious work of art.

To appreciate how painting is displayed, it helps to understand that the city houses both frescoes, otherwise known as murals or wall paintings, and portable panel paintings on wood or canvas. Frescoes rank as one of the city's greatest achievements, because of the sustained effort that artists poured into creating them. The only other city whose frescoes vie with those of Florence is Rome, where they range from third-century catacombs to Michelangelo's decoration of the Sistine Chapel and beyond. But, as would be expected considering Rome's brutal history, there are long periods when the arts languished. In Florence, excepting a few scattered decades, frescoes can be found from their beginnings in the first decade of the 1300s up to 1570 when the last important one was completed.

Panel paintings that once hung over church altars, on the other hand, have largely been moved to the city's three major museums: the Uffizi, Accademia, and Pitti Palace, the last two specializing on specific periods. Some stunning paintings can still be found in churches and small tucked-away cloisters, however.

The Addendum includes a discussion on various technical aspects of panel painting and fresco, on modeling, color, light, and shadow that will prove especially helpful before visiting the early fresco cycles in Santa Croce and the Brancacci Chapel.

The Sites

The most important sites are the first five and of these the first three are intimately linked. **Santa Croce**'s Giotto represents the first of a line of painters that led directly to Masaccio, painter of the **Brancacci Chapel**, and through him, to Michelangelo, two hundred years later. Like Giotto, the sculptors at **Orsanmichele** influenced Masaccio and played a pivotal role in shaping the styles of other Renaissance painters. These three sites can comfortably be visited in a morning. The first five sites also rank at the top of every guide's list of the city's most important art sites, except, astonishingly, the Brancacci Chapel, the site where Renaissance painting begins.

Consider visiting the first three sites in order. They allow you to become acquainted with technical concepts at a more leisurely pace than confronting them for the first time at the Uffizi.

But before you enter Santa Croce, prepare yourself for what lies ahead by reading the opening chapter, "The Origins of Florentine Painting", an abbreviated walk through the thousand years of painting that laid the foundation to Florentine art.

Site 1 Santa Croce Church and Museum

(estimated time: one and a half hours)

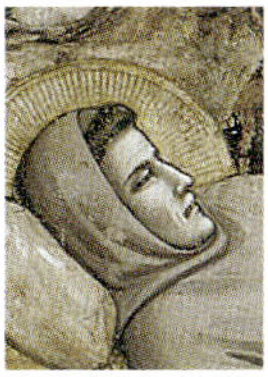

The Franciscan church is home to the beginnings of the city's grand tradition of wall painting. Here Giotto and his followers discover how to model the human figure, to place it in a space that makes sense, and to plant its feet firmly on the ground. We take these things for granted today, but to early Florentine artists they posed great challenges, and in surmounting them, they paved the way for all Western art. To the uninitiated eye, these paintings can seem dry, a bit foreign, and difficult on first encounter. Florentine art, especially evident in the earlier formative periods, is first and last an intellectual art based on perfecting the drawing that underlies the color. Only then did it move onto the lush sensuality that marks later periods.

Site 2 Orsanmichele

(est. time: half an hour)

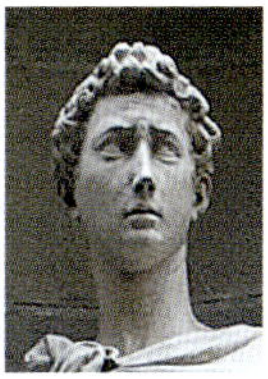

The site provides a simple, outdoor access into the world of Florentine sculpture. The statues adorning the building's niches represent several competing styles and one marks the beginning of the Renaissance, setting the stage for the Brancacci Chapel. (Many of the sculptures are copies; the originals are either in the Museo di Orsanmichele or the Bargello.)

Site 3 Brancacci Chapel

(est. time: 20 min: small charge).
In high season the chapel should be booked ahead online.

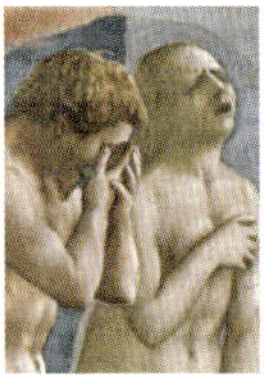

This is the most important site in Florence for painting, after the Uffizi. The time allotted in the chapel itself is limited to fifteen minutes. The Addendum offers a brief explanation of space and perspective on which these scenes are organized. Masaccio and Masolino have painted nine frescoed scenes chock full of groundbreaking innovations, so you may want to read ahead. Above the altar hangs one of the city's oldest paintings still in its original location.

Site 4 Uffizi Gallery

(est. time: 2 to 3 hours or more). Book ahead

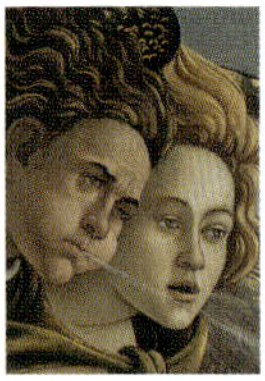

Can the world's greatest collection of Florentine masterpieces be seen at warp speed? Yes, if that means around two hours, although three to four hours would be preferable. Pace yourself, take breaks, sit out in the hall and collect your thoughts. Some forty Florentine paintings are discussed in detail (the Romans, Germans, and Venetians will have to wait another day.) For the two hour limit, I've starred the twenty most important works. They are in rooms devoted to the greatest painters of their era, including the Medievalists Cimabue, Duccio, Giotto; Botticelli, foremost master of the linear style; Leonardo da Vinci and Michelangelo (and their face-off); High Renaissance artists, and finally the magnificent Mannerists, who develop a highly sensual style.

Site 5 Santa Maria Novella Church and Cloister

(est. time: one and a half hours)

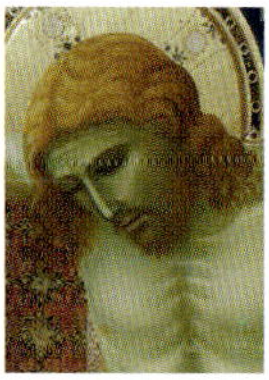

This Dominican church is deservingly famous, for it contains major frescoes and paintings from all periods, including Masaccio's famous *Trinity* and Giotto's monumental crucifix. In a chapel off one of Florence's many beautiful cloisters are huge frescoes that reflect the Dominican's obsession with preaching their severe doctrinal views within a framework of childlike, sumptuous Gothic art.

THE FOLLOWING FIVE SITES ARE FIVE MINUTES APART

Site 6 San Marco Convent and Museum

(est. time: 1 to 2 hours)

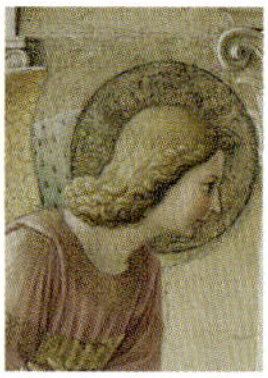

A one man show devoted to the beloved Fra Angelico, plus works by Fra Bartolomeo, a principal artist of the High Renaissance, and Ghirlandaio's famous *Last Supper*. Despite the charm of Angelico's paintings, they don't influence future styles as much as the paintings in other sites do.

Site 7 Santa Apollonia Refectory

(est. time: 30 minutes)

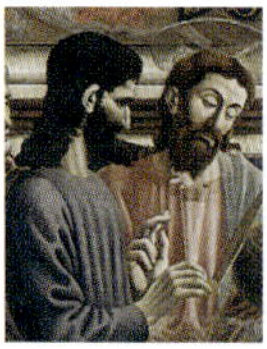

The refectory houses Andrea del Castagno's riveting *Last Supper*. Its elusive perspective construction is devilishly difficult to untangle.

Site 8 Accademia Gallery

(est. time: one and a half hours)

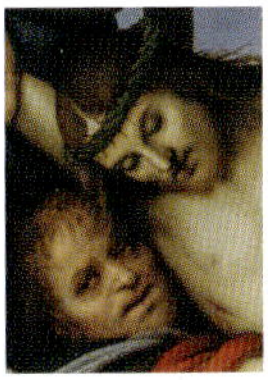

For painting, the museum's collection specializes in works from the thirteenth and fourteenth centuries. As beautiful as they are, the major paintings from this era can be found in Santa Croce, Santa Maria Novella, and the Uffizi. A large room on the entrance floor contains a group of early sixteenth-century paintings that sit on the cusp between the Renaissance and High Renaissance styles. One in particular is fascinating for its juxtaposition of two different styles.

Site 9 Santissima Annunziata

(est. time: 45 minutes)

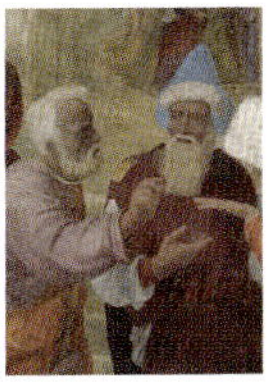

I never fail to visit this church when in Florence. Guidebooks barely rate Santissima Annunziata a mention, so it is seldom visited by tourists. It is also a very active church, and even though it is open in the morning and from four to seven, there are often services in the church itself. The real interest is in the atrium where Andrea del Sarto, Jacopo Pontormo, and Rosso Fiorentino work out in fresco at eye level the concepts that would define the High Renaissance, an area where the Uffizi's collection is lean. It is best to visit when there is strong sunlight. Otherwise, you can ask the nice sacristan to turn on the lights.

Site 10 San Michele Visdomini

(est. time: 15 minutes)

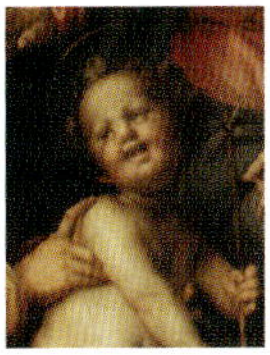

A modest church a half block from the Duomo, it is home to only one major artist, Jacopo Pontormo, who is the first to take the decisive step beyond the High Renaissance style to Mannerism. If the painting is not lit, ask the sacristan to turn on the lights.

Site 11 Santa Felicita

(est. time: 30 minutes)

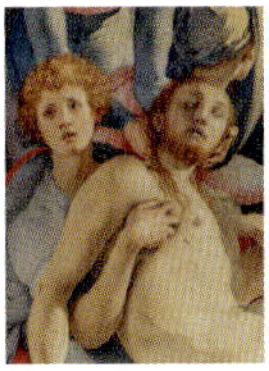

Amazingly, tourists don't seem to know this little church, which lies in the Oltrarno just beyond the Ponte Vecchio on the left. You must squeeze a visit into your schedule no matter what. The site chronologically follows site 10, although nothing you have seen can prepare you for the chapel's single hidden jewel, Pontormo's *Deposition*, perhaps Florence's finest hour. Open until noon and after 4:00. Bring some coins for the lights.

Site 12 San Lorenzo

(est. time: 45 minutes)

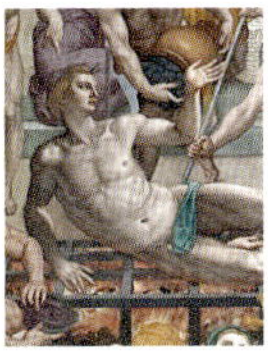

Florence's last Mannerist fresco, executed by Bronzino, and one of Rosso's most luxurious paintings make this site worthy of a visit.

Site 13 Pitti Palace Museum, Galleria Palatina

(est. time: one and a half hours)

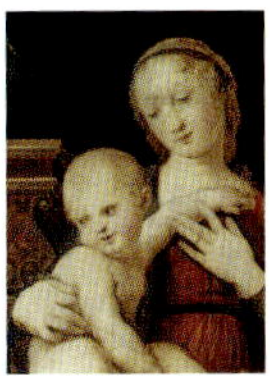

The Palatine Gallery houses large-scale paintings from the High Renaissance, some too large for the Uffizi's smaller rooms.. Among them are two of Fra Bartolomeo's most celebrated altarpieces, Raphael's first major work, a number of paintings by Andrea del Sarto, a splendid Rosso Fiorentino, and other greats. Here, in rooms rarely visited by more than a few people at a time, you have an opportunity to study paintings in depth. Consider a visit to the Boboli Gardens which can be entered from the Pitti courtyard.

SITE 14 PALAZZO VECCHIO

(est. time: one and a half hours)

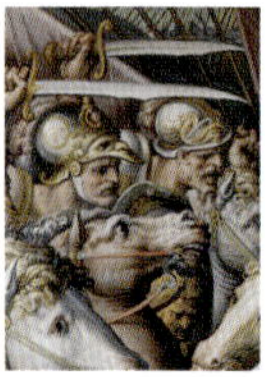

The palace's grand state rooms and private chambers were decorated in the 1540s by Bronzino in a distinctive brand of Florentine Mannerism, and by Salviati and Vasari in a Roman-inspired Mannerist style. The majority of its painting is devoted to propagandistic, ducal art that the average working class Florentine could never have seen. As exquisite as these works are, they sadly represent the waning years of Florentine dominance in the arts.

AUTHOR'S TOP SEVEN PAINTINGS

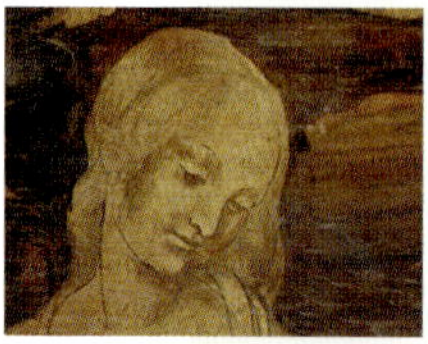

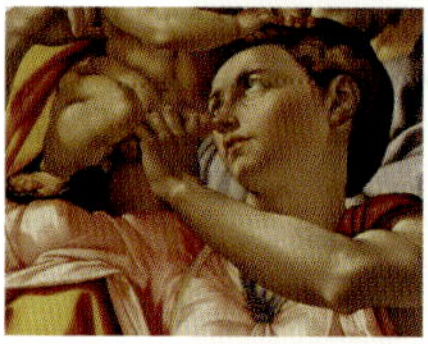

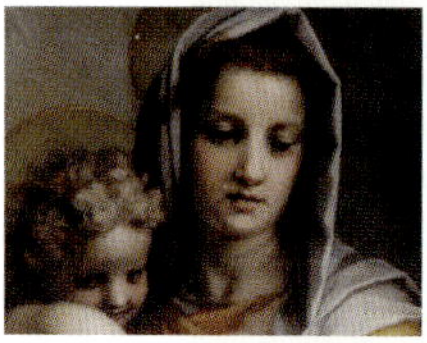

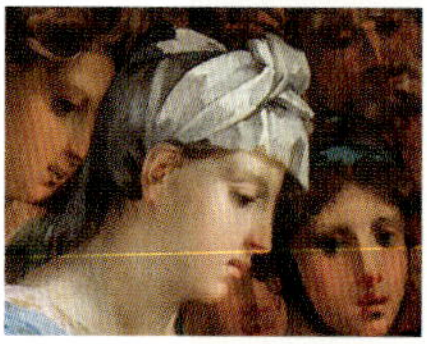

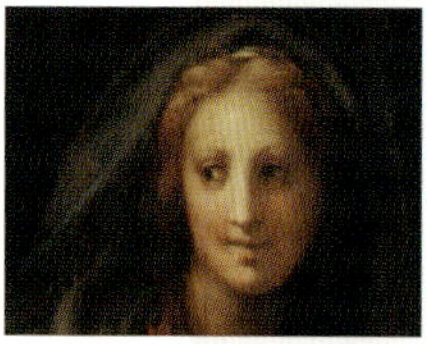

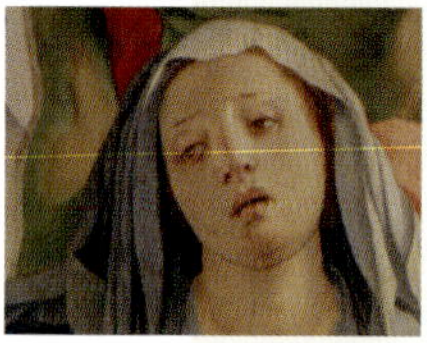

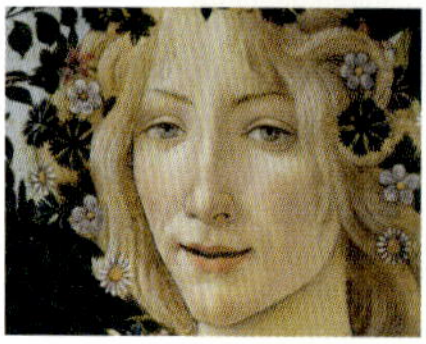

Leonardo's *Adoration* (fig. 87) for the shear effort that he put into it. Michelangelo's *Doni Tondo* (90) for its influence on all that follows it. Andrea del Sarto's *Harpies Madonna* (93) and Rosso Fiorentino's *Marriage of the Virgin* (128) for their colors. Pontormo's *Visdomini Madonna* (126) because it broke the rules, and his *Deposition* (127), because its sadness is matched by its beauty. And Botticelli's *Primavera* (80), because of Flora.

The Origins of Florentine Painting

Florentine art, like all European art, was ultimately rooted in ancient Rome. But a Florentine living in the 1100s would not have known this, nor would he have known that Caesar had founded the city as a colony in 59 BC. And were he willing to venture to the Holy City (the rigors of such a trip would have been formidable) he would have been shocked to see how little of the ancient monuments was left.

Rome still dominated its vast frontiers when Constantine the Great came to power in AD 312 and imposed on history one of its defining moments: an edict that legitimized Christianity. A decade later he commissioned Saint Peter's to be built on state property where its renovated version still stands. But once the Emperor moved the imperial seat of power to Constantinople, site of the ancient Greek city of Byzantium (present-day Istanbul) in 330, Roman influence began to decline on the Italian peninsula. In the ensuing centuries, the ancient city's architectural and sculptural wonders crumbled to ruins, and its naturalistic wall paintings, like the charming scene of a woman playing a lyre (fig. 1), lay buried beneath centuries of accumulated earth.

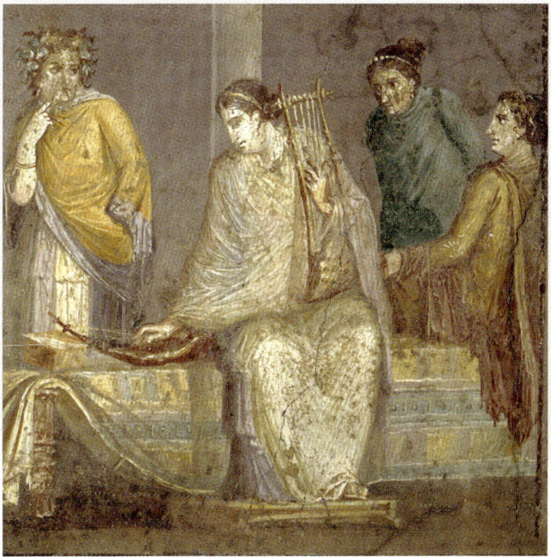

1. *The Concert*, frescoed wall painting from Pompeii, AD 30, National Archeological Museum of Naples. Covered by the eruption of Mount Vesuvius in AD 79; not unearthed until mid-1700s.

Roman frescoes of the first century are remarkable for depicting fully rounded figures sitting and standing in easy postures within a credible space. Each form is rendered impressionistically in loose brush strokes that leave no trace of an outline.

But if our Florentine had stood before one of the few intact monuments left in Rome, the Arch of Constantine (315), he would have been perplexed. Above the two side arches were (and still are) two pairs of roundels containing sculpted reliefs that had been scavenged from imperial monuments of two centuries earlier and patched in place by Constantine's own craftsmen (figs. 2 and 3).

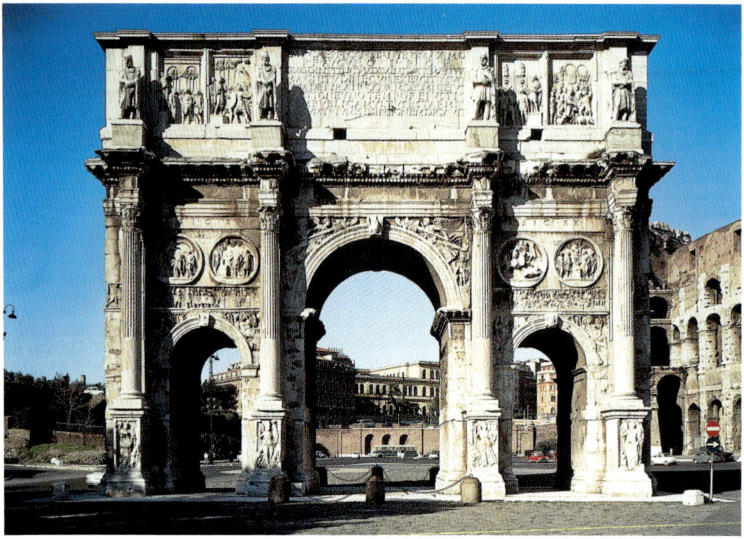

2. Arch of Constantine, 315 AD.

Emperor Hadrian and his hunting companions are standing over a dead lion.

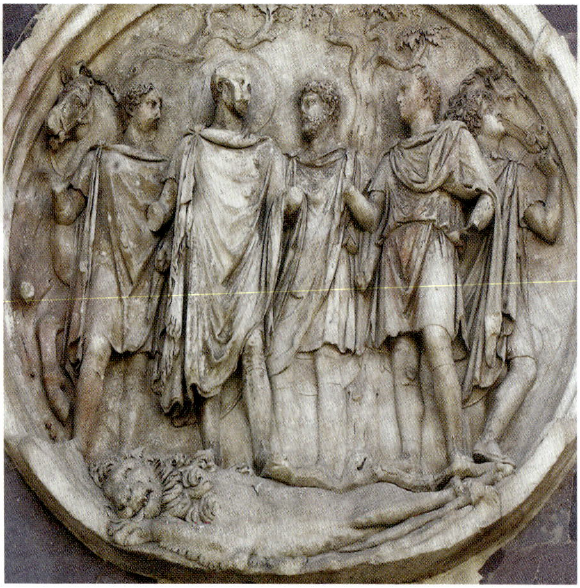

3. *Imperial Lion Hunt*, roundel scavenged from one of Emperor Hadrian's monuments, mid-second century, Arch of Constantine.

Within each roundel, well-proportioned figures stand freely in open space (fig. 3). Such stylistic features, along with the individualistic portraits and great wealth of descriptive detail, date the carving near to the time of the wall painting from Pompeii. Below the roundels is a long frieze, expressly sculpted for the Arch of Constantine (fig. 4). In the center section of the frieze, arranged in two compact rows, the citizens of Rome are depicted receiving largess from Constantine. Their repetitive sameness forms a jarring geometric pattern in violent contrast to the realism of the older roundels. Linked en masse, these flat hard-edge abstractions would have proclaimed raw imperial power to Roman subjects of Constantine's day.

4. Detail of the arch's frieze, 315 AD.

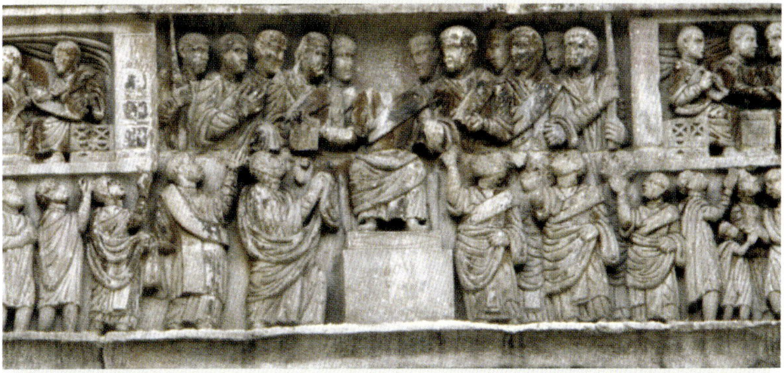

Constantine, his head missing, sits in the center on a throne with his court seated to either side. His subjects are kneeling below with out-stretched hands. Suffice it to compare the naturalistic, looping folds in the tunics of the roundels with the schematic patterns in the folds of Constantine's frieze.

In a single stroke (and a broad one as we shall see) Roman artisans had reshaped the human figure, which had been so naturalistically portrayed two centuries earlier. (Much the same occurred at the beginning of the twentieth century when Picasso rejected the naturalism conveyed in French Impressionism by reassembling the human face.) What is telling, however, is that the Florentine could have related to Constantine's figures, which were not so dissimilar in style from paintings then in Florentine churches (fig. 5). But the same cannot be said of the naturalistic renderings in the roundels. These would have simply been unfamiliar.

Although it is clear that the level of skill required to produce a figure in Constantine's frieze is less than what was required for the earlier roundels, skill alone is not sufficient to account for the radical reversal of aesthetic values. Indeed, the reason for the differences is far more complex. As Rome began to expand its empire over the known world—over Gaul, Egypt, Mesopotamia, Syria, and Persia—the art of its outlying provinces opened up starkly appealing alternatives to artistic expression.

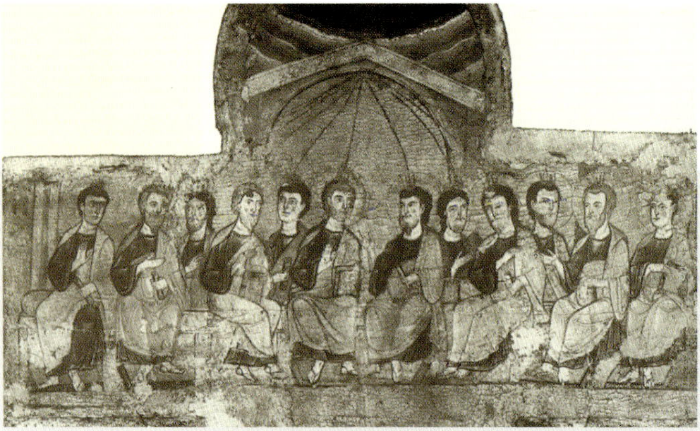

5. Pisan painter, detail of an upper plaque on a painted crucifix, early 1100s, San Frediano, Pisa.

Even though we are comparing panel painting to relief sculpture separated by eight hundred years, we still see the same simplified, severe frontal image of the human figure.

Even though the figure stands as a stiff, squat block, the fully rounded form and the drapery type are still derived from Roman naturalism. By Roman standards the carving would have been labeled 'primitive.' But by Gallic conventions the carving captured Apinosus' strength and dignity.

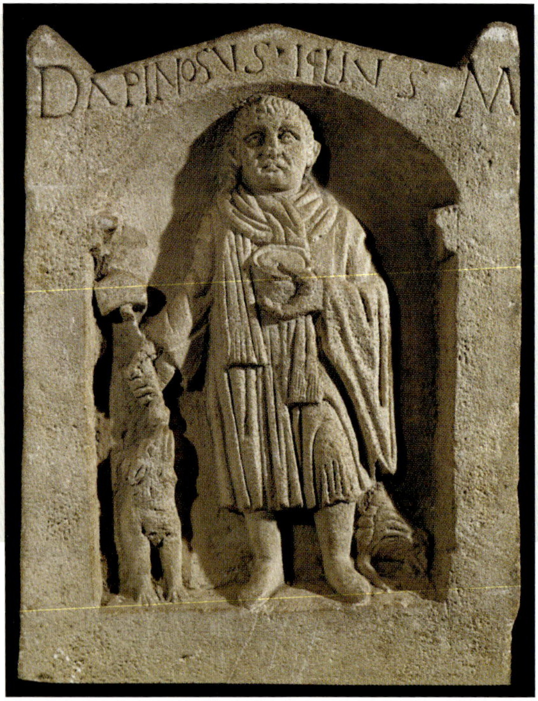

6. Apinosus Iclius with a hammer and cup in his hands, Gallo-Roman tomb relief, second century, Musée d'Archéologie Nationale, Saint-Germain-en-Laye, France.

The human image depicted in these cultures, whether in tribal art, folk art, or burial art, was often rigid and two-dimensional, more abstract and more symbolic, and therefore better suited for expressing themes central to their heritage than Roman naturalism (fig. 6). In short, its relevance threatened, Roman naturalism had all but suffocated in the embrace of the art of its provinces.

The Arrival of Christian Art

Briefly, then, this was the face of Roman art in the fourth century, precisely the period when Christianity and its artistic culture began to find its place in an unraveling society. The shift in power to the Byzantine East, the demise of Rome's ruling class and its pagan traditions, and the sacrifice of history's first art capable of describing the natural world all took place within a few decades. Less than a century later (476), a succession of barbarian sieges finally left Rome a destitute and isolated city. Rarely did the papacy, as the head of the new Church and the only effective power remaining in the city, have the resources to decorate churches. Consequently, from the collapse of the Roman Empire to its eventual resurgence in the 1200s, it fell on the Byzantine East to foster the evolution of Christian art, and, indeed, to ensure its very survival.

From its inception, Christianity, in need of its own artistic means of expression, usurped the scenes glorifying imperial exploits or chronicling domestic life for stories with religious themes. At root, these scenes, like the emperor with his entourage depicted in c. 547 (fig. 7), showed traces

7. *Justinian and His Entourage*, c. 547, San Vitale, Ravenna. Emperor Justinian is standing in the center with church clergy on his left and an imperial body guard on his right.

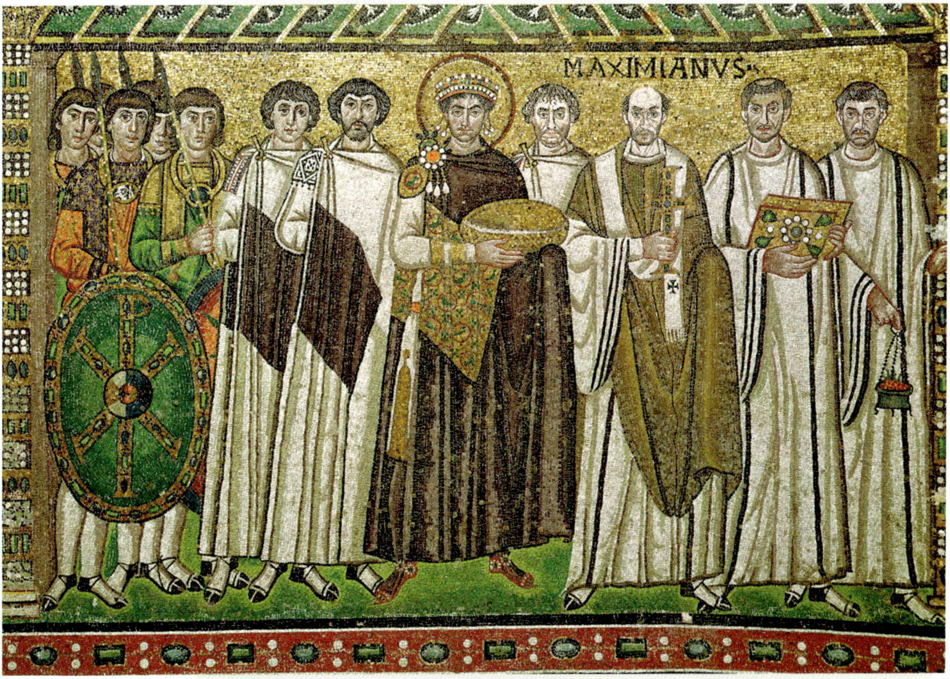

Wall paintings surviving from these centuries, like this picture, are mosaics—tiny tiles, called tesserae, set in mortar, whereas what has been lost are frescoes like fig. 1—paintings done on wet plaster.

of Roman naturalism (as all Byzantine images did to some degree). One of the last Byzantine-inspired wall paintings in Italy to touch upon the visual world, it is justly famous for the distinctive, individualized portraits of the haloed Emperor Justinian and the bald-headed bishop to his left. Staggered one by one behind the emperor and the bishop, various members of the imperial bodyguard, ministers of state, and the clergy appear to be occupying varied points in space. Still, with the gold background and the figures' stiff frontal stance, feet hovering above the green ground, the overriding impression remains one of an elegant wall decoration. The loss of interaction between figures, the absence of space and of three-dimensionality all conspire to evoke the simplified forms conceived during the

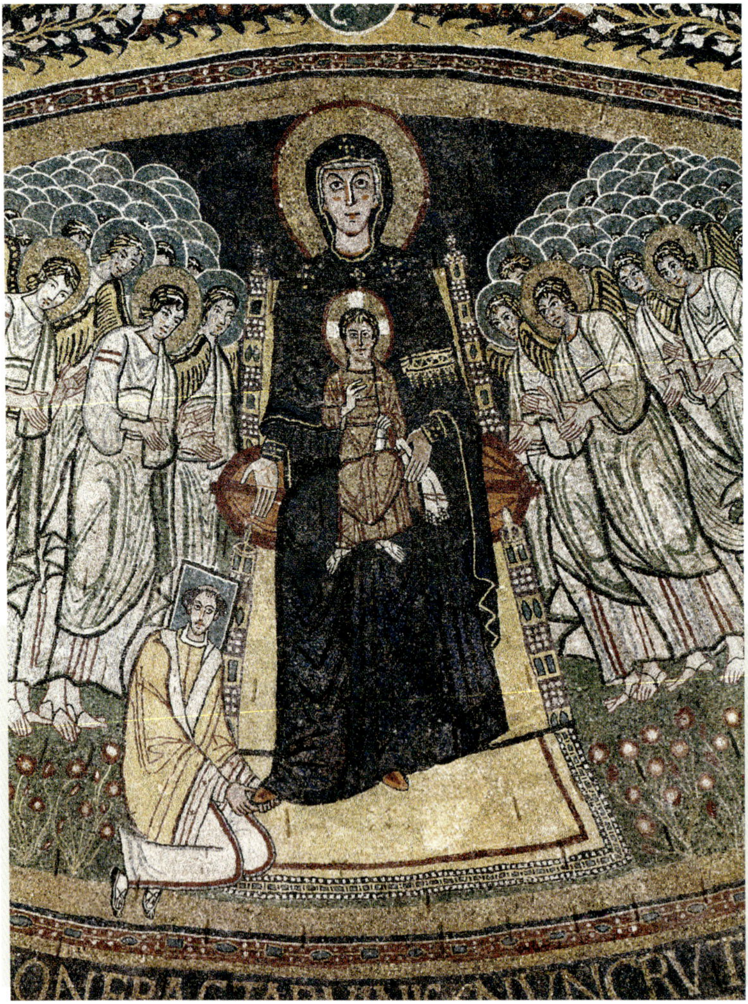

8. *Madonna and Child with Angels and Pope Pascal*, c. 818, apse mosaic, Santa Maria in Domnica, Rome.

The difference in the size of the figures indicates their importance in the Divine Order. The pope's square halo means he was alive at the time the mosaic, which he commissioned, was completed.

9. *Empress Irene*, twelfth-century portrait in mosaic of a Byzantine empress. Hagia Sophia, Istanbul.

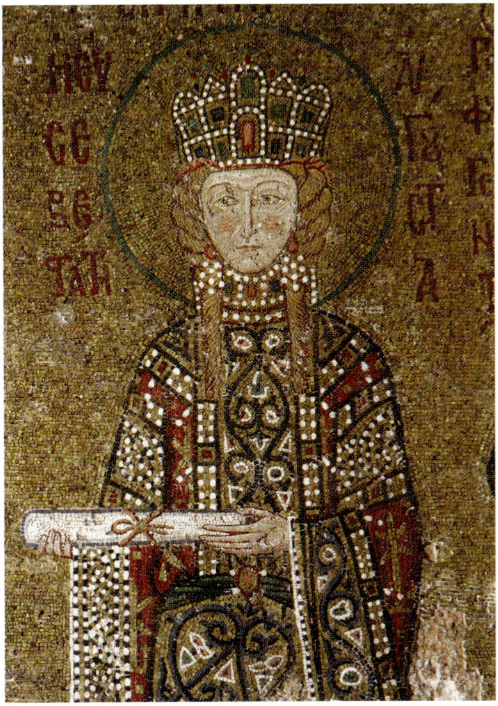

10. *Madonna and Child*, icon painted on wooden panel, early fifth-century, Santa Francesca Romana, Rome.

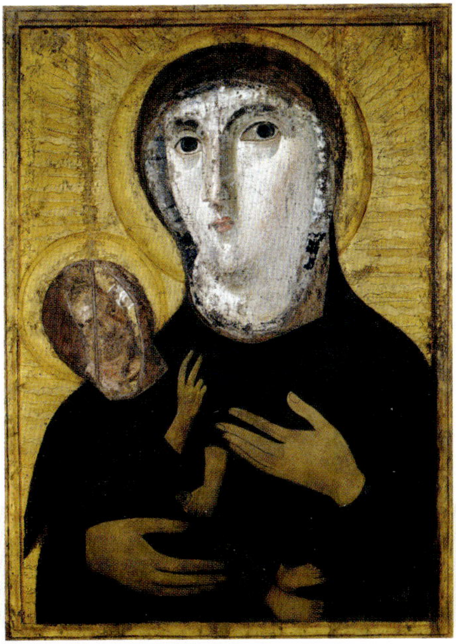

time of Constantine's rule.

Less than three centuries later, in a large heavenly scene that decorates the apse of a church in central Rome (fig. 8), the retreat from naturalism reached new heights. In the stacked choir of angels, the frozen, out-sized image of the Virgin with her Child, and in the abbreviated drawing of the pope kneeling in homage, the sense of art on a human scale has given way to a highly decorative, otherworldly art.

A second type of image proved to be even more pivotal in the development of Christian imagery than wall paintings: the official, half-length portrait of a pagan emperor or empress. Mass produced with little individuality, these painted wooden panels were dispatched to government centers throughout the empire until Constantine abandoned Rome for Byzantium

Not surprisingly, none has survived, but their legacy lasts in the portrait of a Byzantine empress done in mosaic (fig. 9) and in the half-length icons of the Madonna painted on wood (fig. 10). The development over the centuries of both types of images, the one a wall painting with multiple figures that matured into a kind of pictorial biblical story, and the other imperial portraiture that became the icon, formed the basis of Roman and Byzantine painting from the seventh through the thirteenth centuries.

The basic formula of the half-length image of the Virgin cradling her infant as represented here continued on through fourteenth-century Florentine painting.

The Arrival of Florentine Painting

Isolated from Rome and Byzantium, Tuscan artists attempted none of the complexity of storied wall paintings, which in ancient Rome had been especially suited to fresco. Surprisingly Tuscan artists did not produce frescoes. What they did produce were simplified equivalents of both icon and wall painting, which took the form of painted wooden panels depicting a Madonna or shaped as a cross (fig. 11).

Crosses had been depicted in Roman fresco as early as 700. A cross allowed artists to depict an iconic image, usually little more than an outline of a crucified Christ with expressionless eyes wide open. In side panels, artists introduced into Tuscan painting a modest storytelling art, where stubby creatures with schematic features enacted the story of the Passion (fig.12). Fewer than a dozen of this type of crucifix have survived. Their style is Romanesque, as was all art north of Rome in that period: figures are flat, firmly and simply outlined, and as yet untouched by the Byzantine style.

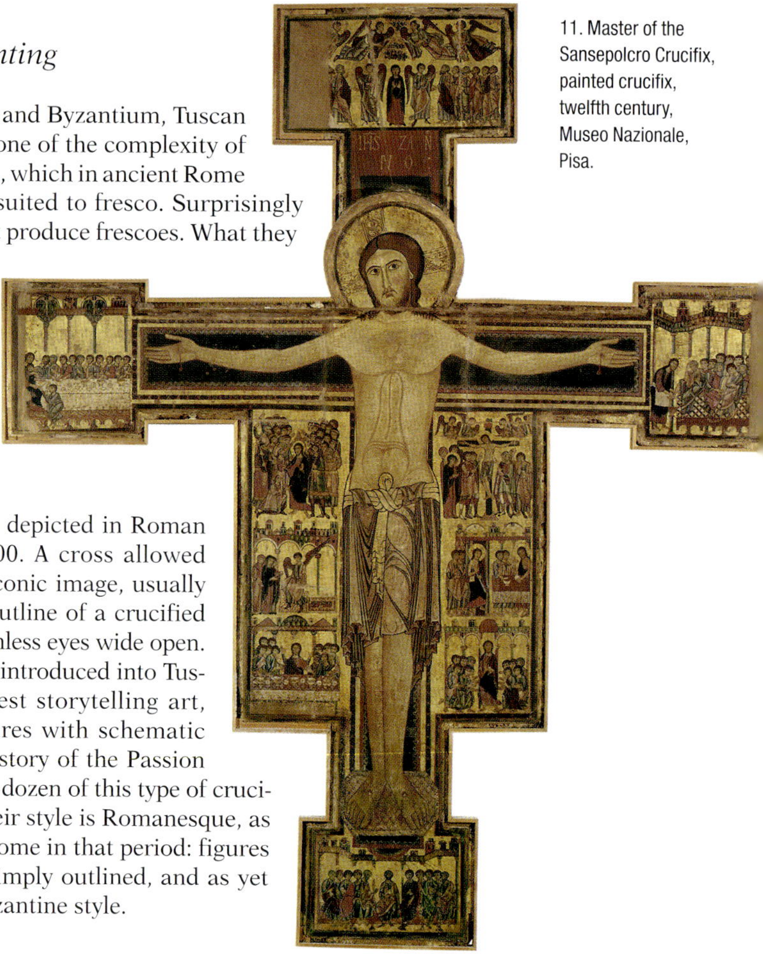

11. Master of the Sansepolcro Crucifix, painted crucifix, twelfth century, Museo Nazionale, Pisa.

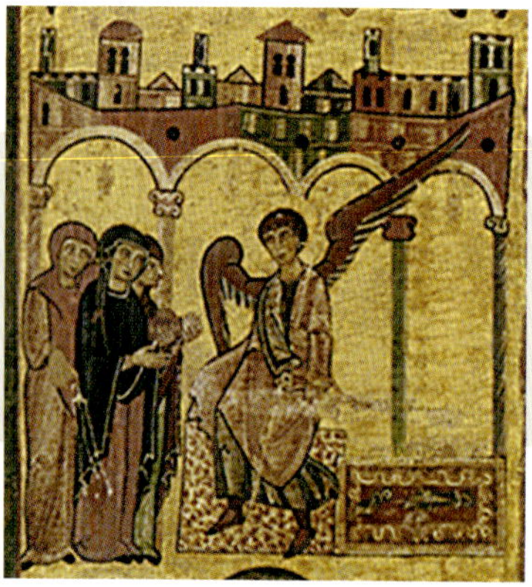

12. *Three Marys at the Sepulcher.* Detail of fig. 11, mid-left side panel showing three female mourners, including the Virgin in blue.

Sitting on an empty sepulcher in the center is the angel who announces that Christ has risen. Side stories, unlike the iconic image of the figure of Christ on the cross, allowed the artist more latitude in depicting interaction between figures.

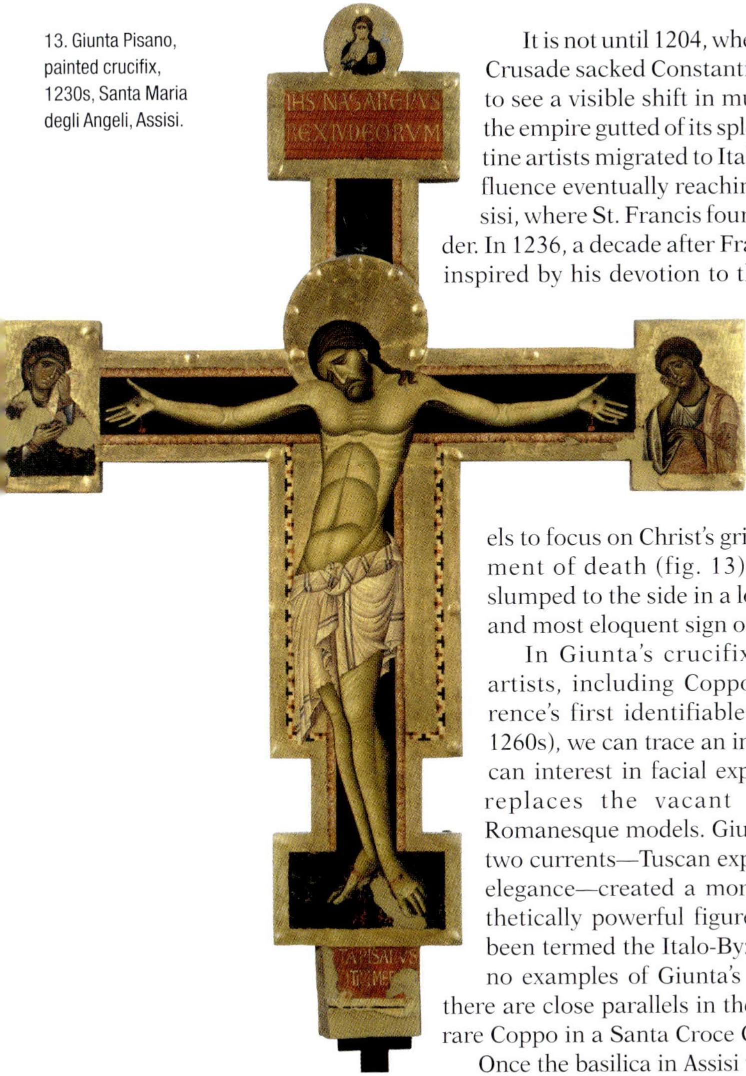

13. Giunta Pisano, painted crucifix, 1230s, Santa Maria degli Angeli, Assisi.

It is not until 1204, when knights of the Fourth Crusade sacked Constantinople, that we are able to see a visible shift in much of Italian art. With the empire gutted of its splendid treasures, Byzantine artists migrated to Italy's art centers, their influence eventually reaching the little town of Assisi, where St. Francis founded the Franciscan order. In 1236, a decade after Francis's death, the order, inspired by his devotion to the poor and suffering, commissioned the Tuscan painter Giunta Pisano to paint a crucifix that would reflect human suffering in the true Franciscan spirit. Giunta omitted the side panels to focus on Christ's grimacing face at the moment of death (fig. 13). His elongated body slumped to the side in a long, gentle arc is a first and most eloquent sign of Byzantine influence.

In Giunta's crucifix and works by later artists, including Coppo di Marcovaldo (Florence's first identifiable painter, active in the 1260s), we can trace an increasingly intense Tuscan interest in facial expression, where pathos replaces the vacant faces of the older Romanesque models. Giunta's synthesis of these two currents—Tuscan expression and Byzantine elegance—created a more convincing and aesthetically powerful figure that led to what has been termed the Italo-Byzantine style. (We have no examples of Giunta's work in Florence, but there are close parallels in the Uffizi Museum and a rare Coppo in a Santa Croce Chapel.)

Once the basilica in Assisi was completed in 1253, painters from all over Italy were summoned to decorate its bare walls in the grand tradition of Roman frescoes. Among them were students of Rome's foremost master, Pietro Cavallini. Like Giunta in Tuscany, Cavallini was Rome's conduit to the new Italo-Byzantine style. His investigations into the secrets of his city's early Christian mosaic cycles led him to reintroduce in his own frescoes a vision of the human figure unseen for centuries. His austere yet fully rounded figures, implying mass and not simply shape, are an amalgam of early Roman naturalism and the formality of the Byzantine (fig. 14).

Note the similarities in the soft modeling in this scene with that of the early Roman fresco in fig. 1. Like that image, this is a true fresco and one of the earliest to have survived from the Christian era.

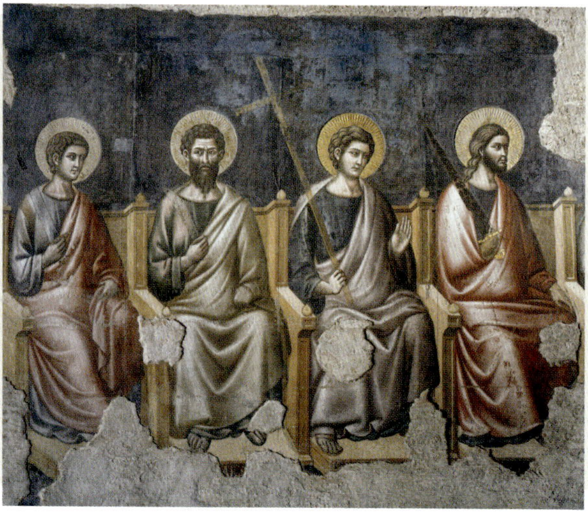

14. Pietro Cavallini, *Last Judgment*, detail, 1290s, Santa Cecilia in Trastevere, Rome.

From Cavallini it is but a short hop to the young Florentine Giotto. To study Cavallini's breakthroughs, Giotto traveled to Rome and established the first links between Florentine art and Roman art.

At the Threshold of Two Centuries, a Turning Point

Giotto (c. 1267-1337) is by history's consensus the founder of modern art. He pulled painting out from under the Byzantine eclipse by endowing his figures with a convincing sense of relief and placing them in a credible space, when space had been lost to Western art for a thousand years. (Note that the Byzantine and Florentine images in figs. 7 through 11 are flat and stylized, in total disregard for volume or space.) In his late work in Florence's Santa Croce, his figures stood for embodiments of humanity—piety, pathos, and dignity—but his compositions were always crystal-clear dramas stripped to their essence (fig. 15).

If the first half of the fourteenth century belonged to Giotto and his followers, the second half saw the gradual unraveling of their influence. When the bubonic plague struck Florence in 1348, killing over half its population of one hundred thousand, terror gripped the survivors. Convinced of God's wrath over their prideful ways, Florentines retreated from Giotto's earthly world to the safety of a medieval church whose doctrines stressed God's hierarchy in a heavenly world.

In the half century following the plague, Florence produced no major painters, and those it did produce painted in the spirit of the times, turning out serious, pious, and spiritually charged Gothic art. With the Gothic we firmly confront the linear style, a markedly decorative art form suited to depicting scenes of mystical ecstasy, but one that had little point of contact with Giotto's relief system (fig. 16). (A century later, Botticelli will emerge as the greatest and last of the famed linear school of Florentine painting.)

Amid this religious fervor, a breach to the watertight bulkheads of Christian orthodoxy ushered in the spirit of Giotto's humanity once again. In the mid-1300s, the famed Italian poet Petrarch discovered the writings of ancient classical literary giants previously known only to monastic communities. Resolute in his faith that man's dignity was rooted in the culture of ancient Rome, Petrarch challenged Florentines to look to the glorious past, when Cicero, Virgil, Caesar, and Ovid wrote triumphantly of moral philosophy, rhetoric, literature, and art that revered man's earthly life.

For the Florentines, this message was an epiphany. As true Roman descendants, their humanity was linked to the dignity of a mighty race. For decades, the study of that distant epoch had been confined entirely within the city's humanist literary circles. But Petrarch's bold challenge planted the seeds for a cultural reawakening in art, law, and civic virtue.

This "reawakening" ignited a revolution in the first decades of the fifteenth century unseen since ancient Rome. Spawned by the humanists, the artists and their patrons threw off the yoke of pestilence and suffering and united to finance a breathtaking series of projects to decorate their

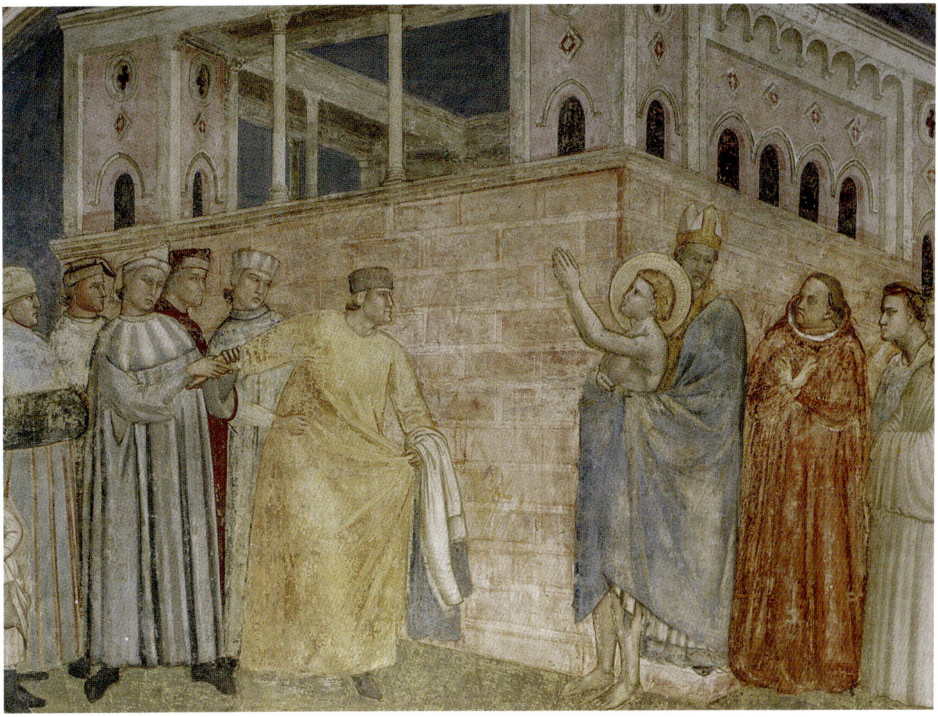

15. Giotto, *Francis's Renunciation of His Possessions*, detail of fig. 22, c. 1305-15, Santa Croce, Florence. Note how the artist frames the interaction between complex figure groupings with architecture.

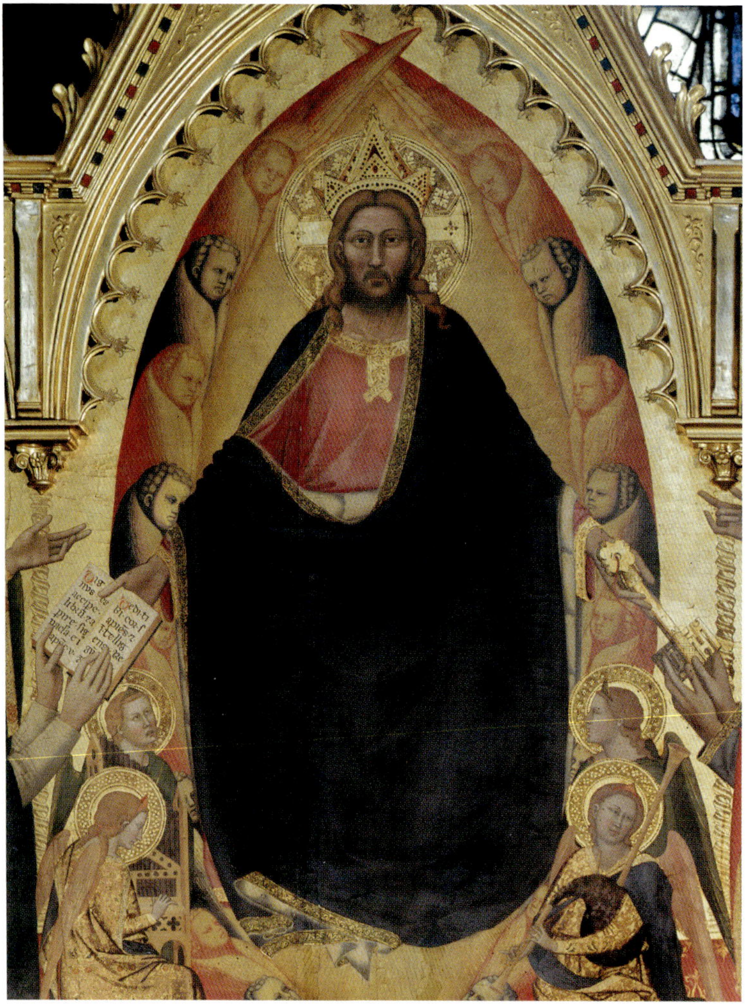

16. Orcagna, *Redeemer Enthroned with Saints*, detail, 1357, Santa Maria Novella, Florence. Note the highly ornate form enclosing the severe frontal image of Christ.

city. Scores of major painters—and unknown minor ones—labored to capture the human figure in all its variety. Sculptors cast bronze doors for the Baptistry and carved statues to embellish the churches, and architects designed chapels on a more human scale. Were it not for the sustained genius of these men, the miracle of Florentine art might never have taken the rest of Europe by storm.

The Survival of Medieval Florence, 1000–1348

In the tenth century, Florence was nothing more than a village of a few thousand people encircled by old Roman walls. The major families of Tuscany, some with connections to Frankish barons, lived protected in vast estates in the countryside and had their winter homes in towered fortresses inside the city walls of Florence. (By the end of the twelfth century, towers numbered 150, with most rising to 250 feet.)

In the eleventh century, two events signal Florence's growing prominence. The first, the consecration of the Baptistry (c. 1059) and the construction of the church of San Miniato (begun in 1013), both built on the old foundations of Roman or ancient Christian structures. The second event proved to be more portentous, as it marked the beginning of Florence becoming deeply implicated in the strife between the papacy and the Holy Roman Emperor. In 1075 Pope Gregory VII challenged the German Holy Roman Emperor Henry IV to stop his investiture of bishops. When Henry fired back his refusal, Gregory excommunicated him. Two years later, in January, a humbled Henry crept through the snows to meet Gregory and ask his forgiveness at Canossa, the castle of Countess Matilda of Tuscany, the king's most important vassal in Italy. The Countess sided with the papacy to free her lands from foreign rule and refortified Florence with a new ring of walls. When she died in 1115 and left her lands to the papacy, the Florentines were free to form a commune headed by the most distinguished one hundred men in the city.

A Factious Society: the Guelfs and Ghibellines

Here begins a period marked by struggles between opposing factions: the urban worker against the rural nobility, city against city, but most conspicuously, the supporters of the papacy (the Guelf party composed of minor nobility) against supporters of the German Holy Roman Empire (the Ghibelline party of landed feudal nobility). These struggles occurred in all Tuscan cities, but in Florence they were particularly contentious.

In 1216 a young Guelf nobleman, Buondelmonte dei Buondelmonti, reneged on a marriage proposal to a woman whose family was aligned with powerful Ghibellines. To avenge her humiliation, on Easter morning as the young man rode his horse across the Ponte Vecchio, the family jumped him and hacked him to pieces.

With Buondelmonti's death, the threat of Ghibelline dominance strengthened the city's resolve to remain aligned with the papacy. Yet the conflict between Guelfs and Ghibellines continued to be a major political undercurrent, fueled by the antagonism between the papacy and the German Empire. Not much was built, sculpted, or painted during this period—at least, little remains. The only artists known by name were a Lucchese family of painters and a Pisan family of sculptors.

In the mid-1200s, as German influence in the region began to wane, the Guelfs strengthened their position by appealing to a broader group of classes. In forming a "republic of the people," the city built the Bargello, the first public palace. This new government represented an increase in the influence of the merchants, the professional classes, and the artisans, who were represented by their respective twenty-one guilds.

Survival of the Fittest

During this same decade, Siena was striving for dominance over Tuscany. Allied with a force of Ghibellines from all over the province, its army massacred the Florentines in 1260 at the battle of Montaperti. Ten thousand died and twenty thousand were imprisoned. Among their numbers was none other than Florence's first identifiable artist, Coppo di Marcovaldo, who paid for his freedom by painting a Madonna that still hangs in one of Siena's churches. (Freedom for painting says something about the esteem in which artists were held.) Hoping to inflict a merciless blow, the Ghibelline forces plundered the Guelf properties and exiled their leaders.

Six year later, Clement IV, a pope with deep antipathy toward the German dynasty by virtue of his French birth, called upon the brother of the King of France, Charles of Anjou, to finally expel the Ghibellines. Not long after, the Florentines threw up the Ordinance of Justice, disenfranchising the 150 uppermost noble families and truncating their towers.

A Golden Age

The years between 1266 and 1337, the span of Giotto's life, saw Florence thrive as a prosperous republic governed by middle-class tradesmen and an upper class of wealthy merchants. By now, its population exceeded 100,000 citizens (only Paris, Milan, Venice, and Naples were larger—not Rome). Despite wars with Siena and Pisa, the enterprising Florentines established a banking system favored by the papacy, an international trade system, guilds that funded the major civic projects, and cloth manufacturing that sent fine textiles all over the Western world. In short, affluence was widespread and artisans had plenty of work. The Duomo (begun in 1296—but not yet its dome), Santa Maria Novella (1270s), Santa Croce (rebuilt larger in 1294), and Palazzo Vecchio (begun by Arnolfo in 1299) were all built during this period. As much as these monuments were revered, the spotlight fell on Giotto's frescoes in Santa Croce (c. 1315-1330) and Dante's *Divine Comedy* (likely written in the years 1304-1321), the first literary masterpiece written in the Tuscan vernacular. One of the most audacious treatments of the human being in history, the poem follows Dante's tour through the *Inferno, Purgatory*, and *Paradise*. Finally, in 1337, the year of Giotto's death, the Florentine guilds began building Orsanmichele, as a combination of granary and oratory. Yet, catastrophic events would soon force the city to wait another sixty years before anything else of note was built or decorated.

1. Santa Croce Church and Museum

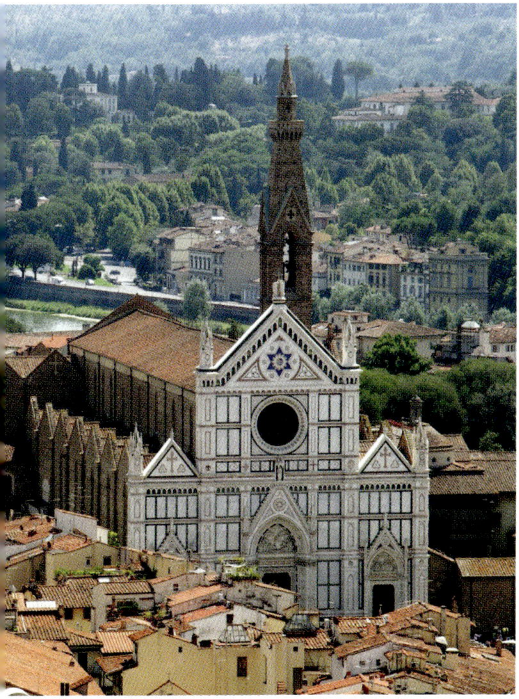

Santa Croce was built over an earlier church by the Franciscan order in 1294, two years before work was begun on the Duomo. It is a Gothic church, the city's answer to the monumental Gothic cathedrals of Notre Dame, Chartres, and others in northern France. But, in contrast to their towering spires and rows of saints, standing stiff and straight as soldiers over their portals, Santa Croce was built in a different spirit. Instead of the transcendent stained glass of French cathedrals, Santa Croce's walls were left bare to be painted in frescoes that would tell the stories of the lives of Christ, the Virgin Mary, and Saint Francis of Assisi (1181/82-1226), who, as a young man, gave up his worldly goods to devote his life to the poor.

Here, then, is the glorious Florentine equivalent to stained glass, the fresco. Giotto and his followers begin the fourteenth century with a stunning achievement that explores man's earthly domain for the first time in Florentine painting.

The Chapels and Their Patrons

Although the church was financed by the commune, the earliest chapels to be frescoed were commissioned by powerful banking families: the Peruzzi, Bardi, and Baroncelli. Since chapels had traditionally been financed by mendicant orders and lay fraternities, Francis would have frowned on families buying chapels. But later, when banking began making usurious profits, these families saw their patronage as a public sacrifice for the expiation of their sins.

Medieval Notions of the Human Figure

Coppo di Marcovaldo, active 1250-76, *Saint Francis Altarpiece*, Bardi Chapel, c. 1250-60

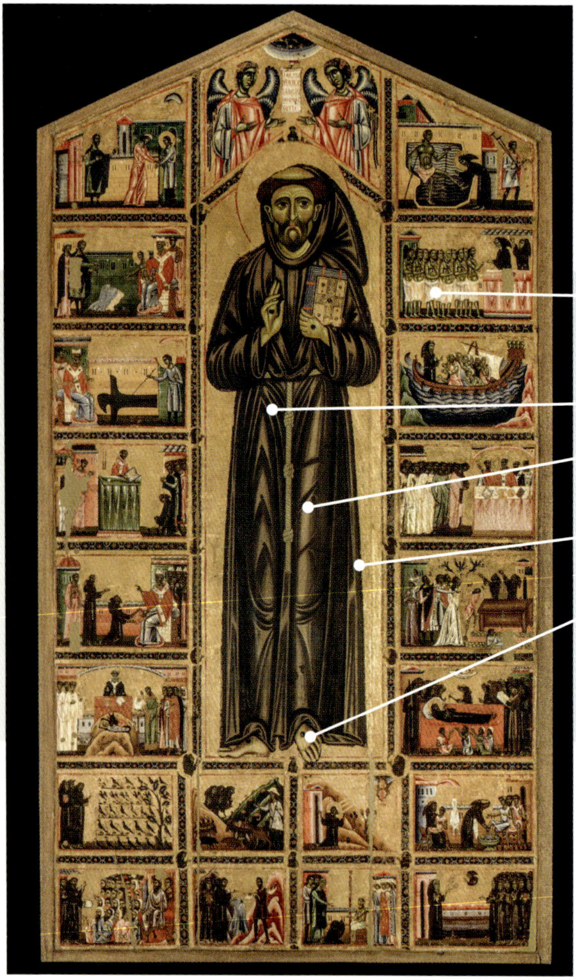

17. Coppo di Marcovaldo, *Saint Francis Altarpiece*, c. 1250-60, Bardi Chapel. As a sacred image meant to be venerated, the patron, one of the ten richest men in Florence, spared no expense in commissioning such a large, gold-leafed, and richly detailed painting.

Stacked figures fail to suggest space, and instead emphasize the flatness of the panel's surface.

Lines denote drapery folds.

Highlights suggest the prominence of the legs.

Black outline accents the figure's outer shape.

The foot pushing forward to the border suggests a hint of three-dimensionality. It also calls attention to the stigmata, the nail holes in Francis's feet and hands.

Coppo di Marcovaldo is Florence's first identifiable artist, and this is one of Florence's earliest paintings still hanging in a church. In its day, this severe, schematic image would have been viewed by a spectator as an accurate depiction of the human figure. The rudimentary side stories of Saint Francis's life begin the Florentine tradition of narrative art, which Giotto would continue on the surrounding walls sixty years later in the demanding medium of fresco. These scenes are characterized by the absence of spatial effects, archaic architecture, and diagrammatic compositions.

The altarpiece's c. 1250-60 dating corresponds to the period when Florentine painting still relied on Byzantine formulae, forming a hybrid commonly referred to as the Italo-Byzantine style (see fig. 13). In Byzantine fashion, the artist paints lines on Saint Francis's drapery to denote folds and adds highlights to denote the roundness of the legs. He also outlines the figure in black. The question of outlines, a matter of little consequence we might think, occupies center stage in Santa Croce's frescoes. Heavy outlines reinforce the appearance of a schematic two-dimensional shape. By the early Renaissance, commentaries on art railed against the use of outlines, since they create an artificial boundary that seals the figure from its surroundings.

Despite the fact that Francis is painted on a flat, reflective gold background, his image projects a measure of non-Byzantine naturalism in the offset eyes and furrowed brow and a hint of incipient space where his toes push forward to the ribbon-like border.

Coppo's notion of space here is a product of the time: the essential quality we must bear in mind when looking at a painting from the thirteenth century is its over-riding flatness.

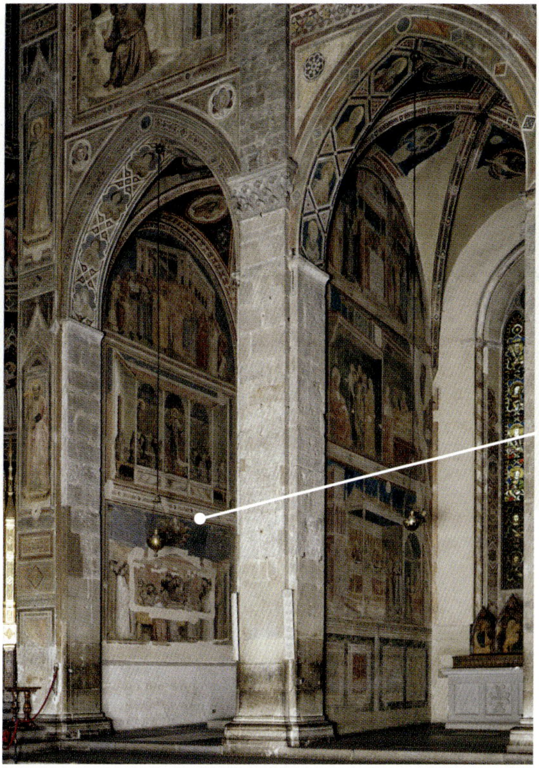

18. Bardi and Peruzzi Chapels, showing Giotto's frescoes.

The off-set views of the chapels shows us the angle at which Giotto intends us to see his scenes.

Giotto also bathes his figures in a pictorial light that corresponds to the natural light streaming in from the stained glass windows at the end of each chapel.

Giotto, c. 1267-1337, *Life of Saint Francis*, Bardi Chapel, c. 1315-20

In *A Room with a View*, E.M. Forster's 1908 novel, a group of English tourists tail a strutting Anglican pastor from chapel to chapel through the church of Santa Croce, craning their necks as he points out the Giotto's. These frescoes had been discovered under a layer of whitewash only a few decades earlier, and it was as hard to imagine then as it is now how Florence's earliest wall paintings could have succumbed to the whims of taste.

19. Giotto, *Apparition of Saint Francis*, c. 1315-20, Bardi Chapel, left wall.

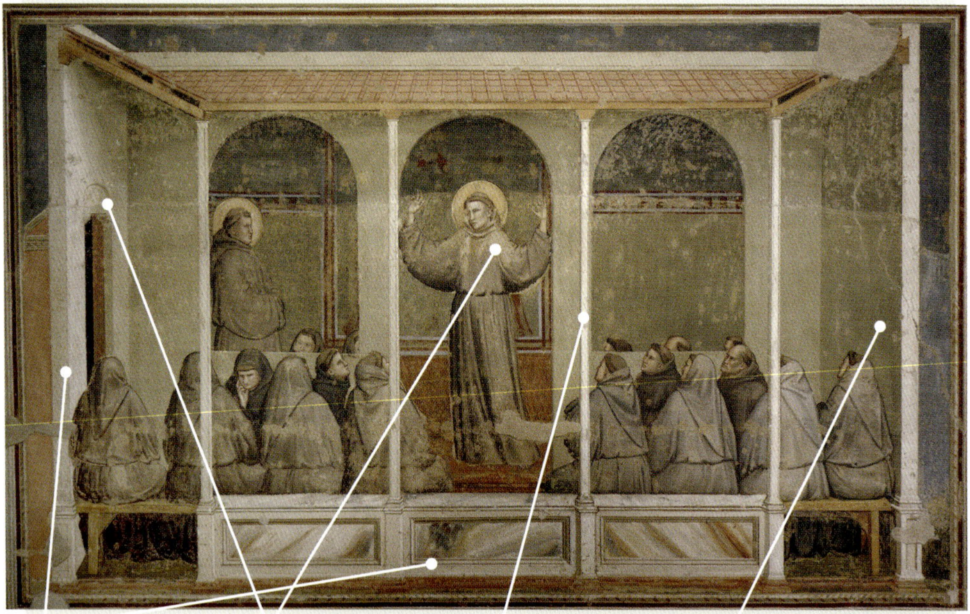

Giotto, who is often called the father of Western painting, has embodied a remarkable array of different talents to different people: storyteller, Christian spiritualist, psychologist, naturalist painter, dramatist. Where he learned to paint isn't certain, though it's likely that in the 1290s he visited the basilica in Assisi, where he would have studied the techniques employed in Rome's ancient fresco tradition.

The first observation to note is that Giotto confronts the problem of depicting the three-dimensional world on a flat surface by relating the scenes to architecture. All but one of the structures depicted are interiors, with forward walls sliced off to show us characters anchored to a clearly defined space. Indeed, the creation of plausible space is one of Giotto's great contributions to Western painting. Space provided Giotto the means to delineate the human figure, his overriding focus, as an isolated mass with breathing room around it. This is a dramatic departure from the simple stacking of flat figures that characterizes the scenes in the Saint Francis painting (fig. 17).

Giotto's use of space is still primitive. None of these frescoes depicts a space governed by true perspective, which became an obsession with Renaissance artists of the next century. And unlike those painters, who create a space contiguous with the viewer's space, Giotto pushes his interiors some distance inside the scene. We stand outside his little dollhouses, gazing in.

Giotto intends for the frescoes to be seen from an oblique viewpoint that corresponds to the chapel's entrance as in the *Apparition* (but also in the *Funeral,* fig. 20).

20. Giotto, *Funeral of Saint Francis*, c. 1315-20, Bardi Chapel, left wall.

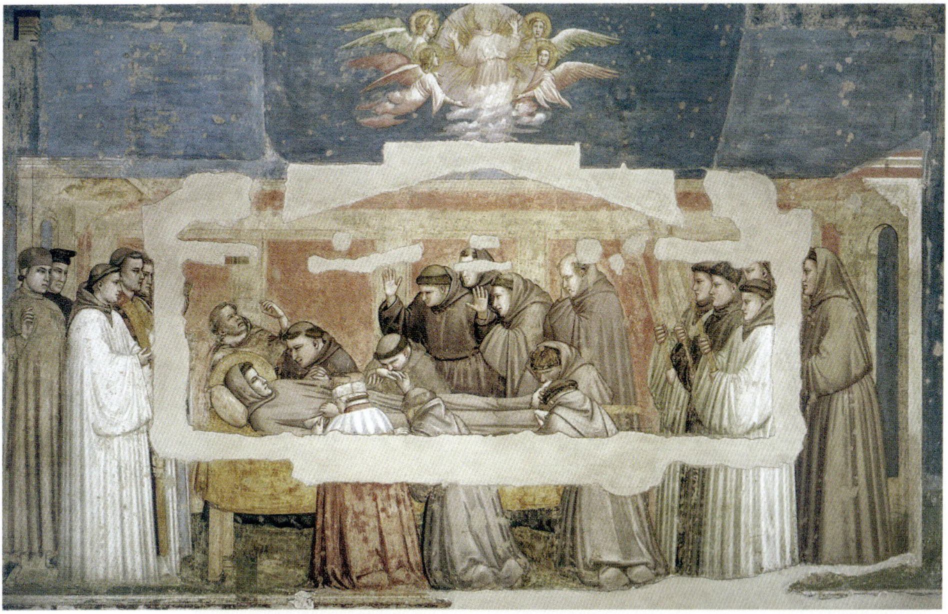

Where the paintings are disfigured tombs were at one time attached to the walls.

Notice how he shows us a greater expanse of the far right wall of the room more than of the near wall, and shifts the spindly forward columns off center. In other words, Giotto sets us obliquely to and simultaneously dead center in front of the building. The attention Giotto gives to the role of light in defining the shape of objects—for example, those lumpish monks sitting in the refectory—is even more critical for future painting than his demonstration of space.

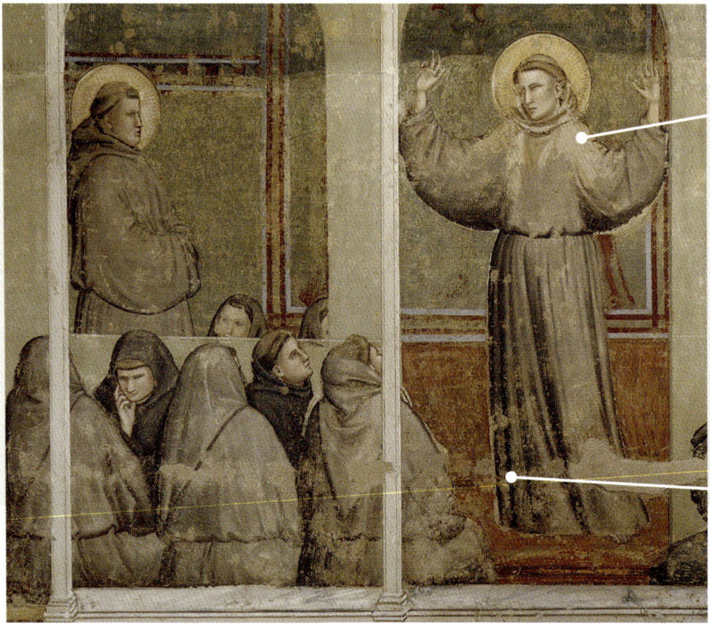

21. Giotto, detail of fig. 19.

We perceive the massiveness of the monks not only because of their silhouettes, but also because of the way Giotto's directed light shapes their volume. The parts that protrude toward us are bathed in *highlights*, while the opposite, receding sides are *darkened* by shadow.

Giotto directs his light from an overhead angle that corresponds to natural light emanating from the window. This light bleaches color on the figure's illuminated side, while its absence deepens color on its backside. Since our eye perceives that pale colors on a flat wall visually jump forward and darker ones recede, the graduated transition of pale to dark simulates a figure's rounded mass. (Pale colors come forward because they reflect light back to the eye.)

Giotto's treatment of space and light is unquestionably a supreme technical achievement, but what puts him in the company of the finest painters of any century is his intuitive ability to strip a story to its bare essentials. He paints expressive faces in scenes depicting despair but prefers gesture as a means to focus on the moment. For example, in the *Apparition of Saint Francis* the neatly ordered architecture imparts a sense of calm that accents the mysterious apparition of Francis to his fellow friars. His arms, raised in salutation, complete the circle begun by the arch overhead; interaction with the architecture directs our eye to Francis.

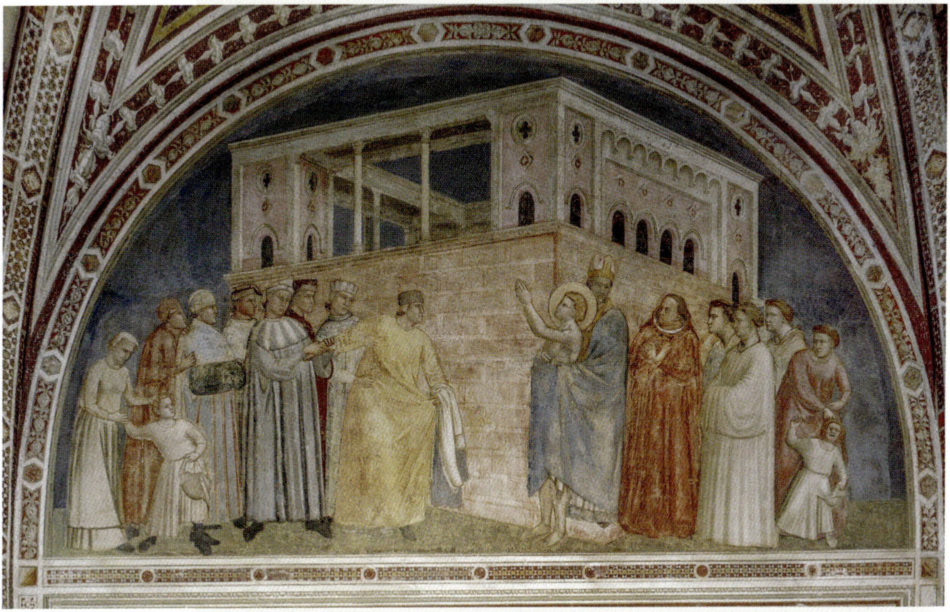

22. Giotto, *Francis's Renunciation of His Possessions*, c. 1315-20, Bardi Chapel, left wall

The corner of the masterfully foreshortened building accents Francis, while the receding wall underlines the father's outstretched arm.

The *Renunciation* captures the moment when young Francis, whose body is draped by the bishop behind him, renounces his possessions before his father. The father rushes forward to rebuke Francis, but is restrained by his respectable colleagues. Again, Giotto uses architecture for dramatic effect: the strong vertical of the imposing building marks Francis and a telling space separates father from son, implying the isolation of the humiliated parent.

Note that Giotto marks the father in yellow, a color by convention reserved for morally weak adversaries. Yellow is normally a bright color that pops forward, especially as its paler version moves toward white, but Giotto deepens it with shades of umber brown to match the richness of the other colors. Thus, we read all colors as having the same muted midrange intensity.

Trial by Fire is the simplest of the Bardi frescoes structurally, but the most sophisticated psychologically and chromatically. Francis traveled to Egypt to convert the sultan and to prove the truth of Christianity. Here, he is about to step into the bonfire. Opposite Francis, the monarch's attendants, resplendently robed in deep yellow, white, blue and red, their faces and dark complexion drawn from life, shrink back in disbelief. Our eye goes first to the sultan, next to the attendants and then to Francis, back and forth and back in taut suspense.

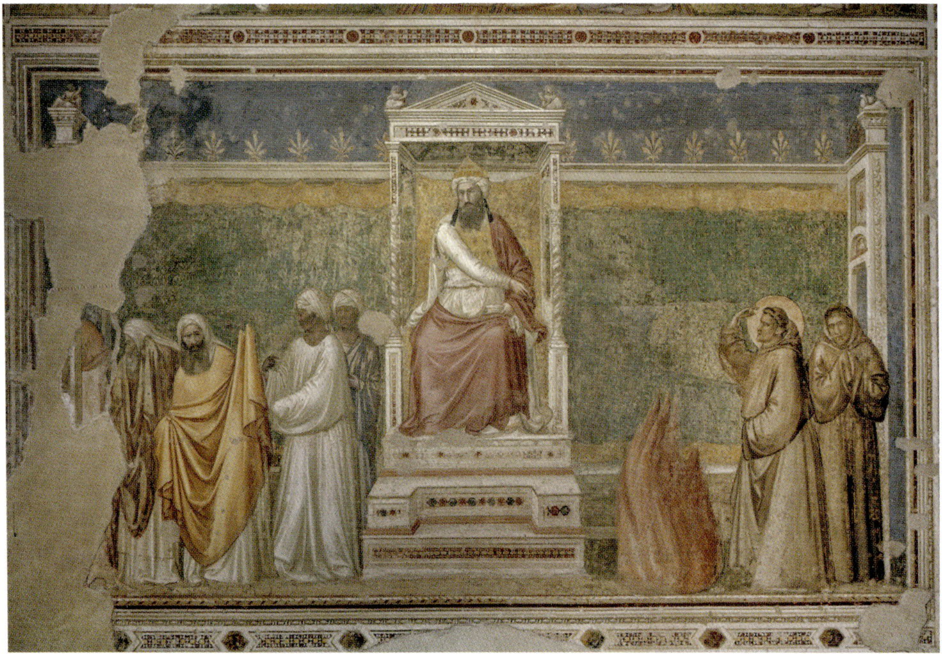

23. Giotto, *Trial by Fire*, c. 1315-20, Bardi Chapel, right wall.
24. Giotto, detail of fig. 23, *Trial by Fire*.
25. Giotto, detail of fig. 20, *Funeral of Saint Francis*.

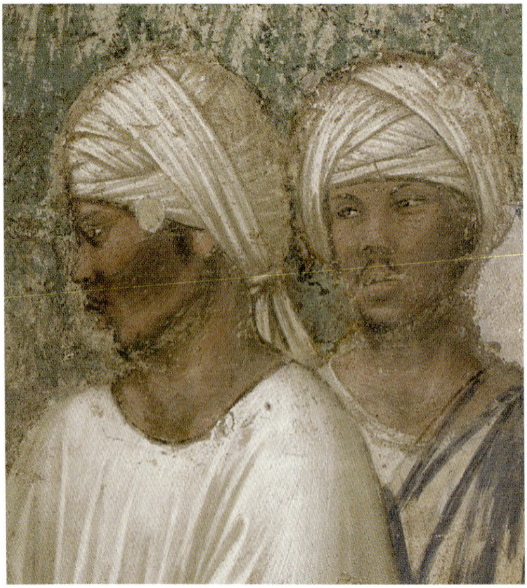

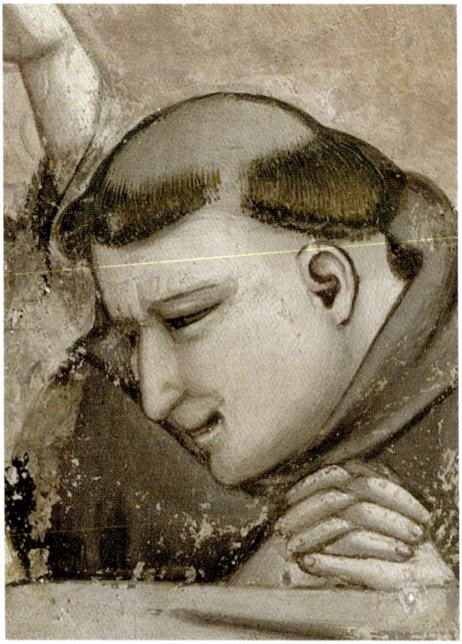

If we look more closely at this scene we see that something compelling is going on in the way Giotto models these characters. In comparing their faces (fig. 24) with those in the *Funeral of Saint Francis* (fig. 25), we note that no definitive outline surrounds their silhouettes, whereas the features and tonsured scalps of the friars are outlined by a dark color.

If we can fix in our minds the difference between the two—the edges in one painted loosely with an open brush, creating soft contours that endow the figure with relief, and the edges in the other demarcated by a line that emphasizes its silhouette, that is, merely its shape—we will have come a long way toward tracking a major feature that will divide Florentine painting in the coming centuries. The linear style with its stress on picture surface leads to Botticelli, while the relief style with its stress on space leads to Leonardo da Vinci.

Giotto, c. 1267-1337, *Lifes of John the Baptist and John the Evangelist*, Peruzzi Chapel, c. 1320-30

The frescoes are badly damaged because Giotto painted them *a secco*, that is, on dry plaster, which doesn't absorb and protect the paint the way wet plaster (the usual medium for frescoes) does.

The figures in the *Raising of Drusiana from the Dead* (fig. 26) are less tightly grouped, more distinctly individual, with garments that are fuller, with softer edges than the sharply outlined ones in the Bardi's earlier scenes. In this fresco, Giotto conjures up his most daring use of architecture: the high walls and towers of a fortified city run diagonally beyond the frame to reinforce our sense of the city's great size. Giotto's

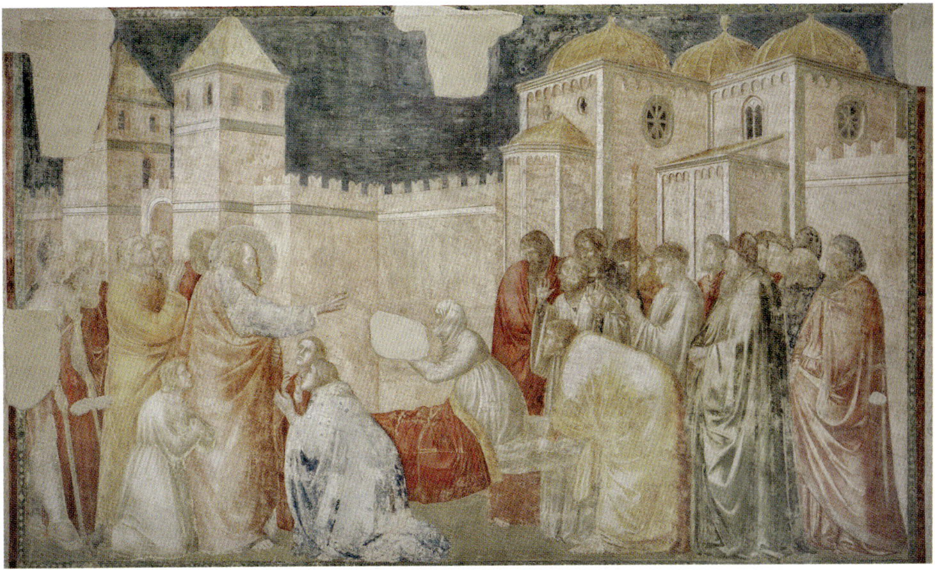

26. Giotto, *Raising of Drusiana from the Dead*, c. 1320-30, Peruzzi Chapel, right wall.

depiction of John bringing Drusiana back to life captures a solemn, deeply human moment. He marks it with the long, bare wall bordered by two monolithic towers. The noble figures stand before the wall, full-bodied and dignified in heavy drapery that Giotto would pass on to Masaccio, and through him, to future generations of painters.

Beyond Giotto

Taddeo Gaddi, c. 1300-1366, *Life of the Virgin*, Baroncelli Chapel, 1330

With Giotto working in Naples, Taddeo Gaddi, his pupil for many years, chose to probe a pictorial world where naturalism and ornamentation coexist.

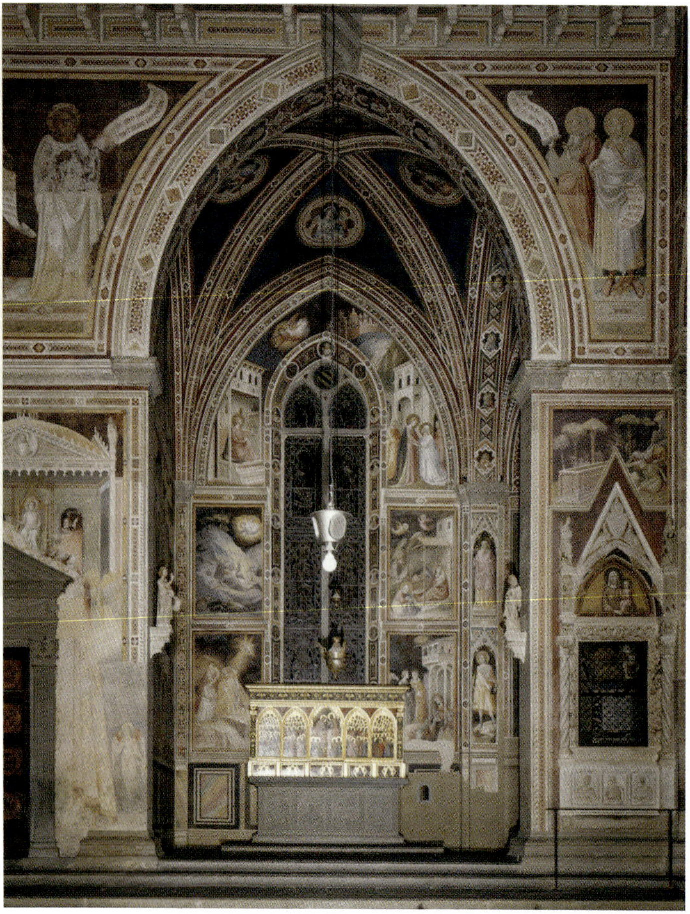

The two scenes depicted in the next pages (figs. 28, 29) are painted on the left wall and therefore perpendicular to the altar wall, where a stained glass window bathes them in an iridescent multi-colored light. Gaddi takes advantage of this light by deploying colors in these frescoes that pick up the various hues cast upon them.
The scenes are in chronological order and meant to be read from top to bottom.

27. Baroncelli Chapel, view of back wall from the chapel's entrance.

In comparing pupil to master, we begin by noting that these are night scenes distinguished by large voids of darkness set against a palette of lustrous pastels. The *Expulsion of Joachim,* in the lunette at the top, is divided into two scenes (fig. 28). On the left, stands a tall spindly temple set in an oblique view that underscores its three-dimensionality. Inside the temple, an imposing rabbi has just expelled Joachim as unworthy because the elderly future father of the Virgin has yet to father a child.

28. Taddeo Gaddi, *Expulsion of Joachim from the Temple*; *Annunciation to Joachim*, 1330, Baroncelli Chapel, left wall.

On the back of the figure leaning through the temple's columns, a rose robe turns to silver-green, an unnatural yet beautiful embellishment. Such artificial color shifts, found throughout these scenes, signals us that Taddeo is moving away from Giottesque naturalism (Giotto always insists on naturalistic single colors) towards an ornamental art.

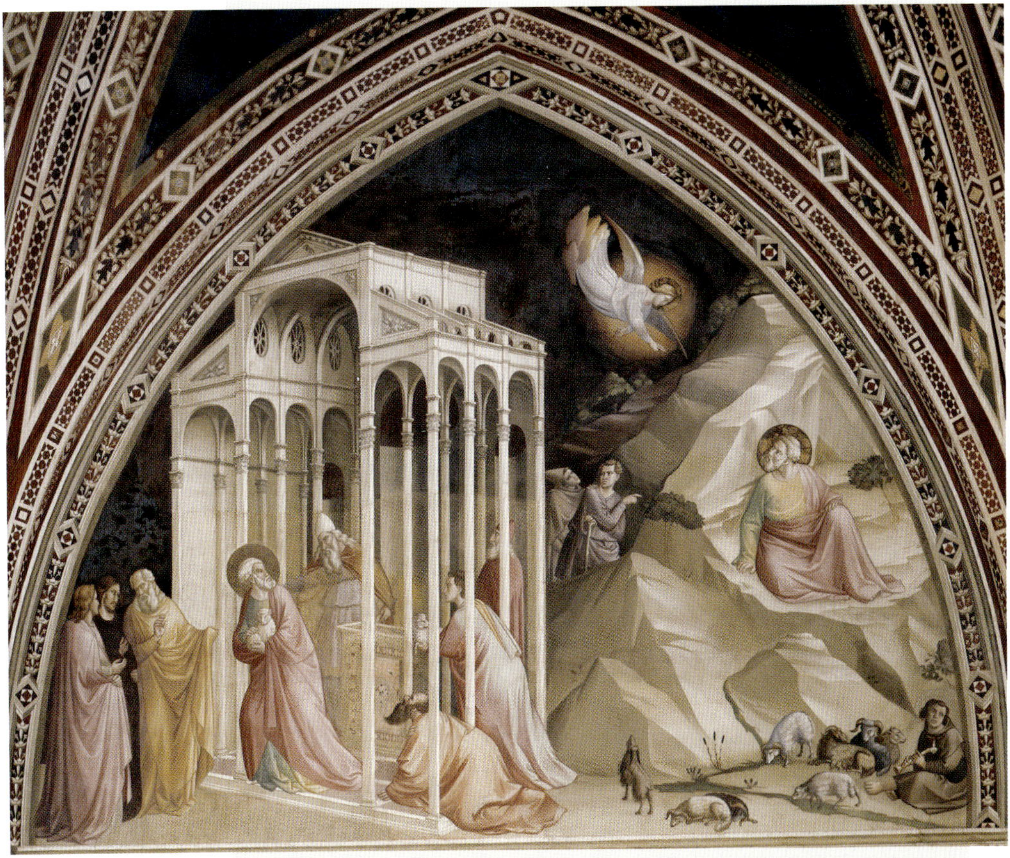

On an adjacent rocky hillside in the same scene, isolated by deeper space than Giotto had conceived, Joachim appears once again, startled by an angel's message that his wife is to bear a daughter.

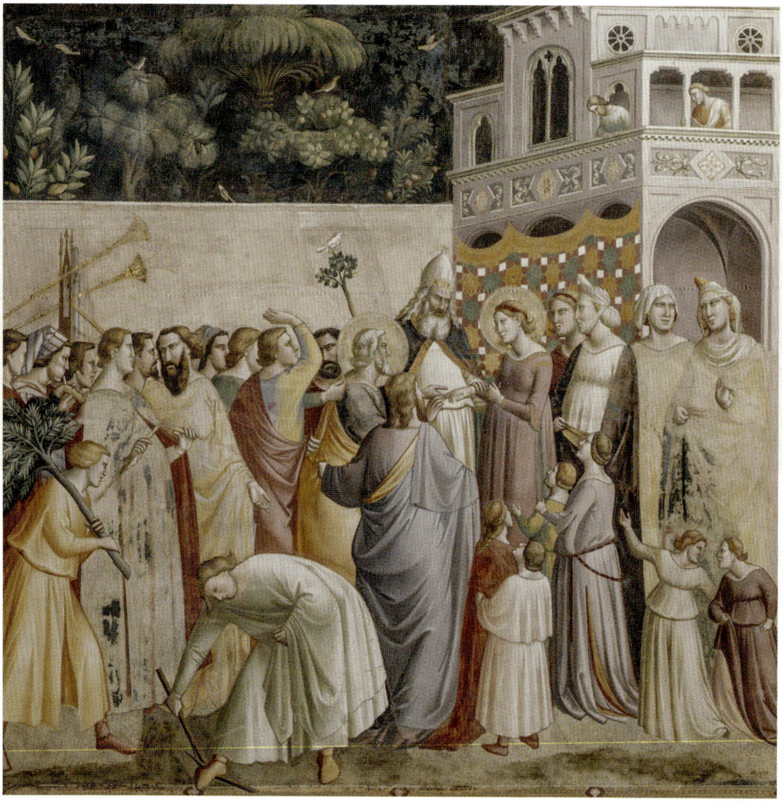

Note the decorative details on the building and the vivid depiction of birds perched in the lush foliage in the background. Such eye-catching diversions never appear in Giotto's frescoes.

29. Taddeo Gaddi, *Marriage of the Virgin*, 1330, Baroncelli Chapel, left wall.

In the *Marriage of the Virgin* (fig. 29) Taddeo follows Giotto's conventional placement of figures across the foreground and bathes them in a light that simulates the natural light that streams in from the window. The brash rainbow of colors, the linear treatment of the figures—many are outlined—and the patterned tapestry hung on the façade of a building all point to Taddeo's continued interest in probing the decorative side of a scene. What's more, this riot of fanciful, elongated characters threatens to distract from the marriage ceremony itself, an unholy transgression of Giotto's simplicity and focus, but delightful nonetheless.

ON THE ALTAR WALL NEXT TO THE STAINED GLASS WINDOW

In the *Annunciation to the Shepherds* (fig. 30, also shown in fig. 27), Taddeo confronts the knotty problem of choosing a light source for a scene next to a window. Since the ambient light admitted from the window leaves the surrounding wall in comparative darkness, Taddeo can't deploy natural light to mimic his pictorial light. Instead, he illuminates the two shepherds in the foreground by a supernatural light that we can see emanates from the angel. The intensity of this light bathes the shepherds and the rock in an unnatural golden glow rendered with remarkable realism. But the absence of cast shadows that could anchor these figures to the rock leaves them floating above. An explicit outline that defines the figures' edges—natural light does not reveal outline—further seals these figures from the light cast upon them.

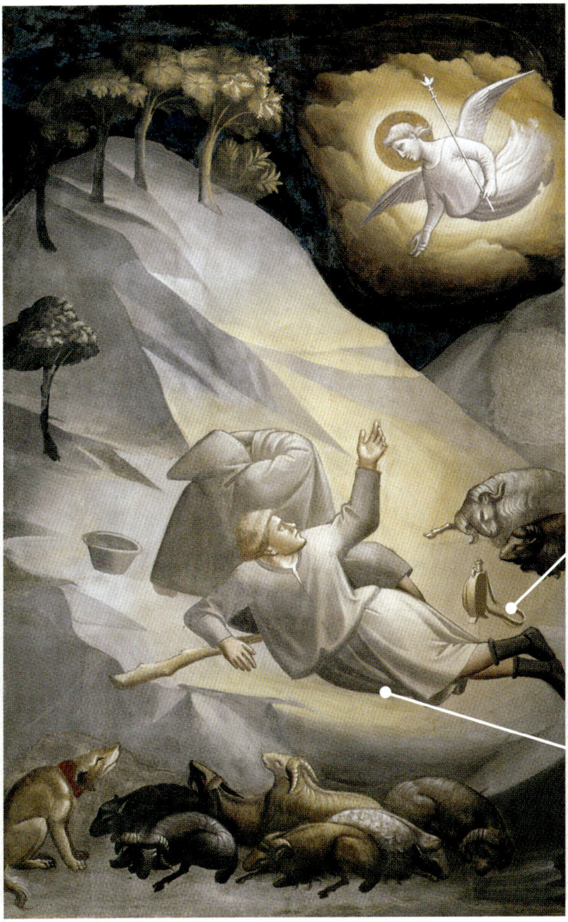

30. Taddeo Gaddi, *Annunciation to the Shepherds*, 1330, Baroncelli Chapel, altar wall.

Note: the only shadow that appears is the one left by the strap of the canteen sitting on the rock.

The absence of cast shadow gives the sense that the figures are suspended above the rock.

To reiterate the distinction between this treatment of the figure and Giotto's later style in *Trial by Fire,* we must think in terms of silhouette. Every painted object, whether its borders are blurred by open brushwork or incised by line, has a silhouette. A silhouette that has blurred (we can also say feathered) contours implies bulk; a silhouette that has hard-edge contours emphasizes shape, especially if darkly outlined. Once we distinguish the difference, we have our finger on a principal stylistic feature that divides the naturalistic relief style from the linear ornamental style (again Leonardo vs. Botticelli).

Earliest Florentine Last Supper

Taddeo Gaddi, c. 1300-1366, *Last Supper*, former refectory, 1335-40

On the former refectory wall in the last room of the museum

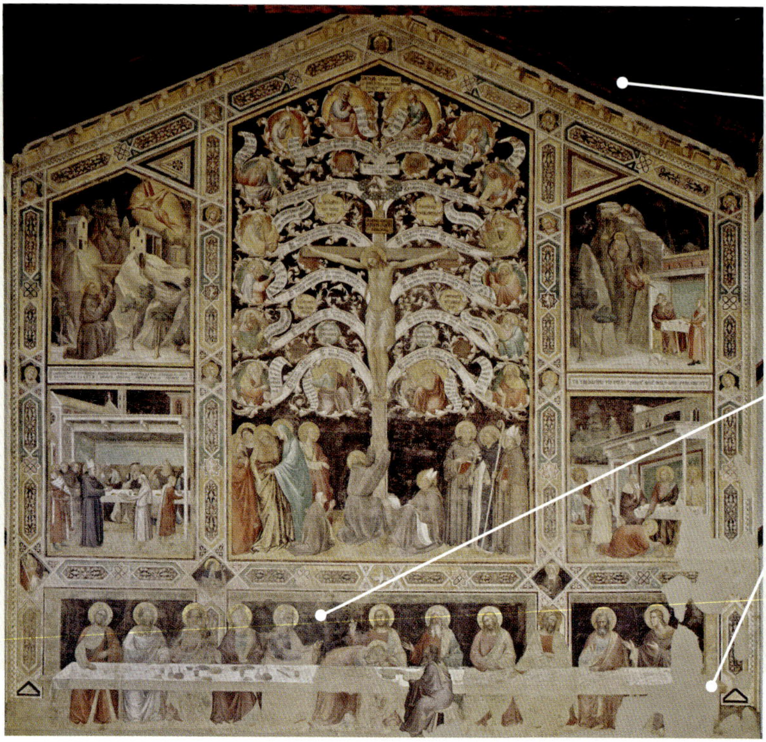

Painted corbels appear to support the refectory's roof beams.

The apostles are clearly depicted sitting in front of the decorative borders.

The top and sides of the table have been foreshortened.

31. Taddeo Gaddi, *Last Supper*, 1335-40, former refectory.

The earliest *Last Supper* in Florence follows the tradition of its being depicted on the end wall of refectory halls where monks dine in silence before scenes of Christ and the apostles. Compared to the fanciful figures and gay pastels that graced the Baroncelli frescoes, the mood here shifts back to Giotto's solemnity and earth colors.

Taddeo has set the *Last Supper* below four lateral scenes and the *Crucifixion,* which occupies the center of the *Tree of Life*. In the latter, Christ's ancestors foretell his birth, passion and resurrection. Although these scenes evoke deep space, Taddeo clearly means for them to be seen as painted decoration on the wall behind Christ and the Apostles. By placing the life-size figures in front of the decorative scenes and by foreshortening the table top, Taddeo has created the illusion of a scene that projects beyond the wall into the refectory, an important advance since rational perspective had yet to be discovered.

The subject of the *Last Supper* can be found as early as AD 200 on the walls of Roman catacombs. According to the Gospels, Christ's farewell to his apostles occurred on the night before his crucifixion when he announced that he would be betrayed by one of them and sacrificed for the absolution of humankind's sins. It was at that moment he took bread and wine, proclaiming, "This is my body and blood. Do this in commemoration of me," thus establishing the sacrament of the Eucharist reenacted in Catholic masses.

To identify the various characters, Taddeo employs traditional symbolic references. By convention, the swarthy betrayer, Judas, has black hair and lacks a halo; he is isolated across the table facing Christ. John, the youngest apostle, who stands for innocence, is always seen sleeping by Christ's side. Peter, the favored apostle who will lead the Church after Christ's resurrection, commonly sits on his other side.

Anticipating International Gothic

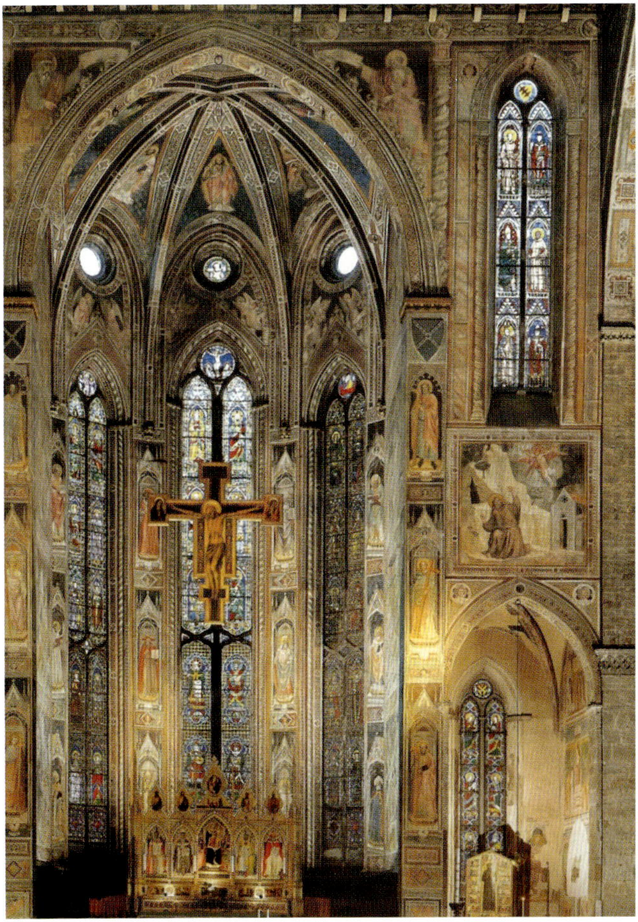

32. Cappella Maggiore (main chapel), Agnolo Gaddi's stained glass windows and *Legend of the True Cross* on the side walls. At the right is Giotto's Bardi Chapel, and on the wall above is his *Saint Francis Receiving the Stigmata.*

Agnolo Gaddi, c. 1350-1396, *Legend of the True Cross*, Cappella Maggiore, c. 1380-90

ON THE SIDE WALLS OF THE CAPPELLA MAGGIORE

These works have been under restoration from 2005 through 2013, the date of the book's printing. The chapel's fresco cycle underscores the church's dedication to the Holy Cross, in Italian, Santa Croce. It tells an apocryphal story taken from popular legend about the finding of the buried True Cross by Saint Helen, Emperor Constantine's mother, and its recovery by Emperor Heraclius after being stolen by the Persian king Chosroes. In composing his scenes, Agnolo, the son of Taddeo, dismisses Giotto's spatial organization and emphasis on the single figure in favor of a scene crammed with animated figures that enhance the wall's surface excitement.

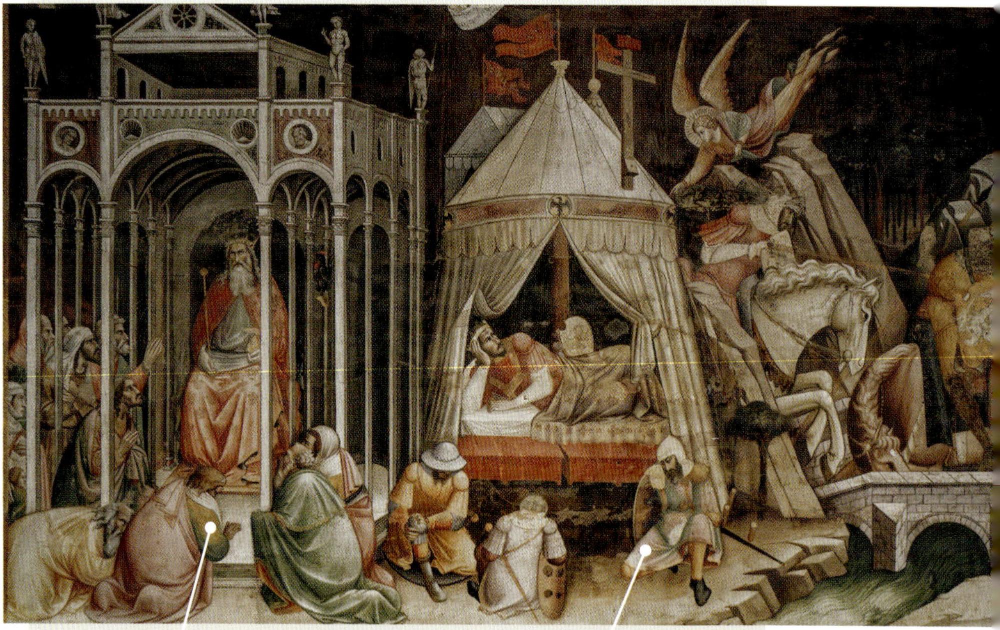

On the middle figure, a yellow sleeve shifts to green.

On the right, the soldier's green tunic shifts to violet.

33. Agnolo Gaddi, *Dream of Emperor Heraclius*, c. 1380-90, Cappella Maggiore.

The *Dream of Emperor Heraclius* is representative of the rest, but slightly less cluttered: the idolatrous king Chosroes sits enthroned in his spindly architecture, the emperor in his tent dreams of the cross's whereabouts, and finally the emperor charges on his white stallion to battle the king for its possession.

Giotto's realism plays no role in this charming, fairy-tale fantasy of heroes and villains, but the joy of color does. Here, we see for the first time a palette generously mixed with whites. The color chord itself—

green, rose, and yellow—is closer to Taddeo's palette than to Giotto's earth colors. In his modeling, he follows both artists' technique of concentrating colors in their purest state in the shadows of the folds; to connote the light that bleaches out puffed-up contours, he mixes white in his colors. The richness in the soft contrasts within a single robe and between robes of different colors yields a broad field of pastel patterns of tapestry-like beauty. In contrast, Giotto emphasizes the single figure. In some passages, Agnolo follows his father's artificial color shifts, most notably in the middle figure in rose robe kneeling before the king where a yellow sleeve bleeds to green, and in the soldier sleeping on bended knee where the same green turns to light violet.

Agnolo's frescoes bring to a close a tradition that history describes as the Age of Giotto. In point of fact, they are far removed from Giotto. More so than his father's art, Agnolo's is ornamental and nothing suggests visual reality.

Even though Agnolo is not an essential stepping-stone from Giotto to artists of the Renaissance, we must judge him only partially as the exhausted finale to the century. Rather, his art anticipates the coming International Gothic style, of which his pupil, Lorenzo Monaco, was Florence's chief exponent.

PAINTINGS IN THE NAVE

The paintings in the nave represent the waning years of Florentine creativity, a period called the Counter Reformation. In the mid-sixteenth century, some clerics of the newly emerging Protestant faith denounced images in churches as idolatrous. To appease the reformers, Pope Paul IV forbade church painting that did not naturalistically depict the messages of Christian stories. Consequently, in 1565, Duke Cosimo de' Medici commissioned the paintings to accord with Church doctrine. The blatant artistic excess—artificial color and provocative nudity—that had been so fundamental to the art of the previous period, a style called Mannerism, were left entirely to the private domain, which in the main meant art of the Medici Court. We will explore the art of the Counter Reformation more thoroughly at Santa Maria Novella, and we will study in detail two variations of Mannerism in the museum here, as well as a whole range of subspecies of this highly complex, often troubling art in museums, palaces, and churches throughout Florence.

HIGH MANNERISM

IN THE LAST ROOM OF THE MUSEUM

Francesco Salviati, 1510-1563, *Deposition*, Santa Croce Museum, c. 1550

The two massive panels in the center of the museum's last room were painted for the nave before Church reformers fought to stifle Mannerism's artful extravagance. Heavily damaged in the 1966 flood, they were not restored until 2006. The results reveal a color brilliance that will challenge scholars to rewrite color's vital role in this period. Mannerist color can lead the eye across the canvas by its dazzlingly chromatic surface patterns, as it does in the Salviati, or it can focus the eye on characters central to the story, as it does in the Bronzino.

Salviati is not trying to paint a realistic picture. Like many Florentines who worked in Rome, he contributed to the formation of a relief-like style that pushes figures close to the foreground in the manner of Roman relief sculpture. Figures take on the look of effervescent pastel patterns—blues, roses, oranges, greens—dispersed across the can-

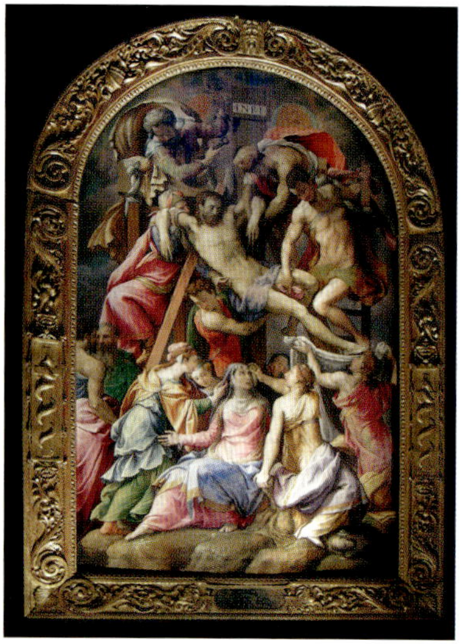

34. Francesco Salviati, *Deposition*, c. 1550, Santa Croce Museum.

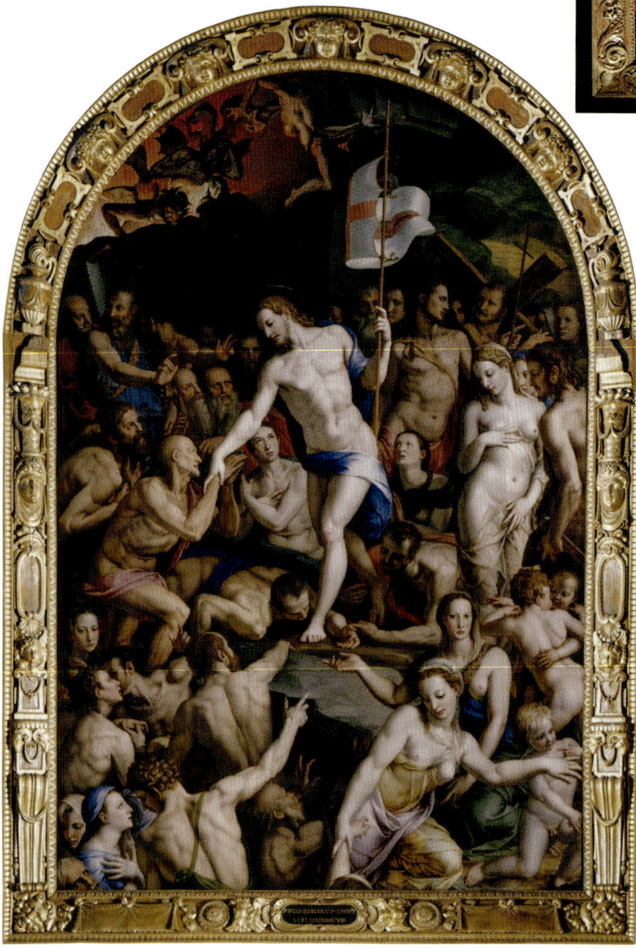

35. Agnolo Bronzino, *Descent of Christ in Limbo*, 1552, Santa Croce Museum.

vas. No shadows are permitted to subordinate their splendor. In passages these colors artificially bleed to other colors for purely ornamental effect, as they did in the Gaddi frescoes. For a scene depicting tragedy, the mood seems emotionally cool, an essential characteristic of the late Mannerist style. For no other reason than that Salviati was seen as an outsider, his picture received a cool reception in his native city.

Agnolo Bronzino, 1503-1572, *Descent of Christ in Limbo*, Santa Croce Museum, 1552

Florentines preferred their art to be conflicted with layers of meanings and images of people from history mixed with contemporary life, and Bronzino has served his audience brilliantly. Below Christ's elbow is a portrait of Bronzino's young protégé, Alessandro Allori, in the guise of the nude Isaac. Although both pictures share a tangle of contorted poses, this isn't Salviati's relief-like style. Instead, Christ occupies a centered space surrounded by a multitude of figures. Color plays a subordinate role, but where it exists, it leads the eye around the picture surface to patterns of flesh modeled into polished hardness. In this sense, Bronzino creates a tension between deep space and surface pattern that Salviati's style lacks.

Although many figures are no longer known, Florentines then could have identified all of them. On the upper left, dressed in blue, is Bronzino's self-portrait in the guise of King David. Beside Allori-Isaac, the voluptuous nude on the right is taken from the ancient statue, *Venus Pudica,* then in the Medici collection. The old man Christ raises from Limbo is the picture's patron. At the lower border, a woman pulls up a figure we can't see, but her sensual pose, legs spread and breasts pushed up to the picture plane, make us wonder why the Church waited so long to clamp down on wayward art. Mannerist artists, however, were pretty deft at such passages, inviting their audience to untangle complex inferences. To us it may seem strange that Florentines would have seen this sensual creature as a manifestation of divine beauty on earth.

Counter-Reformation Restraints

Alessandro Allori, 1535-1607, *Deposition*, Santa Croce Museum, 1571

Caught in the vice of the restrictions on antinaturalism imposed by the Reform movement, Allori is searching for a voice he could adapt to Church dictates. What remains of the High Mannerist style is subtly suggested in the lower zone where the glassy gray iridescence of the Roman soldier's skin-tight jersey conflicts with the picture's more sober colors.

The picture's pervasive shadows and its rich, golden light that evocatively models the soft borders of the flesh tones extend a lineage begun by

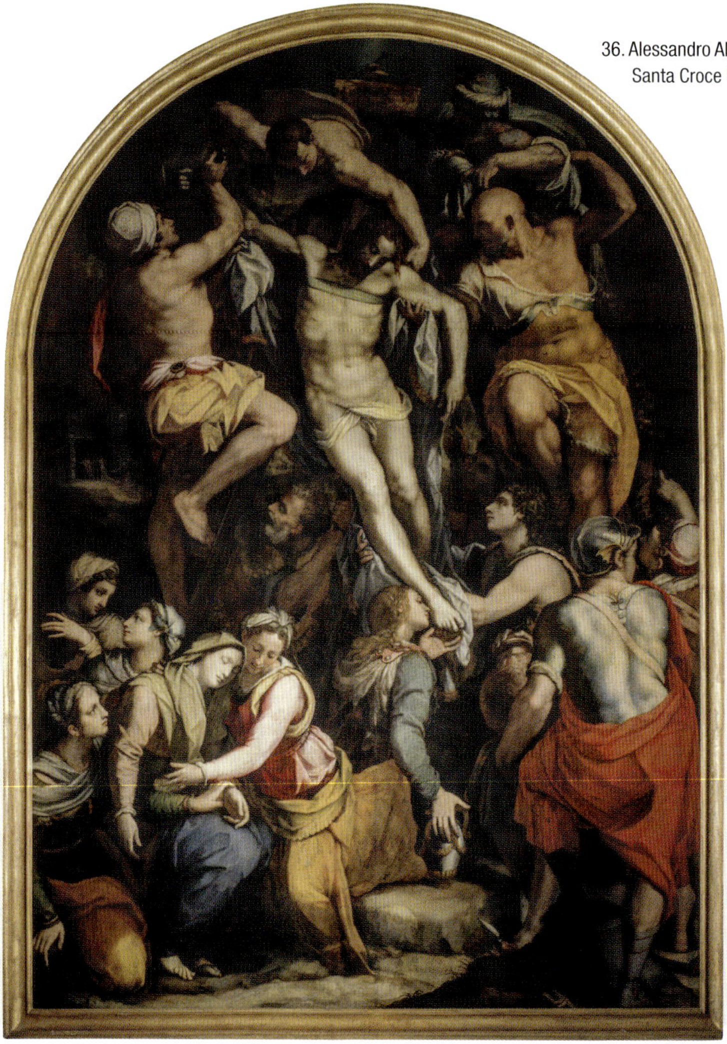

36. Alessandro Allori, *Deposition*, 1571, Santa Croce Museum.

The subject of Christ being lowered from the cross appears at the very beginning of Florentine art in the tiny side panels of a painted Crucifix (figs. 11, 55, 57). Four hundred years later, Allori's version is representative of the best art of its time.

Leonardo da Vinci. Ever since Leonardo, most artists, excepting Michelangelo, had experimented with the potential of the interplay between shadow and light to evoke a mood or to highlight a scene's protagonists. But the massively muscled figures lowering Christ show the powerful influence of Michelangelo. In a scene describing the death of a loved one, the mourners' expressions and gestures lack the simple conviction that Giotto captured in the monks' mourning of Saint Francis. We get the feeling that Allori is uncomfortable depicting scenes of tragedy, having spent his formative years under the tutelage of Bronzino, whose Mannerist style stressed the elegance of the human figure rather than emotional states.

Cimabue, c. 1240-1313, Crucifix, Santa Croce Museum, c. 1280-85

This too suffered the indignities of sixteen feet of water lapping at the minute, laboriously applied, seven-hundred-year old brushstrokes of once-luminous flesh tones. The image hovers between tragic corporeal death and spiritual triumph, and between remote Byzantine elegance and forceful Tuscan expression. Of the Byzantine, there is the sweeping arc of a slender body and the elongated arms abstracted from nature. Of the Florentine, there is the agony of the face and the anatomical demarcations painted in soft tones across the torso, a technique that Giotto would improve on. Like no other painting of its era, this Cimabue crucifix stands as the last expression of a towering master who captured the moment when an enduring medieval spirit intersected a timeless human one.

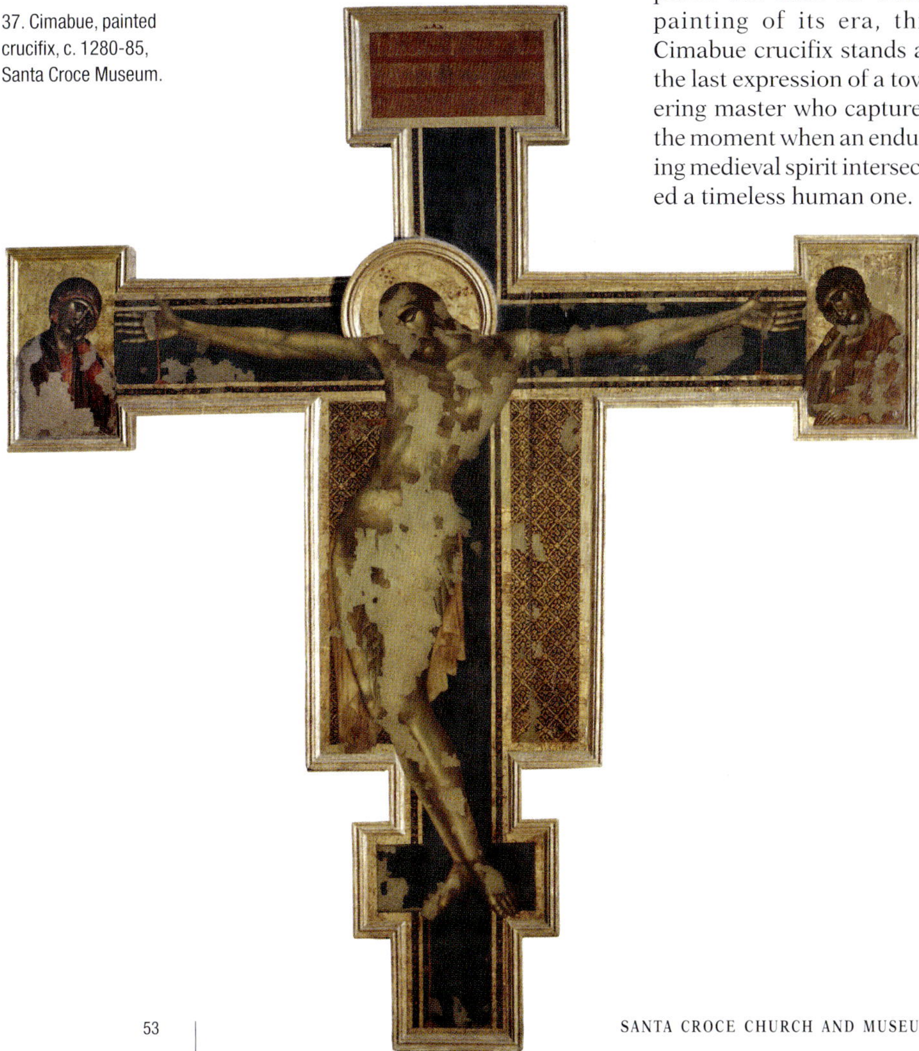

37. Cimabue, painted crucifix, c. 1280-85, Santa Croce Museum.

PLAGUE, REVOLT, HUMANISM, THE MEDICI, 1348–1433

The first quarter of the fifteenth century has always been singled out for the burst of artistic activity that laid the foundation for the Renaissance. But a closer look at Florentine society brings into view a sorrier picture. In 1344, the Bardi and Peruzzi banking families, whose burial chapels in Santa Croce bear their names, went bankrupt on bad loans to the king of England, nearly bringing down the economy of the whole city. In 1348 the Black Death struck. Killing half of its population of roughly one hundred thousand, with survivors throwing the corpses of their loved ones out onto the street, the plague ranked as the city's worst disaster. Uncertain when the next plague would strike—and it did, repeatedly—the populace submitted to religious obsession. Not surprisingly, no top-flight artists emerged in the next half century. One of the few commissions during this period was the decoration of the Strozzi di Mantova Chapel in Santa Maria Novella (1357), which reveals the dark side of church doctrine.

REVOLT

Some scholars see these years as a period of opportunity. A smaller population meant cloth workers were in high demand. Wages rose, and immigrants flooded the city, creating a greater need for basic goods. By the 1370s the population had grown to seventy thousand. But a series of plagues and famines cut the population to around forty thousand. The streets had become contracted, pestilent, and crowded with a desperately impoverished populace. With competition rising from the English and the Dutch, the wool industry, which had provided wealth for decades, sank into a deep depression, making work scarce. The messy plight of the lowly cloth workers, who had been forbidden their own guild, finally forced a series of violent strikes, culminating in 1378 in what is called the Ciompi revolt. It is here that the Medici name first turns up. One Salvestro de' Medici played a role in supporting the demands of all the workers on the bottom rungs of society, a prescient fact that carried far-reaching consequences. Wealth, now obtained through international trade and banking rather than from the wool industry, was concentrated in the hands of the patrician and mercantile families. Yet the specter of social anarchy had a profound impact on the mentality on all sectors above the urban poor. With the support of the population from the shop-keepers on up, the major guilds ruthlessly suppressed the wool workers and took over once again the highest posts of government. After the repression of the Ciompi the city was governed by an oligarchy of the patrician and merchant classes.

In 1400, Florence's population still hovered around forty thousand. With its resources impoverished, Milan was threatening to overtake the city when, in 1402, (the year after the Baptistry door competition), the leader of the Milanese troops, Duke Gian Galeazzo Visconti, suddenly died of the plague. It was in this period that a modest and cautious man, Giovanni di Bicci de'

Medici (1360-1429) amassed a fortune and left a line of descendants who, beginning with Cosimo, overshadowed all political groups to such a degree that the history of Florence is all but subsumed within the history of the Medici.

In 1429, the year that Giovanni di Bicci died, Florence began a four-year campaign against their hated enemy, Lucca. Critical of bungled battles that exhausted the city's treasury, an incensed populous split into two factions: the followers of the patrician Rinaldo degli Albizzi, who had supported the war, against the middle-class followers of Cosimo, who dared not oppose it. Despite his wealth, Cosimo was no match for the ancient dynasty. In 1433, Rinaldo orchestrated his exile.

Status of the Arts

Given that the affairs of the city were so demonstrably fragile, how was it that the city prospered? It did so for two reasons. First, its citizenry believed in the destiny of a Roman birthright, a legacy shaped by a profoundly Christian culture. Second, no other city could boast a sculptor-architect like Arnolfo di Cambio (died c. 1313), a man of letters like Dante (died 1321), a painter like Giotto (died 1337), and a poet like Petrarch (died 1374). These giants of the arts set a standard for later artists and their patrons. And whether by fate or by virtue of intellectual cross-currents germinating within the culture, a new generation revitalized their cause: Brunelleschi, Ghiberti, Donatello, Masaccio, and the humanist scholars could be counted among its number. Financed by the wealthiest guilds in the opening decade of the Quattrocento, the first three of these artists discovered one-point perspective, cast the Baptistry's second bronze doors, decorated the façade of the Duomo with sculptures that were to be the spiritual protectors against forces threatening the city.

Humanism and the Cult of Antiquity

Beginning in the mid-1300s, Petrarch's influence proved seminal for the development of humanism, which in the early Renaissance dominated Florentine intellectual life in ways that never touched other Italian cities. Captivating the Florentine intelligentsia with his devotion to writers of antiquity—to Plato, Livius, Virgil, and Cicero—Petrarch inspired generations of patricians to study the original texts in Latin for their stylistic eloquence and rhetorical force. As a cultural movement centered on learning, humanism promoted an active civic life for the common good. No longer satisfied with strictly Christian solutions to moral problems, humanists searched for a code of conduct befitting of a new age that emphasized the uniqueness of human experiences over the immateriality of the divine.

2. Orsanmichele

Turning Points

In no other place can the pride and competitive spirit of the guilds be better seen than at Orsanmichele. The prestigious Wool Producers and Wool Finishers guilds (Arte della Lana and Arte di Calimala), the wood and stone workers, sword makers, bankers, butchers, and tanners guilds spared no expense in hiring the city's top sculptors. These statues,

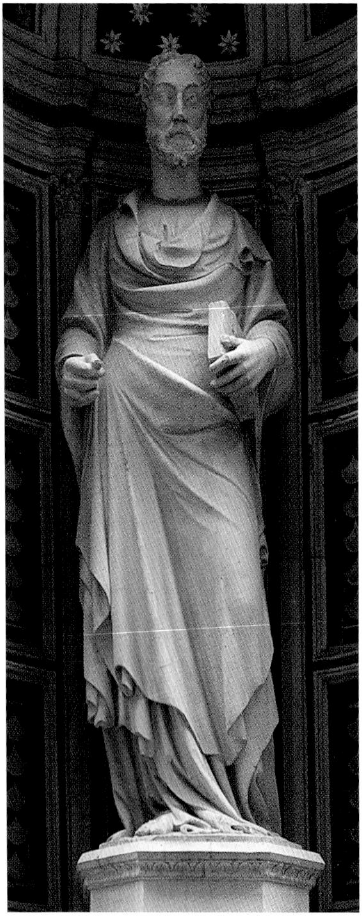

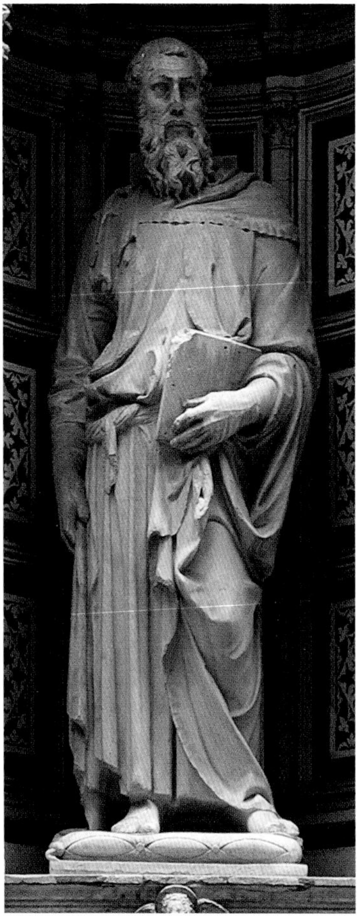

38. Niccolò Lamberti (attributed), *Saint James*, c. 1410, Orsanmichele (original in Orsanmichele Museum).

39. Donatello, *Saint Mark*, c. 1411, Orsanmichele (original in Orsanmichele Museum).

along with those meant for the Cathedral façade, were the first to be created since the Great Plague of 1348. Due to their life-size proportions and easy accessibility in their outside niches, they offered artists—foremost Masaccio, painter of the Brancacci Chapel—an unparalleled opportunity to study the development of the human figure.

The statue to the left of the seated *Madonna of the Rose* (c. 1399), an early fifteenth-century rendering of *Saint James* attributed to Niccolò Lamberti (c. 1370-c. 1425; fig. 38), provides the clearest idea of the late Gothic style: a stiff figure facing frontally like a sentry-box soldier; an indifference to anatomical accuracy; and a limp pose that suggests nothing of the potential for movement.

The statue represents the conservative *status quo* at the turn of the century, the tired end of an era as yet untouched by a new style that would rock convention. Lamberti was scheduled to sculpt the figure for the niche to the left, but was relieved of the honor.

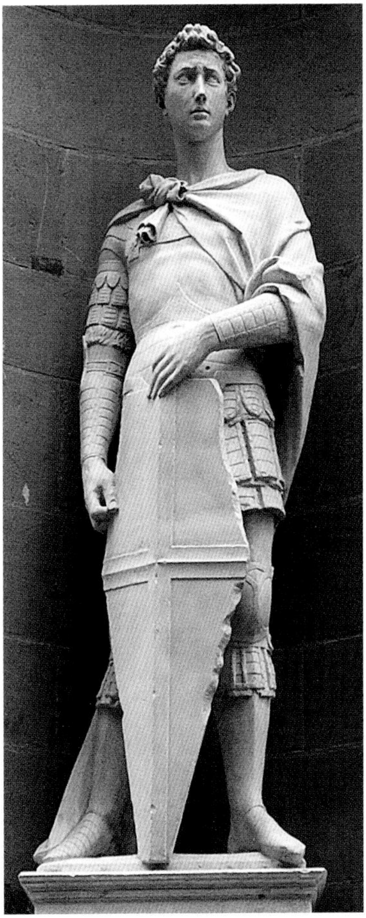

40. Donatello, *Saint George*, c. 1416, Orsanmichele (original in Bargello Museum).

That honor went to the young Donatello (1386-1466), who had been an assistant in Ghiberti's workshop during the early years of crafting the Baptistry's second pair of bronze doors. He began his career in 1408 at the age of twenty-two and ended it sixty years later, as the greatest sculptor of the Quattrocento.

Donatello's *Saint Mark* (c. 1411), commissioned by the Linen Weavers guild, ranks as one the major advances in Western art (fig. 39). Notice how Mark's powerful body confronts us from an angle. His stance is firm and resolute, yet charged with the potential for movement: a perfect equilibrium balancing strength with languid repose. We have no doubts as to how his body works beneath the drapery. He stands on his weight-bearing right leg and slackens the left in a true *contrapposto*, a posture in which one side of the body compensates for the weight of the other. Donatello's mastery of the standing pose forever changed the visual language of the human form and marks the true beginning of the Renaissance.

Around the next two corners is a second work by Donatello, *Saint George*, commissioned by the Armorers and Sword Makers guild in 1416 (fig. 40). His stance, a slight *contrapposto*, is set well forward in the niche so it can be viewed from the sides. His expression and frame are taut with the concentration of one who is about to battle a dragon. His right hand once held a sword or spear. Rivaling the *Saint Mark* for its invention, the advances here lie in the statue's silhouette where the line of the torso continues down the shield.

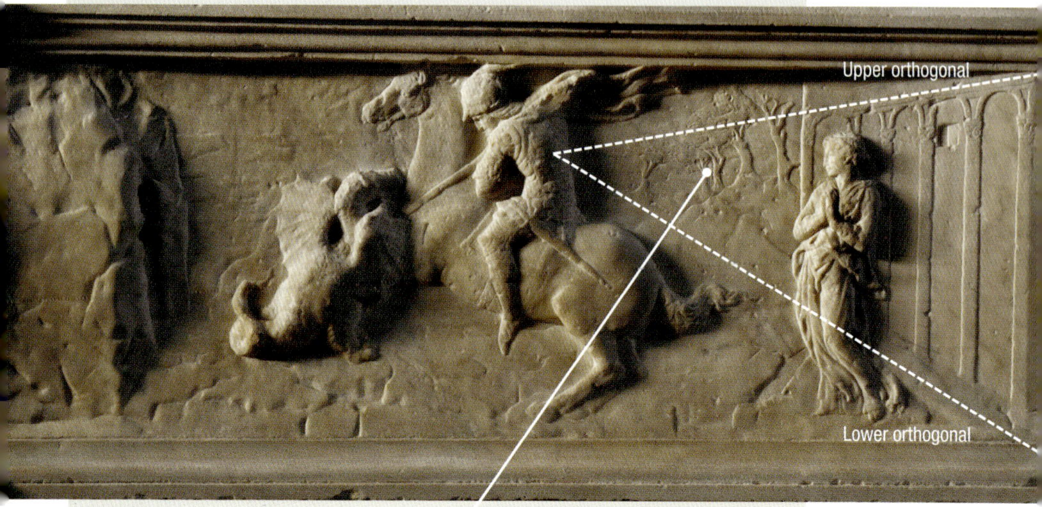

Note (only visible on site) that the surfaces meant to depict distance have been roughly carved, so that the crystalline surfaces break up light, producing the effect of atmospheric haze.

41. Donatello, *Saint George and the Dragon* relief, Orsanmichele (original in Bargello Museum).

Below the statue is a small relief of *Saint George and the Dragon* (the original, in the Bargello Museum, is in better condition); it is inconspicuous and deceptively simple, yet its consequences for painting were enormous. The tradition of sculptural relief dates back to elaborate battle scenes depicted on Roman monuments. The spatial depth of these scenes was limited to the actual size of one or two overlapped figures. Here Donatello confines his carving to its shallowest limits in order to confront the problem of spatial illusion. In the center, we see Saint George, a fourth-century knight, astride his rearing horse at the moment of piercing the dragon with his lance. On the left, an ominous cave; on the right, the lovely princess in her fluttering gown poses in a sinuous Gothic sway—a reminder that Donatello is still working in a Gothic world. Behind the princess is an arcade with columns that allows the artist to carry off, for the first time in art, a radical application of Brunelleschi's newly invented system of one-point perspective. Notice that the arcade diminishes in size as it nears some far-off trees, so that it appears to recede into the deep space. Its roof and base act as diagonals—technically "orthogonals"—aiming right at the center of Saint George, the "single point" here. In a stroke, Donatello has shown painters how to create a coherent space and organize it around a central character.

To better appreciate Donatello's innovation, walk left to the *Four Crowned Martyrs*, sculpted around 1415 by Nanni di Banco (c. 1385-1421). It, too, moves away from Gothic curves and towards figures whose classically idealized heads and careworn, individualized faces look more Ro-

42. Nanni di Banco, *Four Crowned Martyrs*, c. 1415, Orsanmichele (originals in Orsanmichele Museum).
43. Lorenzo Ghiberti, *Saint John the Baptist*, 1413-16, Orsanmichele (original in Orsanmichele Museum).

man than Gothic. Note how skillfully the sculptor captures the tense bond shared by the four figures, as they were to be executed by Emperor Diocletian in the third century for refusing to sculpt a pagan god. In the relief below, we find, in contrast to Donatello's use of perspective, a perfect example of the Roman classical relief style, with space limited by the actual depth of the carved figures. Yet this carving of sculptors in their workshop faithfully replicates how Nanni himself is excavating their forms.

Finally, on via Calzaioli, Florence's first large-scale sculpture in bronze, Ghiberti's *Saint John the Baptist* (1412-16). Commissioned by the powerful Wool Finisher's Guild or Arte di Calimala, this costly statue holds pride of place on the front corner on the building. The figure

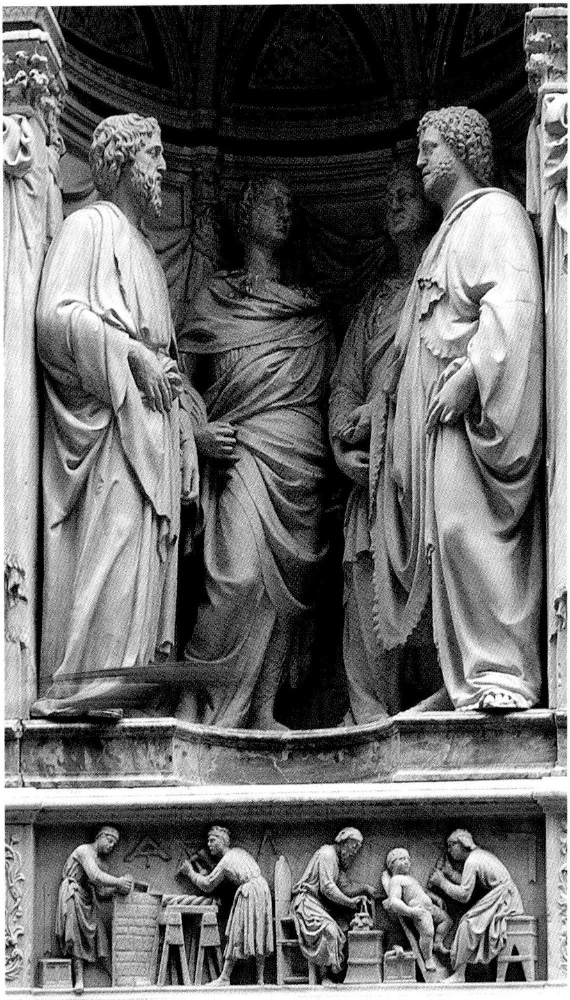

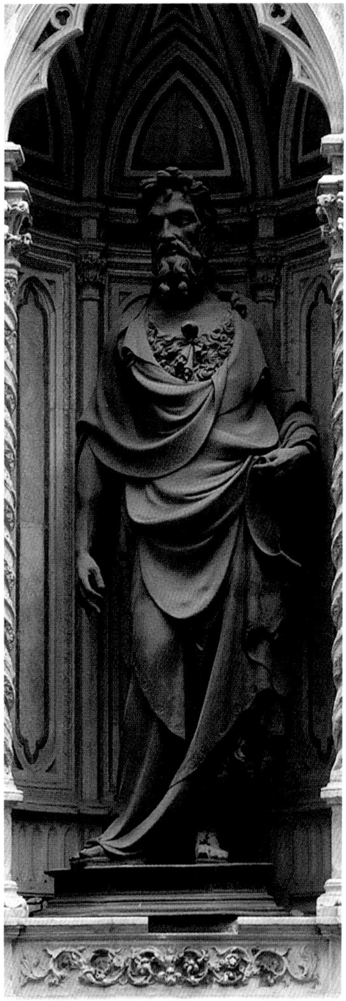

meets us frontally in an S-shaped sway, an essential characteristic of the International Gothic style then sweeping across Northern Europe, and which Ghiberti was then investigating in the Baptistry doors. The emphasis is on the drapery, very bold and deeply modeled, as is the face. The pattern of crisscrossing crisp folds projects a distinct linear quality that doesn't reveal much about the body beneath, but both face and drapery convey something of the wild fanatic who roamed the desert in biblical times. Ghiberti's lively International Gothic elegance, which would soon be deemed old fashioned, contrasts markedly with Donatello's raw physicality. The seeds of these two opposing styles, the one decorative and linear (especially when seen in the context of the painted figure) and the other naturalistic, would define both sculpture and painting for much of the century.

Gothic Sculpture and Painting

Andrea Orcagna, active c. 1344-1368, Tabernacle, Orsanmichele, 1349-59

Orsanmichele Interior

The fourteenth century has been called the great age of painting, but for sculpture it was an age of decline after the plague (1348). Orcagna's extravagantly inlaid marble Tabernacle represents the finest of that era. The façade, carved with spiraling Gothic columns and saints standing guard over its portals, resembles an elaborate Gothic church. Nothing so sumptuous would be carved again. But, in approaching the individual scenes, we must suspend our sense of logic, for they are intricate, fussy, and out of scale with one another. Commissioned after the plague as a thanks offering, it was designed to contain Florence's famed miracle-working image described below.

Bernardo Daddi, c. 1290-1348, *Madonna and Child with Saints*, Orsanmichele, 1348

Daddi, who likely died in the plague just after completing this altarpiece, was one of Giotto's most prominent followers. Though he had earlier worked in fresco in Santa Croce, attempting to interpret the master's sober realism, his talents were best suited to intimate, gentle scenes of the Madonna painted in tempera on wood panels, where color played its role as pure ornament. This elegant, jewel-like example, composed mainly of burnished gold and costly ultramarine blue, is one of the finest paintings in all the Trecento (fourteenth century).

44. Bernardo Daddi, *Madonna and Child with Saints* altarpiece, 1348, Orsanmichele.

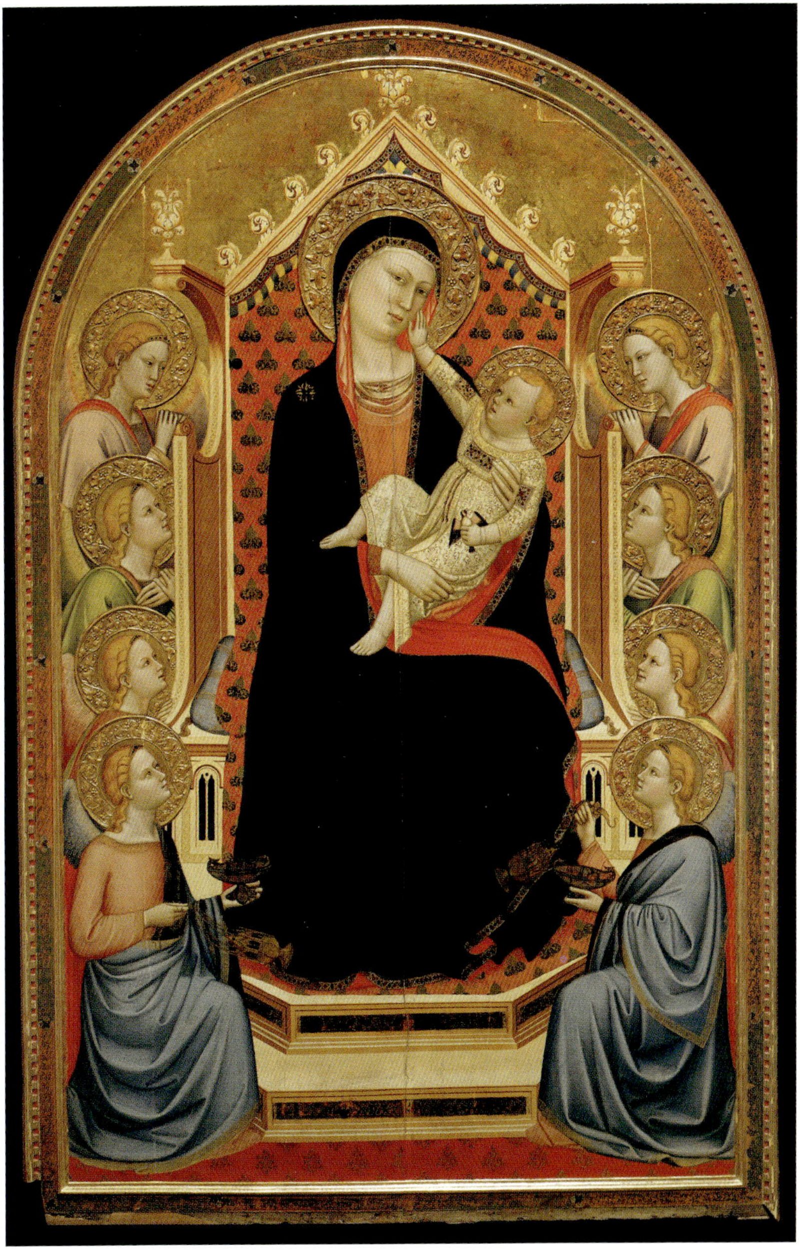

Medici Dynasty, the Rule of Genius, 1434-1492

THE AGE OF COSIMO DE' MEDICI, 1389-1464

In 1434, when Medici followers succeeded in overturning Cosimo's exile, Florence faced threats on all fronts. Venice, with a vast fleet of warships in control of the high seas, was consumed with protecting its trading routes. Milan, under the Visconti dukes, remained a constant danger from the north, while the king of Naples threatened to strike from the south (he died en route). In Rome, the papacy, just recovered from the Great Schism, had begun to wrest control over the city from powerful baronial families.

The Rise of Cosimo de' Medici

Cosimo de' Medici inherited a vast fortune from his father Giovanni di Bicci. On the strength of his business empire, Giovanni had become banker to the papacy in 1415, with funds from interest rates pouring into Medici hands. That Cosimo became the richest man in Europe was due chiefly to this connection. But Giovanni left more than wealth, bequeathing to his son the Medici Party, which Cosimo expanded by slow, inconspicuous, and illegal manipulation. Formed of the lesser ranks of the political class, whose allegiance he had cultivated over many years, the Medici Party under Cosimo began to control the pulse of Florentine political life. With the instincts of a feudal lord, Giovanni had married off Cosimo to Contessina Bardi, the daughter of the poor but prestigious family whose ancestors owned Santa Croce's Bardi Chapel. To elevate his son's status further, Giovanni employed the finest humanist tutors to educate him in the classics.

The year of his return from exile, Cosimo at first moved cautiously. But events soon propelled him to virtual leadership of the city's political machinery. His strength among the voting members of the commune provided the support he needed to exile his arch-enemy, Rinaldo degli Albizzi, and seventy members of his clan.

In diplomatic affairs, Cosimo was a master strategist. One of his most important achievements was the choice of Florence as the seat of the Ecumenical Council of 1439 which was also attended by members of the Eastern Orthodox Church. With the death of the last of the Visconti dukes, defeated by the Florentine army in the battle of Anghiari (1440), the mercenary soldier Francesco Sforza stepped in as leader of Milan. Soon in need of funds, he signaled Cosimo, who saw an opportunity that his father would never have risked: the funding of a potential enemy. In making the loan, he formed a workable alliance that tipped the balance of power in northern Italy in favor of Florence. In 1453, the loss of the eastern Mediterranean to the Turks forced the Venetians to advance onto the Italian mainland. But the Milan-Florence axis proved decisive, forcing Venice into a treaty that lasted forty years.

Character and Interests

Little is known of Cosimo in his youth. He doesn't make his appearance on the public stage until his father's death. He was then forty. Representations of him in works of art reveal an old man with a gaunt, careworn face. He suffered greatly from gout, a crippling affliction that he passed onto his son, Piero, and his grandson, Lorenzo. When not submerged in his business affairs, he nurtured his passion for ancient classical literature, particularly Plato and Aristotle. Contemporary humanists who were his social equals portray him as a man who balanced an active life with a contemplative one.

Cosimo's interest in the arts was restricted mainly to architecture and sculpture. When the time came to build a larger palace on present-day Via Cavour, he hired Michelozzo, instead of Brunelleschi. Brunelleschi made certain that his buildings broke new ground. Cosimo wanted his architect to design something that wouldn't call attention to his wealth. He turned to Brunelleschi for the renovation of San Lorenzo's nave, however. For the decoration of the church's Old Sacristy, Cosimo sought out Donatello. Their relationship lasted thirty years. In the last decade of his life, he hired his friend to cast bronze pulpits for San Lorenzo. Cosimo died during their construction, at the age of seventy-five. Donatello died just as they were completed, at the age of eighty. Both men are buried in the church, Cosimo in the floor in front of the main altar, side by side with Donatello.

Beyond doubt, Cosimo's business and political prowess contributed greatly to Florence's stability during the mid-Quattrocento. While he strongly encouraged the leading humanists of the day, he had little influence over the direction of the arts. And although he oversaw the renovation of San Marco, patronizing Fra Angelico, and funded more projects than his contemporaries had, he did not fund Santo Spirito, Brunelleschi's masterpiece.

THE AGE OF LORENZO THE MAGNIFICENT, 1464-1492

When Cosimo died his son Piero walked into the leadership of the Florentine state. But Piero did not possess the kind of charisma, cunning, and foresight that his father had exhibited. Stricken with gout, he lived only five years after his father died. Yet his legacy is remarkable in several respects, not the least of which was his marriage to Lucrezia Tornabuoni, a shrewd and highly intelligent woman with whom he bore a son, Lorenzo. Considering his sickly nature—he died at age fifty-three—Piero successfully fought off the only threat to his regime, which came from families dispossessed by Cosimo.

In the arts his tastes were capacious, spending lavishly on painting that ran mainly to the precious. His major project was the decoration of the chapel in the Medici Palace, for which he hired Fra Angelico's student, Benozzo Gozzoli, the last to paint in a style reminiscent of the International Gothic.

Consolidation of a Regime: Lorenzo de' Medici

When his father died, Lorenzo, at age twenty, was prevailed upon by a group of six-hundred citizens to step in as ruler. Almost immediately, he discovered that the Medici bank had made bad loans to the Duke of Burgundy through an unscrupulous agent. Seizing on Lorenzo's vulnerability, Pope Sixtus IV severed relations with the Medici bank and transferred the papal treasury to a rival firm run by the old aristocratic Pazzi family. The move forced Lorenzo to borrow funds, and when he was unable to repay them, he had to turn over country palaces and large tracts of land.

Like his grandfather Cosimo, Lorenzo

was a keen observer of the political landscape. Knowing the pope had ambitions to see his own family in control of central Italy, Lorenzo recognized his life was in danger. Minor attempts to unseat him came to nothing until 1478, when the Pazzi conspiracy was unleashed with the support of the pope. During high mass in the Duomo, at the moment the host was elevated, members of the Pazzi jumped on Lorenzo and his younger brother Giuliano. Giuliano died on the spot of multiple knife wounds, but Lorenzo, with a slash in his neck, fought off the attackers with his sword and fled the cathedral. Outraged citizens soon hacked many of the conspirators to pieces and hung others, including the bishop of Pisa, from the Palazzo Vecchio. After the plot failed, the pope excommunicated Lorenzo and, with the backing of Naples, sent his armies to menace Florence. Seeing the tide of the conflict turn in favor of his enemies, Lorenzo struck out on a mission, whose failure would have changed the history of Florence. Passing alone through enemy lines, Lorenzo arrived at the court of Naples in 1479. So captivated was the king by Lorenzo's charm and his knowledge of the arts, that he decided to withdraw his troops from Tuscany, and the pope, who lost his strongest ally, made peace. Lorenzo returned to Florence a triumphant savior. But with France on the rise, Lorenzo spent his last years mediating between Italy's warring city-states to deprive the French forces of an excuse to cross the Alps.

When the time came to arrange their son's marriage, Piero and Lucrezia chose a member of the great Orsini family. The Orsini ranked as one Rome's oldest families, with large landholdings throughout Italy. Because they were soldiers, their alliance would secure Lorenzo's position. By upper class standards, Lorenzo's marriage to Clarice Orsini appeared to be correct and dutiful. If he wasn't devoted to her, he was loyal. They raised eight children, one of whom, Giovanni, the future Pope Leo X, was appointed cardinal at age thirteen, an uncontroversial decision with far-reaching implications.

Lorenzo's Character

Lorenzo the Magnificent was an extraordinary and complicated man. Not only did his accomplishments place him at the top of the political hierarchy in Italy, his public persona and private life today merit the label, Renaissance man. He excelled at falconry and horsemanship, engaging in jousts amidst lavish public fanfare. Although Lorenzo did not directly patronize the major arts, he did commission Andrea del Verrocchio, Botticelli and Filippino Lippi to decorate the banners and standards that attended these events. He also recognized the young Michelangelo's genius and invited him to study the sculptures in the gardens of the Medici palace.

Above all, he was an esteemed poet and an intellectual who surrounded himself with the most gifted humanists in Italy. This was no small matter, for this group founded the Neo-Platonic Academy. It was their theories on beauty and love that profoundly influenced Michelangelo and formed the philosophical basis for Botticelli's *Primavera*.

So long as Lorenzo lived, Florence stood as a beacon of intellectual inquiry bright with optimism. But when he died at the age of forty-three from the effects of gout, Florence lost its way as Western culture's arbiter of taste.

3. Santa Maria del Carmine, Brancacci Chapel

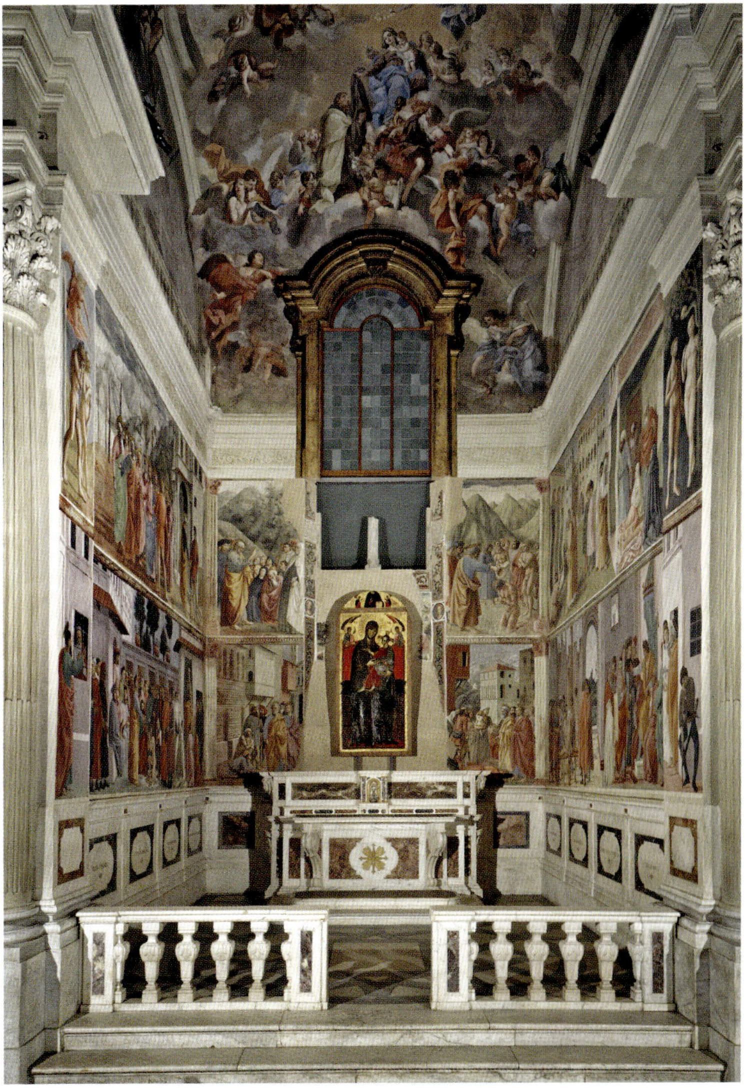

45. Brancacci Chapel with the thirteenth-century altarpiece.

The Brancacci Chapel was part of a Gothic church built in 1268, adjacent to a still-existing convent of Carmelites, and frescoed by some of the same artists who had worked in Santa Croce. The church's founders were the Carmelites, a cloistered monastic order whose roots by tradition lay in the Holy Land from the time of the Old Testament prophet Elijah (their actual origins likely date from the times of the First Crusade of 1096). Legend has it that Peter preached to the Carmelites, which accounts for their presence in several of the frescoed scenes (they are the figures in white robes). The present church, built in the Baroque style, dates from 1771 when the original structure was destroyed by fire, except for this chapel and its soot-covered frescoes, which were not cleaned until 1990.

Pietro Brancacci was the founder of the Chapel in 1367, but it was his descendant Felice Brancacci, a rich cloth merchant, who commissioned the frescoes to honor Saint Peter as the namesake of his ancestor. At one time he had been a friend of the Medici, but when he married into the archrival Strozzi family, the Medici banished him to exile, where he died in poverty. No member of the Brancacci was ever buried in their chapel.

Birth of Renaissance Painting

Masaccio (1401-1428) and Masolino (1383-c. 1440), *Life of Saint Peter*, Brancacci Chapel, c. 1424-27

It wasn't until about fifteen years after Donatello completed his *Saint Mark* on Orsanmichele that an artist managed to accomplish in paint what the sculptor had done in stone. When one finally appeared—Tommaso di Giovanni, commonly called Masaccio—he revitalized Giotto's entire pictorial language by giving a new scale and dignity to the human condition, and set painting on a course we call the Renaissance—all before his death at twenty-six. It took Masaccio and his older collaborator, Masolino, three years to fresco the *Life of Saint Peter* on the walls of this modest chapel. Seeing the work of these two masters side by side, it is easy to contrast Masolino's courtly International Gothic style, then sweeping across Europe, with the bold new realism of Masaccio.

Adam and Eve: Archetypes of Two Styles

The two scenes depicting Adam and Eve, the first sinners, in the upper left and right corners would have reminded the viewer of the reasons for Christ's sacrifice and the founding of his Church upon Peter, the ultimate redeemed sinner who had denied knowing his Lord the night before his crucifixion. In Masolino's *Temptation*, the dark background of the Garden of Eden frames the frontal poses of a lean and sensual Adam and Eve. Eve coyly sidles up to the tree as the serpent glides over her, signaling us she is

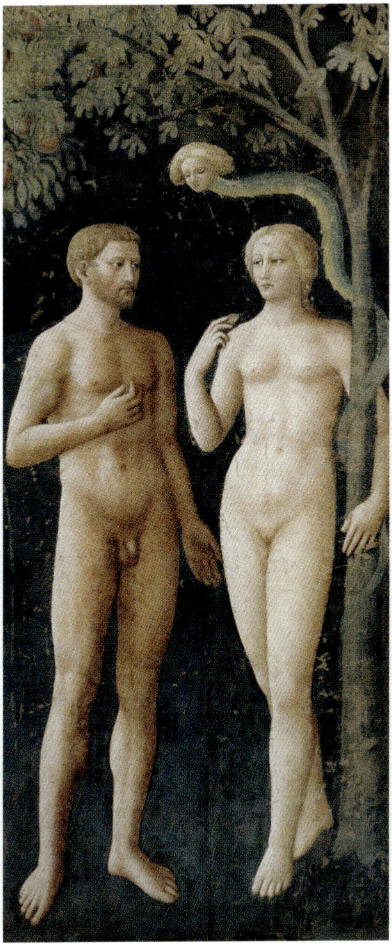

Because of the lack of cast shadows in the *Temptation* scene, Adam and Eve appear to be floating above the ground. In the *Expulsion*, the cast shadows indicate that the figure's feet are planted firmly on the ground, and that the light, as for all scenes, falls from the chapel's window on the right.

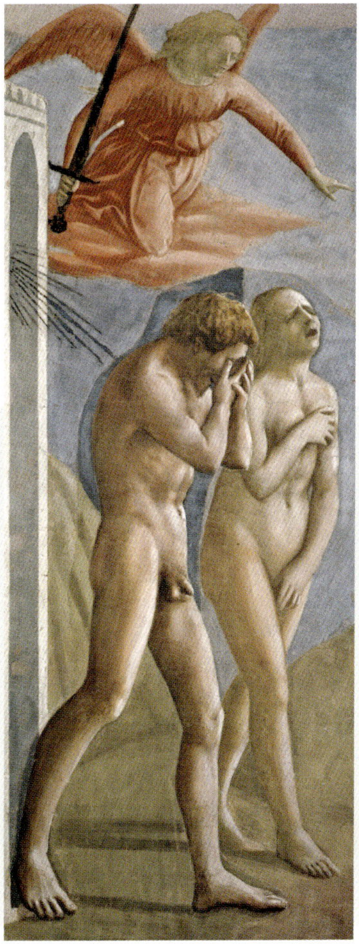

46. Masolino, *Temptation of Adam and Eve*, c. 1424-25, Brancacci Chapel.

47. Masaccio, *Expulsion from the Garden of Eden*, c. 1424-25, Brancacci Chapel.

already its captive. Delicately painted leaves provide the embracing canopy as metaphor for the sexual charge of Adam and Eve's shared disobedience. The painting is a perfect example of the International Gothic tradition: static, weightless figures with elegant silhouettes bear vacuous expressions that could stand for any willful state, such as pride or indifference.

In marked contrast, the figures in Masaccio's *Expulsion* seem almost painted in haste. Eve's eyes are little more than slits made with a stroke of the brush, and yet they, like the rest of the image, convey raw emotional power. Striding forward, Adam covers his eyes while Eve, shamed by her body, covers her breasts and genitals and howls in despair. A woeful angel hovers above, uniting them in their self-revulsion. No doubt their nudity astounded the clergy; in the next century, their genitals were covered with fig leaves until the frescoes were cleaned in 1990.

Organization of the Two Large Scenes

Viewed from the chapel's center, the space depicted in the two scenes below appears to be an extension of the space in which we are standing. The scenes share a similar color chord, which, like Giotto's, runs to earth

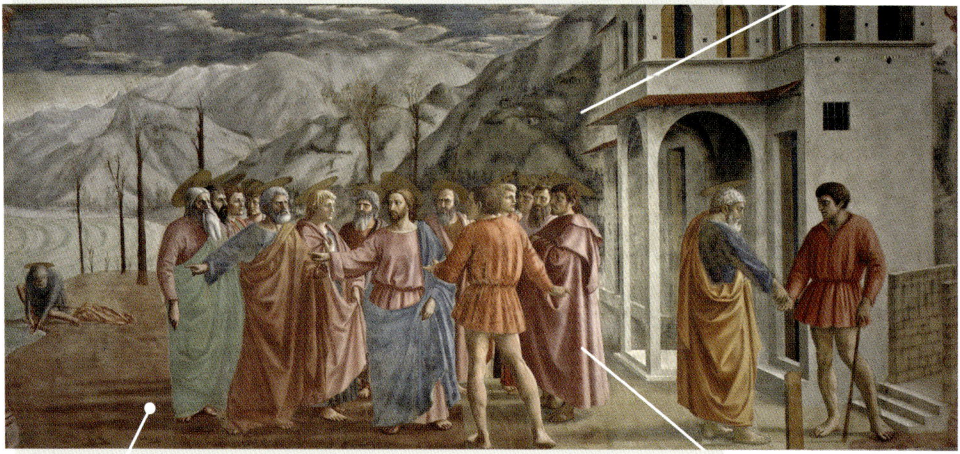

Masaccio's directed light records shadows on the ground, marking each figure's place in space. Cast shadow, lost to painting for centuries, establishes the ground level and anchors feet firmly to earth.

48. Masaccio, *Tribute Money*, c. 1425, Brancacci Chapel.

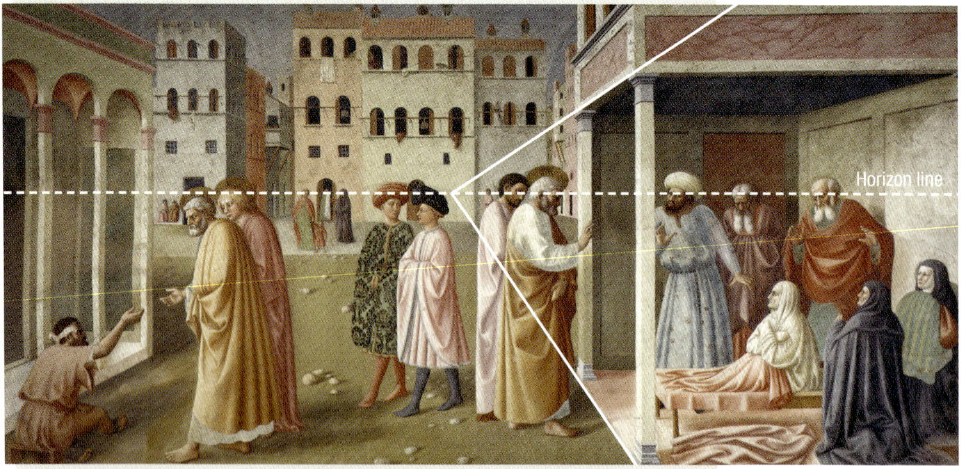

Note in both pictures how the imaginary orthogonals establish both the vanishing point and the horizon line, which in turn, corresponds to the height of the heads.

49. Masolino, *Peter Cures the Cripple and Raises Tabitha*, c. 1424-25, Brancacci Chapel.

colors. They are also linked by a common horizon line (figs. 48, 49), which corresponds to the level of the heads of all of the figures—even the tiny characters in Masolino's distant cityscape. The horizon line is established by the vanishing point, here determined by the intersection of the imaginary orthogonals that continue on from the receding top and bottom borders of the buildings in the foreground.

Masaccio and Masolino, for the first time in painting, are aligning their scenes to the same single-point perspective.

Masaccio, *Tribute Money*, Brancacci Chapel, c. 1425

In this stunning scene (fig. 48) Masaccio resurrects Giotto's vision of the grand narrative tradition he'd frescoed in Santa Croce. But Masaccio's rendering of a story set within a vast landscape was absolutely novel in the history of painting. The picture describes three moments in the life of Peter as if they were occurring simultaneously. In the center, a Roman tax collector confronts Christ and his party, demanding payment for passage across the Lake of Galilee to enter a Roman controlled town. Unperturbed, Christ directs an outraged Peter to the lake on the left to fetch a coin from the mouth of a fish. While Masaccio marginalizes the famous miracle—the coin in the fish—he does not marginalize the figure of Peter. He directs our eye to both Peter and Christ (the vanishing point coincides with Christ's head), who are surrounded by a semicircle of powerful disciples to emphasize the real theme of the story: the relationship of trust and obedience between two men, decisive leader and uncertain follower. Lastly, on the right, we see Rome's craven agent in his flimsy tunic collecting payment from a powerful Peter, monumentalized by the sweeping folds of his robes and framed by the arch overhead.

Perspective

The arch on the right, part of a custom house, plays the same role that Donatello's arcade does in the *Saint George and the Dragon* relief. Both create a convincing space for the actors to live in. The portals of Masaccio's buildings, like Donatello's, diminish in size with distance, providing an imaginary, horizontal grid that allows him to fix his actors in space and determine accurately their relative size: thus we see Peter in perfect scale at three distances. Masaccio could have nailed down more diagonals by constructing a second building on the left, but he understood (as many subsequent artists did not) that providing too many clues to a composition's perspective results in a rigid and obvious design. So he's sparing in their use, instead letting our eye meander over the distant landscape.

Masolino, *Peter Cures the Cripple and Raises Tabitha*, Brancacci Chapel, c. 1424-25

Masolino's companion piece to the *Tribute* is the most effective urban space painted in Florence (fig. 49). The two entirely separate episodes in the life of Peter flanking a superfluous pair of figures at the center are sure signs of Masolino's handiwork. And the two buildings Masolino used to establish perspective—again, follow the roof lines—suggest an all too rigid approach to Masaccio's more skillfully disguised system of perspective. Most scholars see the hand of Masaccio in the townspeople in and around those four sturdy Florentine palazzi just beyond the piazza. These figures are the first to be painted in deep space according to the rules of perspective. That said, only Masolino would have painted those dandies in their flat pinks and brocaded outfits sashaying across the piazza. Appealing as they are, these two characters steal the show—a show whose theme is the life of Peter.

The Small Frescoes: Strides in Naturalism

In Masolino's *Peter Preaching* and Masaccio's *Peter Baptizing the Neophytes* a massive Peter ministers to a crowd of the faithful before a mountainous landscape. Masolino packs his characters in tight, spaceless rows, while Masaccio poses his loosely in a circle.

Spatial depth is perfectly clear in Masaccio's painting, even with no architectural diagonals to guide us. And then consider the nudes, for

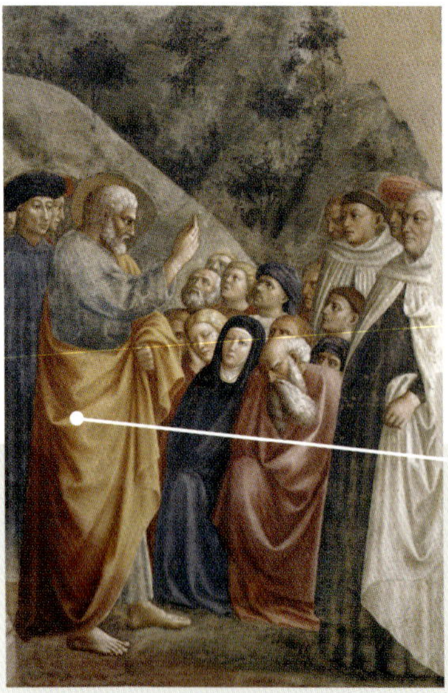

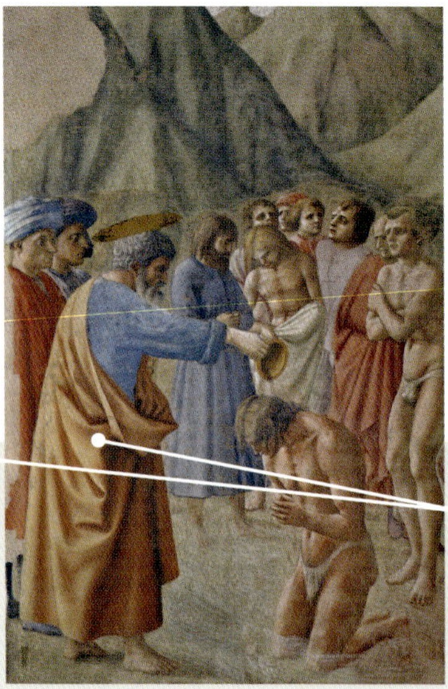

50. Masolino, *Peter Preaching*, c. 1424-25, Brancacci Chapel.

51. Masaccio, *Peter Baptizing the Neophytes*, c. 1425-26, Brancacci Chapel.

Both artists deploy rich middle tones to mimic the prominence of a figure's bulk.

example, the young man shivering in the early morning cold. There is nothing in Western painting to equal the realism of these nudes until the arrival of Michelangelo eighty years later.

Light, Shadow, and Color

To monumentalize the figures, Masaccio endows them with a greater heft than Giotto employed. The key was a relief system based on strong contrasts between light and shadow, his legacy to future artists. Both Giotto and Masaccio intended their color systems to simulate bulk. Consequently, each system employed a color that appears to visibly come forward from the surface of the wall. The difference lies in their color's intensity and placement.

At Santa Croce, Giotto worked within a narrow range of lights to darks that assumed that drapery colors were illuminated by a diffuse light angled from overhead. Masaccio instead illuminates his figures by a raking light focused from the side. The highlighted pale tones merge to deep darks on the shaded side, with the purest color standing for the figure's protruding volume. In each scene, Peter's robes range from pale yellow to burnt umber, with a deep gold-yellow reserved for the center. This system assures that the richest, most eye-catching middle tones, instead of Giotto's pale ones, simulate the figure bulk.

52. Masaccio, *Peter Healing the Sick with His Shadow*, c. 1425-27, Brancacci Chapel.

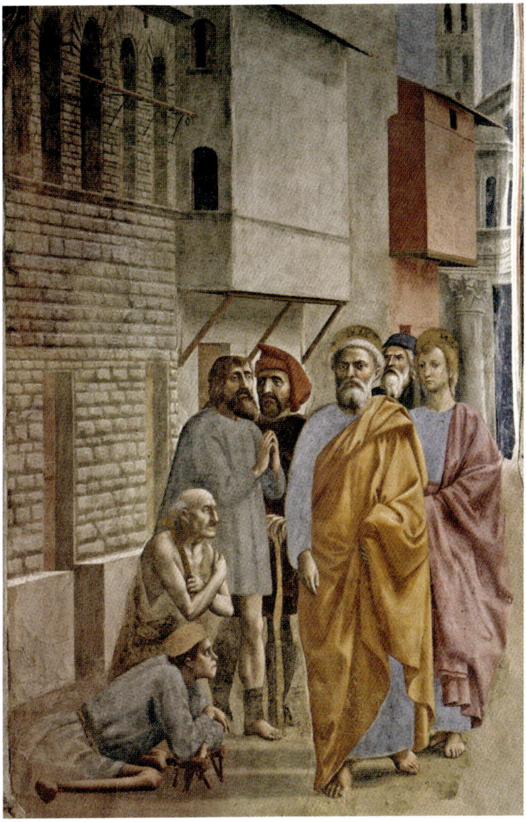

Masaccio, *Peter Healing the Sick with His Shadow*, Brancacci Chapel, c. 1425-27

Masaccio's daring use of a scene set at a diagonal propels Peter down a long Florentine alley toward us. We catch Peter at the moment of his miracle, just as his shadow is cast over the old man blessing himself and is about to fall on the lame man propped on his wretched legs. The individuality of characters from the lower strata of society reaches far beyond anything yet attempted in painting.

Masaccio, Filippino Lippi (1457-1504), *Raising of Theophilus's Son* and *Peter Enthroned*, Brancacci Chapel, c. 1427, 1480

The picture shows the right side and central section of a scene on the lowest tier painted by Masaccio. The central portion and the left side (not shown) was left unfinished at Masaccio's death, until Filippino Lippi completed it sixty years later. Lippi, a late Renaissance master, was able to replicate every aspect of Masaccio's style. The importance here lies in Masaccio's exquisitely life-like self-portrait staring out at us and those of his friends, Brunelleschi and Masolino (the three men standing to the right).

53. Masaccio, *Peter Enthroned*, detail of Masaccio, Filippino Lippi, *Raising of Theophilus's Son* and *Peter Enthroned*, Brancacci Chapel.

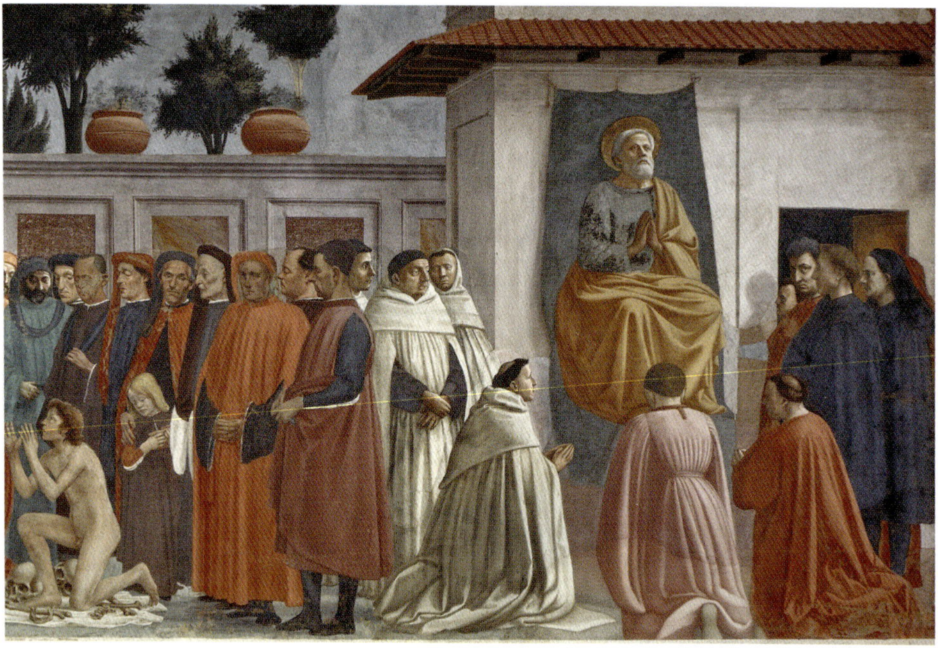

The Chapel's Legacy

The Brancacci frescoes prove Masaccio the heir of Giotto, who, painting a century earlier, had initiated the push toward realism. The powerful bodies he owes to Donatello's heroic statues, his revolutionary depiction of space to Brunelleschi's discovery of perspective. But beneath Masaccio's pictorial language unfolds a new conception of the role of art in the interpretation of man in nature. Although he lived in a profoundly Christian world, his art represents a visual and philosophical shift from a God-centered universe. Christ appears only once in these frescoes. It is, rather, the fully human Peter who emerges as the center of a gloriously familiar world.

Symbolism

A painting devoted to the life of Saint Peter was replete with possibilities of religious and political symbolism. With the end of the Great Schism, papal authority had been reestablished in Rome for the first time in over a hundred years. After pope Martin V entered Rome in 1420 and wrested control of the city from the old aristocracy, he faced an even greater challenge, one to his spiritual authority. A kind of populist uprising amongst church clergy that declared bishops equal to the pope, it threatened to undermine the legitimacy of papal succession and the authority inherited directly from Peter. The choice of Peter as the protagonist of these pictures, therefore, would have signaled the Carmelites' belief in a strong papacy whose authority began with Peter.

On the Altar

A Baseline

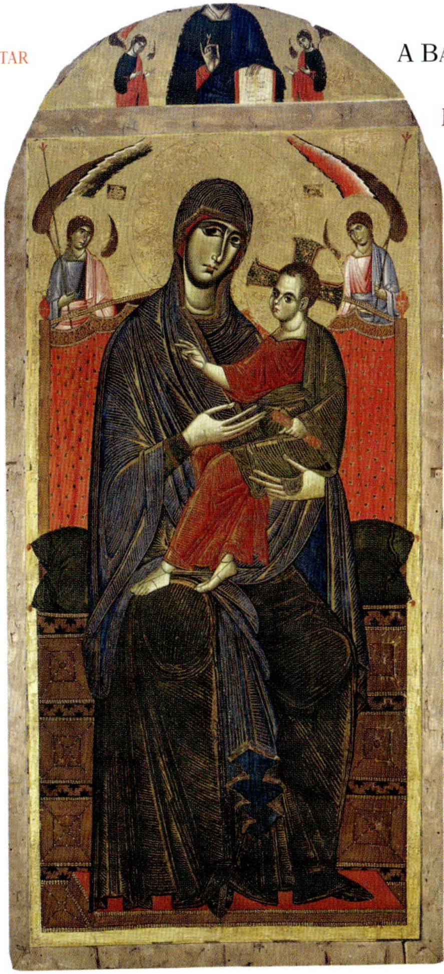

54. Master of the Saint Agatha, *Madonna Enthroned*, 1260s, Brancacci Chapel.

Master of the Saint Agatha (Master of the Madonna del Carmine), *Madonna Enthroned*, Brancacci Chapel, 1260s

The panel on the altar, one of the oldest portable paintings still in a Florentine church, marks the threshold where the Byzantine and the Italian meet. It is the critical precursor to the Madonnas in the Uffizi that we will study shortly.

The Madonna's tiny mouth, incised nose, almond eyes, and tendril-shaped hands all reflect Byzantine tradition. The gold zigzags and the background that implies divine light derive both from the conventions of indigenous Italian painting and the Byzantine.

An important distinction separates this image from the Saint Francis icon of roughly the same date in the Bardi Chapel of Santa Croce (fig. 17): because the figure has not been circumscribed with a black outline, the shape of the

Madonna appears fuller than that of Saint Francis. We also see fullness in the face, indeed pliancy, here conveyed by the dark-light modeling that shapes the underside of the jaw where it meets the neck.

Unlike a typical Byzantine face, which stares out blankly, this face communicates with us, possibly a soulful message of sadness. We also see in the angels an awareness of the presence of the Madonna: they stand stolidly behind the cloth hung from a back support and gaze forward toward the Virgin, implying separate spaces. Even the little detail of the fabric falling from the Child's mantle over the Virgin's right hand implies space and a material substance not seen in the Byzantine style.

Masaccio's Legacy

Despite his age—he arrived in Florence in 1422 in his early twenties and immediately joined the painter's guild—Masaccio was one of the earliest artists to document the conflicts inherent in his society. We have only to look back to his *Peter Healing the Sick with His Shadow* (fig. 52) on the streets of Florence to support this view. Although he would have had little association with Ghiberti, whose precious International Gothic style ignored the city's realities, he counted among his friends Brunelleschi and Donatello, whose influence can be seen in his paintings. Yet, before Brunelleschi had constructed a single building, before Donatello had been recognized for his pioneering efforts in sculpture (that honor went to Ghiberti), before admiration for the International Gothic style had withered, in short, before medieval Florence had become Renaissance Florence—Masaccio was dead.

His remarkable achievements in accurately depicting the natural world were honored in the writings of the architect-scholar, Leon Battista Alberti, and Leonardo da Vinci. The historian, Giorgio Vasari, who described Masaccio's monumental breakthroughs in terms of Giotto's rebirth in his 1550 *Lives of the Artists*, ranked him as the necessary stepping stone to Leonardo and the "divine" Michelangelo. Twenty years later, in 1570, an immense altarpiece designed by Vasari was installed in front of Masaccio's fresco, the *Trinity,* in Santa Maria Novella.

4. Uffizi Gallery

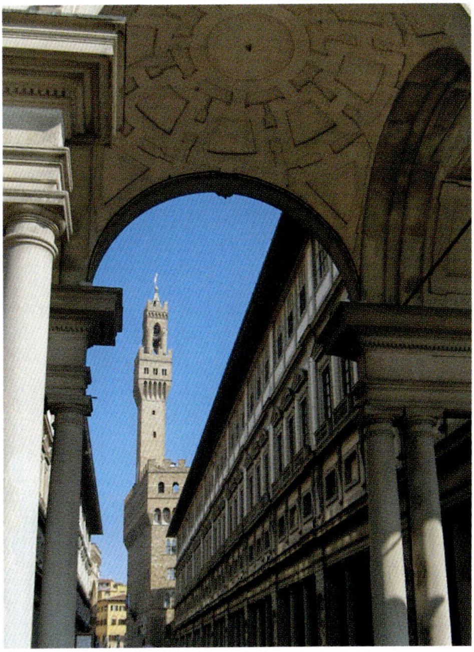

The Uffizi's collection is the most succinct and comprehensive tribute to Italian painting anywhere in the world. And because the museum specializes in the painting of its own city, this portion of its collection is particularly dense with Renaissance masterpieces. A detailed discussion of each artwork is impractical, of course. Happily, it is also unnecessary, for the essentials of the Florentine style can be grasped without dissecting every work. Our focus is limited to about forty paintings and their role as beacons for all that followed. Of the thirty-some painters responsible for creating this majestic body of work, most we will meet again in the churches and cloisters where their works still stand in the sites for which they were intended. But crucial works by Leonardo da Vinci, Botticelli, and Michelangelo can be seen in no place but the Uffizi. Many of the works we will see are altarpieces. While many altarpieces may seem to look the same, their differences are significant. Despite a tradition-bound format, the religious subject left the artist a great deal of latitude to demonstrate his understanding of the human form and the space it inhabits, to probe the mystery of light—or lack of it—and to experiment with color. Thus we can see in even the simplest altarpiece something of the foundations of Western painting unfold.

A word on the relationship between altarpieces and museums: As magnificent as they are, altarpieces were not painted to be hung on museum walls, but rather to adorn an altar. The purpose of their splendor was to remind the faithful that the means to salvation lay in the celebration of the Mass, at which Christ's passion was reenacted. This was the common man's only opportunity to see, whether in a soaring cathedral or a modest little chapel, the mystical purity of color and gold lit by the flickering glow of candlelight.

Pisan School, Crucifix with Scenes of the Passion (Crucifix no. 432), Uffizi, last quarter of twelfth century

The beautifully preserved wooden crucifix on the far right wall is the Uffizi's oldest picture. Like the Madonna Enthroned, it represented the most common pictorial theme suitable to hang above the altar of a church in the twelfth century.

Most painted crucifixes come from Tuscany, and those showing a wide-eyed Christ triumphant over death were largely painted before 1250. In Romanesque fashion, the figure of Christ is forcefully outlined, straight-up and frontal, with few internal demarcations denoting anatomy. In the side panels, gnome-like creatures with protuberant almond-shaped eyes, set in heads that dwarf their tiny bodies, dart about enacting the story of Christ's passion. But there is nothing comical

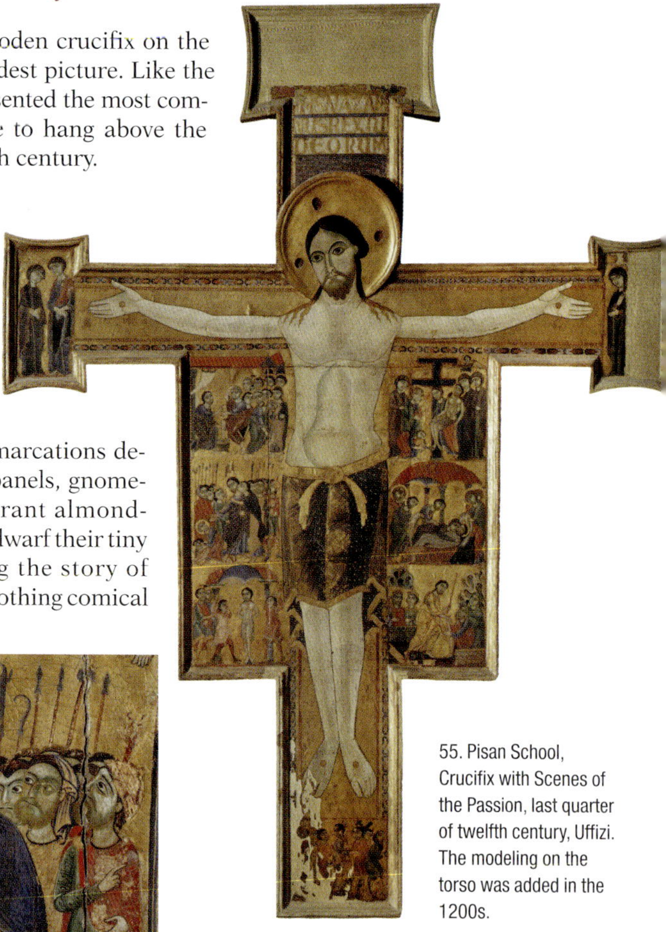

55. Pisan School, Crucifix with Scenes of the Passion, last quarter of twelfth century, Uffizi. The modeling on the torso was added in the 1200s.

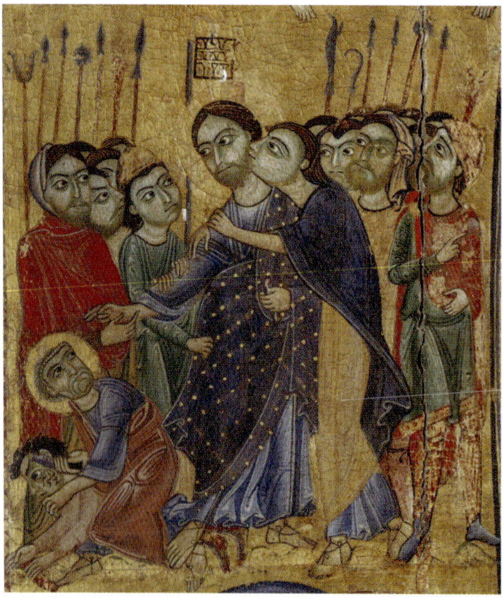

56. *Betrayal*, detail of fig. 55.

about these odd little fellows; their expressions and body language are deadly serious. In the *Lamentation* (middle right), Mary's grief is ingeniously invoked by the geometry interlocking her prostrate body with her son's. With very little variety in facial expression, the artist pulls a great range of emotion from his actors. No figure in painting can be as creepy as Judas in the scene of the *Betrayal* (middle left, fig. 56) in which the long reptilian slope of his slimy body sidles up to the noble figure of Christ for the "kiss."

Master of 434 Crucifix, Crucifix with Eight Scenes of the Passion (Crucifix no. 434), 1250s

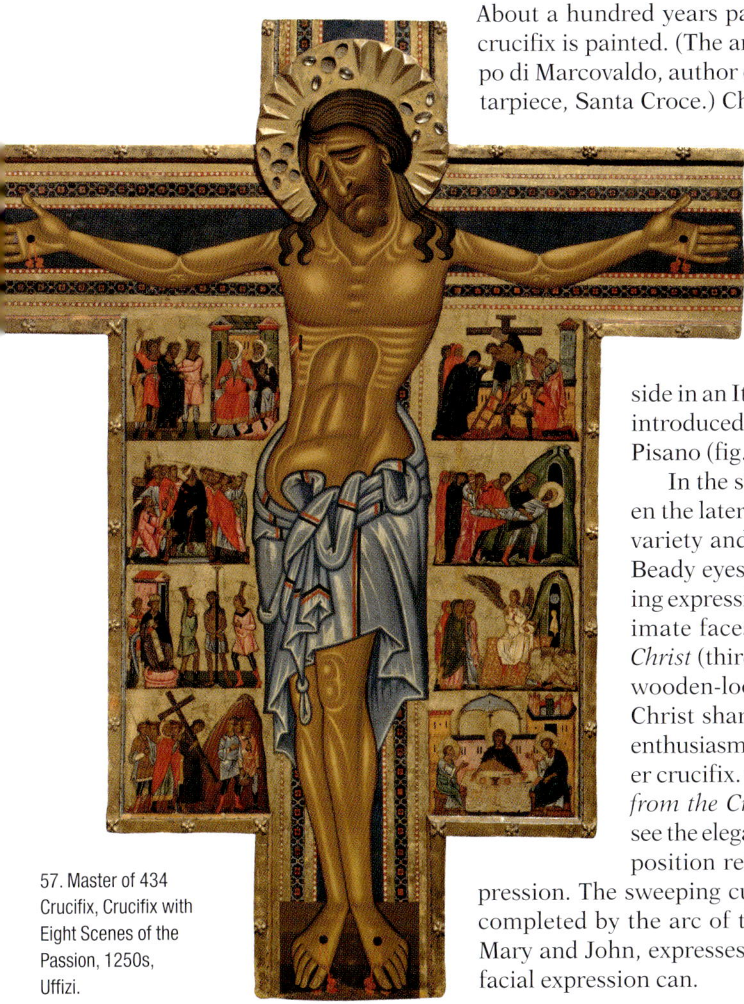

57. Master of 434 Crucifix, Crucifix with Eight Scenes of the Passion, 1250s, Uffizi.

About a hundred years pass before this second crucifix is painted. (The artist likely taught Coppo di Marcovaldo, author of the *Saint Francis* altarpiece, Santa Croce.) Christ's face is now contorted in death; in an early example of plastic modeling, muscles and joints are delineated by light and dark contrasts instead of by line; and the limp body swings to the side in an Italo-Byzantine fashion introduced to Tuscany by Giunta Pisano (fig. 13).

In the side panels, where, given the later date, we might expect variety and vitality, we find less. Beady eyes incapable of registering expression are set within inanimate faces. In the *Scourging of Christ* (third down on the left) the wooden-looking soldiers flailing Christ share none of the sadistic enthusiasm of the group in the older crucifix. Only in the *Deposition from the Cross* (top right) do we see the elegance of Byzantine composition reinforce Florentine expression. The sweeping curve of a lifeless body, completed by the arc of the grieving figures of Mary and John, expresses pathos far more than facial expression can.

At this point, having examined two of the rarest storied crucifixes in the entire repertoire—only about nineteen have survived—it is worth noting what features they share. First, the artists who created them did not conceive of anything other than that the image and the surface of the panel were one and the same. Second, many of these panels were prized as precious, miracle-performing objects to be venerated.

Tuscan Painter, *Madonna Enthroned with Child*, Uffizi, c. 1230-40

The most common altarpiece throughout Tuscany was the cult image of the Virgin, originally derived from the portable Byzantine icon. Painted around the 1240s, this elegant little *Madonna Enthroned* relies heavily on Byzantine models from the 1100s, a period noted for its severely schematic rendering of the human form. The rigid frontal view of the Virgin and Child, the almost total flatness of forms meant to indicate the cushion, throne, and footrest, and the absence of modeling in the diagrammatic facial features, all represent Byzantine features. By contrast, Tuscan traits exist in the way the head and halo rise above the rectangular frame, giving the Virgin a measure of sculptural presence. Similarly, the cushion stretches beyond the borders of the frame, suggesting a degree of three-dimensionality. Decidedly Florentine, a vibrant color chord contrasts a shrill tomato red and maroon to the deep blue of the skillfully modeled robe.

The small *Annunciation* below, a direct quotation of Byzantine formulas, underscores the artist's ability to depict figures moving and posed within a rudimentary space.

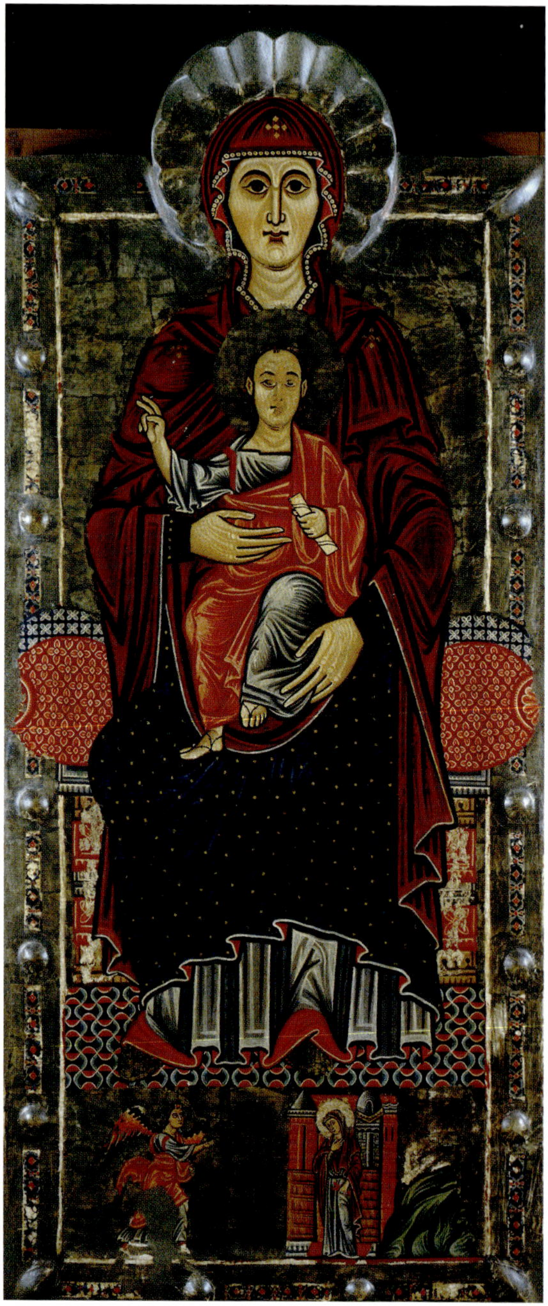

58. Tuscan painter, *Madonna Enthroned with Child*, c. 1230-40, Uffizi.

HANGING IN THE CENTER OF THE ROOM

Cimabue, Duccio di Boninsegna, Giotto, *Madonna Enthroned*

With these three magnificent works, we witness a major revolution in the history of the arts. Each is named for the church whose chapel it was meant to adorn. Today there is talk of returning them to their original sites.

59. Cimabue, *Santa Trinita Madonna*, c. 1280-85, Uffizi.

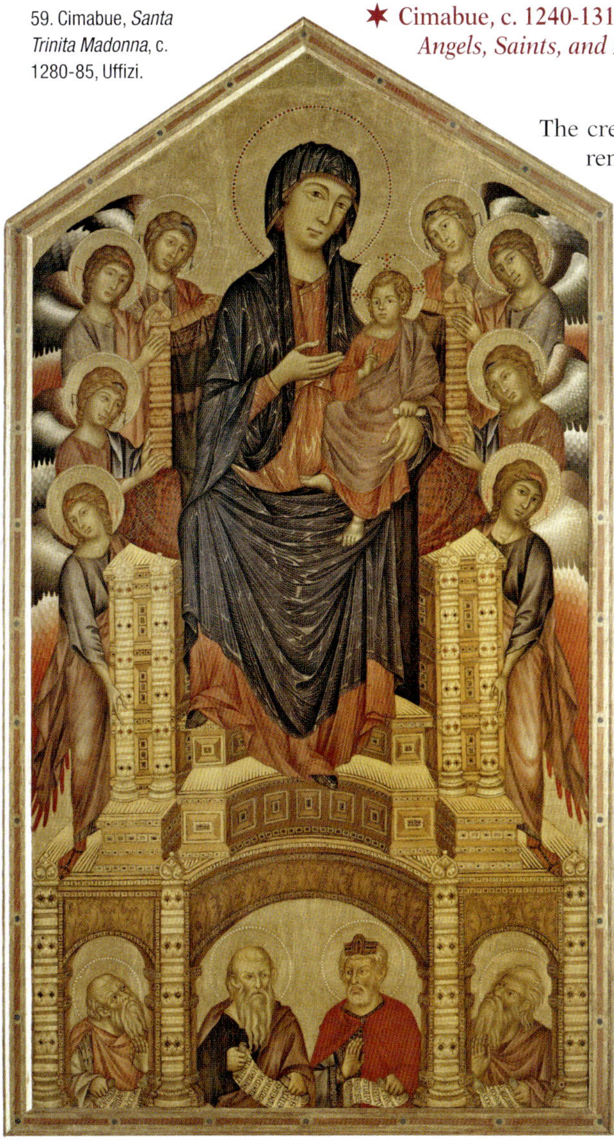

✶ Cimabue, c. 1240-1313, *Madonna Enthroned with Child, Angels, Saints, and Prophets (Santa Trinita Madonna)*, Uffizi, c. 1280-85

The creator of the oldest panel, the Florentine Cimabue, the greatest painter of the thirteenth century, brought the Italo-Byzantine style to perfection and to a final conclusion.

To better establish our bearings in confronting this magnificent, otherworldly image, it is worth referring back to the famous *Madonna Enthroned* in the Brancacci Chapel (fig. 54). It was painted a mere twenty years earlier, yet the differences are striking. For one thing, Cimabue has placed his monumental Madonna on a solid wooden throne, albeit unwieldy with the missing back legs. Larger and more splendidly bejeweled than anything that had ever been executed, this throne faces us frontally. Side arms flare outward in a rudimentary display of perspective, giving it depth enough for the Madonna to occupy it. Only such a throne could suit a Madonna who looks more human than the Brancacci's more Byzantine version. Her face seems more vital, because Cimabue has modeled her flesh with long parallel filaments of color. Black, white, umber, and red appear in compact combinations that give it a plausible texture and pliancy. The almond-shaped eyes staring out blankly from inexpressive iconic features—long nose, defined eyebrows, small mouth—are what remain of centuries of Byzantine convention. Her gown is the last we'll see in which the zigzag lines of the Byzantine hardly hint at the body's contours. Despite the considerable innovations in space, the gold glitters, and with the gold background, the eye reads the image as splendidly flat.

And then there is the corps de ballet of eight angels arrayed at her side, tightly stacked one behind the other. With their softened and endearing features and their abundant plumage in iridescent red, white, and blue, they are as delightful as any creatures in Italian art.

Before passing to the next Madonna, we may wonder whether Cimabue foresaw that his work would close the glorious epoch of Byzantine virtuosity and herald currents of an entirely new style. An air of purposeful conservatism, even intransigence, is evident in the way he evokes in his Madonna the severe side of the Italo-Byzantine style. If we had only the upper zone to judge, we would never appreciate his skill at portraying expression as he does in the small petulant prophets peering from beneath the throne. Perhaps Cimabue saw that inevitable changes were about to come, and holding firm against the future, displayed for the last time the monumentality of a heritage in decline.

✶ Duccio di Boninsegna, c. 1255-ante 1319, *Madonna Enthroned with Child and Angels* (*Rucellai Madonna*), Uffizi, 1285-86

Not long after Cimabue completed his *Madonna*, Duccio, the father of Sienese art, painted this altarpiece for the Rucellai chapel in Santa Maria Novella (where it stood until 1937: it has been in the Uffizi since 1948). Rooted in a different heritage, Duccio conveys a very particular sentiment in his Madonna, and his depiction of space, rudimentary as it is, sets the stage for the Madonna in the center of the room. By turning his four-legged throne at an angle, Duccio conveys its spatial depth. Unlike Cimabue's throne, which corresponds to the picture surface, this throne is pushed back into the scene so that we perceive the illusion of space beyond the picture surface. Duccio establishes a pronounced ground level and plants the angels' feet solidly on it. These little creatures, lovingly wrapped in tunics and filmy robes, would have looked magically lifelike to a thirteenth-century spectator. He doesn't crowd them. We see them whole and isolated, leaving the background field of gold visible as atmosphere that could take on any color in nature—sky blue, for example. Duccio sacrifices the austerity of Cimabue's *Madonna* for delicacy, informality, and tenderness. His Madonna rests her hand gently on the child snuggled into her lap—a sure sign of Duccio's Sienese roots. Her shape is softer, her outline more agile than those of the other Madonnas here. Only the line of the gold hem that courses lyrically down and across the deep blue expanse of her gown, perhaps the most beautiful

60. Duccio di Boninsegna, *Rucellai Madonna*, 1285-86, Uffizi.

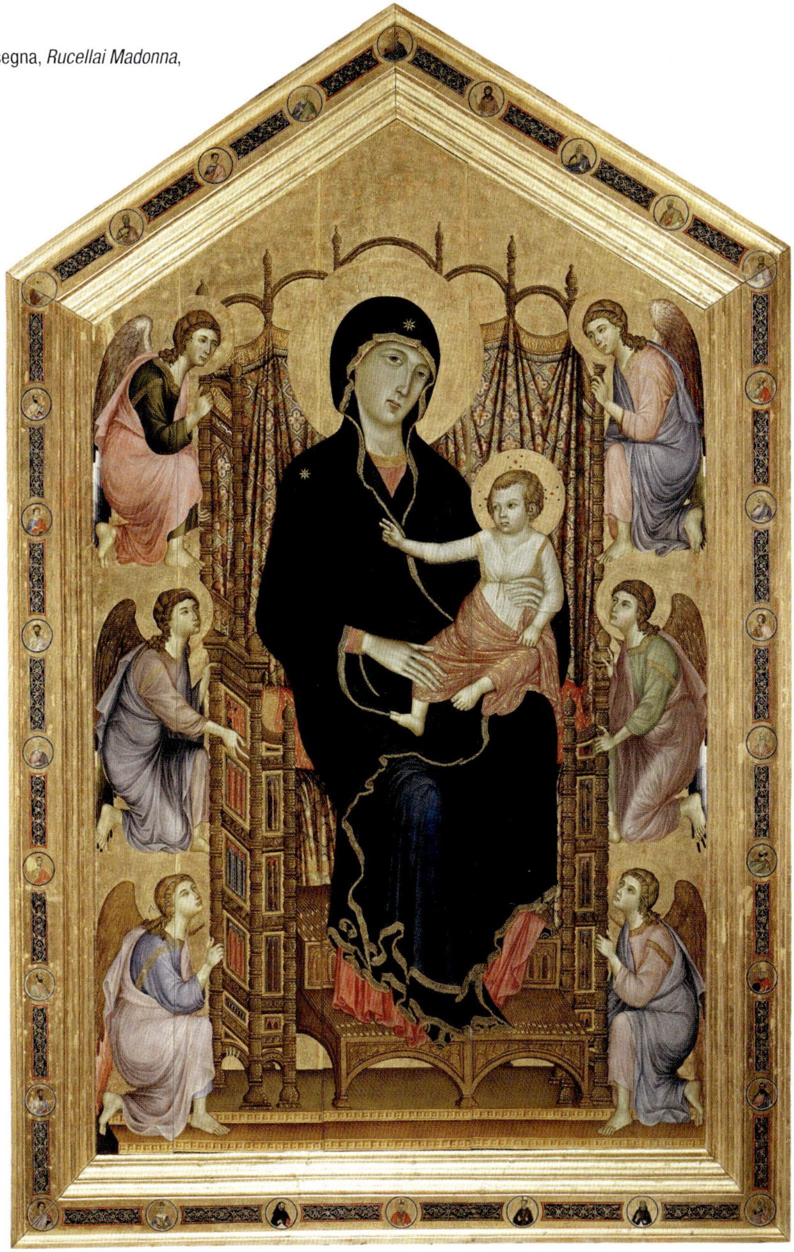

line in Italian art, hints at the body's contour beneath. Less functional than artifice, this line creates an elegance that forecasts the coming Gothic style for which the next generation of Sienese painters would become famous.

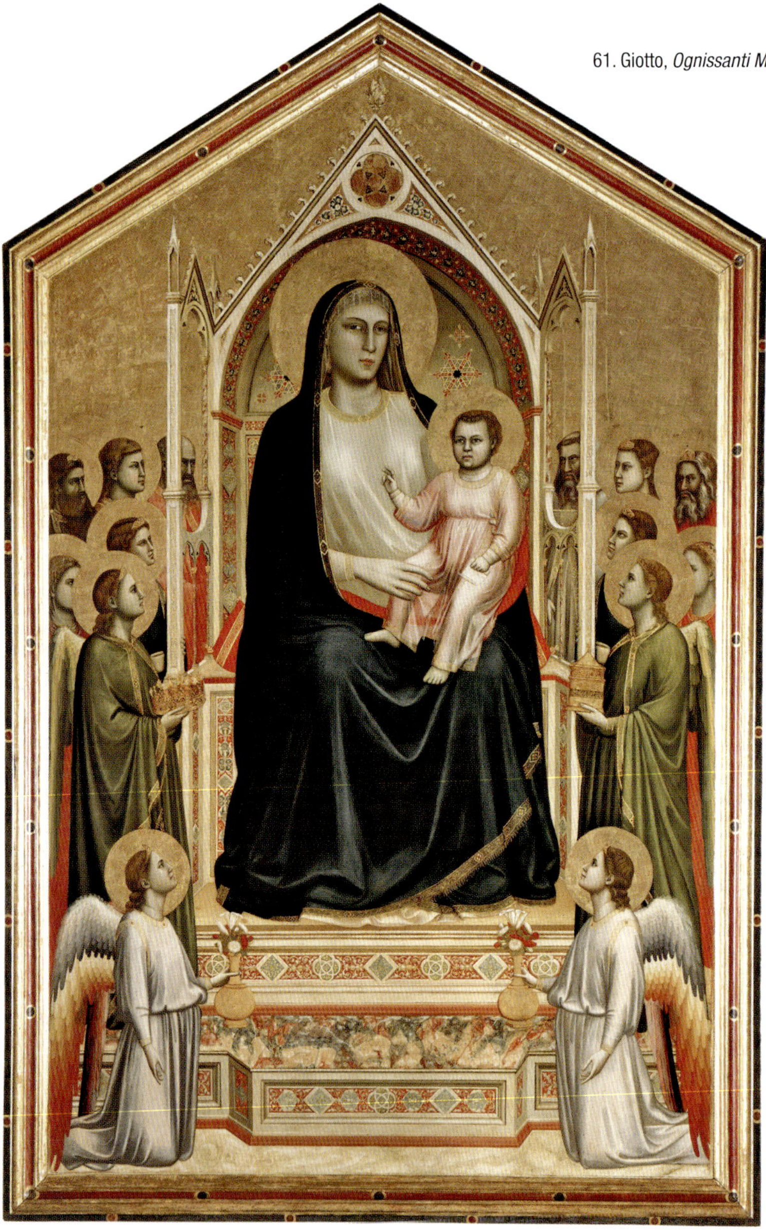

61. Giotto, *Ognissanti Madonna*, c. 1310, Uffizi.

★ Giotto, c. 1267-1337, *Madonna Enthroned with Child and Angels (Ognissanti Madonna)*, Uffizi, c. 1310

The change in styles that takes place in the twenty-five years that separate this panel from the Cimabue and Duccio marks a decisive advance in

Western art. Giotto's Madonna arises out of an altogether different concept. She is full-figured and bears features that suggest consciousness, qualities that will not be addressed again for another century. Rejected here and forever hence in Florentine art are the gold linear striations in the drapery. In their place are broad fluted folds that reflect the body's contours beneath.

Giotto constructs her throne in marble and introduces Florence to Gothic ornamentation—arches on the sides of the throne and delicate pinnacles decorating the top. Gothic decoration was unusual for Giotto; he never would have embellished the Madonna with gold, as did Duccio. Again we see the split perspective that he employed in the Santa Croce frescoes to suggest spatial depth—the inside of the throne's canopied arch is narrower on the left—implying a side view, yet we see the throne straight on.

Everything about this painting reinforces the illusion of space. Giotto plants his contingent of angels, rendered in sober earth tones, in front of and around the throne. Thus we view these figures as standing in different planes in space. Giotto also implies space by creating figures bulky enough to fill it. Instead of using the flat patterns that describe the Cimabue and Duccio figures, he models their draperies in lights and darks that suggest how natural light searches out volume (for example, the highlighting of the Madonna's knees), an effect we call *relief*. While Giotto's treatment of space constitutes an essential achievement, it is his exploration of the human form in relief that will forever set Florentine painting on its course.

Before passing on to another kind of art, several fundamental features that these three images share must be stressed. Foremost, the fronts of all three thrones face the planar surface of the picture, in spite of Duccio's additional side view and Giotto's oblique view of the canopy's interior. The backgrounds are of reflective gold leaf, the placement of the angels is strictly symmetrical, and the bright colors form beautiful patterns.

These compositional elements all emphasize the picture surface. Of course, this runs counter to the idea that the spectator looks past the surface into a deeper space that the artists have contrived to create. This interplay, or tension, between surface organization and the illusion of space ranks as one of the defining characteristics of Florentine art.

ROOM 3 SIENESE INFLUENCE

The two painters in this room, both artistically descended from Duccio, collaborated to formulate the great stylistic tradition of Siena. Sienese artists were keenly aware of the sensuous possibilities of the picture surface and the tensions created in apposing this surface to the illusion of space. Here, we examine two paintings that had a profound influence on Florentine art.

Ambrogio Lorenzetti, c. 1290-1348, *Presentation at the Temple*, Uffizi, 1342

For all of Giotto's research into space, it was the Sienese who made the next advances. Here, we see the outside of a highly ornate church that hugs the picture surface and, for the first time, an inside space deeper than it is wide. However, because the tiled pavement appears to recede steeply to a vanishing point deep within the church, the space is subverted by the forward placement of the altar and the priest.

Although this space represents a significant leap forward, it is not constructed according to the rules of mathematical perspective formulated in the next century, which keyed the architecture to the height of the figures. The scale of the figures here is at variance with the church, which after all remains a dollhouse refuge. The fully rounded figures, placed near the front, we can attribute to Giotto's influence. But the portraits of the matronly Prophetess Anna on the right, of the sad mother of Christ holding an empty cloth (a premonition of her son's sacrifice), and of the oblivious baby sucking on its thumb all represent the kind of poignant details particular to a Sienese sentiment.

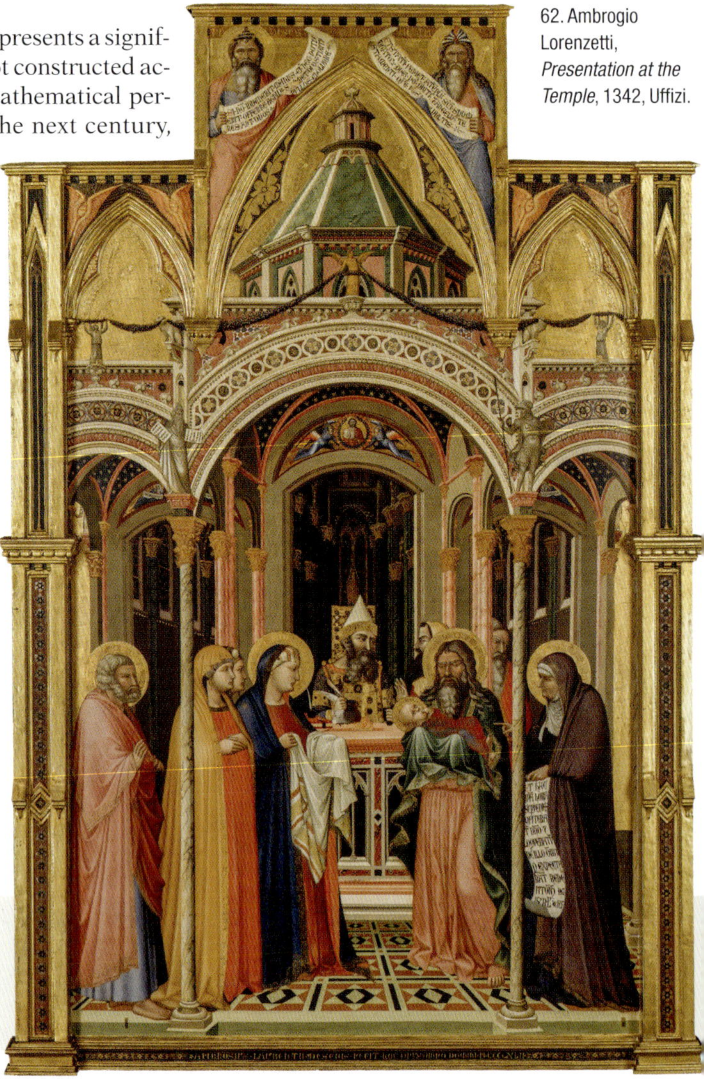

62. Ambrogio Lorenzetti, *Presentation at the Temple*, 1342, Uffizi.

The architecture reflects the interior of the Sienese cathedral, for which the picture was originally intended.

63. Simone Martini, Lippo Memmi, *Annunciation with the Saints Ansano and Massima*, 1333, Uffizi.

✶ Simone Martini (c. 1284-1344), Lippo Memmi (c. 1285-1356), *Annunciation with the Saints Ansano and Massima*, Uffizi, 1333

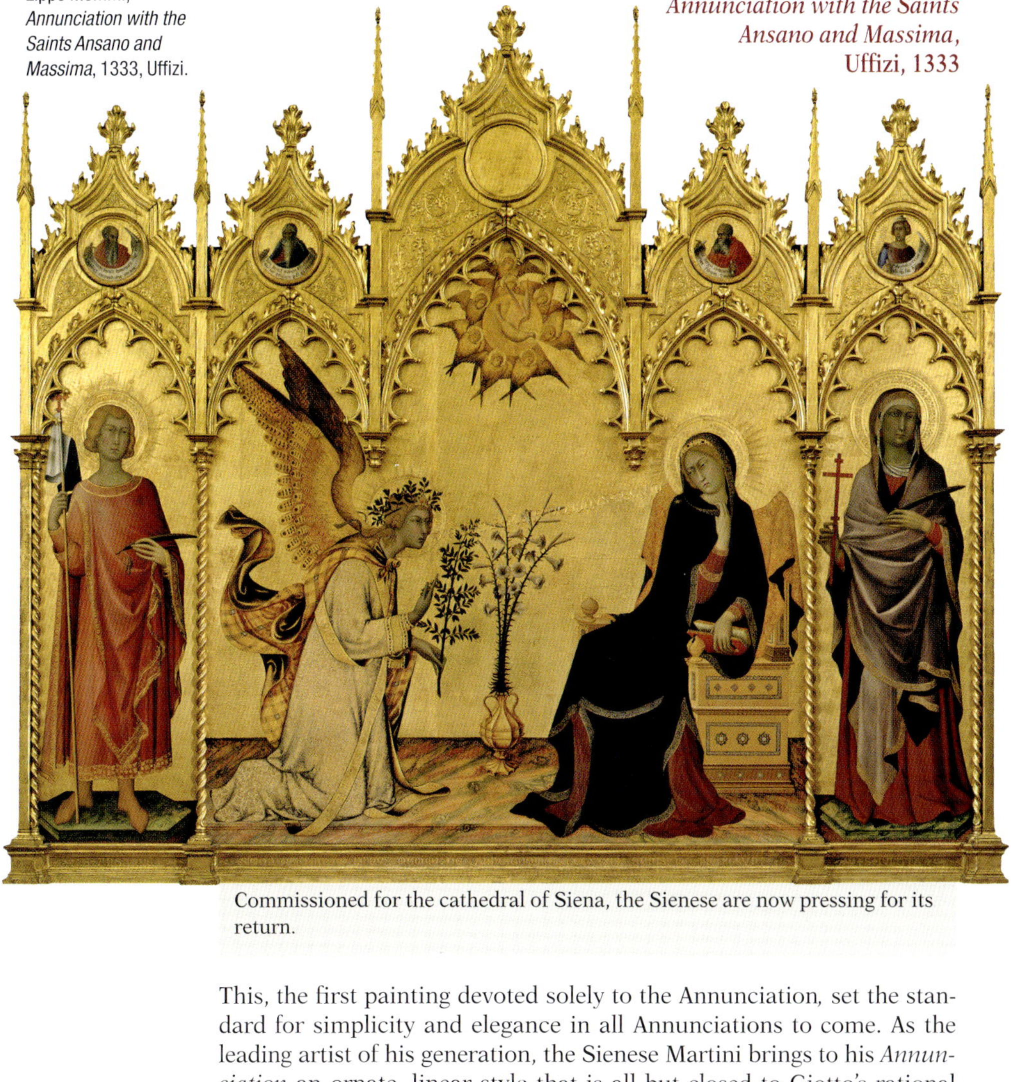

Commissioned for the cathedral of Siena, the Sienese are now pressing for its return.

This, the first painting devoted solely to the Annunciation, set the standard for simplicity and elegance in all Annunciations to come. As the leading artist of his generation, the Sienese Martini brings to his *Annunciation* an ornate, linear style that is all but closed to Giotto's rational relief style.

We are present at the instant Gabriel, with wings still a-flutter and draperies in commotion, alights just beyond the truncated Gothic column into the sanctity of the Virgin's space. The marble pavement that runs to the glittery gold background and the placement of the vase of lilies and solid throne just short of that background give a measure of dimension to this space. In the profile of the angel we also see dimension, more precisely, a third dimension, especially prominent where shadow separates one wing from the other. Mary's shape, by contrast, is flat, a most eloquent sign of the linear style, the essential component of early Gothic art.

With his eye to hers, Gabriel announces the will of God, spoken for all eternity in the gold-tooled script that issues from his mouth: "Hail Mary, you shall give birth to a Son." In rhythmic excitements, her figure answers his in recoil, which Martini marks just at the point where the line of her knee abruptly turns upward.

Fourteenth-Century Gothic Painting

ROOM 4

In the broadest sense, the whole Trecento reflects the influence of Giotto, and in another, it marks the gradual unraveling of his style. The Black Death divides the century at the midpoint, and the art of either half is only meagerly represented in the Uffizi. To follow Giotto's immediate disciples in the first half of the century, we must look to Santa Croce's great fresco cycles or go to the Accademia. For the painters of the second half, we will go to Santa Maria Novella to see a more severe art, but an art nonetheless still born from the seeds of Giotto's style. Here, we examine one picture each from the early, middle, and latter century to see the era in microcosm.

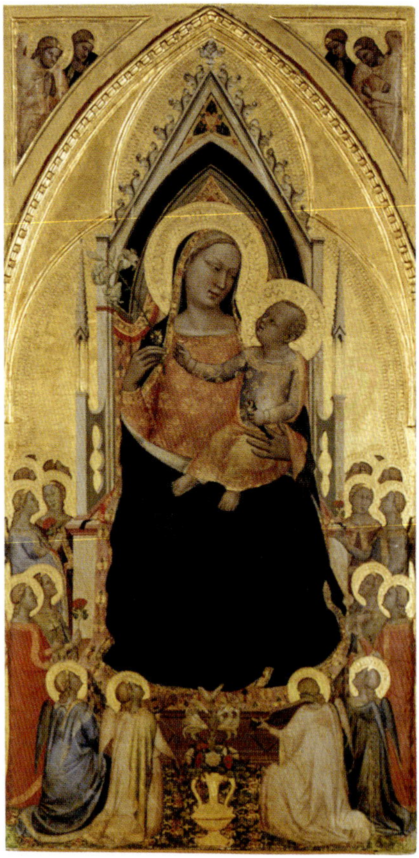

64. Bernardo Daddi, *San Pancrazio Polyptich*, central piece, 1336-38, Uffizi.

Bernardo Daddi, c. 1290-1348, *Madonna Enthroned with Child, Angels and Saints* (*San Pancrazio Polyptich*, central piece), 1336-38

Among Giotto's followers, Daddi is acclaimed as the most influential painter in the first half of the fourteenth century and this altarpiece is the finest example of his mature style. Here, we are in the full flowering of the early Gothic style: the spindly throne and the gay palette—in fact the gaiety of the whole ensemble—deployed in a decorative balance that would have been unthinkable to Giotto but would nevertheless form the color key in devotional works for the rest of the century.

The embroidered gold hem of her drapery—decorative rather than descriptive of a body beneath—we can attribute more to the linear style of the Sienese masters than to Giotto, who would have insisted that the draperies reflect the source of light.

65. Giottino, *San Remigio Pietà*, 1340s, Uffizi.

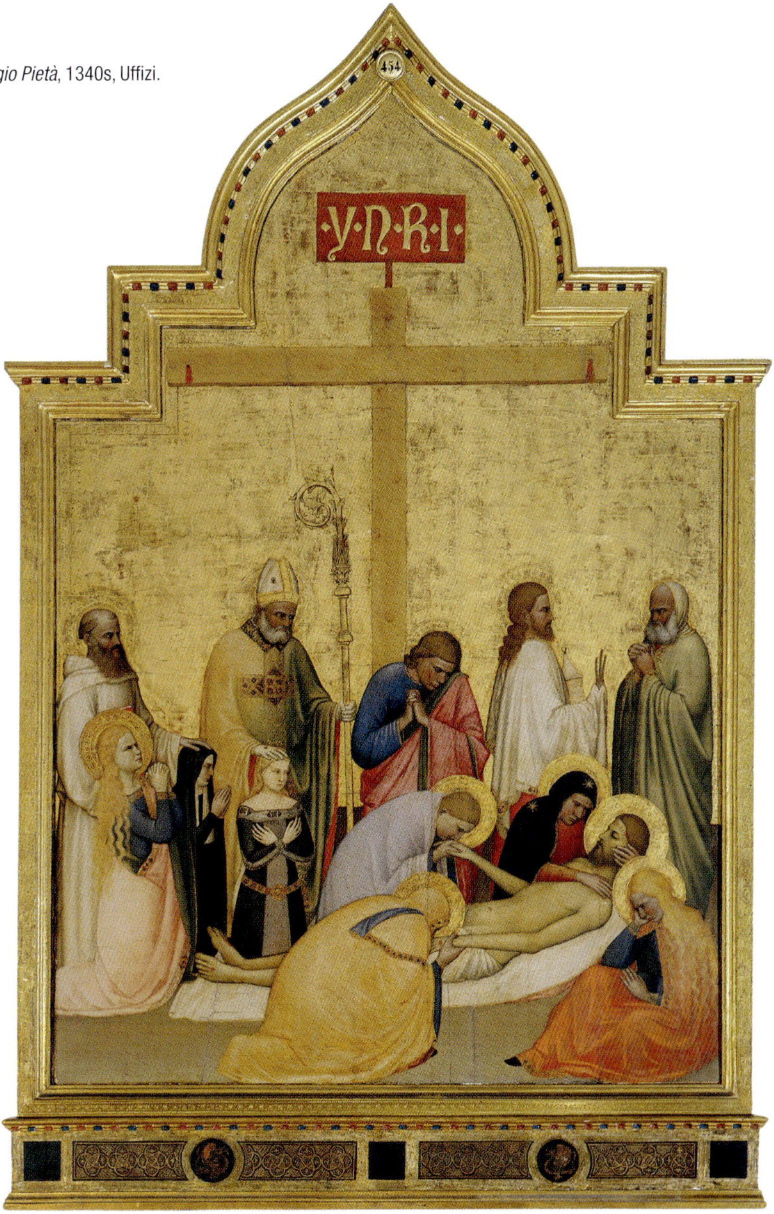

Giottino, active 1324-1369, *Lamentation over Christ* (*San Remigio Pietà*), Uffizi, 1340s

The picture is the work of an artist that history has named Giottino because of his affinity for Giotto's style. Although finding no need to frame his scene with architecture, he is very much Giotto reborn in the monumental figures inhabiting a clear space. The figure whose back is to us provides the heft that Giotto conveyed in the Santa Croce frescoes. But Giottino handles individual facial expressions better than Giotto. Look to the sensual Mary Magdalene with flowing golden tresses, her face flushed with despair, slumped in the corner; or to the Virgin cradling the pliant body of her son. A Benedictine nun kneels next to a stunning young woman; the blessing conferred by the bishop's hand placed gently on the woman's head signals she is the picture's donor. Female donors were rare in this period.

How much more intense this group would be without the unfortunate placement of the two characters in stiff profile on the right. Giotto, with his gift for dramatic impact, would never have allowed anything so distracting to interfere with the story's pathos. Yet this picture's silent grandeur survives the disruption, standing as a timeless depiction of a mother's sorrow over her son's death.

66. Andrea Orcagna, *Saint Matthew Tabernacle*, c. 1367, Uffizi.

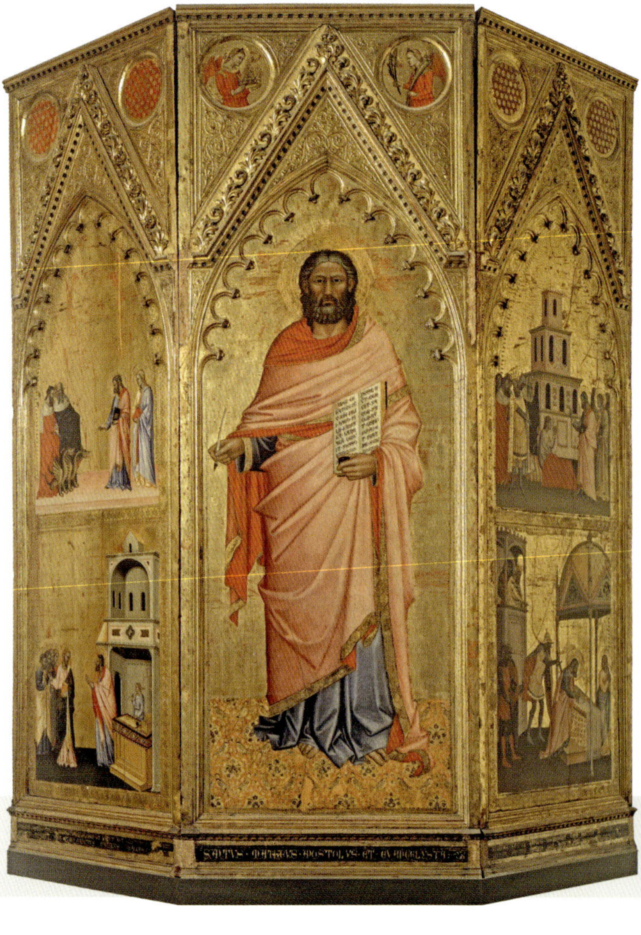

Andrea Orcagna, active c. 1344-1368, *Saint Matthew and Scenes from His Life (Saint Matthew Tabernacle)*, Uffizi, c. 1367

The picture reflects the pious sober side of Gothic painting in the last half of the fourteenth century, and the artist, Andrea di Cione, otherwise known as Orcagna, is Florence's chief representative of that period. His paintings are few and rare, considering he and his three brothers operated the largest workshop in Florence. The artist is better represented in Santa Maria Novella where his masterpiece resides in a small chapel beautifully frescoed by his brother.

The tabernacle was probably mounted on a pier at Orsanmichele.

ROOM 5 INTERNATIONAL GOTHIC

During the fourteenth century, Gothic art flowed over Europe like a great wave, yet had only a timid impact on Florentine painters still working under the shadow of Giotto. But from the brief period of 1400 through 1424, the year Masaccio's style burst onto the scene, Florentine painting was entirely Gothic, specifically, International Gothic. A late variant of the Gothic style, International Gothic evolved in the courts of France in the late fourteenth centu-

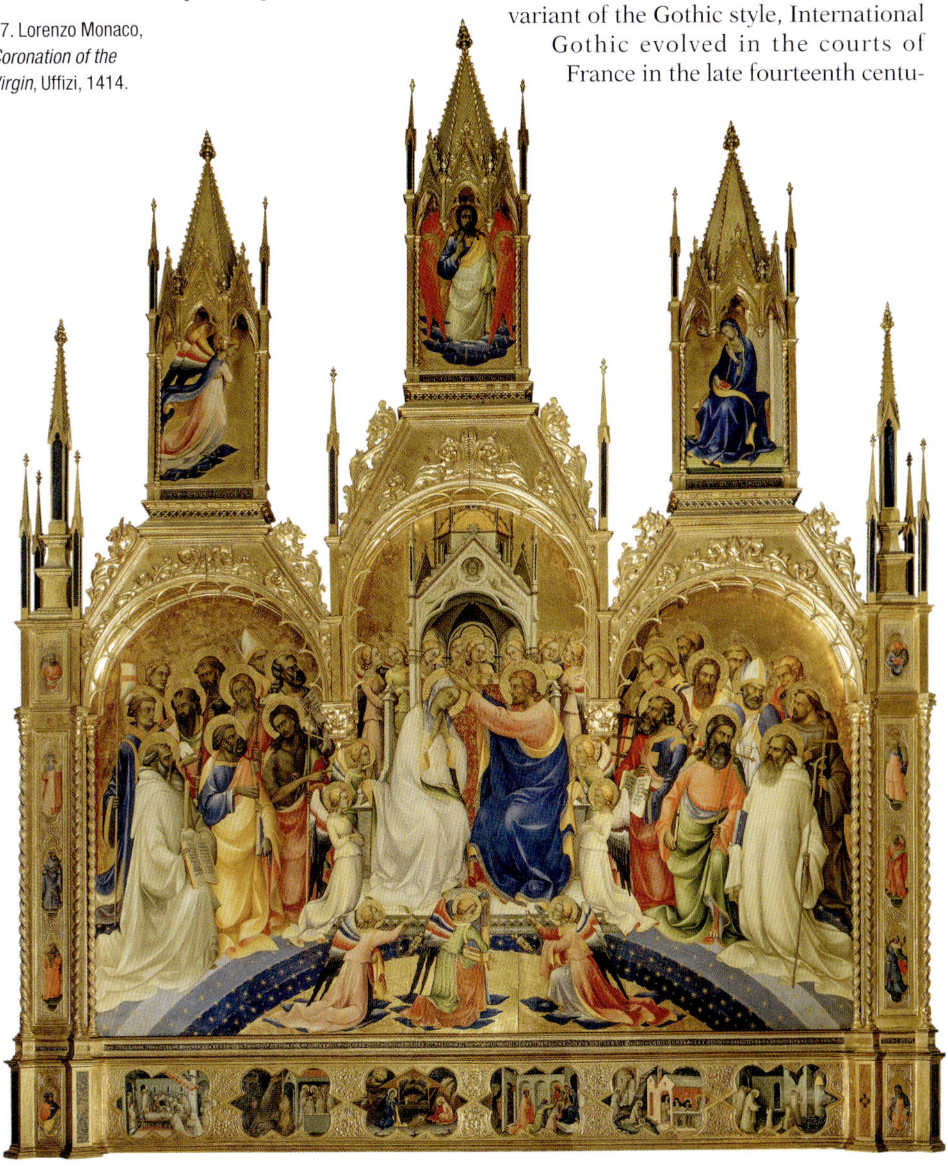

67. Lorenzo Monaco, *Coronation of the Virgin*, Uffizi, 1414.

ry under the influence of Simone Martini, who had worked there decades earlier. In this room are several of Florence's finest examples from that brief period, each illustrating a distinct strain of International Gothic.

✶ Lorenzo Monaco, c. 1370-c. 1425, *Coronation of the Virgin*, Uffizi, 1414

The Camaldolese monk was the dominant painter in Florence in the first quarter of the fifteenth century, and the *Coronation* represents his greatest masterpiece. In style, it largely rejects earlier Florentine traditions by discarding the naturalism that Giotto and his followers had strived toward early in the last century. Rather, the scene means to encourage the viewer to move from a perception of the familiar to the divine. In other words, the picture is not bound by optical reality.

A resplendent Gothic frame shoots upward, its half-columns partially dividing a unified scene depicting the heavenly court into thirds. At the center, the Virgin Mary, draped in the white robes of the Camaldolese order, is being crowned in heaven by Jesus, while diminutive angels and a retinue of bulky saints in high-keyed colors look on. (Bulk is the only evidence of Giotto.)

All these figures, their draperies trailing off in wisps of decorative swirls, especially the S-shaped angels, introduce us to motifs of the International Gothic style, thus far only employed in Florence by Ghiberti in the Baptistry's north doors. But what foremost distinguishes this style as International Gothic is that the drapery is all and the underlying structure little or nothing. Giotto's style, where the drapery says something about the articulation of the body beneath, now seems like the distant past. (The palette is briefly discussed in the Addendum.)

✶ Gentile da Fabriano, c. 1370-1427, *Adoration of the Magi*, Uffizi, 1423

Palla Strozzi, the richest banker in Florence, commissioned Gentile to paint this splendid panel because of the artist's particular ability to render intricate detail with extravagant materials. Wealthy Florentines of the time such as Strozzi were caught at the cross roads of a medieval chivalry declining in the face of a newly emerging humanism (Strozzi patronized humanist circles), and Gentile describes both.

As Gentile is one of the few non-Tuscan painters to work in Florence, there are qualities in this painting that would have impressed the Florentines—certainly the novelty of the crowded deep landscape and much of the non-religious detail. Consider, for example, the delicate modeling of the face of the middle king, the skillful depiction of the foreshortened horses, the page kneeling to remove the spurs of the younger king, and the rich array of exotic animals. This was fine stuff.

But Florentines would have bickered over other characteristics, mainly the light-hearted spirit within a religious scene (indecorous), the monkeys (sin!), and the gold tooling that reflects light instead of a penetrating

68. Gentile da Fabriano, *Adoration of the Magi*, 1423, Uffizi.

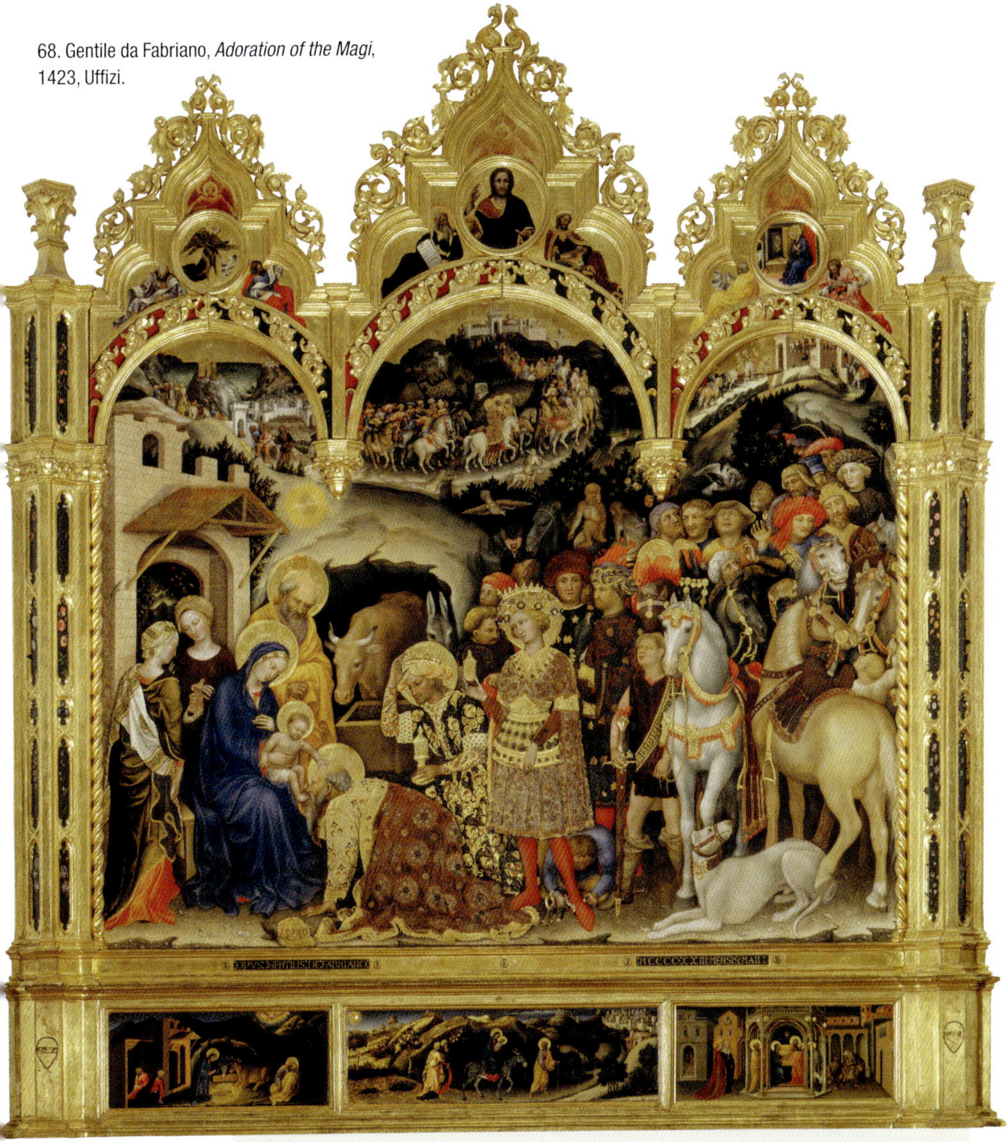

Although Gentile's visit to Florence was short, with this painting, a paradigm of the International Gothic style, his reputation eclipsed even that of Lorenzo Monaco.

Giottesque light that spells out the volume of objects. Yet how could a spectator not be drawn by this extravagant painting with its fine, brocaded outfits and minutely drawn detail of wealth righteously obtained?

Gentile's *Adoration* differs from later versions in that it marginalizes the holy family and instead concentrates on the kings and their retinue.

Like the grand public festivals that the Florentines enjoyed, it depicts the passing of the great feudal tradition of knighthood and chivalry fleshed out with the crowded abundance of detail that characterized the style of International Gothic.

Lorenzo Monaco, c. 1370-c. 1425, *Adoration of the Magi*, Uffizi, 1420-22

Lorenzo painted the *Adoration* toward the end of his life, and he most likely completed it before Gentile's version. More so than his *Coronation*, the picture exhibits elements that fall under the broad label of the International Gothic. The figures have lost their bulk to slimness and towering height. Their elegant swaying postures create rhythms that respond to and echo the curvilinear forms throughout the scene. The form of the bearded man in yellow repeats in the turban, in the scimitar, and in the robe, their curves mirroring those of the horse, dog, and rock. In fact, every form moves in curves.

69. Lorenzo Monaco, *Adoration of the Magi*, 1420-22, Uffizi.

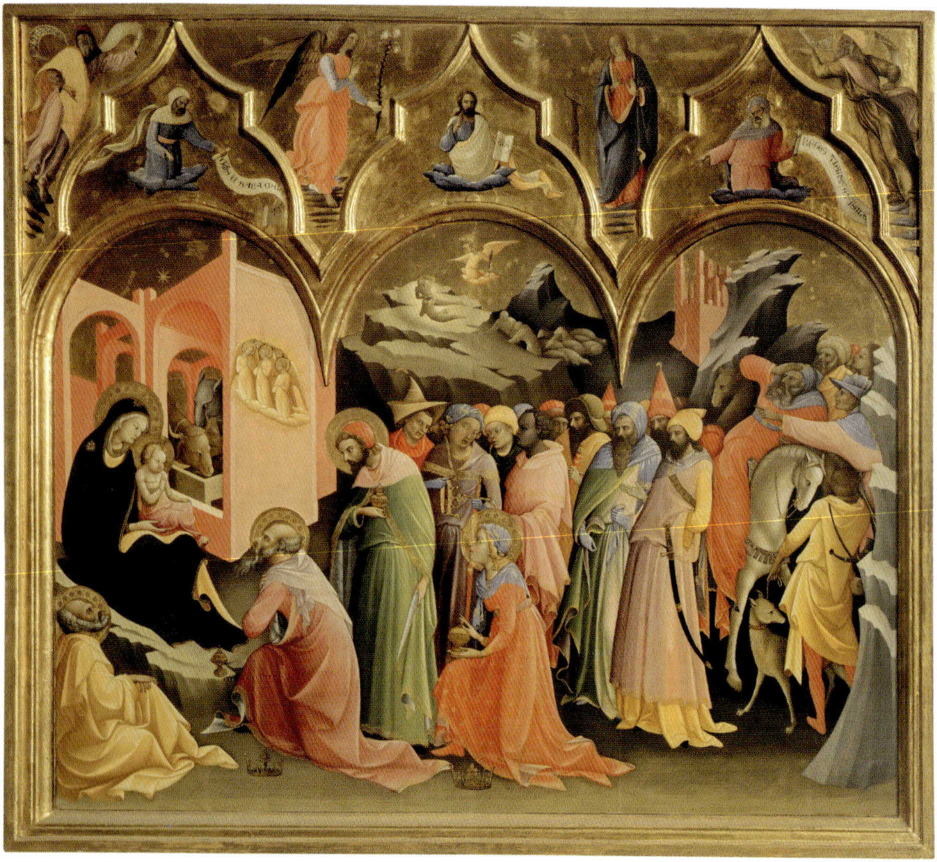

Only three years later, as he was beginning his last picture, Lorenzo was replaced by his young protégé, Fra Angelico (whom we'll meet in the next room). The patron had decided his style had grown stale.

ROOM 7 EARLY RENAISSANCE INVESTIGATIONS INTO NATURE

The painters in this room ushered in the first phase of the Renaissance at a time when Lorenzo Monaco's linear style still dominated Florence. Before his death in 1428 at age twenty-six, Masaccio laid the foundations for the new era with the earliest painting here, the *Virgin and Child with Saint Anne*. What separated this painting from the International Gothic was a system of graduated light and dark tones that imitated how natural light defines an object's relief. Ten years later, the humanist architect Leon Battista Alberti provided a scientific basis to painting in an influential treatise that urged painters to "imitate nature." Masaccio's relief, with its rejection of outlines, had proved to be the essential first step. Alberti also described a system of rational perspective that Masaccio employed to create the illusion of space on the walls of the Brancacci Chapel. He devised a rational color scheme. Ever sensitive to the potential of the eye-popping brightness of Gothic color, he advised painters to mute their colors with the addition of black. But his last prescription, which challenged painters to render their figure's emotional state through movement and facial expression, proved for decades to be beyond the painters' skill, until the arrival of Leonardo da Vinci.

Not all painters were disposed to Masaccio's relief, seeing his figures as blocky and lacking in liveliness. For these artists, most notably Botticelli, the line of a silhouette was everything. It offered possibilities for depicting forms enlivened by grace and un-weighted by bulk—traits fundamental to the linear style. The precision of lines and outlines versus the spatial solidity of relief—of linear versus tonal painting—became the critical measure by which these artists and their successors judged one another.

★ Masaccio (1401-1428), Masolino (1383-c. 1440), *Virgin and Child with Saint Anne*, Uffizi, 1424-25

The contrast between the late International Gothic style of Masolino and the bold new style of the young Masaccio portends a critical shift in Florentine art. Masolino's contribution—Saint Anne and four of the angels (you might hazard a guess as to which are his)—endows the painting with sumptuous passages we have come to expect in International Gothic painting. He drapes his figure of Anne in brilliant red-orange and sits her on something we can't see, possibly a two-tiered throne, but here the spatial relationship isn't clear. She looms majestically over her family, yet she seems at odds next to her daughter. In part, she is hesitantly drawn and out of scale. More suitable to his style are the bold colors he sets out on the upper left: black in the angel's wings, yellow shifting to orange in his tunic, muted reds and greens in the cloth of honor decorated with pomegranates.

By contrast, Masaccio reaches back to Giotto for inspiration, blocking his Madonna out in the same severe pyramidal shape. More so than Giotto's, her face is nobly human, even heroic, as she contemplates her child's grim future. The powerful baby would have been beyond Giotto's vision.

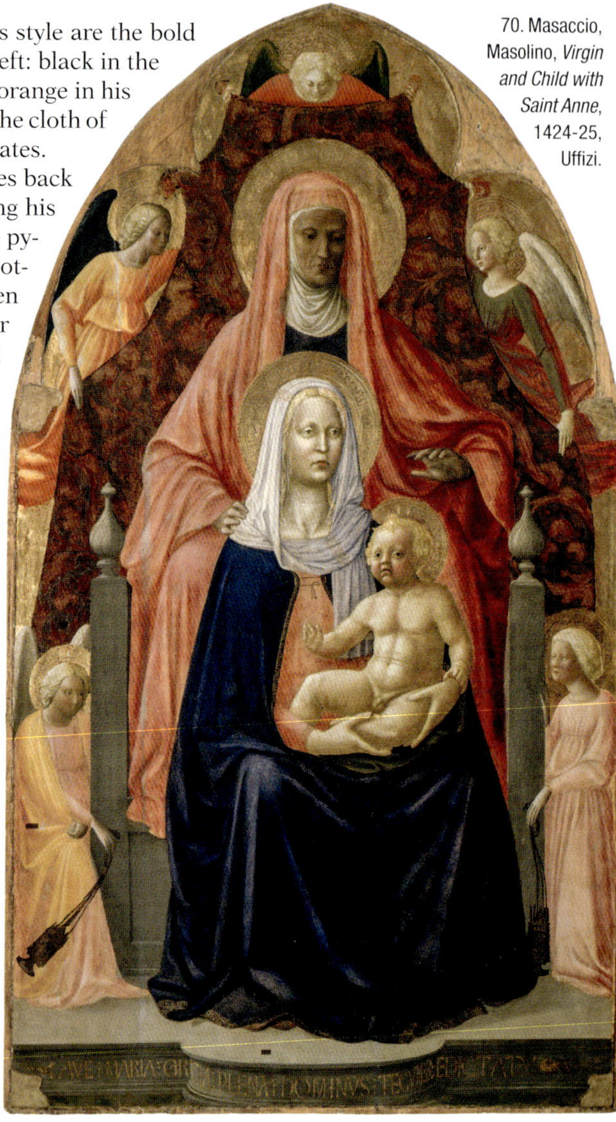

70. Masaccio, Masolino, *Virgin and Child with Saint Anne*, 1424-25, Uffizi.

But something more compelling than figural design is happening here. The key to Masaccio's figures lies in the directed light that streams in from the upper left and discriminates, especially apparent in the flesh tones, between highlights and shadows, thus distinctly evoking the illusion of relief. Masolino's indifferent light is the principal reason his figures appear soft and flatter than Masaccio's. Most conspicuous are the features of his angels (Masaccio's is on the upper right) where the notion of light is inconsistent, leaving the shading dispersed in random patches, like facial makeup enthusiastically applied by a young child. The contours are explicitly clear in the features of Masaccio's angel. But just as remarkable in this tiny creature is the precision he invests in the eyes. With a few dabs of paint, he brings to life an intelligence that Masolino could never have envisioned.

Fra Angelico, c. 1395-1455, *Coronation of the Virgin*, Uffizi, 1435

A transitional work of art by the Dominican Fra Angelico, the most celebrated painter of his generation, exemplifies his formative period as a decorator of illuminated manuscripts, a taxing skill shared by artists trained in the Gothic era's linear style, including his teacher Lorenzo Monaco.

Fra Angelico's painting represents the last vestiges of an International Gothic style whose splendor he turns into a conveyance for mystical ecstasy. As Christ crowns Mary in a celestial paradise, they sit enveloped by rays of light created by Angelico's masterful gold tooling. Angels, slim and curvilinear in shape, dance in swaying rhythms around the divine couple. Still, in a nod to the onrushing new order, Angelico disperses the heavenly court in rational semi-circles that recede deftly into a deep, clear space.

71. Fra Angelico, *Coronation of the Virgin*, 1435, Uffizi.

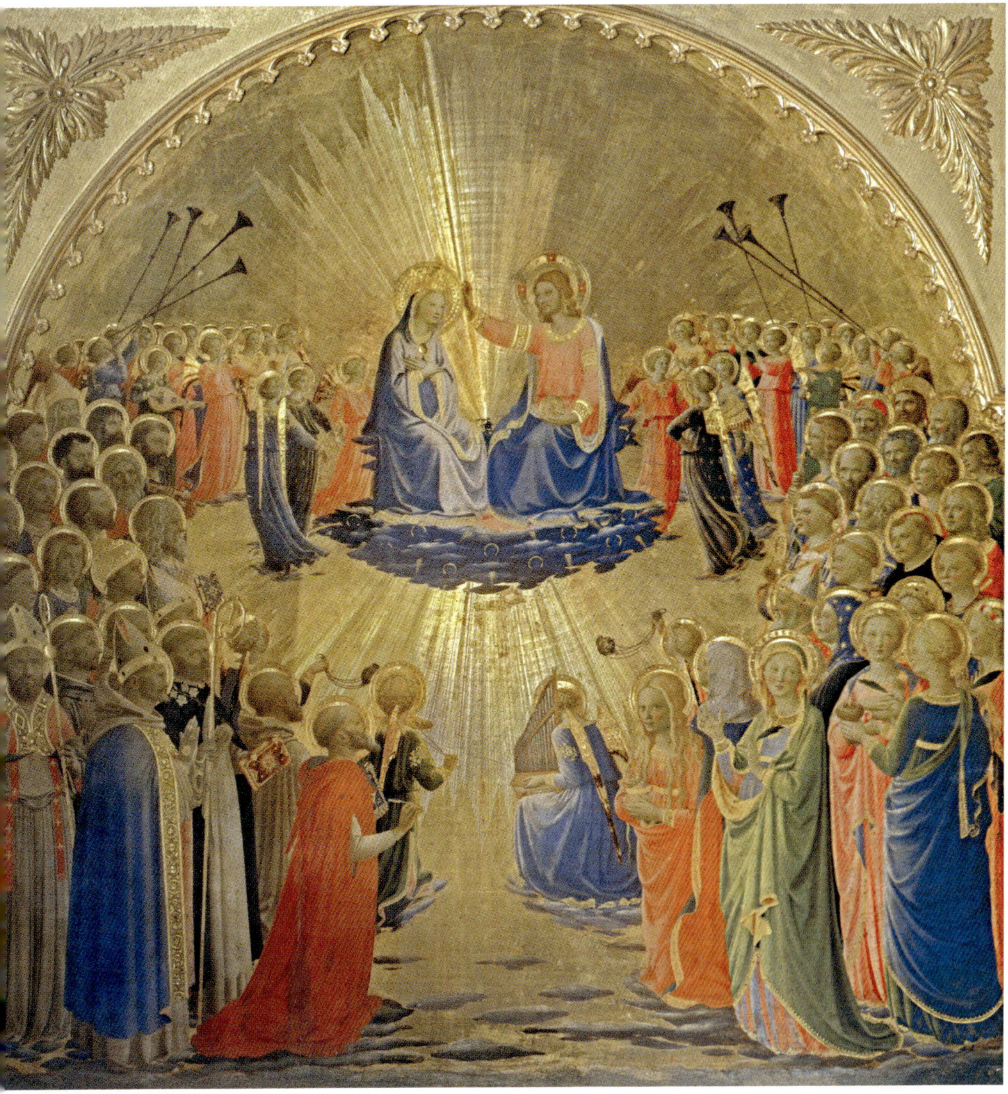

✶ Domenico Veneziano, 1410-1461, *Madonna with Child and Saints (Santa Lucia de' Magnoli Altarpiece)*, Uffizi, 1445

The Venetian Domenico spent much of his career in Florence. Little remains of his work, but this, his masterpiece, expands on the concepts of space, color, and light.

The panel is an early example of an altarpiece in which saints are no longer isolated from each other by Gothic pendants, but instead share the same space and take notice of us in ours. On the right stand Saint Zenobius and Saint Lucy, who contemplates Saint Francis and John the Baptist while holding her eyes on a gold plate—they were gouged out at her martyrdom. John, in turn, implores us to recognize the mother and child.

The architecture is ordered by perspective in typical early Renaissance fashion. The columns diminish in size and recede toward the center to give us a sense of the loggia's depth. Behind is an open-aired alcove whose diagonal side walls are topped with pinkish ribbing to create orthogonals that intersect at the womb of the Virgin.

But for all its rationality, something else is going on in the space. Notice that the forward arches of the loggia are placed at the picture's surface, giving the impression that the saints are inside even though we see they are standing on the pavement in front of the loggia. Manipulating the

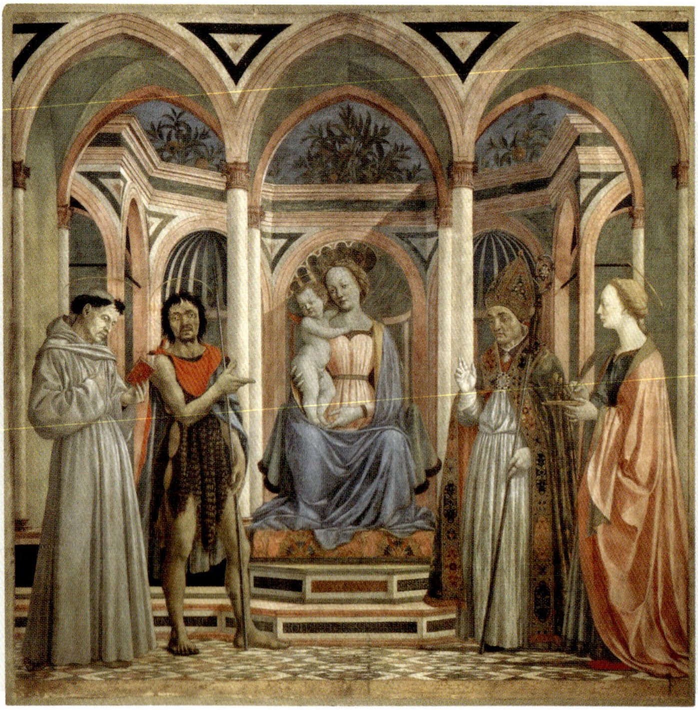

72. Domenico Veneziano, *Santa Lucia de' Magnoli Altarpiece*, 1445, Uffizi.

Line versus Relief. The borders of the figures are crisply contoured; a dark outline circumscribes the flesh tones in the forearm and hand of John, though a strong measure of relief is visible in his brawny limbs and rugged features. This emphasis on the explicit delineation of contours seals the figure off from its surroundings. This patched-in-look was much disparaged by critics of the next century.

architecture allows the artist to place his figures near the picture's surface.

In his palette, Domenico employs luminous pastels—pink and rose, lime green, and gradations of gray—to create the feeling of a sun-drenched villa. He restricts the red in John's robe to an isolated field to prevent its popping forward, and thereby contradicting the illusion of deep space. But in his lighting, we see an innovation in the use of black pigment, which had been used only in isolated draperies. To simulate how the pinks and greens in the back wall of the alcove are bleached by sun light or deepened by shadow, Domenico paints with traces of black wash to suggest the shadow that passes diagonally behind Mary's figure. Such atmospheric gradations anticipate the style of Leonardo da Vinci.

★ Paolo Uccello, 1397-1475, *Battle of San Romano*, Uffizi, c. 1436

Paolo Uccello was a guiding light of the early Renaissance made famous by his life-long pursuit of perspective. His panel depicts the battle of San Romano in 1432 between the Florentines and the Sienese. It is the center piece of a set of three (the others are in Paris and London), commissioned by a banker aligned with the Medici, to glorify the only successful battle in an otherwise ill-conceived military campaign.

The subject is unabashedly International Gothic, a battle scene

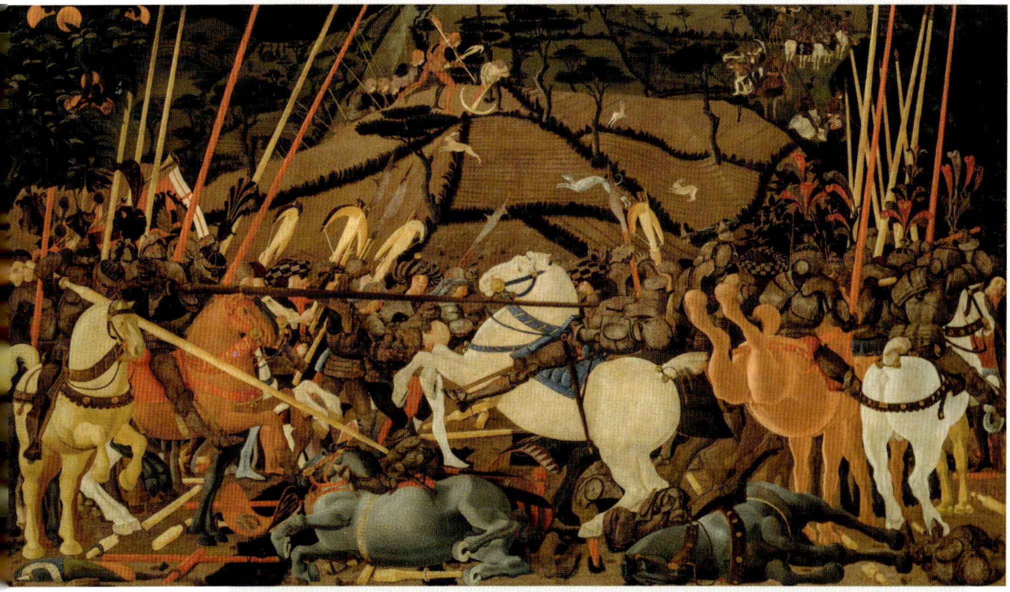

73. Paolo Uccello, *Battle of San Romano*, c. 1436, Uffizi.

The armor is decorated with tarnished silver leaf that once glittered in reflective patterns calling attention to itself—antinaturalistic effect Alberti would have disdained.

memorializing a world of feudal chivalry, still much a part of the times, in a dazzling display of equestrian knights and grand phalanxes of armies entangled in chaos. Bugles, banners, lances, crossbows, and suits of armor derive from the Gothic ideal of the battle as an opulent pageant.

The way Uccello imposes a rational order on the pandemonium is alien to the Gothic, however. Six foreshortened horses and fallen lances, systematically crossed and squared, establish a clear ground plane that directs our eye by a precise perspective grid to the story's focal point, the decisive moment when the Sienese general is toppled from his mount. A scheme so pervasively rational drains the picture of any naturalism, but not its storybook charm. Naturalistic anatomical studies and innovative lighting, which some artists in this room chose to probe, have been eclipsed by geometrically shaped carousel horses frozen in place and featureless comic-book faces peeking out of their helmets. What we have here is an artist who is captivated by the trappings and ritual of battle, creating a stylized parody.

From an aerial view, we note a rural background at odds with the perspective of the foreground scene. It is as if Paolo Uccello sees no place for rationalism in Tuscany's beloved countryside, where scattered hunters chase down rabbits amid hedges and furrowed fields.

Renaissance Colorists

ROOM 8

In a room devoted to the work of Filippo Lippi, we follow the development of a gifted colorist influenced in his early career by Masaccio's relief system and Alberti's prescription to create a pictorial space contiguous with the viewer's.

Lippi was a Carmelite monk very unlike his older contemporary, the pious Dominican Fra Angelico, whose delicate paintings of the Madonna made little reference to Masaccio's style, yet found their way into the young painter's art. Lippi's private life was best remembered for an illicit relationship with his model Lucrezia Buti—a nun in a convent where he was chaplain—which led to a son, Filippino Lippi. For this he was roundly defrocked, but he was allowed to continue his life with her.

Filippo Lippi, c. 1406-1469, *Coronation of the Virgin*, Uffizi, 1444-47

Were it not for the sturdy Masaccio-inspired figures we might mistake this for a Gothic picture: Gothic in the golden frame's hanging arches that imply separation, in the overcrowding of figures and ornamental details, in the over-sized presence of God crowning a timid virgin borrowed from Fra Angelico. The side arms of their throne and the boundaries of the platform below act as orthogonals that direct our eye to the vanishing point at the head of God. Yet the eye-catching seashells on the arms of the throne, jutting out toward where the frame's arches fall, appear to push the daringly foreshortened lower group out in front of the picture's

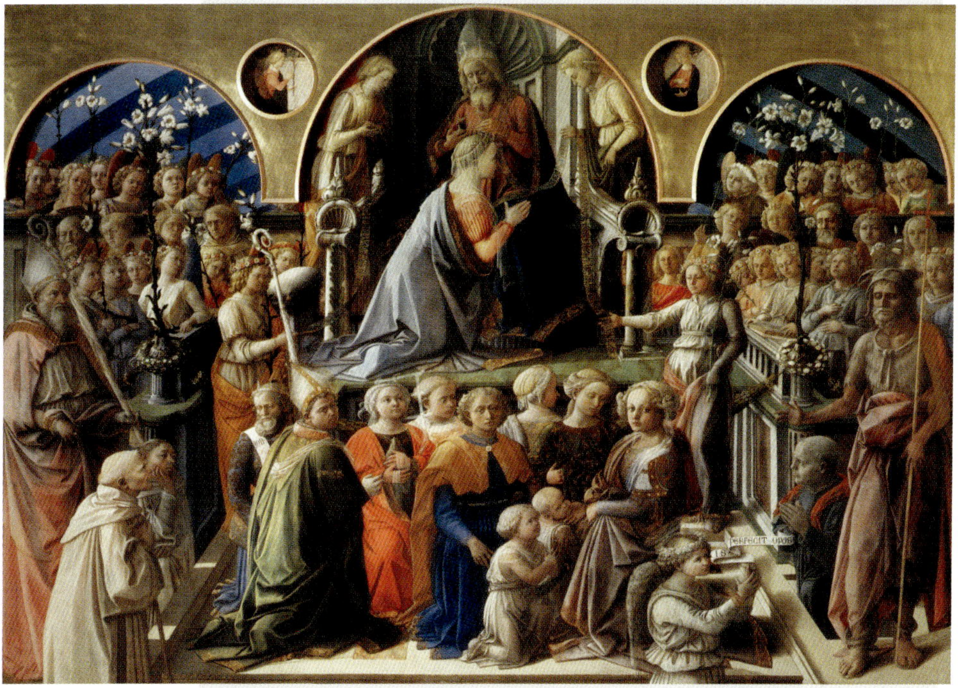

At the far left, the artist himself, staring out, chin cupped on his hands. Opposite him on the right, the kneeling, already deceased patron.

74. Filippo Lippi, *Coronation of the Virgin*, 1444-47, Uffizi.

frame. What results are two separate scenes that disorient our focus: one we view at eye level and the other from above.

But we see progressive features as well: in the light that strikes the foreground figures from the left, in the figures that diminish in size as they push to ever deeper space, in the ambitious yet confused relationship of constructed space, and particularly in the individually characterized portraits of the saints kneeling on a platform in the foreground. (Included here, the lovely woman done up in the latest Florentine finery kneeling next to her two children and her husband, St. Eustace, in royal blue robe. Because Eustace was a Roman general who converted to Christianity, he and his family were martyred by Emperor Hadrian in 118 AD.)

Along with the deep space and varied character studies, Lippi's palette plays a vital role as a touchstone to Alberti's "imitation of nature." Instead of dispersing bright colors in Gothic patterns that emphasize the picture's surface, Lippi reserves his strongest colors for those figures closest to us and uses traces of blacks to grays to neutralize the colors of the background figures. This gradual muting of color with distance, as occurs in nature, creates a sense of atmospheric depth that gives visual unity to the whole. (The palette is further discussed in the Addendum, p. 218, fig. 146).

★ Filippo Lippi, *Madonna and Child with Two Angels*, Uffizi, 1460-65

This half-length Madonna is one of Lippi's last paintings and truly one of the triumphs of the Renaissance. Mary is seated before a window that monumentalizes her spare figure and pushes it into our space without trivializing a landscape that extends into a distance dimmed to a hazy blue. Instead of a Madonna's conventional drapery, she wears a fashionable Florentine gown of dark greenish-blue.

The silhouettes of her head, neck, and hands are described by simple austere contours no longer beholden to Angelico's gentle linearism. The line that creates the contours is for the most part hidden from us by the darks of the landscape and the gown, but a particularly beautiful one clearly distinguishes Mary's jaw from her neck.

Deep in prayer, she is unaware of our presence and unresponsive to the chubby Jesus, who is hoisted to her shoulder by two angels, his mischievous playmates. She is beautiful and elegant, crowned with a tiny string of pearls that encircle her head and a diaphanous veil that gathers in elaborate folds over her golden hair. An alternate reading of her lovely profile might suggest she is a Florentine aristocrat, or possibly, Lippi's beloved Lucrezia.

Lippi's painting made a strong impact on two artists whose work dominated the coming decades. The palette, limited to earth tones—darks, ruddy flesh tones, whites, and rose—equally subdued by mixes of black to pale gray, anticipated the work of Leonardo da Vinci. But the painting's most endearing quality, the linear treatment of the silhouette, leads to his one-time student, Botticelli.

In the Virgin, we finally see beauty well beyond Alberti's prescription for naturalism.

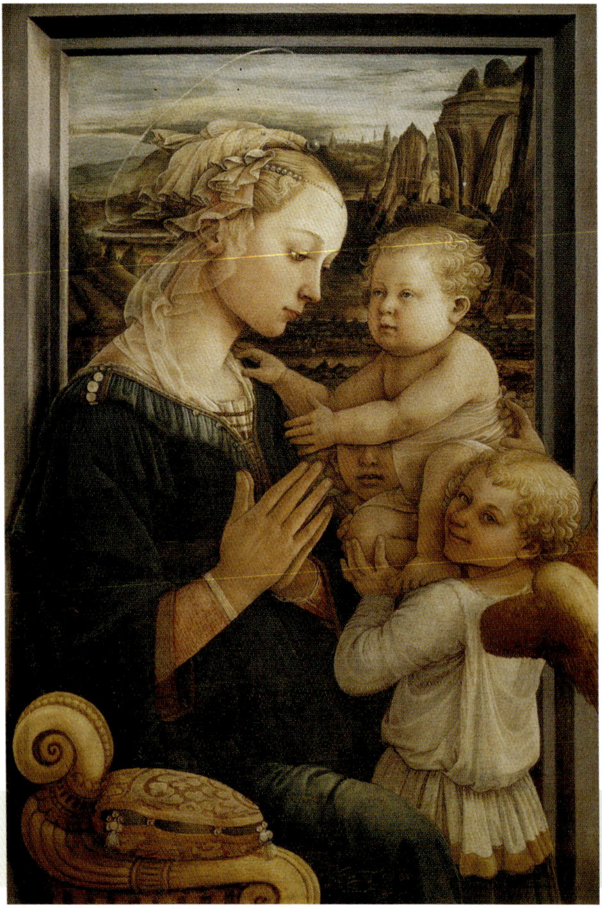

75. Filippo Lippi, *Madonna and Child with Two Angels*, 1460-65, Uffizi.

76. Filippino Lippi, *Madonna Adoring the Child*, c. 1483, Uffizi.

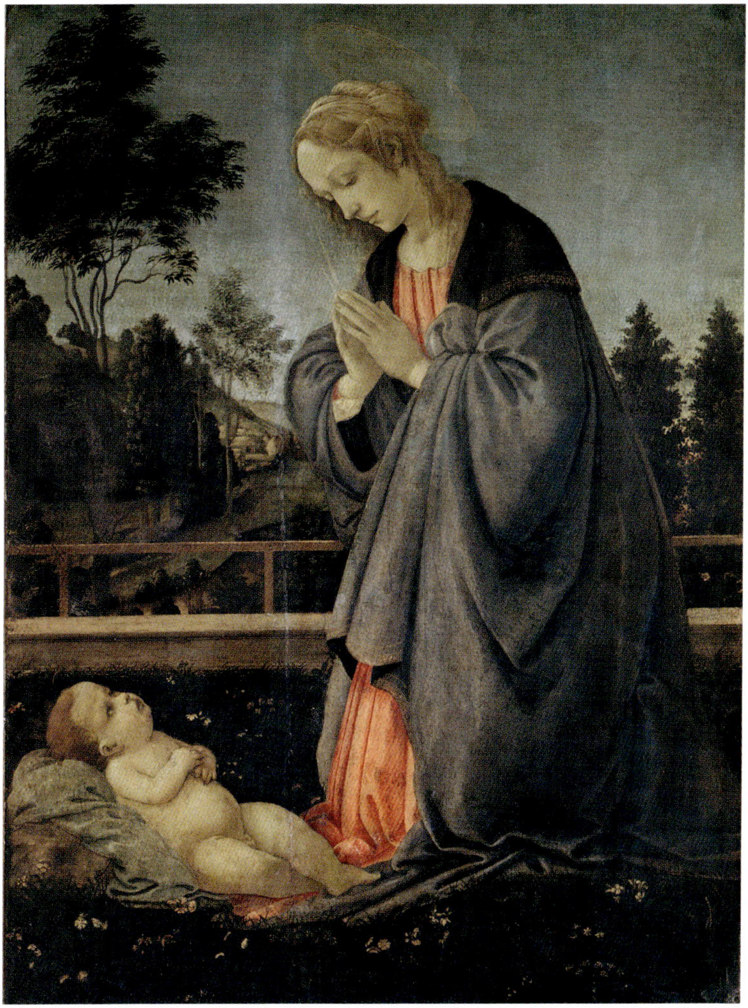

Filippino Lippi, 1457-1504, *Madonna Adoring the Child*, Uffizi, c. 1483

Filippino Lippi was one of a half dozen major protagonists working in a range of disparate styles in the late Quattrocento. Apprenticed first to his father and then to Botticelli, his art culminated in a masterpiece frescoed in Santa Maria Novella. His inclusion here, while chronologically out of sequence, offers us fine comparisons with his father's *Madonna* we just studied. This quiet pastoral scene, one of the earliest of this master's works, is a literal description of nature in the Albertian sense that the background space is a logical extension of the foreground space. The spare palette of blues, greens, and rose merges seamlessly to reinforce a visual unity.

Filippino Lippi, *Adoration of the Magi*, Uffizi, 1496

Unlike Gentile's festive, disorderly *Adoration*, Lippi gives the composition stability by placing Mary at the apex of a pyramid completed by the three kings kneeling before her. He threatens the sanctity of her space, however, with a mix of hyperactive spectators robed in various disquieting colors. Depicted in an array of intricate poses and cocked heads, these characters compete obsessively for our attention.

Lippi's pervasive activity is fresh and provocative, yet, as the picture's only unifying force, it propels his art beyond the bounds of a har-

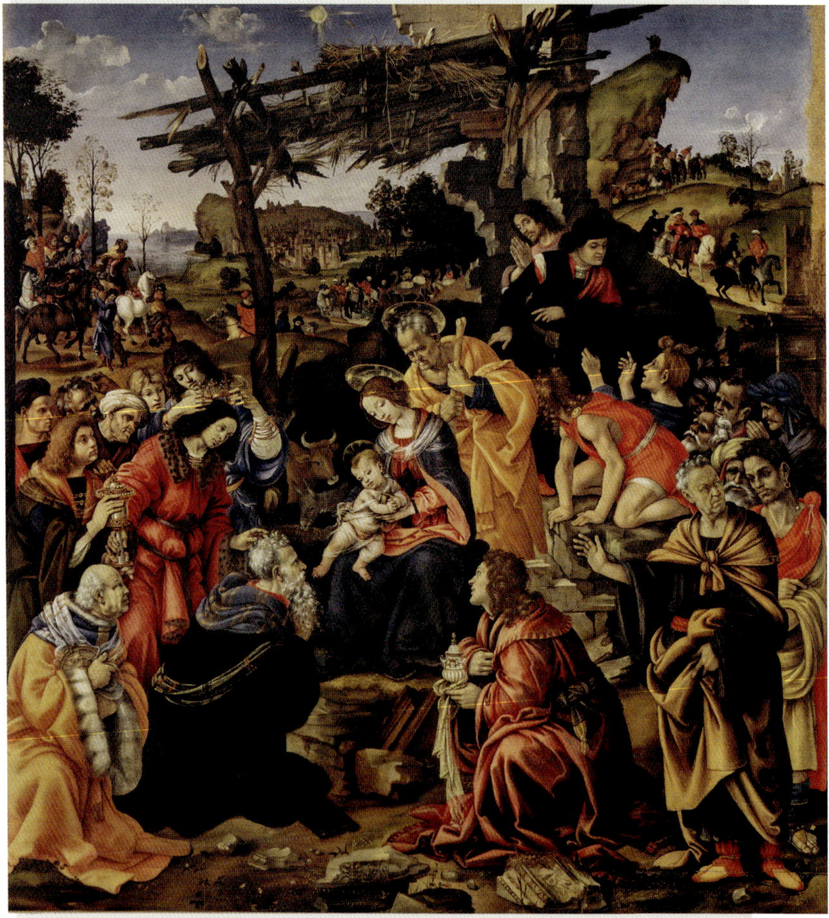

77. Filippino Lippi, *Adoration of the Magi*, 1496, Uffizi.

The features of the faces are coarse graphic characterizations favored by Northern European art, instead of the idealized types that characterized his *Madonna Adoring the Child* and Florentine painting in general in these years.

mony that was just taking shape in Renaissance art. Once Lippi had mastered the "imitation of nature" in his early works, he turned to the language of ornament in an appeal to the senses rather than to the intellect. His style didn't fit Alberti's paradigm; he would have abhorred the bright colors and over-crowded fussiness.

ROOM 9 GESTURE, POSE, AND EXPRESSION

Sandro Botticelli, 1445-1510, *Fortitude*, Uffizi, 1470

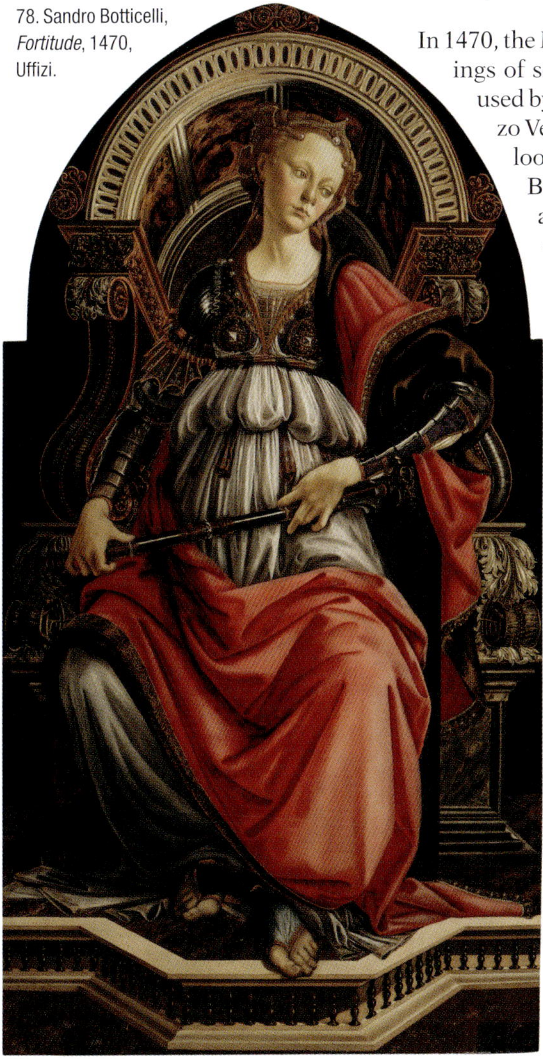

78. Sandro Botticelli, *Fortitude*, 1470, Uffizi.

In 1470, the Merchants' Tribunal commissioned paintings of seven Virtues to hang above the benches used by the judges in their court in front of Palazzo Vecchio, which explains why we seem to be looking at their extended bodies from below. Botticelli's opportunity to wrest *Fortitude* away from Piero del Pollaiolo, who had executed the first six, was pivotal for an artist beginning his career. Along with Leonardo da Vinci, he had worked with Verrocchio as an assistant, where he adopted much of the older master's style in portraying fully rounded figures and faces with broad foreheads and pointed chins. As a youth, he'd studied under the aging Fra Filippo Lippi, whose late style climaxed in the graceful silhouettes that shaped his *Madonna and Child with Two Angels*. Ultimately, it was this style that emerged as Botticelli's most endearing legacy.

Whereas Piero del Pollaiolo's *Virtues* sit like lifeless statues in imperious judgment, *Fortitude* marks the moment when the painted image takes on the look of life, revealing both poise and attitude. She shows us how a simple tilt of the head and, most tellingly, how soft reflective eyes can suggest a mind at work. Her relaxed but firm grip on her military baton closes a line that sweeps down one shoulder and up the next. Such a form is a lyrical manifestation of an expressive state, her sympathetic resolve in her high station.

The Uffizi's collection of Botticelli masterpieces documents every period of a career that at its height epitomized the golden age of Lorenzo the Magnificent. In the beginning, Botticelli was, like other Renaissance painters, preoccupied with describing the physical aspects of natural appearances. In less than a decade he reversed course to become the greatest representative of the linear style, a style which had its foundations in Simone Martini's *Annunciation* (fig. 63). So as unique and beautiful as these paintings are, they increasingly push beyond the bounds of plausibility toward simplified abstractions of the human figure. As a style antithetical to naturalism, this art collided with the art of his contemporary, Leonardo da Vinci. Yet it was precisely this antinaturalism—the supreme indifference to the anatomical realities of the human figure—that played a key part in the art of the next century.

Sandro Botticelli, 1445-1510, *Adoration of the Magi*, Uffizi, c. 1475

The *Adoration* propelled Botticelli into the Medici circle as their favored painter for the rest of the century. Commissioned by a money lender indebted to the Medici for his wealth (we see him as an old, white-haired man gazing out on the right) the picture memorializes the ruling lineage of the city's most powerful family in the guise of the three Magi and their attendants.

79. Sandro Botticelli, *Adoration of the Magi*, c. 1475, Uffizi.

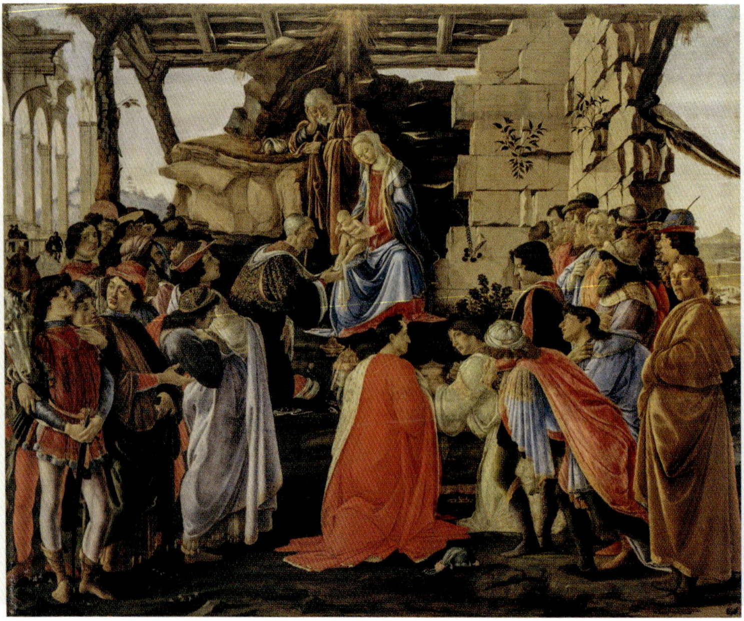

For patron and artist alike, this picture represents a bold, near-sacrilegious act in placing a wealthy, mercantile family in a sacred space. The sixteenth century historian Vasari stated that it was the superb portraits of the Medici clan, the patron, and the artist's self-portrait that prompted Pope Sixtus IV in 1481 to select Botticelli as one of the artists to fresco the walls of the Sistine Chapel.

A timid Mary sits with her tiny baby beneath a rough wooden manger whose roof symbolizes the canopy over the altar of a Christian church. Interrupting this sacred spaceis a portrait of the deceased family patriarch, Cosimo di Medici, depicted as the eldest king, kneeling impertinently close to the Christ Child. Below are his heirs, the Medici clan who take pride of place in this beloved biblical scene. In the center, on axis with Mary, is Piero (also deceased) as the second king, solitary and resplendent in his royal red cloak trimmed with ermine. Two wedges of family and friends direct our eye toward him. Standing to the right in red-trimmed black robe is Lorenzo the Magnificent, Piero's son and de facto ruler of the city. To his left is the kneeling Giovanni as the third king, dressed in white, speaking with his brother Piero. In the left foreground, two jocular lads, preening themselves, add a measure of informality. Among the spectators on the right stands the artist himself, who stares out at us, signaling that we share the painting's space.

The solidly sculptural and plausibly spaced figures represent Botticelli's deepest penetration into naturalism, which is the closest his style comes to that of Leonardo.

✶ Sandro Botticelli, *La Primavera*, Uffizi, 1482

At the time of Botticelli's death in 1510, this extravagant wooden panel, one of the largest to have survived the Renaissance, was considered antiquated—too remote from the styles of Leonardo and Michelangelo.

Like his other paintings, it was forgotten for centuries, until English aesthetes rediscovered it in the nineteenth century.

In a painting alive with sensuality, Venus gazes out, somewhat quizzically, while the three Graces perform a sprightly rondo, a dance then at the height of Florentine fashion. The fluttering filmy drapery, which barely disguises their supple bodies, follows and reinforces their movements, impeded by the almost visible air that surrounds them.

Primavera marks the first appearance of a classically antique allegory in Florentine painting. The subject plays out against a tapestry-like background, yet nature enlivens the painting with a tactile pagan beauty. While Venus is the goddess of springtime and of carnal desire, she is also the goddess of love and marriage, and that is her role here. Modestly dressed in a contemporary white Florentine gown and a rich, red velvet cape, her breasts emphasized by a braided gold cord, she is framed by the myrtle, her special tree. To each side runs a row of orange trees, whose fruits that were known in antiquity and the Renaissance as *medica mala*, may well allude to the name Medici. She stands, in her divinely timeless spring garden, on a carpet of wildflowers; exquisitely painted roses, cornflowers, crocuses, and violets tell us the month is May. And yet, amid this vernal splendor, her face is as cool as porcelain, and the last of Botticelli's female faces to retain the oval fullness that characterized Fortitude.

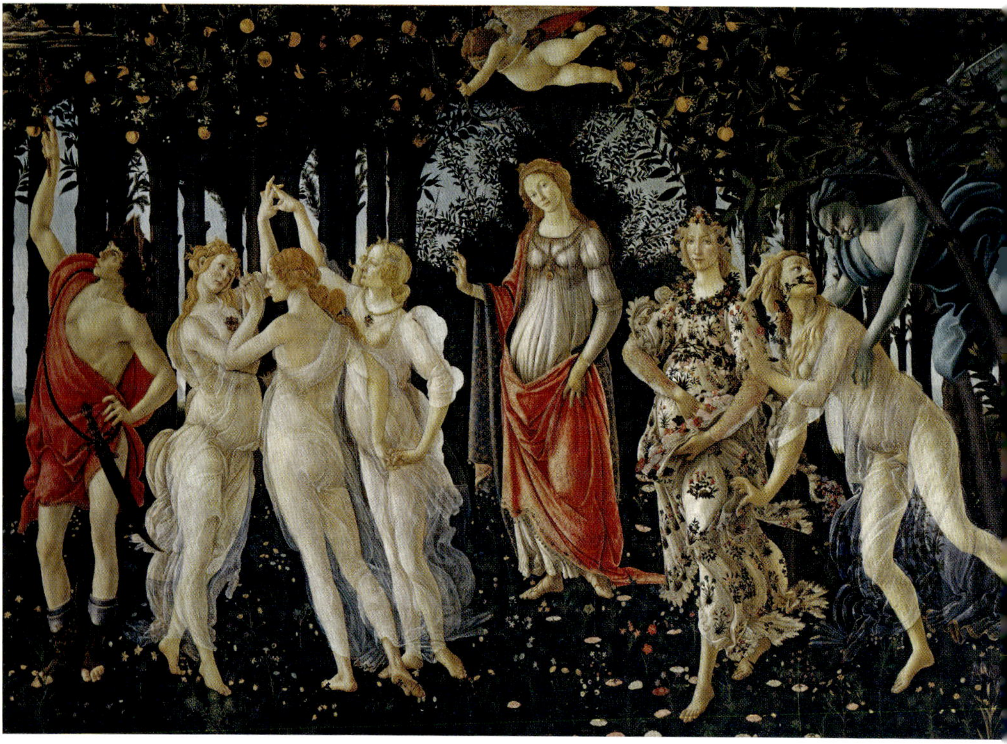

As Venus gazes out aloof, she gestures toward the dancing Graces, each with her single pearl, symbol of virginity, braided into her golden locks. Above Venus hovers her son, Cupid, about to fire his flaming arrow into one of the Graces, hinting at the painting's possible theme. To the left of the Graces is Mercury, in Roman mythology, the lover of Venus, father of Cupid, and god of wisdom and eloquence. Unlike those of the weightless Graces, his statuesque body stands firm, in a sensuous stance reminiscent of Donatello's bronze *David*. Outfitted with the accoutrements of protector—sword, winged helmet, and military cloak—he taps a group of small clouds, which are forbidden in Venus's garden, with his caduceus.

80. Sandro Botticelli, *Primavera*, 1482, Uffizi.

To the right, the gauzily clad virginal nymph Chloris has been spied by Zephyr, god of the spring wind, and is trying to flee as he swoops down, his violently expelled breath a symbol of her rape. She screams in surprise, but only roses fall from her mouth. In the myth, Zephyr repents and marries Chloris, rewarding her by turning her into a goddess, protector of flowers. We see her again in front, awakened and transformed as the married Flora, one of the most hauntingly beautiful creatures in all of painting.

Flora represents a new type of feminine beauty—the culmination of

Botticelli's most sensual style. She strolls languorously forward, sprinkling roses in her path, and, despite the fashionable dress of a married woman, she invites desire. Her blonde tresses fall loosely beneath her garlanded crown. Dark arching eyebrows, a long aquiline nose, a rosebud mouth, and a pretty cleft chin distinguish her narrow, oval face atop her long, supple neck.

She is more finely drawn—more particular, with the lines of a woman who is of our world—than the classically sculpted features of Botticelli's other beauties, as though their physical perfection had somehow failed his ideal. Yet he will not paint a woman like her again. Her gaze transfixes us with an expression as enigmatic as Mona Lisa's. With her lips parted just enough to reveal her white teeth, is she smiling? Or is she about to speak, and, if so, of what?

81. Detail, *Primavera*, Flora.

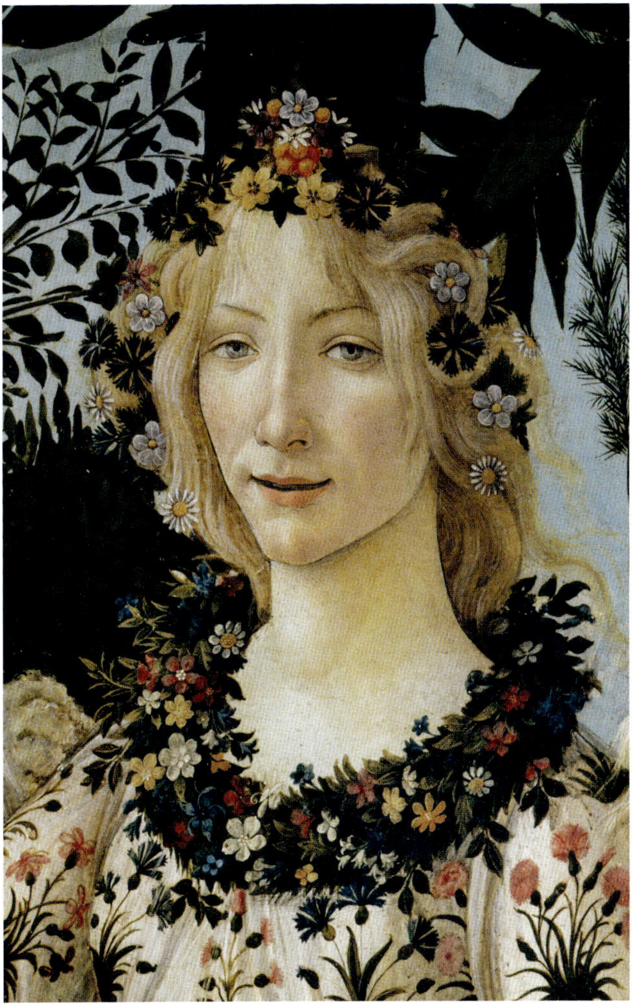

In the *Primavera* Botticelli forges an entirely new Renaissance style. He dismisses coherent space for the Gothic concept of a painting as a surface brought alive by the harmonious patterns placed upon it. He dismisses the psychological interrelatedness of the figural groupings of his earlier *Adoration* for a cadenced rhythm that unites his figures in a splendidly choreographed pagan ritual. He takes liberties with his anatomy, sacrificing modeling and articulated joints for ornamental smoothness. His goddesses spring from the imagination; they are born of artifice, of a supremely confident line that defines with perfect fluidity their graceful silhouettes. Soon, the world of artifice, by means of reshaping or simplifying the human figure for purely aesthetic or other expressive purposes, will be tested by the art of Leonardo, Michelangelo, and the great Mannerists of the sixteenth century.

Botticelli executed the painting for a cousin of Lorenzo the Magnificent, Lorenzo di Pierfrancesco de' Medici, who had recently married—a fact that may hold a clue to Botticelli's intention. Or maybe not: the meaning of the *Primavera* remains a mystery. Quite possibly its origins lie in the cultural atmosphere of the Medici circle, which had embraced pagan antiquity's celebration of human beauty and given it a Christian reading as the visual reflection of the divine. Or is the *Primavera* simply homage to spring, or to youth? Or a lyric love poem in paint? Whatever meaning Botticelli had in mind, his celebration of love and marriage is surely an ode to joy.

✶ Sandro Botticelli, *Birth of Venus*, Uffizi, 1482-85

Close in date to the *Primavera* is one of the earliest paintings on canvas, and the largest that survives from the Renaissance. Botticelli offers us Venus as the goddess of both love and desire, solitary and resplendent in her nudity. She steps hesitantly from seashell to shore, ending a long journey across the sea after being born from the seeds of the god Uranus.

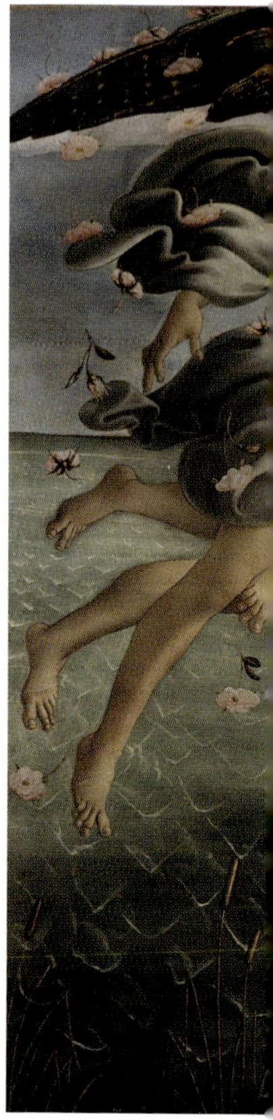

82. Sandro Botticelli, *Birth of Venus*, 1482-85, Uffizi.

She gazes dreamily past us, covering herself modestly with the thick locks of her corn-yellow hair. A series of gentle S curves, from her tilted head to her toes, silhouette her seemingly boneless body—the first female nude in Italian art to be painted solely for its beauty. On either side of her simple form hover the far more intricate figures—their draperies a whirlwind of swirls and smaller arabesques—that attend her arrival. On the left, perhaps the most beautiful rendering of ecstatic movement in all of painting, Zephyr, god of the spring wind, entangled with an amorous nymph, blows Venus gently ashore. On the right, one of the Horae—minor goddesses who attend Venus—springs upward to enfold her in a luxuriant rose-colored robe stitched with primulas and daisies and bordered with gold brocade. Note the rhythmic interplay between these three silhouettes: as always Botticelli places strong emphasis on the line of a beautiful silhouette.

Behind lies the vast sea, painted in luminous aquamarine tones; its ripples, a series of simple Vs, roll gently inland. At the bottom left edge are delicate water reeds—not so crucial to the picture's grand scheme, we might think, yet catching our eye with their simplicity and stillness and serving as a balance to the active forms. On the right, blossoming orange trees announce the arrival of spring. A meandering coastline ends in a long promontory that draws the eye to the distant horizon—a background far different from the shallow, tapestry-like garden of the *Primavera*.

As so often with Botticelli, much of the delight is in the details. Consider, for example, the gold, which no painter had given such prominence since the Gothic era. Botticelli, unlike his Gothic predecessors, deploys it sparingly and subtly. Follow the serpentine border of the rose robe to the right of Venus from the bottom upward and you come upon

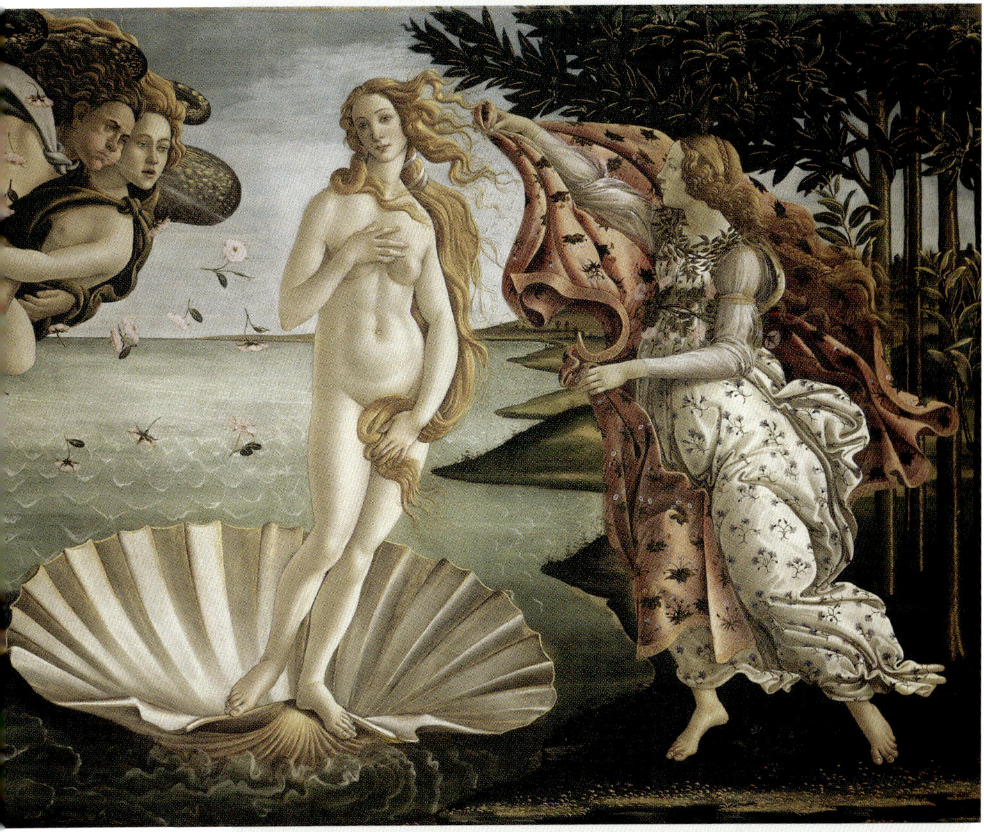

The painting belonged in the collection of the Medici family, as did the statue *Venus Pudica* (now in the Uffizi) which had only recently been unearthed in Rome and after which Botticelli based his figure.

the sharply scalloped golden hem embroidered in exquisite patterns—a beautiful little motif. Elsewhere, gold embellishes the nymph's olive-green cloak; it glimmers behind the schematic pebbles on the beach; it sharpens the dark verticals of the tree trunks and the veins of the leaves.

In no other Italian painting do we find such radiance, such a concentrated splendor of small and large forms. As a celebration of feminine beauty—and of beauty for its own sake—it hides no other meaning. It is as magnificent as any altarpiece, and no doubt its sensuality, even eroticism, raised eyebrows. But because it too was likely painted for Lorenzo di Pierfrancesco de' Medici, it escaped the scrutiny and censure of the larger public. Yet in less than a decade Botticelli would renounce its themes and retreat to the safety of newly emerging currents of Christian mysticism.

✶ Sandro Botticelli, *Annunciation*, Uffizi, c. 1490

In a startling rebuke to the style of his beguiling pagan goddesses, Botticelli turns to a severe and intensely spiritual beauty to describe the mystical core of Christian belief. Such reflects Botticelli's response to the pious preaching of Savonarola, the Dominican monk who was then denouncing the hedonistic ways of the Florentines, specifically of the Medici and their circle. (Savonarola was burned at the stake in 1498.)

He sets his scene in a coldly austere room where a window opens to an enclosed garden—symbol of Mary's virginity. The distant landscape reflects the influence of Northern European views.

Interrupting Mary from her reading at a lectern, an angel alights and crouches in a tightly coiled genuflection to announce God's will. His agitated drapery repeats the nervous advance of his outstretched hand.

83. Sandro Botticelli, *Annunciation*, c. 1490, Uffizi

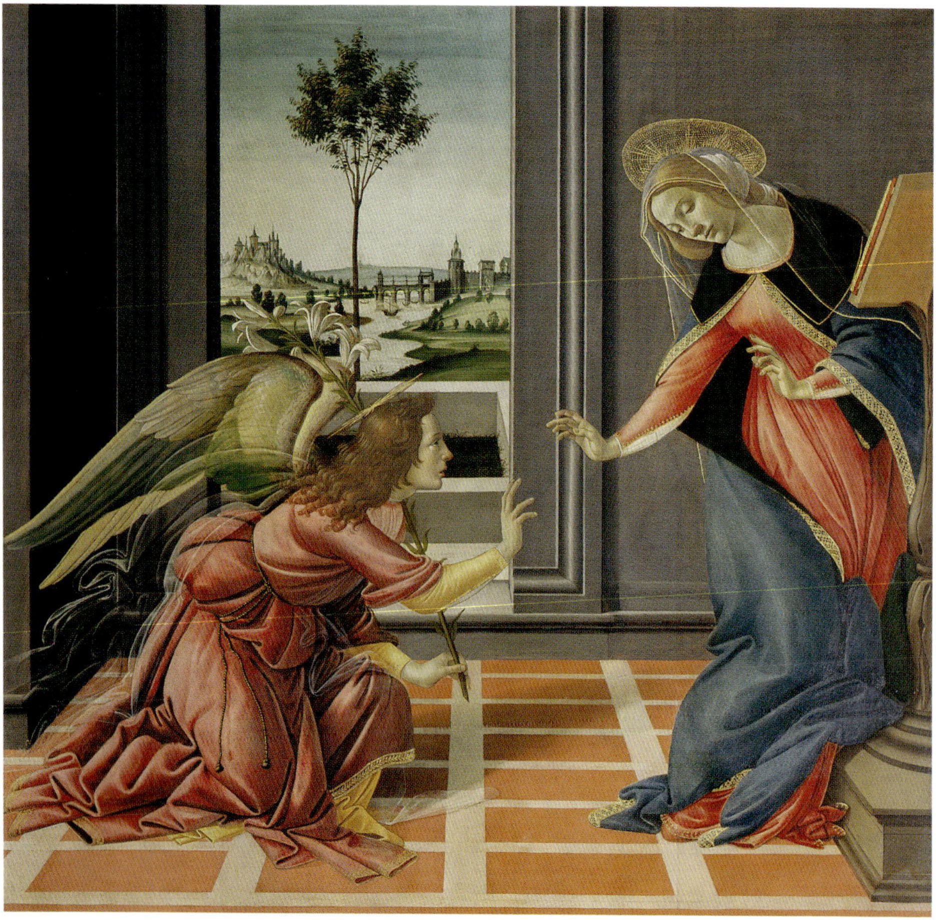

Meeting at the door frame, her hand answers his hand in a tentative pas de deux, powerful for reflecting the torments of her mind. Every sinuous line and sweeping fold of her garments and the incarnate grace of the curve of her elongated body are marshaled as the visual manifestation of the conception of the Savior within her womb. We are present at the moment of her understanding, "Behold, I am the handmaiden of the Lord."

Domenico Ghirlandaio, 1449-1494, *Adoration of the Magi*, Uffizi, 1487

Ghirlandaio ran the most successful workshop in Florence at the end of the century. He is also the Renaissance's most indefatigable practitioner of naturalism in its blandest form, a perfectionist who leaves nothing to the imagination. Whereas Botticelli simplifies his pictures to the point of abstraction, Ghirlandaio explains everything, large and small down to the last detail.

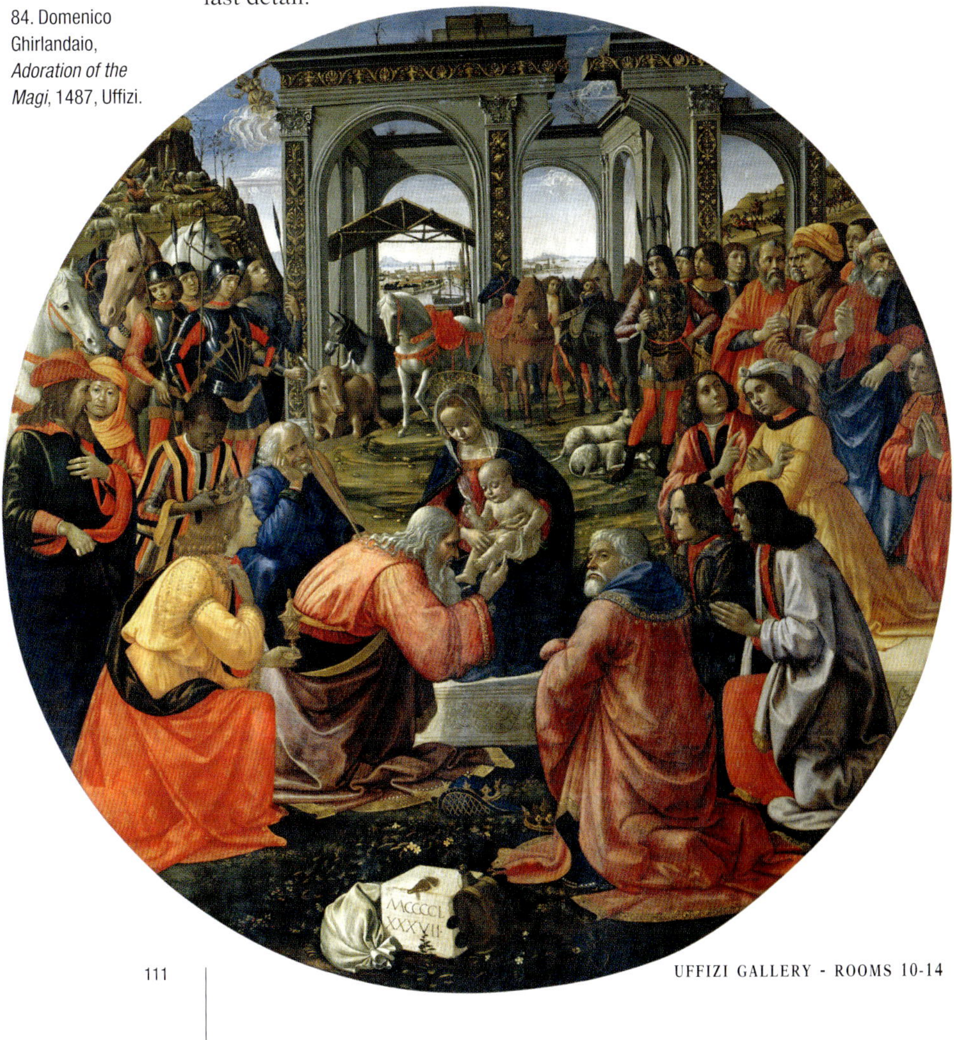

84. Domenico Ghirlandaio, *Adoration of the Magi*, 1487, Uffizi.

This is the style chroniclers of the next century strove to discredit: colors too bright and obsessively dispersed in symmetrical patterns; a space that crowds figures to the side (surprisingly, we find fewer of them here than we do in Botticelli's *Adoration*, fig. 79); and especially the hard, dry finish to the figures and their draperies.

Where Ghirlandaio excels is in the lifelike, individually characterized portraits of contemporary citizens that undoubtedly populate this scene, and we shall see even more stunning examples in Santa Maria Novella. He also gives us what many artists ignore: a foreground space brimming with interesting groupings that continues to a distant, charming seaside landscape, a horizon line just right—not too low or too high—and a ground plane that runs to ours as if we've captured the whole scene through a telescopic lens.

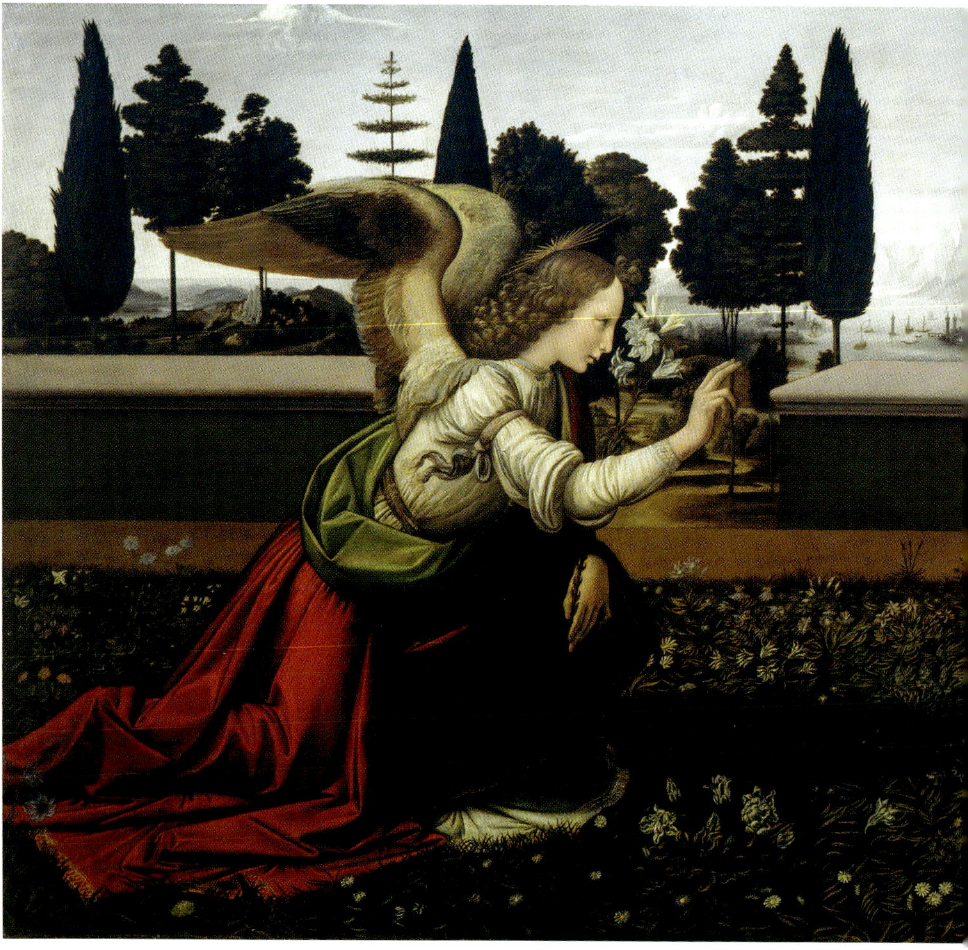

The Conquest of Nature

For all its seeming simplicity, Alberti's prescription to imitate natural appearances did not bear fruit until the year he died in 1472, when it emerges in Leonardo's earliest known work, the *Annunciation*. It is here, near the very beginning of his career, that Leonardo begins to formulate a rational color system. A second picture, a small passage in Verrocchio's *Baptism of Christ,* for most of the past century had been thought to have been his first. Comparisons between the two provide an intriguing lesson in understanding Leonardo's artistic development. Last is the key to the approaching High Renaissance, Leonardo's revolutionary *Adoration* (fig. 87). As a painting of concepts, it is difficult to interpret, and more so to articulate. And this may be one reason that Leonardo never received a

85. Leonardo da Vinci, *Annunciation*, c. 1472, Uffizi.

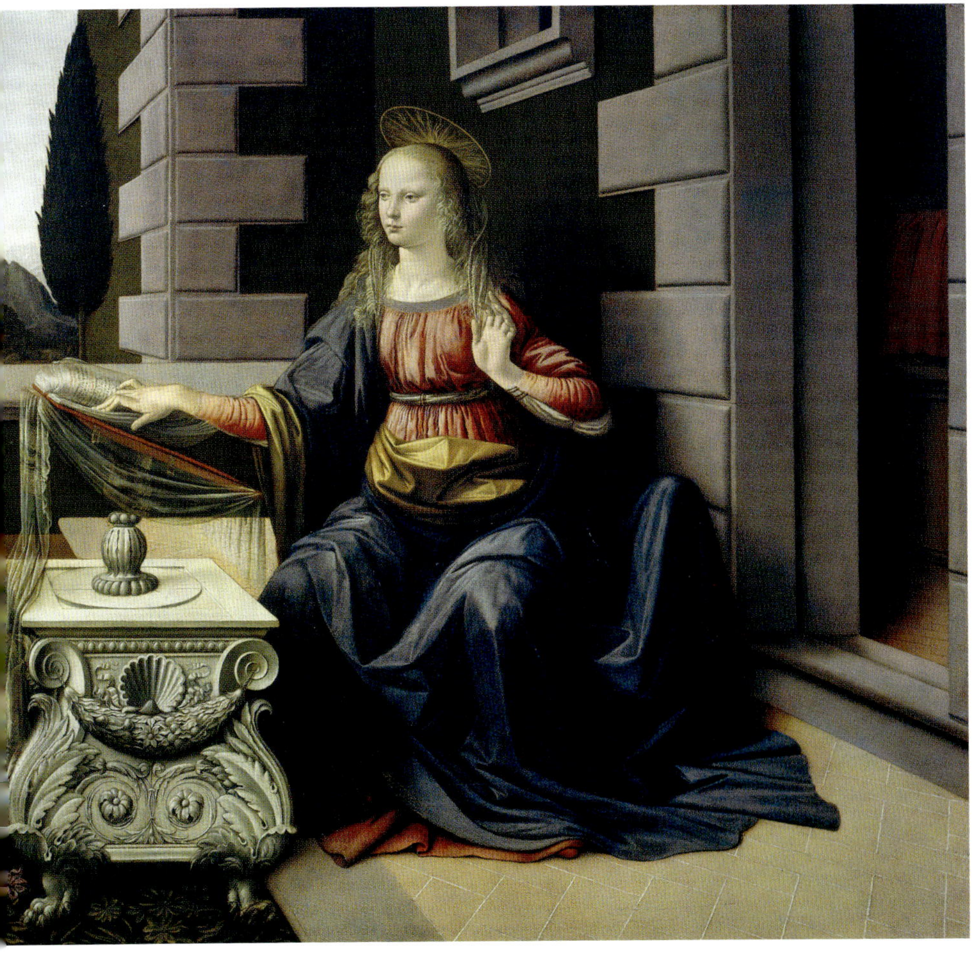

single commission from the Medici clan. On the surrounding walls are altarpieces by major artists whose contrasting styles represent the waning years of the Renaissance proper.

✶ Leonardo da Vinci, 1452-1519, *Annunciation*, Uffizi, c. 1472

Leonardo's picture, the most accurate description of nature we have encountered, is notable for the distant landscape's dim details, the bird-like wings of the angel; and the folds of Mary's drapery—all results of studies he repeated countless times in his drawings.

Although this is widely recognized as the first painting by Leonardo's hand, it comes with caveats. Skeptics point to two hands in the different treatments of the angel and Mary, the one so finely rendered in the rhythms of movement and the other a conventional portrait descriptive of nothing that suggests surprise. In the context of his later *Baptism*, the Virgin's rigid pose, immobile features, and mechanical gestures fail to register a hint of vitality. Also, the architecture recedes too abruptly—how far it extends is uncertain. The building's undefined perspective makes it difficult to fix Mary's position in relation to it. Then there is the odd spatial relationship of her figure to the lectern, which is closer to us than she is. Yet she fingers the near side of the book with her most distant hand, an anatomically impossible gesture.

These we can chalk up to inexperience. But there is no question that the palette, which forms the basis of the color system that will culminate in the *Mona Lisa*, is all Leonardo. He limits his colors to blue, red, and yellow in Mary's robes, and red and green in the angel's. Employed at full strength, each would have a different intensity, but Leonardo neutralizes them to the same intensity by mixing them with black. Thus, in what is called *tonal unity*, no single color is dominant, an unrealistic effect that painters of this period unfailingly continued to employ. But with the gains in naturalism, something of the beauty of pure color has been lost.

✶ Andrea del Verrocchio (1436-1488), Leonardo da Vinci, *Baptism of Christ*, Uffizi, c. 1476

Leonardo's debut onto the art scene of Florence has long thought to have begun here in his deceptively modest contribution to Verrocchio's painting. A talented sculptor with modest experience in painting, Verrocchio assigned his young assistant the task of painting in the distant landscape and the angel at the left, after he had completed the rest himself.

Verrocchio brings a sculptor's mentality to the athletic John the Baptist and scantly draped, meekly pious Christ. Both are boldly modeled and anatomically correct figures, and represent painting's best effort in the 1470s. Yet there remains a statue's hard clarity to the silhouette and a stiff, mechanical quality to their forms. Verrocchio's angel's blocky, flat

86. Andrea del Verrocchio, Leonardo, *Baptism of Christ*, c. 1476, Uffizi.

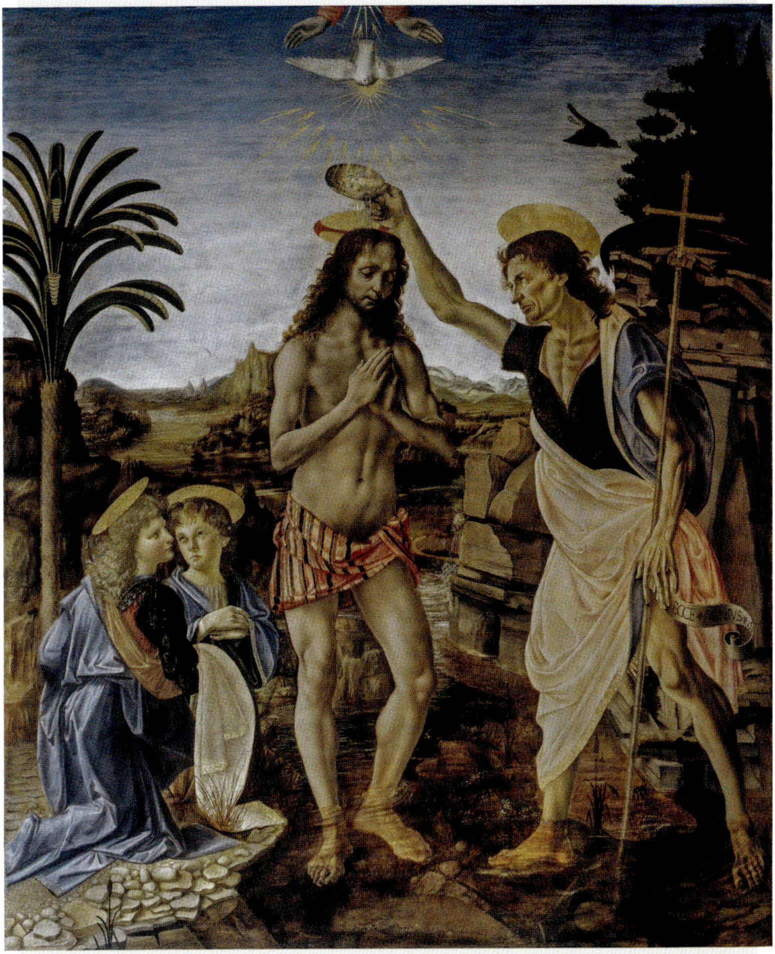

The most important sculptor of the late Renaissance, Verrocchio commanded a large workshop that enlisted the likes of Leonardo, Botticelli, and Perugino. Vasari, the Renaissance's first major historian, recounts – with more than a core of truth – that when the master saw what Leonardo had accomplished, he gave up painting altogether.

face, with its crisp black lines contouring the eyelids and its wiry whirlpool of hair, stares in dumb astonishment at Leonardo's angel as if to say, "Who is this beauty?".

Leonardo's exquisite creature indeed appears to have been sent from the heavens. Its shape, rendered so subtly in oil (Verrocchio used standard egg tempera) and free of emphatic outline, is softened by the same filtered atmosphere that makes objects in the distant landscape lose distinction, especially near the bleached-out horizon line, just as distance would be seen in real life. Verrocchio's figures, in contrast, are contoured so explicitly they look as if they are pasted into the scene, like the schematic rocks in the right foreground and the palm tree on the left.

Leonardo's angel represents his early obsession with matching a body's shape and pose to a facial expression appropriate to the story (notably absent in the Virgin in the *Annunciation*). Seen kneeling from behind, the crouched pose gives the figure fullness, and together with the head—turned enough to reveal the left eye—implies a body coiled at the instant of response to his Lord. Pink, luminous flesh that only oil can suggest overlays features that from chin to forehead are modeled by the subtlest changes in tone.

With a jeweler's precision, he also braves the difficulty of the eyes, those telling windows to the mind, which even the greatest portraitists, such as Raphael and Titian, often render opaquely, in browns or darker, or obscure in shadow. So alive are these eyes with blissful concentration that we can sense the moisture of their tears. Together with the body's pose, they speak of a profound devotion that later masterpieces rarely match.

✶ Leonardo da Vinci, *Adoration of the Magi*, Uffizi, 1481

In 1482, the year Botticelli completed the *Primavera*, Leonardo abruptly departed for Milan, leaving behind an unfinished picture that marks an irreversible shift in the history of painting. If we look around at the static figures and vacant faces in the altarpieces on the adjacent walls, we can see why no previous work of art could have prepared Leonardo's contemporary audience for the breadth of ideas presented here.

Painters looking for the mere "imitation of nature" would find only a wondrously pretentious meditation. The picture's core, however, is simple: a Madonna sitting alone admiring her infant. Although just barely sketched, she is Leonardo's vision of ideal beauty. Only three forms share her space: the submissive kings on the lower right and left. A sense of stability and calm are imparted to the scene by Leonardo's arrangement of their figures in the form of a pyramid.

From here, we are drawn to an undulating arc composed of a disorderly mix of haunted images threatening to violate the stillness of the Madonna's space. Beyond is a distant landscape overrun with a mysterious alchemy of contrasts: the chaos of violent horseback skirmishes alongside the rigid order of unfinished architecture. We are left to wonder what Leonardo conceived, and how much he intended we comprehend. And why, especially, does this picture forecast the High Renaissance?

The answer lies in Leonardo's recognition that the long pursuit of nature had produced artists who were adept at depicting physical "man", but were incapable of endowing him with expressions that reflected something of an inner life. Leonardo's desire to redress this imbalance is the heart of what the *Adoration* is about.

To capture the mood of a story about three kings come to see the newborn savior, Leonardo targets the incredulous spectators gesticulating, crouching, and crawling out of the darkness like amphibians testing the first light of day. He deliberates on each of them—some sixty figures in all—if only for a moment. Even among those just barely suggested we find some of his most beautiful images, such as the youth with wavy tresses to the left of the Madonna, his head cocked toward her. We search them out where they appear and vanish into incompleteness and shadow, as disturbing ghosts of Leonardo's imagination.

Never had such a broad diversity of physical types been depicted. But it is the astonishing variety of *emotional* types that is most significant for those artists who would follow him. He assigns a convincing shape and facial expression to each figure that together reflect the particular state of mind that explains their individual actions. Faces read other faces and interpret their surroundings. Young and old, seekers and doubters, riders on galloping horses are suspended in restless uncertainty.

As the only artist to adopt shadow, rather than light, as the scene's unifying force, Leonardo bathes his arc of images in a common darkened

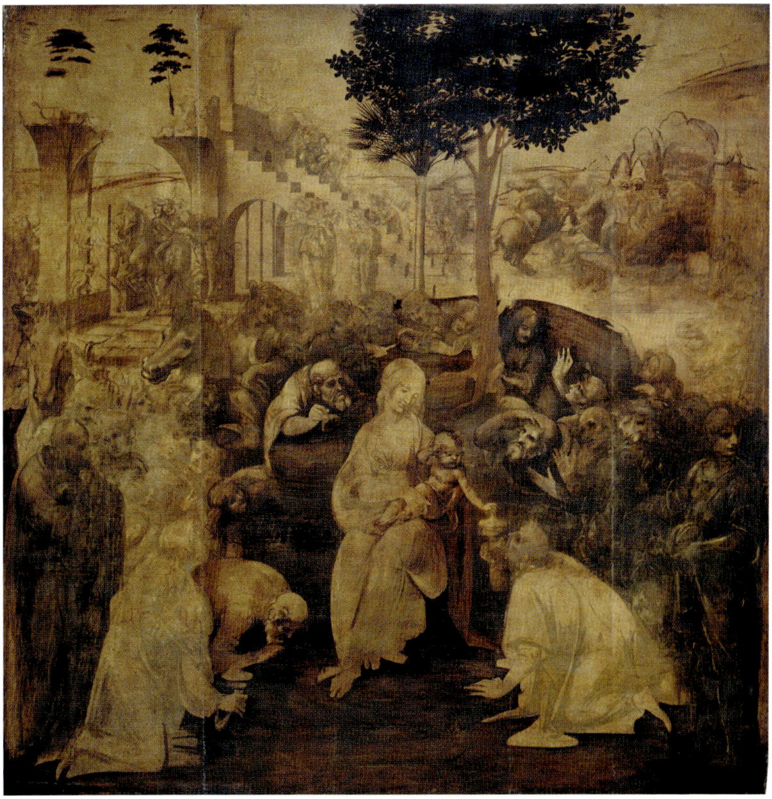

87. Leonardo da Vinci, *Adoration of the Magi*, 1481, Uffizi.

atmosphere. He unites them also by an intensity of movement and ceaseless gesture. In rhythmic sequences, the shifting of one figure counterbalances a complementary shifting of another.

In confronting painting's first exploration of the human psyche, we must ask if Leonardo left the *Adoration* intentionally unfinished. Had he enriched it with color and defined its figures explicitly by subjecting them to light, would the clarity have robbed it of its essence? The answer is yes, because shadow, for all its insubstantiality, veils figures and faces in darkness and uncertainty, an uncertainty that invokes the fragile interplay of a sensible outer world and a sensed inner one.

Leonardo da Vinci, *Mona Lisa*, Louvre, Paris, c. 1503-1506

Leonardo's impact on young painters of the sixteenth century was so profound that we must address one of his last paintings before leaving Florence for good. Much has been said about Mona Lisa's cryptic smile and penetrating eyes. But the portrait's immediate influence lay in Leonardo's continued interest in shadow, light and color, the elements that go into simulating relief. The brightness of late Renaissance color as employed by Filippino Lippi, Botticelli, and Ghirlandaio tended to make forms too pronounced, especially if they were held captive within clearly defined borders. Consequently, in the *Mona Lisa* we see an emphasis on softened contours over explicit contours, a veil of smoky haze (called *sfumato*, an important term we will refer to again) that further blurs contours, and the suppression of light and color toward dark monochrome. This is tonal unity at its most extreme. Although these are superb technical innovations, this is an artificial system that does not account for the brightness of color in nature. As we will soon discover, Michelangelo, Raphael, and other significant painters dealt with color in entirely different ways.

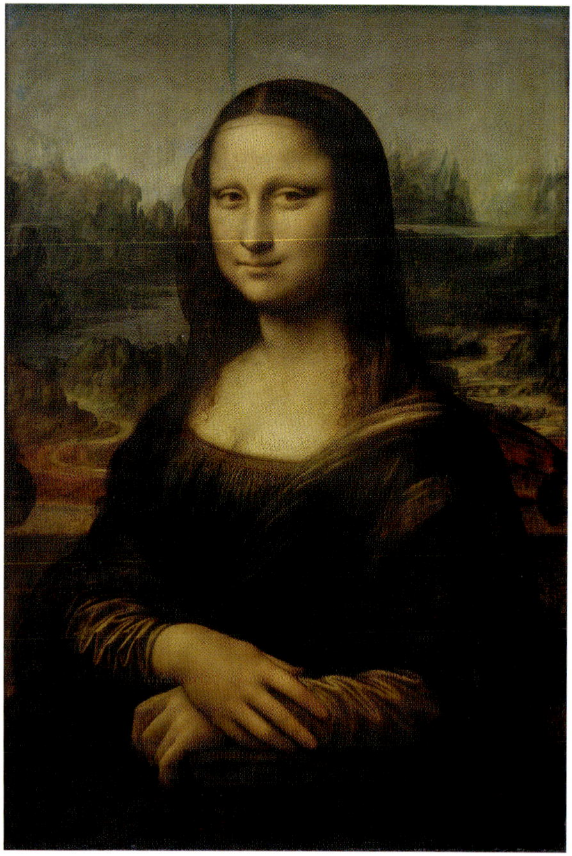

88. Leonardo da Vinci, *Mona Lisa*, c. 1503-1506, Louvre, Paris.

On the wall to the right of the Leonardo's paintings

Pietro Perugino, c. 1448-1523, *Madonna Enthroned with Saints*, Uffizi, 1493

In the last decades of the fifteenth century the Umbrian Perugino belonged to a group of prominent painters working in a number of divergent styles, including those of Ghirlandaio, Botticelli, and Filippino Lippi. Each of these styles, while preceding that of the High Renaissance (which we'll see shortly), never took part in its foundation because they all pushed too far in one direction.

If Leonardo's *Adoration* approximates natural appearances, Perugino's inert images do not. Least compelling are the vacant expressions and the eyes that fail to register consciousness. It is as if Perugino has relaxed both a figure's physical presence and its interior motives in order to avoid exposing his inability to infuse a measure of vitality in either one.

Lest we dismiss this painting out of hand, we must recognize its rather impressive features, namely the unified space uncluttered with fussy details. Most significant are the soft outside contours inspired by Leonardo's *sfumato* technique, which distinguish these figures from the hard contours that characterized the paintings of Perugino's contemporaries. In other words, if we can get beyond the cloying, overly restful figures, we must confess that Perugino has painted a harmonious picture. But because of his style's shortcomings, he left Florence a humbled man, bequeathing his legacy to his pupil, Raphael.

89. Pietro Perugino, *Madonna Enthroned with Saints*, 1493, Uffizi.

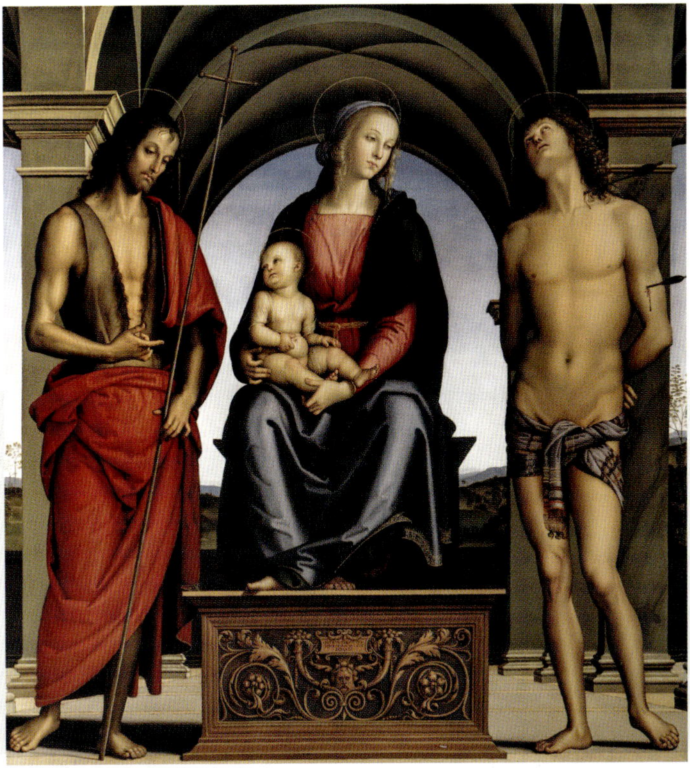

By applying pigmented glazes of oils, layer upon translucent layer, Perugino was able to create deep, resonant colors that don't appear to sit on the panel's surface. Thus, we see in the flesh tones a range of colors that describe what lies beneath the tissue-thin layers of live skin.

In this room we enter a narrow transitional period between the overly emphatic styles of the last decades of the Renaissance proper and a new style called the High Renaissance (next room). This style is based on the idealization of natural appearances, where physical actions reflect a state of mind. The sole exception to past styles and the key to the invention of a High Renaissance style was Leonardo's *Adoration*. But here we find Michelangelo, in his only surviving painted panel, already testing aesthetic alternatives to Leonardo's advances.

✶ Michelangelo Buonarroti, 1475-1564, *Holy Family* (*Doni Tondo*), Uffizi, c. 1504

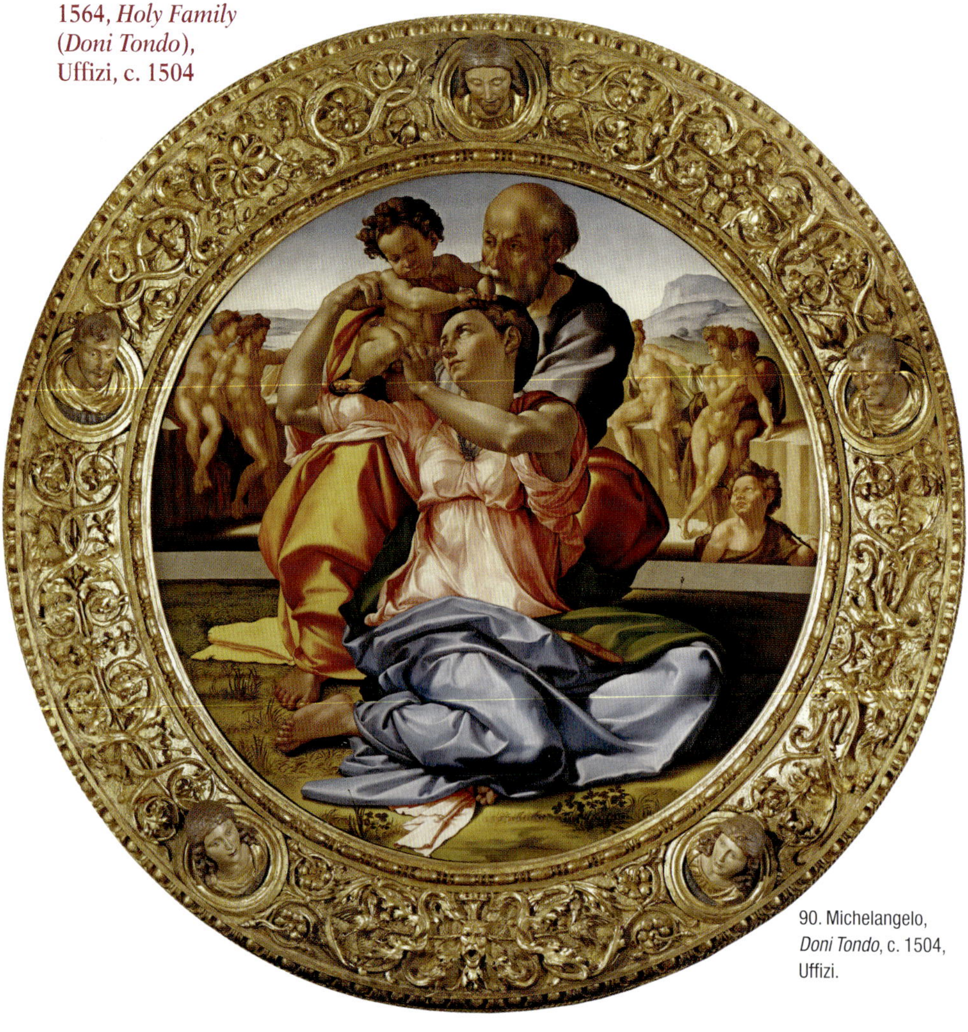

90. Michelangelo, *Doni Tondo*, c. 1504, Uffizi.

By the time Michelangelo painted the *Tondo* for Agnolo Doni, he was legendary. In Rome he'd carved the *Pietà* (1499), in Florence the *David* (1501). In the same year, Leonardo, newly arrived from Milan after a twenty-year absence, placed on the high altar of Santissima Annunziata a drawing that stunned the Florentine community: *Virgin and Child with Saint Anne*. Confronted with the only person who threatened his preeminence, it was inevitable that Michelangelo would take on Leonardo, and the *Doni Tondo* can be taken as his rebuttal of Leonardo's visionary style.

91. Leonardo da Vinci, *The Virgin and Child with Saint Anne.*

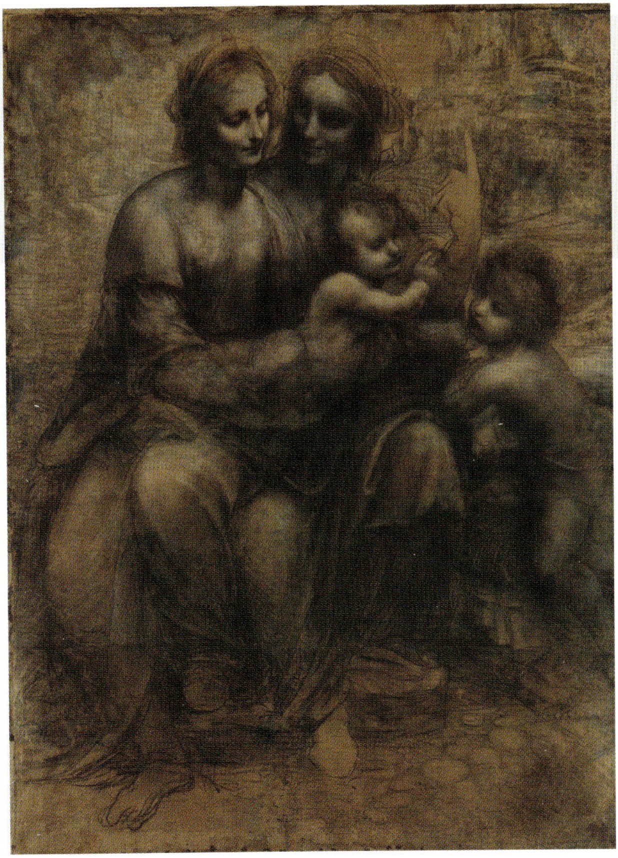

Like so many of Leonardo's masterpieces, this drawing resides abroad, in this case, London's National Gallery. The drawing is five and half by three and a half feet, while the diameter of Michelangelo's painting stands at four feet.

The arrival of the *Doni Tondo* and the *Virgin and Child with Saint Anne* on the landscape of Florentine art is a watershed event in Western art history. Throughout the late Quattrocento, artists had strived to depict the natural world. The aim of Michelangelo and Leonardo, however, was to probe beyond the visible, and they alone had the gift to achieve what others could not.

Although both depict the Holy Family—Michelangelo has substituted Joseph for Anne—the two pictures inhabit different worlds.

Michelangelo borrows nothing of Leonardo's shapes, whose borders are lost in shadowy imprecision. On the contrary, his shapes are sharply drawn. His brilliantly polished surfaces and deep recesses are etched as if carved from a marble block. His high-keyed colors constitute an entirely new invention—saffron opposite salmon is not the only combination that rings with artificiality and with dissonance where the form's hard-edged borders meet. Instead of Leonardo's demure femininity, we see Mary with the neck, shoulders, and bare, brawny arms of a young male, as if sensuality had no place in Michelangelo's concept of women.

But to the extent their manipulation of forms strains natural appearances, both artists have moved toward a new language based on an artifice so highly contrived it left their fellow artists with nothing on which to build. Michelangelo's distortion of Mary's form into a vigorously foreshortened, serpentine *contrapposto* and the exaggerated breadth of Joseph's lower body give the picture a purely aesthetic charge that tests the limits of plausibility. Thus, the expressive power of this picture resides entirely in its artificiality, with no desire to engender an emotional response from the viewer. Although he had proved himself master of describing emotion—determination in the *David,* for example—in the *Doni Tondo* Michelangelo willfully disregards Leonardo's supreme achievement, with facial expressions strictly conventional by Quattrocento standards.

Leonardo's drawing is stamped with artifice of a different character. In contrast to Michelangelo, he has shaped his figures' interlocked bodies to match the sublime expressions on their faces. In short, Leonardo's ability to render a body animated by an intense inner life ranks as one of the crowning events in art.

Without ever acknowledging his debt to Leonardo, Michelangelo would soon begin probing the entire spectrum of human emotion. Within a year of painting the *Doni Tondo*, he was called to Rome by Pope Julius II to unleash his awesome powers of expression in the Sistine Chapel.

Fra Bartolomeo, 1472-1517, *Vision of Saint Bernard*, Uffizi, c. 1506

When the Dominican Friar Savonarola was burned at the stake in 1498 for his religious extremism, Fra Bartolomeo, trained under Ghirlandaio, suffered a spiritual crisis, stopped painting, and entered the firebrand's monastery of San Marco. But by the time Leonardo and Michelangelo had departed Florence in 1506, the monk had once again taken up his brush and quickly emerged as one of the chief inventors of the High Renaissance style.

For Bartolomeo, this painting, the first since his monastic seclusion, represents an ambitious undertaking in search of a fresh style. By balancing the fibrillating motion of a mystical apparition on the left against the quiet simplicity of the earthly figures, Bartolomeo creates a unique aesthetic tension. Mary hovers like the prow of a ship, propelled toward the Dominican monk Bernard by a flotilla of ecstatic angels. These figures, choreographed so preciously, remind us of the agitated lyricism of the later Botticelli, while Bernard recalls the solid figures of Ghirlandaio. In contrast, the voluminously draped figure of Saint John conveys a dignified monumentality that will define the essence of Bartolomeo's style.

The soft modeling of shapes, including a meticulously described landscape in perfect atmospheric perspective, points to Bartolomeo's early allegiance to Leonardo. But the passive expressions and lifeless eyes are only slightly more vital than Perugino's faces, and this too marks this painting as pre-High Renaissance.

A bold palette is dispersed freely throughout in retrograde Gothic fashion. But the fluid passages of pastels blended into the angels' wings of peach, lavender, and aqua are entirely Bartolomeo. Far removed from the Gothic past, the muted skies rendered in pale blues and sepia forecast his stature as one of the most nuanced colorists in the High Renaissance.

92. Fra Bartolomeo, *Vision of Saint Bernard*, c. 1506, Uffizi.

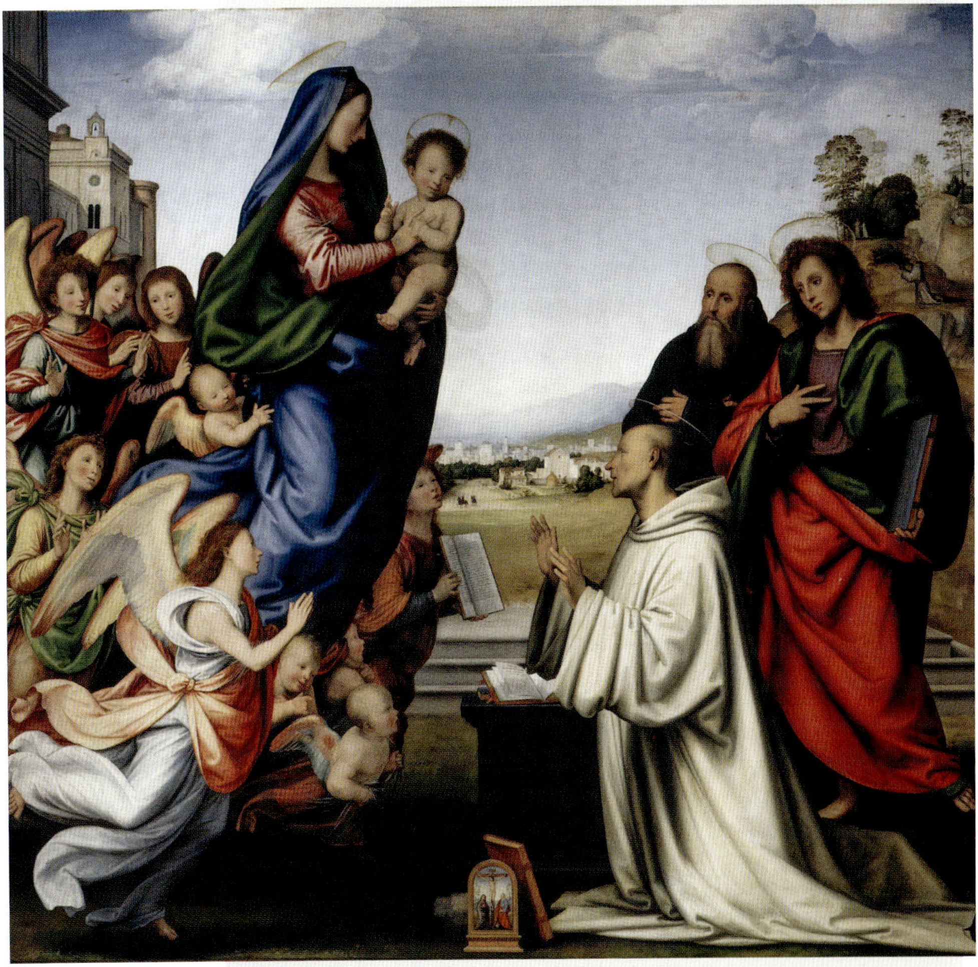

The miniature painting of the Crucifixion placed at the picture's edge is an early Quattrocento motif that interrupts the continuity between the pictorial space and ours, and is but one item that prevents the painting's admission to High Renaissance status.

High Renaissance

The High Renaissance style, or "classic style," can briefly be defined as the "idealization of natural appearances." The period in which the style predominated generally dates from Leonardo's *Last Supper* of 1498 to Raphael's premature death in Rome in 1520. In Florentine painting, the High Renaissance first appears as the core idea of Leonardo's *Virgin and Child with Saint Anne* (fig. 91), a drawing that evokes in the figures an inner life. From around 1503 to 1508, Michelangelo, Leonardo, and Raphael were all competing in Florence to find new ways to elaborate on the new style. By 1508, all three had departed, leaving Andrea del Sarto, Florence's finest colorist, as the artist who carried the new style to its pinnacle and final conclusion. The following two works best represent the Uffizi's collection of High Renaissance painting.

★ Andrea del Sarto, 1486-1530, *Madonna of the Harpies*, Uffizi, 1517

ROOM 58
(First Floor)

A High Renaissance painting par excellence, the *Madonna of the Harpies* is a superbly integrated composition of figures actively turning within a simply defined space. The painting also represents Sarto's break with Leonardo, the only artist to have devised a rational color system.

As we've seen in the *Mona Lisa* and earlier *Annunciation*, Leonardo had muted a narrow range of colors toward a dark uniformity with mixes of blacks. The technique successfully achieved color balance, but failed to mimic the appearance of reality. The *Madonna of the Harpies* is therefore Sarto's attempt to recapture the natural richness of color by rejecting pigments altered by black.

John's drapery is an uninhibited tomato red, Francis's a neutral gray-beige, and Mary's a combination of smoky blue, red, grayish yellow, and white. Depending on where he needs to depict shadows and highlights, Sarto uses a range of dark to light grays obtained from the drapery colors themselves, rather than from black or white. The intensity of red, for example, can be varied by using grays that are mixes of complementary colors, either orange and blue or purple and yellow, because orange and purple contain the color red. (A complementary color is obtained by mixing a primary color with its opposite on the color wheel. The results produce a range of grays from near white to near black, depending on the intensity of the two colors in the mix.) The Virgin's blue robe can be altered by the same color combinations—orange and blue or purple and yellow—because both combinations contain blue.

In other words, *the colors in any one drapery, even Francis's, contain traces of all the other colors* and are calibrated to strike the same light-dark intensity. Thus, our eye sweeps easily across John's drapery and gray-white undergarment, Francis's robe, and Mary's multicolored draperies.

One additional element of this style demands a critical eye. Sarto means to pull us into this space, as if we'd intercepted the saints' private moment.

This casual proximity, however, and the saints' agreeable expressions lead us to consider whether the artist was incapable of depicting intense spiritual states. Many scholars think so. Spiritual fervor and high drama may have been beyond Sarto's reach. His strength lies, rather, in his ability to capture in color an earthbound world suffused with grace and energy, qualities that spring effortlessly from only the most gifted artists.

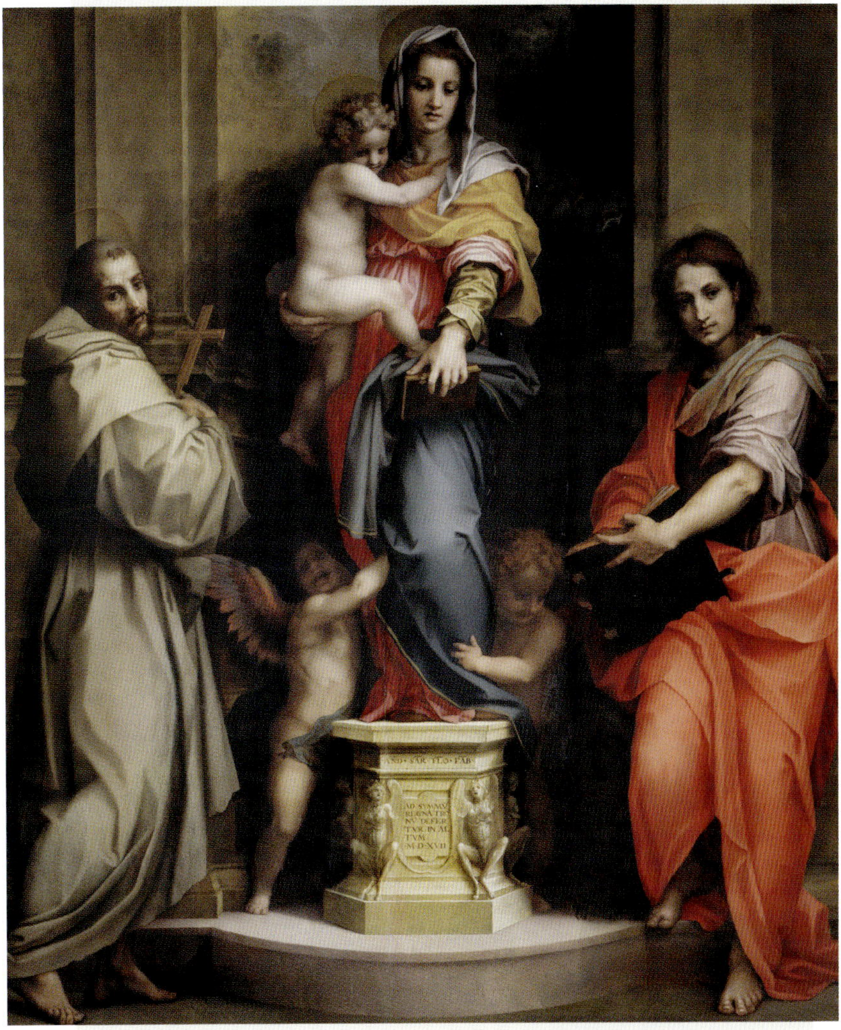

93. Andrea del Sarto, *Madonna of the Harpies*, 1517, Uffizi.

Carved into the pedestal are curious creatures, mistakenly called harpies. They are in fact sphinxes, ancient symbols of wisdom in Egypt that here symbolizes the Virgin's awareness of her child's fate.

Raphael, 1483-1520, *Madonna of the Goldfinch*, Uffizi, 1506

ROOM 68
(FIRST FLOOR)

When Raphael painted this work midway through his four-year stay in Florence, he was beginning to move beyond the influence of the restful style of his teacher, Perugino, toward Leonardo's animated forms. Thus, the picture is a hybrid of both styles. He retains Perugino's soft Umbrian landscape, but he infuses the figures with a graceful vitality and tenderness. The pyramidal grouping of the Virgin with the two children comes from Leonardo's *Virgin and Child with Saint Anne* (fig. 91), but Raphael simplifies the poses, reduces much of the shadow, and emboldens the colors, which Leonardo had subdued as far back as the *Annunciation* (fig. 85). He keeps to the master's simple palette but reduces it to red, blue, and

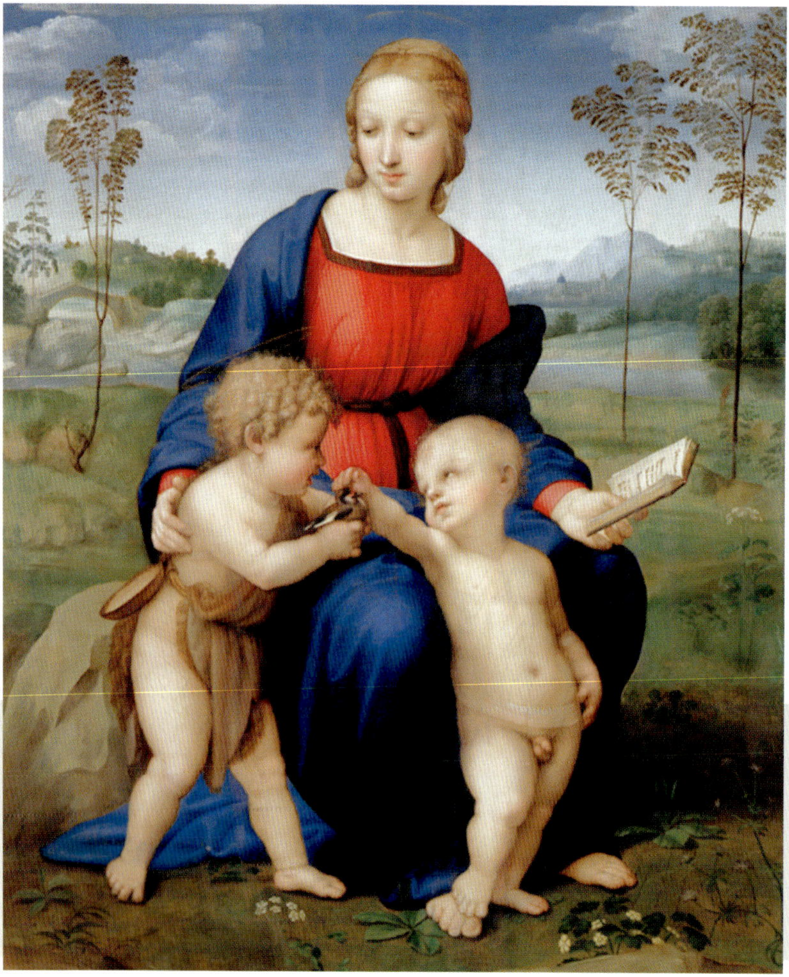

94. Raphael, *Madonna of the Goldfinch*, 1506, Uffizi.

In general, birds symbolize the flight of the soul, but the goldfinch, with its red-crowned head, symbolizes Christ's death.

earth colors. The painting ranks as one of the earliest High Renaissance pictures by virtue of the simple harmony of its parts and the intelligence conveyed in the faces.

Mannerism

The concept of artifice is as fundamental to Mannerism as naturalism is to the Renaissance and idealism is to the High Renaissance. Through an extraordinary range of artistic devices, the Mannerist style could be employed to strike a mood or to provoke an emotional response in the viewer. By mid-century, it had evolved into a highly refined movement, expressive of hidden meanings or of nothing but its own beauty.

95. Rosso Fiorentino, *Madonna and Child with Saints*, 1518, Uffizi.

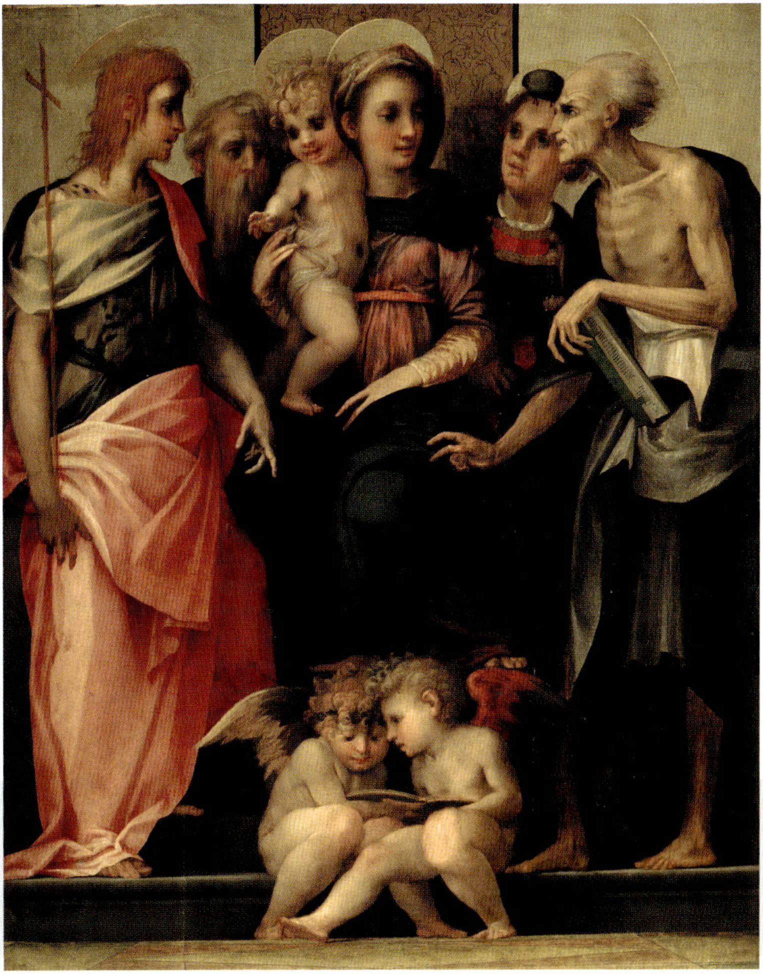

Commissioned by the director of Santa Maria Nuova Hospital for the church of Ognissanti.

Because of its antinaturalism, it was discredited for centuries, but by the early twentieth century Mannerism had been reappraised for its artificial splendor. In chronological order, works by Florence's finest Mannerists, whom we'll meet later on site.

Rosso Fiorentino, 1495-1540, *Madonna and Child with Saints*, Uffizi, 1518

ROOM 60 (FIRST FLOOR)

In one of the earliest paintings to breach Renaissance decorum, Rosso collapses space, crowds figures, and attenuates bodies—all characteristics of early Mannerism which he helped found with this painting. Even the rock dripping with blood sunk into the head of Stephen, the ghoulish attribute of his martyrdom, would have met with approval. But the queer expressions that disfigures the faces—the loony look Rosso plants on the child, and his portrait of Jerome, a venerated early father of the church, as some emaciated mad hermit just back from roaming the desert—would have been over the top. Equally provocative is the excessive prominence he awards the claw-like hands that point downward to the saucy little angels, two of the loveliest creatures in painting.

The mood suggests we are witnessing a scene as mysterious as an unholy apparition, nevertheless one brimming with beautiful passages. Rosso applies his dissonant colors loosely—almost impressionistically—across the canvas, complementing greens with rose, violet, and crimson to pull the eye full circle, even touching upon the angels.

Besides seducing us with color, how do we explain Rosso's intentions? Is he parodying a traditional painting like the *Madonna of the Harpies*, or depicting sincere devotion? Contemporary documents have nothing to say on the subject, other than that the prior who commissioned this altarpiece forbade that the painting ever be hung in the chapel for which it was intended.

Because of his early missteps, Rosso was forced to work in Rome where his extremely refined style helped shape late Mannerism.

✶ Rosso Fiorentino, *Moses Defending the Daughters of Jethro*, Uffizi, c. 1523

In an obscure episode in the life of Moses, seven daughters of Jethro take their flock to water, and when they are attacked by shepherds Moses comes to their rescue.

Rosso's commission, his last before leaving Florence for good, was a private one from a notoriously violent man, which might explain the choice of a subject that became Michelangelo's life-long pursuit, the heroic male nude.

All the hallmarks of Rosso's later style are here: a canvas crowded with bodies (the abbreviated profiles of six of the daughters relegated to a distant, bizarre spacing); a tilted ground plane that spills the figures into the foreground and out of the picture and pulls us into the fight's vortex; a harsh lighting that searches out musculature, but doesn't truly bring bodies into plausible relief.

There is, rather, a dry linear quality, an explicitness to the forms that exposes itself for what it is: pure artifice. Some of this can be detected in the fallen figure in the right foreground, where Rosso exploits a body's sensual contours with an artful line that courses down the stressed borders of the rib cage and protruding hip.

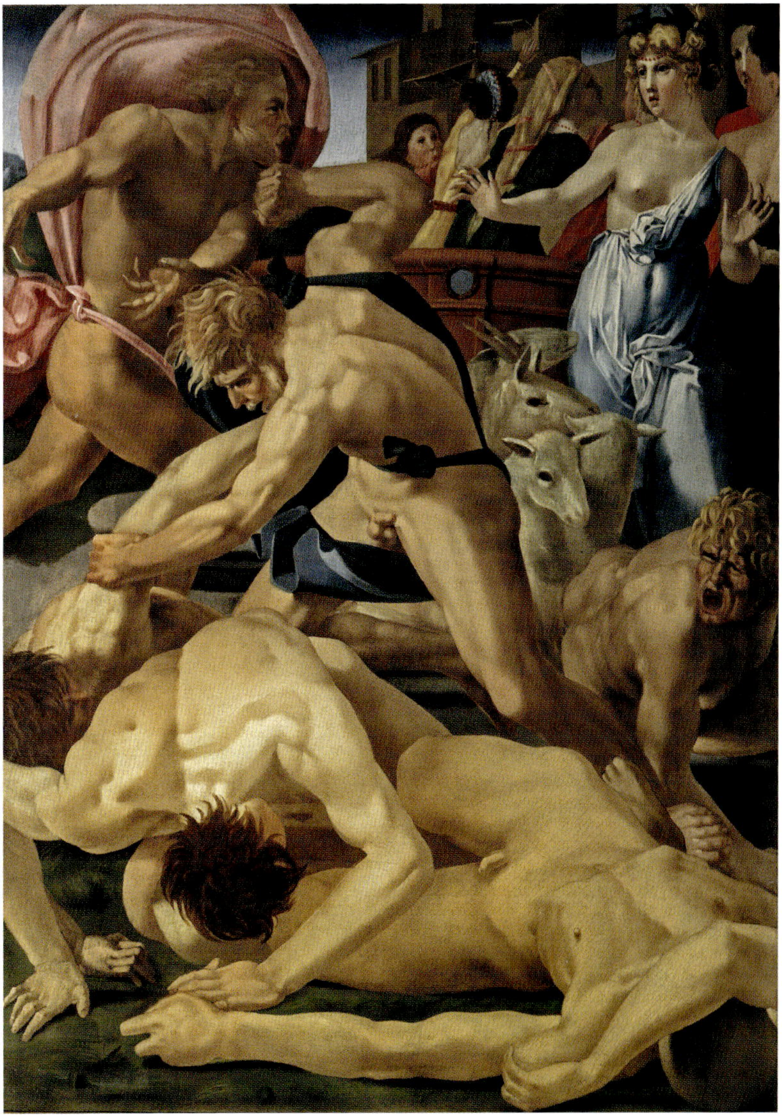

96. Rosso Fiorentino, *Moses Defending the Daughters of Jethro*, c. 1523, Uffizi.

Other than the sweet perfidy of desire, what could Rosso expect his patron to see? A kind of comic-book detachment pervades the sex and violence. A bestial attacker, amplified by a sinister cape in violent motion, rushes the maiden, but her coquettish look of bewilderment does not suit her desperate state. Despite the fever of battle, this struggle feels stylized, with figures highly choreographed in scaffolds of tight geometry.

The nudity here, in its alluring contortions, has the flair of satire. The beauty of the female form reveals itself beneath a filmy gown, while Moses' manhood, piteously emphasized by the girdle that whips through his legs, swings dead center.

Whatever interpretations apply, Rosso's final statement to Florentine posterity rests in figures so provocatively crafted that they lead in the coming decades to a style in which forms, as aesthetic shapes, say all that need be said.

★ Jacopo Pontormo, 1494-1557, *Supper at Emmaus*, Uffizi, 1525

ROOM 61 (FIRST FLOOR)

The biblical story occurred after Christ's Resurrection, when he met two former disciples walking to the town of Emmaus. Because the journey was long and they did not recognize him, they invited Christ to join them for supper. The picture captures the moment when one of them recognizes their companion as the risen Christ.

Sometime after Pontormo completed it, the picture was cut back, altering its original appearance. It had been placed within a door frame on the wall of the monastery to create the illusion of an opening into an adjacent room. Visitors wandering past would see Christ breaking bread (sign of the Eucharist) among monks and disciples.

Pontormo, one of the most gifted artists of his era, meticulously renders a rustic setting of everyday objects: animals peer out from beneath the table; feet reveal the grime of a day's journey; a pewter plate casts a soft shadow; a rough hand grasps a bread roll. Such realism—unprecedented in Florentine painting—anticipated Caravaggio's paintings in Rome of seventy years later.

But what really distinguishes this work from its High Renaissance predecessors is the tension between the illusion of normalcy and the forms and colors that stand out as excessive, artificial, and decorative, that is, the "art" of the work of art. For these we need only to look at the monk's strangely elongated shapes and small heads, the umber-black background and the disorienting space, and the dissonant color combinations in the seated guests' garments.

Pontormo clothes these two figures in ruffled drapery embellished with zigzagging folds. On the figure at right, lemon yellow competes with mottled green. His cinnabar shaded back catches the orange in his companion's robe, its swirling folds modeled in bleached pink—lovely, superfluous, and conspicuously at odds with the picture's otherwise sober colors.

Much of the picture's strength is invested in these characters. They anchor the broad diagonals that run from the monks' diminutive heads downward and through their exquisite shapes. Like reverse orthogonals, these diagonals converge toward a point that corresponds to the object of Christ's riveting stare. Standing just beyond the scene, we are the focal point that completes this picture, complicit protagonists compelled to acknowledge the presence of the risen Savior.

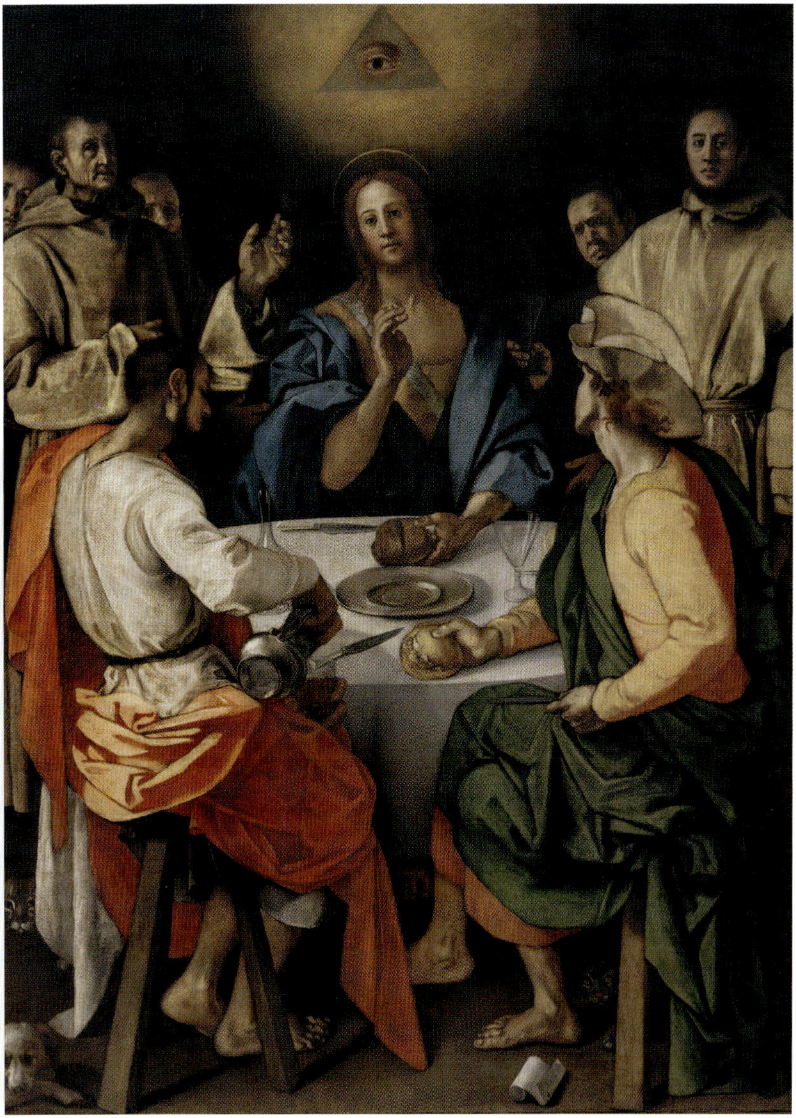

97. Jacopo Pontormo, *Supper at Emmaus*, 1525, Uffizi.

The obtrusive triangle with the eye representing the Trinity at the top of the picture was unfortunately added by a later artist.
The monks pictured here are real life portraits painted while Pontormo was staying at the Certosa di Firenze, the Carthusian monastery nearby the suburban village of Galluzzo, to escape the plague.

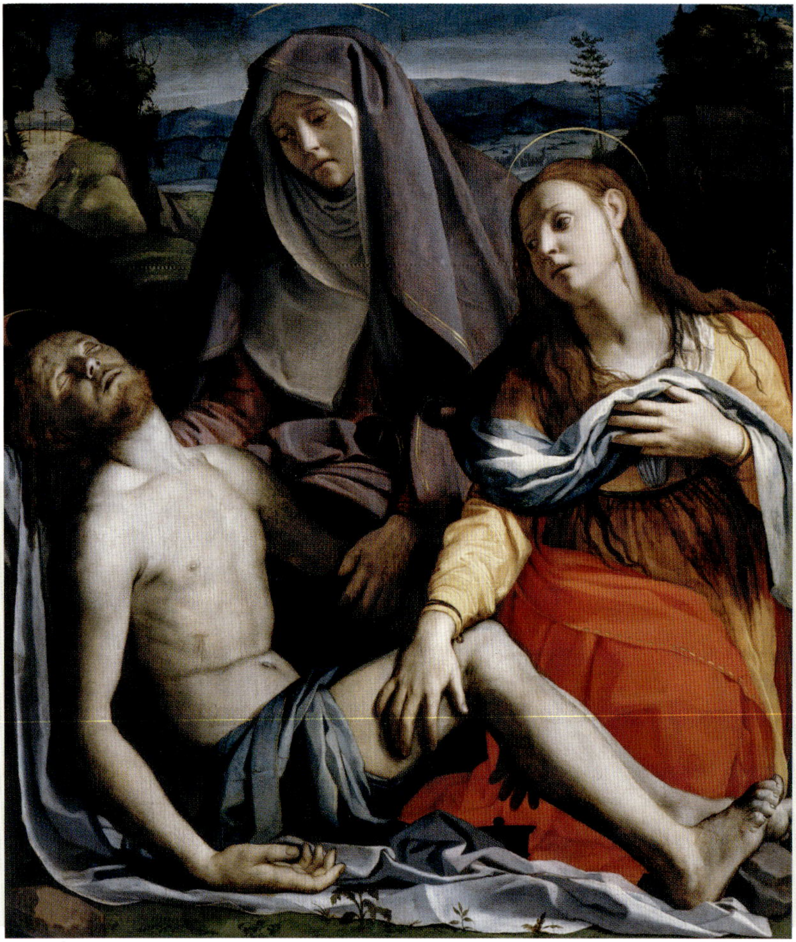

98. Agnolo Bronzino, *Lamentation with Mary Magdalene*, c. 1529, Uffizi.

Being forced to engage a dead Christ at arm's length and to intrude on the mourners' last moments with his grimy body would have been piteously troubling to a sixteenth-century viewer.

Agnolo Bronzino, 1503-1572, *Lamentation with Mary Magdalene*, Uffizi, c. 1529

ROOM 64 (FIRST FLOOR)

Bronzino, pupil and lifelong friend of the older Pontormo, grew to become the most eloquent exponent of late Florentine Mannerism. The *Lamentation*, one of his earliest altarpieces, is also one of the few to evoke intense emotion. Curiously, given that he was deeply familiar with Pontormo's style, Bronzino's only Mannerist inclinations are the glowing colors borrowed from *Supper at Emmaus*. Otherwise, the classical proportions of the figures and their spacing embrace High Renaissance standards as practiced by Andrea del Sarto.

Mary Magdalene's forward position, her iridescent colors, and the placement of her hand on Christ's mid-thigh identify her as the picture's protagonist. Bronzino, however, refuses to subordinate the Virgin, despite her sober gown and rear position. Occupying the picture's apex, she registers her own prominence, conveyed by the prism of light along the line of the nose and at her temple. Bronzino treats her gown like Sarto did his color mixtures in the *Madonna of the Harpies*, blending the three primaries of Mary Magdalene's garments—red, blue, and yellow— to give the Virgin's robe that resplendent brown-purple, symbol of mourning.

✶ Agnolo Bronzino, *Holy Family*, Uffizi, c. 1541

To a sixteenth-century viewer accustomed to High Renaissance decorum, a painting such as this, where figures are open to close examination, would have been seen as a bold act. With all the detachment of statuary, this bareheaded porcelain goddess and her consensual husband observe a child's natural, erotic curiosity about the soft texture of the flesh of the sleeping baby.

99. Agnolo Bronzino, *Holy Family*, c. 1541, Uffizi.

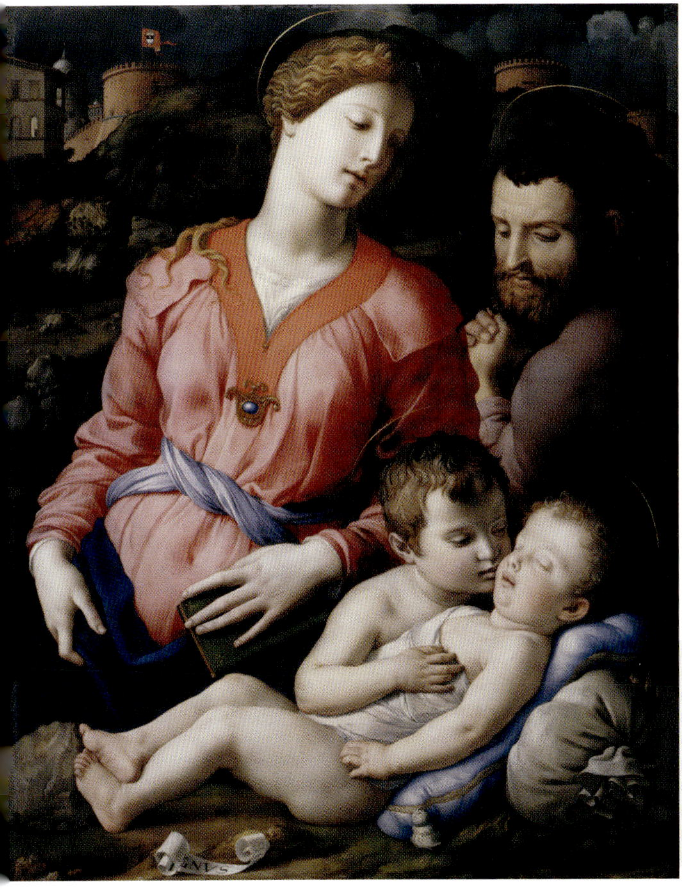

It cannot be lost on us that we, too, are complicit voyeurs in observing the children, but more so in scrutinizing the parents. Bronzino's ability to pull an unwitting spectator into the dialogue, his willingness to dismiss emotional content, and his exploitation of sensuality inherent in the nude body, become increasingly characteristic of his style and lead to a notable variant of late Mannerism (also called High Mannerism).

The picture was a devotional work for the wealthy Florentine Panciatichi family. Their coat of arms can be seen on the banner flying over the castle in the background.

5. Santa Maria Novella Church and Cloister

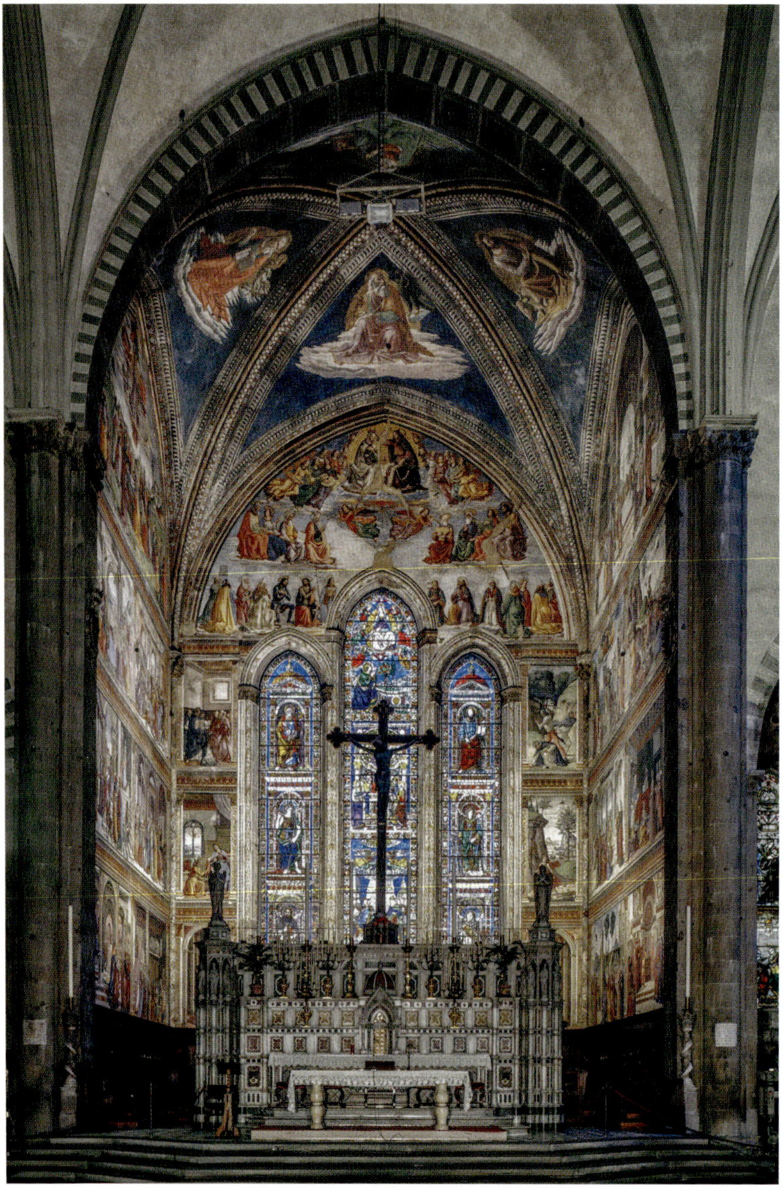

100. Santa Maria Novella, view of the nave and the major chapel.

The home of the preaching Order of the Dominicans, first established in the Gothic style in 1246, Santa Maria Novella is the only church in Florence whose art traverses four centuries, and virtually every piece is masterfully representative of its era. Beginning the chronology is Giotto's thirteenth-century crucifix, which established the pre-eminence of the Florentine style. In the Strozzi di Mantova Chapel, frescoes and a single altarpiece represent the only significant works of art in the period immediately following the plague. In the Spanish Chapel off the cloister, one of the most sumptuous fresco cycles in all of Italy.

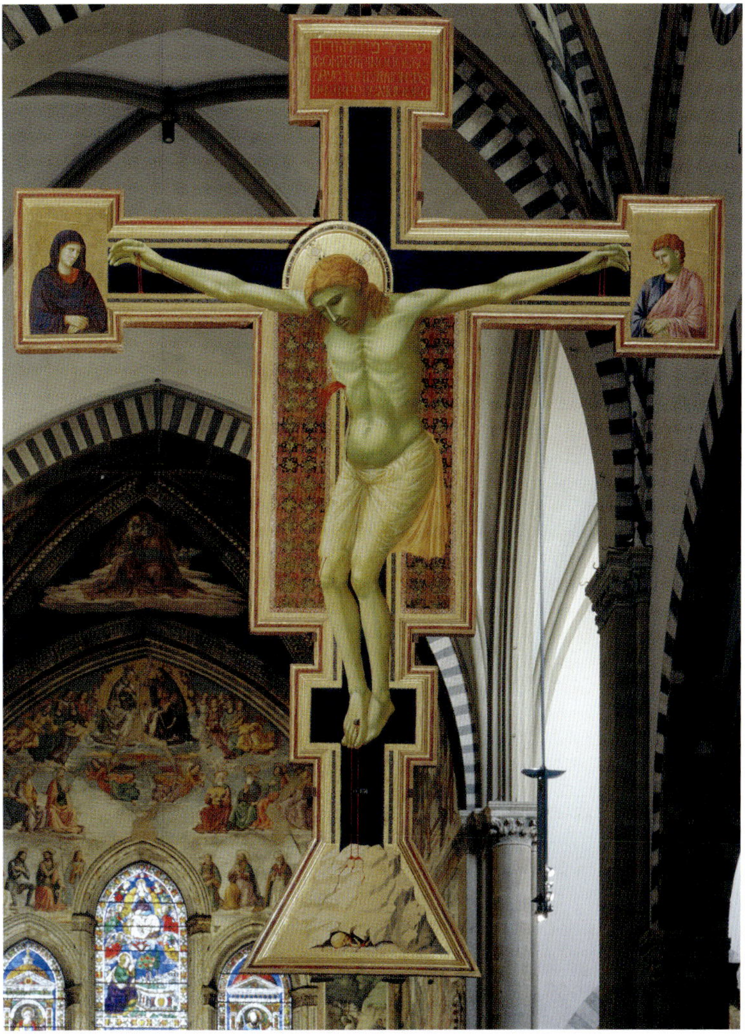

101. Giotto, Crucifix, c. 1290, Santa Maria Novella.

The Painted Crucifix, End of a Tradition

In the nave

Giotto, c. 1267-1337, Crucifix, Santa Maria Novella, c. 1290

The precedent for this crucifix is Cimabue's crucifix in Santa Croce. But placing it in the context of Giotto's Uffizi *Madonna* (fig. 61), the only other large-scale painting by this master, is more difficult. The Madonna is draped and seated in a tradition-bound format among a choir of angels. Here, we have an isolated, full-figured nude and, because of its stark realism, appears more advanced than the *Madonna*. Yet it was painted twenty years earlier, which provoked skeptics in the early twentieth century to suggest it was the work of an unknown artist.

Because of recent restorations, it is all but certain that this image has been brought to life by the brush of Giotto, who was the only artist of his era to have observed nature's laws of light and shadow, its ability to stress physicality by distinguishing a body's contours. We sense this physicality at the instant a person becomes a silent mass, and witness the tissue-thin flesh pulled tight over the rib cage, the pliant musculature, and lost muscle tone in the protuberant abdomen. Gravity pulls the weight of this corpse downward, as art draws Cimabue's Christ to one side. Even the tentative foreshortening of hip and head and the combed beard and coiffed hair we can dismiss as a stage in a style of a young artist still tied to an older tradition.

Giotto's crucifix, the first realistic portrait of Christ in the history of painting, effectively brings to an end the tradition of one of Tuscany's first painted subjects. No one ever bettered it. In the future, the painted crucifix will be left to more complex themes, like the *Trinity* by Masaccio on the wall to our left, to whom Giotto, over a hundred years earlier, bequeathed a language at once powerful, succinct, and timeless.

Gothic Masters Interpret Dante, Dominican Dogma

Nardo di Cione, active 1343-1366, *Last Judgment, Paradise, Hell,* Strozzi di Mantova Chapel, 1350-57

Strozzi di Mantova Chapel, left transept

The Strozzi Chapel is dedicated to St. Thomas Aquinas (1225-74), the Dominican's leading theologian and codifier of Church dogma. The historical context in which the works of art were created was the devastating effect the Black Death had on a profoundly Christian, medieval culture that saw it as an act of divine punishment. (It killed its victims in three days.). The Dominicans, as the self-proclaimed guardians of the faith, commissioned the frescoes to juxtapose, in vivid detail, to what end the Last Judgment leads.

Less than a decade after the plague struck, Nardo Cione, brother of

102. Strozzi di Mantova Chapel, (built c. 1340-1350) showing frescoes of the *Last Judgment*, 1350-57.

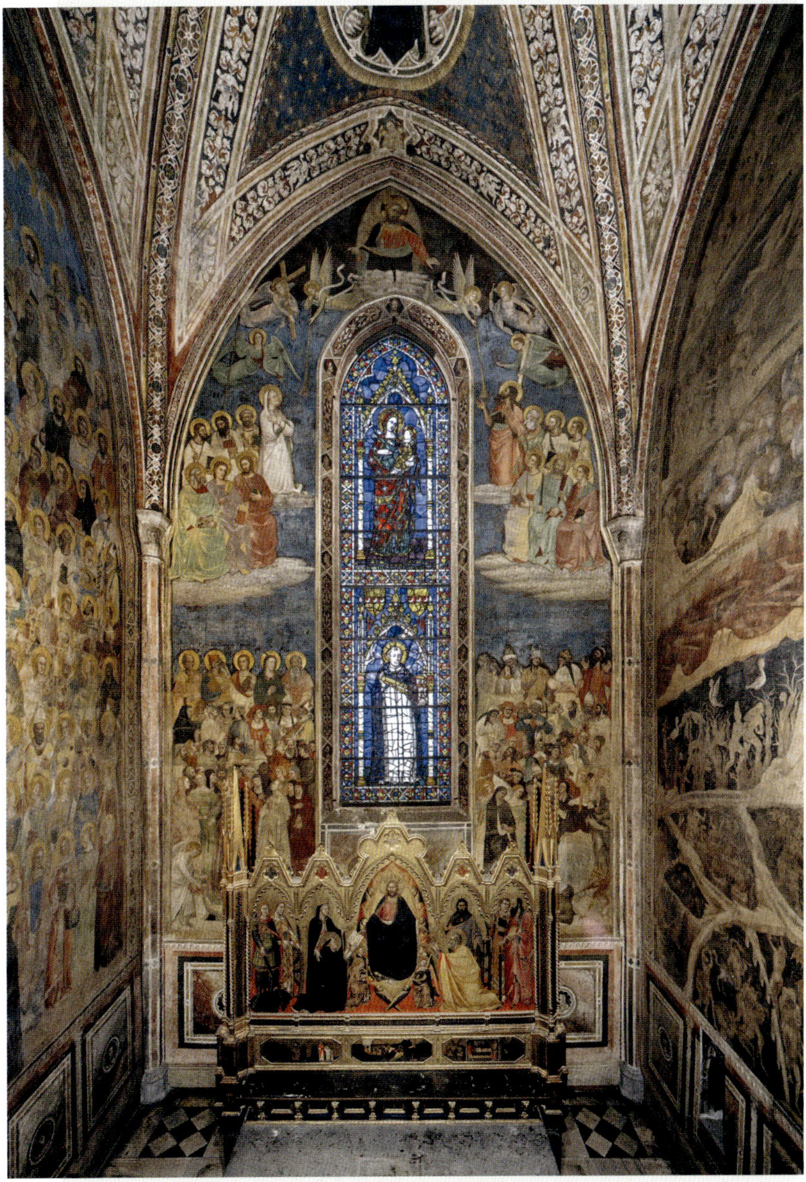

On the far wall, left of the stained glass window are the *Blessed*; on the right of the window, the *Damned*; *Hell* is on the right wall and *Paradise* on the left. Above the window, Christ, accompanied by wisps of angels depicted in the Gothic style. In the foreground, Orcagna's altarpiece, the preeminent masterpiece of the Gothic era.

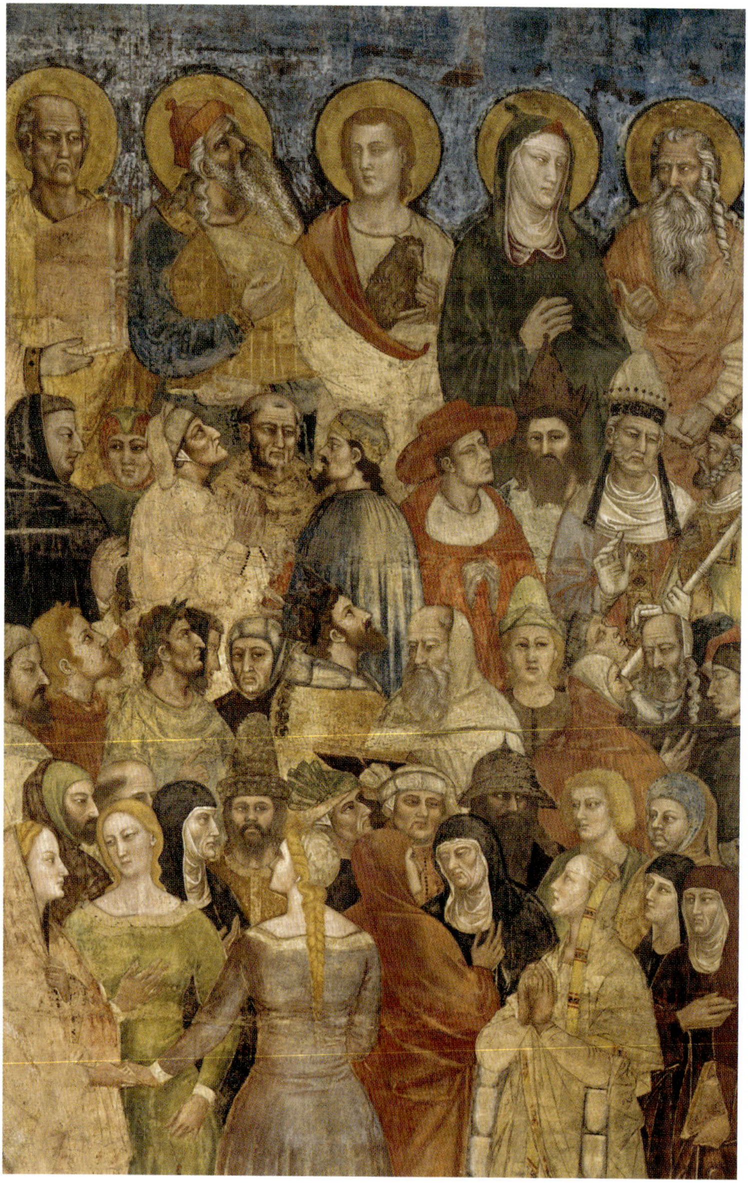

103. Nardo di Cione, *The Blessed, Last Judgment*, detail fig. 102.

Andrea Orcagna, painted these scenes in a severe, antinaturalistic style that is said to have reflected the period's morbid preoccupation with death and afterlife. What gave structure to these scenes was Dante's *Divine Comedy*, written early in the century. The frescoes on the wall behind the altar depict the *Last Judgment*. In the scene to the left of the

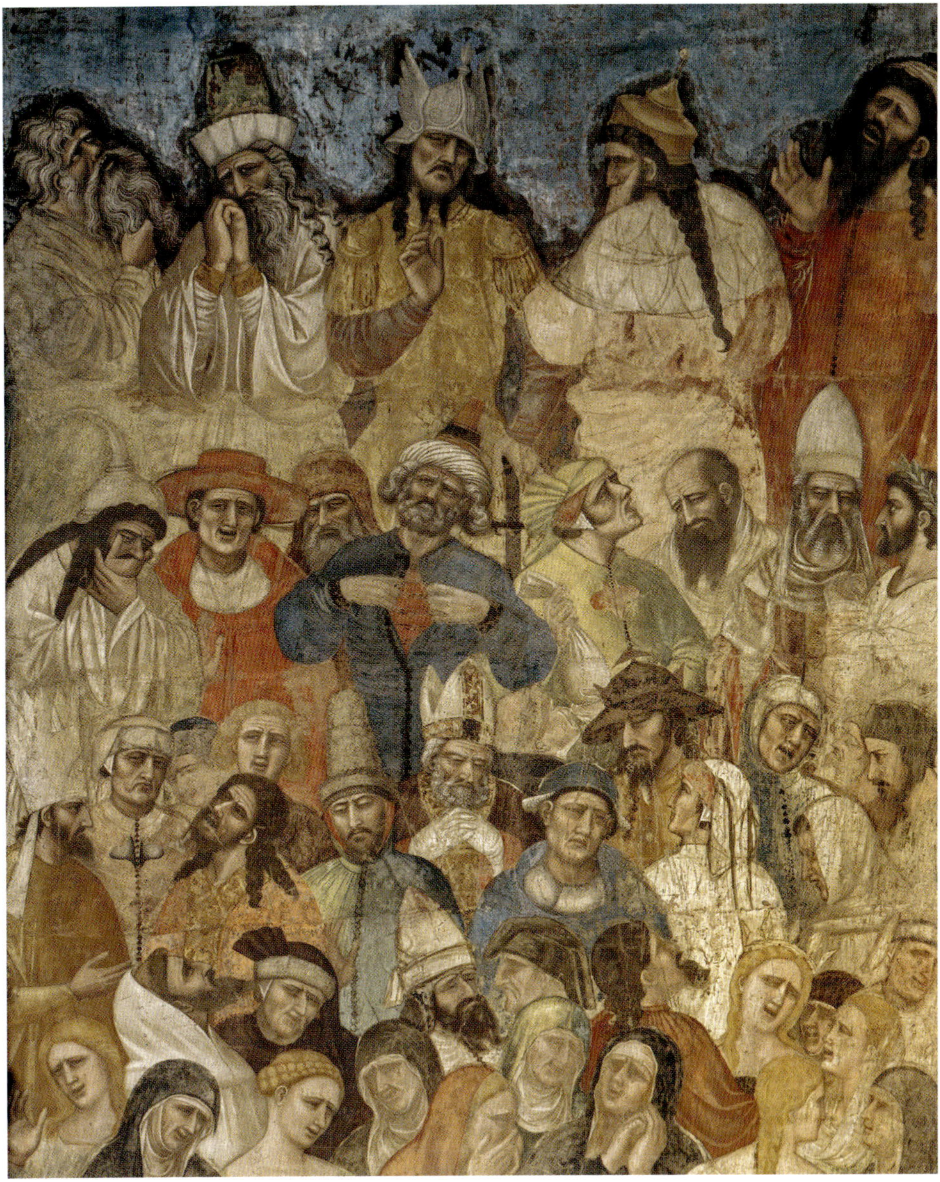

104. Nardo di Cione, *The Damned*, *Last Judgment*, detail of fig. 102.

stained glass window (fig. 103), there is an air of appealing orderliness to the rows of the Blessed. A lush palette of slate blues and forest greens, burnt orange, and yellow and whites modeled in umber highlights the entire wall's beautifully decorative, tapestry-like pattern. A close look beyond the pattern reveals a group of highly individualized characters with features skillfully modeled in soft contours. The kind of hard-edged figures that we saw in Giotto's earlier scenes in the Bardi Chapel do not appear here. What's more, some of these characters stand in profile or toward the wall, creating the very real sense they are fully rounded figures occupying an upward receding space much like the bleachers of a sports arena. Just below the top row of over-sized, haloed saints, the figure of Dante, dressed in white and wearing his tell-tale cap, gazes upward to catch a glimpse of the Lord in the arch above the window.

To the right of the window (fig. 104), a frenzied hoard of the Damned gesture vehemently, straining against any order imposed upon them. Within this group, which includes a fair share of church clerics and exotic pagans, Florentines could have identified the various social ranks by their costumes and headgear. In the lowest rows a group of disheveled nuns weep in despair.

Paradise, left wall. Painted in faded pastels and earth colors and graced with gold halos, the figures represent the Gothic artist's deep commitment to a pure, linear-based art. Individual passages are remarkably beautiful, but matter less than the power of the whole. *Hell*, right wall, is too ruined to make out the details, but it is known that the public was terrifyingly fixated on the visual manifestation of Dante's descriptions of Hell. The scene as a whole has the appearance of decaying organic life painted in blacks and burnt reds, and nakedness is the theme.

Andrea Orcagna, active c. 1344-1368, *Redeemer Enthroned with Madonna and Saints*, Strozzi di Mantova Chapel, 1354-57

On the altar

Orcagna was the most prominent painter in the second half of the century and this is the finest example of his work. It is also an accurate reflection of the distance painting had traveled in the space of the twenty years since Giotto's death. The richly decorative scheme, with tooled gold background, costly ultramarine blue, and brilliant metallic coloring, sets a tone for a world that exists beyond visual reality. Thus we see, suspended in the center of the picture, an iconic image of an enthroned Christ in a rigid, frontal pose enclosed in a *mandorla*, an almond-shaped form composed of morbid-looking seraphim. Staring blankly ahead, Christ hands the keys to Peter, founder of the Church, and a book to Saint Thomas Aquinas. Peter is paired with John the Baptist just behind him, an austere image by any measure, while Thomas, as the patron of the painting, is paired with the Virgin who commends him to Christ. A brocaded orange carpet pitched vertically anchors the figures in the middle three arches to a space that makes no rational sense.

The edgy austerity of the picture is forbidding. But to suggest that it represents a decline in artistic standards by radically deviating from naturalism overlooks Orcagna's sophistication in posing elements of Giotto's figure canon against the irrational and abstract. Just look to the soft, graduated tones he employs in modeling the features of Saint Thomas and

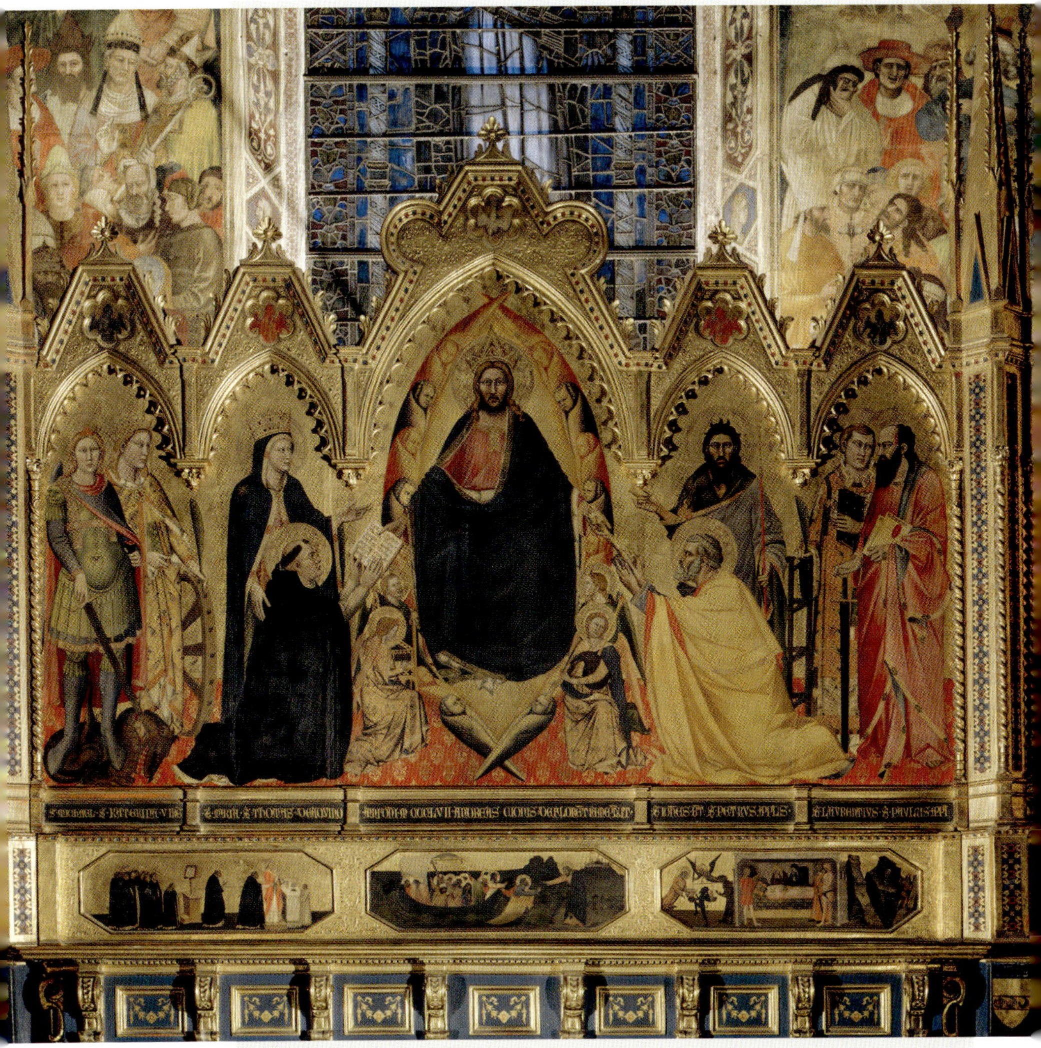

105. Andrea Orcagna, *Redeemer Enthroned with Madonna and Saints*, 1354-57, Strozzi di Mantova Chapel.

The picture's donor, Tommaso di Rossello Strozzi, was a member of a lesser branch of the Strozzis, one of the oldest patrician families in Florence.

the Virgin, or to the credible space that the archangel Michael and Saint Catherine inhabit on the left, or to the simple sweep of the figures' draperies. Each of these features, along with the sumptuous details, reflects an artist supremely at the forefront of the major stylistic trend in Florentine art. Foremost, Orcagna makes the picture's message perfectly clear. The pathway to redemption leads through the papacy as represented by Peter and guided by Christian dogma as purposed by the Dominicans.

Masaccio, 1401-1428, *Trinity*, Santa Maria Novella, c. 1426

Painted about a year before he died, Masaccio's *Trinity* is the most rational and mathematically based painting in all of Florence. By applying Brunelleschi's perspective system, he has created a perfect illusion of a barrel-vaulted chapel projected beyond the wall on which it was painted. The longitudinal ribs of the foreshortened vault provide orthogonals that recede to a vanishing point whose horizon line corresponds to the steps where the two patrons kneel. This line in turn approximates the height of the average viewer's eye level. Thus we look slightly down on the tomb at the base of the scene and up to the vault above. The distance between the cross ribs of the vault determines the ideal distance the viewer must stand from the wall in order to be correctly aligned with its perspective (approximately fifteen paces). The life-sized donors (likely already dead when the picture was painted) kneel on a step that is contiguous with our space. Their foreshortening accurately corresponds to the distance from which we view them. The skeleton that lies below on the tomb, and by tradition refers to Adam, the first human, is the most anatomically accurate rendering for its time. The inscription above reads, "I was once as you are; as I am, you also will become."

John the Apostle and Mary stand foreshortened in the chapel's forward space. These are massive and heroic figures and are linked to the donors and to God by color and gesture. Mary's portrait, in particular, of an elderly woman whose face has been worn by years of sorrow, is unprecedented for its time. Such a likeness will not be repeated until Ghirlandaio painted the women of the Tornabuoni family in this church's main chapel.

Farther back in the chapel, God the Father, the first member of the Triune God, stands behind his crucified Son, the second member. The third member, the Holy Spirit, is depicted as a dove, but appears as a white scarf tied at God's neck. Unlike the other figures, Christ and God, as divine figures, are not foreshortened according to the rules of perspective. For all of its mathematical certainty, Masaccio doesn't give us the coordinates to determine accurately the position of God with respect to his space. (The difficulty in determining God's position in the vault arises from the fact that Brunelleschi's perspective system was based on a figure standing on a grid of receding square tiles. A figure's height and place in the space could then be determined by the horizontal and vertical lines that the tiles create. But in this painting, God is not standing on the grid, but on what appears to be Christ's tomb.) If Christ's tomb on which God stands is on the back wall, as it appears to be, then it conflicts with the perception that God and Christ are positioned just behind Mary and John. Such minor ambiguities are meaningless in the face of the picture's overall perfection. The logic of the scene refers to the perfection of God's domain and our understanding of it reflects our potential for salvation.

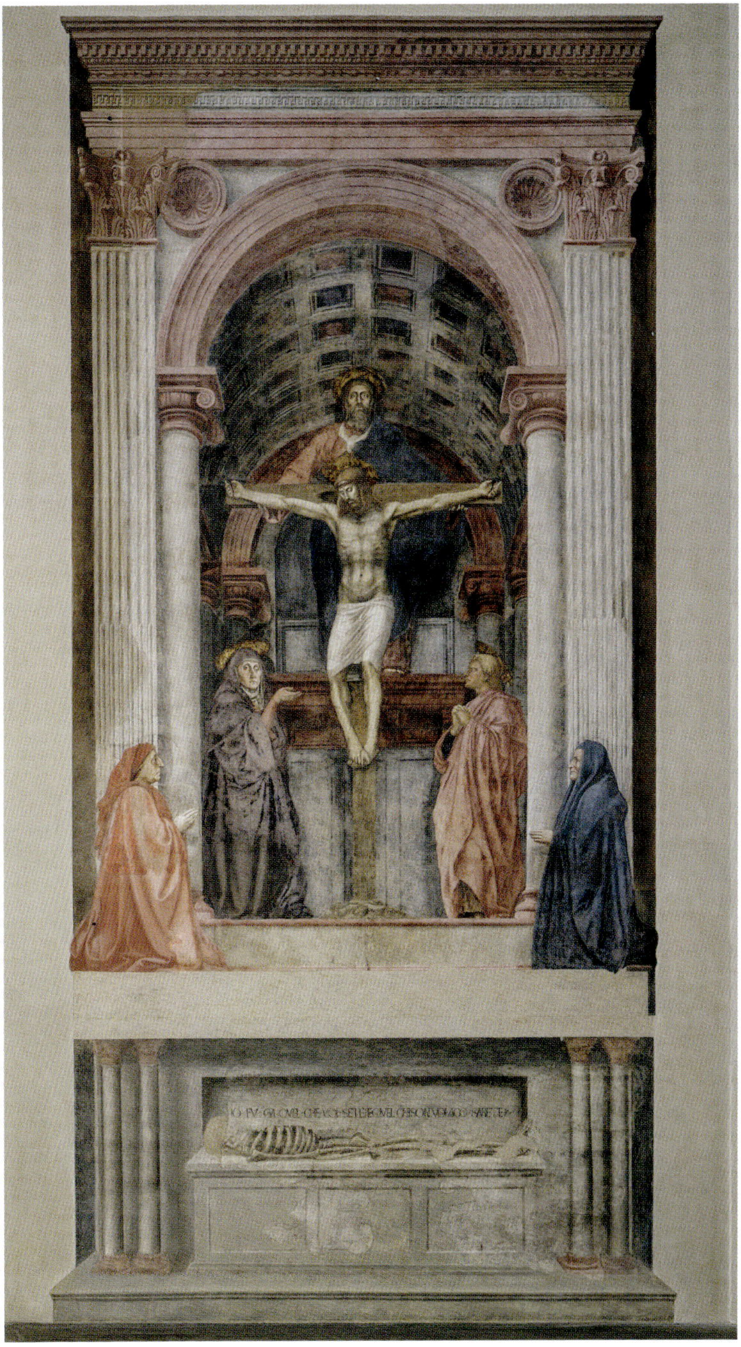

106. Masaccio, *Trinity*, c. 1426, Santa Maria Novella.

Domenico Ghirlandaio, 1449-1494, *Birth of the Virgin*, *Birth of John the Baptist*, Main Chapel, 1485-90

MAIN CHAPEL (CAPPELLA TORNABUONI), SCENES FROM THE LIFE OF JOHN THE BAPTIST AND LIFE OF THE VIRGIN

With Leonardo in Milan in the last decade of the fifteenth century, the pace to the stylistic inventions that had prevailed earlier in the century had stagnated. Instead, a number of diverse styles were being practiced by the city's leading artists. In the most ambitious fresco cycle painted in the Quattrocento, Ghirlandaio's descriptive detail and clear, accessible style represent one of these major lines of development.

The scene devoted to Mary's birth shows a wealthy family's bedroom where a baby has just been born. By the standards of previous paintings, this room is spacious and scrupulously measured out by the rules of perspective. Columns, meticulously detailed with motifs of antiquity, partially divide the scene into separate episodes in the life of the baby's mother, as if they were occurring at the same time. Atop the lavender tinted steps, then, we see Saint Anne nine months before giving birth to Mary, embracing her husband over the news of her conception.

The range of pure colors and the figure's crisp contours signal us that Ghirlandaio is not of Leonardo's camp. (Leonardo loathed this kind of painting. Having had no patience with scenes stacked one upon another on a chapel wall, he urged his fellow painters to create a single scene, using the upper section of the wall to depict a deep landscape or an atmospheric sky.)

107. Domenico Ghirlandaio, *Birth of the Virgin*, 1485-90, Main Chapel.

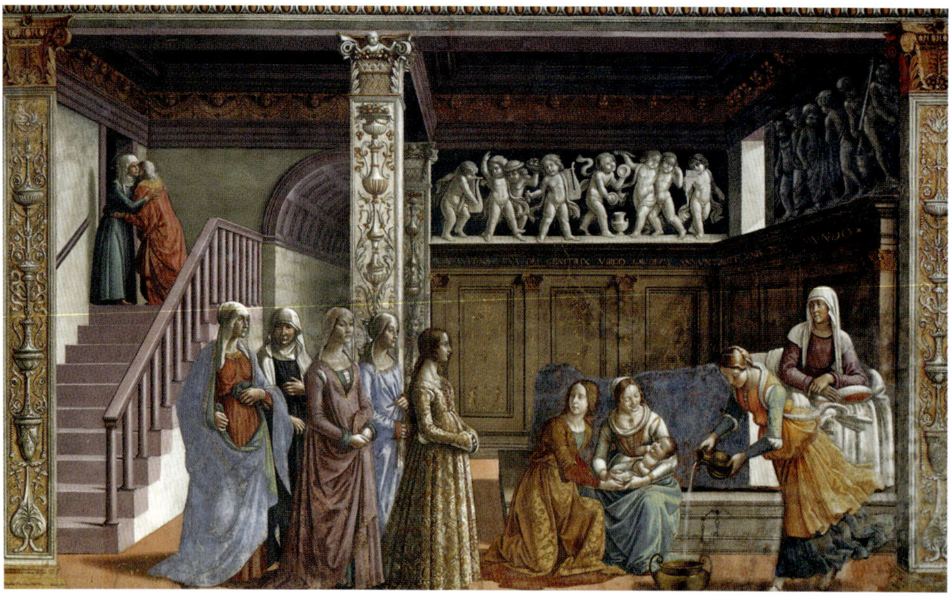

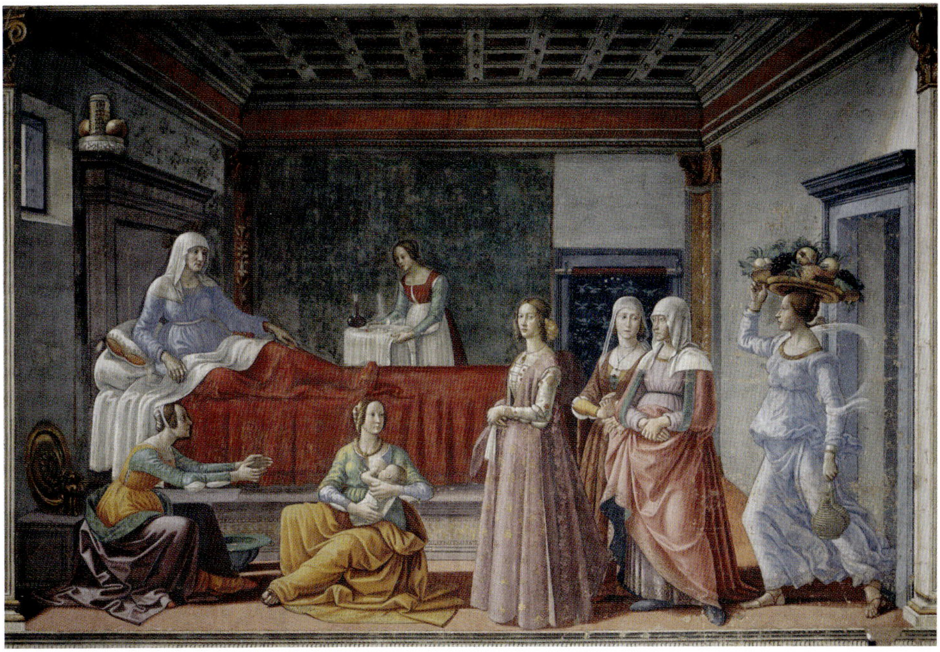

108. Domenico Ghirlandaio, *Birth of John the Baptist*, 1485-90, Main Chapel.

Master of the busiest workshop in Florence, Ghirlandaio was famous as an accurate chronicler of Florentine city life. His restrained storytelling catered to a conservative clientele not looking for novel effects in their paintings. His patron was Giovanni Tornabuoni, head of Florence's powerful banking family, and we see a whole gallery of lifelike portraits of the Tornabuoni family. Standing stiffly in pride of place, and expressive of no particular sentiment, this group has no equal in the fifteenth century. Countering their stated dignity, a nursemaid rushing in from the right, her skirt trailing in exaggerated swirls that follow her spirited motion, suggests an artist confident in his newly acquired and still precarious skills in depicting movement.

Birth of John the Baptist is close in format to the *Birth of the Virgin*. But the maid prancing in with fluttering draperies, charming in Botticelli fashion, looks haplessly misplaced in a scene of utter calm. Despite her singular appeal, not every artist appreciated the lack of vitality in Ghirlandaio's style. They had a point. In fact, of those styles at the end of the century with the potential to cross the divide to a deeper probing of man's inner life, especially Botticelli's and Filippino Lippi's (see adjoining chapel), Ghirlandaio's simple narratives had the farthest distance to travel. Yet, the precision of his draftsmanship and the clarity of his colors place Ghirlandaio as one last great exponent of the Giottesque tradition, the essential step to the art of his young student: Michelangelo, in a little more than a decade, transformed ceilings into explosive dramas.

Filippino Lippi, 1457-1504, *Saint Philip and the Dragon*, Strozzi Chapel, 1495-1502

STROZZI CHAPEL, TO THE RIGHT OF THE TORNABUONI CHAPEL

The chapel's decoration, which took Lippi the better part of a decade to complete, represents the final triumph of his short career. The lower right scene illustrates an episode in the life of Saint Philip (namesake of the donor, Filippo Strozzi) when the saint is coerced by the priest at

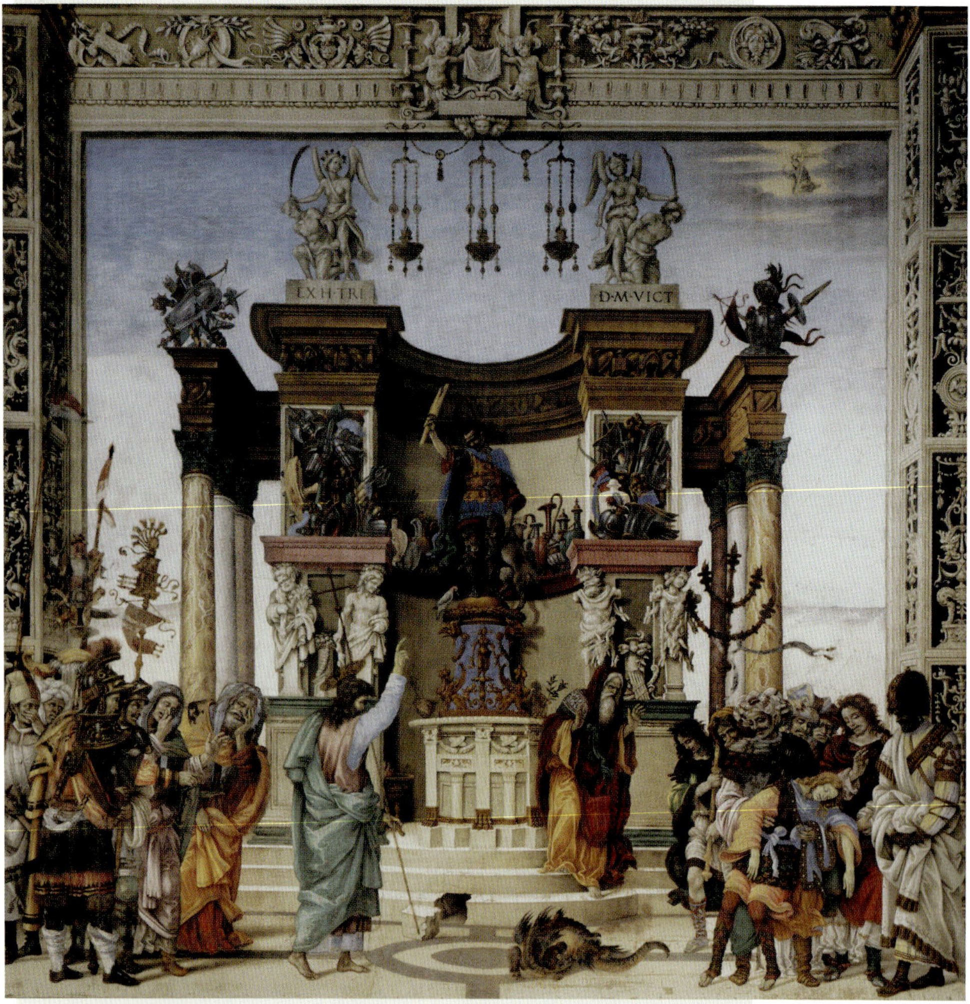

Florentines would have been unfamiliar with the antique ornamental details that embellish this fresco. Lippi, however, while working in Rome in the 1490s, would have seen similar extravagant motifs in Nero's newly unearthed "Golden House".

109. Filippino Lippi, *Saint Philip and the Dragon*, 1495-1502, Strozzi Chapel.

center to make a sacrifice to the pagan idol. At the moment of the priest's command, his son falls dead from the noxious fumes of a dragon that has just slithered out from beneath the pagan altar. After exorcizing the demonic dragon, Philip cures the slouching body of the son at the right.

Lippi projects the full powers of his eccentric temperament onto a religious scene in the guise of an orgiastic operatic stage flushed with classical pagan antiquity: various in the extreme, copious, fanciful, and manically out of control by some standards. Standing atop a pedestal above the altar is the idol, Mars; below him are the four statues of his attendants: frenzy, violence, irrationality, and bestiality. To the left are Roman soldiers decked out in armor, a priest, and various barbaric characters holding their noses from the stench; to the right, a dynamic group of exotic Arabs in turbans and furred helmets, who wince at the slinking dragon. Exquisite portraits by any measure, their delicate skin tones creased with uncertainty, mustaches meticulously detailed, and eyes riveted downward show Lippi's remarkable sensitivity in capturing the likeness of various facial types.

Lippi's style is the polar opposite to Ghirlandaio's prosaic realism and now even far removed from the linear rhythms of his former teacher, Botticelli. Lippi's line is quick, sharp, and abrupt, emphasizing action and ornament shimmering to excess with bizarre details. As such, his picture is a triumph. Master of a uniquely vibrant style, Lippi flaunts precedent. So apparently does his wealthy patron, Filippo Strozzi, scion of the powerful Strozzi family whose tomb shares space with the altar, an audacious contrivance, but an increasingly common one at a time when the wealthy thought themselves virtuous enough to be the chapel's focal point.

In the nave

The Decline of Mannerism

Giorgio Vasari, 1511-1574, *Resurrection with Saints*, Santa Maria Novella, 1568

Here, the illustrious biographer of Florentine artists offers his rendition of a Counter Reformation altarpiece (first discussed in Santa Croce). Vasari, a vociferous advocate of late Mannerism, is no longer considered one of the city's top tier artists, even though he had managed to wrest the position of court painter to Duke Cosimo I from the revered Bronzino.

Taking care to purge excessive nudity from his picture, as dictated by papal reformers, Vasari's wiggly forms reflect Mannerist tastes. His is also dry academic formalism, especially in the positioning of the two saints in the foreground, a formula he repeats many times. He was roundly criticized by the reformers for their inclusion (not realistic—these saints weren't present at the Resurrection) and for their contorted poses (impossibly strained), and for the aggressive distortion of the soldiers' poses in the background (after all, this wasn't a battle field). And while the angels are tour de force creations, these kinds of passages came easily to Vasari who repeated them everywhere, since borrowing from himself and other artists was not considered plagiarism in late Mannerist circles.

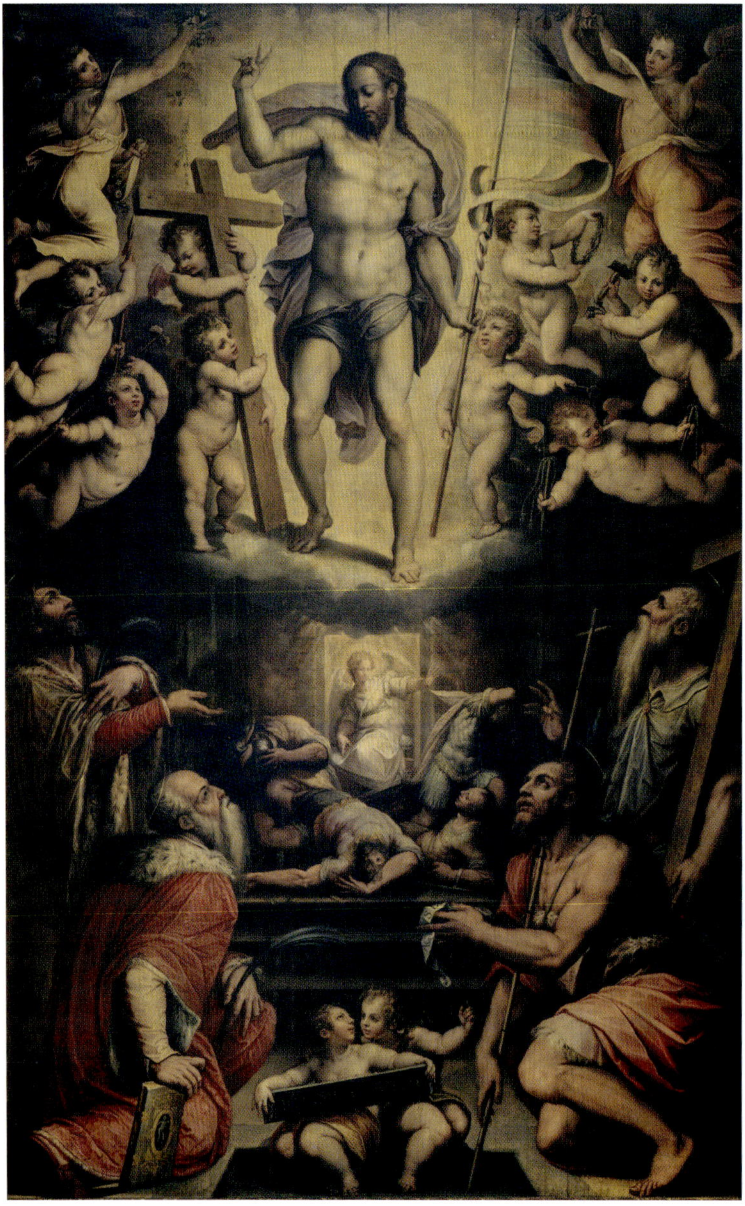

110. Giorgio Vasari, *Resurrection with Saints*, 1568, Santa Maria Novella

In the Spanish Chapel adjoining the cloister

Dominican Dogma, Gothic Fantasy

Andrea da Firenze, 1343-1377, *Path to Salvation*, Spanish Chapel, 1365-67

The frescoes in this chapel are the most impressive works of the Gothic period and unique for their size as single, tapestry-like fields covering an entire wall. The cycle represents the theme of the *Exaltation of the Dominican Order,* which played a major role in the fight against heresy. On the altar wall are the scenes of the *Crucifixion, Passion,* and *Descent into Limbo*. As does every scene, the *Path to Salvation* reflects the troubling times after the plague when Florentines were desperate for spiritual guidance and this painting lays it out as a road map to heaven.

Painted a decade later than those in the Strozzi di Mantova chapel, the style of this scene is more lively and the mood less morbid.

Set in a garden landscape, the scene begins unfolding on the lower

111. Andrea da Firenze, *Path to Salvation*, 1365-67, Spanish Chapel.

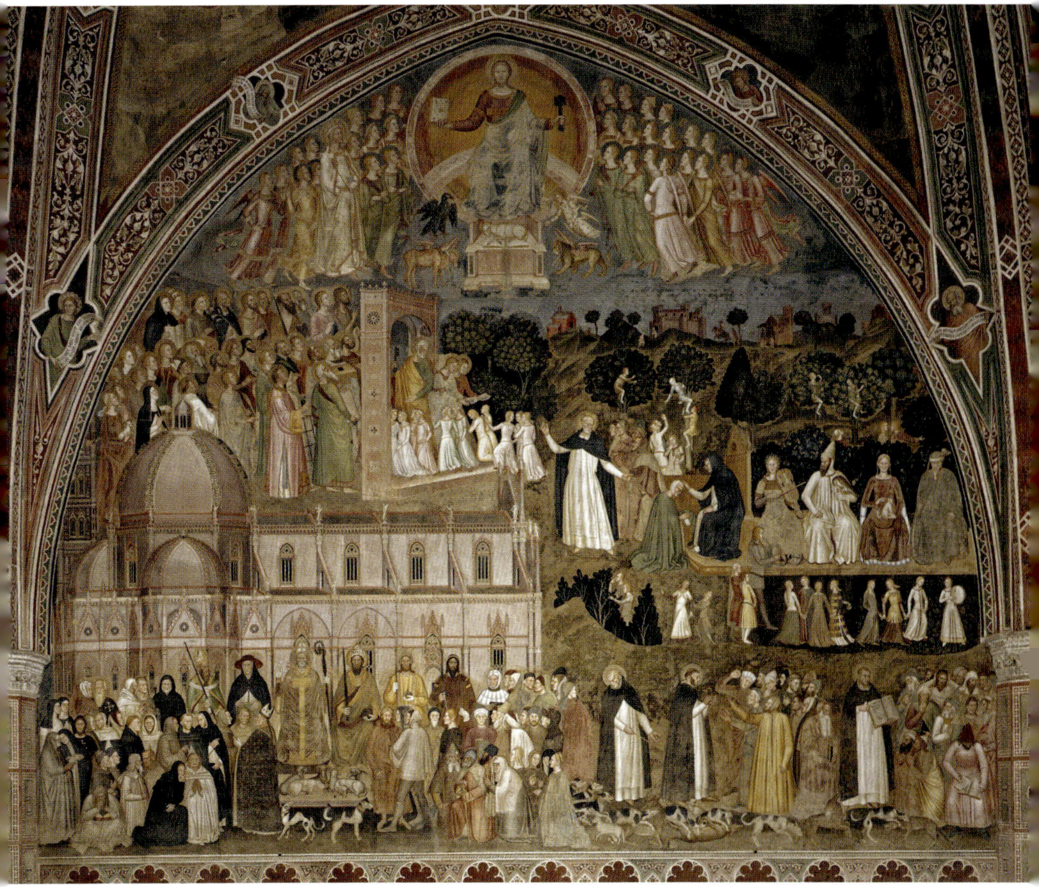

left where the pope sits enthroned between emperors, kings, and bishops. Behind is an imagined view of Florence's cathedral topped with a dome that would not be designed for another sixty years. Below the pope, a crowd of religious clerics reflects on the words of a bishop robed in exquisite plaid. To the right, a grim motley group—grim is the fashion throughout—prays on their knees for salvation. Expressions vary little throughout, but a rich diversity is found in garments and headdresses. Further right, a Dominican sics the "hounds of heaven," dogs spotted in Dominican blacks and white, on a pack of heretical wolves. At the far right Saint Thomas Aquinas, the chief doctrinal authority of the Dominicans and of the Church in general, holds a book of scripture before a converted group of heathens, including two kneeling Jews. Above, a group of

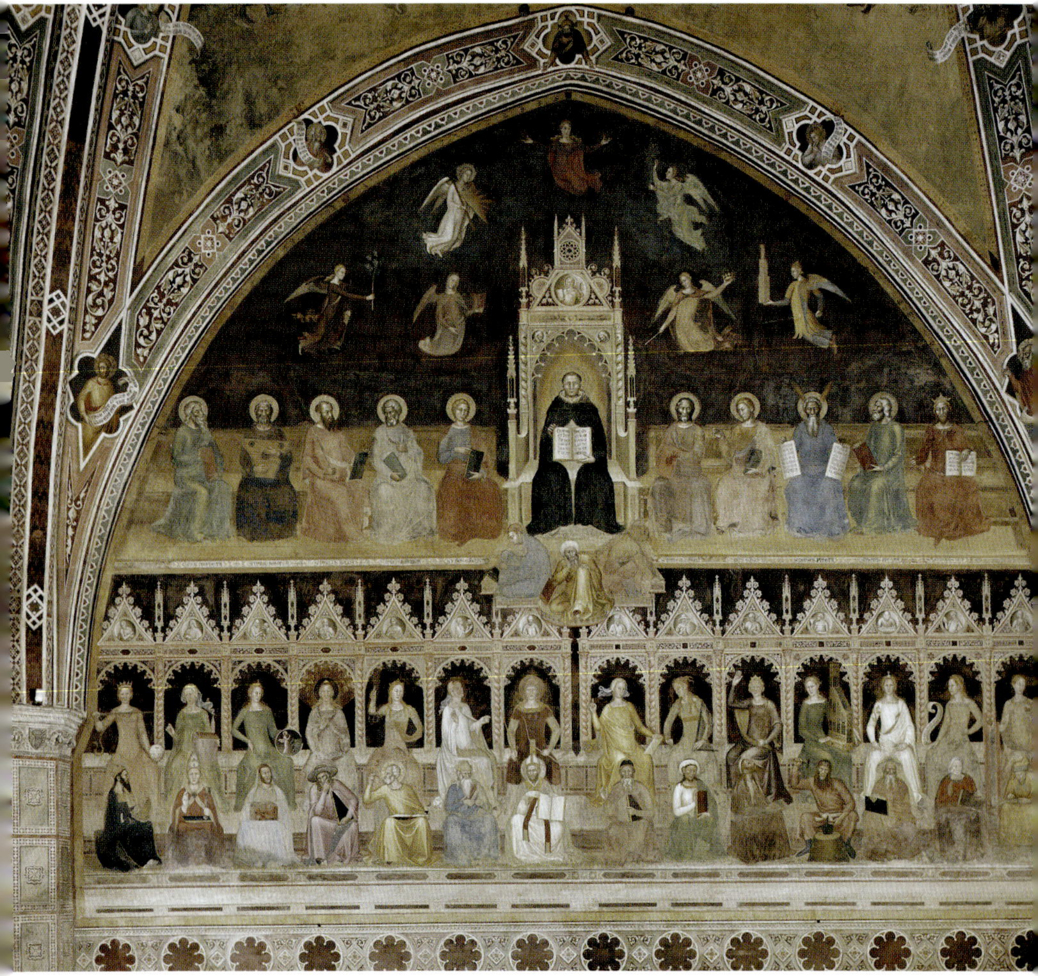

112. Andrea da Firenze, *Triumph of Saint Thomas*, 1365-67, Spanish Chapel.

maidens dance in lovely rhythms before four stern adults, who look on with disapproval. In the center, given prominence, Saint Dominic directs the saved toward the Gates of Paradise where Saint Peter ushers in a group of children to join those in heaven, who, rapt in adoration, gaze at a Christ in glory attended by a host of angels.

By disassembling Giotto's rational space and dramatic focus, Andrea has created individual passages of undeniable charm. And if we can get beyond the heavy rhetoric, we see quaint scenes rendered like a child's book of cautionary tales in lively patterns rich in earth tones and pastels.

Andrea da Firenze, *Triumph of Saint Thomas*, Spanish Chapel, 1365-67

On the opposite wall, a rigidly schematic scene in perfect symmetry evokes the doctrinal austerity of the Dominican hierarchy. Centered in the top row, Saint Thomas, enthroned between prophets, holds open the Book of Wisdom. Above, personifications of the Seven Virtues float against a deep purple background. At Thomas's feet, sit three miserable heretics. In the middle register, seated on exquisitely detailed Gothic thrones, fourteen beguiling females personify the liberal arts—rhetoric, grammar, logic, and so on. Slim, elegant, boneless forms, these beauties represent the epitome of the linear style. At their feet are their pre-Christian delegates, including Euclid, Aristotle, and Pythagoras. The whole wall demonstrates the Gothic artists' penchant for order and balance, for patterns, ornamental details, and the beauty of a broad palette. Somewhat at odds with their reputation as vigilant guardians against heresy, the Dominicans have created one of the most exquisite chapels in all of Italy.

Spellbinding Perspective

On the walls of the Green Cloister, outside the church, part of Santa Maria Novella Museum

Paolo Uccello, 1397-1475, *Temptation of Adam and Eve, Deluge*, Santa Maria Novella Museum, 1425-30

Paolo Uccello painted the series of frescoes over a twenty year period. In the earliest scene, the *Temptation* on the left (no photo), he poses the slim and seemingly boneless Adam and Eve in a perfect example of a Gothic "sway." As flat patterns of conspicuous elegance, an essential feature of the International Gothic style, they are far less natural than Masolino's version of the subject in the Brancacci Chapel, painted during these same years.

In the *Deluge* to the far right (the last painted), Uccello has completely transformed the human figure. The monumental form of the male in the foreground (his purpose is unknown) and the skillful rendering of the struggling nudes can be traced back to Masaccio's figures in the Brancacci Chapel.

The *Deluge* exposes Paolo Uccello's macabre obsession with demonstrating a spellbinding ability to create a spatial world that sucks us into a nightmarish void that the vanishing point dictates. Two opposing, acutely foreshortened views of Noah's Ark instantly funnel our eye toward a storm about to sweep upon us. At points, our eye encounters revolting scenes of panic and despair: desperate human beings with animal instincts clubbing one another to death, floating dead babies, a vulture pecking rotting flesh. The only solace is the image of Noah at the window on the right, receiving a plant sprig from a bird, the sole sign that life still exists on earth.

113. Paolo Uccello, *Deluge*, 1425-30, Green Cloister, Santa Maria Novella Museum.

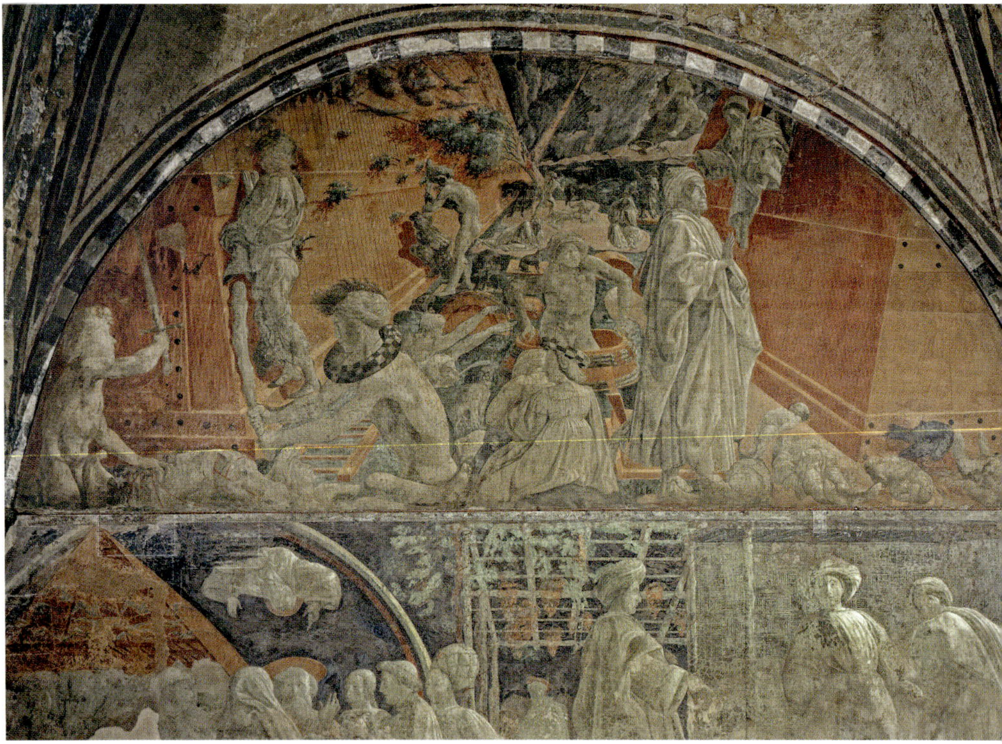

Medici Exile, 1492-1512

With Lorenzo gone, his spoiled and arrogant son Piero failed to inspire the loyalty of the aristocracy's rank and file. When his father's worst fears came to pass and French forces under Charles VIII swept down the Italian coast in 1494, Piero was forced to cede Pisa. Condemned as an act of treason, Piero fled the city. The French marched in and occupied the Medici Palace and other private homes, until the threat of battle convinced them to head for Naples. Once in Naples, Charles pronounced himself king. When his supply lines began to thin, he headed back to France, his journey hastened when his troops were defeated in a battle by a coalition promoted by Venice, Milan and Mantua.

With Piero in exile, Girolamo Savonarola, a Dominican friar from San Marco, stepped in and set the stage for a revival of a Medici-free republic. Described throughout the ages as a non-Florentine religious zealot, Savonarola has garnered much attention by modern historians. He first appeared on the scene in 1489, when Lorenzo invited him to preach. Seemingly, his anti-materialist exhortations to commit to a life of deep religious devotion were directed to a lower class audience. But with Lorenzo in his grave, Savonarola's blistering sermons began gaining force, railing against opulence gained at the expense of the poor and at lewd paintings in churches—images that incited sin. Warning that Florence deserved punishment, the mood of the elite grew grim. But more than a kernel of truth lay at the bottom of his message. An effete, exclusionary caste who patronized the arts solely for their own private use and who flagrantly displayed their wealth had grown out of touch with the common man's core values. The calls for reform found a hungry audience among the lower classes. But once Savonarola began savaging the Pope for his worldly splendor, his fate was a forgone conclusion. When the pope summoned him, he refused to go. Opposition to him by the Medici supporters grew until he was arrested. First tortured for treason, Savonarola was burned at the stake in 1498. A plaque embedded into the stony pavement of Piazza della Signoria marks the spot.

Savonarola's long travail carried profound consequences. Michelangelo was deeply affected; his later depictions of humankind's struggle against sin testify to that. Botticelli abandoned his nubile nymphs for a tortured, religious art. Fra Bartolomeo cloistered himself at San Marco in 1500, where he took the vows of the Dominican order.

With Savonarola and Piero de' Medici gone—he drowned at age thirty while attempting to reenter the city—the Great Council of Five Hundred, which Savonarola had a part in creating, elected Pier Soderini as the head of state in 1502. Soderini's appointment for vice chancellor was Niccolò Machiavelli, the great political theorist and eventual author of *The Prince*.

The New Republic and the Arts

Several avant-garde works of art were executed during the republican regime, most notably by Michelangelo and Leonardo, who had returned to Florence by the end of the century. In Leonardo's *Virgin and Child with Saint Anne* (1501; fig. 91), it was Anne—her feast day falls on the date an early tyrant was expelled from the city—who stood as a protector of republican liberty. In Michelangelo's *Doni Tondo* (1504; fig 90), the Holy Family has been interpreted as a foundation of the ideal state. The regime itself hired Michelangelo and Leonardo to paint famous battle scenes on the walls of the Sala Grande in the Palazzo Vecchio. (Michelangelo's reached only the drawing stage; ruined remains of Leonardo's mural likely lie beneath Vasari's battle scenes.) Last, Michelangelo's *David* (1504) was hauled to Piazza della Signoria as a conspicuous symbol of republican triumph over a tyranny.

Collapse of the Republic

But with the fierce antagonism rising between the common people and the pro-Medici upper classes, the social fabric was corroding. Without the guiding hand of Lorenzo, the republic faced threats from within and grave military threats from without. France had once again taken Milan in 1499 and was expanding throughout much of northern Italy. Ever since the French king Charles VIII had entered their city in 1494, the Florentines had to face the chilling reality of just how fragile their republic had become. It was in this state of heightened insecurity that Soderini, against all precedent, pursued an alliance with the French as a source for trade. Seeing the alliance as a threat, Pope Julius II decided that the hated French must go and organized the Holy League, comprised of the papacy, Spain, and Venice, to drive them out. The outbreak of war placed the fledgling republic in a terrible dilemma. With both sides demanding loyalty, Soderini chose to remain neutral. When the Holy League succeeded in forcing the French to withdraw, a vengeful pope, on the advice of Cardinal Giovanni de' Medici (remember, son of Lorenzo the Great), decided upon Soderini's future. With events beyond his control, Soderini fled in 1512. On the same day, Giovanni's brother, Giuliano, entered the long-neglected Medici Palace.

Florence under the Medici Popes, 1513–1534

The years following the ouster of the republican government were shaped by Lorenzo's shrewd foresight in procuring an appointment for his second son, Giovanni, to the College of Cardinals. Since an early age, Giovanni had pursued a fluency in canon law that assured his election to the papacy as Pope Leo X on the death of Julius II in 1513. Identified with Rome at the height of the Renaissance, cultured in Greek and Latin letters, a patron of the arts, an opulent entertainer, Leo was masterfully ruthless. With his younger brother, Giuliano, ensconced in the Medici Palace as the nominal head of government, Leo ran Florence with an iron scepter.

His immediate task was to flood the city with professional soldiers from the papal ranks, while flattering the leading families who hoped to take part in the new regime. To that end, he doled out Vatican ceremonial posts to members of the city's ranking families. To Filippo Strozzi, Medici archenemy, went the head of the exchequer; to a Pazzi, a treasury position.

When Giuliano proved to be insufficiently political, Leo married him off to the daughter of the Duke of Savoy. In his place, Leo installed Lorenzo, the twenty-year old grandson of Lorenzo the Great. He then appointed his cousin Giulio a cardinal, whose responsibility was to oversee Lorenzo, who was ambitiously pursuing a program of more overt control of the government than had any previous Medici. He died in 1519, age twenty-six. (It was for this Lorenzo that Machiavelli wrote the *Prince*.)

When Pope Leo died in 1521, a Flemish was elected as Pope Adrian VI. A priggish puritan who neglected the arts, Adrian was wildly unpopular when he died a year later, opening the way to a second descendent of Giovanni di Bicci de' Medici as pope. To Florentines, Giulio's modest lifestyle, piety, and illegitimacy proved less threatening than had Lorenzo's. But his move to Rome left a vacuum that was filled by the thirteen year-old bastard son of Giuliano, Ippolito, who quickly took on princely airs. Events in Rome mercilessly overshadowed his reign.

From the start, Giulio, as Pope Clement VII, faced one long reign of uninterrupted humiliation. The French Francis I continued to fight Charles V for dominance in Italy; King Henry VIII of England bullied for divorce; the Protestant Reformation fanned out all over Europe; the Turks defeated Hungary, in Charles's own backyard. These events imposed on the pope the most pervasive crisis Europe had seen. When Clement's most pressing need called for a quick decision in favor of Francis or Charles, he hesitated. Charles responded with speed. Already head of Germany, Spain, Naples, and the Netherlands, Charles sent troops against the French, capturing Francis I in Pavia and imprisoning him.

Sensing that Clement lacked the forces to protect Florence, anti-Medici groups speedily ushered the petty tyrant Ippolito out of Florence, including his cousins Alessandro and the three year-old Caterina, the future queen of France. For a third—and final time, a republic was reinstated.

The Sack of Rome

Within days, the suspicions of the new republic proved to be onerously correct, when the imperial army swept into the Holy City in May, 1527, to unleash the utterly brutal carnage in what has become known as the "Sack of Rome." From the nobility to the poor, many died and many fled, including most of the city's artists. Hundreds of churches were pillaged. Clement escaped through a passageway to his fortress at Castle St. Angelo.

Once word spread that Clement had little choice but to capitulate, surrendering territories and funds, but gaining Charles's support for a Medici return to power, the Florentines began to fortify their city against imminent attack. Michelangelo was put in charge of fortifications. The attack came in 1529 in the form of a siege by imperial troops. The Florentines held out for a year until many citizens had been killed in battle, or had died of the plague or starvation. Under the direction of both Clement and Charles, Alessandro, the bastard son of Lorenzo the Younger, was installed at age twenty as duke. Ippolito's jealousy festered until he died five years later at age twenty-three.

Like Ippolito's, Alessandro's character ran to the perverse. An authoritarian ruler and skilled politician, he mixed with the poor and privileged. He roamed the city streets at night, incognito. Sexually the most voracious of the Medici, his seduction of women from all classes earned him a grim end. Baited by a woman he expected to conquer, he was trapped alone and held down by Lorenzino de' Medici, a distant relative and procurer of his mistresses, while an assassin bludgeoned him to death at age twenty-five. Lorenzino was tracked down in Venice and stabbed to death.

6. San Marco Convent and Museum

From 1434 to 1441, years in which he was quickly gaining power over the city, Cosimo de' Medici contributed the funds to refurbish San Marco and to enlarge its monastery as a public act of penance. During construction, the Dominicans inspired one of their own, Fra Angelico, the most revered painter of his generation, to render a series of works for the church and to decorate the monks' cells. Cosimo had a double one reserved for his private use. Sixty years later, a second Dominican, Fra Bartolomeo, grew to become one of the masters of the Renaissance. San Marco was also home for ten years to Savonarola, the fiery Dominican who was burned at the stake in 1498.

Gothic Relic or Innovator, the Elusive Artist

Fra Angelico (c. 1395-1455), Lorenzo Monaco (c. 1370-c. 1425), *Deposition* (*Santa Trinita Altarpiece*), San Marco Museum, early 1440s

Because Angelico inherited the Gothic frame and the saints in the gables above from the recently deceased Lorenzo Monaco, the picture begs comparison with the styles of both Lorenzo and Masaccio. In place of the gold background normally associated with a Gothic frame, he paints his signature blue sky and decorates it with two attendant wisps of angels. Instead of Lorenzo's swaying Gothic figures wrapped in their voluminous draperies, he poses his subjects straight up and drapes them in robes with vertical folds. These are slim figures that he will not alter over the course of his career. We do see some of Masaccio in the lifeless body of Christ and in the splendid portraits of the bearded figures on the ladder, including the haloed Nicodemus and Joseph of Arimathaea. The same cannot be said of the honey-smooth faces of the other mourners, even of Mary Magdalene kneeling to kiss Christ's feet.

Although sensitive to rapidly developing advances, Angelico is one of the few artists who could never conform to Masaccio's relief system, which he thought robbed a picture of the visual splendor necessary to convey a spiritual scene. On that score, he is the one great artist unwilling to employ Alberti's system of muting drapery folds with mixes of blacks. What Angelico is after is brilliance, even though dominating colors deny the picture its spatial qualities and contradict the mood of a pathos better suited to a more sober palate. (For more on this picture's color, see Addendum, fig. 145).

A curious final note commends Angelico to the highest rank of painters. When we think of his peers, Domenico Veneziano, Filippo Lippi and Paolo Uccello, we attribute to their figures' borders a certain hard-edged quality. Yet, without ever approaching Masaccio's relief, Angelico, with the subtlest touch of the brush, gently softens the borders of his draperies and flesh tones to correspond remarkably to the natural appearances evoked by a later generation of painters.

114. Fra Angelico, Lorenzo Monaco, *Deposition*, early 1440s, San Marco Museum.

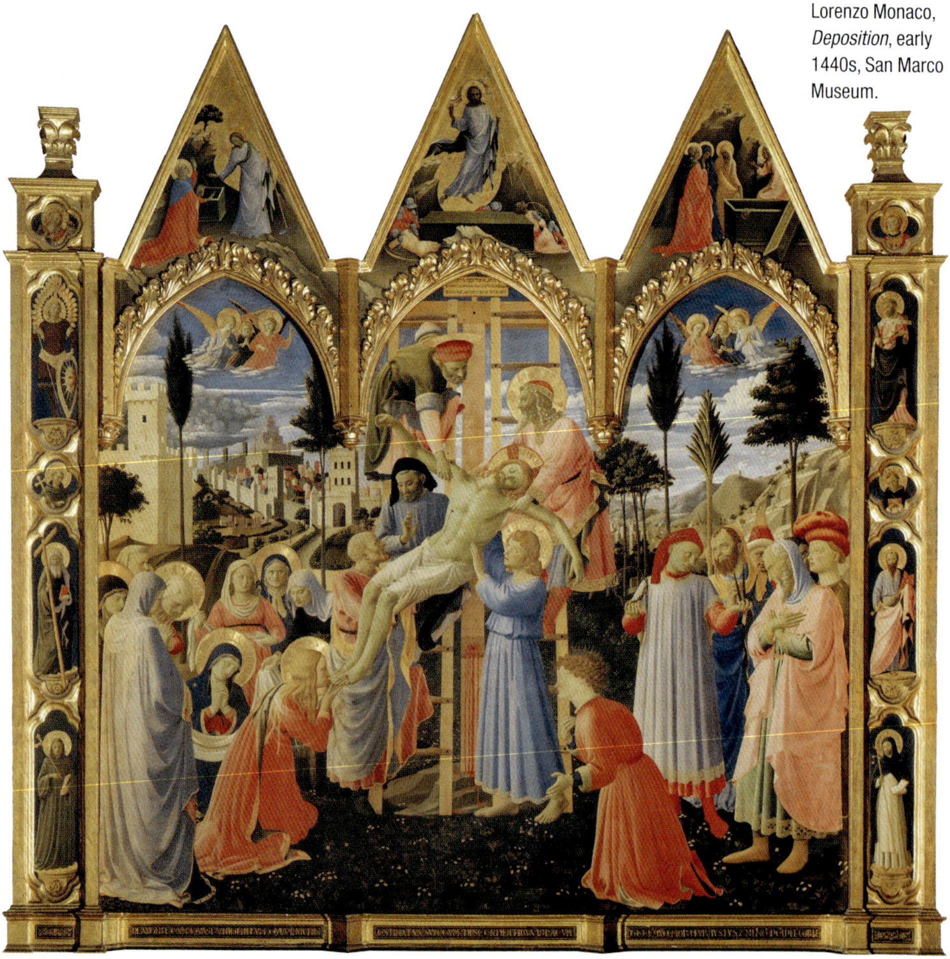

Palla Strozzi commissioned the work to hang as a pendant to Gentile da Fabriano's *Adoration of the Magi* in the Strozzi Chapel. Together, they would have commemorated Christ's birth and death.

IN THE MONASTIC CELLS ON THE SECOND LEVEL, NORTHERN CORRIDOR FACING THE STAIRCASE

Fra Angelico, *Annunciation*, San Marco Convent, 1440-50

Fra Angelico's achievement in each of these frescoes is profound, but none is a more poignant meditation than this scene. Here is an Annunciation reduced to its simplest essentials, with none of the theatrical commotion and fluttering draperies that other Annunciations deemed integral to describing the Virgin's startled recoil. In the silence of her monastic cell, this Virgin is at peace.

Even though Angelico throughout his career acknowledged Masaccio's technical advances in the rational exteriority of life, we still see an artist very different from Masaccio. Angelico does so much with so little. What other artist could depict so beautifully the delicate slope of Mary's fragile body and render her eyes so sensitively, adjusting their tiny blues and whites to convey the intensity of her interaction with the angel?

115. Fra Angelico, *Annunciation*, 1440-50, San Marco Convent.

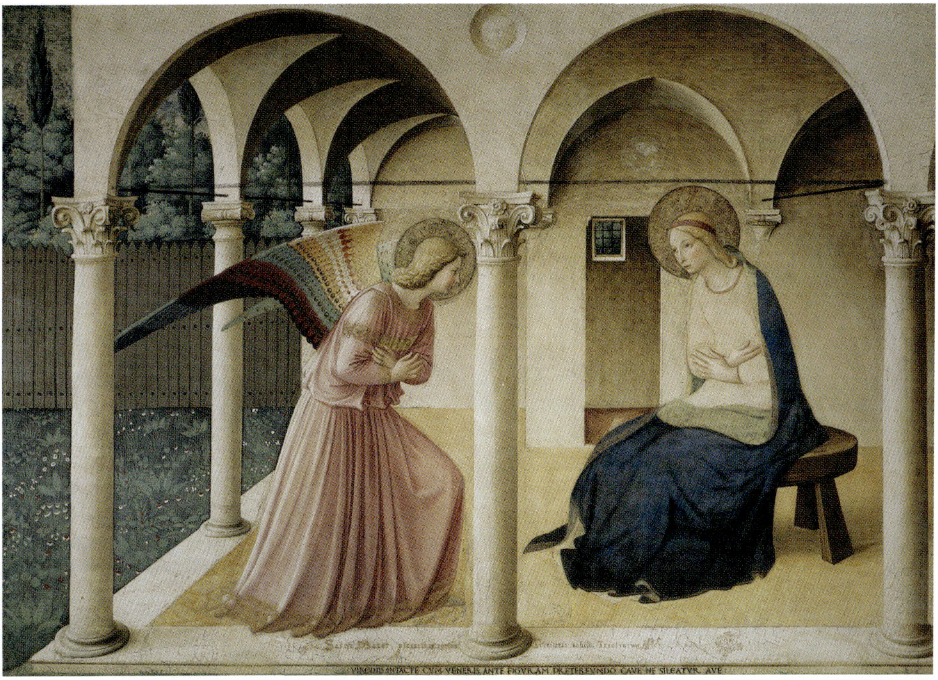

IN THE REFECTORY INSIDE THE BOOK STORE

QUESTION OF STANDARDS IN LAST SUPPERS

Domenico Ghirlandaio, 1449-1494, *Last Supper*, San Marco Convent, c. 1485

In the most general sense, Ghirlandaio's *Last Supper* recalls Andrea del Castagno's c. 1447 version (fig. 118). Both artists evoke a rigorous sense of space, but, as would be expected considering the later date,

Ghirlandaio's is more convincing. By setting the scene in a loggia whose lunettes open to a garden, the artist conveys the feeling that we are looking into a sun drenched villa. With the loggia's pair of vaults appearing to be supported by the refectory's actual corbel in the center, and with the U shaped table, there is little doubt that this space means to be contiguous with ours. Critical to this illusionism, the shadows that the figures project against the wall and the shadows on the hanging tablecloth reveal that the light directed from the left is an interior light shared by the actual space of the refectory.

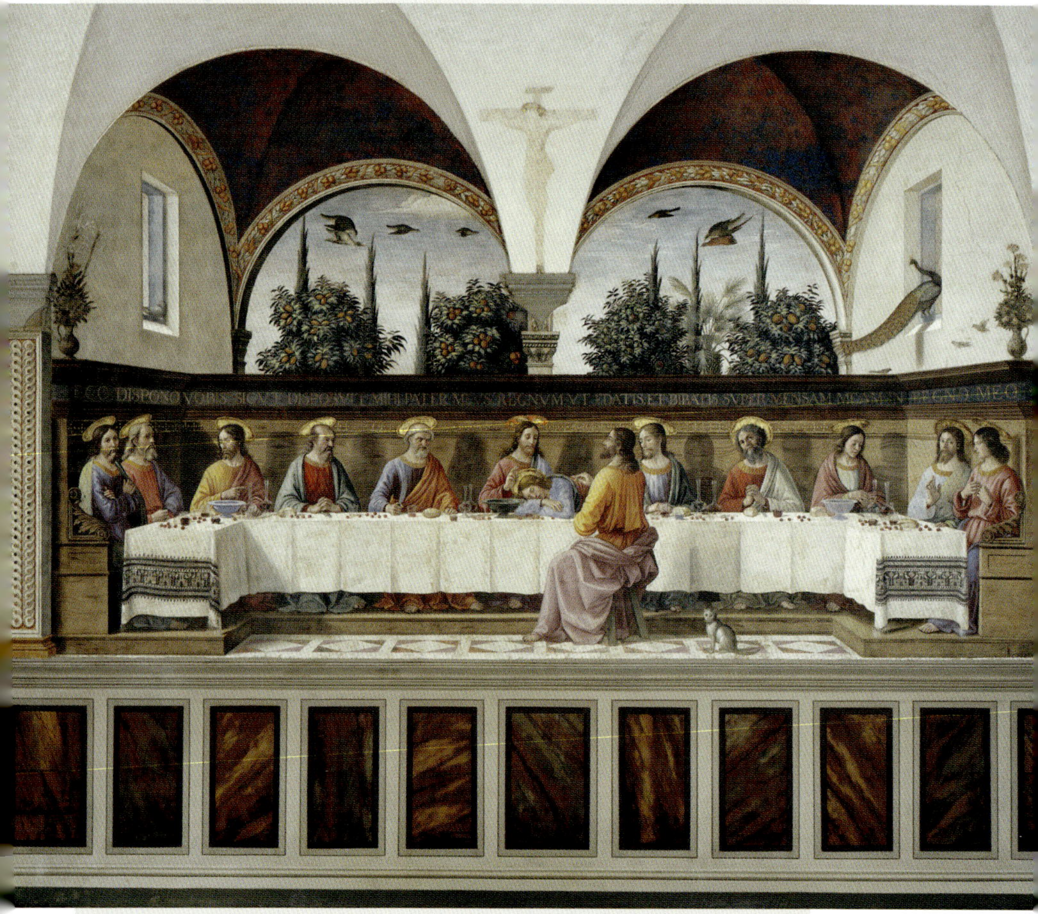

Symbolism: palm trees, stand for Christ's passion; cypress trees, his death; orange trees, regeneration; birds, liberated souls; dove, the Holy Spirit; peacock, immortality; bowls of water, baptism; bread and wine, the Eucharist.

116. Domenico Ghirlandaio, *Last Supper*, c. 1485, San Marco Convent.

Although the artist has a flair for a calm, rational space, he doesn't have much flair for angst. Judas is benign. In fact, given the scene's potential for explosive power, the participants project little animation. Ghirlandaio's figures sit stiffly upright, isolated and immobile in gesture and expression, and this static quality remains a constant throughout his career. He never seemed capable of evoking a figure's interior life by means of its actions and expressions.

On the other hand, he shows skill in depicting in vivid detail the symbolic value of the stuff of daily experience. For example, Judas is juxtaposed to a cat, the enemy of God's dogs, the Dominicans. He also sits opposite the faithful, sleeping John and holds the bread that Christ will bless, designating he is the betrayer. Peter holds a knife, foretelling he will slice off a soldier's ear when Roman troops come to arrest Christ that night.

The San Marco School

On the vaulted wall just inside the entrance room to the museum. A detached fresco from Santa Maria Nuova

Fra Bartolomeo (1472-1517), Mariotto Albertinelli (1474-1515), *Last Judgment*, San Marco Museum, 1499-1501

This little known and inconspicuous fresco (not illustred) is Bartolomeo's last painting before he cloistered himself for five years in the monastery of San Marco because of the execution of Savonarola the year before. The date of 1499 marks the uneasy state of art in the city, with Leonardo still in Milan and Michelangelo in Rome. Dominating the art scene were Botticelli, whose searing spiritual states had lost touch with reality; Filippino Lippi and his agitated art; and Perugino, who seemed incapable of depicting emotion. Yet, it was Perugino who most influenced Bartolomeo at the beginning of his career.

Bartolomeo's upper half of the *Last Judgment* (the ruined lower half is by his workshop partner Mariotto Albertinelli) offers the first hint of a High Renaissance style in its simplest form. Like Leonardo's ring of incredulous spectators in the *Adoration* (fig 87), Bartolomeo sets his apostles in a semicircle and links them by rhythmic gestures and poses. Masterfully foreshortened in their ponderous drapery, these monumental figures peer down on us from their lofty perches in the heavenly ferment.

In the room opposite the refectory

Fra Bartolomeo, *Virgin and Child with Saint Anne and Saints*, San Marco Museum, c. 1510

The unfinished, monotone under-painting emphasizes the precision of the drawing that underlies Bartolomeo's style and the importance that formal relationships play in his compositions. The figures are as geometrically ordered as is the deeply spaced architecture that frames them. Figures dispersed in diagonals, triangles, pyramids, and semicircles continually dominate his style. But, while the calm, measured discipline of this kind of art is undeniably elegant, it sacrifices the charm and easy naturalness of the style of his peer, Andrea del Sarto.

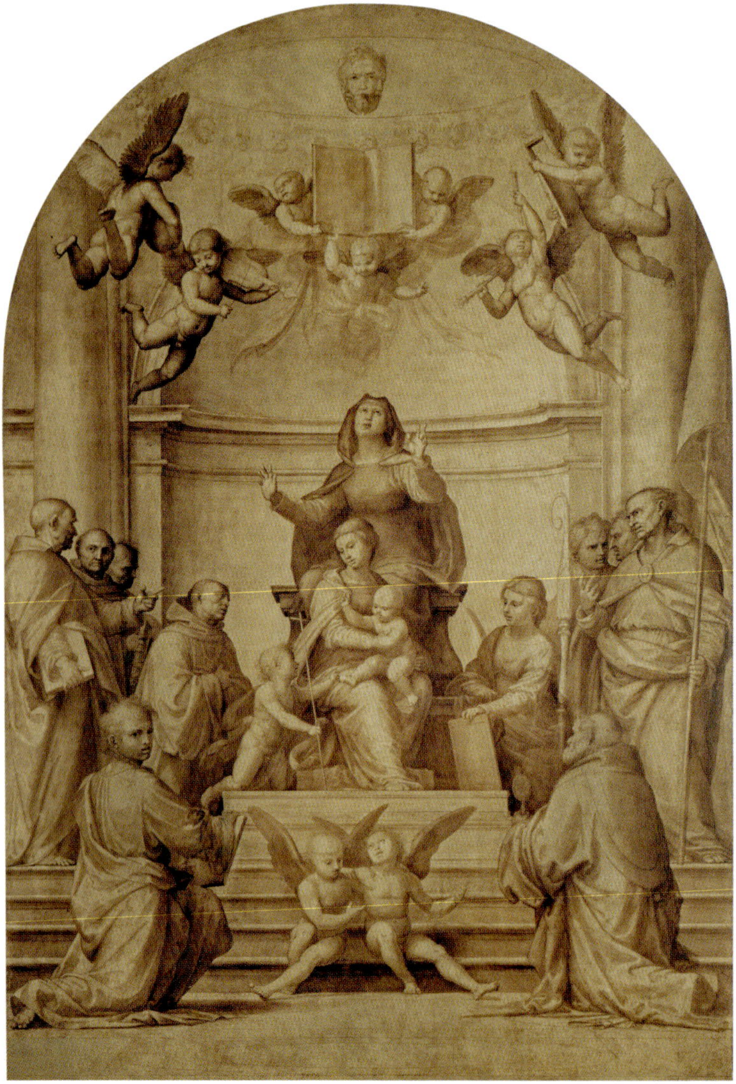

117. Fra Bartolomeo, *Virgin and Child with Saint Anne and Saints*, c. 1510, San Marco Museum.

7. Santa Apollonia Refectory

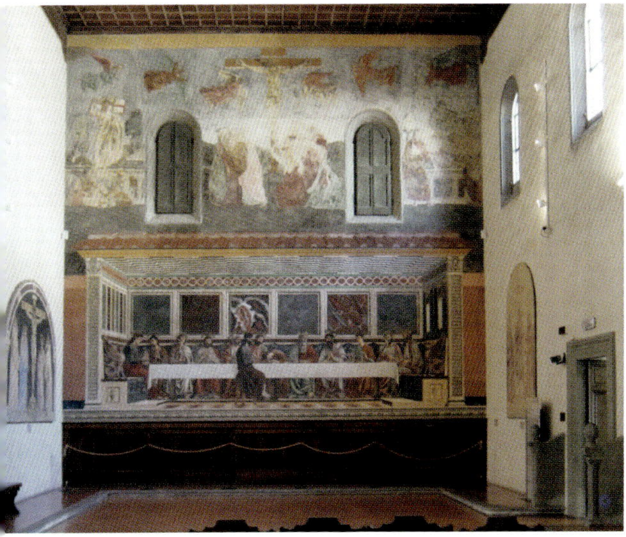

Brutal Realist

Andrea del Castagno, c. 1422-1457, *Last Supper*, Santa Apollonia Refectory, c. 1447

Of the dozen depictions of Last Suppers in Florence, Castagno's is the most structurally taut and mysteriously tense drama. His is also the most illusionistic to date and the first to follow the rules of perspective, which are established by the orthogonals derived from the tiled roof, the floor pavements, the marbled side-panels, and the black and white tiles of the ceiling. Instead of leading to Christ, each of these orthogonals points toward John who sits at the center of the table. Although side benches recede inward to reinforce this perspective, Castagno doesn't provide us with enough information to configure how far back this space extends. The ceiling tiles all have an equal depth from front to back, instead of diminishing with distance. In the same manner, the six marble panels, which we see from an extreme oblique view at each end of the room, are of an indeterminable width; we don't know whether they are as wide as the six back panels or not.

Oddly, considering his rigorous illusionist treatment of architecture, Castagno sets his room apart from the refectory. We see the pillared end walls and some kind of an adjacent outdoor space, which means we are outside looking in, just as we were in Giotto's Santa Croce frescoes. But Castagno isolates this space in a manner that forces us to face a mind-altering, claustrophobic stage setting that threatens intensely.

The strip of stark white table cloth, laid out like an altar covering, set against the veneered marble panels painted in swirls of dissonant colors foretells of betrayal and human sacrifice. Like Taddeo Gaddi (fig. 31),

Castagno places the halo-less, swarthy, black-haired and bearded Judas isolated and opposite John and Christ. Faced off, the protagonist and antagonist form an axis metaphorically marked by that particular marble panel painted in black-dominating, hostile colors just above their heads. These colors are repeated by degrees in the other panels, the roof and

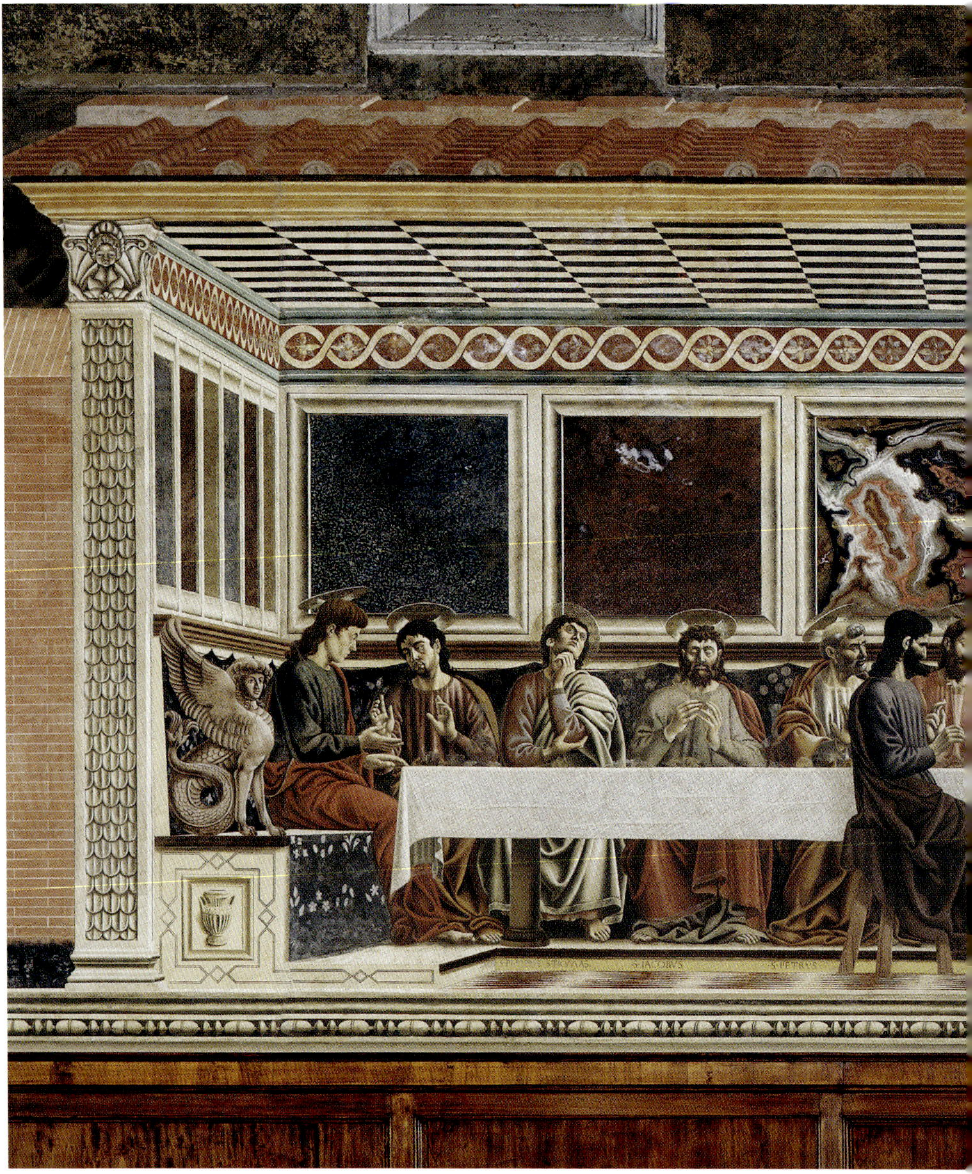

118. Andrea del Castagno, *Last Supper*, c. 1447, Santa Apollonia Refectory.

ceiling tiles, and in the participants' robes. Unlike the sweet pastels employed by Angelico, Castagno follows Alberti's dictum by mixing his colors with black to deepen the shaded tones that give to drapery and facial features the same severely faceted, sculpture-like quality that he does to the architecture.

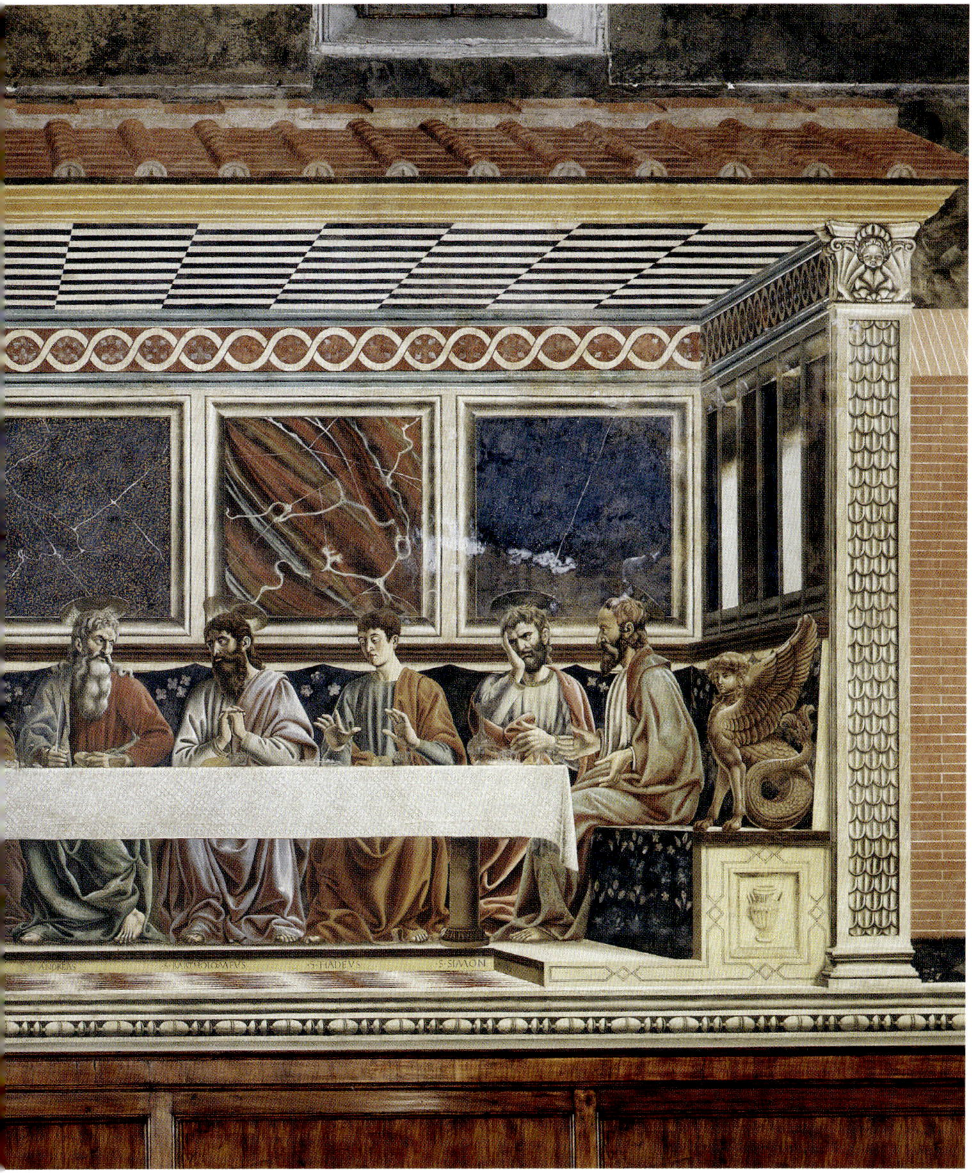

8. ACCADEMIA GALLERY

In addition to Michelangelo's *David*, the museum specializes in paintings from the fourteenth century (where the Uffizi's collection is notably lean). It also houses a group of paintings from the fifteenth century that, for one reason or another, fail to cross the divide between the Renaissance and High Renaissance styles. The painting below represents the most intriguing of that group.

FLAWED?

Filippino Lippi (1457-1504), Pietro Perugino (c. 1448-1523), *Deposition*, Accademia Gallery, 1504-5

The Servites hired Perugino to complete this piece when Filippino Lippi suddenly died at just forty-seven. Although two more incompatible painters can not be found, the juxtaposition of their styles affords us an opportunity to address what keeps each from breaching the divide between the Renaissance and High Renaissance.

The upper section, almost entirely by Filippino, depicts three vigorous, anatomically correct figures in difficult poses lowering the body of Christ. The variety and individuality of their facial expressions rank as some of the finest portraits of the period. But Filippino failed to shed his obsession for fussy details, namely the copious draperies flying about and the precious ties hanging in swirls from the cross. These essentially decorative elements, interlocked with the outstretched arms of the agitated bodies on the ladder, read as one ensemble of lively, two-dimensional surface patterns. Filippino's mature style, then, can be described as a composite of the ornamental and the realistic.

By comparison, Perugino, the most popular artist at the turn of the century, fails mightily. He did the body of Christ and the figures in the lower zone in his typical bland, enervating style. The juxtaposition of his contribution to the animated movements and expressions of Filippino's figures emphasizes his formulaic faces and dainty, effeminate gestures. Even more damning, it is clear from a study of Filippino's preparatory drawings that Perugino erased an area of dramatic focus. Changing Mary Magdalene, who now kneels inertly, from the original version in which she desperately clutches the cross, earned Perugino nothing but scorn.

In sum, both artists remained intractable, unwilling or unable to make any concessions to what by now had become the standard: Leonardo's idealization of natural appearances. Still, Filippino Lippi and Perugino both rank as top tier Renaissance artists, each carving out a uniquely memorable style.

119. Filippino Lippi, Pietro Perugino, *Deposition*, 1504-5, Accademia Gallery.

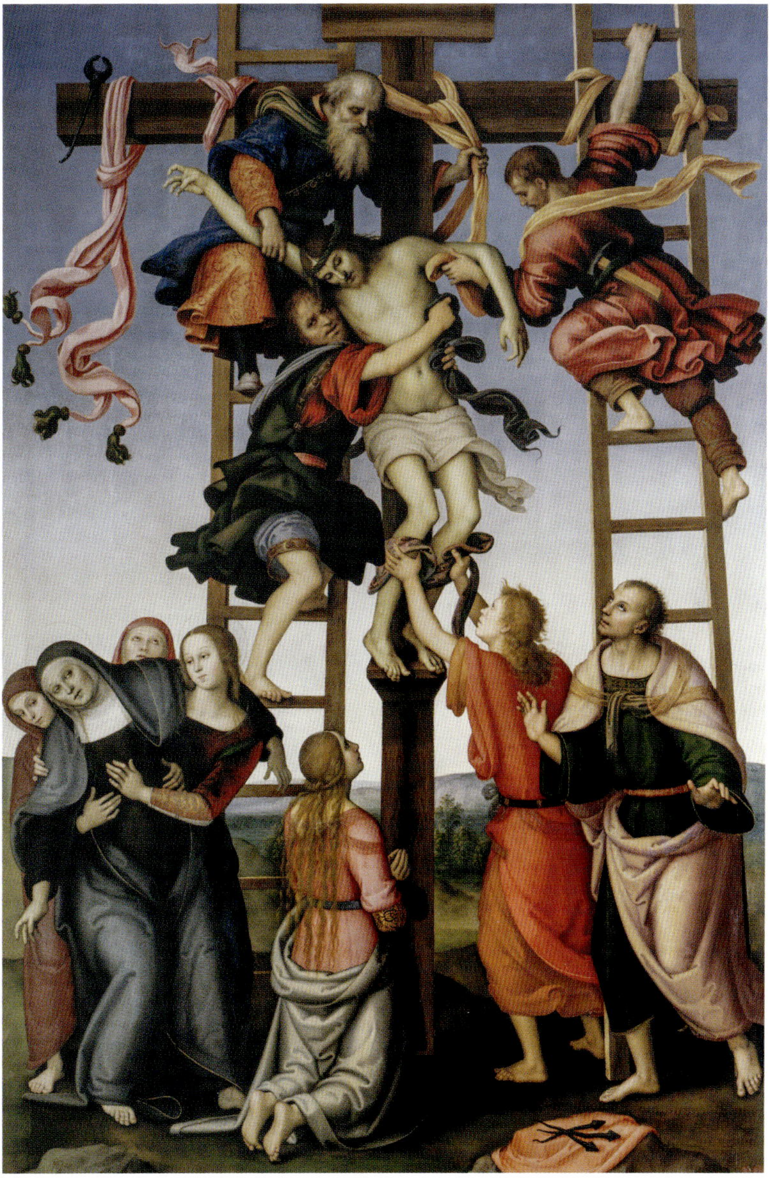

9. Santissima Annunziata Church and Cloister

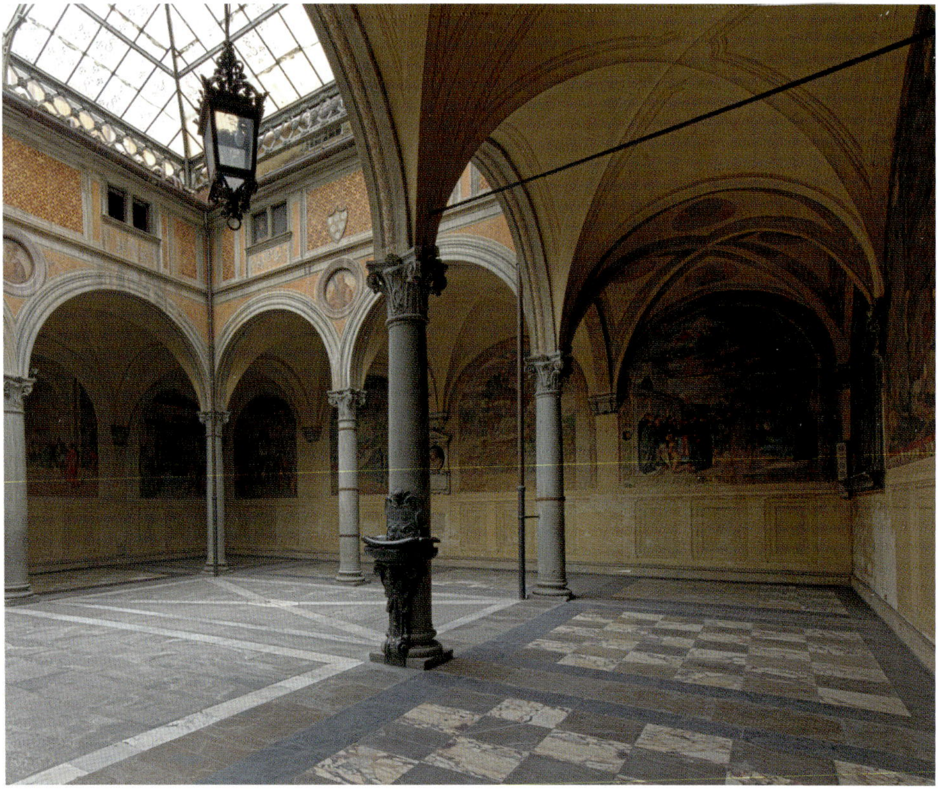

Santissima Annunziata basilica, Chiostrino dei Voti.

Throughout the seven years (1509-1516) it took artists to decorate its atrium, or Chiostrino dei Voti, because of the number of life-size votives that once packed the space, Santissima Annunziata, church of the Servite Order, was the city's hothouse of creativity. Getting to know one of them, Andrea del Sarto, represents the clearest opening in Florence to understanding the development of the early High Renaissance. Here, too, we meet Sarto's brilliant young pupils, Jacopo Pontormo and Rosso Fiorentino, making their first entrance onto the public stage of Florence's fiercely competitive art world.

120. Andrea del Sarto, *Curing of the Possessed Woman*, 1509-1510, Chiostrino dei Voti.

Andrea del Sarto, 1486-1530, *Curing of the Possessed Woman*, Chiostrino dei Voti, 1509-1510

With Leonardo in Milan and Michelangelo in Rome, Andrea del Sarto's successful execution of these prestigious commissions would have insured him a place second only to Fra Bartolomeo in artistic stature (see

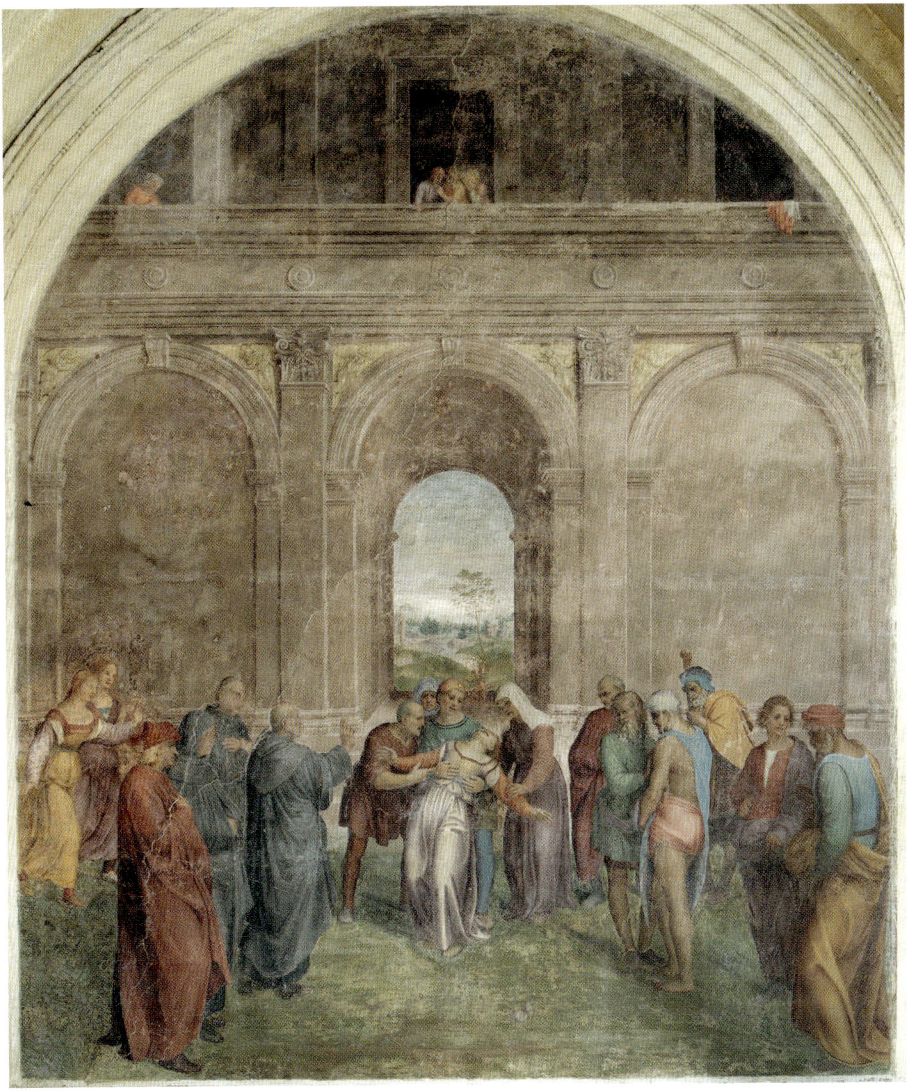

San Marco, fig. 117). In three frescoes by Sarto we will primarily focus on his advances in color manipulation. The problem of color brilliance or of diverse colors that fail to confer a uniform volume on a figure or on a group of figures was not truly confronted until Leonardo began suppressing color toward a uniform intensity by the addition of black. The technique, fully developed in the *Mona Lisa*, was ingenious, but failed to accord with natural appearances.

The earliest three frescoes, just to the right of the entrance, depict the life of Filippo Benizzi, founder of the Servites. They share a common scheme: a group of characters set variously upon a stage as if they were giving a performance. They also share a common palette, which Sarto limits to the conventions of the late Quattrocento, dispersing strong hues of inherently different intensities about the scene for chromatic balance: yellow here, red there, and so on.

In the most daring scene and the first completed, the *Curing of the Possessed Woman*, many of the figures are clumsily proportioned. The man in yellow at the lower right, for example, appears too tall to be capable of centering weight over feet. More importantly, the fullness of his lower body does not conform to his upper body because the colors of his various garments are not uniformly modeled. Where the yellow gown has been modeled by an artificial shift to deep umber brown to confer roundness (a direct quotation of Masaccio in the Brancacci Chapel), the light blues and greens covering his upper frame are barely modeled and therefore appear flatter. The same holds true for the tall figure wearing red short pants. This fabric, modeled in near-white pink to fuller red, gives shape to his body, whereas the light blue drapery does not. In contrast, the slumping pose of the possessed woman appears remarkably lifelike because of her rounded out volume. Here, the artist employs a combination of colors favored in the Gothic era, but will soon reject as optically unnatural. Look to the folds of her cream-white gown, which he models in purple—a beautiful effect, but an artificial one. Purple, we know from experience, does not exist in the shadows of white fabric.

At this stage of his development, Sarto has yet to discover the key to describing a fully developed figure that will mark the beginning of his mature style in the next painting. To do so, he must amplify his figures and employ colors of equal intensity to confer equal volume.

Andrea del Sarto, *Journey of the Magi*, Chiostrino dei Voti, 1511

To the right of the church entrance are five frescoes depicting the Life of the Virgin

Rather than depicting an Adoration of the Magi, Andrea del Sarto concentrates on the rich pageantry of their journey as the procession winds down a deep countryside to the immediate foreground. In place of figures staged against an architectural backdrop, he balances the animated gathering against a palace in steep recession that continues beyond the picture frame. He divides the crowd in two, integrating the smaller group to the palace and the larger group to the landscape.

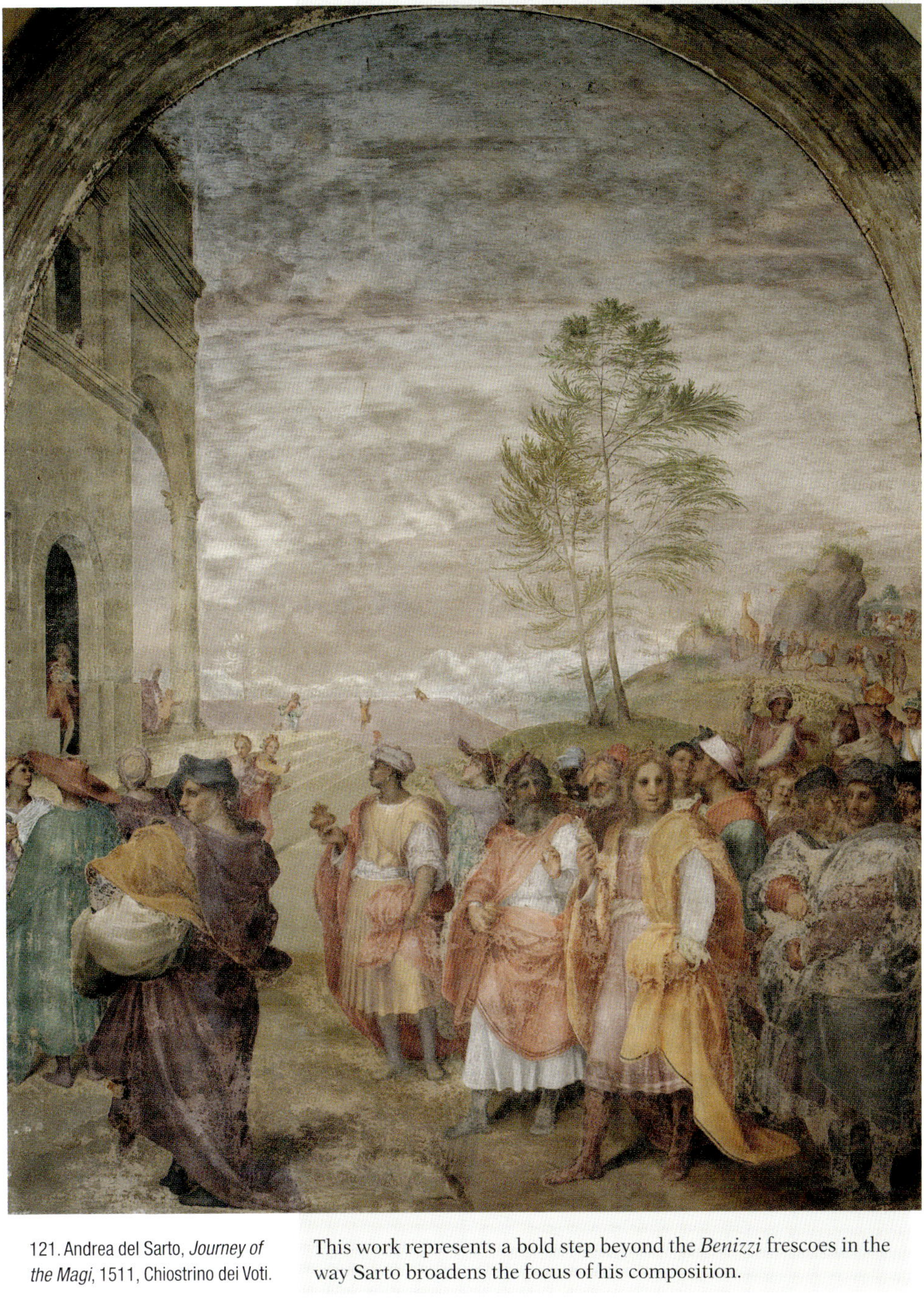

121. Andrea del Sarto, *Journey of the Magi*, 1511, Chiostrino dei Voti.

This work represents a bold step beyond the *Benizzi* frescoes in the way Sarto broadens the focus of his composition.

To this side of the smaller group stands a ponderous character who twists to his left, as if he senses someone. His body is lost to the puffed-out, voluminous drapery, yet his form's monumentality effectively compensates for the massed gathering and anchors the vertical axis of the composition established by the corner of the building.

The draperies reflect the unified treatment of color intensity that Sarto was searching for in the *Benizzi* frescoes. Each is painted in a soft, muted color, which he skillfully manipulates to bring out the rich gradient of tones in the shadows and highlights of the folds. Here, no color competes and none dominates.

In the scene's uncanny naturalness, color, in all its subtle variations, is Sarto's unprecedented protagonist: in the prominence he gives the freely painted sky, the beautiful wisps of two lone trees, and the landscape that dims at the horizon. Sarto's ability to integrate a large crowd, an abbreviated piece of architecture, and an open, almost infinite space into a harmonious whole, yet keep the look of informality, is absolutely novel in Florentine painting. To Leonardo or Michelangelo, whose tight analytical designs were the antithesis of this style, such informality would have represented a lack of dramatic focus that could only rob a picture of its gravitas.

Andrea del Sarto, *Birth of the Virgin*, Chiostrino dei Voti, 1513-14

In the vault of this handsomely appointed room, angels frolicking above the bed canopy signal that this is no ordinary event. A baby girl has just been born, and women of the household, family and friends in contemporary Florentine dress attend to the mother, while a midwife prepares the bath for the newborn child. The comfort of a fire where a young boy warms his hands, sculptured putti above the mantel, the carved cornices of the settee and the canopy of the master bed, suggest a home of civilized, patrician prosperity. This is a space in which we can place ourselves, but only as observers who might otherwise intrude on the tranquility of this time-honored celebration shared among women.

Artfully arranged in easy poses, they appear to have come together for an intimate family portrait intended for posterity. In slow measured rhythms a group of eight women weave a sweeping S-shaped arabesque that turns on the woman in red until it trails off to the last woman standing at the fireplace.

What pulls the eye across this pattern are not the individual figures, but an aesthetic of a different order, as yet unseen in Florentine painting, that arises from the graceful harmony of their colors. As a rhetorical flourish, Sarto sets them out plainly at the right, where the explicit whiteness of the bed sheet, repeated as accents in the costumes of all the women, leads the eye to soft variations of the three primary colors: blue in the blanket, yellow in the woman in profile, and red in the woman facing us. From these, spring a range of half colors that merge seamlessly in combinations among the various tunics and gowns.

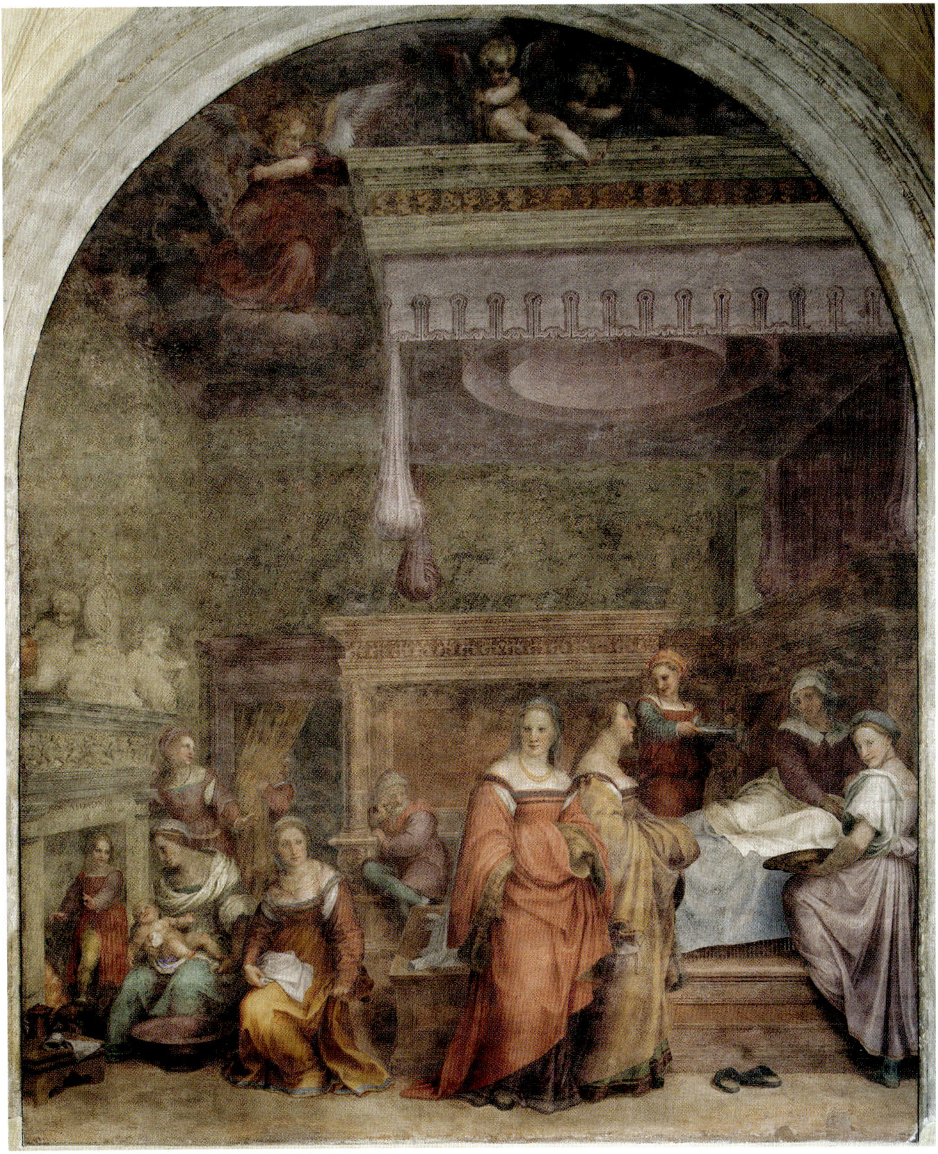

122. Andrea del Sarto, *Birth of the Virgin*, 1513-14, Chiostrino dei Voti.

Look once again to this line of eight women, which offers us little interest in physical or psychological interconnection, and follow the flawless fluidity in the succession of their colors: cream-lavender, purple, mahogany, muted yellow, red, golden yellow, aqua green, and lilac. Colors are precisely adjusted to the same tonal intensity, with rich variations in the highlights and shadows of the folds. The whole color chord is repeated throughout the room in various mixtures in the teal green of the walls, the lavenders of the decorative furnishings, and the faded burnt orange in the curtains by the door, even touching upon the husband who sits in solitude on the settee.

In a last vestige of his dependence on Leonardo's sfumato, a crutch he would discard in *Madonna of the Harpies* (fig. 93) for its suppression of color's natural intensity, Sarto mutes his tones by drawing a veil of smoky atmosphere over the scene. But, here, in an interior space dimly lit by a diffuse source high overhead, sfumato works, allowing light to be cast on nothing in particular—even faces—other than the knee of the woman sitting.

Even so, yellow against red, the picture's visual punch in the two magnificent central women, is a daring juxtaposition that should bring the red to prominence and the yellow to recession, and the way Sarto handles the combination is beyond the vision of any painter in Florence. Employing the artificial color shifts he'd investigated in the *Possessed Woman* but rejected as optically unnatural in the *Journey*, Sarto, by the subtlest variations, links these two women's colors to those of the women on either side. The folds of the yellow gown he enriches with shades of lavender that visually engage the lavender gown of the woman opposite, while the sleeves of the sitting woman's golden yellow gown he shifts to red that repeats the red of the woman standing. In both cases the colors are so integral to the forms they describe that the difference between their combination—yellow against red and yellow against lavender—is so small as to be barely perceptible.

The difficulties Sarto addresses in the *Birth* are entirely aesthetic ones, resolving one of the last imbalances in Florentine painting. He does not probe emotional states or grand drama. By High Renaissance standards his picture runs dangerously close to the reportage that the Northern Europeans were so skillful at depicting in their domestic scenes. Yet the *Birth of the Virgin* is as suave an aesthetic triumph as would ever be painted, resolving finally, the awkward opposition of the naturalism of color and its artistic manipulation. Neither he nor any successor ever attempted to repeat it.

Franciabigio, c. 1482-1525, *Marriage of the Virgin*, Chiostrino dei Voti, 1513

A respected colleague of Sarto in the early years of their careers, Franciabigio completed this fresco just before he had seen what his friend was doing with the *Birth of the Virgin*. In its stage set design and dispersal of figures, the picture stands somewhere near the level of Sarto's *Curing of the Possessed Woman* of four years earlier. Unlike that scene, however, no figure, in movement or at rest, stands in an effective contrapposto, with body centered over feet, the basic proposition of Renaissance painting. Although the figures are monumentalized and pulled up to the picture plane, they don't move with the easy naturalness that characterized the

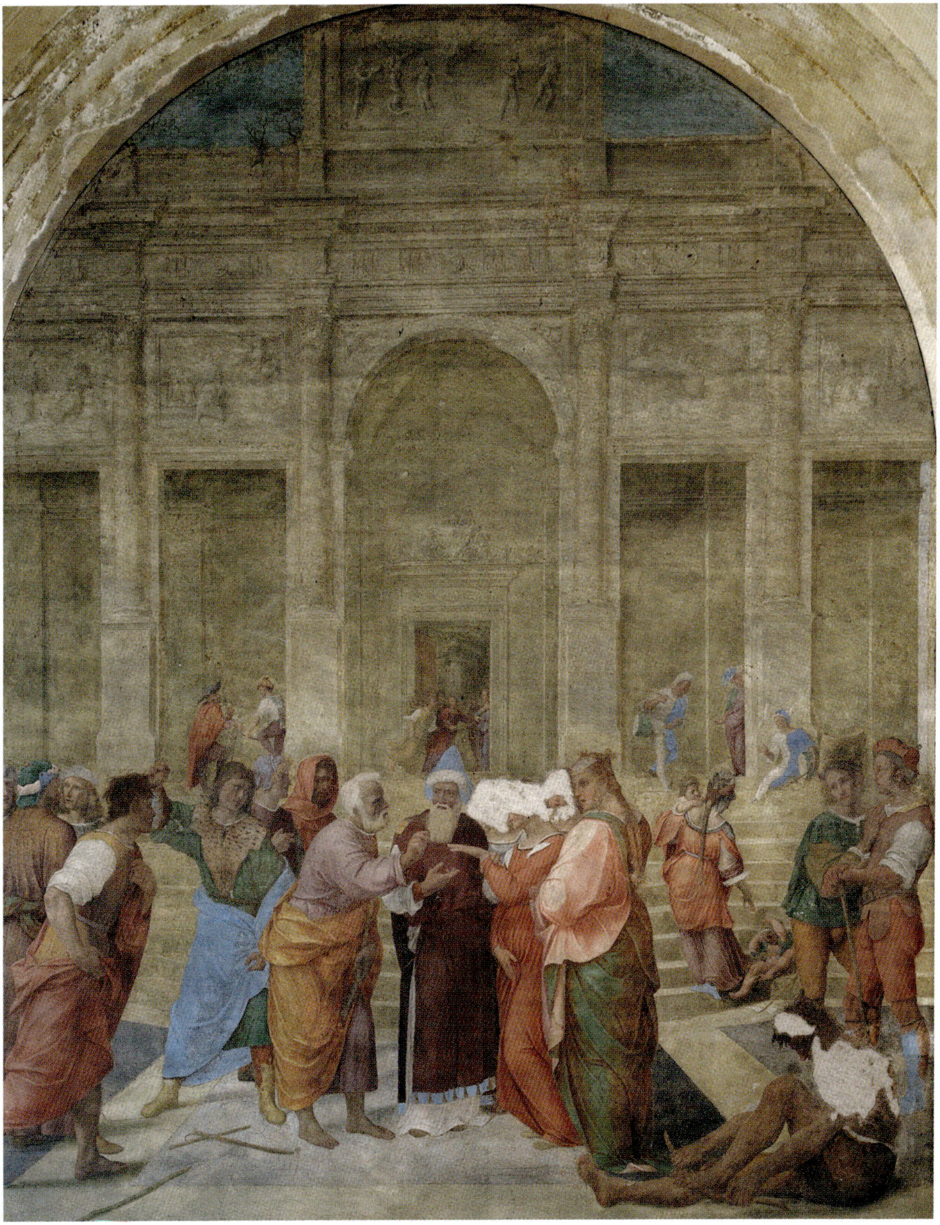

123. Franciabigio, *Marriage of the Virgin*, 1513, Chiostrino dei Voti.

figures in Sarto's *Journey of the Magi*. Nor do they pose in the rhythmic interconnections that describe the groupings in Sarto's *Birth* and *Journey*. Despite the theatrical gestures of the disappointed suitors, who are threatening to intrude on the marriage ceremony itself, the whole appears to be more a lively Quattrocento projection of isolated parts than a harmonious whole directed toward a single end.

When Sarto unveiled the *Birth of the Virgin*, the impetuous Franciabigio took a hammer to the face of the Virgin, and the picture has stood ever since as we see it now.

Jacopo Pontormo, 1494-1557, *Visitation*, Chiostrino dei Voti, 1514-16

Pontormo was twenty when selected to depict one of the most beloved themes in the religious repertoire. Since comparisons with Andrea del Sarto's *Birth of the Virgin* would inevitably come, he faced formidable challenges. The size of the lunette would require that he paint a more elaborate version of the *Visitation* that traditionally had been managed by a simple scheme: two women, Elizabeth and Mary, embrace over the news that each had miraculously conceived a son.

Steeped in the artistic traditions of his native city, Pontormo turned for inspiration to Leonardo's *Adoration* (fig. 87), where figures are cast in deceptively simple geometric forms: a pyramid encircled by an arc. Applying the same scheme, he stations a gathering of animated individuals before a semi-circular, shallow apse. What attracts these characters to this space isn't certain; perhaps they come and go in their daily routine on what appears to be a church portico.

Lounging on the steps is a curious woman who engages us, while opposite sits a self-absorbed naked boy. Her foot, resting on the ground plane that runs to our space, signals she is our entrance to the picture. She sits in a sensual S-shaped pose that pulls our eye upward to her exquisite portrait framed by a white head scarf, and then to deeper space, where it meets the woman with the bundle. It next follows the semicircular plane of the apse into deep shadow, until finally, the eye swings forward to rest on the naked child.

The child and the seated woman are essential to the composition; they direct our eye to the two women in the center by completing the pyramid where Mary greets her older cousin, as if quite by accident. Elizabeth bends on one knee and looks to Mary, who places one hand on her cousin's shoulder and reaches with the other as if to raise her for the embrace that Florentines know from their *Visitations* is about to come. Elizabeth's genuflection is such a natural gesture that no figure appears to take notice. Nor did Leonardo, Michelangelo, or any lesser artist foresee the power that underlies her form. A simple diagonal, beginning at the child's extended leg and coursing through her kneeling figure, thrusts her upward along its trajectory toward Mary in a compelling act of love.

With Pontormo's description of an extraordinary moment, the two cross currents of High Renaissance art converge for the first time. The appearance of informality that Sarto brought to his painting is here more finely disciplined by the highly contrived, rigorous design that has defined the Florentine tradition since Giotto. Pontormo does not reveal

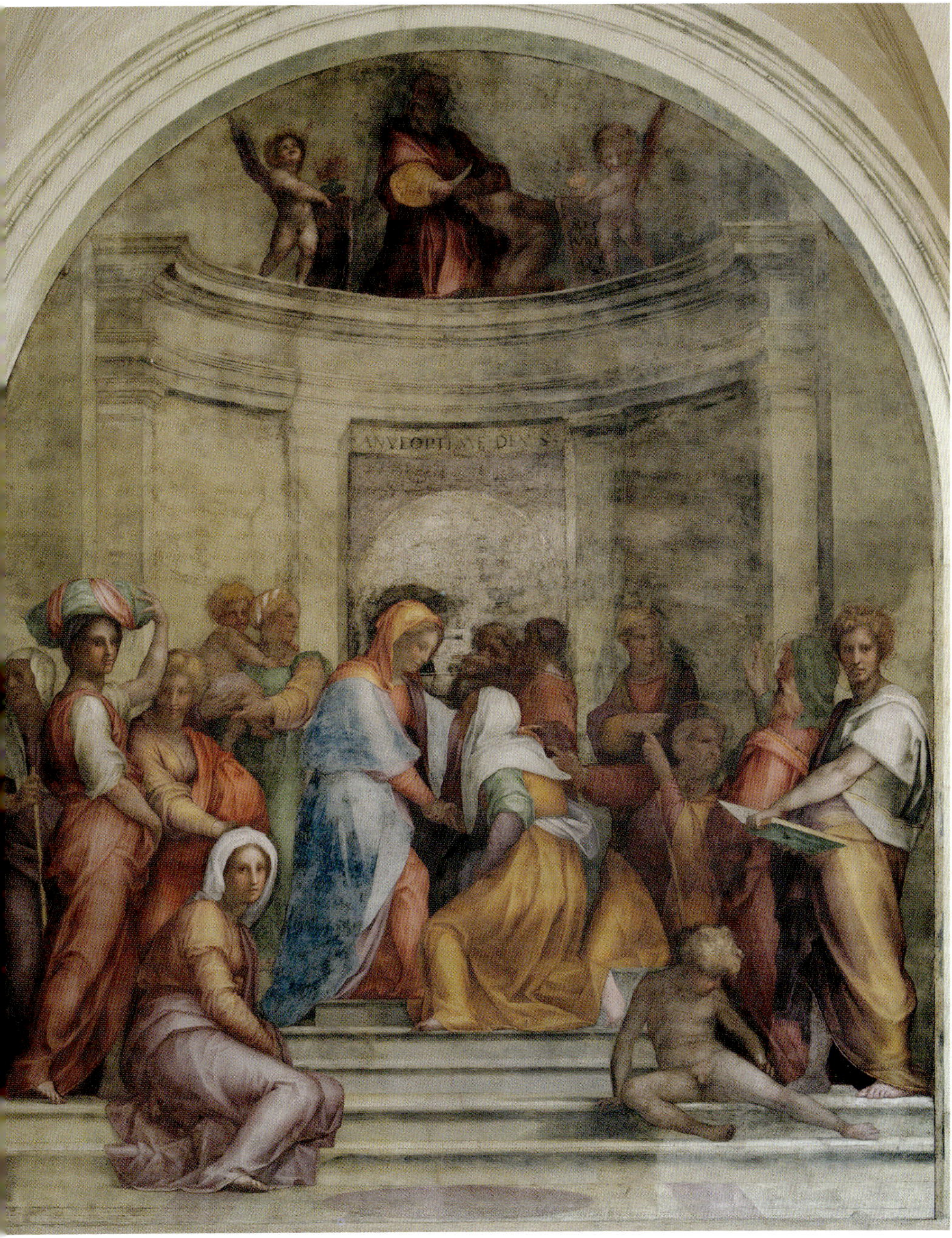

124. Jacopo Pontormo, *Visitation*, 1514-16, Chiostrino dei Voti.

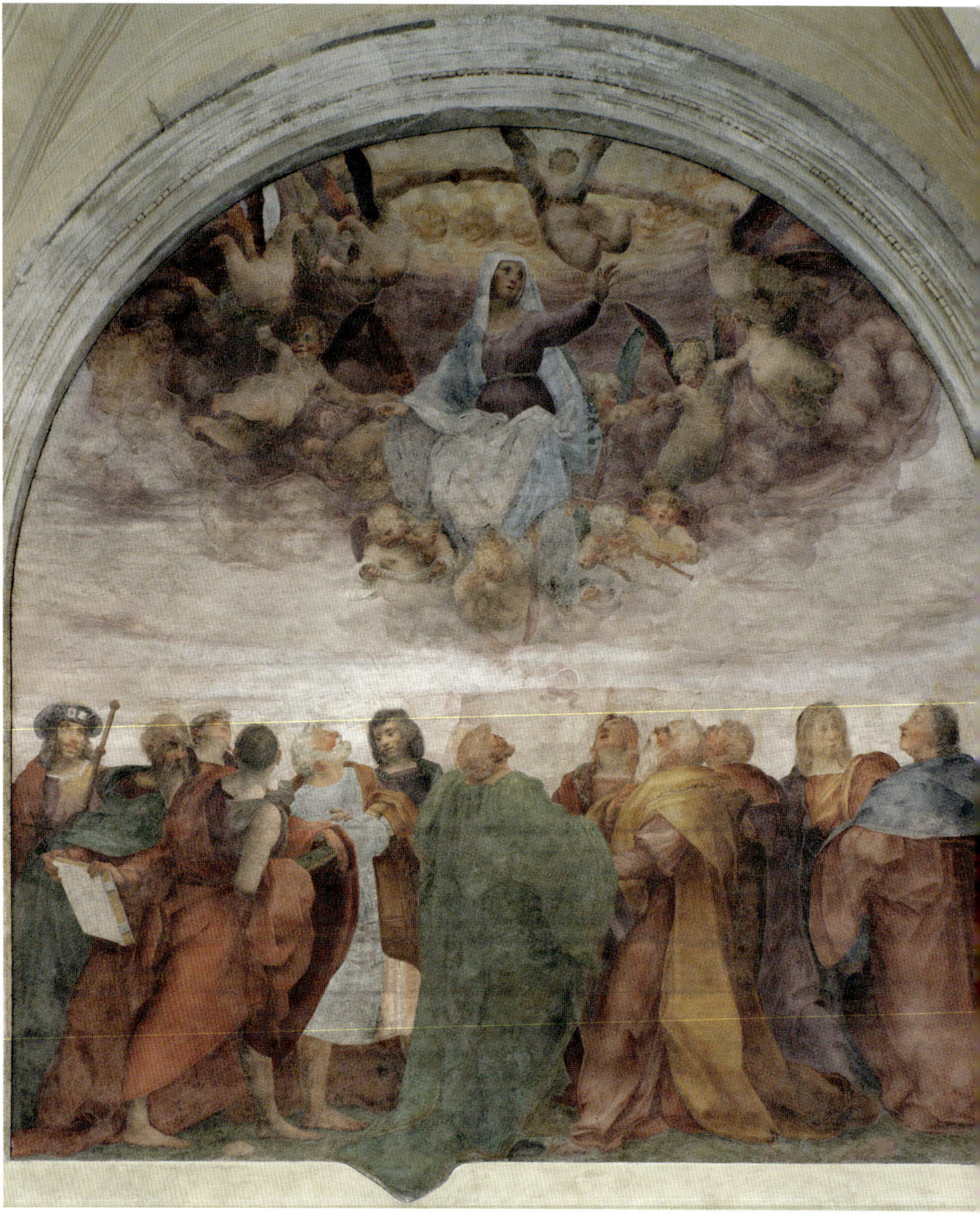

125. Rosso Fiorentino, *Assumption of the Virgin*, 1517, Chiostrino dei Voti.

Elizabeth's face. Rather, he shapes her poignant gesture and Mary's response by the clarity of plain geometry.

Rosso Fiorentino, 1495-1540, *Assumption of the Virgin*, Chiostrino dei Voti, 1517

Neatly fitted to the arched wall is a hemispherical scene in turbulent commotion, where the Virgin ascends through lavender clouds to a golden heaven, accompanied by a flotilla of ecstatic, somersaulting angels. Below, apostles gaze upward to watch Mary leave this earth, but appear in their agitation to have only a tenuous connection to reality. These characters met with strong disapproval—so strong that the Servites wanted Sarto to repaint Rosso's picture. But Sarto was on to bigger commissions. Certainly the undignified grimace of Saint James at the far left and the vacant expressions on the pliant faces of the others would have been disturbing. And perhaps the Servites would have been disoriented by the compressed space, the absence of the Virgin's tomb, and the disproportionately small heads atop massive draperies shoved so close to the picture's threshold that a robe spills over the edge.

Much speculation has focused on Rosso's motives in the *Assumption*. Is he rejecting the classical sensibilities that Sarto had perfected in the *Birth of the Virgin*? Is he an eccentric twenty-year old in search of a voice? Or, perhaps the answer lies in two distinct views of color. Other than the rectangular scheme comprising the apostles, a pronounced absence of formal structure challenges the eye to adjust to broad fields of deeply resonant color. In this sense, Rosso's picture offers an alternative to Sarto's clarity of colors. For Sarto, the role of color in defining forms lies in its response to the action of light. For Rosso, color is an aesthetic end it itself, obscuring form rather than defining it, blurring boundaries between naturalism and artificiality.

10. San Michele Visdomini

Andrea del Sarto and Jacopo Pontormo, who lived in the Visdomini neighborhood, attended this church. Francesco Pucci, a banker aligned with the Medici, commissioned the work for the family chapel where the picture has stood ever since.

Discovery of Mannerism

Jacopo Pontormo, 1494-1557, *Virgin and Child with Saints* (*Pala Pucci*), San Michele Visdomini, 1518

As Leonardo's *Adoration* opened the way to the High Renaissance, Pontormo's painting marked the decisive step to a new style called Mannerism, a style that soon took Florentine art by storm.

The Madonna sits within a shadowed niche above a retinue of family and saints, including a kneeling Saint Francis, Saint John with his open gospel, and the rambunctious angels, all of whom we have met in the *Harpies Madonna* (fig. 93). The chapel is dedicated to Joseph, Mary's husband, who Pontormo places on Mary's right. He supports an ebullient Christ Child holding a reed cross symbolic of his fate. On either side of Francis are the child John the Baptist, and Saint James. Pontormo distributes all of these saints loosely to form two sides of a triangle that leads upward to Mary, at the apex, the composition's only stabilizing scaffold. The painting's mood and by extension its meaning are perplexing.

For one, the puzzling expressions: Mary, unexpectedly smiling, points beyond the picture's boundary to the church's high altar, symbol of her Son's coming sacrifice, as if sharing a simple pleasure. Judging from their tormented, open-mouthed expressions, John and Joseph appear to be consumed by intense, spiritual yearning. Only the strangely elongated Francis engages another figure, gaping rapturously at the Christ Child, whose own expression of giddy ecstasy borders on the abnormal. James stares out at us, as if caught in a momentary lapse of concentration. None of the expressions seem appropriate to an altarpiece, as spiritual decorum collapses into unlicensed religious fervor.

Similar contradictions undermine our expectations of classical repose. Space is collapsed, with participants stacked upwards. The triangle supporting Mary is subverted by an inverted triangle that Pontormo shapes with two diagonals created by linking the attenuated bodies of the saints. Both run from the Baptist through the saints to the right-and left-hand angels. Color is rich, but muted by the strong shadows and a sfumato reminiscent of Leonardo. What light there is isolates crooked limbs and torsos in up or down V shaped configurations that project an agitated pattern across the canvas. This pattern echoes the figures' tremulous, visibly charged expressions in what could well be their contemplation of redemption through Christ's death.

To charge Pontormo with parodying Sarto's complacent mood in the *Harpies Madonna* is tempting, but fails to acknowledge Pontormo's own subjective identification with what he has created. He was an intensely spiritual man and the subtlety with which he creates a like intensity in this painting would have been beyond anything the Florentines had ever seen.

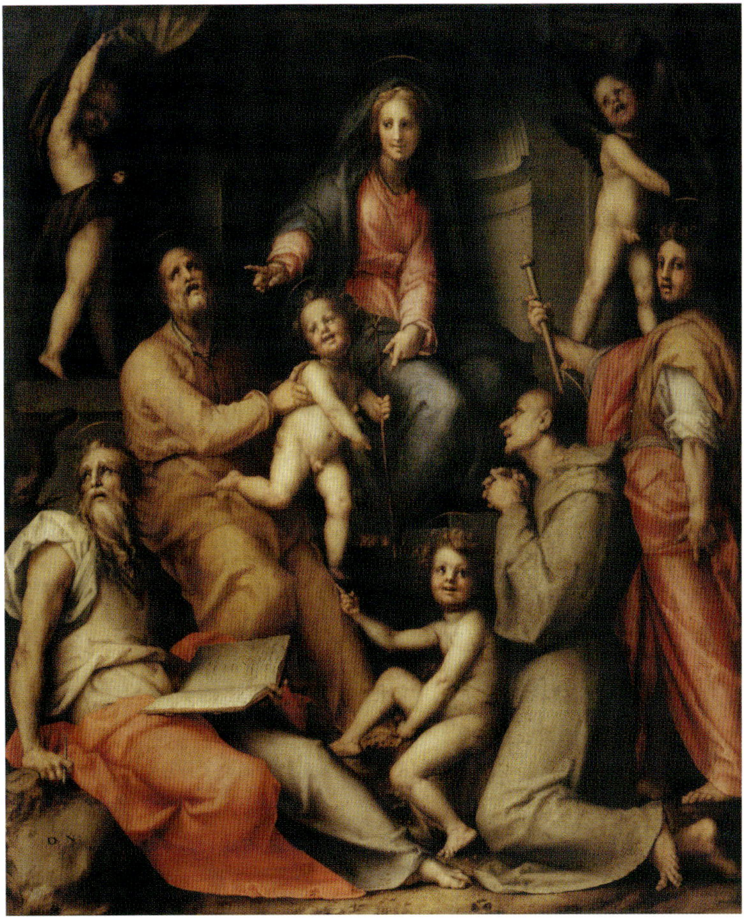

126. Jacopo Pontormo, *Madonna and Child with Saints*, 1518, San Michele Visdomini.

11. SANTA FELICITA

In 1525, the banker Ludovico Capponi commissioned Pontormo to paint the *Deposition* nine years after the painter had made his first Mannerist statement in the San Michele Visdomini altarpiece.

TRIUMPH OF MANNERISM

Jacopo Pontormo, 1494-1557, *Deposition*, Capponi Chapel, c. 1527

Though the history of Florentine painting is a history of supreme achievements, only Leonardo's *Adoration* and Pontormo's *Deposition* caught the Florentine community wholly unprepared for the range and depth of expression their pictures evoked. Pontormo's endless struggle, like Leonardo's, to find new forms as a conveyance for human emotion, places him in the company of the finest painters in Western history.

The origin of the style is uncertain. Neither Leonardo's nor Sarto's influence plays a role here. And but for the odd spacing, Pontormo has abandoned all traces of the style that defined his earlier Visdomini altarpiece, foremost his painterly treatment of color, light, and shadow. Yet, there is plenty of fuel for Pontormo's style in the distorted figures' explicit contours and acid coloring in Michelangelo's *Doni Tondo*. Otherwise, for the contemporary viewer, the origins of the style's blatant antinaturalism appear to have no precedent.

The stunningly haunted expressions lay bare a bitterly disturbing scene, disturbing in its subject, but all the more so for its paradoxically exuberant color. We recognize the dead Christ and his mother, but their relationship to the surroundings and to the whole cast of sensual athletic extras is unclear. A painful rift signals he has just been taken from Mary's lap, as she sadly waves him off in a final parting. But, if this were a traditional Deposition it would have a cross, a ladder, and at least some sense of solid ground, but here no such points of reference fix the scene. Instead, we gaze up to tortured bodies piled up close to the picture plane, spaced in difficult-to-read relationships. The two hands holding Christ's left arm make sense only when we recognize that one of the arms belongs to the woman turned away from us. Together, the whole weightless ensemble of interlocked bodies seems to rest on the big toe of

127. Jacopo Pontormo, *Deposition*, c. 1527, Capponi Chapel.

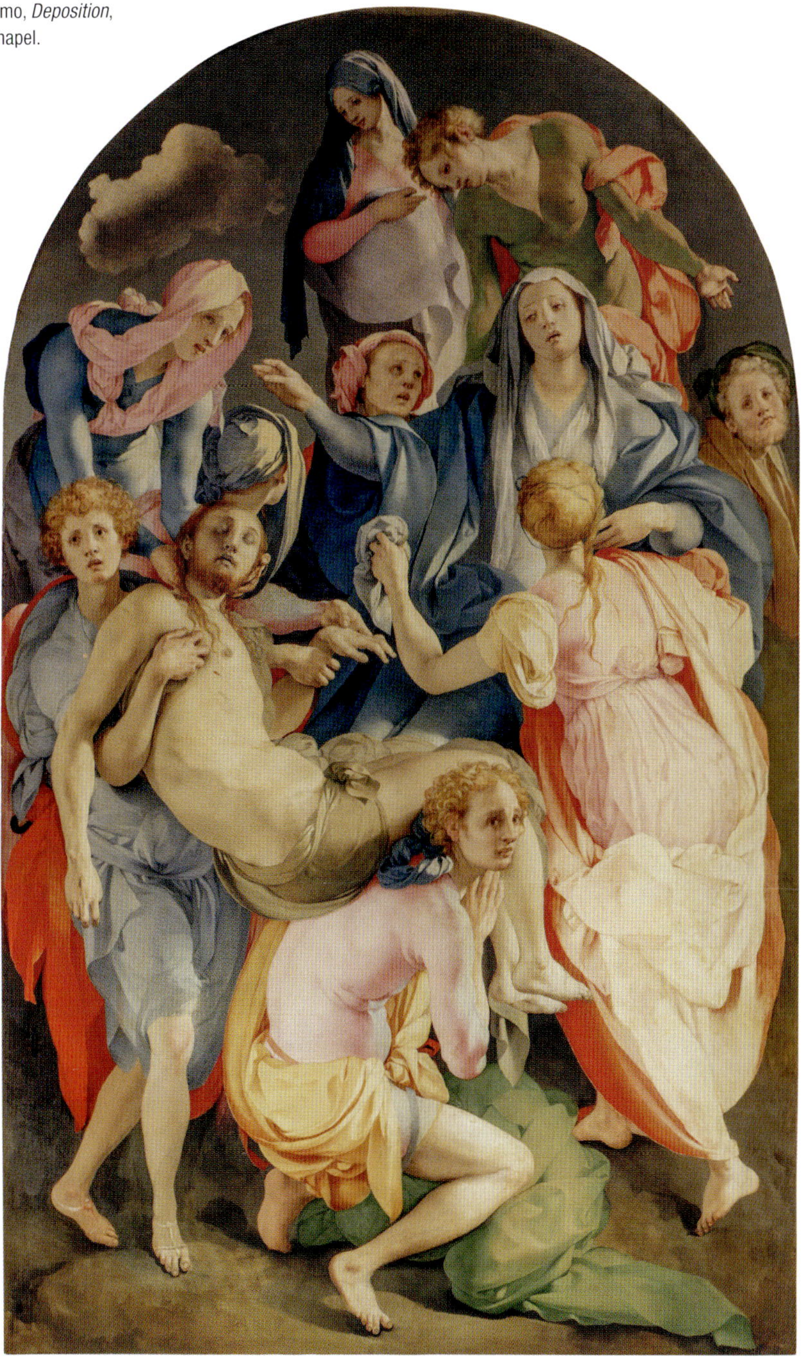

the crouching figure supporting Christ, leaving us with the feeling we are looking into an aberrant world.

Our eye enters the apparition by following the woman in voluptuous pink (Mary Magdalene?) rushing toward Mary, then upward to pursue the forms round and round counterclockwise, captured by the oval whirlpool of the picture's surface. Small forms echo this oval shape in exquisite counterpoint to the suffering: the looping folds of Mary's outstretched arm, the pink head scarf of the woman who tenderly supports Christ's head, the green hair-tie of the crouching figure, the thin ribbon lacing through the hair of the woman in pink, about to offer a handkerchief to Mary.

Pontormo's colors are not descriptive of anything seen before; nor are the shapes that are pumped into translucent tissue-thin skin in a puzzling interplay with fabric (look to the pink jerkin of the crouching figure). The painting's luminosity and unnatural, high-keyed colors stress the virtual absence of shadow and the lack of internal modeling that belies each body's sculptural plasticity. Instead, Pontormo rounds out a figure's volume with colors that rarely stray to darker tones, emphasizing surface pattern over spatial depth, even though an impression of space between figures is clearly evident. In places these colors bleed into alternate colors, like the pale blue that runs to pale pink in the arm holding Christ's hand, and similarly, the faint aqua that embellishes the lower belly of the crouching figure. The colors themselves repeat in rhythms. Neon pinks and ice blues dominate iridescent oranges and yellows, all intensified in the few recesses or bleached out where bodies are most pronounced.

For Pontormo's anguished identification with a mother's grief (he has painted himself staring out past us on the right), no aesthetic order based on visual experience would do. Only an entirely new canon of forms and colors, arising from no shared reference, extravagant, abstracted, and artificial, could capture deep emotion and still retain the disciplined, formal order that marked his style. This is the exquisite language of artifice that, by different means and intentions, Leonardo brought to the *Virgin and Child with Saint Anne* and Botticelli to his simplified silhouettes in the *Primavera*.

In this sense only, Pontormo returns to the principles he had explored in the *Visitation*, where forms are worthy of and intrinsic to their meaning. But in a more critical sense, the forms in this picture convey a dimension of power and visual splendor that speaks of human suffering so painfully beautiful that it almost cannot be visually realized.

As the last and purest essay in Florentine painting to provoke intense feeling, the *Deposition* marks the finale to Pontormo's long research into how the manipulation of aesthetics controls the expressive content of a work of art, and conversely, how the beauty of human emotion generates aesthetics. It remains the definitive masterpiece of a style called Mannerism, the period occupying some twenty years between the High Renaissance and High Mannerism.

12. San Lorenzo

The church of San Lorenzo, consacrated in 393 AD, contains two of the finest Mannerist paintings in Florence. It was the parish church of the Medici Family

Crisis of Mannerism

Off the right nave

Rosso Fiorentino, 1495-1540, *Marriage of the Virgin* (*Pala Ginori*), San Lorenzo, 1523

Because Rosso had received a hostile reception for his critical role in the formation of Mannerism, he tempered his unorthodox style to compete for Florentines commissions. Here Rosso has produced a composition that seemingly accorded with "good taste". Otherwise Mannerist devices are deftly written all over this painting.

An undercurrent of puzzling sexual tension pervades the young couple's marriage ceremony. No longer the paternal type, Joseph appears as a man who might signify a potent threat to the bride's virginity. Young and viral, he sports corn yellow locks in a wavy coif, a loose open shirt, a short tunic revealing bare flesh atop a dandy's flashy pink boots.

Then there is Rosso's odd fixation on the assemblage of pincer-like hands, where the rabbi's are about to join those of the betrothed. Their fingertips are tantalizingly close, yet they don't meet; a trace of open space reflects the poignancy of a physical union unrealized, especially in the context of his youthful beauty. These strange, aberrant hands we find elsewhere, and not just as aesthetic motifs. The Dominican friar's finger pointing upward to the ceremony reads more as a scarcely veiled phallic sign that marks Joseph's manhood. Below, the lovely Saint Apollonia, breasts and midriff exposed beneath her filmy gown, seems transfixed by the friar's gesture. She too is marked by provocative hands, the one holding a book of unknown significance, and the other fingering the attribute of her martyrdom, pincers locked onto a single tooth. Opposite is the marvelous portrait of Mary's aging mother, robed in a range of ochre to creams that match her tawny flesh tones.

If we must identify the one trait that distinguishes Rosso style, it would be his relish for the sumptuous physicality of the brushstroke. In other artists' paintings, were we to isolate any single passage for close examination, we'd likely gain information because of the precision of the drawing. But with Rosso we'd lose ourselves in the exquisite patterns of mark making. So, in scanning the painting as a whole, what best comes into focus is the artifice of a thickly painted, continuously shifting, iridescent palette, shimmering at luscious full value, with whites forcing a sheen that resonates across the canvas.

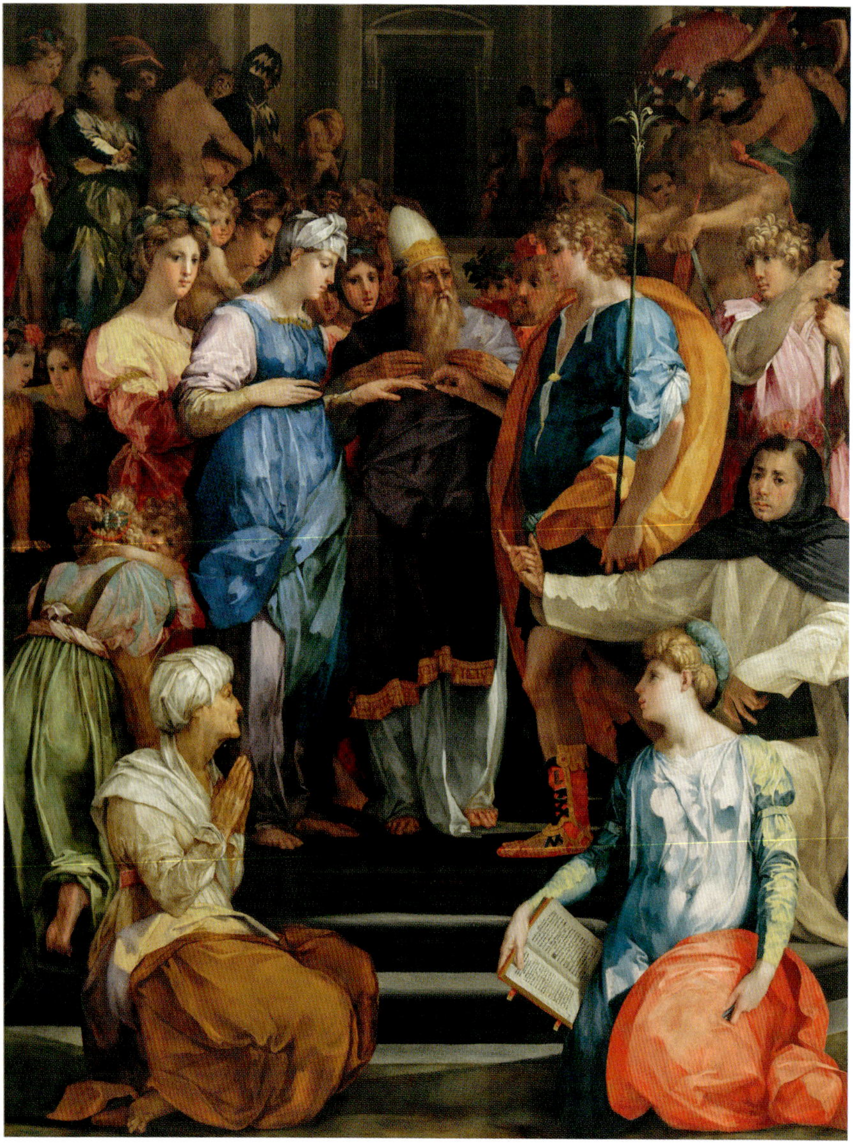

128. Rosso Fiorentino, *Marriage of the Virgin* (*Pala Ginori*), 1523, San Lorenzo.

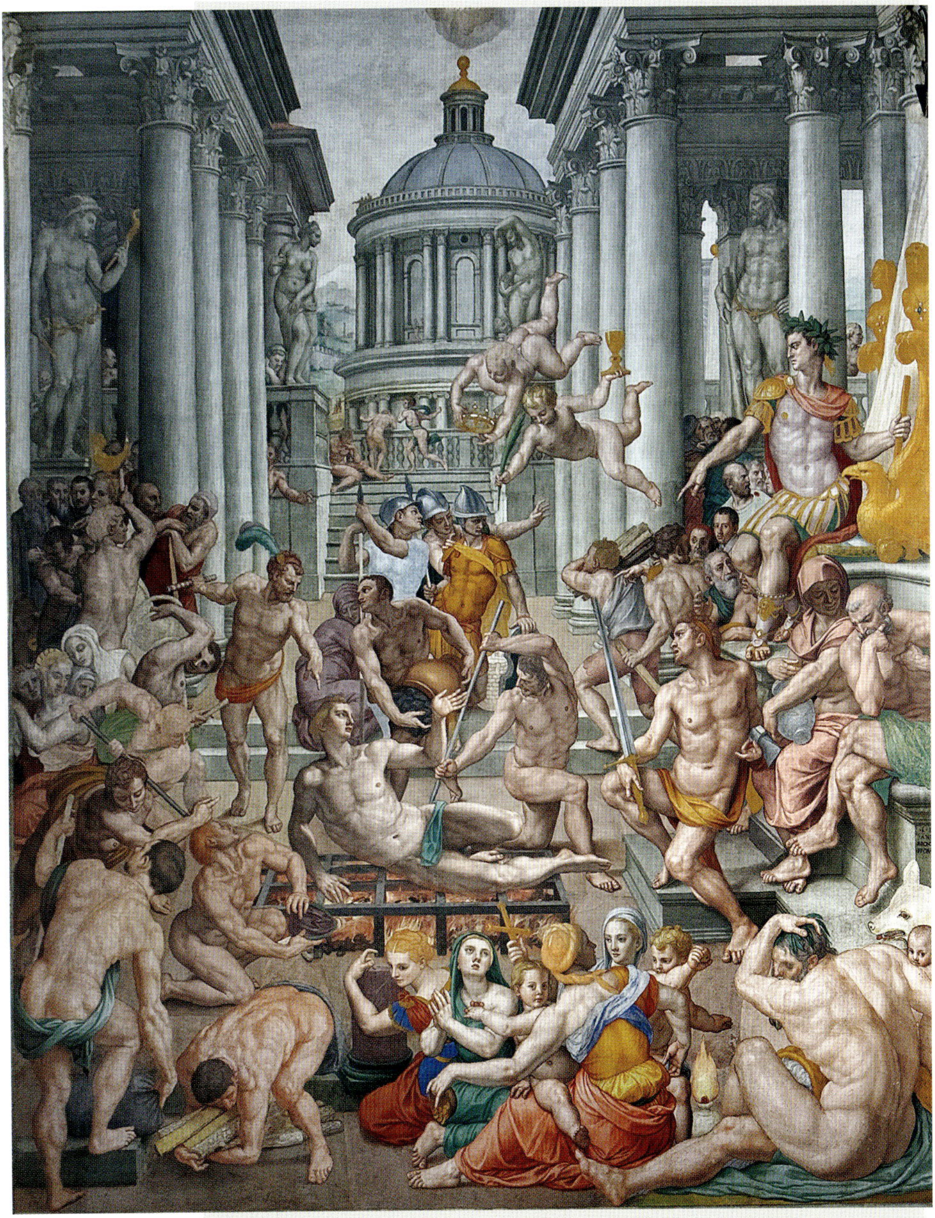

129. Agnolo Bronzino, *Martyrdom of Saint Lawrence*, 1569, San Lorenzo.

To celebrate the Florentine lineage, Bronzino has included the portrait of the deceased bearded Michelangelo below the Emperor's knee at the far right, and his own self portrait at the painting's left edge, standing between those of his beloved deceased mentor Pontormo and his young protégé Allori.

Agnolo Bronzino, 1503-1572, *Martyrdom of Saint Lawrence*, San Lorenzo, 1569

IN THE NAVE, ON THE LEFT

The aging Bronzino painted his final fresco when the Protestant Reformation was in full force in Florence. Duke Cosimo commissioned the work to prove he was on board with Pope Pius IV's church dictates. We have addressed the Counter Reformation in Santa Croce, but what is significant in 1569 is that, as proof of his aversion to nudity, the pope was threatening to tear down Michelangelo's *Last Judgment* only five years after he had died.

In response, this fresco is, in fact, a sly appeasement to Vatican conservatives—no female nudes, males modestly draped—and at the same time, it is a defiant homage to the style of Michelangelo, which Bronzino had seen as the apotheosis of the Florentine tradition.

When completed, church spokesmen attacked it as unbecoming of church art, and as bad art altogether for its blatant anti naturalism and weak color. As to antinaturalism, nothing could be closer to the truth, as Bronzino never aspires to imitate nature. As to bad art, it is today considered the finest example of late Mannerism.

Here Bronzino fully exploits the visual appeal of Mannerist artificiality: a chilling reduction of reality orchestrated in the icy atmospheric clarity of a classical courtyard, pumped up flesh in Michelangelesque disturbing poses, impassive emotion. A lurid orange keyed off the burning embers leads the eye across the whole pictorial patterning of squirming forms. Lawrence lying on his grill is lost to the picture's utter sameness.

We don't sense human suffering within this frenzy of contorted nudes, the raw material that marked late Mannerism. As such, his bloodlessly dispassionate chronicle of sadism, conceived in a coldly schematic style by any standard, is closed by dimensions to a "reformed" art drained of a power that only art that belongs to artists can convey.

His triumphant last call to younger artists to imitate the style of the late Michelangelo would have been unthinkable in the Rome of the Counter Reformation. Sadly and inevitably, perhaps, younger painters never took to the style of Bronzino or of Michelangelo. Vatican conservatism proved too much for them.

13. Pitti Palace, Galleria Palatina

The Pitti Palace possesses the most complete collection of large scale altarpieces from the High Renaissance in Florence. By comparison the Uffizi possesses one, the *Madonna of the Harpies*, albeit the finest in the entire repertoire. Many of these masterpieces have undergone extensive restorations that have brought to light just how skillful the artists who painted them were as colorists. The museum is also home to smaller, more private works by the major painters who were active in the first decades of the sixteenth century. The following six paintings have been selected for their pivotal contribution to the Florentine style.

Large-scale High Renaissance Paintings

Sala di Saturno

Raphael, 1483-1520, *Madonna enthroned with Child and Saints (Madonna del Baldacchino)*, Galleria Palatina, 1507-8

The twenty-four year old Raphael left his only major Florentine commission unfinished when he was summoned to Rome by Pope Julius II in 1508 to fresco Vatican apartments. Having studied the "sweet style" of Perugino as a student, Raphael came to Florence anxious to profit from the city's progressive art scene. Within three years, he had mastered enough of the essentials of the Florentine style to produce a picture that would set the precedent for the monumental High Renaissance altarpiece.

Except for the scene's calm order, there is nothing of Perugino here, none of his limp poses, vacant faces, and formulaic eyes. In his own small Madonnas, Raphael had learned from Leonardo the secrets of depicting the intelligent look of an engaged eye. And, despite having assimilated Leonardo's complicated system of shadow, light and color, Raphael avoided the master's unnatural color restraints and shadowy atmosphere. Raphael's warm color chord has no equal. His black, white, plum, and teal green, which in another artist's hands would compete for attention, here seem utterly natural.

In dignified poses, these statuesque saints stand within a clear space monumentalized by classical columns and a semicircular niche. A simple baldachin curtained in a green enriched by yellow frames a mahogany throne where a proud mother shares an intimate moment with her child.

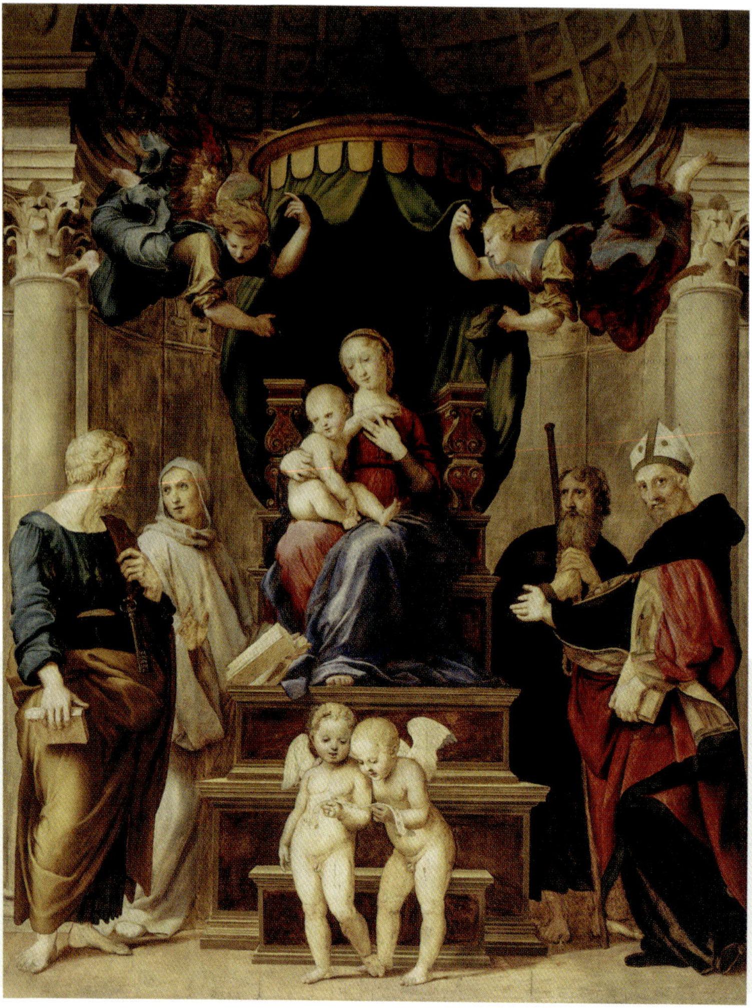

130. Raphael, *Madonna del Baldacchino*, 1507-8, Galleria Palatina.

Commissioned for the Dei Chapel in Santo Spirito, but because the painting was left unfinished, it was later purchased by the Medici for the Pitti collection.

Two child-like angels in the foreground sing from a musical score, while the baby, absorbed by the discussion between Saints Peter and Bernard, tugs at his toes.

Saint Augustine gestures us forward to share in a cocoon of tranquility warmed by the ecru colors of the pavement and the marbled architecture. And, indeed, our inclusion completes a space whose natural appearances are conceived at an aesthetic and intellectual level as yet unknown in Florentine painting. Brief though his stay was, he left the city's future masters, Fra Bartolomeo and Andrea del Sarto, a model of grace and vitality.

The following two altarpieces, representing Fra Bartolomeo's mature style as head of the School of San Marco, were painted after Leonardo, Michelangelo, and Raphael departed Florence, leaving him as the principle innovator of the High Renaissance style. Early in the second decade his authority was shared by Andrea del Sarto until the monk's early death in 1517.

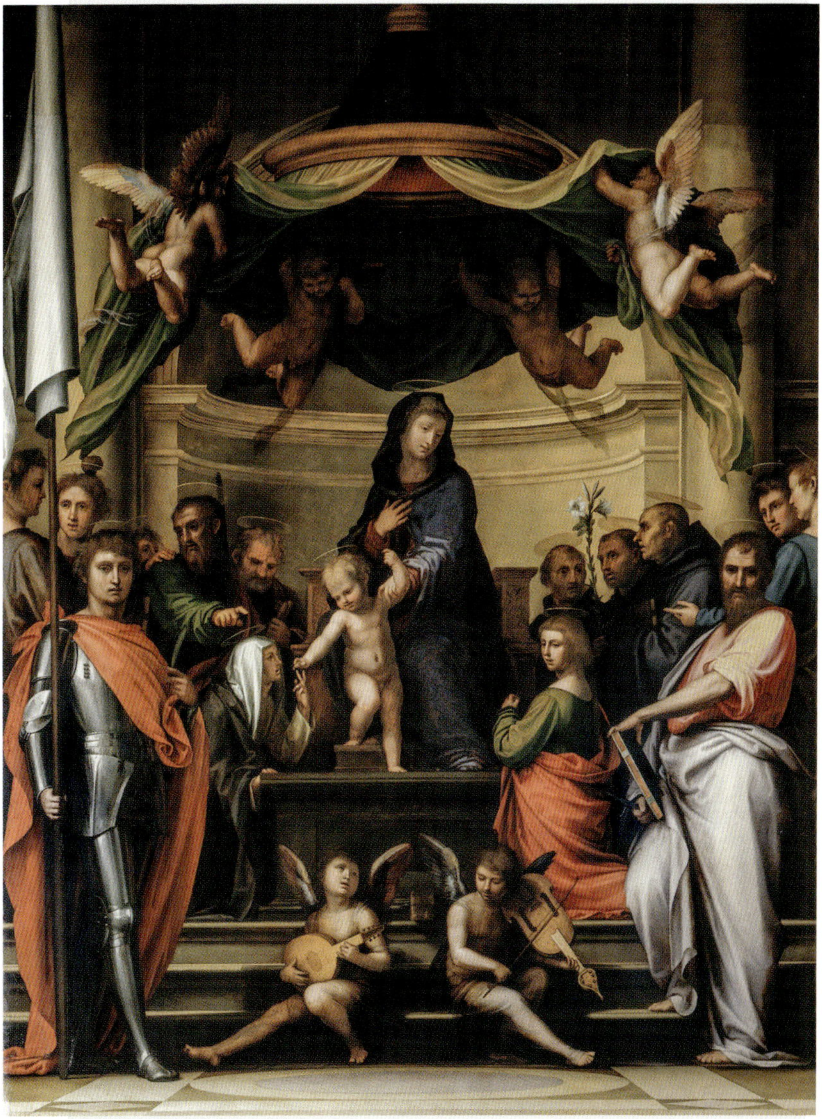

131. Fra Bartolomeo, *Mystic Marriage of Saint Catherine*, 1512, Galleria Palatina.

Commissioned for church and convent of San Marco.

Fra Bartolomeo, 1475-1517, *Mystic Marriage of Saint Catherine*, Galleria Palatina, 1512

Sala dell'Iliade

Fra Bartolomeo's magnificent altarpiece is a direct descendent of Raphael's *Madonna of the Baldachin* in terms of its monumental structure and the positioning of the various actors. But there the similarities end. The spatial clarity and the actors' vitality in Raphael's *Madonna* now register as imposingly formal and remote. The saints have tripled in number and the relationship between them is static. Poses here are strictly conventional and expressions uncommunicative and compromised in those figures with the lifeless black eyes.

In the manner of his shadows, Fra Bartolomeo comes closest to Leonardo, but employs them more insistently, limiting light to focus on isolated patches of brilliant color. Such a scheme, for example, allows him to focus on the white headscarf of Saint Catherine, who is about to receive the wedding ring from the Christ Child; or to backlight the luminous niche; or to highlight the beautiful passage where the intense yellow turns to blood orange in the tunic of the saint standing on the right.

If the provocative interplay between shadow and color provides the picture's aesthetic charge, the rigorous geometry of large forms—the steps, the monolithic columns, the circular baldachin, and the semicircular niche that shapes the saints' grouping—provide the dignified formality that always lies at the core of Fra Bartolomeo's paintings.

Fra Bartolomeo, *Christ Resurrected with the Four Evangelists* (*Salvator Mundi*), Galleria Palatina, 1516

Return to the Sala di Saturno

Fra Bartolomeo's last major painting was completed the year he died at the age of forty-two. The formal relationship between figures and architecture found in the *Salvator Mundi* ("Savior of the World") reflects one strong current of a High Renaissance style which he founded and continued to refine throughout his short career. The strong shadows that isolated color in the *Mystic Marriage* he abandons in favor of Leonardo's filmy *sfumato* whereby colors are tempered by a softer light. Fra Bartolomeo stands apart from other Florentines, because he learned to enrich his colors to a deep resonance while studying in Venice. Indeed, he ranks as one of the finest colorists in the sixteenth century. Strong Venetian influence turns up in the luminosity of the apse with its subtle gradations of light to dark beiges and grays. Similar gradations can be found in the blends of lilacs and the traces of greens and faint yellows that enliven the white in Christ's draperies.

The relationship of figures to architecture comes from Sarto's *Harpies Madonna* (fig. 93) with which Fra Bartolomeo's picture will inevitably be compared and found wanting. Where Sarto's figures are animated by poses linked in effortless, artful rhythms, Fra Bartolomeo's figures are

132. Fra Bartolomeo, *Salvator Mundi*, 1516, Galleria Palatina; commissioned for Santissima Annunziata.

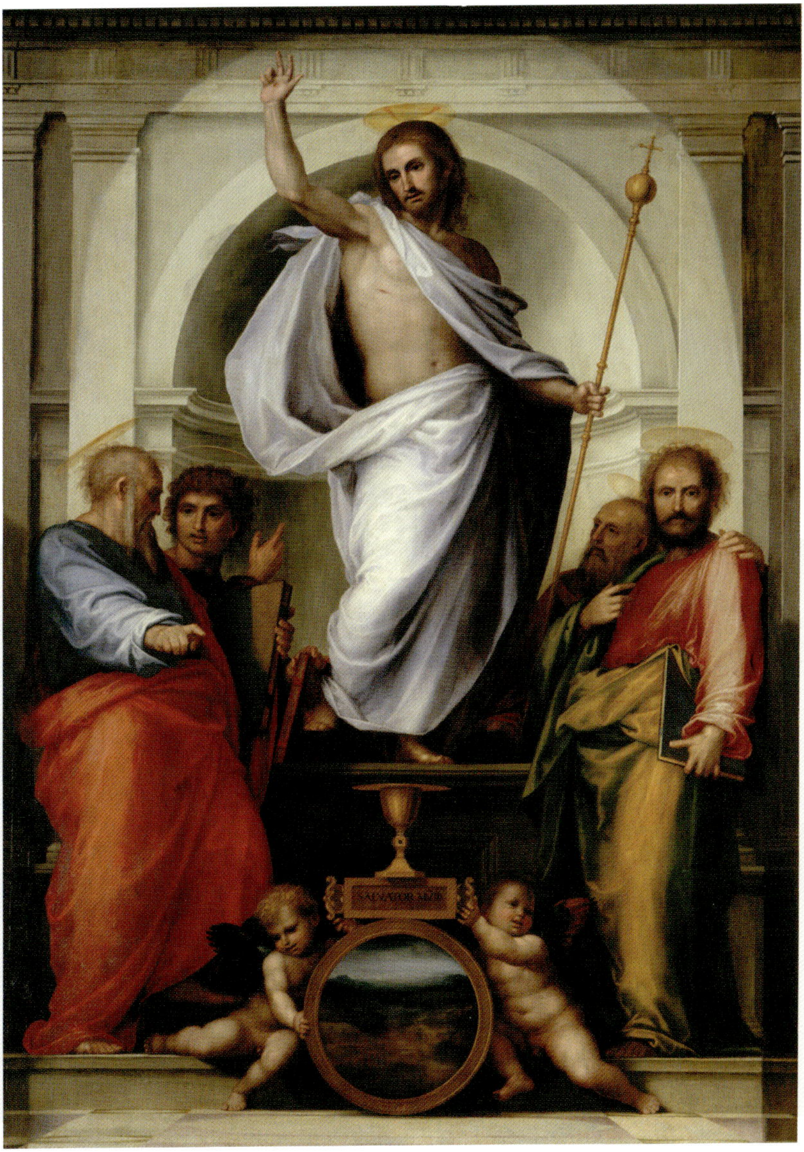

The picture's Latin title, meaning "Savior of the World," is a common epithet for Christ. At his feet the chalice of the Eucharist rests on a round picture of a landscape that represents the world and is supported by exquisitely rendered putti.

characterized by rhetorical gestures and stiff poses that give to their forms the appearance of statuary.

Fra Bartolomeo has never been seen in terms of the gifts that have made Sarto's art so endearing over the centuries; he doesn't project the quality of easy accessibility and informality. But in his art we find a sincere piety, spiritual fervor and gravitas that Sarto never seemed to aspire to.

Rosso Fiorentino, 1495-1540, *Madonna with Child and Saints* (*Pala Dei*), Galleria Palatina, 1522

On the window wall of the Sala dell'Iliade

In its present state, Rosso's altarpiece describes a gathering of saints and a Madonna and Child staged before an insignificant niche that has none of the grand manner of a Fra Bartolomeo. But Rosso's intentions have been subverted. In the following century, his canvas was fitted within a surrounding canvas that now expands the scene to its present state (the demarcations are clear). The original visual experience would have been

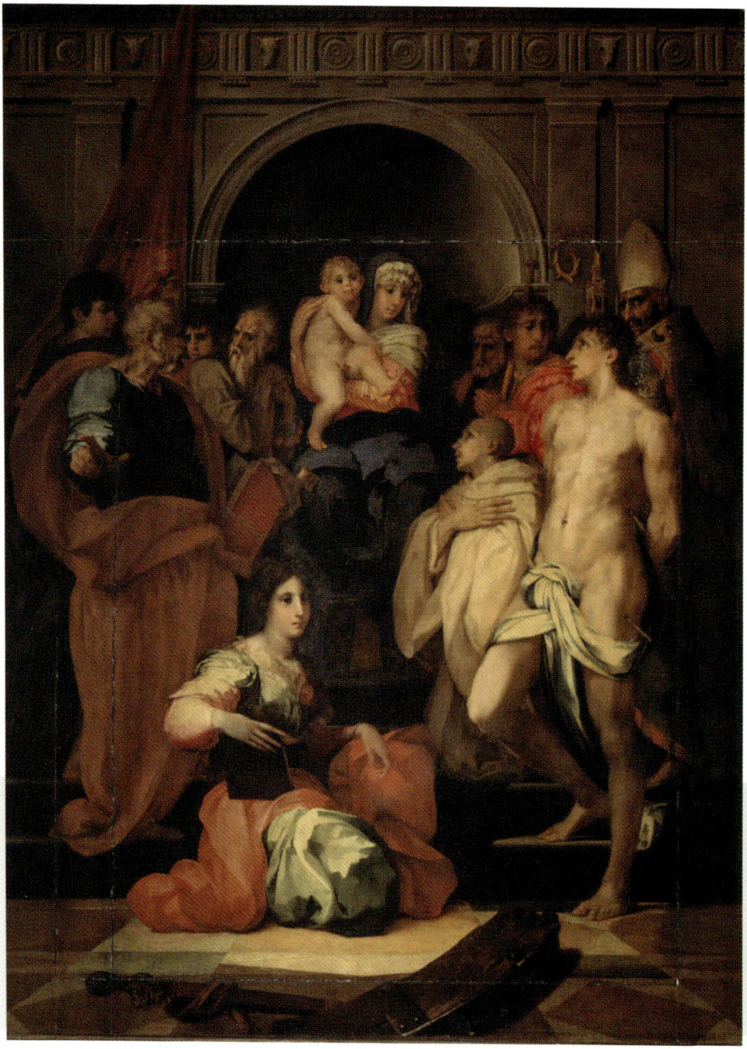

133. Rosso Fiorentino, *Pala Dei*, 1522, Galleria Palatina.

The patrons are the same Dei family who commissioned Raphael's unfinished *Madonna of the Baldachin*. This is its replacement.

more immediate with the scene collapsed into a tighter format. So we shall imagine away the outer and concentrate on the inner picture where bodies are now crowded into a compressed space, constants of the Mannerist style Rosso helped invent. But when space compresses colors in dissonant juxtapositions, we have a different aesthetic that can't be explained by terms that characterize other styles. Formality-informality, naturalism-idealism, that define an Andrea del Sarto or a Fra Bartolomeo or the probing psychological states that define a Pontormo simply don't apply to his style. What does apply, however, is his innate sense of what makes art in the purely material terms of painted brushstrokes on a flat canvas.

Characteristically, Rosso limits his major colors to blues, reds and a green which, when mixed in their lightest values with white, produces the icy iridescent greens in the draperies of Saint Catherine kneeling in the foreground, the bleached blue in Saint Peter's thrust out forearm, and the hot reds in the swirling robes that function purely as delicious ornament. Beiges, so subtly at variance, suggest in the nude the softness of flesh or the textured fabric of the robe worn by the kneeling monk.

On opposite side walls

Andrea del Sarto, 1486-1530, *Assumption of the Virgin* (*Panciatichi Assumption*), Galleria Palatina, c. 1522
Andrea del Sarto, *Assumption of the Virgin* (*Passerini Assumption*), Galleria Palatina, 1526

Of the two altarpieces hanging on opposite walls, one is considered to be a distinguished product of the High Renaissance. The other is considered to be derivative. Both were painted by Andrea del Sarto sometime in the pivotal 1520s. With Pontormo producing little in the late twenties, Rosso and Michelangelo in Rome, and Fra Bartolomeo deceased, the competitive atmosphere that once challenged artists, perhaps, left Sarto answerable only to himself, resulting in a slackening of energy in his style. So the question becomes, with the smallest details bearing the weight of scrupulous attention, which ranks as the stronger piece.

At first glance the two pictures appear to be nearly identical. An enormous scene showing the Virgin and a flotilla of baby angels rising to heaven with the astonished apostles left standing around her empty tomb. Both scenes also share the vibrant color combinations of the earlier *Harpies Madonna* (fig. 93), but their metallic sheen and brittleness of the fabric does not appear in that painting. In the foreground of the *Panciatichi Assumption*, an apostle looks out, startled by our sudden appearance. Likewise, the spontaneous gestures of the other apostles are caught midstream, reflecting an impulse of movement. Faces express shocked wonderment.

By contrast, in the *Passerini Assumption*, the forward figure (now dressed in bishop's robes) stares out at us languorously. The once-active gestures of the other apostles have come to rest. The apostle in yellow, for instance, rests his book at his side, while the apostle standing at center gestures calmly with outstretched arm. Admittedly, the variations are subtle, but taken together they project two distinct sensibilities. The *Panciatichi Assumption* is infused with the vitality of credible human action, urgent and tense, and characteristic of a miraculous event. Throughout the *Passerini Assumption*, the full import of the

134. Andrea del Sarto, *Panciatichi Assumption*, c. 1522, Galleria Palatina.

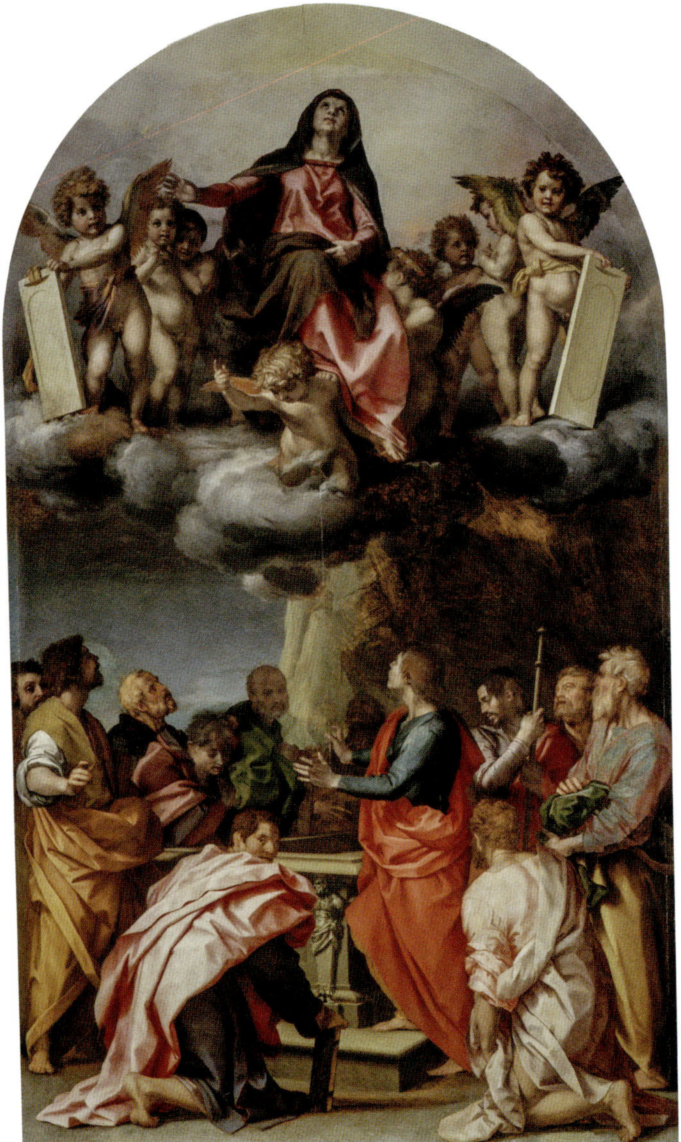

moment has given way to listless grace and tepid emotion, hallmarks of late Mannerism, a style that Sarto never probed further. That said, in the last four years he had to live, Sarto also never returned to the rigorous forms that shaped his most dramatic material, notably, his *Madonna of the Harpies*.

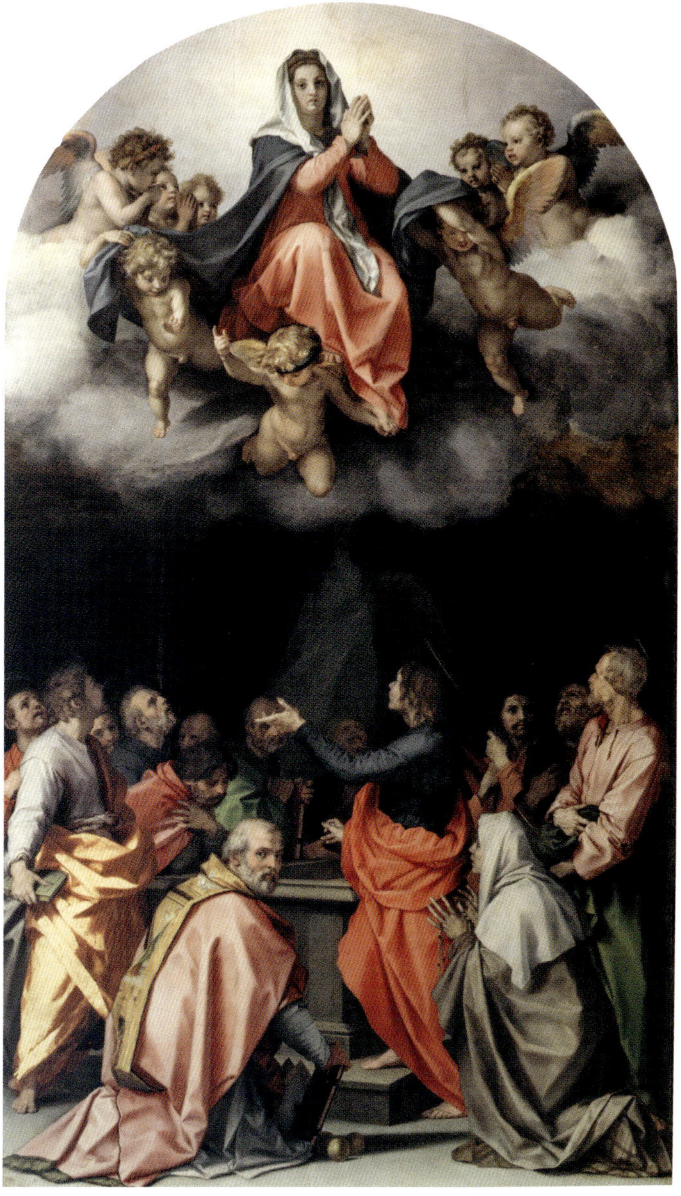

135. Andrea del Sarto, *Passerini Assumption*, 1526, Galleria Palatina.

FLORENCE UNDER THE MEDICI GRAND DUKES, 1535-1587

COSIMO I DE' MEDICI, 1535-1572

In the four decades since the death of Lorenzo the Great, the world order had changed on a level not seen since the fall of ancient Rome. A divided Italy lay exposed to the harsh realities of kingdoms ravenous for the fruits of her soil. The Americas were discovered; Spain, under Isabelle and Ferdinand, became a seafaring power; the French no longer competed with the Holy Roman Empire under Charles V; the African continent was circumnavigated, opening up trade routes to the Far East; Venetian power was stripped by Turks; the future of Christianity teetered under the Protestant Reformation, while the Papacy shepherded in a cultural shift from Florence to Rome.

With the assassination of Duke Alessandro, Florence ran the risk of submitting to absolute control under Charles V. However, with his troops spread thinly across Europe, Charles wasted no time in nominating a member of the predictably controllable Medici: the obscure eighteen year-old, Cosimo, son of Giovanni de' Medici "dalle Bande Nere" (of the Black Bands), a great-grandson of Cosimo the Elder's brother. Little interested in Florentine affairs, Giovanni had been a professional soldier. Highly successful in military campaigns, he had achieved folk-hero status when he was killed at age twenty-seven fighting imperial forces moving on toward Rome.

The young Cosimo's ambitions were unknown. Although descended from a different branch of the family, he had received the usual elite education and had accompanied Alessandro on diplomatic missions.

Contrary to expectations, Cosimo's goals and his capabilities in achieving them appeared when the anti-Medici exiles, in alliance with the powerful banker Filippo Strozzi, mounted an attack. He defeated them at the battle of Montemurlo, executed the leaders, and imprisoned Strozzi, who then committed suicide. From that moment forward, Cosimo's hold on power went unchallenged. The pope conferred on him the title of duke, later followed by Charles's investiture of him as Grand Duke of Tuscany. To give weight to the title, Charles advised the twenty-year old to marry the daughter of the Spanish viceroy to Naples, Eleonora of Toledo.

Consolidation of the State

With the exiles shattered, Cosimo's first objective was to move Florence away from imperial bonds. Caught in the crosshairs of financial distress over his grandiose plans to dominate Europe, Charles sacrificed strategic territories that his forces had earlier captured in return for Cosimo's funds. Although independence from Charles came by degrees, (Cosimo remained loyal to Charles throughout his career) this exchange signaled the last of Charles's physical connection to Florence. Finally free from outside scrutiny, Cosimo invested heavily in arming the city and the

Tuscan countryside. Under the wary eye of Spain, he dared to enlarge the navy, placing ships at key points along the coast. With Pisa, Pistoia, and Arezzo already under his control, in 1555 with Hispanic-Medicean troops Cosimo laid siege to Siena, an ally of France, starving its citizens into submission. Thus, through Cosimo, Charles V was able to retain a foothold in Tuscany.

That Florence survived as an independent state was due to Cosimo's machinations on all fronts. His spies were everywhere, in monasteries, in Venice, Naples, and the papal Court. Disapproval met with imprisonment and any hint of conspiracy with execution. The details of business affairs and diplomacy he managed from his desktop with the supreme confidence of a true professional. In short, the hand of a despot reached over all levels of society.

It comes as no surprise that Cosimo's taste in art ran to whatever celebrated his own glorious achievements. Here, he spent lavishly, hiring the court artist, Vasari and an army of assistants to decorate the walls and ceiling of the Sala Grande, the Great Council Room in Palazzo Vecchio. For the decoration of the upper rooms and Eleonora's private chapel, he assigned Bronzino and Francesco Salviati. With pressure mounting from the pope, he oversaw the installation in Santa Croce and Santa Maria Novella of paintings in the Counter-Reformed style by the leading painters of the time, including Vasari and Bronzino. He also commissioned Bronzino's *Martyrdom of Saint Lawrence*, the last great fresco in sixteenth-century Florence (1569).

Physically, the duke cut a fine figure. Endowed with a powerful body, Cosimo lifted weights and engaged in feats of swimming, fishing, and the hunting of wild boar and sparrows. These were the moments when he mingled with his subjects, feigning to an easy, if somewhat tiresome, informality. At all other times, he closed off, cloistering himself with his family. His marriage to Eleonora proved to be a happy one. They had many children. When she died in 1562, Cosimo was stricken. Sunk in depression, he married a mistress and surrendered the reins of government to his eldest son, Francesco (but not yet his title). Partially paralyzed, he died in 1574 at age fifty-four.

Francesco de' Medici, 1572-1587

Francesco did not thrive in his new position as Grand Duke. Melancholic, insular, and effete, he became the first Medici to refuse to thrust himself before the public eye. When he was young, his father had Vasari construct the private corridor that allowed his son to pass undetected from the Uffizi to the Pitti Palace. With five workers dying in the process, the project destroyed a number of towers, houses, and, most notably, Pontormo's fresco in the dome of the Capponi Chapel in Santa Felicita.

Francesco spent his time in secluded spaces experimenting with chemical reactions, poisons and gunpowder. In 1570, the duke hired Vasari to construct one such space. Perhaps the city's most unusual room, the dark and windowless Studiolo houses rows of cupboards that once held his most prized artifacts. On the door of each cupboard hangs a painting in the late Mannerist style by one of the city's leading artists.

The affairs of state Francesco left to ministers who grumbled that he gave them no direction. In any case, he never faced the military challenges that his forebears had to confront, since Florence no longer posed a threat to surrounding states.

Francesco was best known for two very public acts, one scurrilous even by Medici standards, the other an act of seemingly uncharacteristic magnanimity. The first consisted in the messy entanglements over his long affair with the beautiful Venetian noblewoman Bianca Cappello while married to Joan of Austria, the ignorant and boorish daughter of Emperor Ferdinand (the affair was conducted openly at Bianca's house on Via Maggio). The marriage with Joan produced eight children, but left no heir. When she died in childbirth in 1578, Francesco married Bianca, who then became the Duchess of Tuscany. Since the marriage was barren, Francesco understood that on his death the duchy would pass onto his younger brother, Cardinal Ferdinand I, whom he despised.

But the second act is the source of Francesco's fame. In the 1570s, he installed his prized collection of precious gems and paintings in the Uffizi's Tribune Room. The act set a remarkable precedent, for it began a long line of bequests by subsequent Medici in what has resulted in the grand collections that now make up the Uffizi and Pitti Palace.

Others who followed—Ferdinand I, Cosimo II, on to Gian Gastone, the last Medici Grand Duke (died 1737)—commissioned grand equestrian monuments and other sculpture, often in honor of themselves. But as for painting, it is the contents of the Studiolo that marked the summation of the major cross-currents of the Florentine style in the final years of the sixteenth century.

14. Palazzo Vecchio

When Cosimo I de' Medici, Grand Duke of Tuscany, and his wife Eleonora of Toledo, moved from their old palace (on present day Via Cavour) to Palazzo Vecchio in 1539, the duke commissioned three leading artists to decorate the state rooms and private chambers.

High Mannerist Court Art

As a state room where the duke could receive illustrious visitors from the courts of Europe, the Salone dei Cinquecento was meant to rival the grand audience rooms in the Vatican and the Doge's Palace in Venice. And it's true that the room competes magnificently. But we cannot forget that the Vatican rooms were decorated by Raphael and the Doge's palace by Titian, Veronese, and Tintoretto.

Salone dei Cinquecento

Giorgio Vasari, 1511-1574, and Workshop, *Battle Scenes*, Salone dei Cinquecento, 1566-71

The wall paintings celebrate the city's purportedly everlasting Golden Age under the Cosimo's reign by depicting battles in which Florentine armies defeated their enemies. The self-aggrandizement of artist and patron alike could not be better displayed in what they had conceived as the perfect vehicle to project the primacy of Florence in the visual arts.

Foremost, Vasari means the battle scenes to be read as art, and specifically an art based on an effete artificiality. The primary conventions introduced here come from Michelangelo, whose massively brawny figures fulfill the ideal of human beauty that no painter of the period could ignore. But like other contemporary Mannerists, Vasari ignores the master's passionate spiritualism to concentrate on the figure's pure physicality, which he amplifies beyond plausibility and repeats endlessly in the overwrought, lumpish muscular torsos.

At pivotal points, he sets the heroic figures close to the picture plane and paints them in pale, dissonant pastels that by now are the trade mark of High Mannerism. Otherwise, an utter uniformity pervades the entire picture surface—all counterintuitive to Florentine tradition.

Vasari's style is based on the Roman relief-like style of Salviati's battle

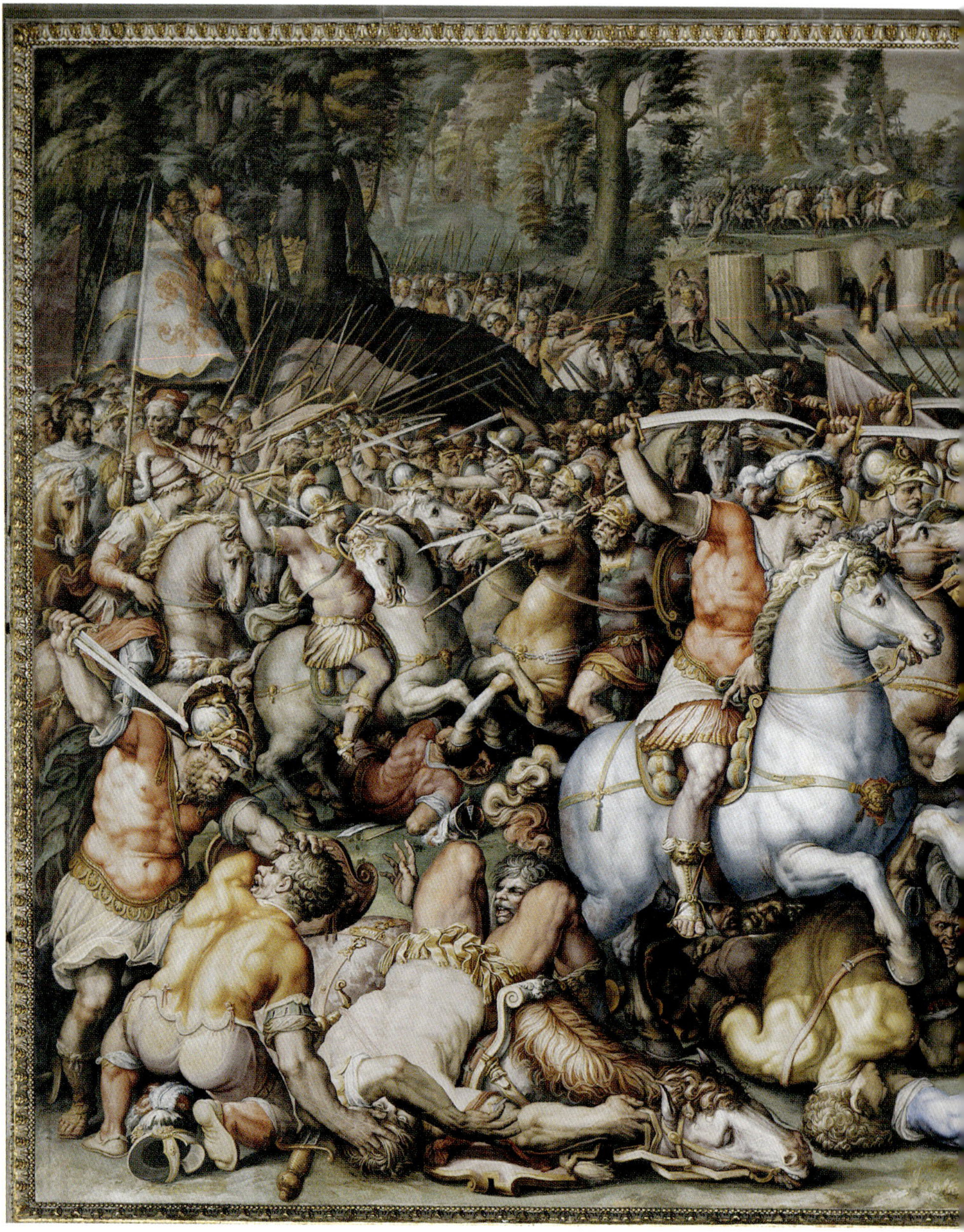

136. Giorgio Vasari and Workshop, *Battle Scenes, Taking of the Tower of San Vincenzo,* 1566-71, Salone dei Cinquecento.

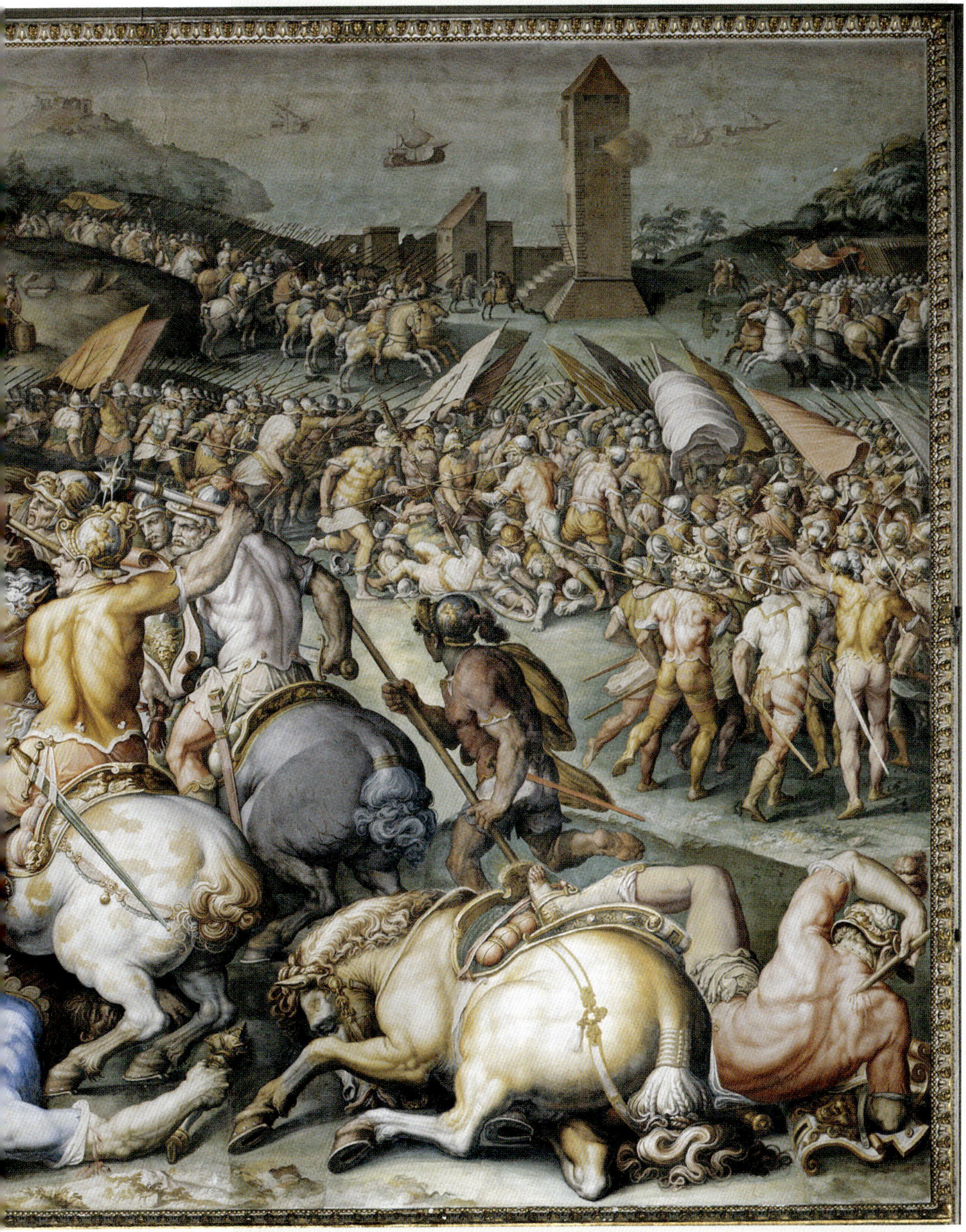

So complex are these scenes that Vasari had a court scholar explain the hidden references to the duke's teen-age son, Francesco I.

scene (fig. 137). But Vasari captures none of that work's flare, charming parody and inflated pomp.

Like his patron Cosimo, Vasari valued the grandiloquence of ancient Rome and its love of the multitudinous trappings of battle accoutrement, all of which he has faithfully reproduced in tapestry-like monotony. But, what Vasari prized most was efficiency. Astonishingly, Vasari's army of painters completed the Salone dei Cinquecento in a matter of about two years.

137. Francesco Salviati, *Triumph of Furius Camillus*, c. 1545, Sala dell'Udienza.

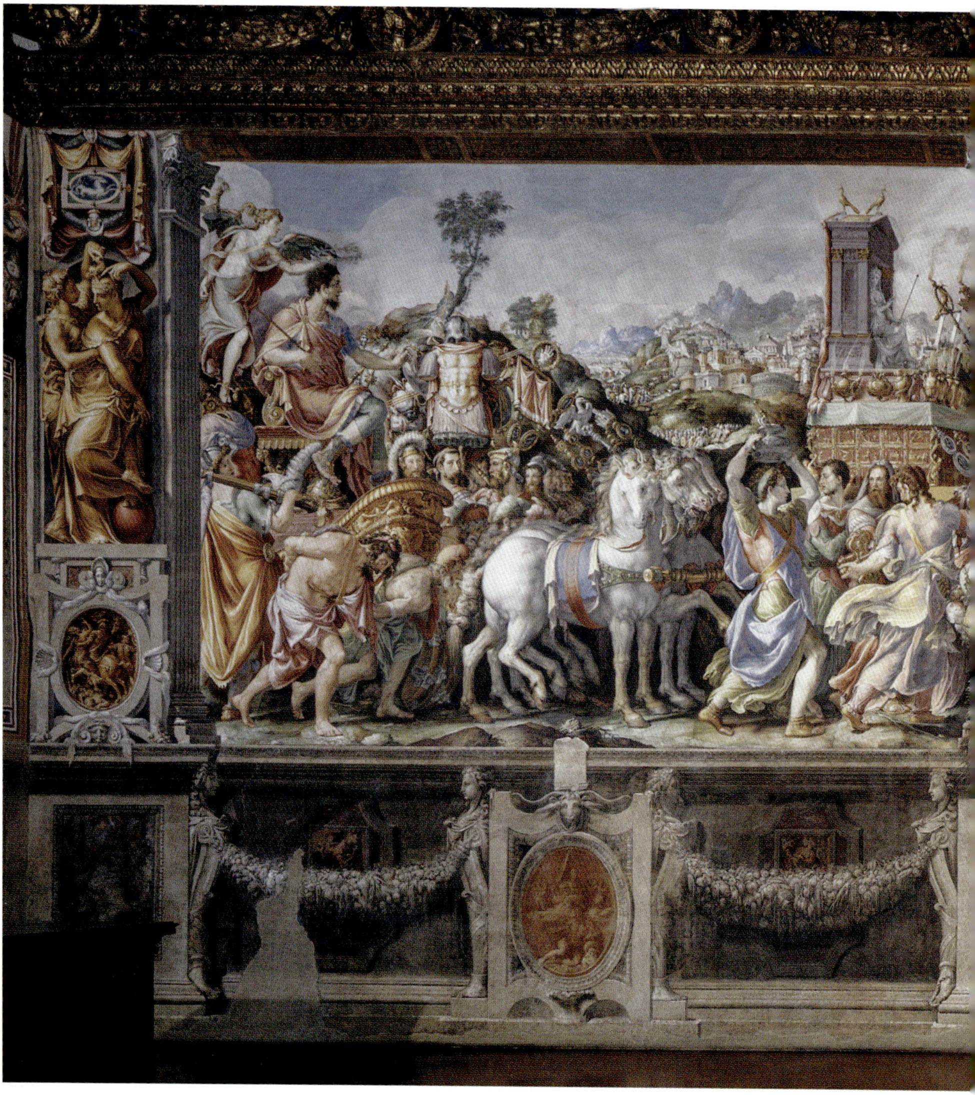

Francesco Salviati, 1510-1563, *Triumph of Furius Camillus*, Sala dell'Udienza, c. 1545

Salviati's dazzling fresco is a splendid hype in homage to Duke Cosimo, who had recently led his forces in a minor victory over the French. In an allegorical reenactment of the battle, Cosimo chose to be portrayed as a famous Roman general. Such over-the-top propagandistic art was meant to be taken with a sly sense of humor.

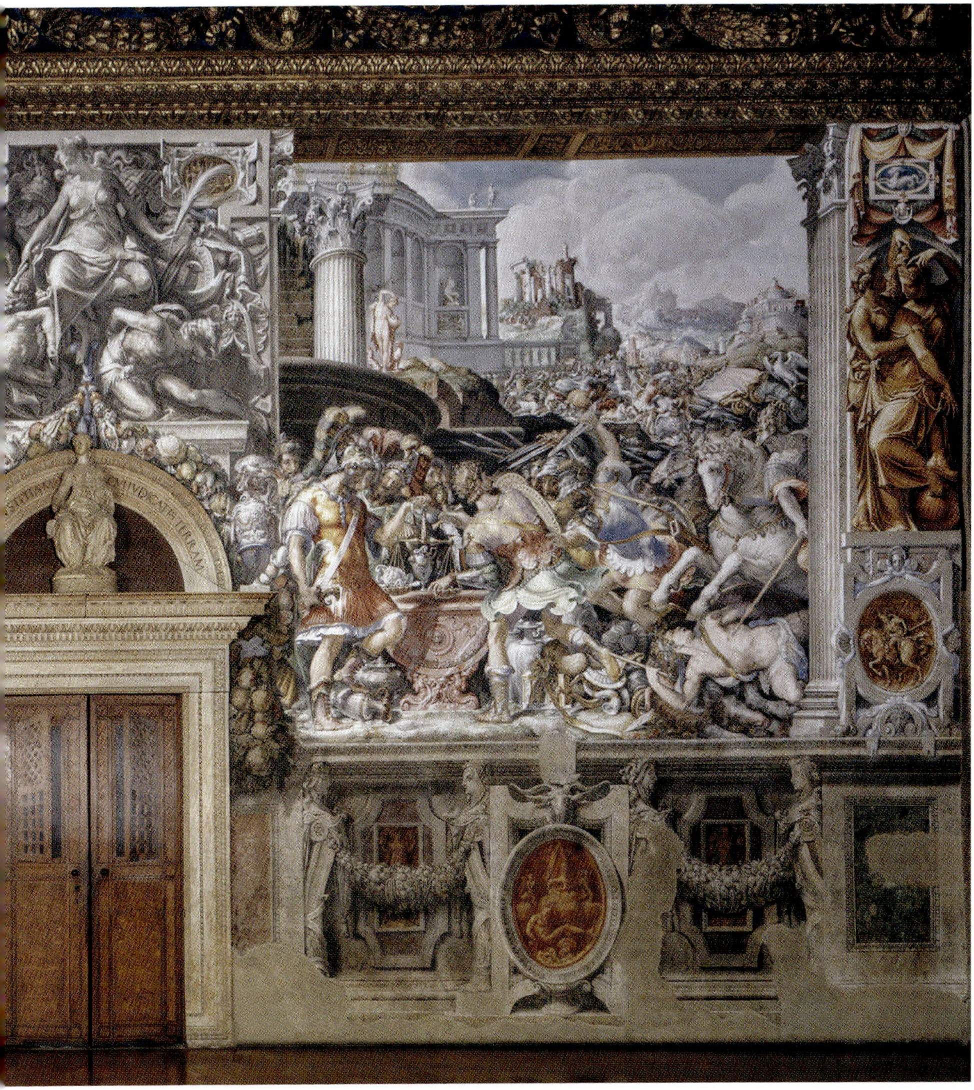

Compared to Vasari's murals, this wall sparkles with pageantry. A procession of Roman troops is returning home with their gallant general, Furius Camillus, in the chariot on the left, who had been recalled from exile to lead them in a victorious battle with the Gauls in 390 BC. The procession marches to the right in a splendid rhythmic cadence, passing behind a broad pier on which is depicted an exquisite trompe-l'oeil painting of the Roman relief sculpture of *Peace Burning Arms* that symbolized the Golden Age of Caesar Augustus. Left of the pier is the famous seated statue of the goddess, Juno, protector of marriage, which the Romans had captured. Thus, all of Cosimo's righteous attributes have been elaborated upon in the thrill of a visual display: a new Augustus who leads the city to a golden age, faithful husband and leader of a Medici dynasty that had been brought out of exile.

Like all court art, this is a version of High Mannerism called the relief-like style, a decorative surface-loving style which Raphael invented for the Vatican apartments just before he died. Similarly, Salviati pushes everything up front parallel to the picture plane, leaving no perspective or focal point to guide the eye. The color scheme, a range of pastels, grays, and beiges, has been aptly described as the "blond manner."

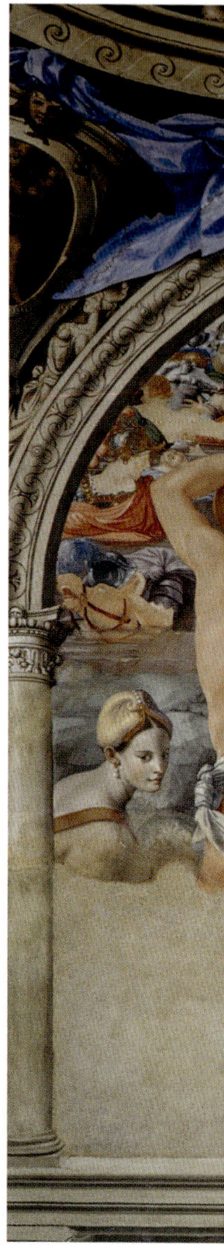

CHAPEL OF ELEONORA OF TOLEDO

Agnolo Bronzino, 1503-1572, *Crossing of the Red Sea*, Chapel of Eleonora of Toledo, 1540-46

Cosimo awarded the decoration of his wife's private chapel to Bronzino, the principal innovator of High Mannerism. A decade later, the duke unceremoniously (and contemporary artists thought unjustifiably) stripped him the honor of court artist and handed it to Vasari. All of the chapel walls were decorated by Bronzino with scenes from Biblical stories. This particular scene describes the Biblical story of Moses leading the Israelites across the Red Sea to safe ground, leaving the pursuing Egyptians to drown in the waters behind them. The gray bearded Moses is seen directing his followers at the right, and we can assume he stands for Cosimo, since a likeness of his pregnant wife, Eleonora, sits nearby. The *Crossing of the Red Sea* attests to Bronzino admiration for Pontormo's *Deposition* and Michelangelo's Sistine Ceiling, where each figure's explicit borders reveal the precision of the drawing that lies at the root of the Florentine tradition.

But in pursuing the High Mannerist ideal, Bronzino reaches further in the shear effect of the picture's artifice. He twists poses to parallel the picture plan to suggest their flatness, such as the broad torso of the nude at the lower right. He models some figures, while others he paints in a thin, flesh-tone wash—like the stunning figure carrying a burden on his head. Seemingly at random, Bronzino scatters the Gothic painters' bright red and precious ultramarine across the wall—even on the fictive deep space—irrespective of the spatial conflicts that come with their brilliance.

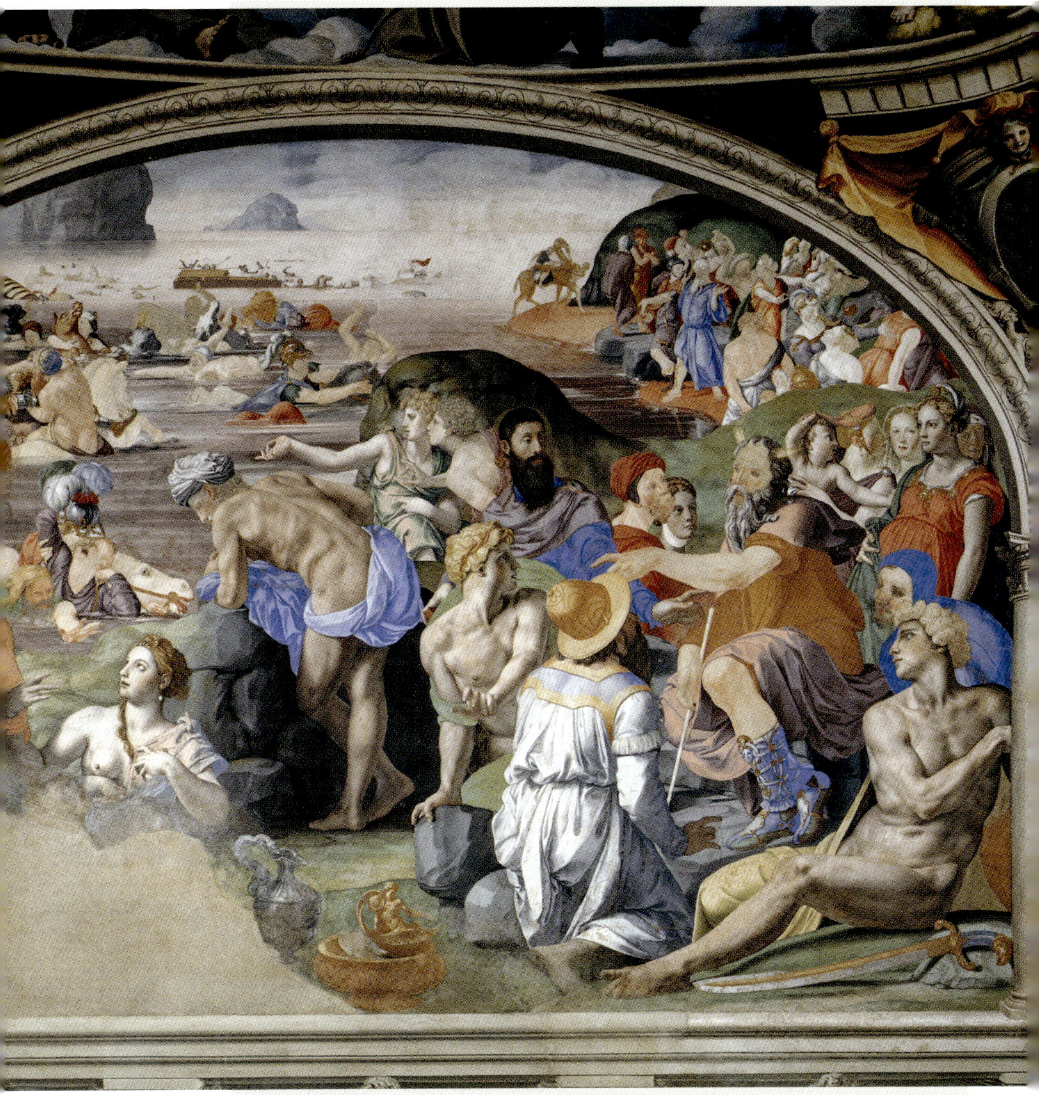

138. Agnolo Bronzino, *Crossing of the Red Sea*, 1540-1546, Chapel of Eleonora of Toledo.

The symbolic implications are clear: water as the substance of spiritual salvation through baptism, and the parallels inferred by the story of Moses saving his people and the pretensions of Cosimo saving the Florentines.

In short, forms read as having equal importance, teasing the eye to dart about, or cagily misdirecting the eye to a figure that has no other purpose than to insist on its artful virtuosity.

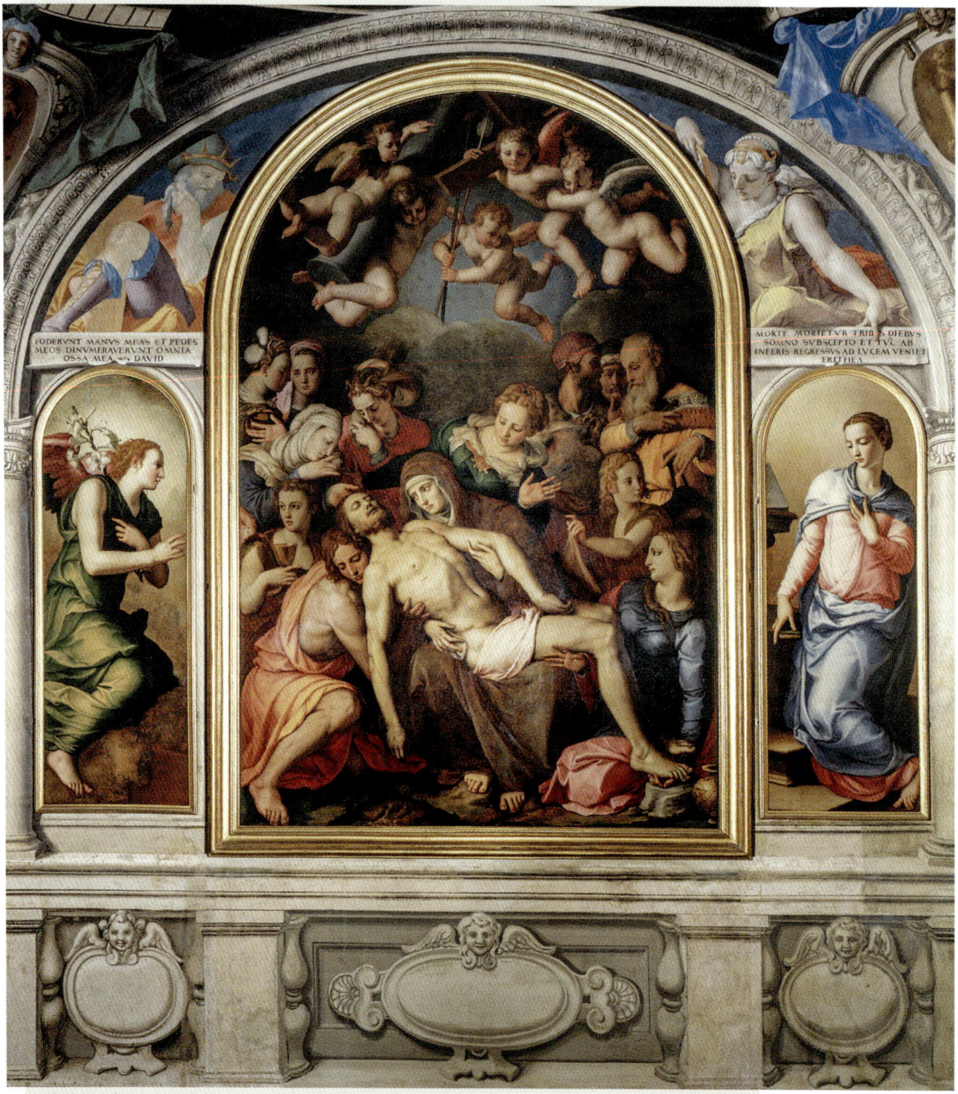

In the side panels, an exquisite *Annunciation* painted in the High Mannerist style. Paired with the *Lamentation*, the scenes mark the beginning and end of Christ's life.

139. Agnolo Bronzino, *Lamentation*, 1553, Chapel of Eleonora of Toledo.

Agnolo Bronzino, *Lamentation*, Chapel of Eleonora of Toledo, 1553

A *Lamentation* painted in 1553, a year in which the Counter Reformation was beginning to spread its influence, demanded unambiguous, straightforward storytelling, unencumbered with Mannerist excess. Consequently, Bronzino, the preeminent High Mannerist, has had to suppress his propensity toward overt sensuality and artificial color.

The scene relates closely to Pontormo's *Deposition* (fig. 127). The figure supporting Christ's body crouches in a nearly identical pose, bearing the weight of the body on his toes. But instead of the space that isolates Mary from her son, here she supports his torso, while Mary Magdalene cradles his feet. And unlike Pontormo's seemingly weightless grouping, these figures can be located on a firm ground plane, though neither painting offers clues as to the nature of the space.

The composition is structured around two diagonals. One diagonal traverses from the upper left through Christ to the lower right; the other traverses from the crouching figure to the gray-bearded man to the upper right (who is Bronzino himself). Where they intersect coincides with the space between Christ's shoulder and Mary's lips. This space represents a variation of the diagonal rift that in Pontormo's composition metaphorically and physically implied separation, a final leave taking of a son from his mother. This emphasis on shaping the composition, organizing the figures around a specific focal point—the space between mother and son—is a quality that distinguishes both Pontormo's *Deposition* and Bronzino's *Lamentation* from the relief-like style's uniformity.

Beyond the two pictures's similarities are the striking differences in their treatment of color and shadow. Pontormo paints his *Deposition* in luminous pigments that give it an ethereal, shadow-free quality that no altarpiece since has approached. Bronzino, in contrast, brings his *Lamentation* to earth, deploying deep shadows and a more somber palette. Where Pontormo's work is a drama of despair so intense it compels the spectator to participate, Bronzino's is a mute meditation on the power of aesthetics to elevate the spirit through its beauty. Yet it is one of Bronzino's few paintings to project a measure of pathos in the figures's expressions, a sure reference to a more sober naturalism about to pervade Church painting.

Studiolo of Francesco I, constructed 1570

In a small room on the main floor off the Salone dei Cinquecento

In one of his rare commissions, Grand Duke Francesco, son of Cosimo I, hired Vasari to design his private studiolo to house his vast collection of precious art objects in cabinets adorned with paintings that obliquely refer to their contents. Vasari employed twenty-two of the city's younger painters (all born in the 1530s), whose styles range from hyper-refined late Mannerism to a naturalism largely purged of capricious Mannerist devices or references to past masters, notably, Michelangelo. In short, these paintings constitute a retreat from decades of Mannerist artificiality and languid grace.

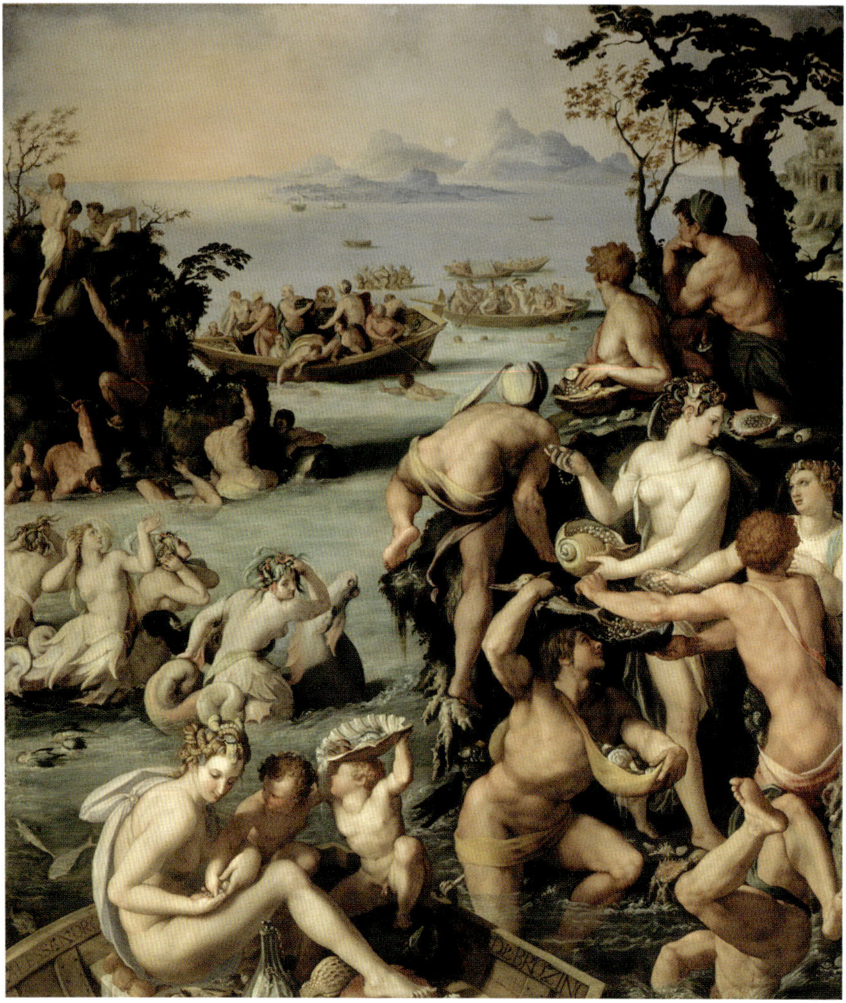

140. Alessandro Allori, *Pearl Fishing*, 1570-73, Studiolo.

Alessandro Allori, 1535-1607, *Pearl Fishing*, Studiolo, 1570-73

An exception to the other paintings is the Mannerist *Pearl Fishing* by Alessandro Allori. In the unbridled nudity, Allori shows his allegiance to his teacher, Bronzino, and through him, to Michelangelo. In fact many figural traits are direct quotations of both artists.

This small work (46 by 40 inches) is one of the gems of the Florentine tradition. We could choose any one of these erotic creatures and their exotic motifs—pearl conchs as headdresses on the females—and consign it to our memory as the fitting end to centuries of Florentine painting. Florence was never again to dominate the European stage.

EPILOGUE

No longer an economic power or an important political player, Florence suffered the indignities of provincialism and its art the failings of old age. With the death of Bronzino, the city's last great Mannerist painter, no fresh talent rose up to take his place. Evidence of this decline can be found in a number of paintings we have seen: Allori's tepid naturalism in Santa Croce or Vasari's impoverished Mannerism in Santa Maria Novella. Rome's Counter Reformation had proved too much for Mannerist art, with all its aristocratic refinements, sensuality, irrationality, and teasing metaphorical puzzles. Mannerist art had been marked by excess, and aside from the semiautonomous principalities of Roman cardinals and the Medici Court, excess was no longer the fashion. It was least of all suited to the piously rational temperament required of religious art, which began to emerge in Bologna and Rome in the last decades of the century.

Aside from the academic paintings he commissioned for the city's churches, Duke Cosimo's tastes ran solely to art in honor of himself, often in the guise of Caesar, Hercules, or of some other heroic figure. Thus, by mid-sixteenth century, art in Florence was pure court art, calculated to celebrate his reign. Although Cosimo was an acknowledged benefactor of the arts, his personal wealth was no match for the power of the purse that the Vatican wielded.

Virtually all of the Florentine artists born in the late Quattrocento spent either their formative or final years studying in Rome, where the big commissions lay. And it was always so. Fra Angelico, Masaccio, Pollaiuolo, Raphael, to name just a few, worked in Rome, died there, and were buried there. Michelangelo died there too, but the city of Florence managed to have him interred beneath a monumental tomb in Santa Croce. The artists who stayed behind in their native city fared worse. Andrea del Castagno died at around thirty-five, Ghirlandaio at forty-five, Filippino Lippi at forty-six, Fra Bartolomeo at forty-four, all most probably of the plague that continuously swept the city streets. Verrocchio died and was buried in Venice. Leonardo and Rosso spent their last years working in France, where they were buried. Botticelli died a broken man, certain that his art would pass to oblivion, and for over three hundred years he was right. According to Vasari, he was buried near Ognissanti on grounds now paved over with streets and buildings. Andrea del Sarto died of the plague at the age of forty-four. He asked to be buried in

Santissima Annunziata, where it was said that a plaque commemorating his soul was affixed to a pillar. It was removed eight years later. Ten years after he died, Pontormo's last frescoes, which had covered the entire choir walls of San Lorenzo, were destroyed by Church reformists. We know only a little of what they looked like, but judging from his drawings in the Uffizi, they were sumptuous and nothing was ever painted to equal them. He is buried in a side chapel of Santissima Annunziata closed to visitors.

Bronzino and Allori asked to be buried in San Cristofano, a church long ago destroyed to make way for petty shops. Giotto was said to have been ceremoniously buried in the crypt of Santa Reparata, the early cathedral that was later reconstructed as Santa Maria del Fiore, but a tour of this site yields only the tomb slab of Brunelleschi. In any case, we know that sometime after his death, his frescoes at Santa Croce were covered in white wash to provide space for more fashionable altars and tombs, whose occupants believed they were assured salvation in the chapel. Masaccio's *Trinity*, the most celebrated fresco of the Quattrocento, met the same fate when Vasari had an altar installed in front of it in 1570, only fifteen years after he had ranked the artist as essential forerunner to the "divine" Michelangelo in the *Lives of the Artists*. What these men had contributed to their city for artisan wages was not recognized until 1563, when Vasari instituted the *Academy of Design,* with the approval of Grand Duke Cosimo I. At last, their status was raised to the level of those practicing the literary arts. Michelangelo was voted its spiritual guide the year before he died.

It is fitting that when Cosimo died in 1574, his son, Francesco, who was a prodigious collector more than a patron of the arts, left the most precious paintings, sculptures and art objects in his beloved Studiolo to what is now the Tribune room in the Uffizi (then, the city's administrative offices) for all to see. The last Medici, Anna Maria Luisa de' Medici (d. 1743), daughter of Cosimo III, bequeathed the family's entire collection to Florence on the condition that no part of it be removed from the capital of the "grand ducal state of Tuscany." Thus was established the legacy of Florentine art in what we now know as the Uffizi Galleries and the Pitti Palace Museum.

More recently, in the 1960s, in a secluded little church not twenty miles from Florence, a historian stumbled onto a painting that bore the unmistakable imprint of Masaccio's style. It turned out to be the earliest of the artist's four surviving paintings.

ADDENDUM

The following three primers, Modeling, Color, and Paint, are an introduction to the challenges Florentine painters faced in depicting the human figure. Pivotal to an understanding of the Florentine style is recognizing that its foundation lay in the primacy of drawing, or *disegno* in Italian. (Venetians, in contrast, placed greater emphasis on color.) But what constituted bold, skillful drawing for one artist might well mean precious, fussy drawing to another. And although Florentine painters viewed color as secondary to the drawn image, they revolutionized how it was applied and how it was interpreted over the course of three centuries. What we are talking about is the stuff of painting: lines, brushstrokes, pigments, and a flat surface.

MODELING

On the next page is a photo of a statue now in Florence's Cathedral Museum (fig. 141). If we look at the statue's external **borders**, we note its **silhouette** has **contours** that curve. Within the borders, we can also see contours that define the statue's drapery folds. More importantly, we note that the figure is **three-dimensional**. How do we know this? Because the photographer has directed his lighting from the left so as to pick up the statue's **highlights** and **shadows,** which distinguish its protruding surfaces and deeply carved recesses. So this sculpture can be seen in terms of both its silhouette and its three-dimensional bulk. **The distinctions between silhouette and three-dimensionality are important when it comes to painting, because a painter can purposely emphasize one over the other.** Botticelli (fig. 82) emphasized silhouette; Leonardo (fig. 86) emphasized three-dimensionality.

The picture depicted in fig 142 is a fresco from the Renaissance. Here the artist is using the photographer's tools to make the figure look like a statue. He paints his figure a uniform grayish-beige, but he employs light and dark variations to mimic the highlights and shadows necessary to convey its three-dimensionality. In painting, we say a figure that projects the illusion of three-dimensionality has **relief**, that is, prominence, or volume. The ability to render the illusion of relief on a flat wall was one of the great discoveries in Florentine painting.

The dark and light variations of a single color used to render relief are

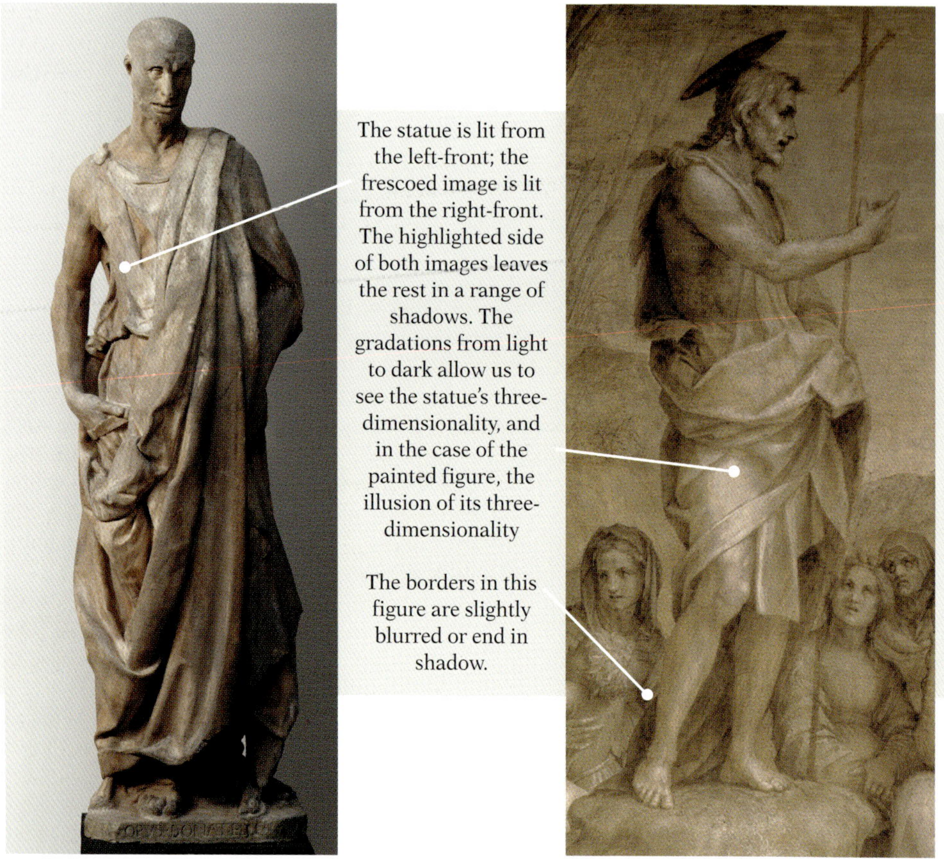

called **tones**. Like the photographer with his lighting, this painter **models** his figure in gradations of light and dark tones that mimic how light strikes a figure, highlighting part of it and leaving part of it in shadow. The statue's similarity to a real draped body is strong by virtue of its deep carving, but to achieve the same effect on a flat wall is another matter altogether. If we look closely at the painting, we can see that the artist, in addition to modeling the figure in darks and lights, has also taken pains to **blur** (soften, smudge) the figure's inside and outside contours by graduating his lights and darks. He has done this so minutely that **the contours do not end in an explicit line**, or they are obscured by shadow. Sharp borders, especially if heavily outlined, emphasize silhouettes, as in a Charlie Brown cartoon. In painting, a figure with sharp borders takes on the look of **flatness**, as if it is pasted into the surrounding scene, a technical problem that Renaissance painters confronted when trying to achieve relief. **Paintings that emphasize the flatness** of their figures call attention to the wall's flatness, that is, to its surface.

141. Donatello, *The Prophet Abacuc* (*Zuccone*), 1432-35, Museo dell'Opera del Duomo.
142. Andrea del Sarto, *John the Baptist Preaching*, c. 1520, Chiostro dello Scalzo.

Paintings that evoke the illusion of depth encourage the viewer to look beyond the wall, as if he were looking through a window into deep space. Paintings in which a figure's outer edges are defined by lines (Botticelli's *Venus*, fig. 82) come under the heading of what we call the "**linear style.**"

Paintings in which figures are modeled to look three-dimensional, belong to the "**relief style.**" These two styles, the linear and the relief, form the basis of Florentine painting from the thirteen through the early fifteen hundreds.

COLOR

Color can lead the eye across the canvas by its dazzlingly chromatic surface patterns or it can focus the eye on characters central to the story. Color can create a dramatic effect, a realistic one, or a purely artificial effect that professes nothing other than its pure beauty. The following, then, is intended to simplify a very complex subject, and to give you the basic tools to evaluate the role of color in the context of the modeling techniques just described.

Fig. 143 is a picture of a spectrum of colors organized within a color wheel. If we look at the second row in (the outer row has been lightened with white), we can see the three primary colors in their purest state—red, yellow, and blue—and the color gradations from one to the other as we move around the wheel. We can also see that blue and red have a broad range from light to dark.

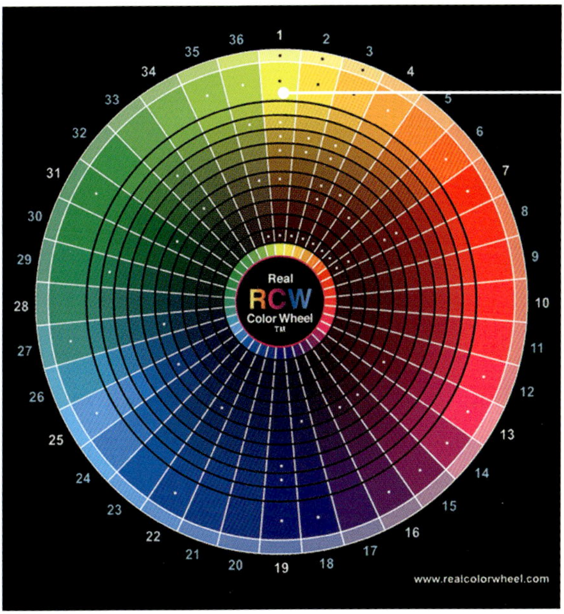

143. Color Wheel.

Pure yellow, on the other hand, is limited to a single unit of the spectrum, and therefore cannot be made any more or less intense.

As we move further toward the center, we note that the colors begin to look the same because they have been mixed with increasing amounts of black. For this reason artists in the fourteenth and early fifteenth century avoided the use of black to model a figure because its opacity would mute color. (Black and white both block out color.)

Instead, these artists preferred painting with pure colors to obtain an effect similar to the radiant clarity that stained glass windows produced. However, because of the wide discrepancies in the intensity of colors across the spectrum, pure color had its limitations when it came to modeling in lights and darks, the essential ingredient, as we've seen, in obtaining the sense of relief. For example, yellow could not be modeled without corrupting its purity, while blue in theory could be modeled with a lighter version in its spectral range. But painters were primarily limited to natural dyes obtained from earth pigments, only a fraction of what appears in the color wheel. Consequently, in order to model a figure's base color, artists turned to white.

How Painters Applied Color

The three paintings discussed here (figs. 144-146) are analyzed in detail in their respective sites. At this point, we are concerned only with how their colors work.

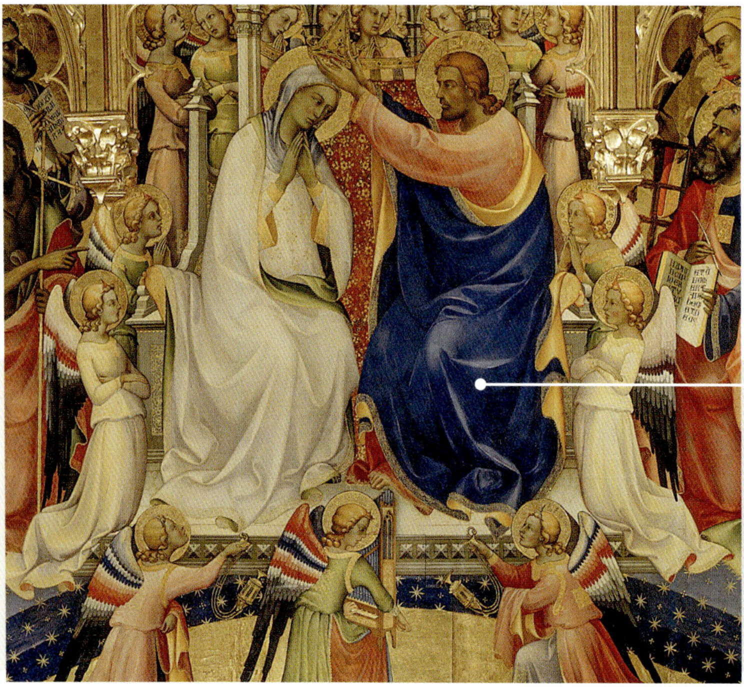

144. Lorenzo Monaco, *Coronation of the Virgin*, 1414, detail of fig. 67.

Ultramarine blue, made from the finely ground mineral lapis lazuli, had to be imported from the mountains of Afghanistan and ranked second only to gold in cost.

Around 1390, the painter Cennino Cennini recorded the modeling technique employed throughout the century, beginning with Giotto's innovations. Pigments were separated into three bowls, one containing the basic color mixed with white, the second with less white, and the third, the pure, most intense color. The lights were placed on the figure's highlighted side, the mid-tones in the center, and the pure color on the opposite, shaded side. This system had the advantage of creating plausible relief and a convincing illusion of a directed light. The primary disadvantage to Cennini's system arose from the fact that when figures were draped in colors of varying intensity, inevitably one would still dominate (blue next to yellow, for example).

The color combinations in Lorenzo Monaco's *Coronation* (fig. 144) make no claim to reality, but rather to a color brilliance that stands for celestial splendor. In Christ's and Mary's draperies, the artist has kept the modeling to a few cursory folds in order to emphasize the flat, decorative quality of the broad expanse of blue and white. This blue, more than any other drapery color, reinforces the perception of flatness.

The picture also illustrates how color variance is interpreted by the eye. The white of Mary's drapery stands out in prominence, that is, it appears to come forward, because white and any color approaching white reflects light back to the eye. By comparison, dark colors absorb light and therefore appear to recede. But in this particular picture, we note that the pure ultramarine blue of Christ's drapery is equally dominating, perhaps more so, because of its appeal to the eye. Thus both pale colors and deep, rich colors like ultramarine blue (or scarlet red) can visually jump forward.

Fra Angelico's painting illustrates both the Cennini system and its manipulation (fig. 145). If we examine the figure kneeling in the foreground, we see that the pure red tones meant to denote the shaded, receding side have also been carried over onto the frontal side protruding toward us. In contrast, the lightest tones meant to represent the illuminated side barely suggest the minimalist of recession. As a result of the broad expanse of intense, un-modeled red, the figures appear flat. The rest of the figures represent Cennini coloring precisely.

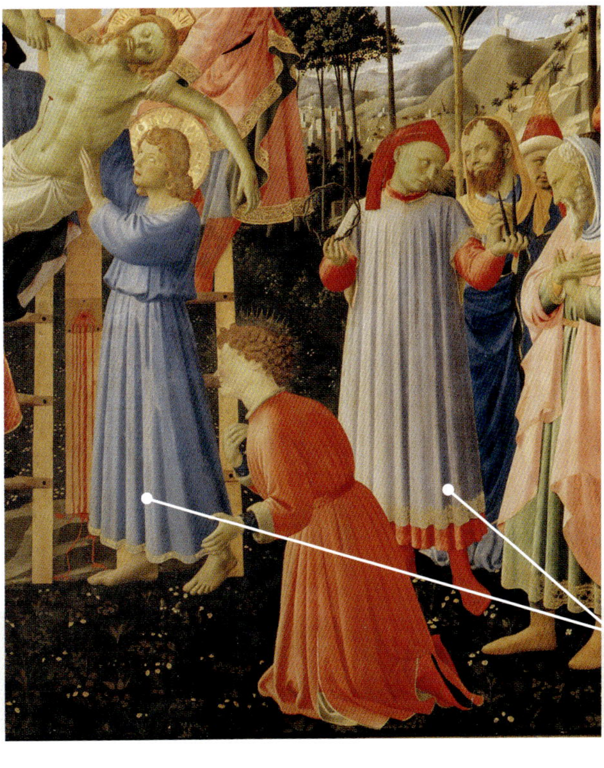

145. Fra Angelico, with Lorenzo Monaco, *Deposition*, early 1440s, detail of fig. 114.

These two figures are modeled according to Cennini's progression of lights, mid-tones, and pure color.

All this began to change in the 1430s with the discovery of a perspective system that could convey deep space. A picture attempting to capture an illusion of deep space now demanded a more modulated color system, especially one that could account for the fact that colors appear more faded according to where they are placed in the distance. To meet these needs, the architect Leon Battista Alberti advised painters to mute their colors to a more uniform intensity with the judicious addition of black. This system allowed colors, as seen in the color wheel, to be deployed over the entire dark to light scale by adding black. Now the pure, most attractive color could stand for the figure's protruding center, the color mixed with black, the shaded side, and the color tinted white, the illuminated side.

In the picture below, a transitional work in terms of color handling, we can see elements of both the Cennini and Alberti systems.

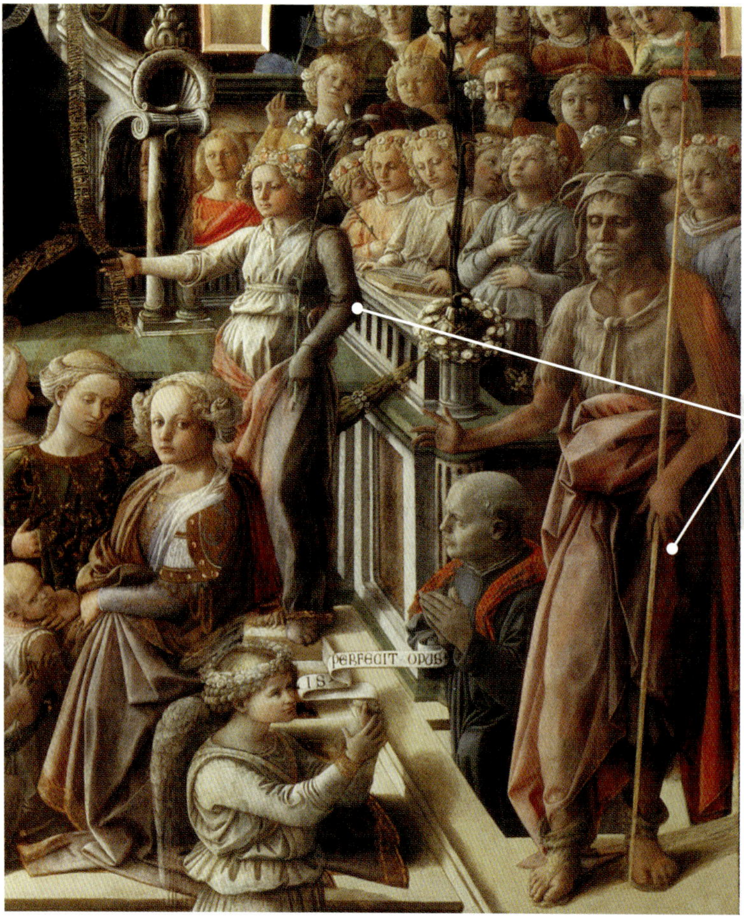

146. Filippo Lippi, *Coronation of the Virgin*, 1439-47, detail of fig. 74.

The shaded side of these two figures have been modeled in black.

In the full picture (see fig. 74) the Virgin's draperies best illustrate the Cennini system, with the pure blues standing for the shaded side, the blue mixed with white, the illuminated side, and the mid-tones the protruding frontal side. The figures standing further in deep space have been dimmed with traces of black, according to Alberti's prescription. Even the whites of the children in the foreground have been grayed down, as have the colors of the figures placed on either side of the platform.

But with the gains in naturalism, something of the jewel-like quality that comes with pure color has been lost. Perhaps the artist, in a final salute to the old Gothic order, added the bright reds and blues of the two figures kneeling in the foreground. How later artists exploited the beauty of color while at the same time harnessing it to the look of life we will study in detail when we move through later styles.

One final point. The bishop robed in green has been modeled with dashes of yellow, an unnatural yet beautiful embellishment. Such artificial color shifts had been deployed since the mid-fourteenth century. The technique would be deployed at full-force by Michelangelo in the Sistine Ceiling.

Paint

Egg Tempera

The three pictures above were executed in egg tempera. Because egg is viscous and dries quickly, the technique necessitated small brushes and small brush strokes, which tended to favor the look of a painted drawing. Depending on the pigments employed, tempera could produce either a mat or a glossy finish. Painting in tempera was a laborious, painstaking technique, but had the ability to produce pure color, fine details and layered modeling.

Oil

Pigments in an oil binder were probably introduced in Florence around the mid-1400s. Like tempera, oil can be applied in layers, usually one at a time because it dries slowly. This feature allowed the artist to use large brushstrokes as a means of feathering a figure's borders or of blending adjacent colors. Once a layer had dried, the artist could apply multiple layers of translucent glazes, allowing the undertones to show through.

Fresco

The city contains some of Italy's finest frescoes, including those of Giotto, who was the first to pioneer the technique in Florence. Of all the forms of painting, true fresco is the most noble. It is also the most difficult. It makes no concessions to the faint-hearted; it offers no refuge to mediocrity. Yet, during the period that fresco was in full bloom (about 1300 to 1550) virtually every painter rose to the challenges that this taxing medium imposed. The sole exception was Leonardo da Vinci.

Frescoes are wall paintings in which the artist applies water-based pigments to freshly spread plaster. As the plaster dries, the color bonds with the lime in the plaster, making it highly durable. The results yielded an eggshell surface of bright, luminous fields of color. Because plaster dries quickly, the artist must confine his work to patches that he can complete in a day. A particularly taxing section, say, a figure or even a face, may take an entire day, while large simple areas, like a sky, could take far less. There are several ways in which a painter could map out his composition before-hand, the most common of which involved painting a rough sketch on the wall before covering it with plaster. This of course meant that the painter had to remember the original drawing. If corrections were to be made, the painter had to scrape away the plaster and begin again. Corrections could also be executed in tempera, and applied over the original fresco. Such over-painting, called *a secco*, was less durable. Artificial, metallic pigments that produced luster and brilliance were not used because they did not bind to the plaster. If needed, they were also overlaid later as *a secco*.

The consequences to a fresco's quick drying are: first, as the plaster dries, the colors fade and this was a positive factor. It meant that the differences between adjacent colors of varying intensities, for example, blue next to yellow, were less prominent. Second, when a painter outlined a form, his brushstrokes were the final ones, because the color was so quickly absorbed into the plaster. Any modeling had to take place within the figure's borders.

Perspective

The following observations contributed to Brunelleschi's discovery of one-point perspective in the early 1400s. Were we to stand on a pavement composed of rows of square tiles and follow them into deep space, we'd notice several things that an artist uses to project the illusion of space on a flat surface. 1. The rows of tiles appear to converge in the distance to a single focal point, what artists call the *vanishing point*. 2. The single point lies on the distant horizon, which corresponds to the *horizon line* in the diagram. The building to the right appears the same way, with its top and bottom borders receding toward the same point. 3. The tiles get closer together as they recede into the distance and this change in spacing can be plotted out as a grid on a piece of paper. This grid provides the artist the means to judge the size of any one object relative to its distance in space, and to organize his composition around the vanishing point. For example, if a full scale man were to be depicted near the pic-

147. Perspective Diagram. Horizon Line and Vanishing point (C)

ture's surface, painters would make him three-braccia high as the reference for all of the other figures. 4. As we take in the distance, we'd see that the head of any figure placed on this grid would lie on the horizon line no matter how far back the figure is in the distance.

The man below is measured in *braccia* (in Italian, "arms"). A *braccio* refers to an arm's length, about 23 inches, so the man is five feet, nine inches tall. (See point 3 of description.)

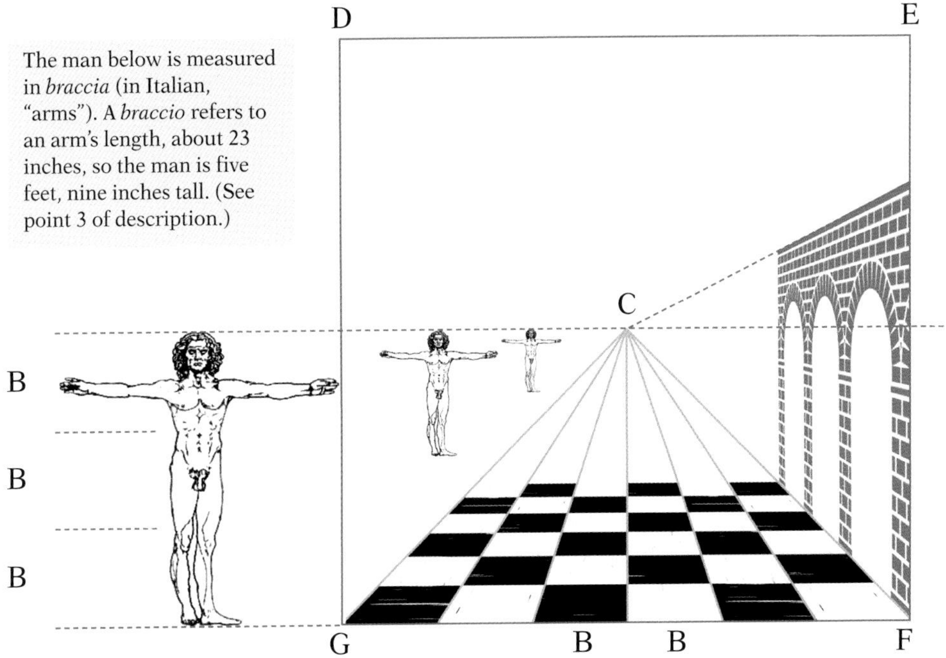

The Medici Family Tree

- **Giovanni di Bicci** 1360-1429 w. Piccarda Bueri
  - PRINCIPAL BRANCH "DI CAFAGGIOLO"
    - **Cosimo the Elder** 1389-1464 w. Contessina de' Bardi
      - **Piero the Gouty** 1416-69 w. Lucrezia Tornabuoni
        - **Lorenzo the Magnificent** 1449-92 w. Clarice Orsini
          - **Lucrezia** 1470-1553 h. Jacopo Salviati
            - **Maria Salviati** 1499-1543 h. Giovanni of the Black Bands
              - **Cosimo I** see cadet branch
          - **Piero the Unlucky** 1472-1503 w. Alfonsina Orsini
            - **Lorenzo Duke of Urbino** 1492-1519 w. Madeleine de la Tour d'Auvergne
              - **Caterina** 1519-89 h. Henry II, king of France
          - **Giovanni** 1475-1521 Pope Leo X s. 1513
        - **Giuliano** 1453-78
          - **Giulio** 1478-1534 Pope Clemens VII s. 1523
            - **Alessandro Duke of Florence** 1511-37 w. Margarethe, Charles V's daughter
  - CADET BRANCH "DEI POPOLANI"
    - **Lorenzo the Elder** 1395-1440 w. Ginevra Cavalcanti
      - **Pier Francesco** 1430-76 w. Laudomia Acciaiuoli
        - **Lorenzo "il Popolano"** 1463-1503
          - **Pier Francesco** 1487-1525 w. Maria Soderini
            - **Lorenzino** 1514-48 Alessandro's killer
        - **Giovanni "il Popolano"** 1467-98 w. Caterina Sforza
          - **Giovanni of the Black Bands** 1498-1526 w. Maria Salviati
            - **Cosimo I Duke (1537) and Grand Duke (1570) of Tuscany** 1519-74 w. Eleanor of Toledo and Camilla Martelli
              - **Francesco I Grand Duke of Tuscany** 1541-87 w. Joan of Austria and Bianca Cappello
                - **Maria** 1573-1642 h. Henry IV, king of France
              - **Ferdinando I Cardinal and Grand Duke of Tuscany** 1549-1609 w. Christina of Lorraine
                - **Cosimo II Grand Duke of Tuscany** 1590-1621 W, Maria Magdalena of Austria
                  - **Ferdinando II Grand Duke of Tuscany** 1610-70 w. Vittoria della Rovere
                    - **Cosimo III** 1642-1723 w. Marguerite-Louise d'Orléans
                      - **Anna Maria Luisa** 1667-1743 h. Johann Wilhelm von der Pfalz
                      - **Gian Gastone** 1671-1737 w. Anna Maria von Sachsen-Lauenburg
                  - **Leopoldo Cardinal** 1617-75

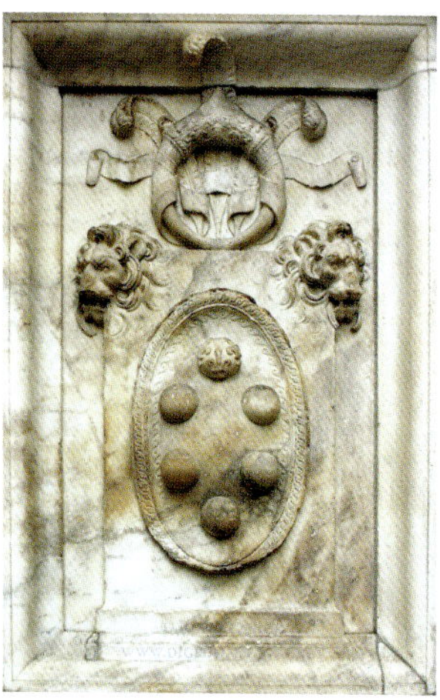

Glossary

Saints, Biblical Stories, Terms

Adoration of the Magi As related in his gospel (2:1-12), St. Matthew describes how three kings (Magi) followed a star to Bethlehem to worship the newborn king of the Jews and to offer him gifts of gold, frankincense, and myrrh. The episode has been considerably expanded in Christian iconography whereby the Magi are depicted as the three ages of man and as the gentiles who came from the three areas of the known world—Europe, Africa, and the Orient. In art, the scene invariably includes Mary, Joseph, and Jesus, usually near or in a wooden manger. This event is commemorated in Western Christianity as the Feast of the Epiphany (January 6).

Annunciation The gospel of Luke describes how the angel Gabriel appeared before Mary to announce the will of God: that she will give birth to a savior. In art, this is one of the most beloved episodes in Christendom because of its simplicity and its openness to elegance. Both figures are depicted parallel to the picture plane, with Mary often reading a book in her bedroom. Behind them is a closed garden, symbol of Mary's unbreached womb. (According to Christian doctrine, she conceived without intercourse). Often, there is a dove, symbol of the Holy Ghost, and a lily, symbol of Mary's purity.

Annunciation to the Shepherds The Gospel of Luke relates that the night of the birth of Jesus an angel appeared to announce to shepherds tending their flocks that a savior had just been born in Bethlehem. The shepherds set out to find the child and when they did they spread the news. Praising God, they became the first evangelists and symbolic of the Jewish people, just as the Magi symbolized the gentiles. The scene is beautifully rendered by Taddeo Gaddi in Santa Croce.

Assumption At Mary's death, her body was transported to heaven. The scene is most often depicted with the apostles standing around her open tomb, while they gaze in amazement at the miracle they are witnessing. In Rosso Fiorentino's version in Santissima Annunziata, the tomb is nowhere to be seen.

Birth of the Virgin One of the most beloved episodes in the life of Mary, mother of Christ, allows Renaissance painters to depict the scene in a contemporary Florentine bedroom where Anne has just given birth. Women in fashionable dresses of the time gather around to pay their respects as midwives and maids attend to the newborn. In Andrea del Sarto's famous version, Mary's father, Joachim, can be seen sitting in the back of the room.

Chiaroscuro Invented by Masaccio, the system of modeling in darks and lights to give the figure the appearance of volume, that is, relief.

Cinquecento The sixteenth century.

Content Refers to what the physical forms imply, that is, the picture's meaning.

Contrapposto Describes the stance whereby a standing figure counterbalances on a weight-bearing leg against the slackened leg. A more detailed discussion occurs in the description of Donatello's *St. Mark* at Orsanmichele.

Coronation of the Virgin Described in apocryphal tracts and the *Golden Legend*, the Coronation takes place after Mary's assumption into heaven when Christ crowns her as queen of the heavens. The scene invariably includes a whole gallery of saints and angels.

Crucifixion Christ's death on the cross at Mount Calvary (also called Golgotha), just outside Jerusalem. The principal figures that attend the crucifixion are his mother, the Virgin Mary, also referred to as the Madonna, the apostle John, Mary Magdalene, and often various Roman soldiers in charge of the execution. In large wall paintings, two other crosses bearing thieves are on each side of Christ's cross. Many Medieval scenes of the crucifixion show only Christ on the cross, often with the images of Mary and John attached to ends of the cross beam.

Deposition Refers to Christ's corpse being lowered from the cross. Depositions usually show the cross, ladders, the Virgin, the apostle John, and Mary Magdalene, who is often seen weeping at the foot of the cross.

Entombment Various members of Christ's intimate circle, including Joseph of Arimathea and Nicodemus carry the body toward a tomb carved into the side of a wall of rock.

Form Refers to what physically sits on the panel or wall, whether it be a simple solitary line or a complex composition.

High Renaissance A style that can be defined as the ideal revision of natural appearances. Among its qualities are decorum, grace, harmony, and balance. As a period, the High Renaissance is generally agreed upon to have begun with Leonardo's *Last Supper* in 1497 and ends with Raphael's death in 1520. In Florence the style was mainly advanced by Fra Bartolomeo and Andrea del Sarto until his death in 1530.

Lamentation After Christ's corpse was lowered from the cross, it was laid on a sheet placed on the ground. Mary is shown weeping while leaning or swooning over the body. Mary Magdalene is customarily cradling the feet while John is supporting the torso. Joseph of Arimathea and Nicodemus, two wealthy followers of Christ, are also often present. Roman soldiers and other onlookers have all left the place of execution.

Last Supper Occurred in a large dining room in Jerusalem the night before Christ's crucifixion when he dined with his twelve apostles to celebrate Passover. During the banquet, Christ announced that one of them would betray him. He later instituted the sacrament of the Eucharist when he took bread and wine, proclaiming, "This is my body and blood. Do this in commemoration of me." Last Suppers can be found in wall paintings in Roman catacombs dating from the second century. By the fourteenth century, Last Suppers were traditionally depicted on the end walls of refectories where nun and monks dined in silence. For more detail about the structure and symbolism of Last Suppers, see Taddeo Gaddi's version, the earliest in Florence.

Mannerism Through an extraordinary range of artistic devices, the Mannerist style, invented by Pontormo and Rosso in 1517, could be employed to strike a mood or to provoke an emotional response in the viewer. By mid-century, Mannerism had evolved into a highly refined movement, expressive of hidden meanings or of nothing but its own beauty. This later stage of Mannerism, as exemplified by Bronzino and Vasari, is termed High or Late Mannerism. The concept of artifice is fundamental to Mannerism. When forms are reshaped beyond the bounds of plausibility, they are defined as "artifice."

Modeling The system of darks and lights that reflects the fall of light, which in turn gives a shape the illusion of mass, commonly call relief.

Pietà takes place after a Deposition and Lamentation when the body of Christ is being cradled across Mary's lap. It is her last intimate and private moment with her son's body.

Quattrocento Means the fifteenth century.

Relief-like style Comes from the term that describes the relief style in the sculpture of ancient Rome that decorates sarcophagi (tombs), and monuments. In painting, the term refers to scenes that through illusion imitate sculptural relief by placing figures close to and parallel to the picture plane. It was first developed by Raphael in painting the rooms of the Vatican apartments and later elaborated in Florence by Bronzino.

Renaissance The Renaissance was first described as a "rebirth" by Vasari in his *Lives of the Artists*. Foremost, rebirth meant a recovery of Latin and Greek texts from antiquity that had long been housed in monasteries. These writings, which included the great historians, rhetoricians, poets, and philosophers from their period, formed the basis of a new way of learning called Humanism. Based on man's dignity in his life on earth, rather than on theological teachings on divinity, Humanism stressed man's duty to civic society. Concurrent with the discovery of ancient classical texts was a new interest in collecting antique art, which in the fourteenth and early fifteenth centuries was limited to coins and to sculptured sarcophagi found on the grounds of churches. The first hints of a new beginning in the arts are considered to have occurred with the competition panels for the Baptistry doors in 1401.

Resurrection The defining mystery of Christianity refers to Christ rising from the dead on Easter Sunday, revealing he was both true man and true God. The scene is represented as Christ bursting from the tomb. The soldiers guarding the tomb are either fast asleep or stricken with terror.

Sfumato A technique developed by Leonardo, in which he added black to colors to create a barely perceptible veil of hazy atmosphere over an entire scene to subdue colors, soften edges, and unite figures to a common atmosphere.

St. Dominic (1170 – August 6, 1221) was the Spanish founder of the Dominicans or Order of Preachers, a militant clerical order, whose task it was to root out heresy and preach mass penitence. Legend has it that before his birth his mother dreamed that a dog leapt from her womb carrying a torch in its mouth, and "seemed to set the earth on fire." This apocryphal story is likely to have emerged when his order became known as *Dominican*, in Latin *Dominicanus,* and by a play of words was interpreted as *Domini canis*: "Dog of the Lord." This explains the presence of spotted black and white dogs depicted in the fresco in the Spanish Chapel of Santa Maria Novella. That he initiated the Inquisition is in dispute, although some of his followers have been associated with the movement. He died in Bologna and was buried in the church bearing his name. He was canonized in 1234.

St. Francis of Assisi (1181/1182 – October 3, 1226), one of the most venerated religious figures in history, founded the mendicant Franciscan Order. The son of a wealthy cloth merchant in Assisi, he lived a high-spirited life until his early twenties when he renounced his possessions to live a life of poverty. Preaching on the streets, he soon amassed a following all over Italy. The order was endorsed by Pope Innocent III in 1210. Francis miraculously received the stigmata, the puncture wounds on his hands and feet that marked Christ's body at the crucifixion. In 1228, two years after his death, he was canonized a saint by Pope Gregory IX. The great basilica bearing his name was begun only a few decades later.

Three Marys at the Tomb The day after Christ's resurrection, Mary Magdalene and the Virgin Mary's two half-sisters went to the tomb to pray when they were met by an angel who told them Christ was no longer in the tomb. In art, the scene customarily appears in one of the side stories in Medieval crucifixes.

Trecento The fourteenth century.

Trinity The Triune God, one of the most mystical doctrines in Catholicism, is composed of Christ, God, his father, and the Holy Spirit as a single Godhead. In pictorial terms, the Trinity is shown as God and the Holy Spirit in the form of a dove gathering up Christ's body and raising it to Heaven. The scene represents Christ's last presence on earth.

Visitation Luke (1:42). When Gabriel appeared to Mary to announce her conception of a savior, he also told her that her elderly first cousin, Elizabeth, would give birth. When Mary went to visit Elizabeth in the town of Nazareth, her cousin was already six months pregnant with a son, who would be called John the Baptist. This too is one the most beloved scenes from the gospels, because of its simplicity. The Virgin and Elizabeth, who was well beyond child-bearing age, greeted each other with an embrace.

Chronology

59 BC. Caesar founds Florence as a colony.

313 Emperor Constantine issues Edict of Milan, ending persecution of Christians.

330 Constantine moves the imperial court from Rome to Constantinople.

476 Fall of the Western Roman Empire. Odoacer, a Germanic chieftain, steps in as ruler.

800 Charlemagne crowned Holy Roman Emperor by Pope Leo III.

1013-50 Baptistry and church of San Miniato built on ancient Roman foundations.

1082 Pope Gregory VII excommunicates the German Holy Roman Emperor Henry IV. Countess Matilda of Tuscany sides with the papacy.

1095 First Crusade opens up trade routes through Florence.

1115 Matilda dies, leaving her lands to the papacy. The Florentines, who also side with the papacy against the German Holy Roman Emperor, are free to form a commune of the most distinguished hundred men in the city.

1210 Francis founds the Franciscan order in Assisi, Umbria.

1216 Dominic founds the Dominican order in Spain. The assassination of a young nobleman in Florence starts a civil war between the Guelfs and Ghibellines.

1240-50 Intense rivalry between the papacy and the Holy Roman Empire played out in Tuscany. Florence, under the Guelf party, continues to side with the papacy.

1246 The existing Dominican church of Santa Maria Novella founded.

1250 Guelfs defeat the Ghibellines. Florence ratifies the "government of the people," an independent commune comprised of a council of elders. This new government increased the influence of the merchants, professional classes, and the artisans, all represented by their twenty-one guilds.

1252 First coining of the Florentine florin. Pope Innocent II decrees torture can be used to extract confessions from heretics.

1255 Bargello, the first public palace built in Florence, is home to the new republic's chief magistrate.

1260 Battle of Montaperti. Siena, aligned with a force of Ghibellines from all over Tuscany and backed by the German emperor, defeats Florence, killing 10,000.

1267 Pope Clement IV, a Frenchman by birth with deep antipathy toward the Holy Roman Emperor, calls for Charles of Anjou, brother of the king of France, who defeats the Ghibellines and is accepted as city's overlord for six years.

1294 Franciscan church of Santa Croce rebuilt larger. Period of great prosperity.

1296 Duomo is begun by Arnolfo di Cambio.

1299 Palazzo Vecchio begun by Arnolfo.

1302 Exile of Dante on trumped up political charges.

1305 In Florentine painting, the birth of naturalism: Giotto paints lifelike figures in Santa Croce.

1307 Dante begins writing *Divine Comedy*.

1321 Dante dies.

1334 Campanile designed by Giotto.

1336 Andrea Pisano begins casting the Baptistry's first bronze doors. Last major sculptural project until 1390s.

1337 Death of Giotto; founding of the existing oratory of Orsanmichele. Beginning of Hundred Years War between England and France. Edward III, king of England defaults on loans from the Bardi and Peruzzi families, forcing their powerful banks into bankruptcy and nearly bringing down the entire economy of Florence.

1348 Black Death: outbreak of the plague in Florence, killing half of its 100,000 citizens.

1374 Petrarch dies, one of the great promulgators of Humanism.

1378 Revolt of the 'Ciompi', disenfranchised day-laborers, who were denied their own guild.

1378-1417 The Papal Schism. Two popes elected by Italian and French cardinals. When a third pope is elected, Council of Constance convened to elect Martin V in 1417.

1400-02 Florence and its territories threatened by Gian Galeazzo Visconti, Duke of Milan, who dies of the plague in 1402.

1401 Competition organized for the second pair of bronze doors for Baptistry; Brunelleschi and Ghiberti the leading Florentine competitors. Ghiberti awarded the commission, begins Baptistry's second pair of bronze doors.

1411 Donatello sculpts *St. Mark* on Orsanmichele, marking what many scholars believe to be the beginning of the Renaissance.

1413 Brunelleschi completes design for the Florentine cathedral's dome.

1425 Ghiberti assigned the commission for the third pair of the Baptistry doors (the 'Doors of Paradise'); Masaccio and Masolino begin frescoing Brancacci Chapel.

1428 Masaccio dies.

1429 Giovanni di Bicci de' Medici, founder of the family's fortune, dies, leaving two sons, Cosimo and Lorenzo, from whom descended two main branches of the family.

1430-40s Period when Fra Angelico, the most revered painter of his era, is active.

1433 Banishment of Cosimo de' Medici from Florence by the oligarchic faction headed by Rinaldo degli Albizzi.

1434 Return of Cosimo from exile. Through the Medici party, he unofficially dominates the republican government.

1440-50s Paolo Uccello, Domenico Veneziano, Filippo Lippi, Andrea del Castagno all active.

1453 Fall of Constantinople, the capital of the Byzantine Empire, to the Ottoman Turks.

1455 First book printed: *Gutenberg Bible.*

1464 Cosimo de' Medici dies; succession of his son Piero as first citizen in Florence.

1466 Donatello dies.

1469 Piero de' Medici dies; Lorenzo il Magnifico confirmed as his successor by a group of leading citizens. Filippo Lippi dies. Marriage of Isabella and Ferdinand in Spain.

1478 The Pazzi Conspiracy against the Medici with the support of Sixtus IV. Giuliano dies, Lorenzo il Magnifico is wounded but survives by escaping to the Duomo's sacristy. Florence is excommunicated by Pope Sixtus IV.

1478 Spanish Inquisition established.

1480 Lorenzo il Magnifico travels to Naples to make peace with its king. Travels to Rome to negotiate peace with the pope. A period of peace in Italy generally follows.

1481 Leonardo paints *Adoration.*

1482 Botticelli paints *Primavera.*

1489 The Ferarrese-born Dominican Fra Girolamo Savonarola, through his preaching, attracts attention of Lorenzo il Magnifico. The foundations of the Palazzo Strozzi are laid.

1492 Lorenzo il Magnifico dies; his position in Florence assumed by his eldest son,

Piero; Christopher Columbus lands in Central America. Jews expelled from Spain, who then migrate to Italy, establishing a large community in Rome.

1494 Invasion of Italy by Charles VIII of France. Charles then enters Florence, but soon withdraws on threat of imminent battle. Flight and subsequent banishment of Piero de' Medici from Florence. Second Republic established under the emotional sway of Savonarola.

1496 The hall of the new governing body, the Sala dei Cinquecento, inaugurated in the Palazzo Vecchio.

1498 Savonarola and two fellow-Dominicans convicted of heresy at the instigation of Pope Alexander VI (Borgia) and publicly burnt at the stake on the Piazza della Signoria.

1502 Under a new constitution, the head of government in the republic to be the *Gonfaloniere di Giustizia*, who would hold office for life. Piero Soderini is the first to be appointed.

1504 Michelangelo's *David* completed and placed outside the Palazzo Vecchio. Under the Soderini republic, Michelangelo and Leonardo da Vinci each receive a commission to execute a battle scene on the walls of the Sala dei Cinquecento, thereby highlighting the opposition of their styles.

1509-24 Andrea del Sarto frescoes the atrium of Santissima Annunziata and the Scalzo cloister.

1512 The republic falls when pro-Medici papal forces agitate for the return of Medici rule. Soderini is exiled.

1513 Election of Cardinal Giovanni de' Medici, son of Lorenzo il Magnifico, as Pope Leo X; Machiavelli publishes *The Prince*.

1515 Triumphal entry of Leo X into Florence.

1517 Luther posts his ninety-five theses in Wittenberg, Germany. Beginning of the Protestant Reformation.

1519 Leonardo da Vinci dies.

1520 Raphael dies.

1522 Election of Cardinal Giulio de' Medici as Pope Clement VII.

1527 Sack of Rome by imperial troops under the Emperor Charles V. The Medici expelled from Florence and the republic restored.

1529 Peace between Charles V and Pope Clement, whose combined forces besiege Florence in the Medici cause.

1530 Florence surrenders. Andrea del Sarto, the preeminent High Renaissance painter, perishes in the plague.

1531 Charles V installs the illegitimate Alessandro de' Medici head of government and declares him the first duke of the Florentine Duchy.

1537 Assassination of Duke Alessandro. The ruling circle in Florence nominates the young Cosimo I de' Medici as head of government, and he is subsequently confirmed by Charles V as duke.

1539 Duke Cosimo marries the younger daughter of the Spanish viceroy of Naples, Eleonora di Toledo.

1540 The duke and duchess leave the Medici palace to live in the Palazzo Vecchio.

1542 Pope Paul III establishes the Roman Inquisition. This court system, based on Canon law, was less conservative than the Spanish Inquisition.

1545 Council of Trent. Established by Pope Paul III as the formal beginning of the Catholic Counter Reformation movement. Bans provocative church painting, which leads to a more naturalistic style that replaces Mannerism by the mid-1550s.

1549 Duchess Eleonora purchases the Palazzo Pitti, subsequently the residence of all the grand dukes.

1550 Vasari publishes first edition of his *Lives* of the artists, dedicated to Duke Cosimo.

1555 Imperial and Florentine troops capture Siena.

1560 Vasari directs beginning of the building of the Uffizi as state offices.

1562 Death of Cosimo I's wife, the duchess Eleonora, and two of her sons.

1564 Duke Cosimo entrusts the regency to his eldest son, Francesco; Galileo born; Michelangelo dies.

1565 Marriage of Francesco de' Medici and Archduchess Joan of Austria.

1569 Pope Paul V grants Cosimo the title of Grand Duke of Tuscany.

1571 Battle of Lepanto: the Ottoman Empire's fleet defeated by a Catholic coalition comprised of Genoa, Venice, the Spanish Empire with the kingdoms of Naples, Sicily and Sardinia, the Papal States, Duchy of Savoy, Grand Duchy of Tuscany, Duchy of Urbino, the Knights of Malta. The victory prevented the Mediterranean Sea from becoming an uncontested highway for Muslim forces, protected Italy from a major Ottoman invasion, and prevented the Ottomans from advancing further up the southern flank of Europe. Lepanto was the last major naval battle in the Mediterranean fought entirely between galleys.

1574 Duke Cosimo I dies; Vasari dies.

1610 Galileo uses telescope to observe the Moon's mountains.

1743 Death in Florence of the widowed Anna Maria Luisa de' Medici, Cosimo III's daughter, who bequeathed the entire Medici collections to the new line of grand dukes as inalienable property of the state.

1769 The Uffizi gallery opened to the public.

Bibliography

The Origins of Florentine Painting

Beckwith, John Gordon. *Early Christian and Byzantine Art*. Harmondsworth: Penguin Books, 1970.

Belting, Hans. *Likeness and Presence. A History of the Image before the Era of Art*, trans. Edmund Jephcott. Chicago: University of Chicago Press, 1994.

Bertelli, Carlo, ed. *La pittura in Italia. L'Altomedioevo*. Milano: Electa, 1994.

Boskovitz, Miklós. *The Origins of Florentine Painting. 1100-1270*. Florence: Giunti, 1993.

Brucker, Gene A. *Renaissance Florence*. New York: John Wiley, 1969.

Carli, Enzo. *Italian Primitives. Panel Painting of the Twelfth and Thirteenth Centuries*. New York: Henry N. Abrams, 1993.

Demus, Otto. *Byzantine Art and the West*. New York: New York University Press, 1970.

Demus, Otto. *Romanesque Mural Painting*. New York: Henry N. Abrams, 1970.

Dodwell, Charles Reginald. *Painting in Europe, 800 to 1200*. Harmondsworth: Penguin Books, 1971.

Grabar, André. *Early Christian Art. From the Rise of Christianity to the Death of Theodosius*. London: Odyssey Press, 1968.

Kitzinger, Ernst. *Byzantine Art in the Making. Main Lines of Stylistic Development in Mediterranean Art, 3rd-7th Century*. Cambridge: Harvard University Press, 1968.

Kitzinger, Ernst. *Early Medieval Art, with Illustrations from the British Museum Collection*. Bloomington: Indiana University Press, 1970.

Krautheimer, Richard. *Rome, Profile of a City, 312-1308*. Princeton: Princeton University Press, 1980.

Oakeshott, Walter. *The Mosaics of Rome, from the Third to the Fourteenth Centuries*. Greenwich: New York Graphic Society, 1967.

Oertel, Robert. *Early Italian Painting to 1400*. New York: Frederick Praeger, 1968.

Petzold, Andreas. *Romanesque Art*. New York: Harry N. Abrams, 1995.

Smart, Alastair. *The Dawn of Italian Painting, 1250-1400*. Ithaca: Cornell University Press, 1978.

Swift, Emerson Howland. *Roman Sources of Christian Art*. New York: Columbia University Press, 1951.

Tartuferi, Angelo. *La pittura a Firenze nel Duecento*. Firenze: Alberto Bruschi, 1990.

Santa Croce Church and Museum

Baxandall, Michael. *Giotto and the Orators. Humanist Observers of Painting in Italy and the Discovery of Pictorial Composition, 1350-1450*. Oxford: Clarendon Press, 1971.

Edgerton, Samuel Y., Jr. *The Heritage of Giotto's Geometry. Art and Science on the Eve of the Scientific Revolution*. Ithaca: Cornell University Press, 1991.

Flores d'Arcais, Francesca. *Giotto*. Milano: Motta, 1995.

Offner, Richard. "Giotto non-Giotto", in *Giotto: the Arena Chapel Frescoes*, ed. James Stubblebine. New York: W.W. Norton, 1969, 133-155.

Poeschke, Joachim. *Italian Frescoes, The Age of Giotto, 1280-1400*. New York: Abbeville Press, 2005.

Smart, Alastair. *The Dawn of Italian Painting, 1250-1400*. Ithaca: Cornell University Press, 1978.

White, John. *The Birth and Rebirth of Pictorial Space*. Cambridge: Belknap Press, 1987.

Orsanmichele

Avery, Charles. *Florentine Renaissance Sculpture*. New York: Harper & Row, 1970.

Poeschke, Joachim, ed. *Donatello and His World. Sculpture of the Italian Renaissance*. New York: Harry N. Abrams, 1993.

Pope Hennessy, John W. *An Introduction to Italian Sculpture*. 3 volumes. London: Phaidon Press, 1955-1963 (I. *Italian Gothic Sculpture*; II. *Italian Renaissance Sculpture*; III. *Italian High Renaissance and Baroque Sculpture*).

Seymour, Charles. *Sculpture in Italy, 1400 to 1500*. Harmondsworth: Penguin Books, 1966.

Santa Maria del Carmine, Brancacci Chapel

Cole Ahl, Diane, ed. *The Cambridge Companion to Masaccio*. New York: Cambridge University Press, 2002.

Hills, Paul. *The Light of Early Italian Painting*. New Haven: Yale University Press, 1987.

Joannides, Paul. *Masaccio and Masolino, A Complete Catalogue*. London: Phaidon Press, 1993.

Meiss, Millard. *The Great Age of Fresco. Discoveries, Recoveries and Survivals*. London: Phaidon Press, 1970.

Stubblebine, James. *Byzantine Influence in Thirteenth-Century Italian Panel Painting*. Washington D.C.: Trustees for Harvard University, 1966.

Uffizi Gallery

Arasse, Daniel, ed. *Botticelli de Laurent le Magnifique à Savonarole*. Milan: Skira, 2003.

Bellosi, Luciano. *Cimabue*. New York: Abbeville Press, 1998.

Blunt, Anthony. *Artistic Theory in Italy, 1450-1600*. Oxford: Oxford University Press, 1962.

Bologna, Ferdinando. *Early Italian Painting. Romanesque and Early Medieval Art*. Princeton: Van Nostrand, 1964.

Brown, David Alan. *Leonardo da Vinci. Origins of a Genius*. New Haven: Yale University Press, 1998.

Cadogan, Jeanne K. *Domenico Ghirlandaio. Artist and Artisan*. New Haven: Yale University Press, 2000.

Chilvers, Ian, ed. *The Concise Oxford Dictionary of Art and Artists*. Oxford-New York: Oxford University Press, 1996.

Clark, Kenneth. *Leonardo da Vinci. An Account of His Development as an Artist*. Baltimore: Penguin Books, 1959.

Crowe, Joseph Archer; Cavalcaselle, Giovanni Battista. *A History of Painting in Italy, Umbria, Florence and Siena. From the Second to the Sixteenth Century*. Vol. 4, *Florentine Masters of the 15th Century*. London: Murray, 1911.

Dempsey, Charles. *The Portrayal of Love: Botticelli's Primavera and Humanist Culture at the Time of Lorenzo the Magnificent*. Princeton: Princeton University Press, 1992.

Freedberg, Sydney J. *Painting of the High Renaissance in Rome and Florence*. 2 volumes. Cambridge: Harvard University Press, 1961.

Goffen, Rona. *Renaissance Rivals. Michelangelo, Leonardo, Raphael, Titian*. New Haven: Yale University Press, 2002.

Gombrich, Ernst Hans. *The Story of Art*. London: Phaidon, 1951.

Henneberger, Melinda. "The Leonardo Cover-up". *The New York Times*, April 21, 2002.

Jones, Roger; Penny, Nicholas. *Raphael*. New Haven: Yale University Press, 1983.

Kemp, Martin, ed. *Leonardo on Painting. An Anthology of Writings by Leonardo da Vinci with a Selection of Documents Relating to His Career as an Artist*. New Haven: Yale University Press, 1989.

Kemp, Martin. *Leonardo da Vinci. The*

Marvellous Works of Nature and Man. Cambridge: Harvard University Press, 1981.

Lightbown, Ronald. *Sandro Botticelli*. Berkeley: University of California Press, 1978.

Maginnis, Hayden B.J. *Painting in the Age of Giotto. A Historical Reevaluation*. University Park: Pennsylvania State University Press, 1997.

Oberhuber, Konrad. *Raphael. The Paintings*. Munich-New York: Prestel, 1999.

Panofsky, Erwin. *Renaissance and Renascences in Western Art*. New York: Harper & Row, 1972.

Ruda, Jeffrey. *Fra Filippo Lippi, Life and Work with a Complete Catalogue*. London: Phaidon Press, 1993.

Schmidt, Victor, ed. *Italian Panel Painting of the Duecento and Trecento*. Washington D.C.-New Haven: National Gallery of Art, Yale University Press, 2002.

Vavalà Sandberg, Evelyn. *Uffizi Studies. The Development of the Florentine School of Painting*. Florence: Leo S. Olschki, 1948.

Vavalà Sandberg, Evelyn. *La croce dipinta italiana e l'iconografia della Passione*. Verona: Apollo, 1914, reprint Roma: Multigrafica editrice, 1980.

White, John. *Art and Architecture in Italy, 1250-1400*. New Haven: Yale University Press, 1993.

Santa Maria Novella church and Museum

Borsi, Franco; Borsi, Stefano. *Paolo Uccello*, trans. Elfreda Powell. New York: Henry N. Abrams, 1993.

Bracco, Paola, in *Giotto. The Santa Maria Novella Crucifix*, eds. Marco Ciatti, Max Seidel. Firenze: Edifir, 2002.

Cannon, Joanna Louise. *Dominican Patronage of the Arts in Central Italy. The Provincia Romana, c. 1220-c. 1320*. London: University of London 1970.

Cole, Bruce. *Giotto and Florentine Painting, 1280-1375*. New York: Harper & Row, 1976.

Goffen, Rona, ed. *Masaccio's Trinity*. Cambridge: Cambridge University Press, 1998.

Poeschke, Joachim. *Italian Frescoes, The Age of Giotto, 1280-1400*. New York: Abbeville Press, 2005.

Roettgen, Steffi. *Italian Frescoes*. 2 volumes, trans. Russell Stockman. New York: Abbeville Press, 1996-1997 (I. *The Early Renaissance 1400-1470*. 1966; II. *The Flowering of the Renaissance 1470-1510*, 1997).

Seidel, Max, in *Giotto. The Santa Maria Novella Crucifix*, eds. Marco Ciatti, Max Seidel. Firenze: Edifir, 2002.

Tartuferi, Angelo. *Masaccio*. Livorno: Sillabe, 2003.

San Marco Church and Convent

Beissel, Stephan. *Fra Angelico*, trans. Chris Murray. New York: Parkstone Press International, 2007.

Danto, Arthur C. *Soul Eyes*. "The Nation", February 6, 2006.

Kanter, Laurence B.; Palladino, Pia. *Fra Angelico*. New York-New Haven: Metropolitan Museum of Art, Yale University Press, 2003.

Spike, John T. *Fra Angelico*. New York: Abbeville Press, 1996.

Santa Apollonia Refectory, Accademia Gallery

Baxandall, Michael. *Painting and Experience in Fifteenth Century Italy*. Oxford: Clarendon Press, 1972.

Santissima Annunziata Church and Cloister

Freedberg, Sydney J. *Painting of the High Renaissance in Rome and Florence*. 2 volumes. Cambridge: Harvard University Press, 1961.

Hall, Marcia B. *Color and Meaning. Practice and Theory in Renaissance Painting* Cambridge-New York: Cambridge University Press, 1992.

Natali, Antonio. *Andrea del Sarto*, trans. Jeffrey Jennings. New York: Abbeville Press, 1999.

Shearman, John K.G. "Leonardo's Color and Chiaroscuro". *Zeitschrift fur Kunstgeschichte*, XXV, 1962, 13-47.

Shearman, John K.G. *Andrea del Sarto*, 2 volumes. Oxford: Clarendon Press, 1965.

San Michele Visdomini, Santa Felicita, San Lorenzo, Palazzo Pitti, Palazzo Vecchio

Brock, Maurice. *Bronzino*. Paris: Éditions du Regard, 2002.

Cheney de Girolami, Liana, ed. *Readings in Italian Mannerism*. New York: Peter Lang, 2004.

Costamagna, Philippe. *Pontormo, Catalogue raisonné de l'œuvre peint*. Paris: Gallimard-Electa, 1994.

Franklin, David. *Rosso in Italy. The Italian Career of Rosso Fiorentino*. New Haven: Yale University Press, 1994.

Franklin, David. *Painting in Renaissance Florence, 1500-1550. "Spirit, Beauty, and Perfection"*. New Haven: Yale University Press, 2001.

Freedberg, Sydney J. *Painting in Italy, 1500-1600*. Harmondsworth: Penguin Books, 1983.

Friedlaender, Walter. *Mannerism and Anti-Mannerism in Italian Painting*. New York: Schocken Books, 1965.

Hall, Marcia B. *After Raphael: Painting in Central Italy in the Sixteenth Century*. Cambridge: Cambridge University Press, 1999.

Hauser, Arnold. *Mannerism. The Crisis of the Renaissance & the Origin of Modern Art*. New York, Knopf, 1965.

Nigro, Salvatore, ed. *Pontormo, Paintings and Frescoes*, trans. Karin H. Ford. New York: Henry N. Abrams, 1994.

Partridge, Loren W. *Art of Renaissance in Florence, 1400-1600*. Berkeley: University of California Press, 2009.

Pilliod, Elizabeth. *Pontormo, Bronzino, Allori. A Genealogy of Florentine Art*. New Haven: Yale University Press, 2001.

Shearman, John K.G. *Mannerism*. Harmondsworth: Penguin Books, 1967.

Smyth, Craig H. *Mannerism and Maniera*. Locust Valley: Augustin, 1963.

Summers, David. "Maniera and Movement: The Figura Serpentinata". *The Art Quarterly*, XXXV, 1972, 265-301.

Summers, David. "Contrapposto: Style and Meaning in Renaissance Art". *The Art Bulletin*, LIX, 1977, 336-361.

Historical Sketches

Berenson, Bernard. *Italian Painters of the Renaissance*. London: Phaidon Press, 1953.

Brucker, Gene A., ed. *Two Memoirs of Renaissance Florence. The Diaries of Buonaccorso Pitti and Gregorio Dati*, trans. Julia Martines. New York: Harper & Row, 1967.

Brucker, Gene A. *Florence. The Golden Age, 1138-1737*. Berkeley: University of California Press, 1998.

Cole, Bruce. *The Renaissance Artist at Work: From Pisano to Titian*. New York: Harper & Row, 1983.

Cole, Bruce. *Italian Art, 1250-1550. The Relation of Renaissance Art to Life and Society*. New York: Harper & Row, 1987.

Kaborycha, Lisa. *A Short History of the Renaissance*. Upper Saddle River: Prentice Hall, 2011.

Kempers, Bram. *Painting, Power and Patronage. The Rise of the Professional Artist in Renaissance Italy*, trans. Beverley Jackson. New York: Allen Lane, 1992.

Levy, Michael. *Florence, A Portrait*. Cambridge: Harvard University Press, 1996.

Shearman, John K.G. *"Only Connect...". Art and the Spectator in the Italian Renaissance*. Princeton: Princeton University Press, 1992.

Vasari, Giorgio. *Lives of the Painters, Sculptors and Architects*, 2 volumes, trans. Gaston du C. de Vere. New York: Alfred A. Knopf, 1996; reprint of 1912 ed.

Index of Illustrations, Photo Credits

Orsanmichele

Santa Maria del Carmine, Brancacci Chapel

Uffizi Gallery

66. Orcagna, *Saint Matthew Tabernacle*. © Studio Fotografico Quattrone, Florence: 88.
67. Lorenzo Monaco, *Coronation of the Virgin*. © Studio Fotografico Quattrone, Florence: 89.
68. Gentile da Fabriano, *Adoration of the Magi*. © Studio Fotografico Quattrone, Florence: 91.
69. Lorenzo Monaco, *Adoration of the Magi*. © Studio Fotografico Quattrone, Florence: 92.
70. Masaccio, Masolino, *Virgin and Child with Saint Anne*. © Studio Fotografico Quattrone, Florence: 94.
71. Fra Angelico, *Coronation of the Virgin*. © Studio Fotografico Quattrone, Florence: 95.
72. Domenico Veneziano, *Santa Lucia de' Magnoli Altarpiece*. © Studio Fotografico Quattrone, Florence: 96.
73. Paolo Uccello, *Battle of San Romano*. © Studio Fotografico Quattrone, Florence: 97.
74. Filippo Lippi, *Coronation of the Virgin*. © Studio Fotografico Quattrone, Florence: 99.
75. Filippo Lippi, *Madonna and Child with Two Angels*. © Studio Fotografico Quattrone, Florence: 100.
76. Filippino Lippi, *Madonna Adoring the Child*. © Studio Fotografico Quattrone, Florence: 101.
77. Filippino Lippi, *Adoration of the Magi*. © Studio Fotografico Quattrone, Florence: 102.
78. Sandro Botticelli, *Fortitude*. © Studio Fotografico Quattrone, Florence: 103.
79. Sandro Botticelli, *Adoration of the Magi*. © Studio Fotografico Quattrone, Florence: 104.
80. Sandro Botticelli, *Primavera*. © Studio Fotografico Quattrone, Florence: 106.
81. Sandro Botticelli, *Flora*, detail of fig. 80. © Studio Fotografico Quattrone, Florence: 107.
82. Sandro Botticelli, *Birth of Venus*. © Studio Fotografico Quattrone, Florence: 108-9.
83. Sandro Botticelli, *Annunciation*. © Studio Fotografico Quattrone, Florence: 110.
84. Domenico Ghirlandaio, *Adoration of the Magi*. © Studio Fotografico Quattrone, Florence: 111.
85. Leonardo da Vinci, *Annunciation*. © Studio Fotografico Quattrone, Florence: 112-13.
86. Andrea del Verrocchio and Leonardo da Vinci, *Baptism of Christ*. © Studio Fotografico Quattrone, Florence: 115.
87. Leonardo, *Adoration of the Magi*. © Studio Fotografico Quattrone, Florence: 117.
88. Leonardo, *Mona Lisa*, Louvre, Paris. © Studio Fotografico Quattrone, Florence: 118.
89. Pietro Perugino, *Madonna Enthroned with Saints*. © Studio Fotografico Quattrone, Florence: 119.
90. Michelangelo, *Doni Tondo*. © Studio Fotografico Quattrone, Florence: 120.
91. Leonardo, *Virgin and Child with Saint Anne*, drawing, National Gallery, London. © National Gallery, London / Art Resource, NY: 121
92. Fra Bartolomeo, *Vision of Saint Bernard*. © Studio Fotografico Quattrone, Florence: 123.
93. Andrea del Sarto, *Madonna of the Harpies*. © Studio Fotografico Quattrone, Florence: 125.
94. Raphael, *Madonna of the Goldfinch*. © Studio Fotografico Quattrone, Florence: 126.
95. Rosso Fiorentino, *Madonna and Child with Saints*. © Studio Fotografico Quattrone, Florence: 127.
96. Rosso Fiorentino, *Moses Defending the Daughters of Jethro*. © Studio Fotografico Quattrone, Florence: 129.
97. Jacopo Pontormo, *Supper at Emmaus*. © Studio Fotografico Quattrone, Florence: 131.
98. Agnolo Bronzino, *Lamentation with Mary Magdalene*. © Studio Fotografico Quattrone, Florence: 132.
99. Agnolo Bronzino, *Holy Family*. © Studio Fotografico Quattrone, Florence: 133.

Santa Maria Novella Church and Museum

100. Santa Maria Novella, view of nave and the major chapel. © Studio Fotografico Quattrone, Florence: 134.
101. Giotto, Painted Crucifix. © Studio Fotografico Quattrone, Florence: 135.
102. Strozzi di Mantova Chapel. © Studio Fotografico Quattrone, Florence: 137.
103. Nardo di Cione, *The Blessed, Last Judgment*, detail of fig. 102. © Studio Fotografico Quattrone, Florence: 138.
104. Nardo di Cione, *The Damned, Last Judgement*, detail of fig. 102. © Studio Fotografico Quattrone, Florence: 139.

105. Andrea Orcagna, *Redeemer Enthroned with Madonna and Saints*, Strozzi di Mantova Chapel. © Studio Fotografico Quattrone, Florence: 141.
106. Masaccio, *Trinity*. © Studio Fotografico Quattrone, Florence: 143.
107. Domenico Ghirlandaio, *Birth of the Virgin*, Tornabuoni Chapel. © Studio Fotografico Quattrone, Florence: 144.
108. Domenico Ghirlandaio, *Birth of John the Baptist*. © Studio Fotografico Quattrone, Florence: 145.
109. Filippino Lippi, *Saint Philip and the Dragon*, Strozzi Chapel. © Studio Fotografico Quattrone, Florence: 146.
110. Giorgio Vasari, *Resurrection with Saints*. © Studio Fotografico Quattrone, Florence: 148.
111. Andrea da Firenze, *Path to Salvation*, Spanish Chapel. © Studio Fotografico Quattrone, Florence: 149.
112. Andrea da Firenze, *Triumph of Saint Thomas*, Spanish Chapel. © Studio Fotografico Quattrone, Florence: 150.
113. Paolo Uccello, *Deluge*, Green Cloister. © Studio Fotografico Quattrone, Florence: 152.

San Marco Church and Convent

114. Fra Angelico, Lorenzo Monaco, *Deposition*. © Studio Fotografico Quattrone, Florence: 158.
115. Fra Angelico, *Annunciation*. © Studio Fotografico Quattrone, Florence: 159.
116. Domenico Ghirlandaio, *Last Supper*. Scala / Ministero per i Beni e le Attività culturali / Art Resource, NY: 160
117. Fra Bartolomeo, *Virgin and Child with Saint Anne and Saints*. © Studio Fotografico Quattrone, Florence: 162.

Santa Apollonia Refectory

View of the Refectory: courtesy Institute for the Study of Western Civilisation: 163.
118. Andrea del Castagno, *Last Supper*. © Studio Fotografico Quattrone, Florence: 164-65.

Accademia Gallery

119. Filippino Lippi, Pietro Perugino, *Deposition*. © Studio Fotografico Quattrone, Florence: 167.

Santissima Annunziata Church and Cloister

View of the Cloister. © Studio Fotografico Quattrone, Florence: 168.
120. Andrea del Sarto, *Curing of the Possessed Woman*. © Studio Fotografico Quattrone, Florence: 169.
121. Andrea del Sarto, *Journey of the Magi*. © Studio Fotografico Quattrone, Florence: 171.
122. Andrea del Sarto, *Birth of the Virgin*. © Studio Fotografico Quattrone, Florence: 173.
123. Franciabigio, *Marriage of the Virgin*. © Studio Fotografico Quattrone, Florence: 175.
124. Jacopo Pontormo, *Visitation*. © Studio Fotografico Quattrone, Florence: 177.
125. Rosso Fiorentino, *Assumption of the Virgin*. © Studio Fotografico Quattrone, Florence: 178.

San Michele Visdomini

126. Jacopo Pontormo, *Madonna and Child with Saints*. © Studio Fotografico Quattrone, Florence: 181.

Santa Felicita

127. Jacopo Pontormo, *Deposition*. © Studio Fotografico Quattrone, Florence: 183.

San Lorenzo

128. Rosso Fiorentino, *Marriage of the Virgin*. © Studio Fotografico Quattrone, Florence: 186.
129. Agnolo Bronzino, *Martyrdom of Saint Lawrence*. © Studio Fotografico Quattrone, Florence: 187.

Pitti Palace, Galleria Palatina

130. Raphael, *Madonna del Baldacchino*. © Studio Fotografico Quattrone, Florence: 190.
131. Fra Bartolomeo, *Mystic Marriage of Saint Catherine*. © Studio Fotografico Quattrone, Florence: 191.
132. Fra Bartolomeo, *Salvator Mundi*. Scala / Ministero per i Beni e le Attività culturali / Art Resource, NY: 193
133. Rosso Fiorentino, *Dei Altarpiece*. © Studio Fotografico Quattrone, Florence: 194.

134. Andrea del Sarto, *Panciatichi Assumption*. © Studio Fotografico Quattrone, Florence: 196.
135. Andrea del Sarto, *Passerini Assumption*. © Studio Fotografico Quattrone, Florence: 197.

Palazzo Vecchio

136. Giorgio Vasari, *Taking of the Tower of San Vincenzo*. Salone dei Cinquecento. © Studio Fotografico Quattrone, Florence: 202-3.
137. Francesco Salviati, *Triumph of Furius Camillus*. © Studio Fotografico Quattrone, Florence: 204-5.
138. Agnolo Bronzino, *Crossing of the Red Sea*. © Studio Fotografico Quattrone, Florence: 206-7.
139. Bronzino, *Lamentation*. © Studio Fotografico Quattrone, Florence: 208.
140. Alessandro Allori, *Pearl Fishing*. © Studio Fotografico Quattrone, Florence: 210.

Addendum

141. Donatello, *The Prophet Abacuc (Zuccone)*, Museo dell'Opera del Duomo. © Studio Fotografico Quattrone, Florence: 214.
142. Andrea del Sarto, *John the Baptist Preaching*, Cloister of the Scalzo. © Studio Fotografico Quattrone, Florence: 214.
143. Color Wheel. Courtesy of Don Jusko, Owner at Real Color Wheel: 215
144. Lorenzo Monaco, *Coronation of the Virgin*, detail of fig. 67. © Studio Fotografico Quattrone, Florence: 216.
145. Fra Angelico, Lorenzo Monaco, *Deposition*, detail of fig. 114. © Studio Fotografico Quattrone, Florence: 217.
146. Filippo Lippi, *Coronation of the Virgin*, detail of fig. 74. © Studio Fotografico Quattrone, Florence: 218.
147. Perspective Diagram: © Francesco Bertini: 221.

Printed in Italy
by Edizioni Polistampa
Florence
2015

hachette
JEUNESSE

Directeur : Antoine Béon
Fabrication : Marine Wiplier
Responsable éditoriale : Adélaïde Lebuy
Responsable artistique : Pauline Ortlieb
Graphiste : Glen Le Boulicaut
Édition : Stéphanie Go
Adaptation des textes : Christophe Rosson
Mise en page : Émilie Laudrin

Les 101 Dalmatiens, d'après *The Hundred and One Dalmatians* de Dodie Smith, publié par *The Viking Press.*

Édité par Hachette Livre - 58, rue Jean Bleuzen – 92178 Vanves Cedex
Imprimé par Rotolito en Italie – Achevé d'imprimer : janvier 2022
ISBN : 978-2-01-714639-1 – Édition : 02 – Dépôt légal : septembre 2021

Loi n°49-956 du 16 juillet 1949 sur les publications destinées à la jeunesse.
Pour tout renseignement concernant nos parutions, nous contacter
par e-mail : disney@hachette-livre.fr

Disney

HISTOIRES à lire avec MON PAPA

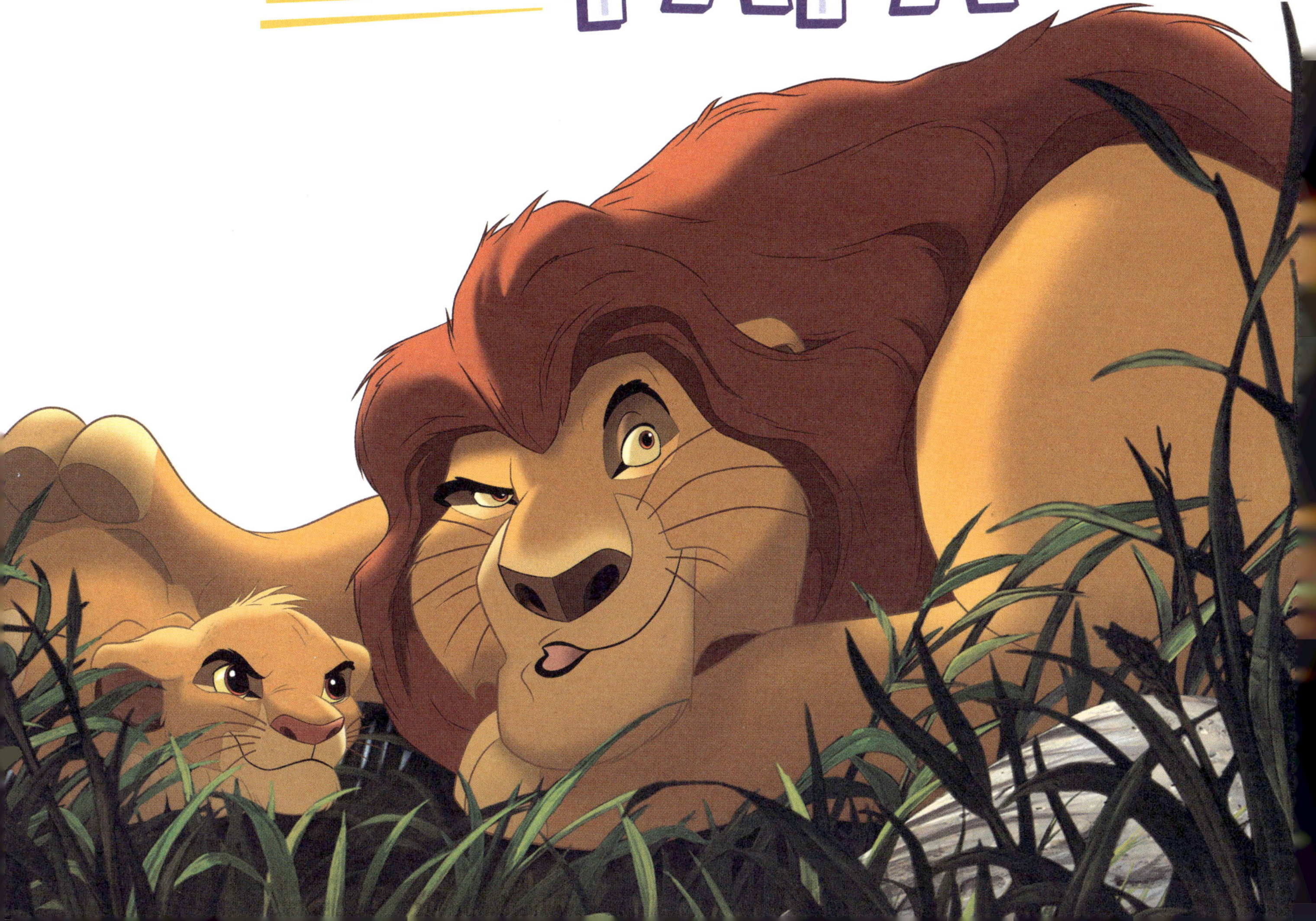

SOMMAIRE

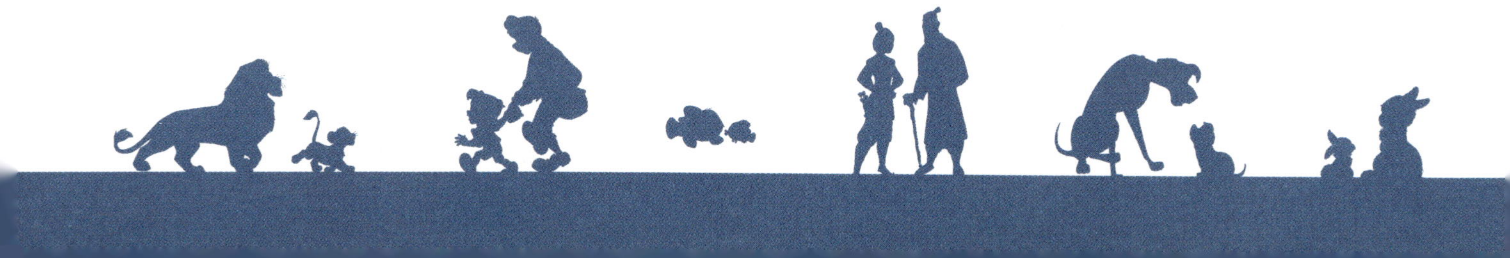

Disney

LE ROI LION

Devenir roi COMME PAPA

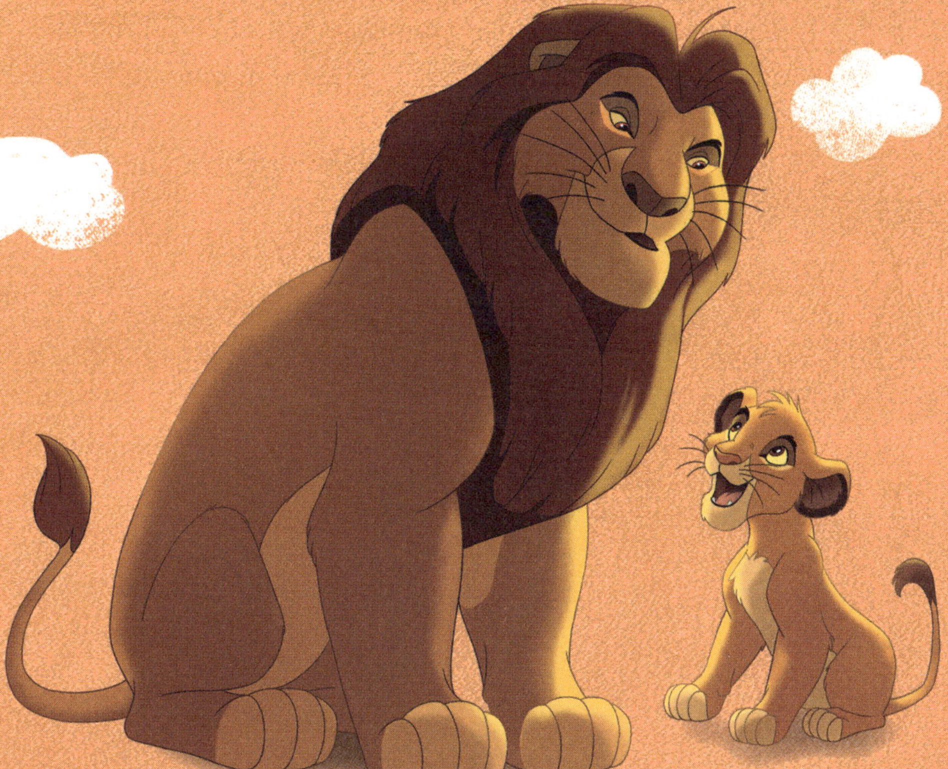

Un nouveau jour se lève sur la Terre des Lions. Simba et Nala ont hâte d'aller jouer.

– Et si on allait se baigner à la rivière ? propose Nala.

– Pas si fort ! lui dit Simba. Si Zazu nous entend, il va m'obliger à faire **mes devoirs de prince...**

Hélas, au même instant, le calao se pose devant le lionceau.

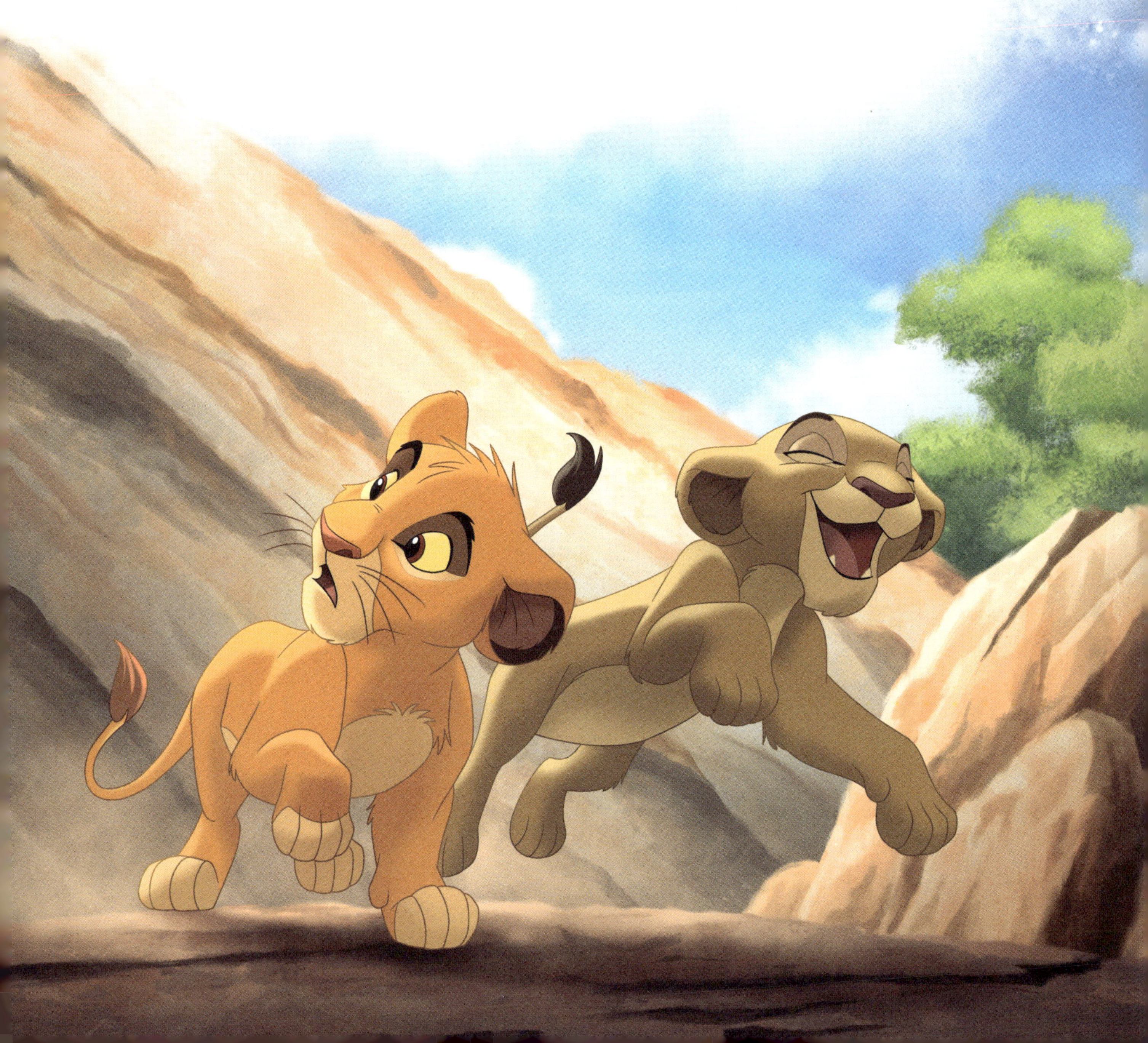

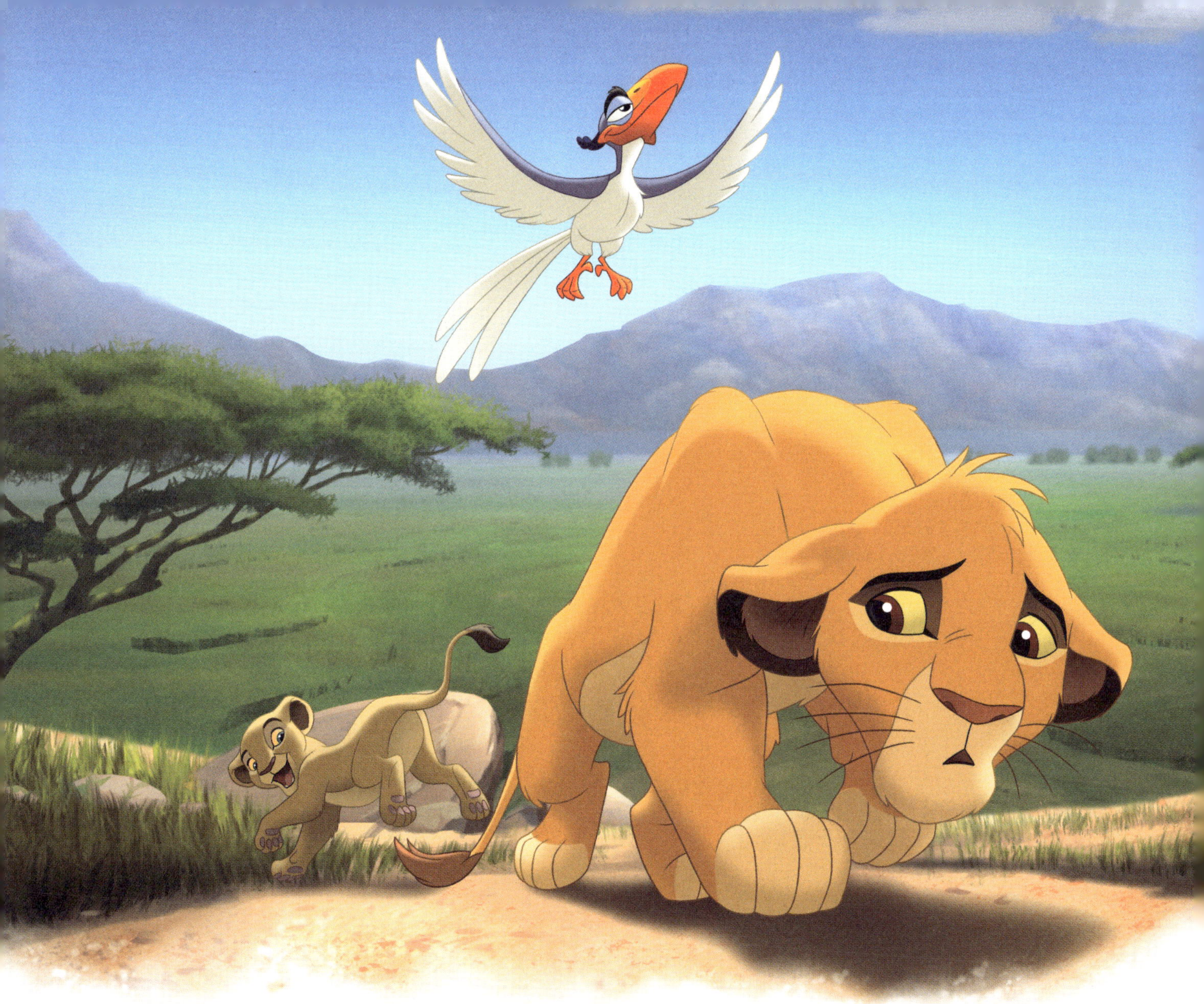

– Suivez-moi, jeune sire, déclare l'oiseau multicolore. Une longue **journée de travail** nous attend.

– C'est que… j'avais prévu de m'amuser avec Nala, râle Simba.

Mais son amie s'éloigne déjà.

– Amuse-toi plutôt avec Zazu ! rigole Nala. À demain, Simba.

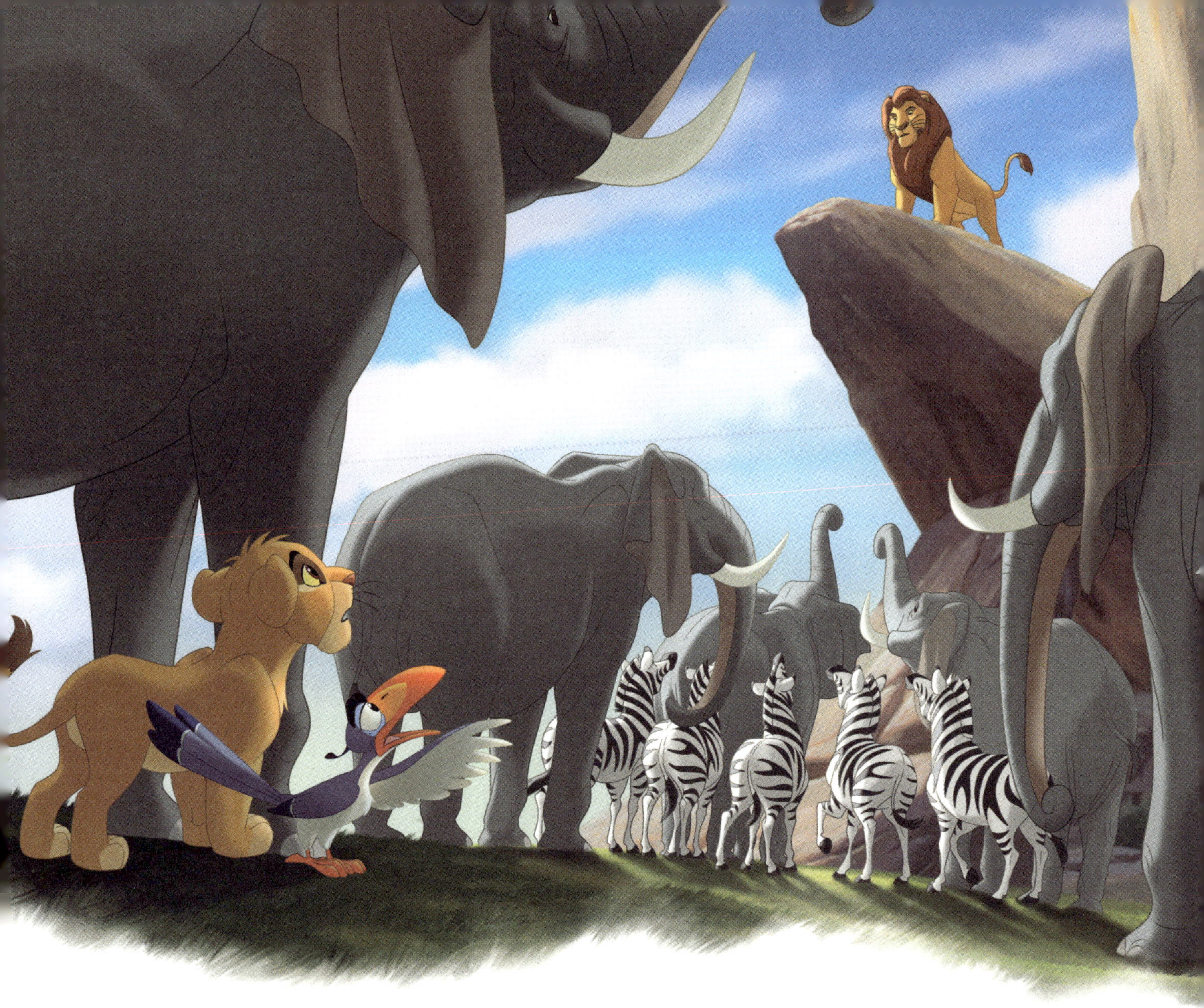

Après avoir réglé une querelle entre les antilopes et les rhinocéros, Zazu conduit Simba au Rocher du Lion. Là, Mufasa est en train d'écouter les problèmes que viennent lui confier ses sujets.

Quoi de mieux, pour apprendre à devenir le roi, que de regarder comment se comporte... **le roi de la savane !**

Au bout de quelques minutes, Zazu explique à Simba :

– Un roi doit écouter tout le monde. Les plus gros animaux comme les plus petits. C'est ainsi qu'il gagne le respect de tous ses sujets.

Simba est émerveillé.

« Quand je serai grand, songe-t-il, j'espère être **aussi fort et respectable** que mon papa ! »

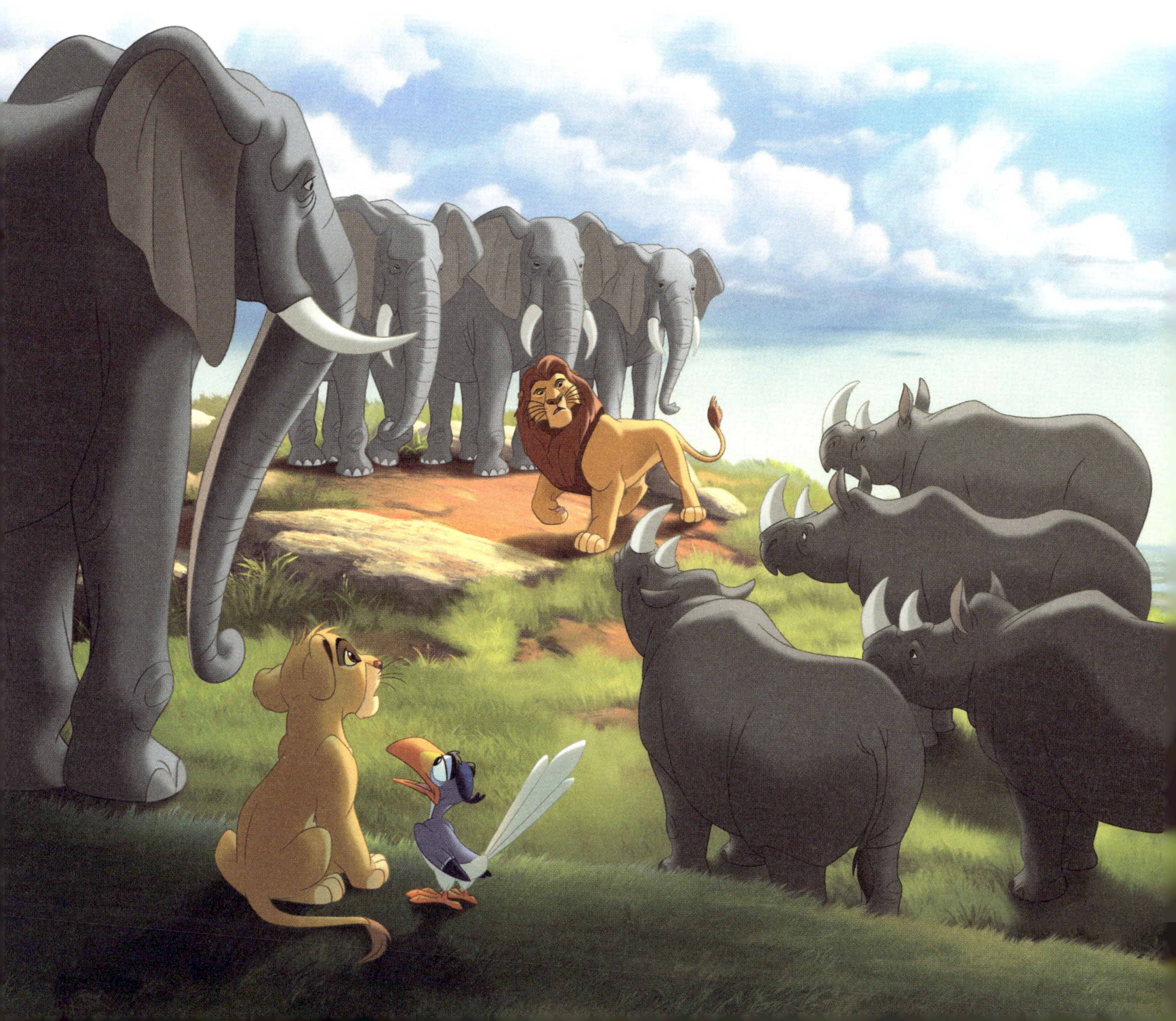

Mais la séance s'éternise... et Simba commence à s'ennuyer. Le voilà qui **se met à bâiller !**

– Cela ne va pas du tout, Votre Altesse, le gronde Zazu. Avez-vous seulement écouté ce que votre père a conseillé aux éléphants ?

– Euh..., hésite Simba. Pas tout...

– Suivez-moi, nous avons encore à faire !

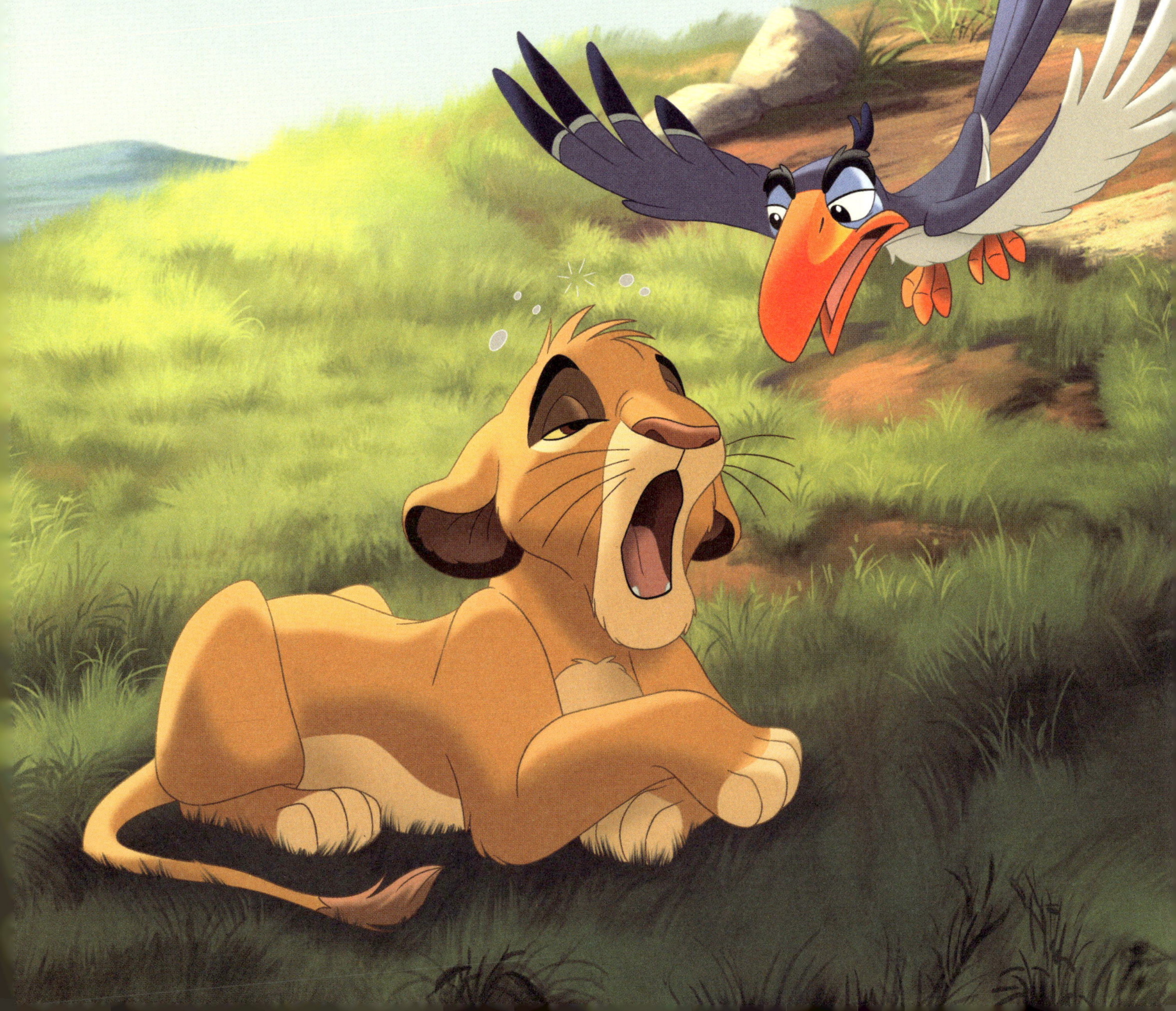

Zazu entraîne Simba vers la rivière, à l'endroit même où le lionceau avait prévu de venir s'amuser avec Nala.

Soudain, **un cri retentit !**

– Tu as entendu ça, Zazu ? s'inquiète Simba.

– Non, quoi ? répond le volatile.

Un nouveau cri résonne alors.

– Ça venait de la rivière, s'alarme Simba. Suis-moi !

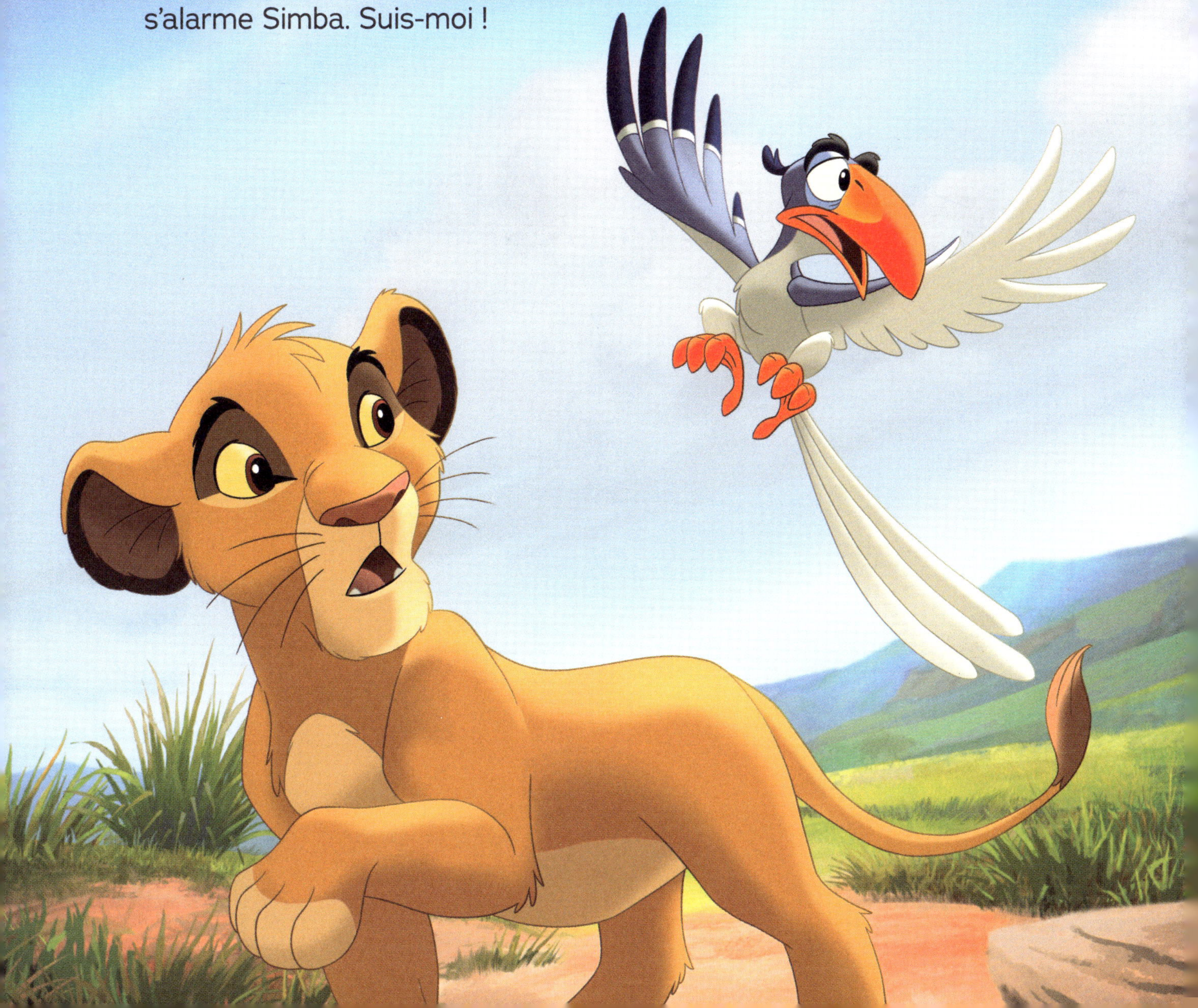

Simba ne s'est pas trompé. Ce sont **les cris de Nala !**

La petite lionne s'est aventurée trop loin dans l'eau.

Et maintenant, le courant l'emporte !

– Va vite chercher mon père, Zazu ! ordonne Simba.

Puis il se tourne vers son amie :

– N'aie pas peur, Nala, on va te sortir de là !

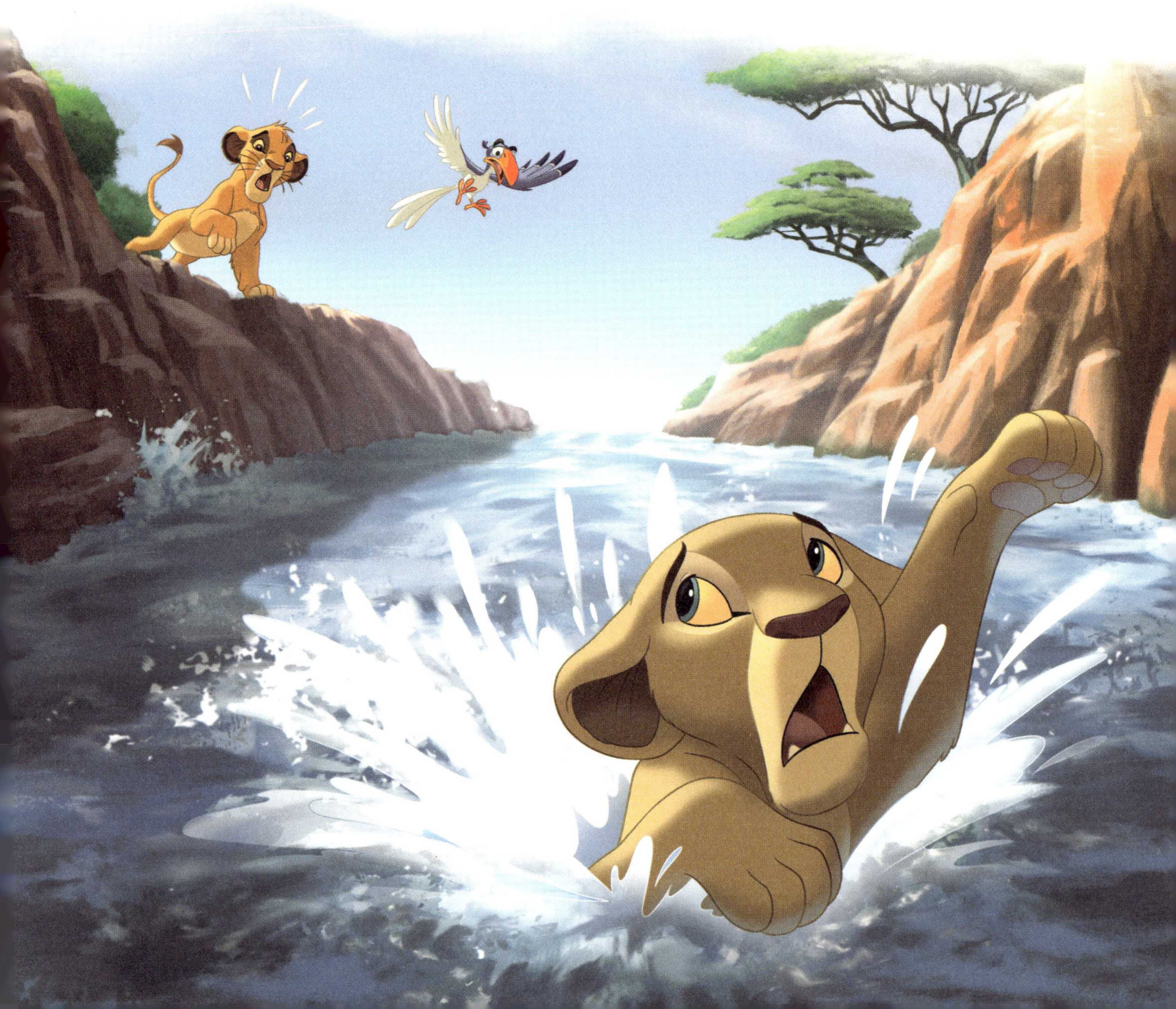

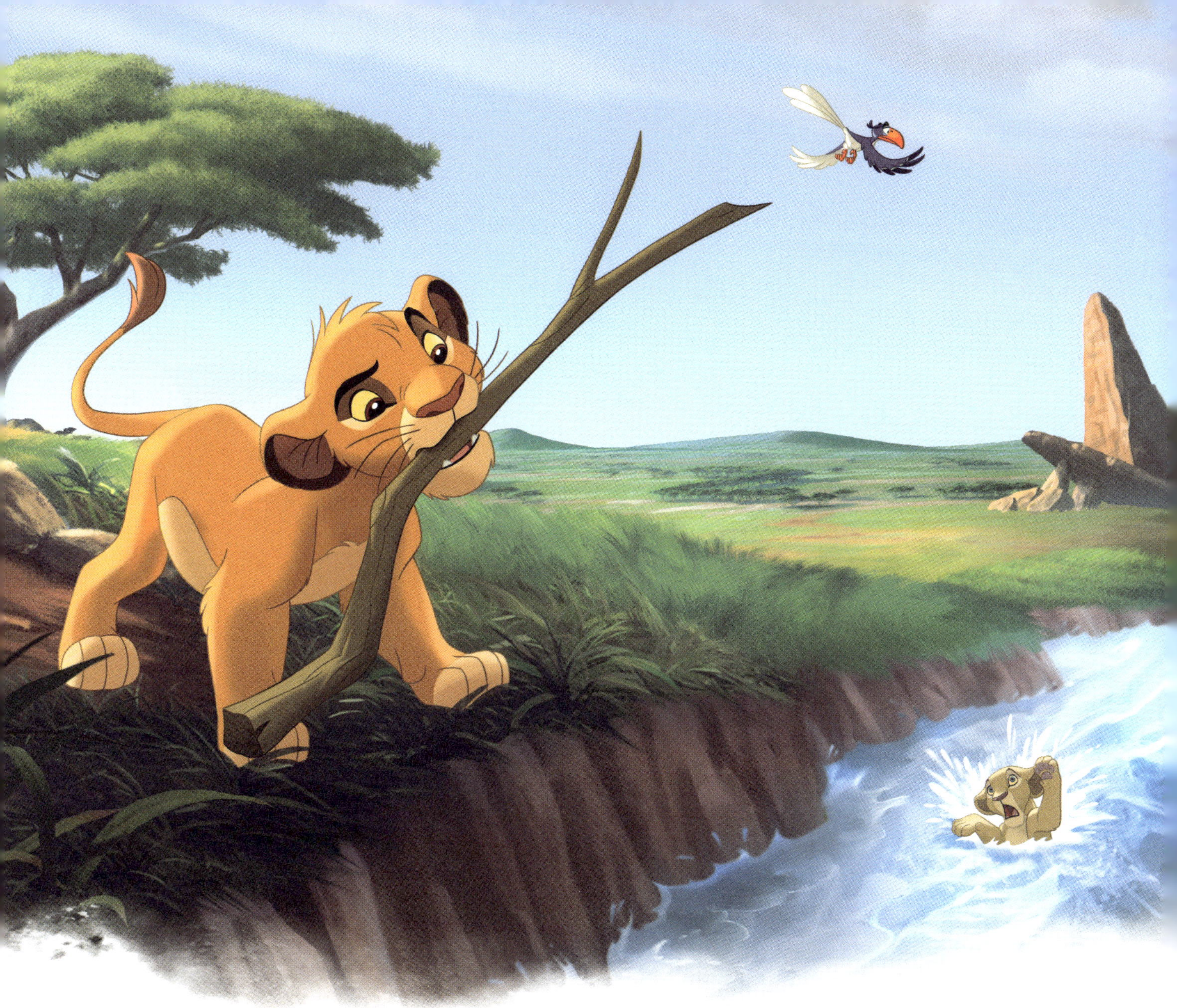

Simba ne reste pas sans rien faire et cherche ce qui pourrait l'aider **à sauver son amie.** Tout à coup, il repère une branche sur la berge. Il court la ramasser puis se précipite au bord de l'eau. Il suffirait que Nala s'y accroche pour qu'il la hisse sur la rive.

Au prix d'un immense effort, Simba réussit à sortir Nala de la rivière déchaînée !

Les deux amis se reposent sur la berge, lorsque Mufasa arrive.

– Simba ! Nala ! s'écrie le roi de la savane. Vous n'avez rien ?

– Non, papa, tout va bien, le rassure Simba.

– **Simba m'a sauvé la vie,** souffle Nala.

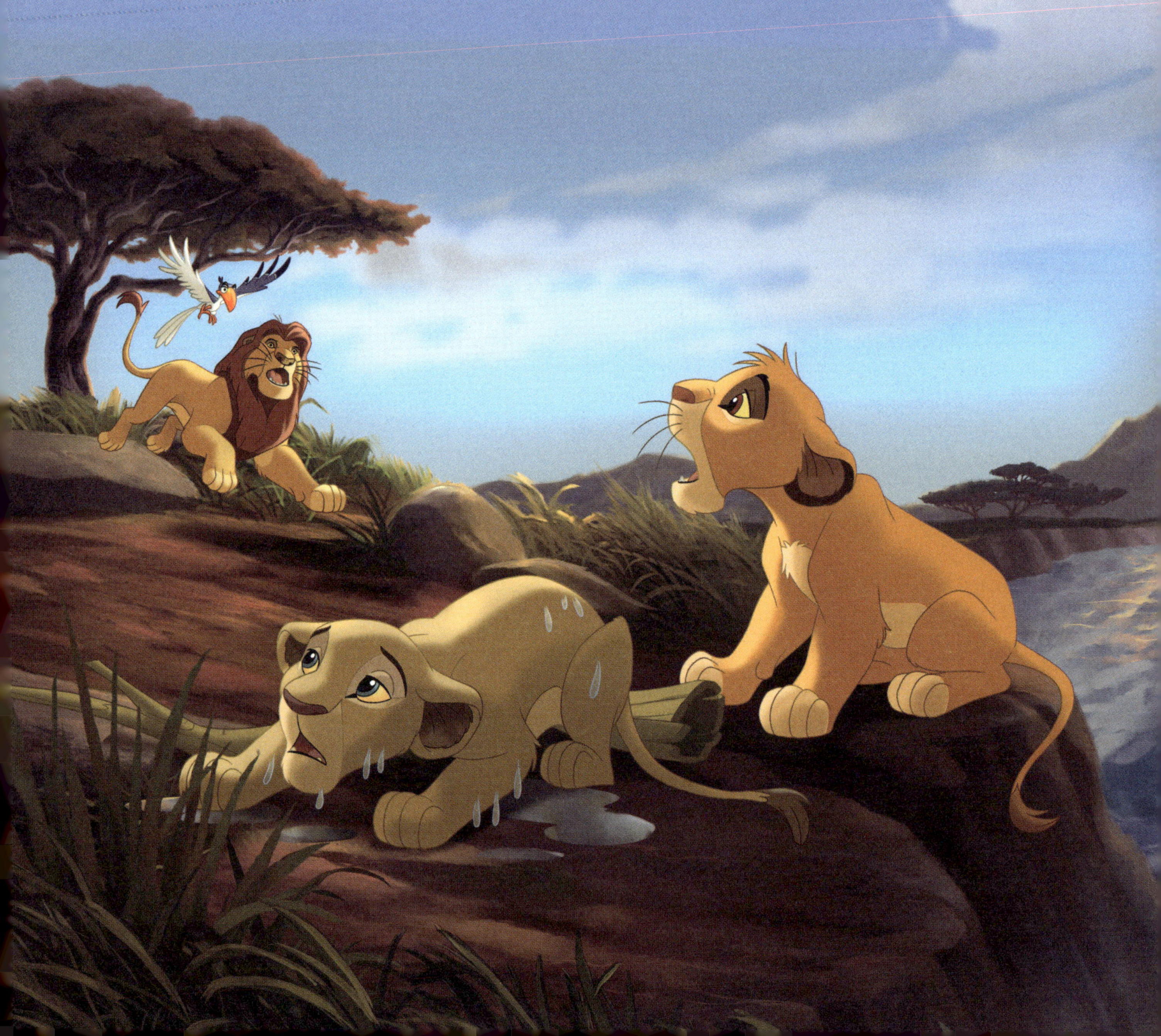

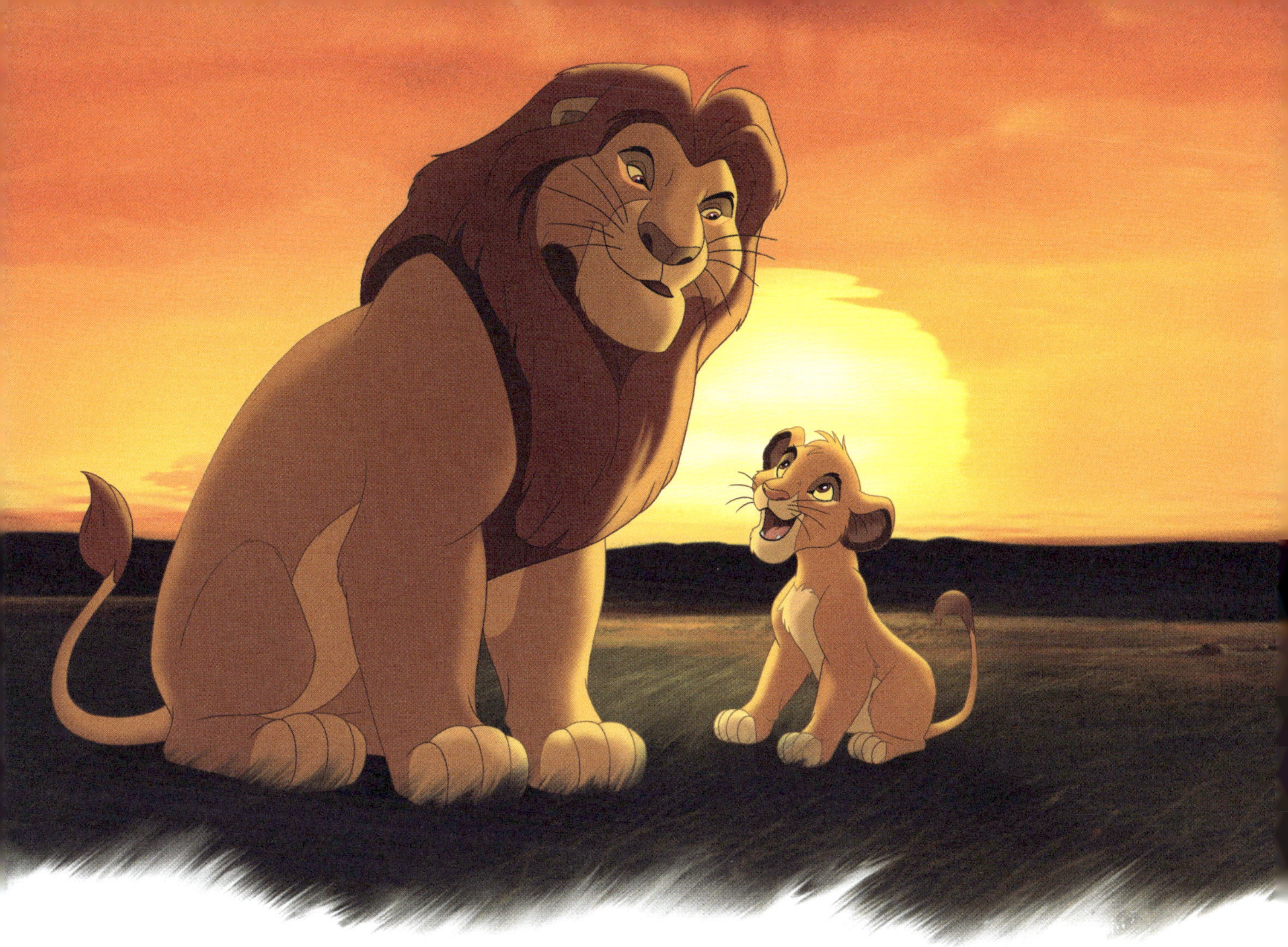

Mufasa, Simba et Nala rentrent ensuite au Rocher du Lion. À leur arrivée, le soleil se couche. Mufasa profite de ce beau moment pour féliciter son fils :

– Simba, aujourd'hui, tu t'es comporté comme un roi. Je suis fier de toi, mon grand.

– Moi aussi, je suis fier **d'avoir un papa comme toi,** déclare Simba.

Disney

Pinocchio

Un vrai PETIT GARÇON

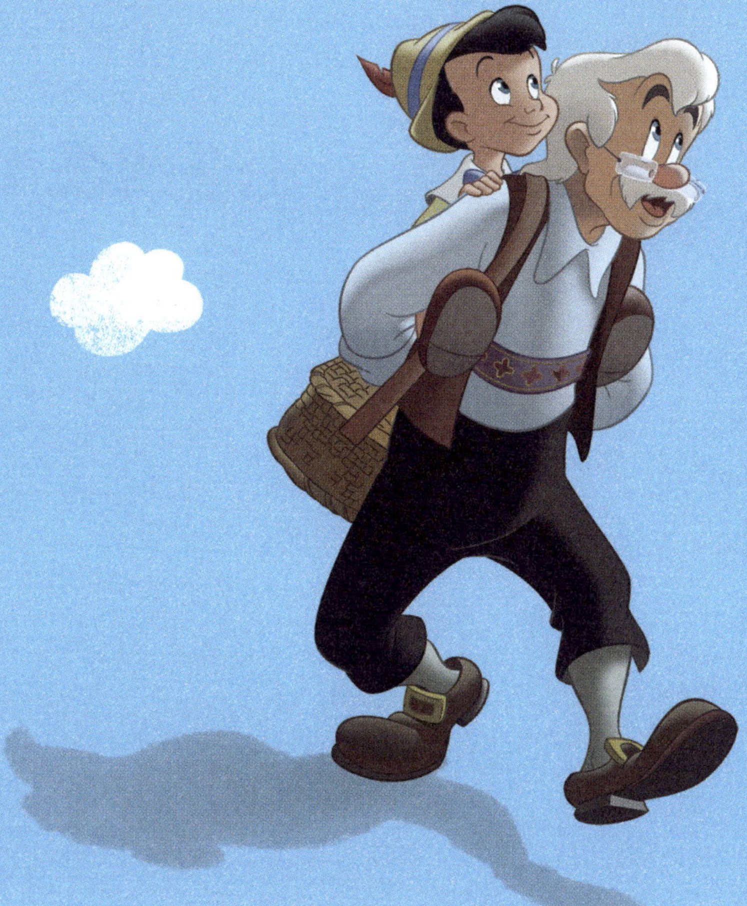

Une nouvelle journée commence dans le petit village où habite Pinocchio. Au saut du lit, la petite marionnette court regarder son reflet dans le miroir.

À sa vue, il éclate de rire : la Fée Bleue a tenu parole, elle a fait de lui **un vrai petit garçon.** Un petit garçon qui est impatient de découvrir sa nouvelle vie !

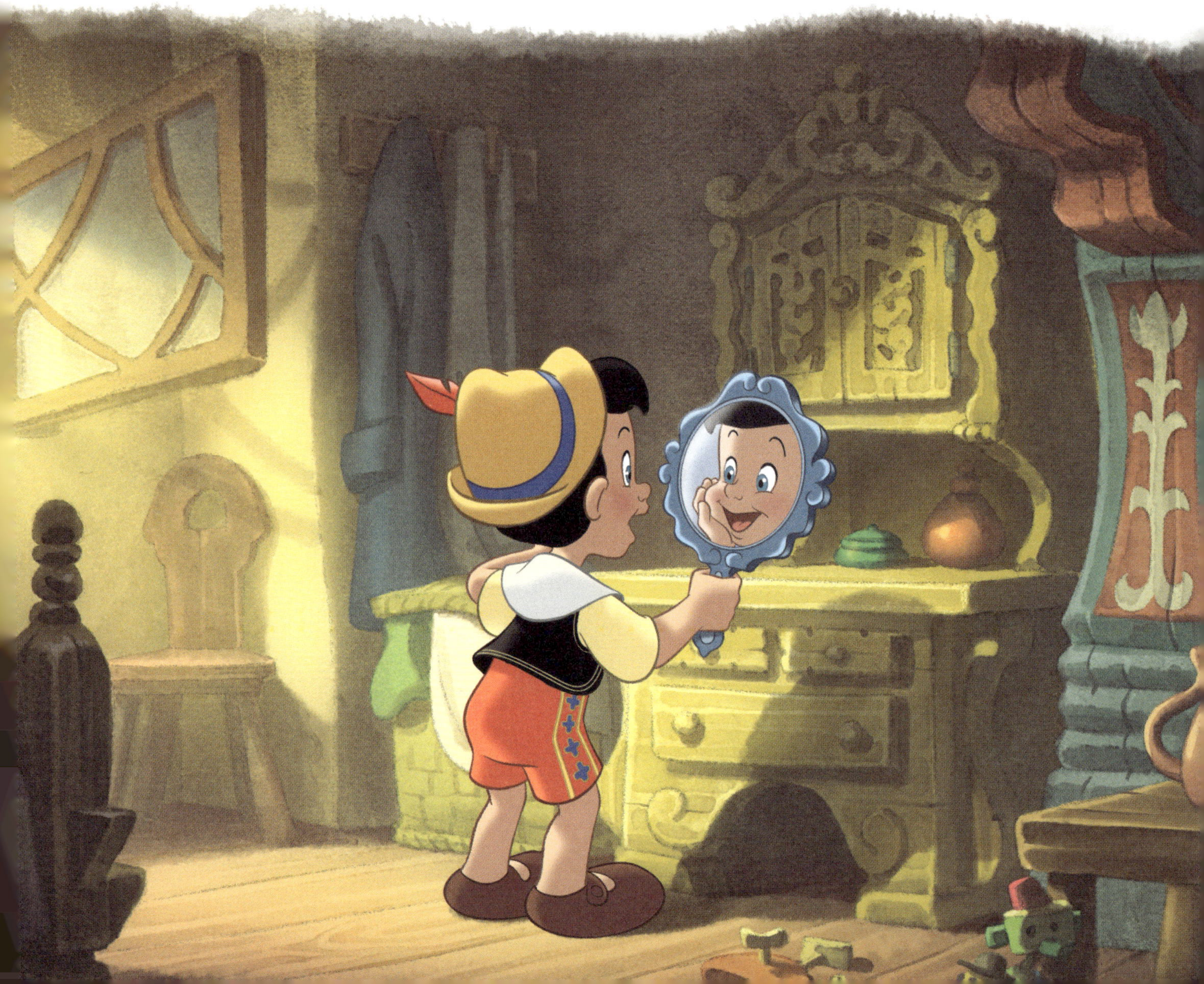

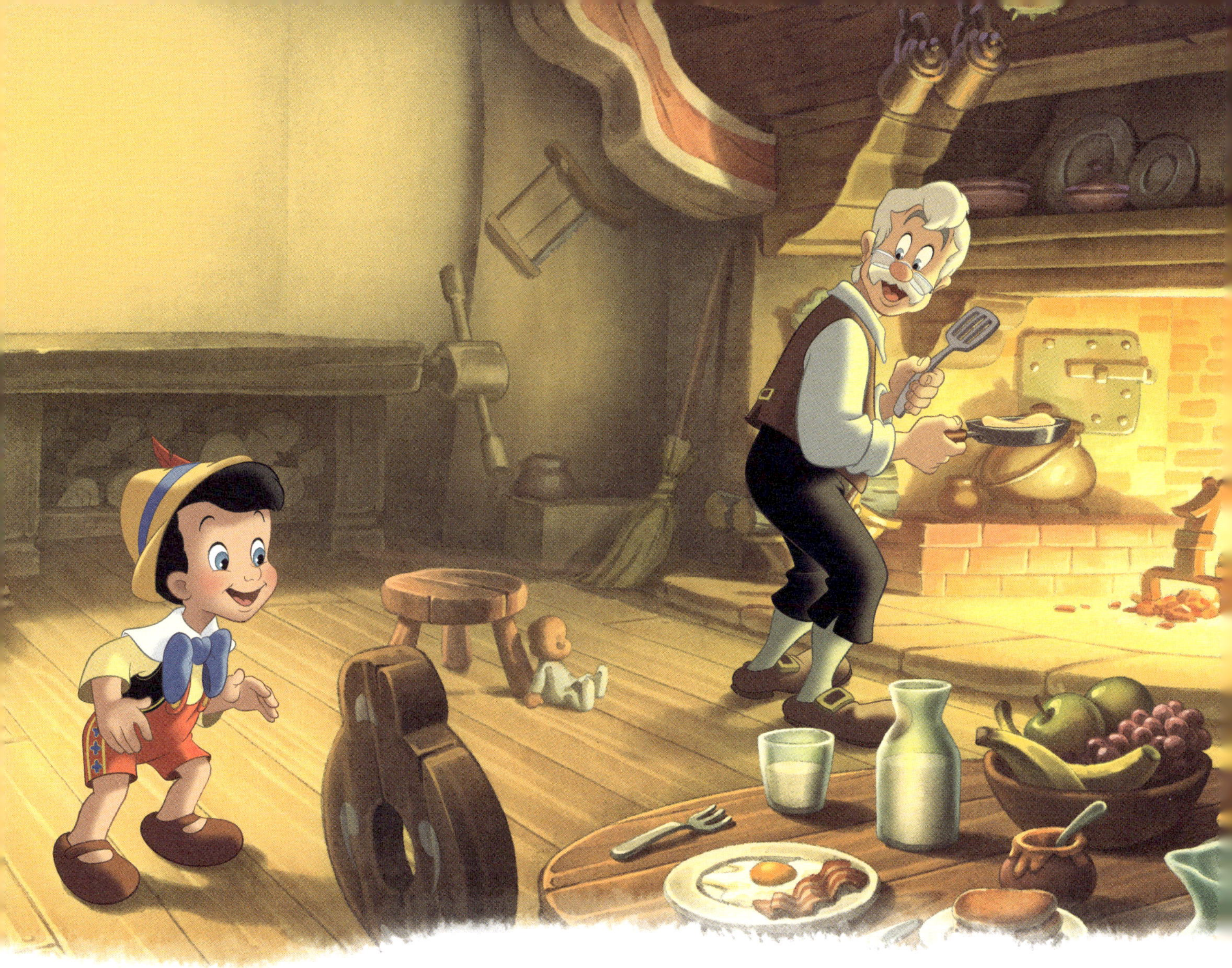

Justement, une délicieuse odeur vient lui chatouiller les narines.

– Pinocchio, à table ! s'écrie alors Geppetto.

Le papa de Pinocchio a préparé **un petit déjeuner de roi :** des œufs, du bacon, des fruits, il ne manque rien !

– Je crois que je vais adorer être un petit garçon ! se réjouit Pinocchio.

– Manger, c'est super ! s'écrie l'enfant. Je pourrais faire ça toute la journée !

Geppetto sourit puis annonce :

– Ça ne va pas être possible, mon fils. Aujourd'hui, j'ai prévu une surprise...

– Une surprise... ? s'étonne Pinocchio.

– Oui, nous allons partir **faire un pique-nique !**

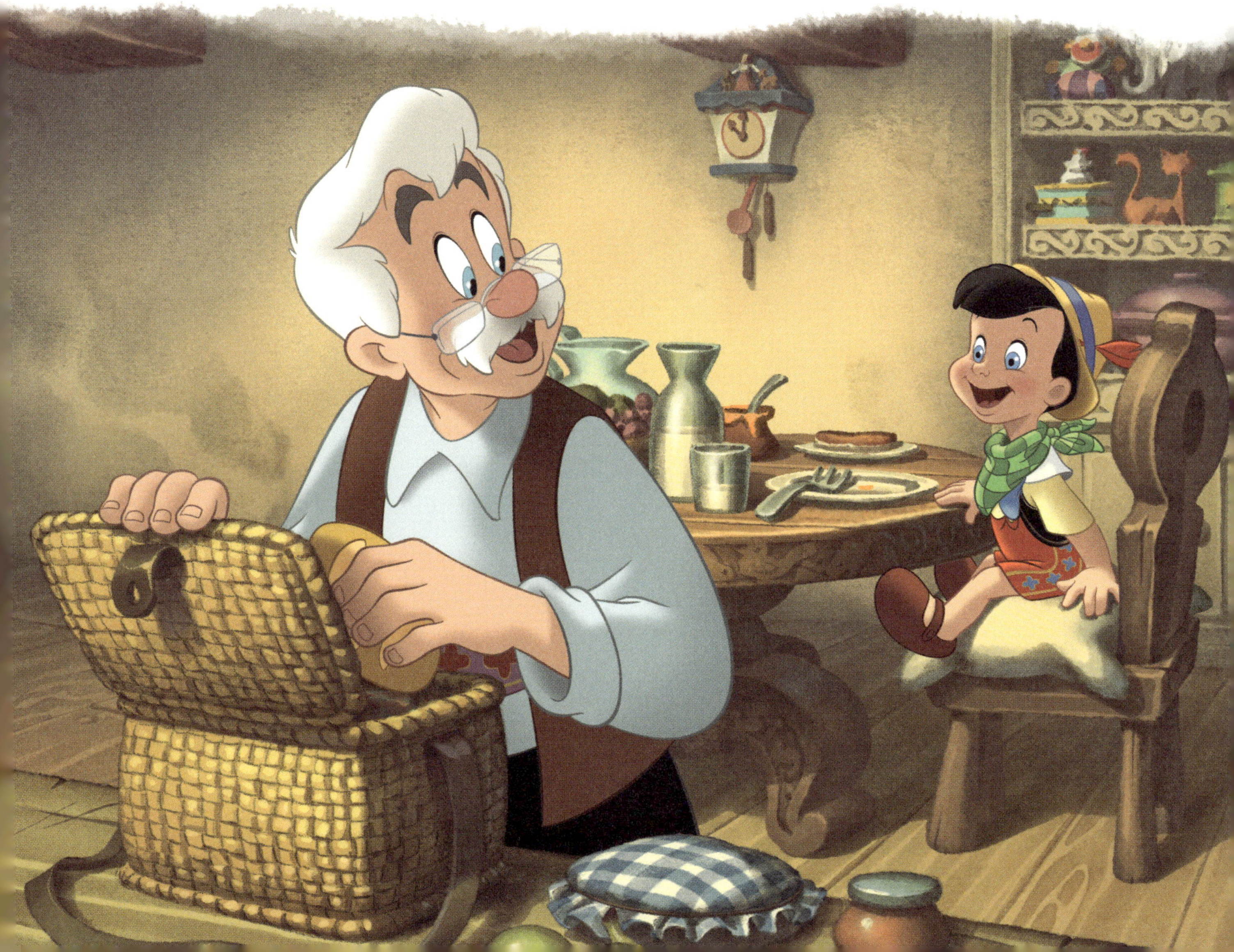

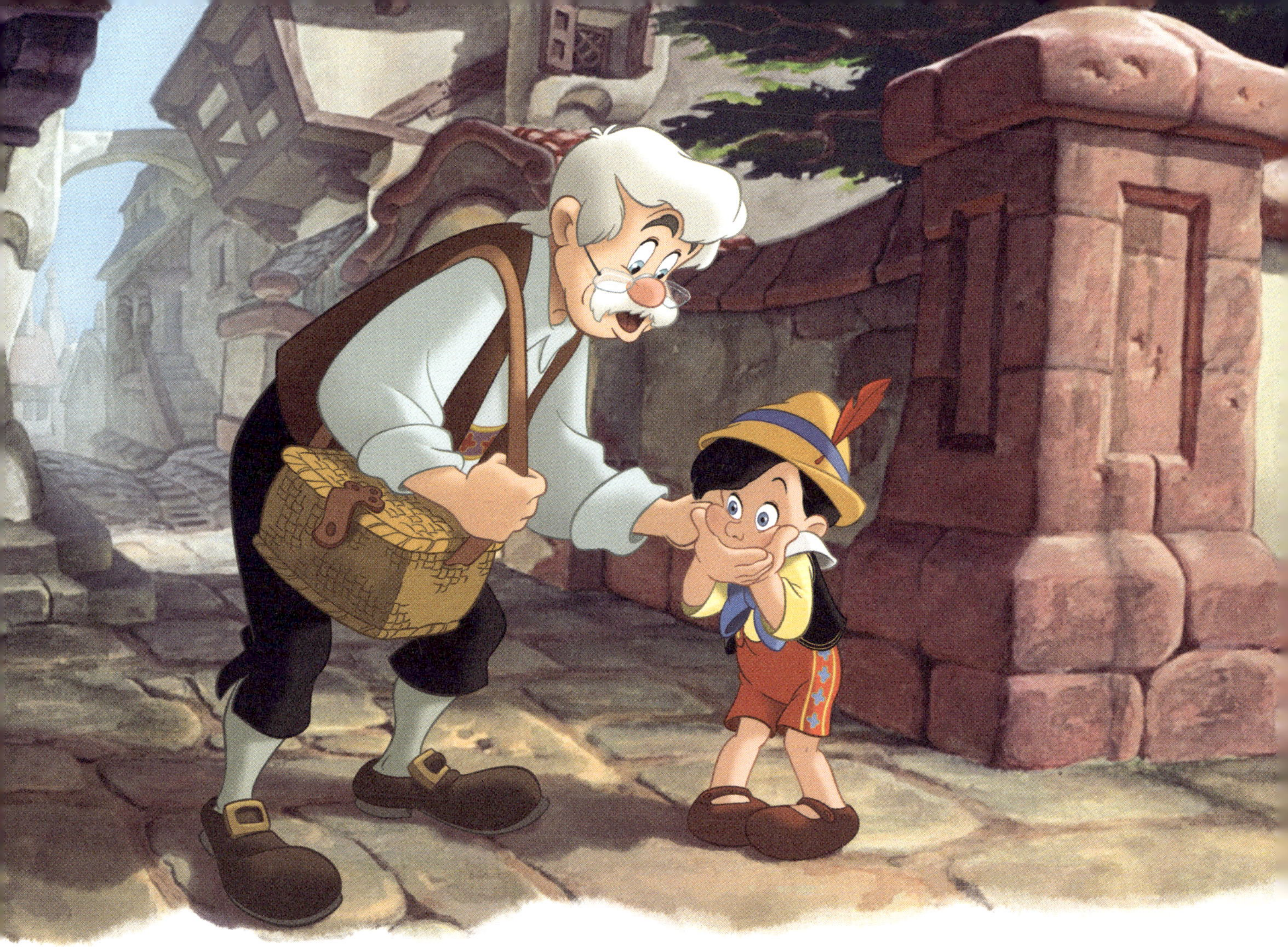

Sur la route, Pinocchio court et bondit dans tous les sens. Il est tellement heureux de **découvrir le monde avec son papa !**

Mais soudain...

– *Hic !* fait Pinocchio. Qu'est-ce qui... *Hic !* m'arrive ? *Hic !*

– Ce n'est rien, tu as le hoquet, voilà tout, le rassure Geppetto. Bloque ta respiration un instant, ça va passer.

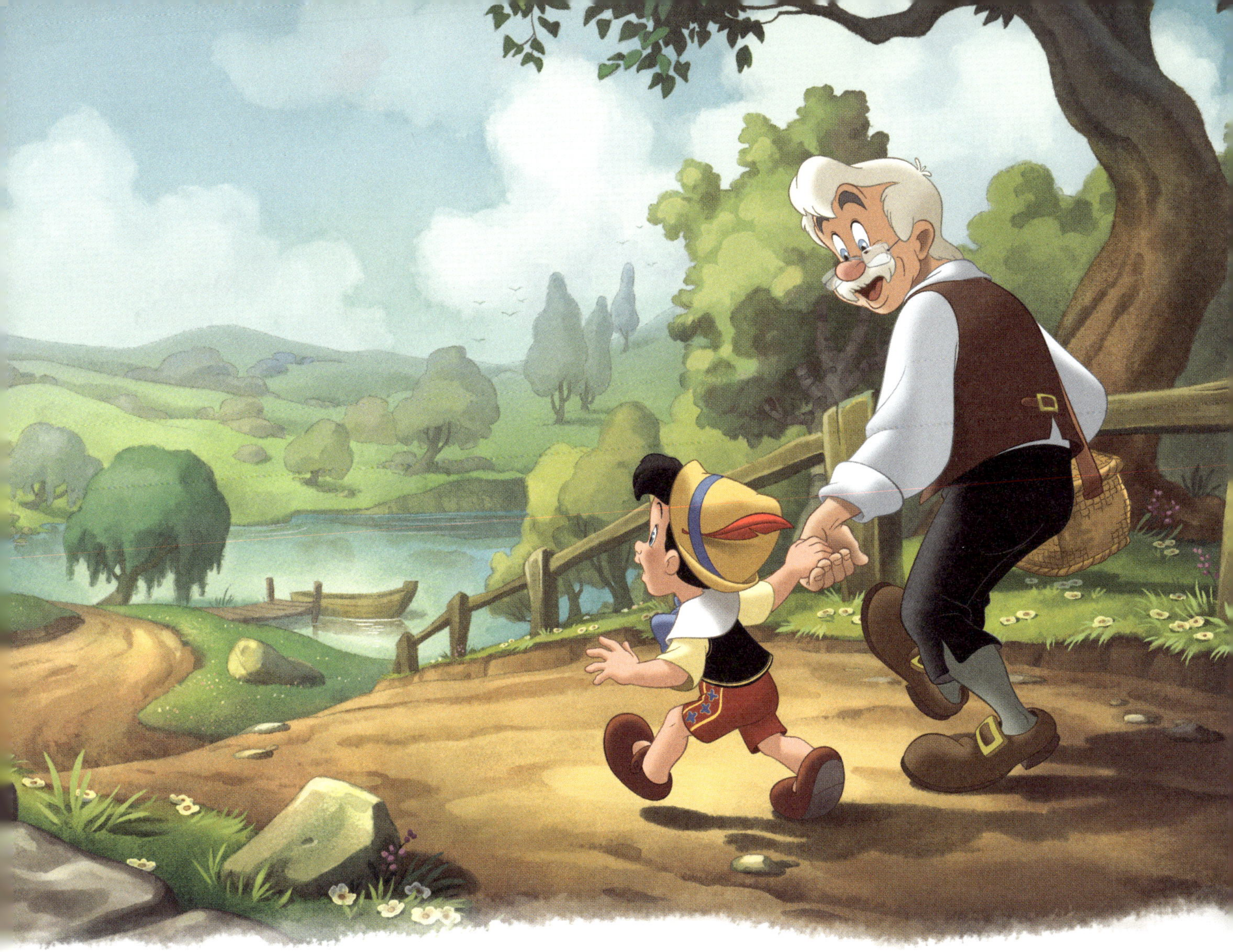

« Être un vrai petit garçon, ce n'est pas toujours rigolo, songe Pinocchio. Heureusement que **mon papa est là pour m'aider…** »

Après avoir marché quelque temps, l'enfant est fatigué.

– On arrive bientôt, papa ? demande-t-il.

– Oui, mon petit, ce n'est plus très loin, lui répond Geppetto.

Le hoquet... la fatigue... décidément, **La vraie vie n'est pas facile !**

Mais Geppetto a prévu un panier rempli de bonnes choses. Le temps d'étaler la nappe par terre, et le papa et son fils peuvent reprendre des forces.

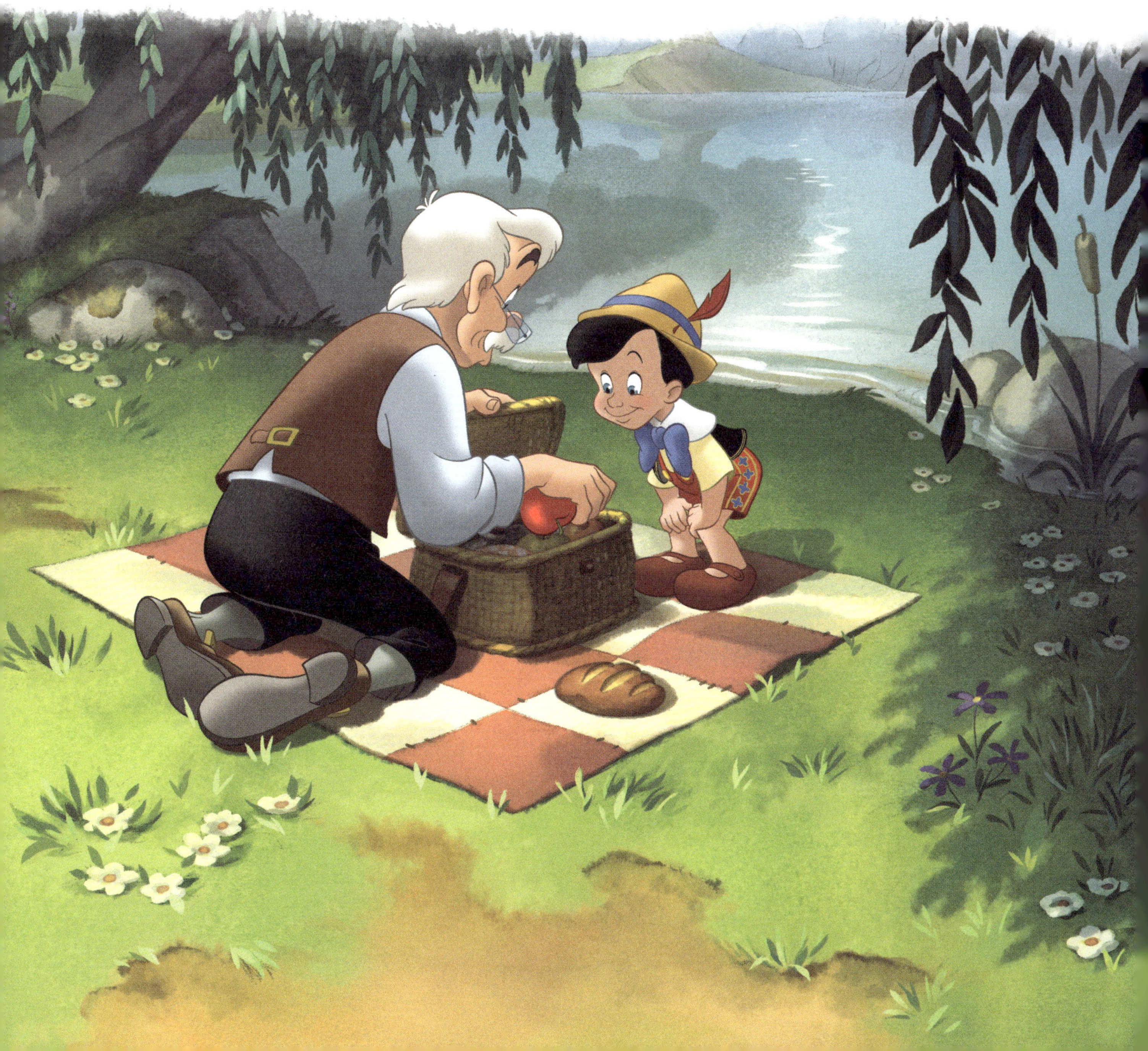

Geppetto et Pinocchio s'amusent ensuite dans la rivière. Ils s'éclaboussent, essaient de pêcher... Quelle journée merveilleuse !

Mais tout à coup, Pinocchio trébuche sur un caillou. Il a les genoux tout éraflés.

Geppetto court aussitôt lui faire **un bisou magique.** La douleur est déjà envolée !

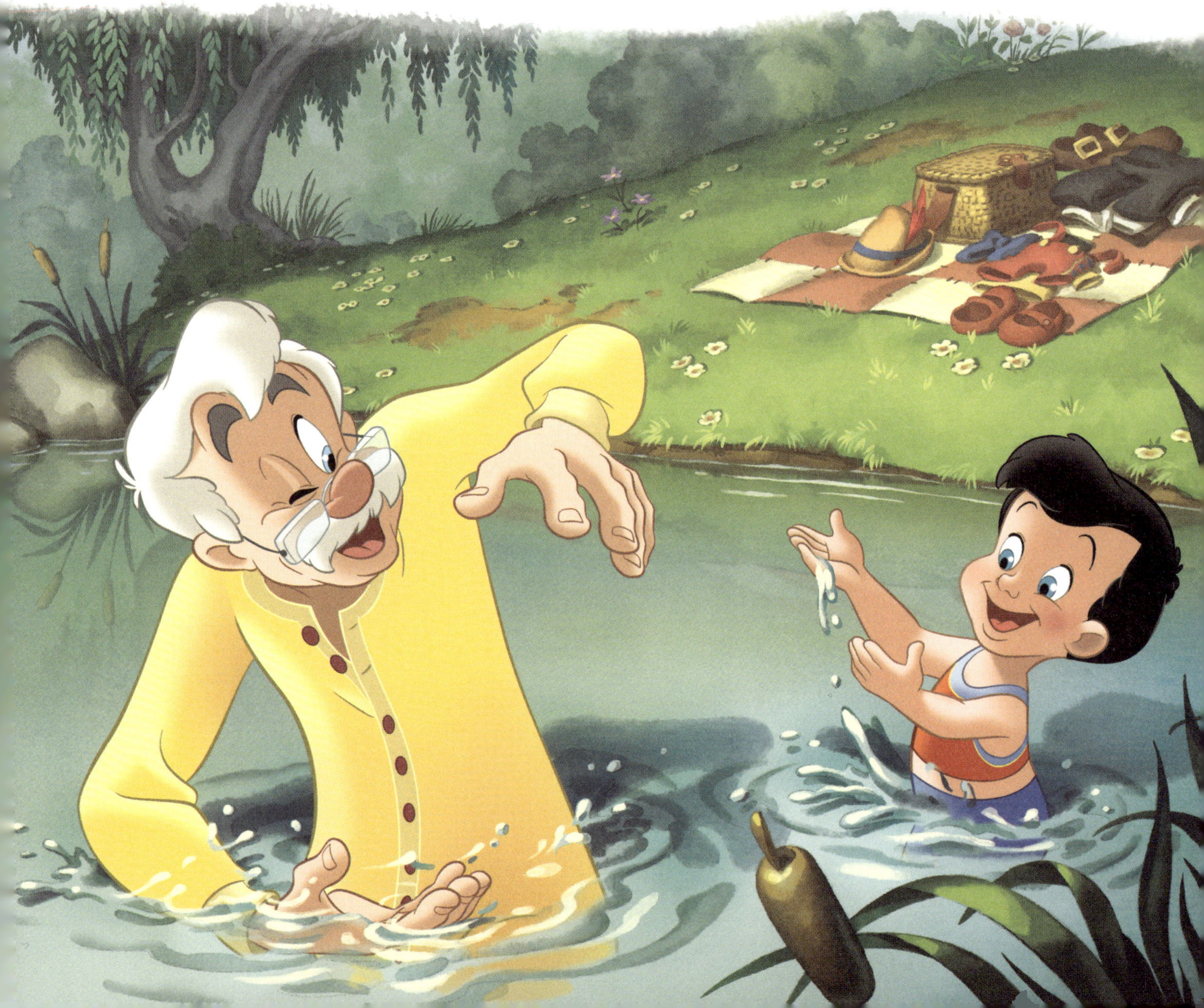

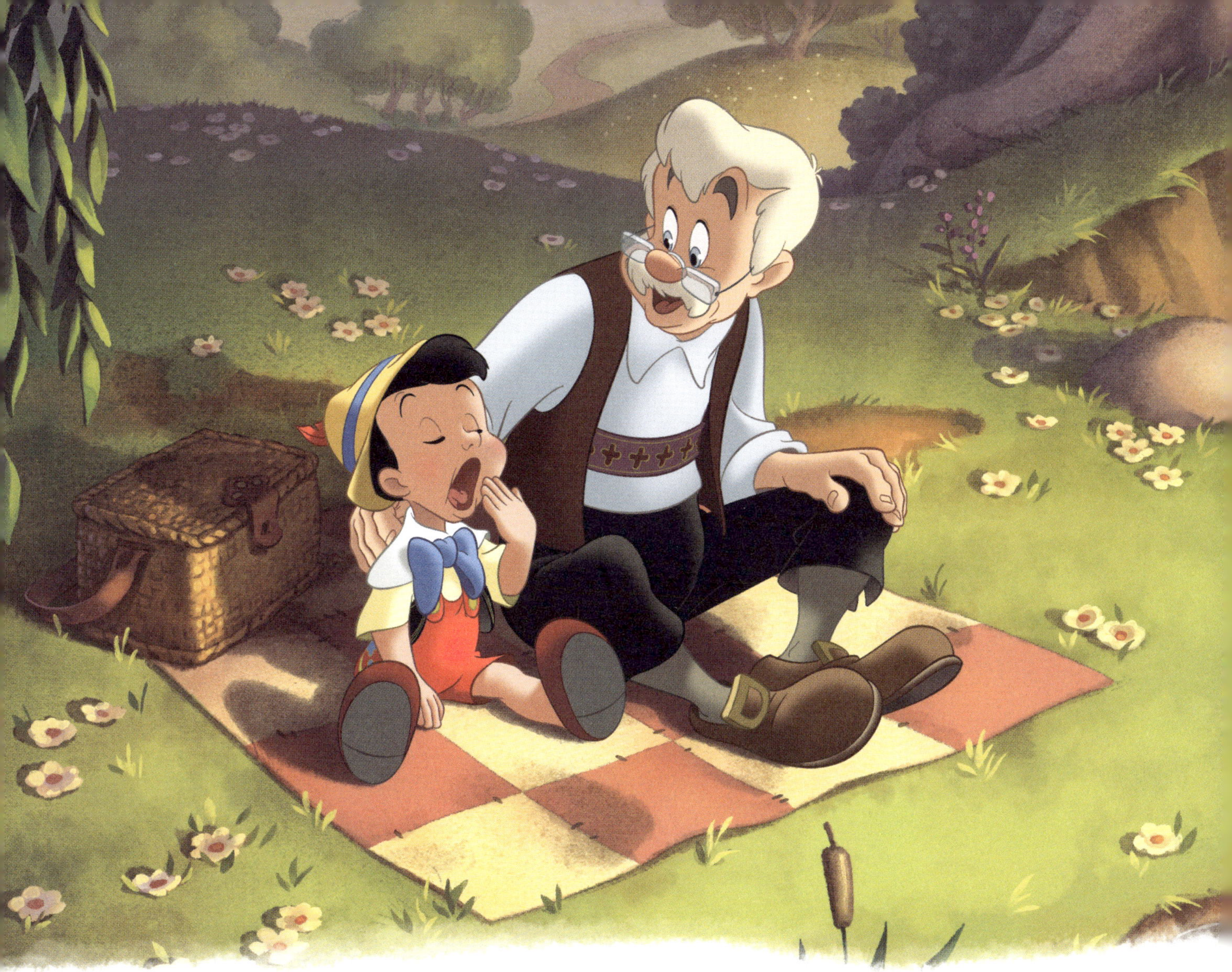

Quand le soleil commence à se coucher, Pinocchio a les paupières lourdes. Le voilà même qui bâille !

– Il se fait tard, estime Geppetto. **Rentrons à la maison, mon petit.**

Malgré la fatigue, Pinocchio aide son papa à ranger les affaires. Ensuite, Geppetto le prend sur ses épaules, et ils se mettent en route.

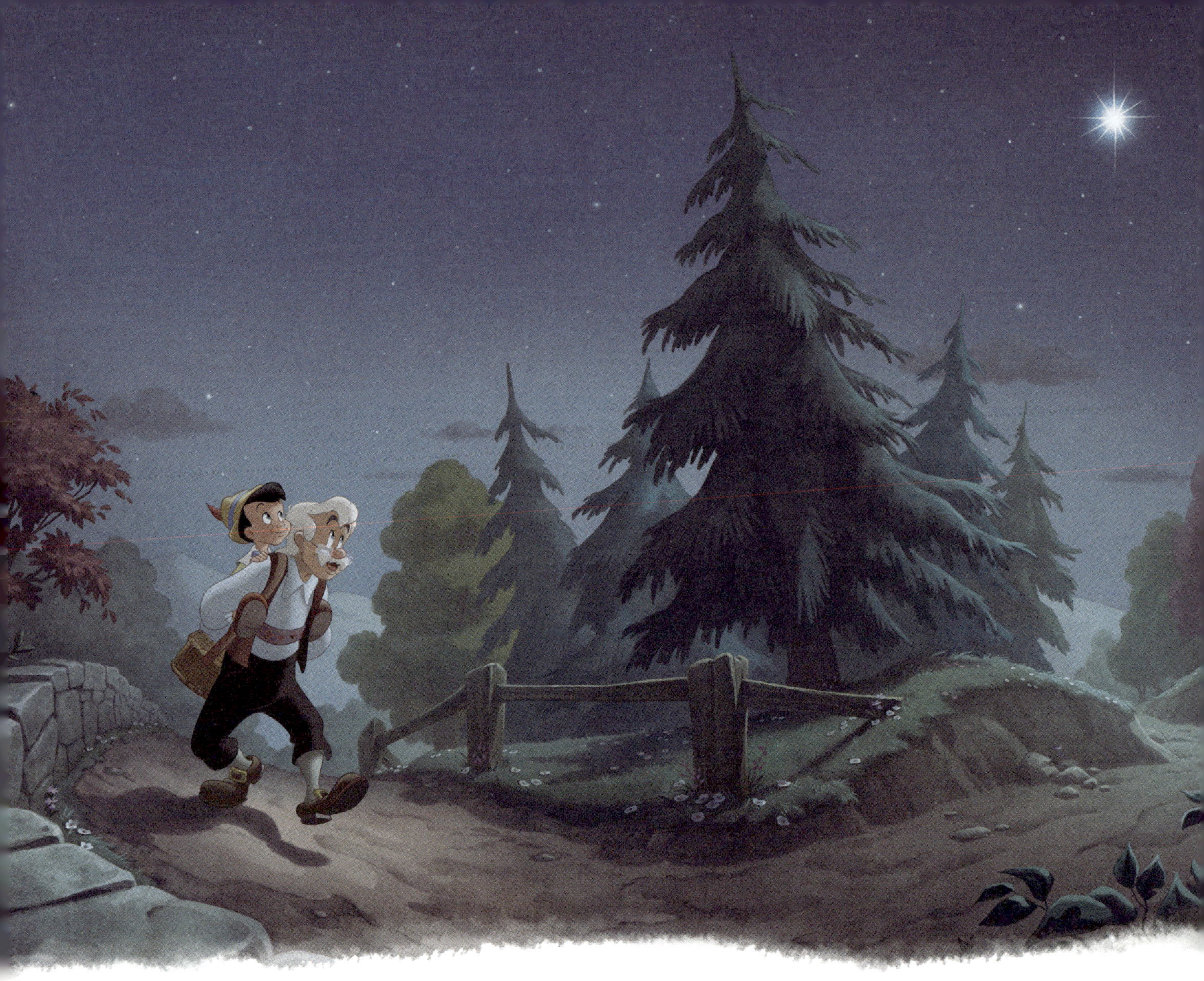

– Je me suis bien amusé, aujourd'hui, dit Pinocchio. Mais être un vrai petit garçon, ce n'est pas simple.

– La vie est pleine de surprises et de difficultés, lui répond Geppetto. Les bons repas et les égratignures ; les jeux et le hoquet… Ne t'inquiète pas, **je serai toujours là pour te protéger.**

Quand le papa et son fils arrivent chez eux, Pinocchio dort déjà. Geppetto le couche dans son lit et le borde. Puis il dépose un doux baiser sur son front et lui chuchote à l'oreille :

– Cette journée a été un rêve, mon fils. J'ai hâte d'en vivre beaucoup d'autres avec toi. Dors bien, **je t'aime, mon garçon.**

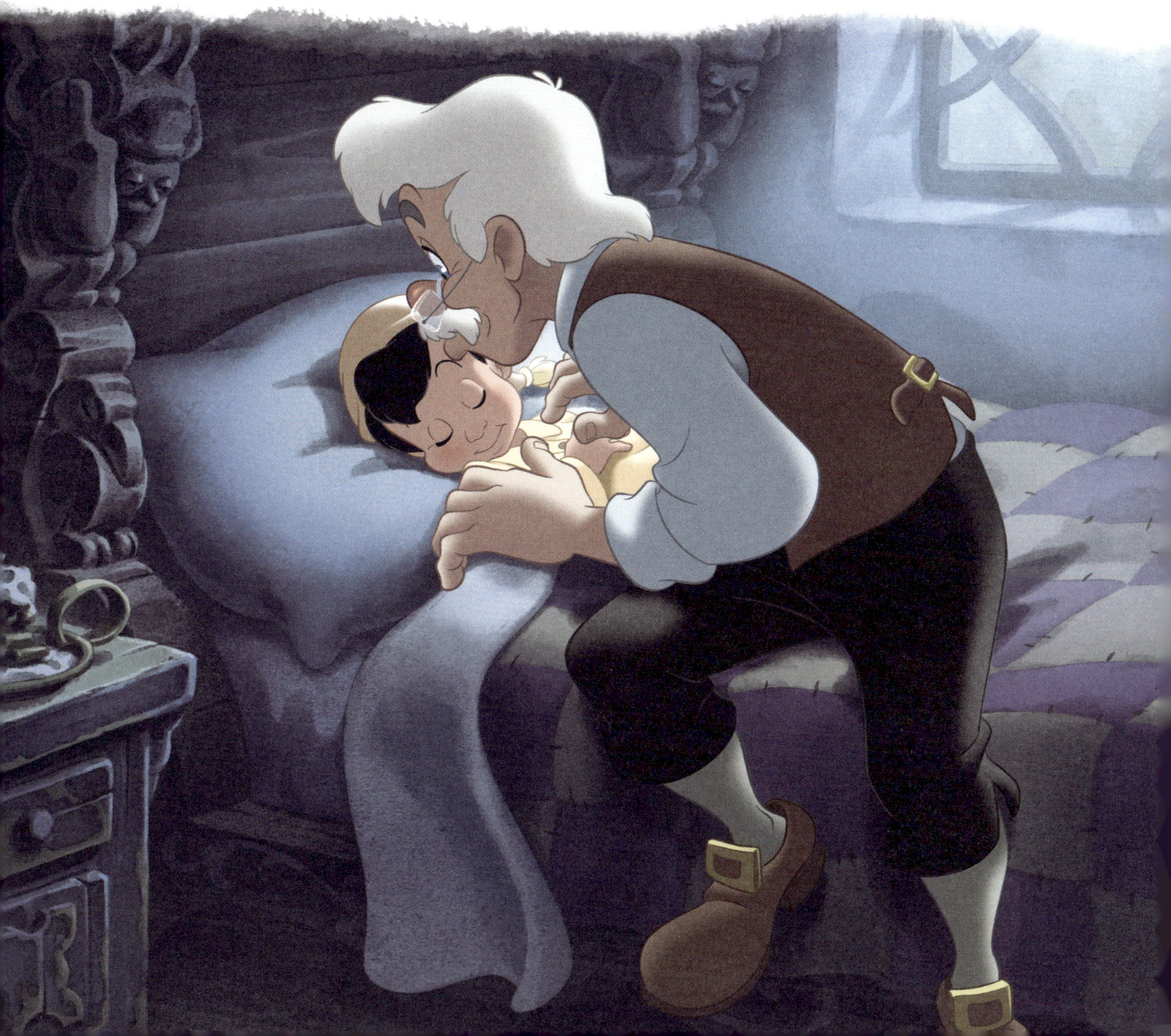

DISNEY · PIXAR

LE MONDE DE NEMO

Balade NOCTURNE

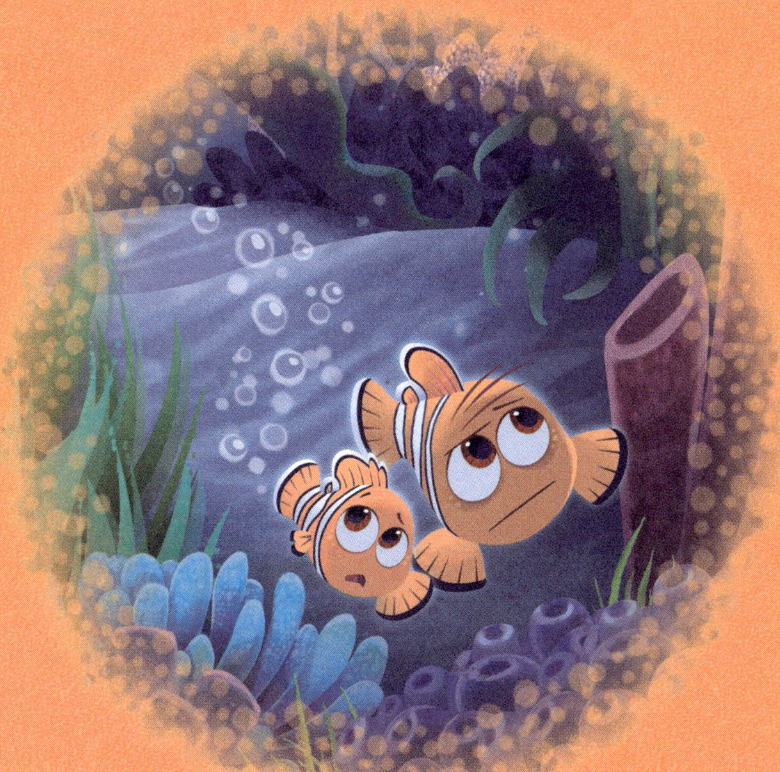

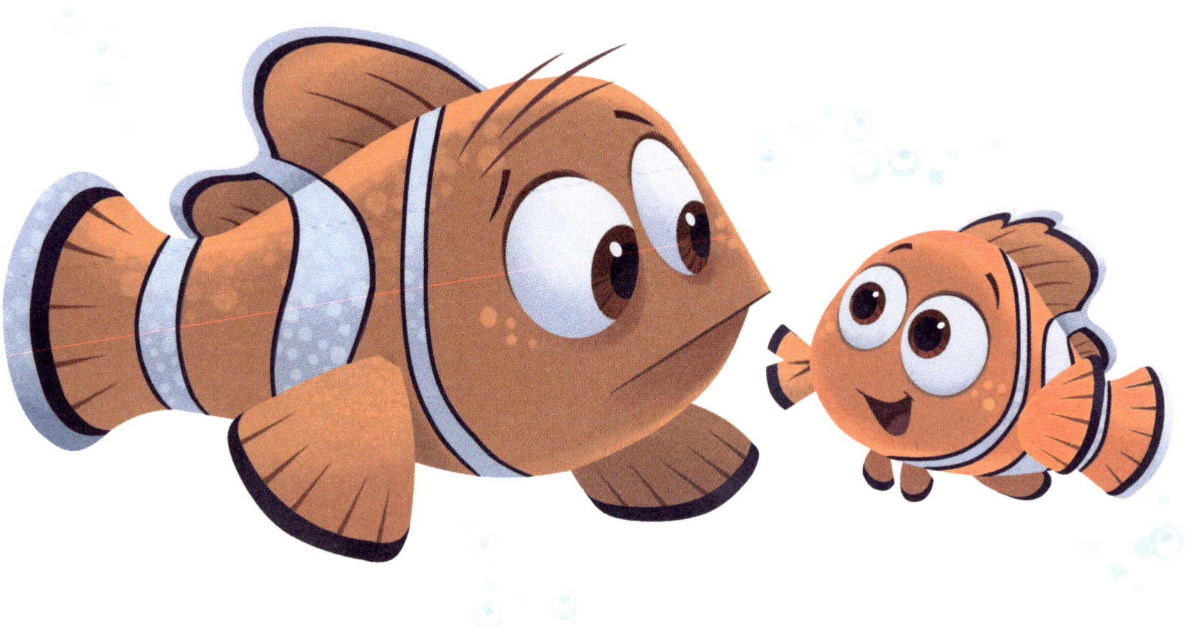

La nuit tombe sur l'océan où vivent **Nemo et son papa, Marin.** Nemo a passé toute la journée avec son amie Perle, la pieuvre... pourtant, il n'est pas fatigué !

– Papa ! s'exclame-t-il. Je peux aller jouer près du corail, s'il te plaît ?

– Non, mon grand, lui sourit Marin. Tu dois aller te coucher, demain il y a école.

Hélas, Nemo n'arrive pas à trouver le sommeil.

– Essaie de compter les dauphins, lui propose son papa.

Nemo essaie... sans succès.

– **Et si on allait se promener un peu ?** suggère alors Marin. Cela t'aidera peut-être à t'endormir après.

– C'est une super idée ! approuve Nemo.

Et les voilà partis en exploration !

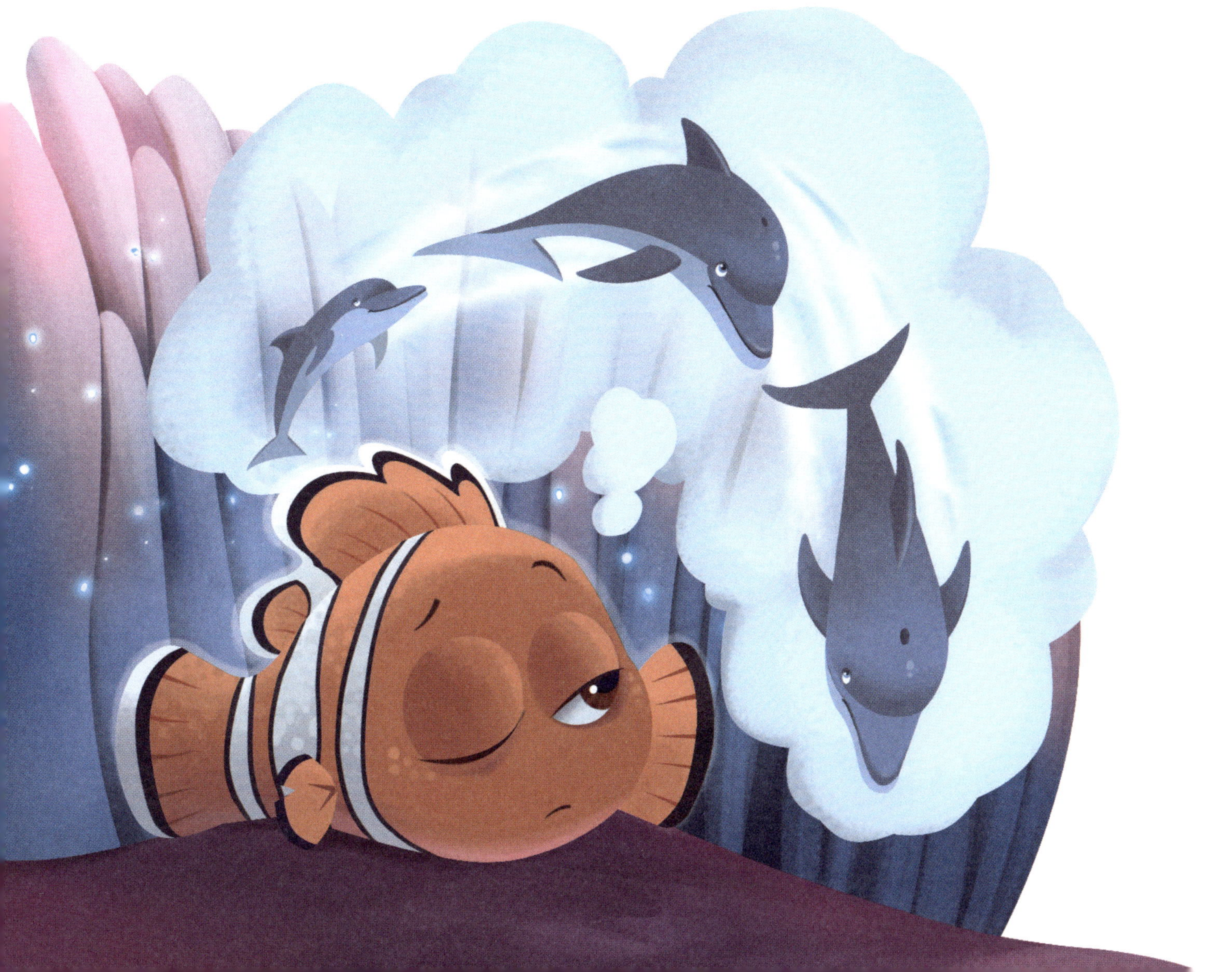

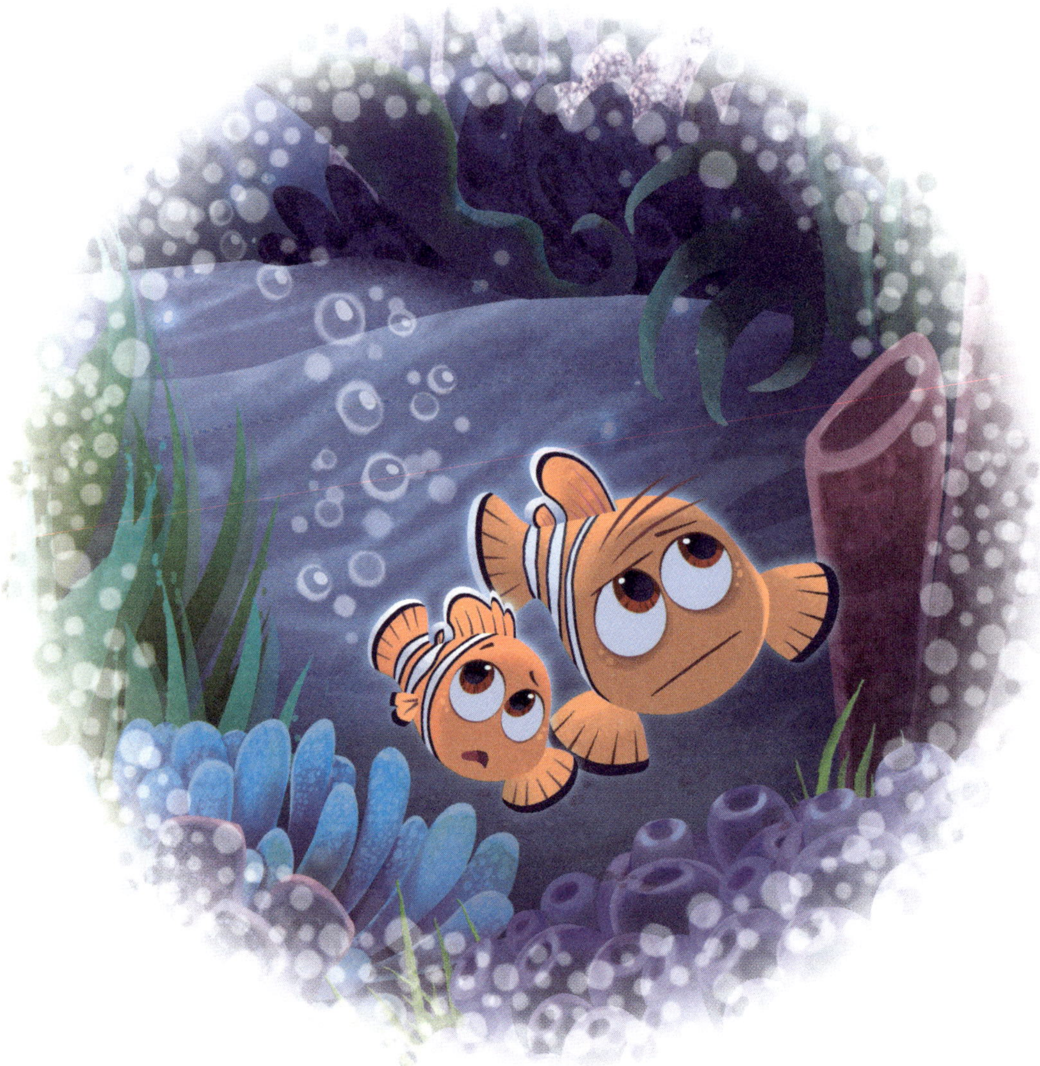

Mais très vite, le papa et son fils regrettent leur décision. La nuit, l'océan n'est pas un endroit très rassurant.

– **Reste près de moi, Nemo,** chuchote Marin. Je ne voudrais pas qu'on fasse une mauvaise rencontre…

– Une mauvaise rencontre ? répète le petit poisson-clown. Comme quoi, par exemple ?

Les deux explorateurs croisent alors un poisson au corps recouvert de plaques lumineuses.

– Bonsoir, **je m'appelle Lumen,** dit le nouveau venu.

– Ravi de te rencontrer, Lumen. Je suis Marin, et voici mon fils, Nemo.

– Je n'avais jamais vu de poisson comme toi, Lumen, comment ça se fait ? demande Nemo.

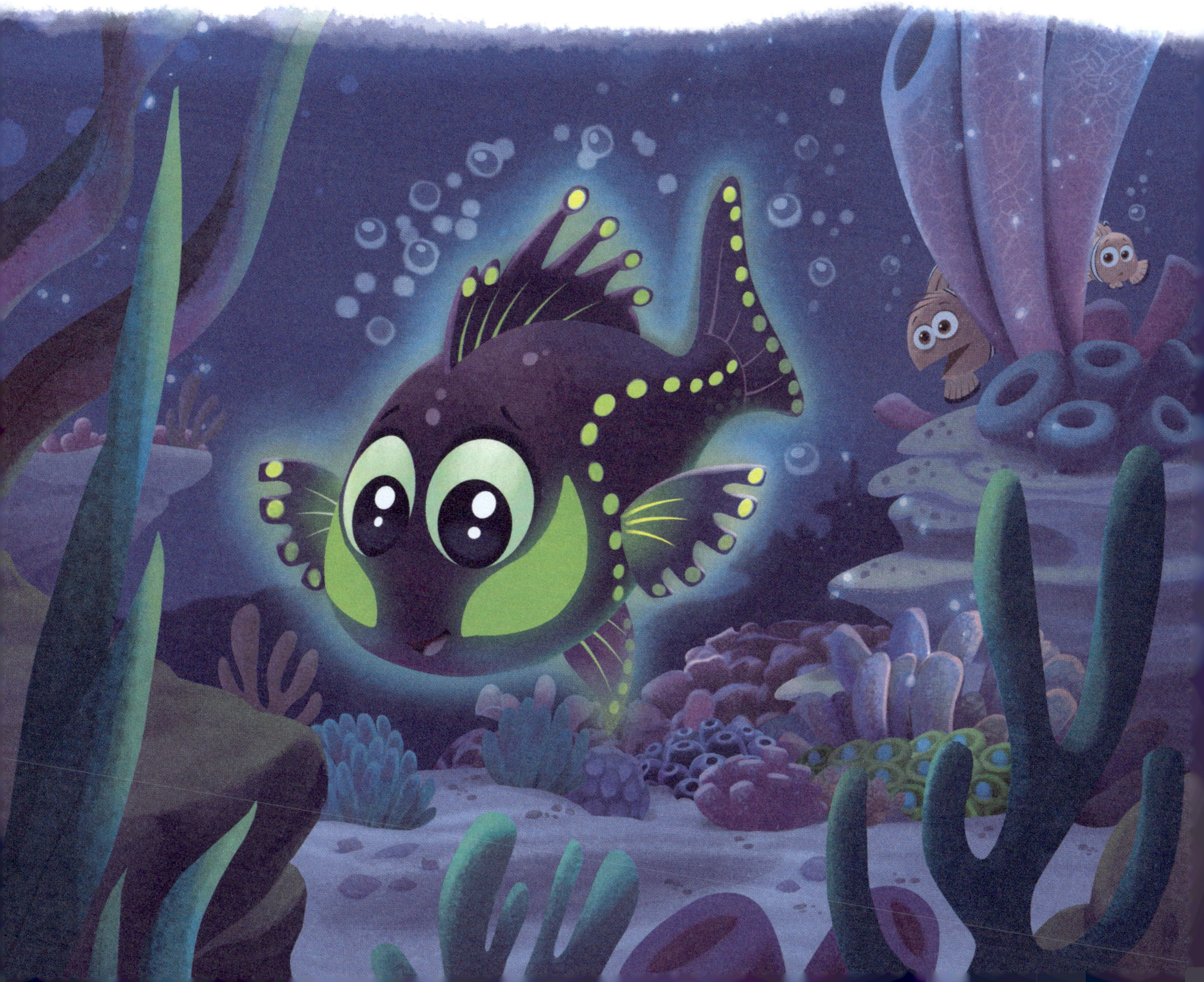

– C’est parce que je suis **un poisson nocturne,** révèle Lumen. Mes semblables et moi, nous nageons et vivons la nuit.

– Mon papa et moi, on est des « nocturnes » aussi, réplique Nemo. Vu qu’on explore l’océan la nuit !

– Ce n’est pas vraiment pareil, mon grand, sourit Marin.

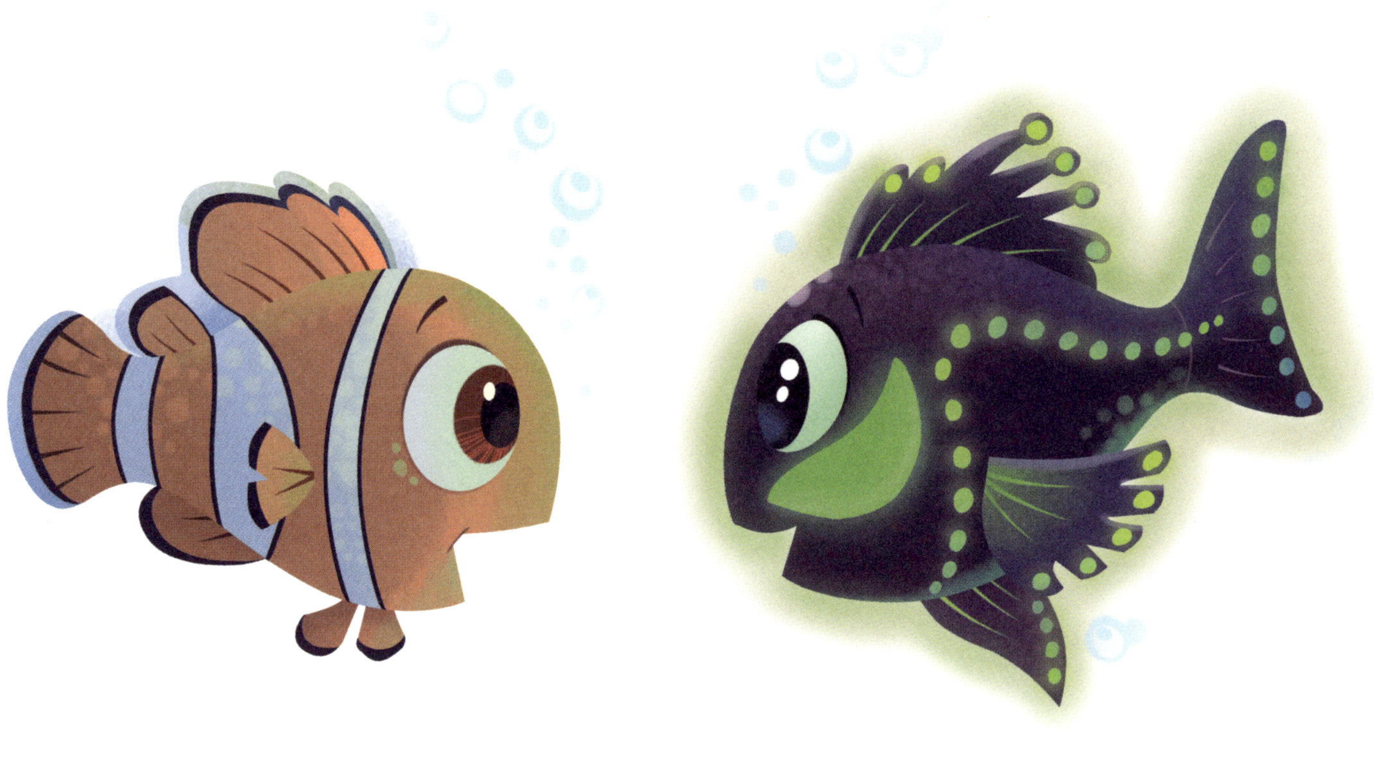

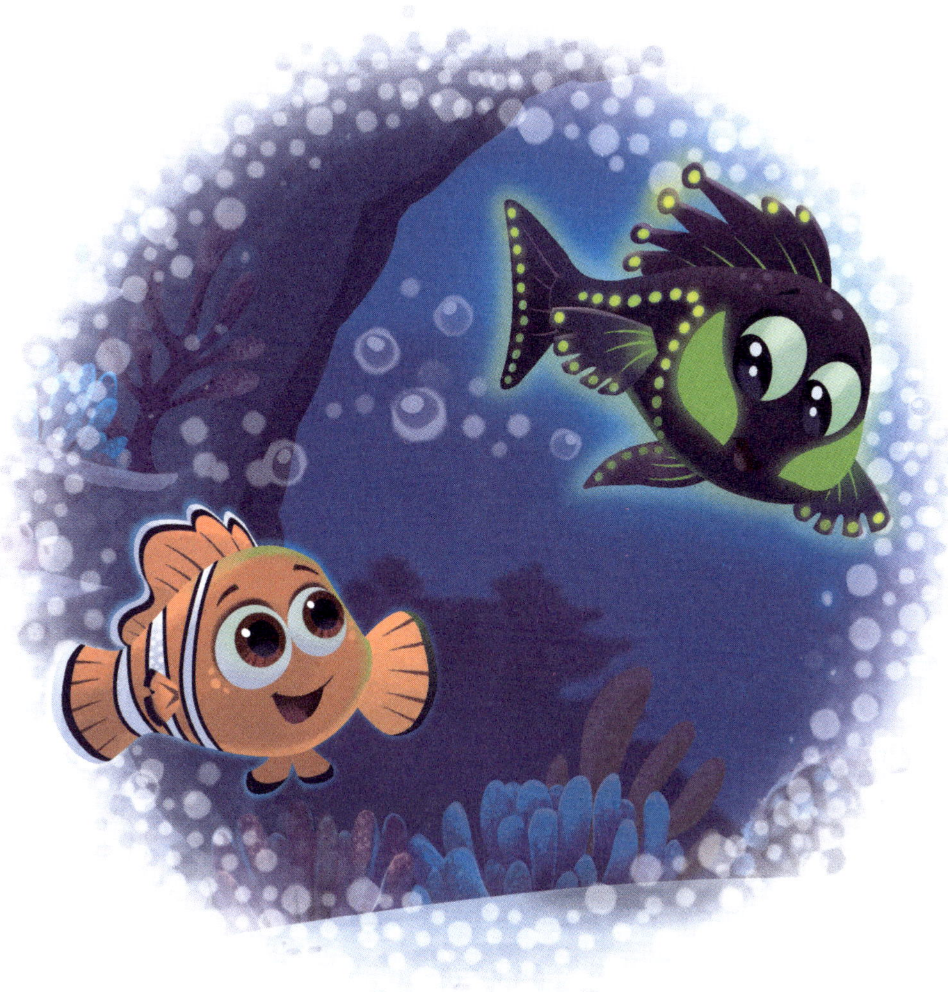

Lumen entraîne Marin et Nemo jusqu'à un banc d'algues.

– Dis, Nemo, ça te plairait de jouer à cache-cache ? propose-t-il ensuite.

– Oh, oui ! s'exclame le petit poisson-clown. Enfin... **si mon papa est d'accord ?**

Marin réfléchit un instant avant de répondre :

– D'accord... mais juste une partie, et après on rentre !

Pendant que Nemo et Lumen s'amusent, Marin inspecte le banc d'algues.

« Il ne faudrait pas qu'un prédateur surgisse par surprise... » frissonne-t-il.

Sa plus grande peur, c'est qu'il arrive malheur à son petit Nemo adoré. Depuis la perte de sa femme, il a juré de **protéger son fils** toute sa vie.

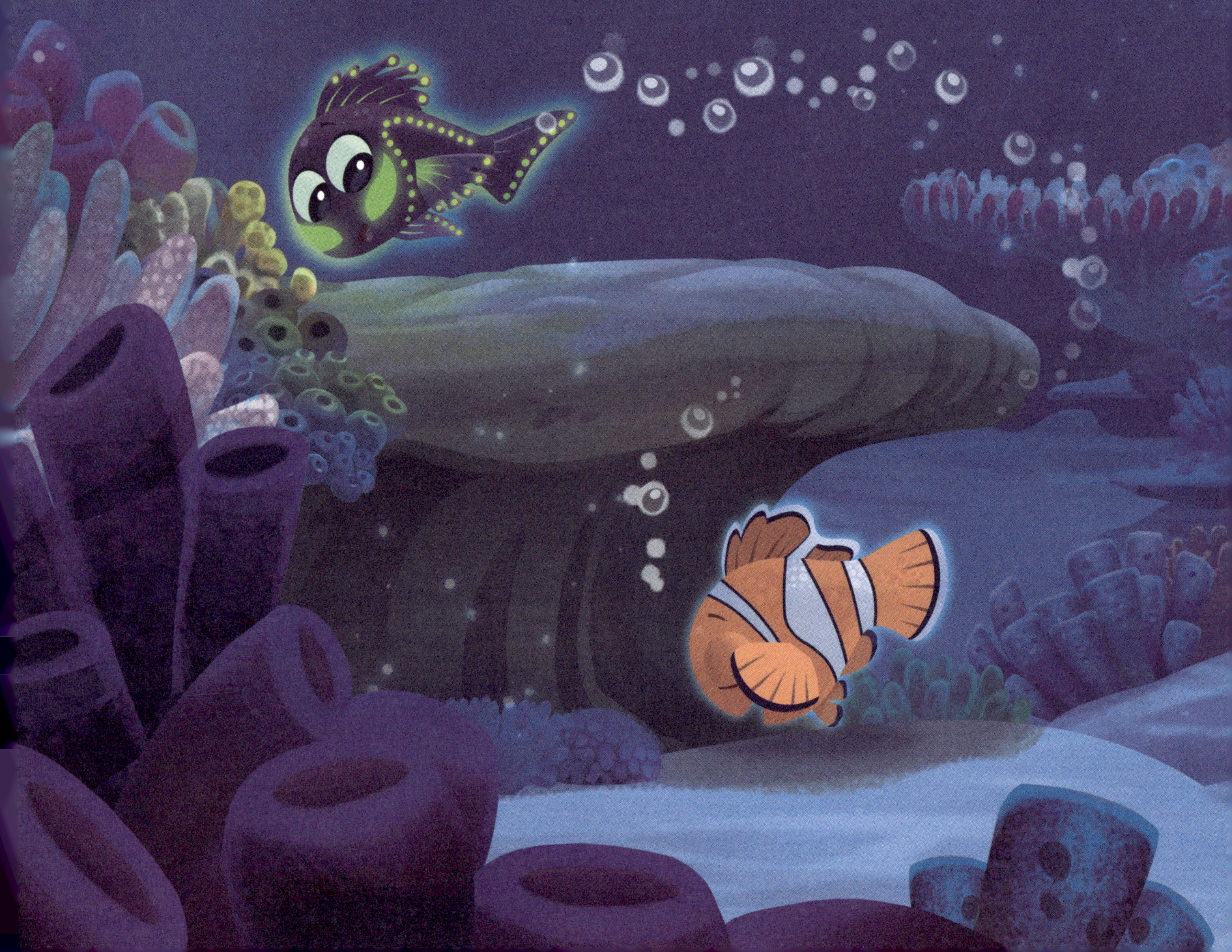

Marin s'enfonce dans ce labyrinthe d'algues. Et bientôt, il n'entend plus les battements de nageoires de son fils... Il ne voit plus les lumières de Lumen non plus...

– Nemo ?! appelle-t-il. Nemo, où es-tu ?

Hélas, aucune réponse ne lui parvient. Marin nage comme un fou pour tenter de retrouver son chemin.

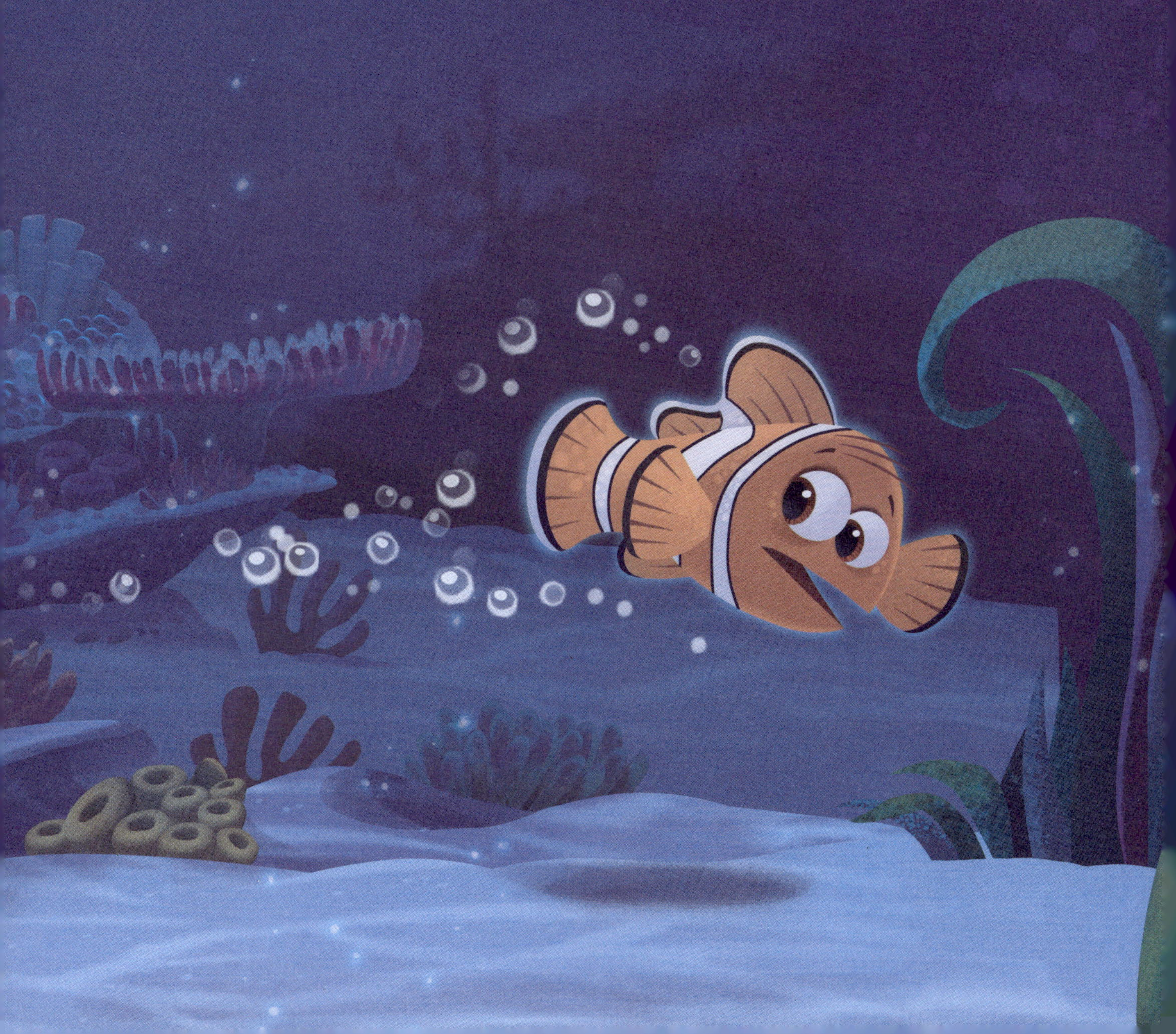

Le pauvre papa commence à paniquer quand, soudain, il aperçoit une lueur entre les algues.

– **Papa !** l'interpelle Nemo. Mais où étais-tu passé ? On t'a cherché partout !

– Moi aussi, souffle Marin. J'ai eu très peur...

Leur frayeur passée, les deux poissons-clowns disent au revoir à leur ami nocturne.

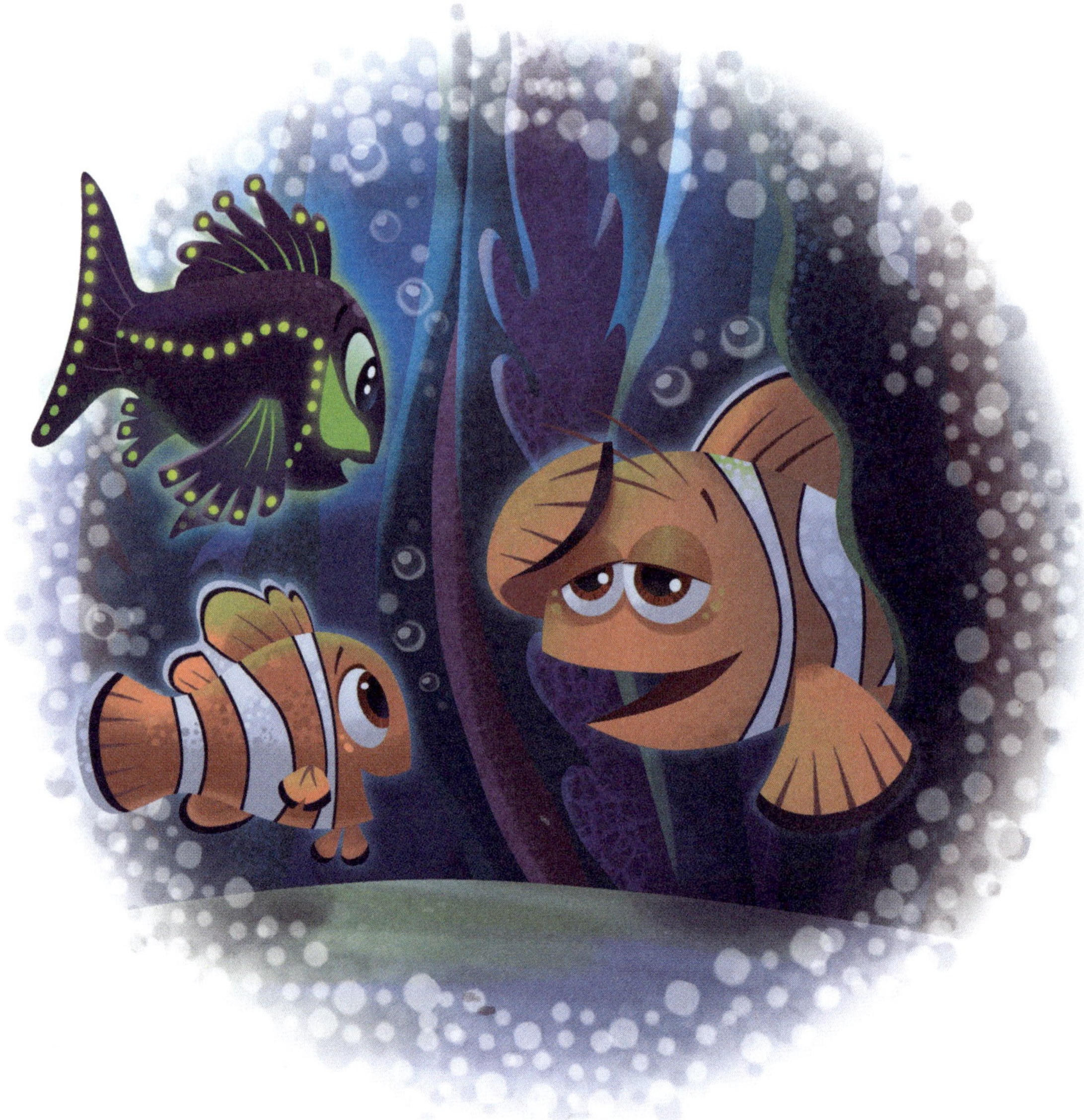

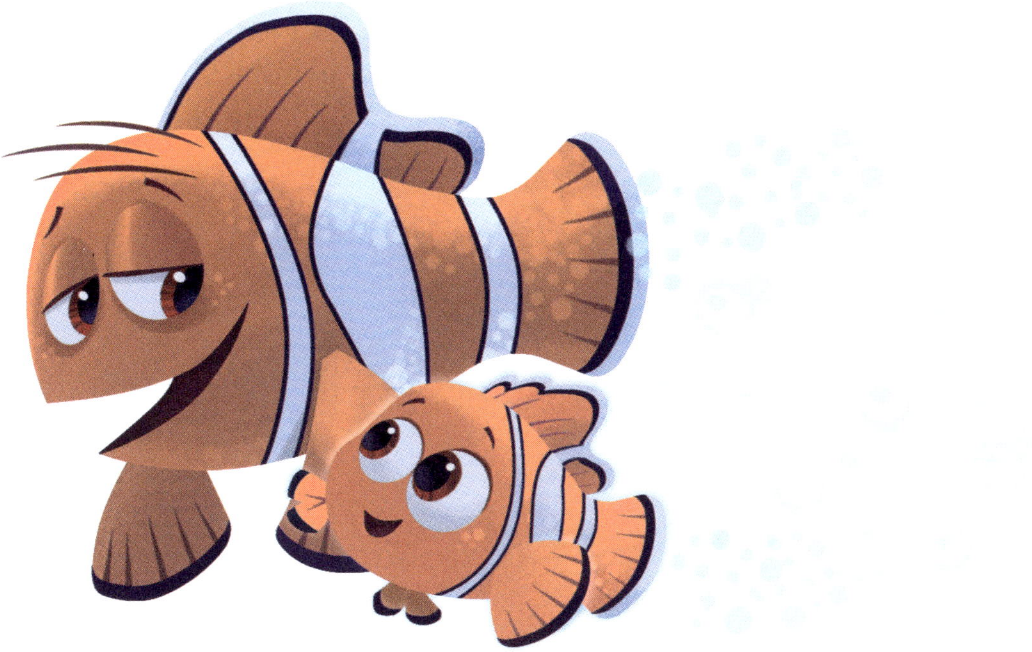

Marin et Nemo regagnent ensuite leur anémone de mer.

– Avec toutes ces émotions, j'espère que tu vas vite t'endormir maintenant, sourit Marin.

– J'espère surtout que je ne ferai pas de cauchemars..., soupire Nemo.

– Ne t'en fais pas, mon grand, **je serai là pour te rassurer. Toujours.**

Disney

MULAN

L'honneur D'UN PÈRE

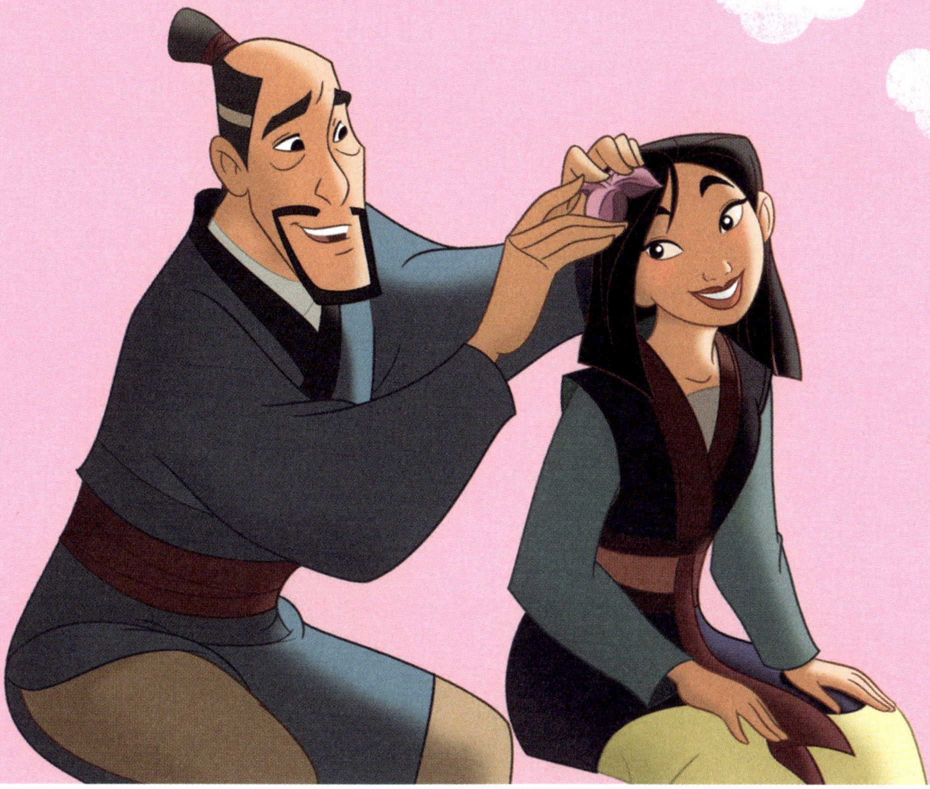

Mulan est tout excitée ! Le jour du Tournoi Impérial approche et, cette année, il tombe en même temps que **l'anniversaire de son père bien-aimé.** La jeune fille ne rêve plus que d'une chose : lui offrir le précieux manuscrit mis en jeu au Tournoi en le remportant !

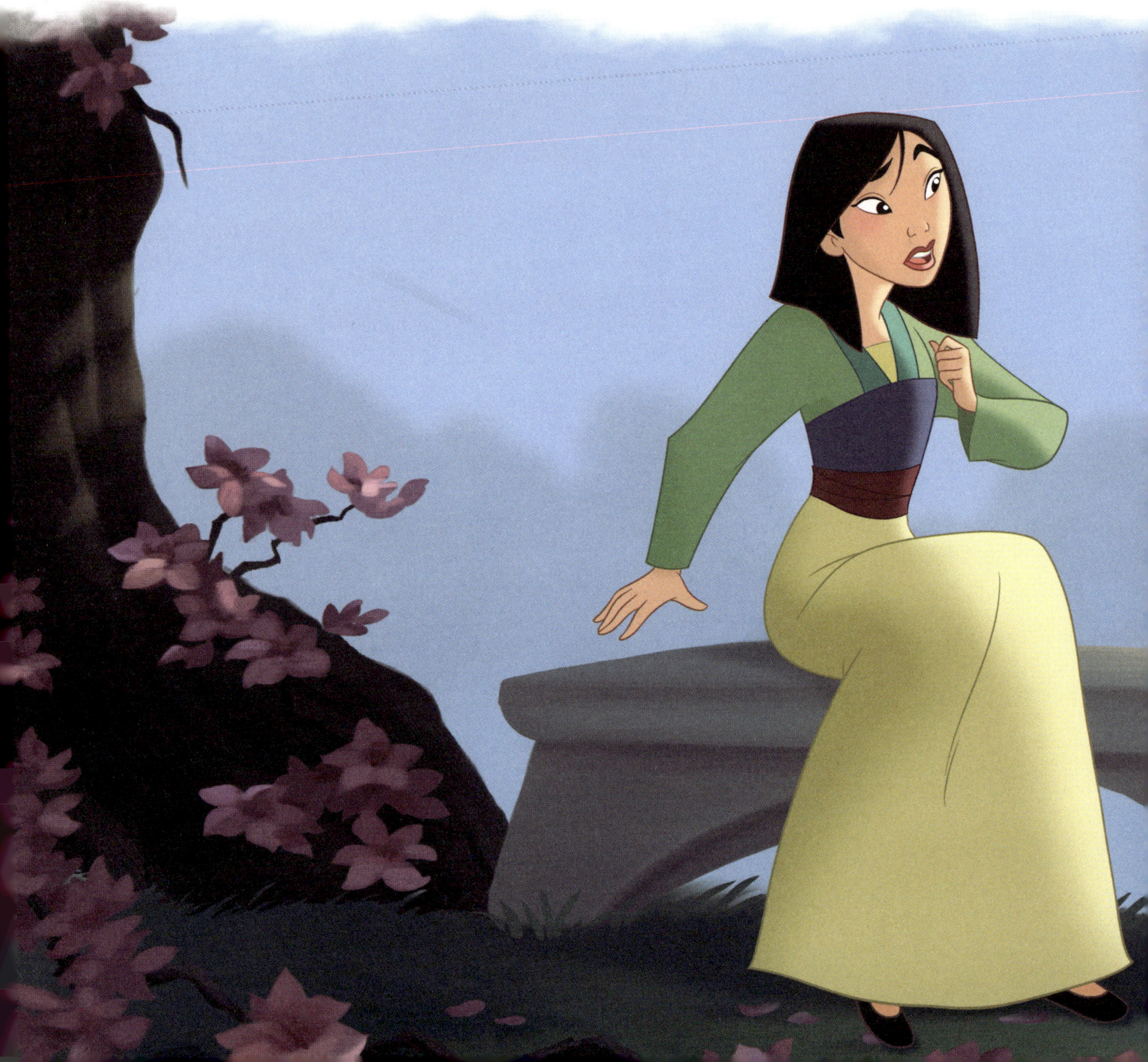

– Penses-tu que je vais gagner, papa ? lui demande-t-elle un matin.

– Mulan, demande-toi plutôt si, par tes efforts, tu vas faire **honneur à ta famille.**

Le père et la fille échangent un sourire, mais Mulan tremble :

« Qu'arrivera-t-il si par malheur j'échoue ? » songe-t-elle.

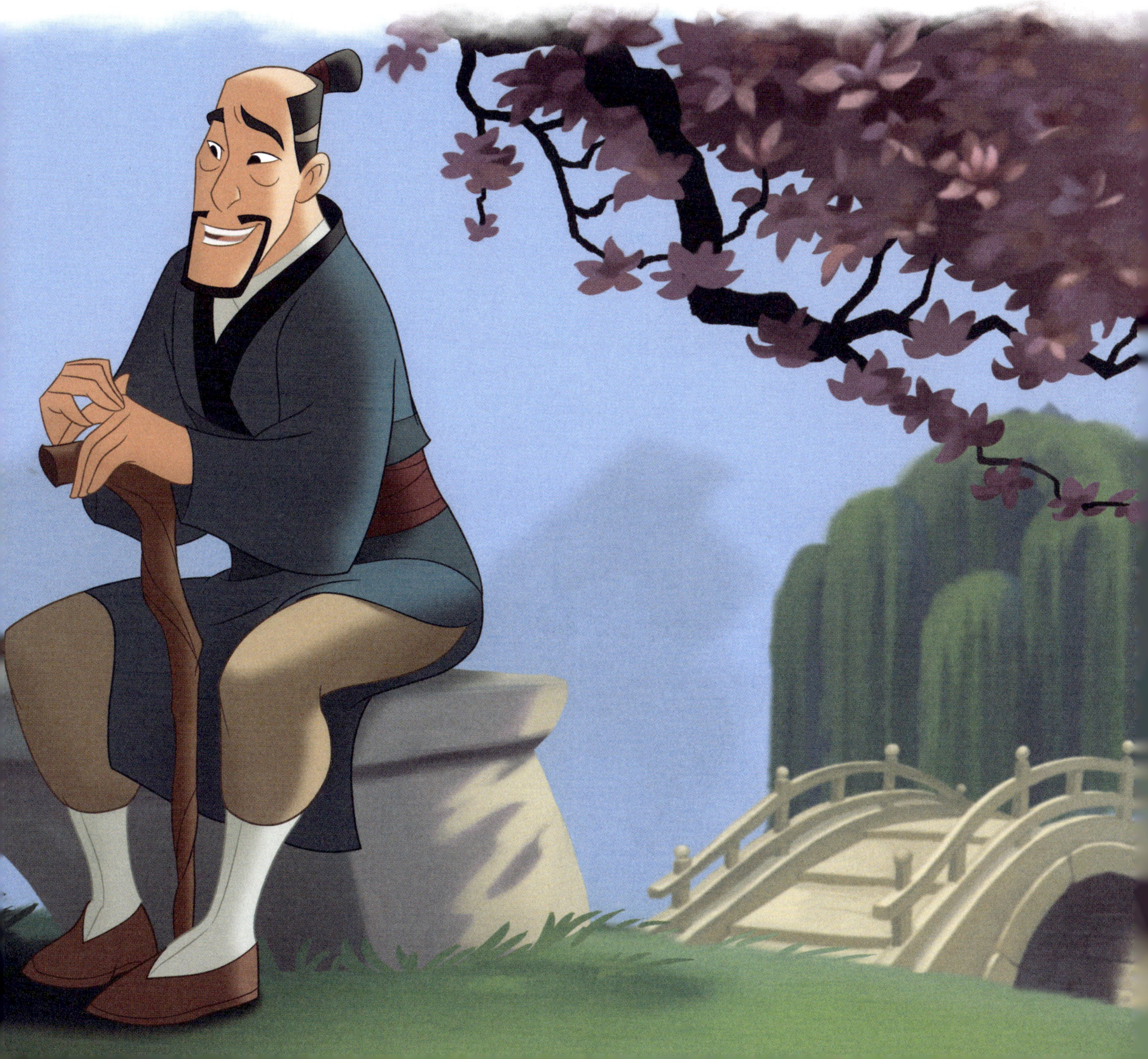

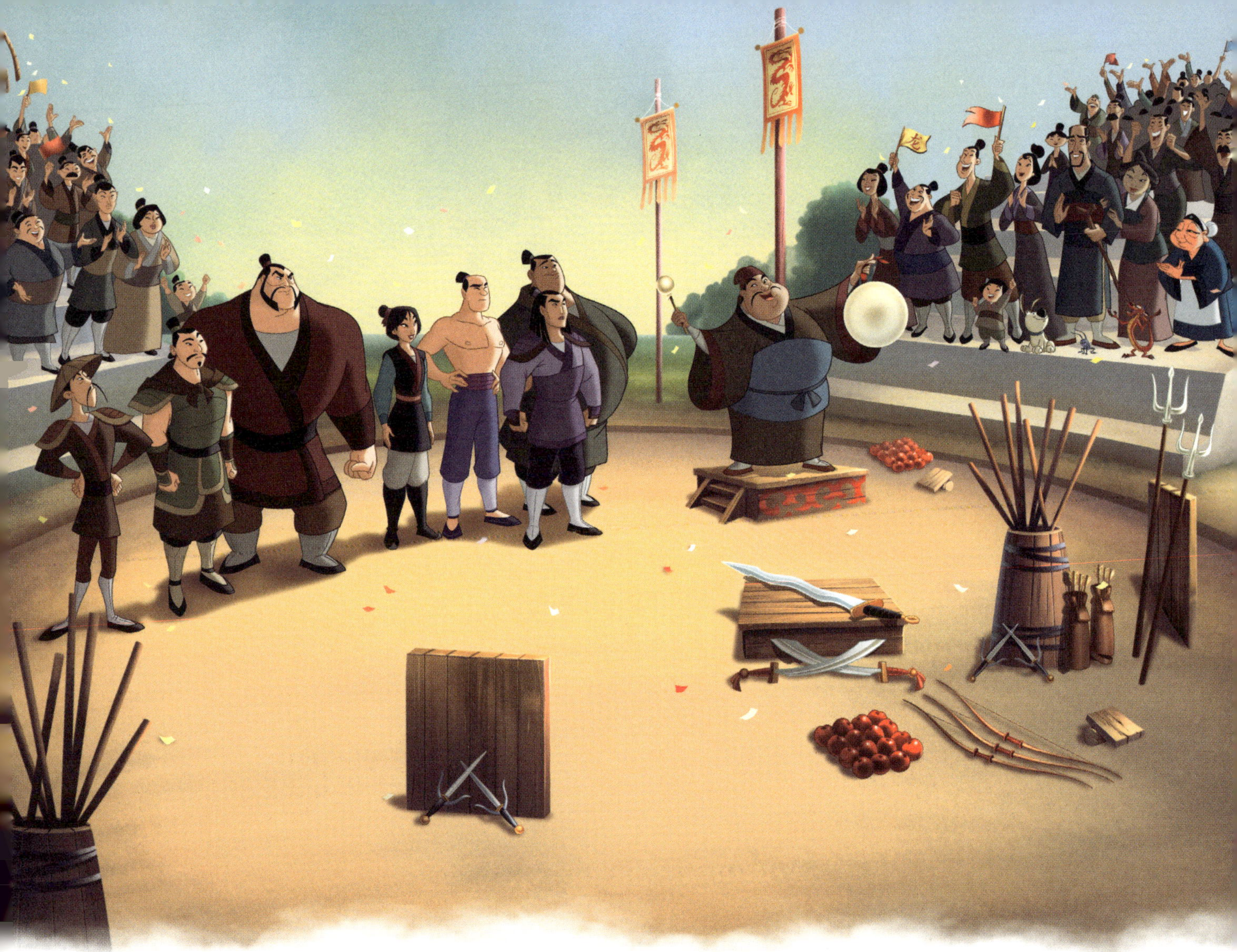

Le grand jour arrive enfin. Mulan se présente aux épreuves avec les plus redoutables guerriers de la région.

Dans les gradins, la valeureuse jeune fille aperçoit toute sa famille venue la soutenir. Son père lui adresse un petit signe de tête.

« Je ne te décevrai pas, papa » s'encourage-t-elle.

Un gong à la main, **le maître de cérémonie** explique comment vont se dérouler les épreuves :

– Les guerriers vont s'affronter en combat singulier. Le vainqueur de chaque manche sera qualifié pour l'épreuve suivante.

Dans sa tête, Mulan se rappelle qu'elle doit faire tout son possible pour gagner.

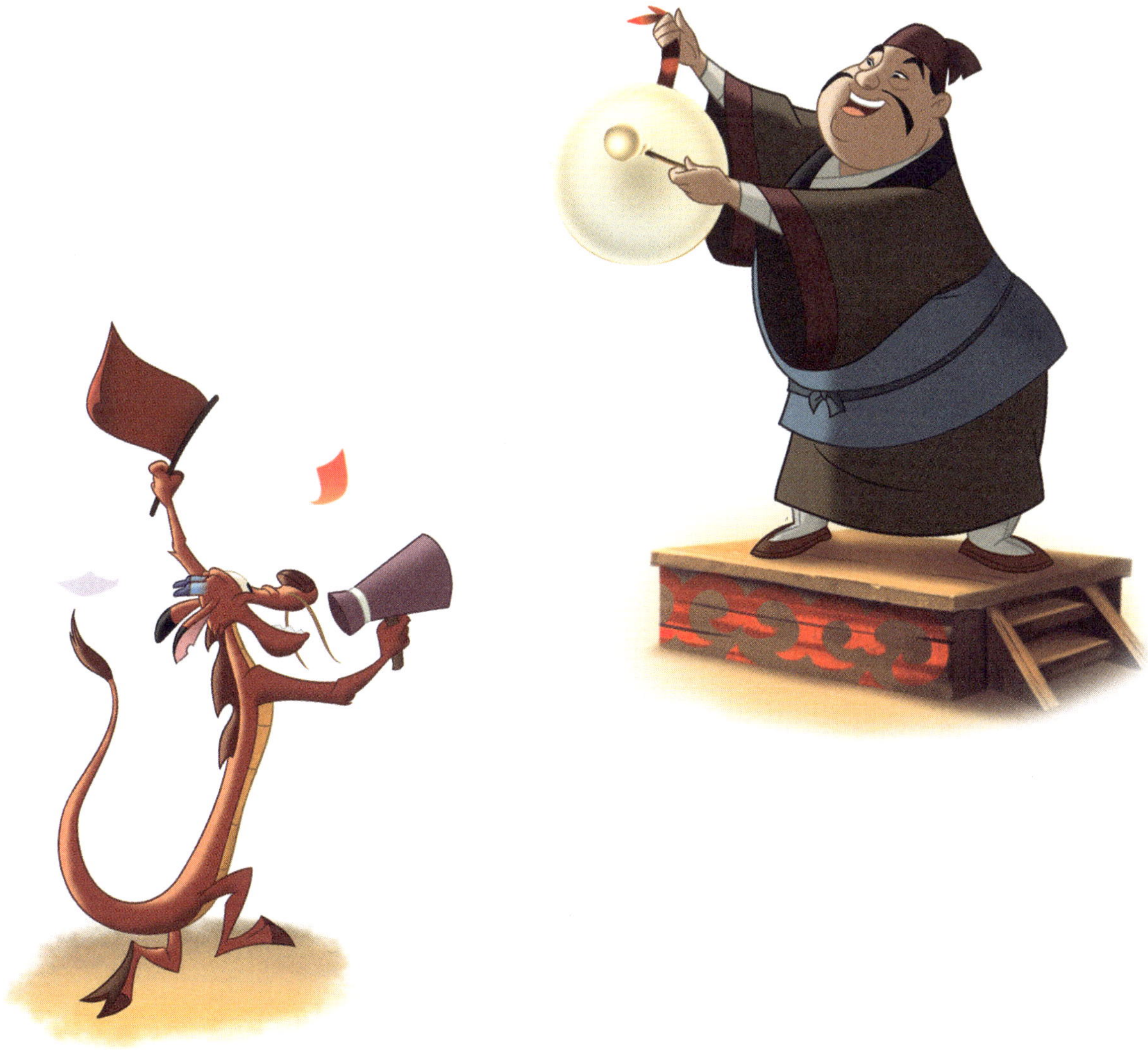

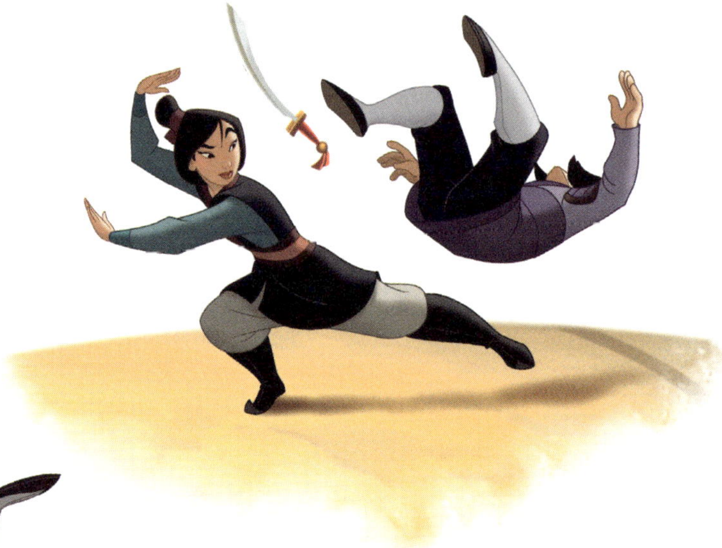
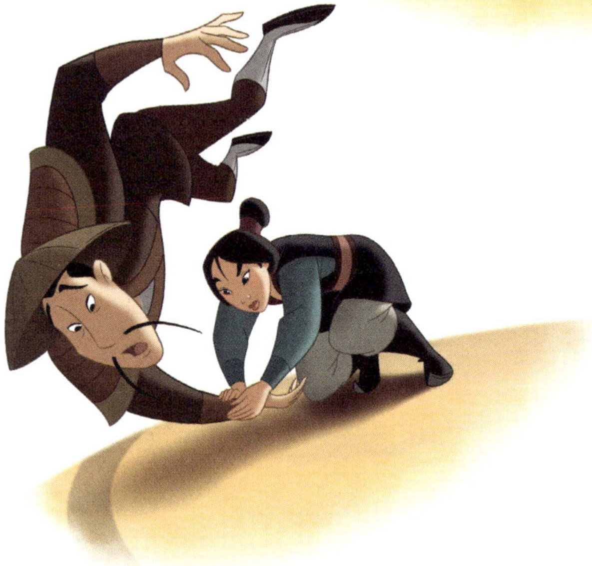
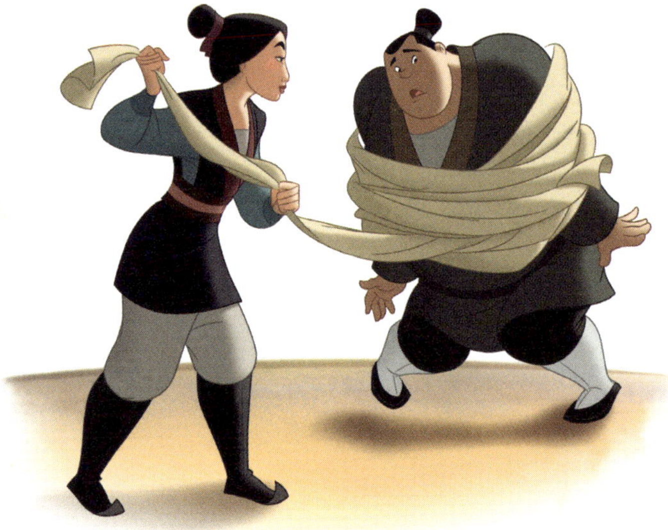

Les épreuves s'enchaînent, et **Mulan triomphe tour à tour de tous ses adversaires.** Que ce soit en combat à l'épée, au tir à l'arc ou en combat singulier, aucun concurrent n'a la force ou l'intelligence nécessaire pour vaincre la jeune femme.

Chaque victoire la rapproche un peu plus de son but !

Et bientôt, **Mulan se retrouve en finale,** face au redoutable Wan Na Pu.

– Pour la dernière épreuve, les candidats ont le choix des armes ! annonce le maître de cérémonie.

Wan Na Pu décide de se battre avec des tridents. Mulan, elle, utilisera l'Épée Impériale !

Wan a l'avantage de la force, mais Mulan résiste grâce à son agilité.

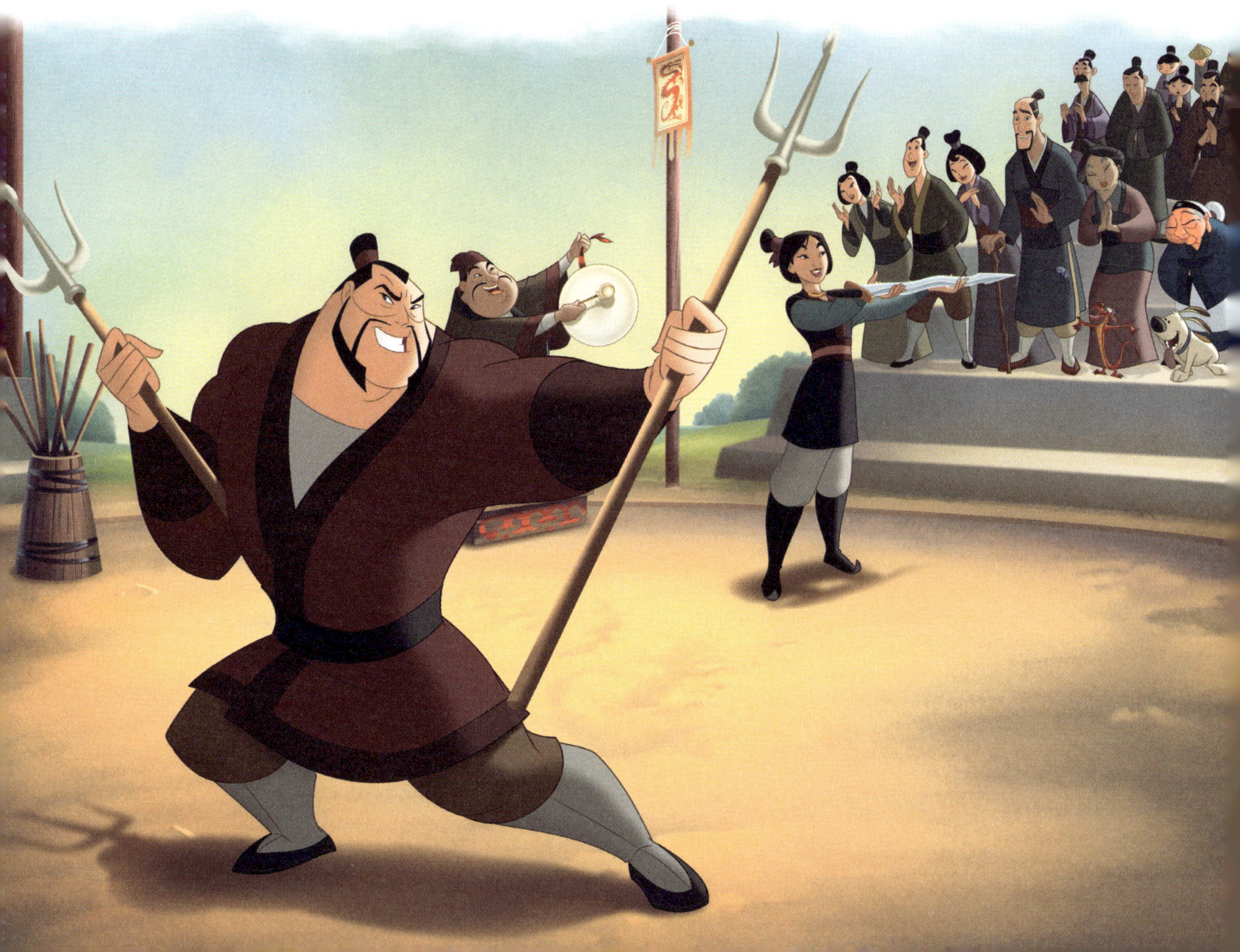

Le duel est serré. Au bord de la piste, Mushu, Cri-Kee et Petit Frère forment une pyramide pour encourager la jeune femme. Quand soudain… **CATASTROPHE !** la pyramide s'écroule. Mais le pire, c'est qu'un des tridents de Wan menace d'atterrir sur les trois compères !

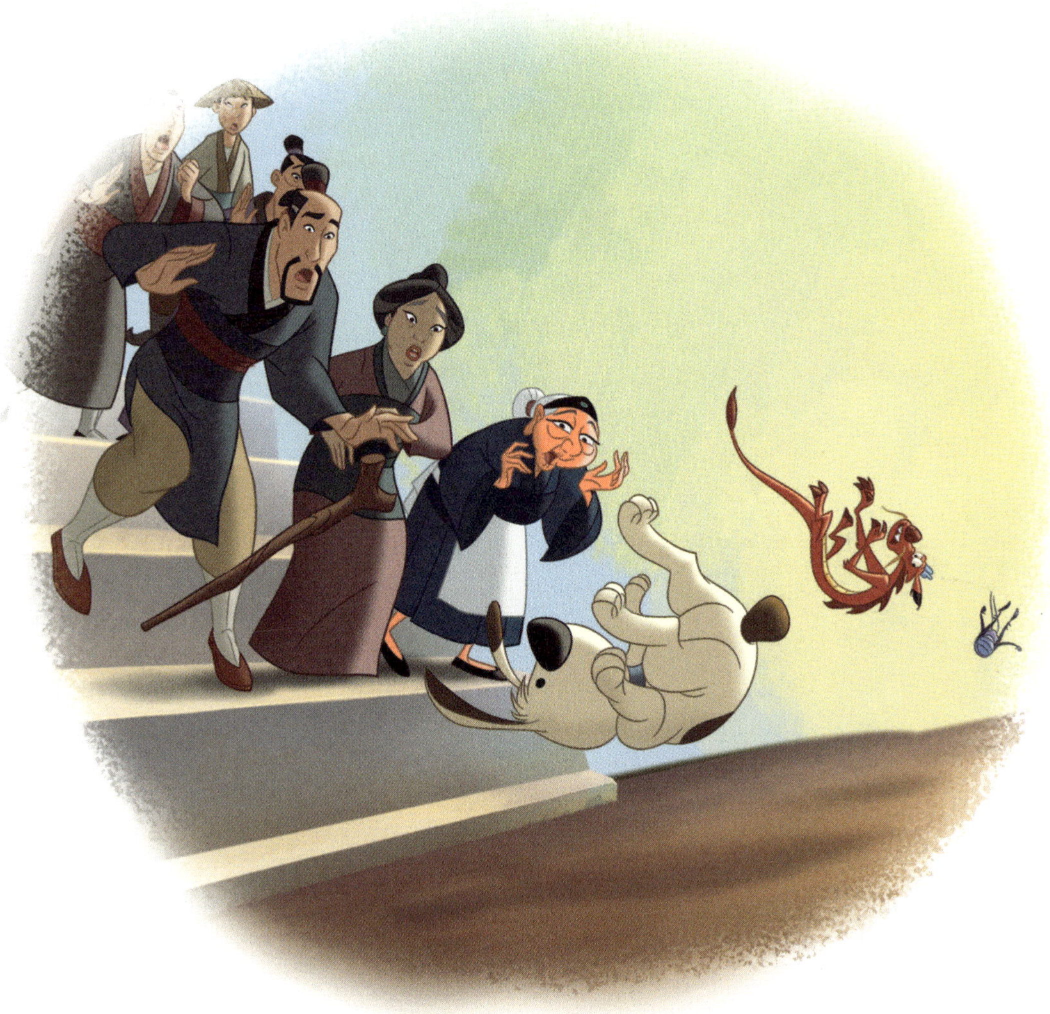

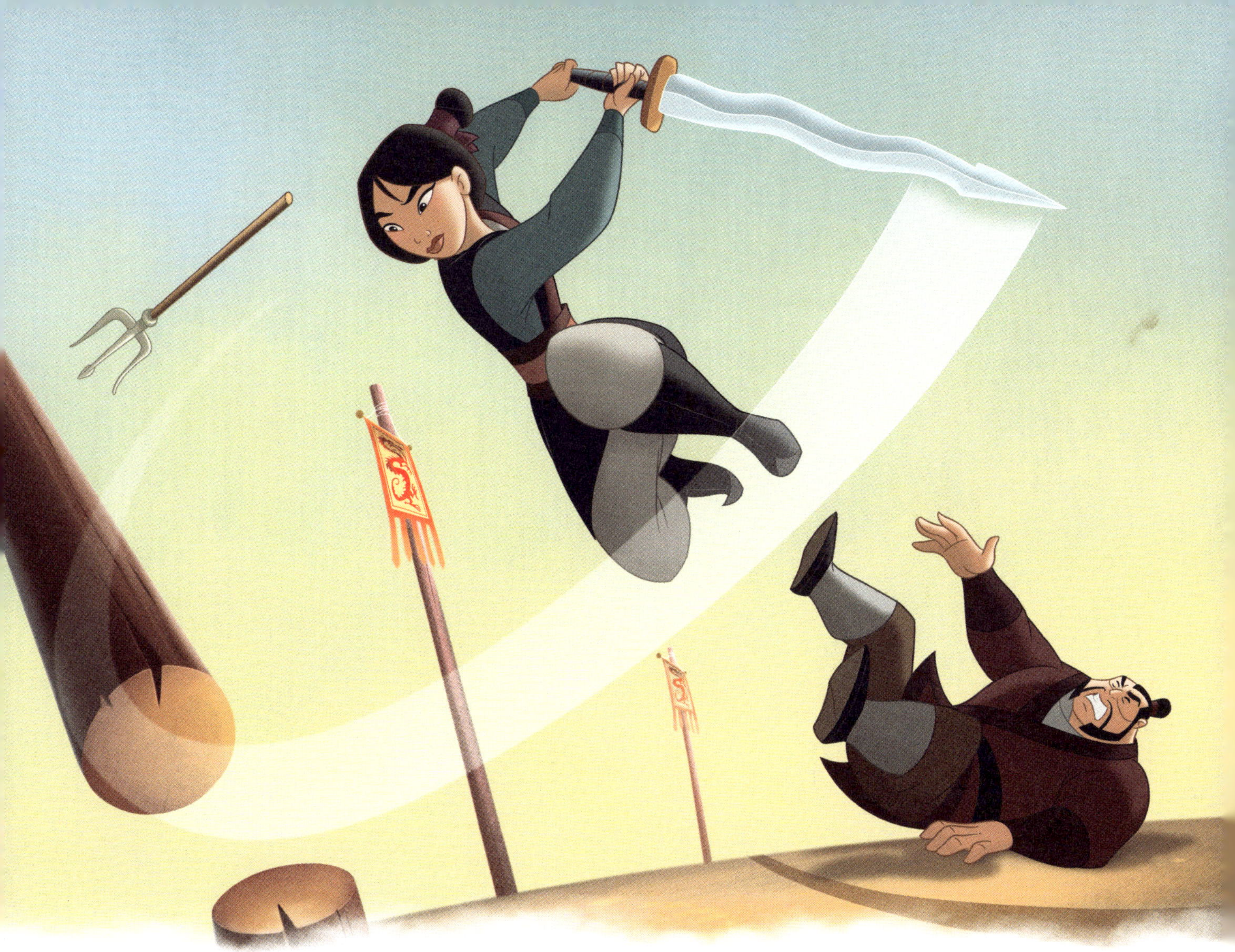

Voyant ses amis en danger, Mulan oublie le Tournoi. D'un coup d'épée, elle abat un poteau qui, en tombant, intercepte le trident de Wan. Mushu, Cri-Kee et Petit Frère ne craignent plus rien !

Hélas, dans la manœuvre, la jeune femme a posé un pied hors de la piste... **Elle est disqualifiée...** Wan Na Pu est déclaré vainqueur du Tournoi !

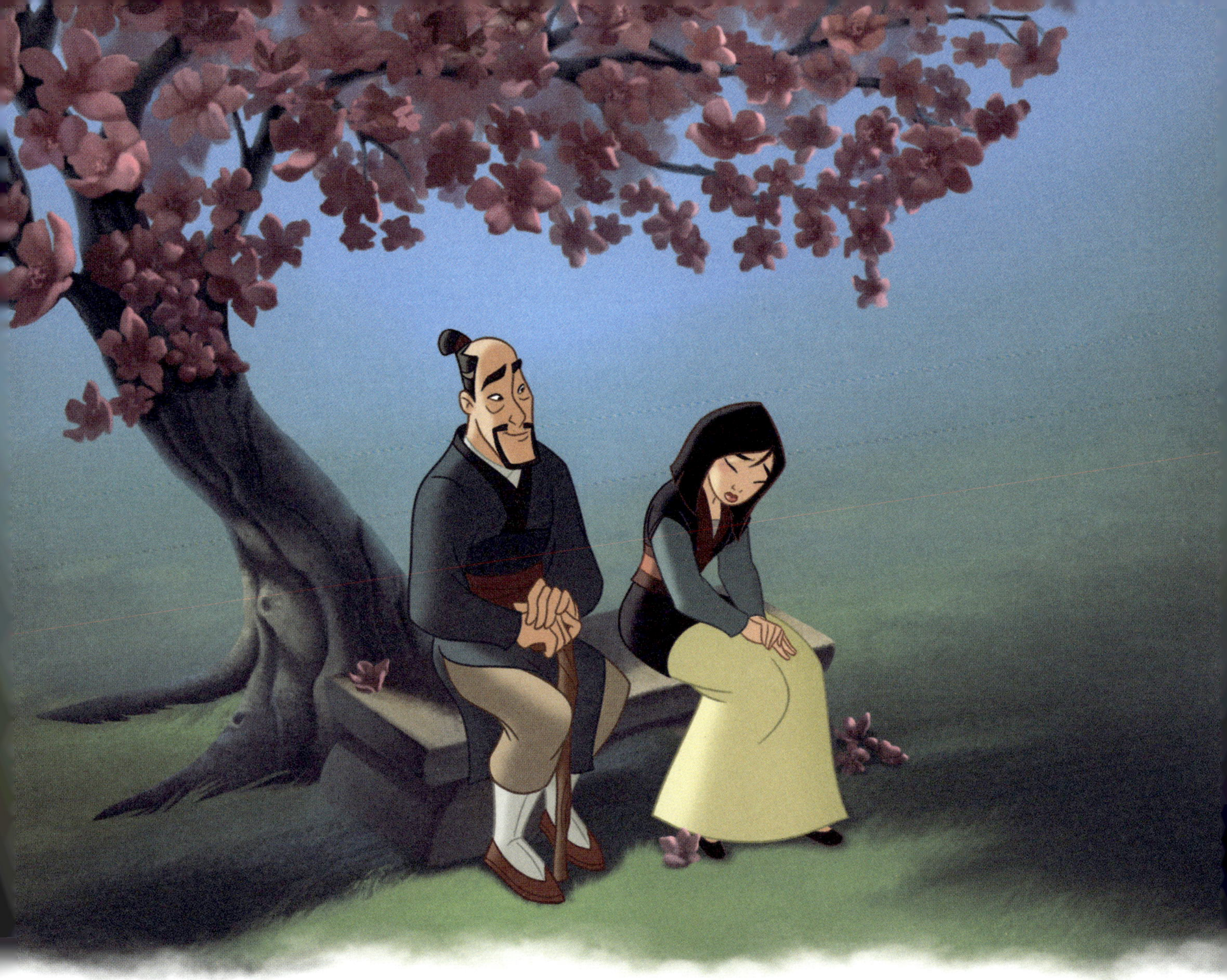

De retour chez elle, Mulan va s'asseoir à l'ombre d'un grand arbre, auprès de son père.

– Cette défaite n'est pas le cadeau d'anniversaire que je souhaitais t'offrir, papa, se désole la courageuse guerrière. **J'ai perdu le Tournoi,** je n'ai pas fait honneur à ma famille...

– Tu te trompes, lui réplique son père. Mulan, tu possèdes un grand cœur et une grande intelligence.

Mulan observe son papa, les yeux pleins d'amour.

– Aujourd'hui, reprend celui-ci, tu as préféré sauver tes amis plutôt que de remporter un tournoi prestigieux... **Je n'ai jamais été aussi fier de toi, ma chérie.**

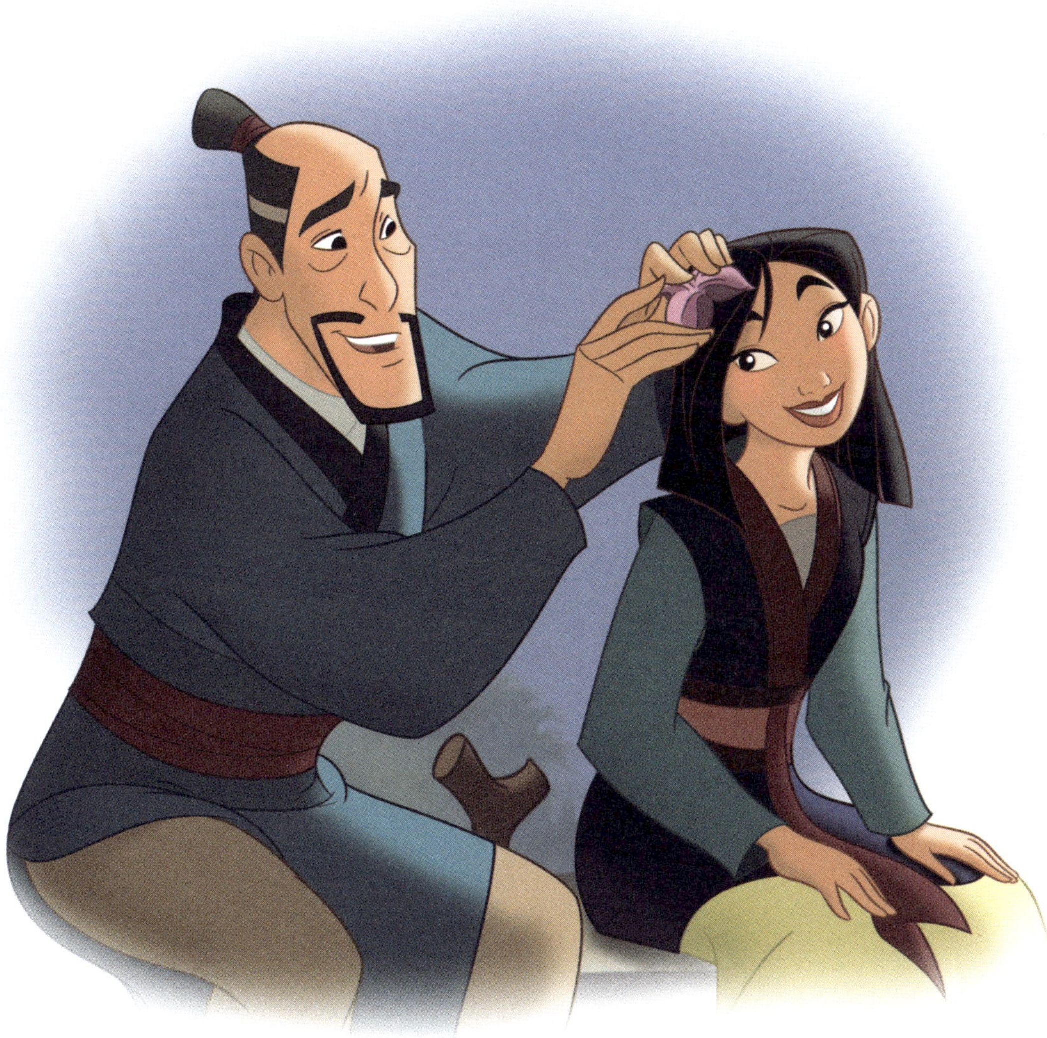

Disney

101 DALMATIENS

Le héros DU JOUR

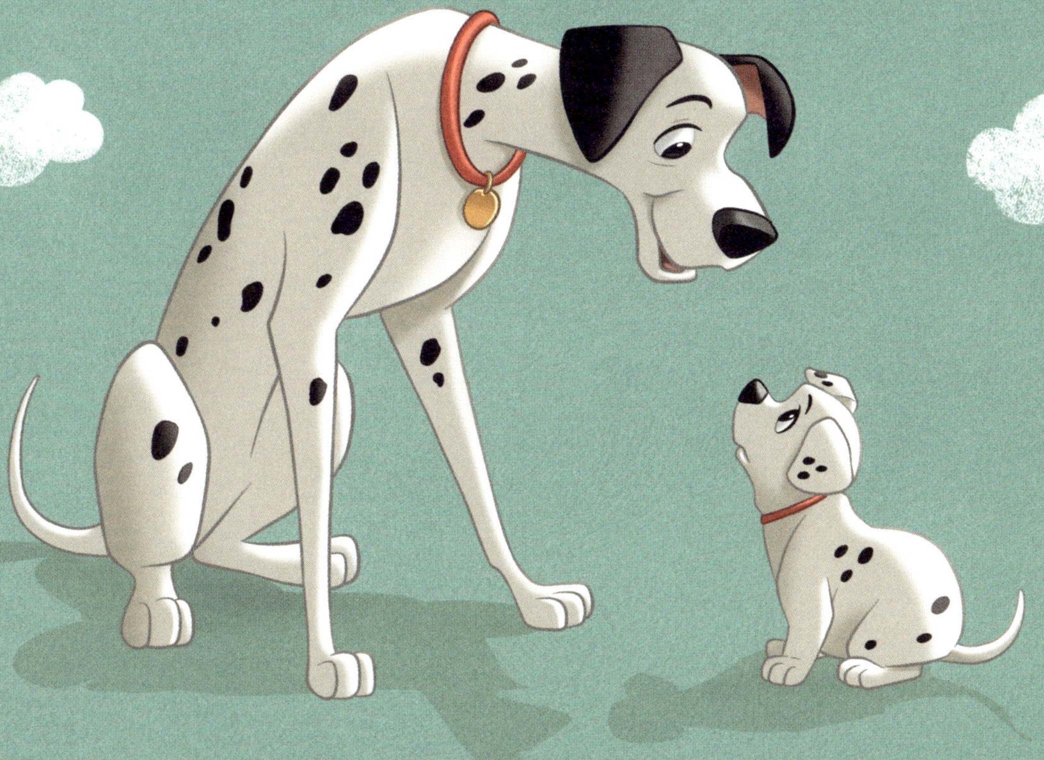

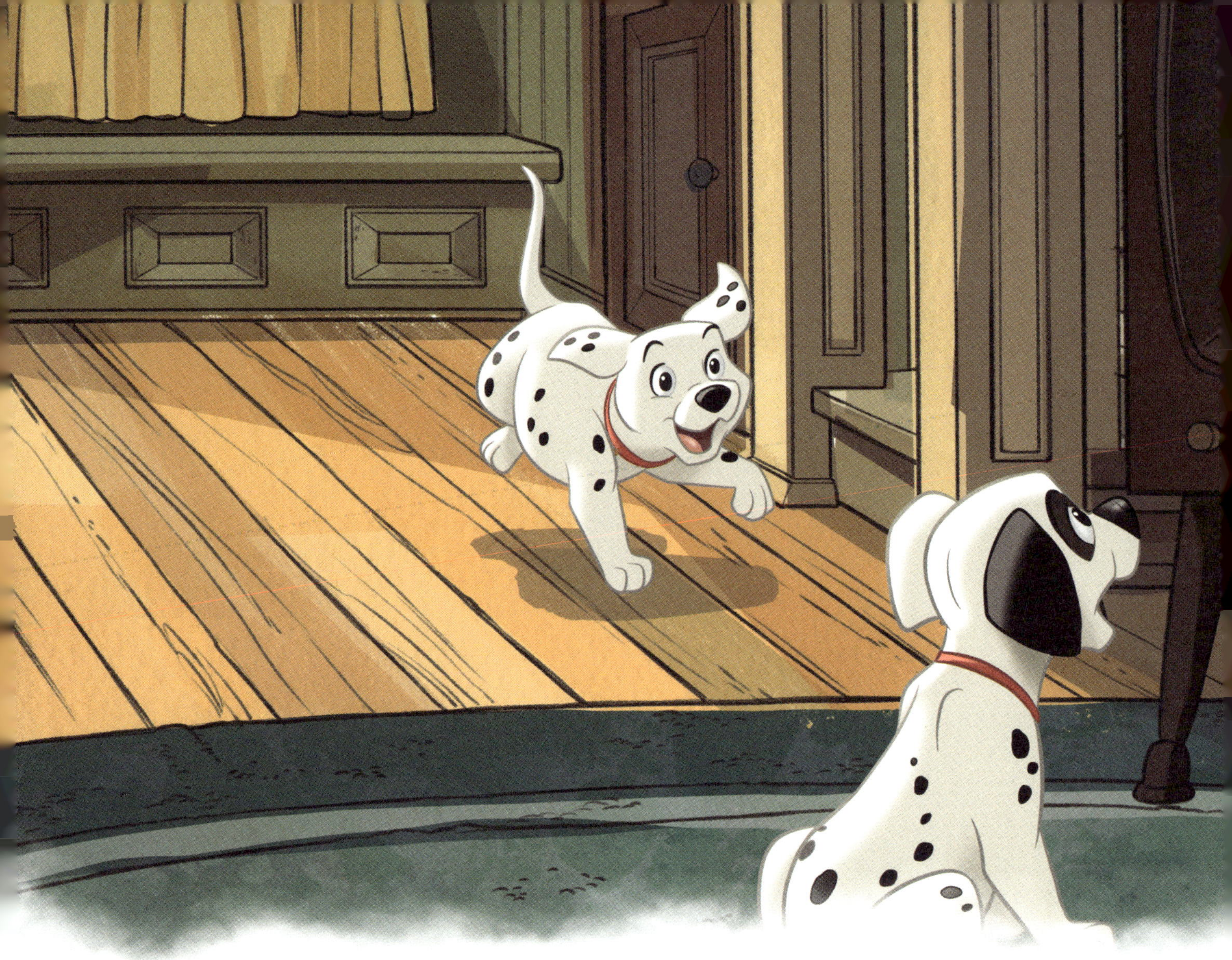

À la ferme des dalmatiens, les chiots de Pongo et Perdita ont une grande passion : regarder *Les Aventures d'Ouragan* à la télévision !

Rolly court retrouver Penny et Patch dans le salon.

Dans l'épisode d'aujourd'hui, le courageux chien policier se transforme **en pompier** pour éteindre un incendie.

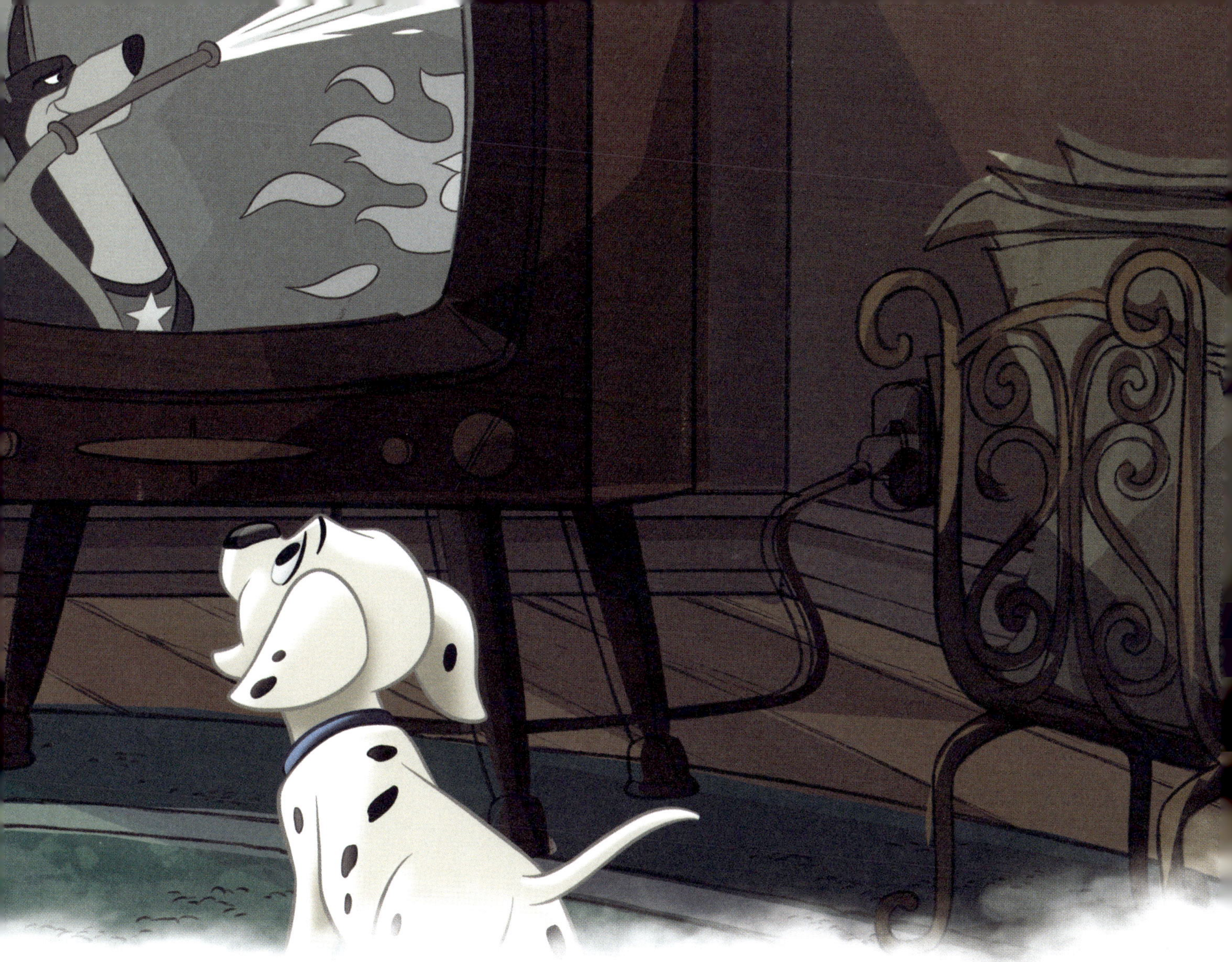

– Quand je serai grand, je serai pompier, comme Ouragan ! s'enthousiasme Patch.

– Moi aussi ! réplique Rolly.

Mais devenir pompier, ce n'est pas si facile... Même quand on est un petit dalmatien plein d'envie. Il faut s'entraîner dur !

– On devrait **demander conseil à papa,** propose alors Patch.

Aussitôt dit, aussitôt fait ! Pongo organise un petit entraînement pour Patch, Penny et Rolly.

– Papa…, hésite soudain ce dernier. J'ai peur de ne pas y arriver.

Le chiot en a presque les larmes aux yeux.

– Ne t'inquiète pas, Rolly, lui sourit son papa. **Le plus important, c'est que tu fasses de ton mieux !**

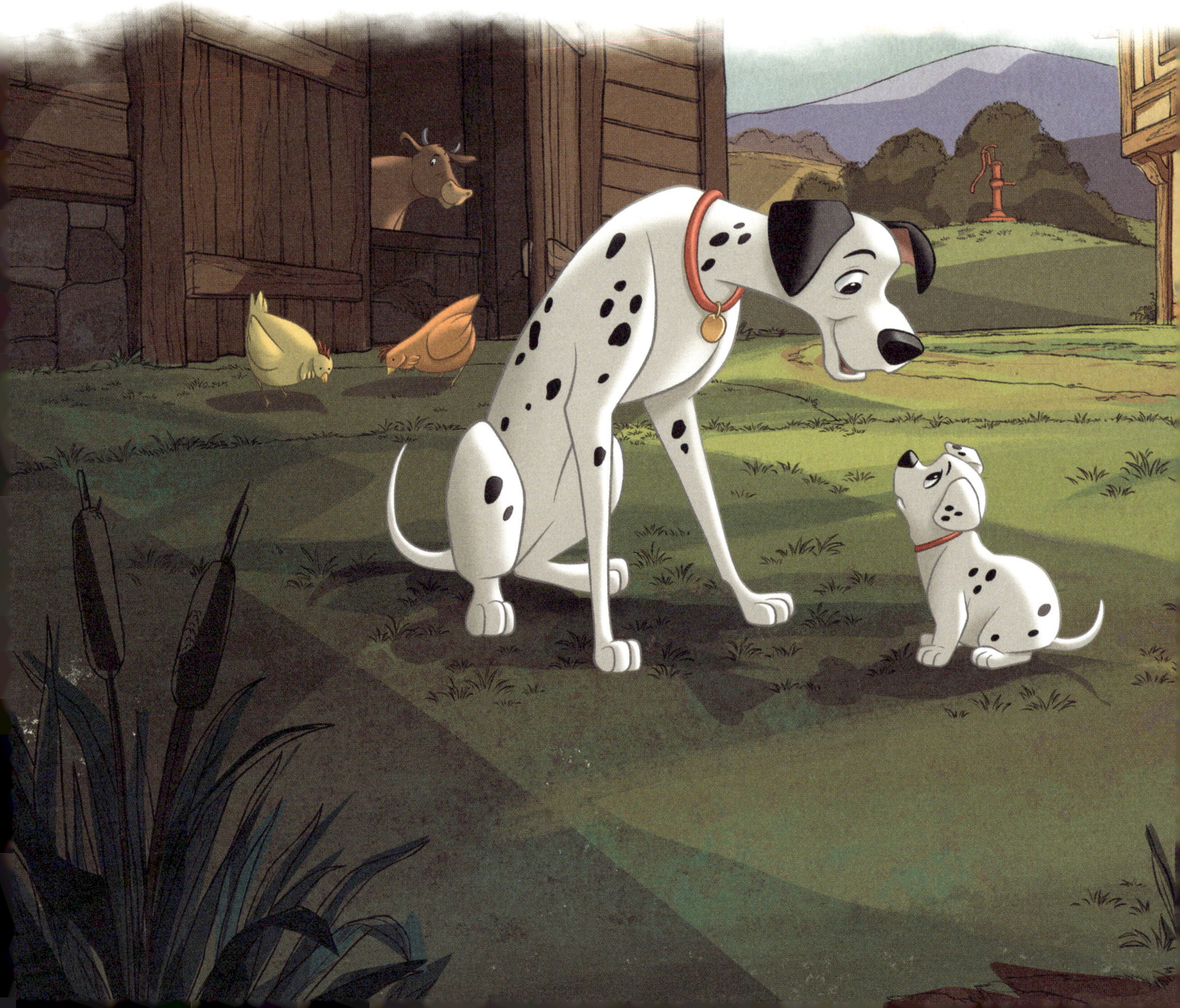

Patch et Penny sont déjà installés derrière la ligne de départ qu'a tracée leur maman. La première épreuve est une course d'obstacles.

– C'est moi qui arriverai le premier ! fanfaronne Patch.

– Sûrement pas ! lui réplique Penny. C'est MOI qui vais gagner.

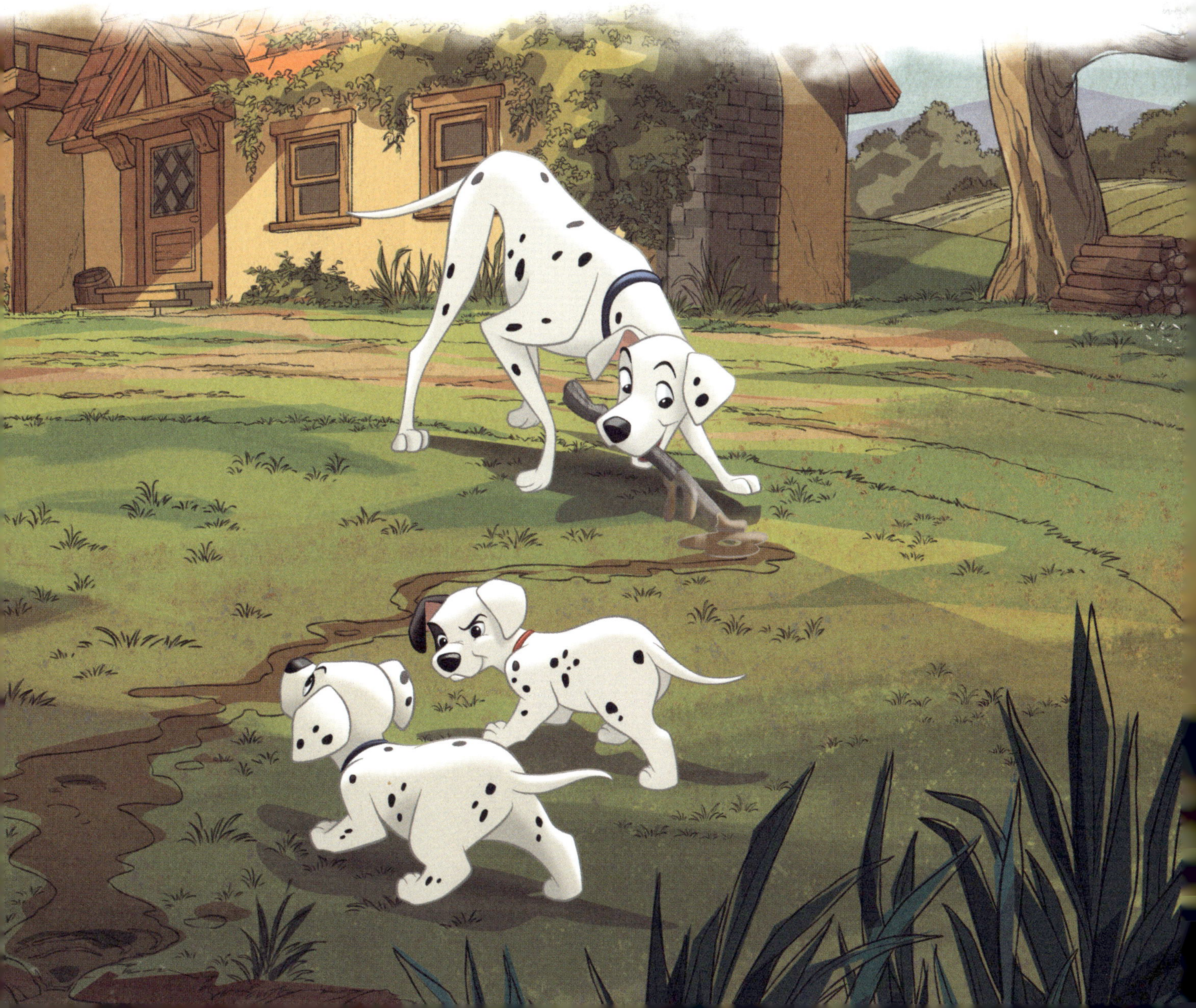

– Trois... deux... un..., c'est parti ! s'écrie Pongo.

Patch et Penny prennent très vite de l'avance sur le pauvre Rolly.

Mais tout à coup, le petit chiot se désintéresse de la course.

Une drôle d'odeur vient de lui chatouiller les narines.

– Tiens, c'est bizarre, ça sent le brûlé, souffle Rolly.

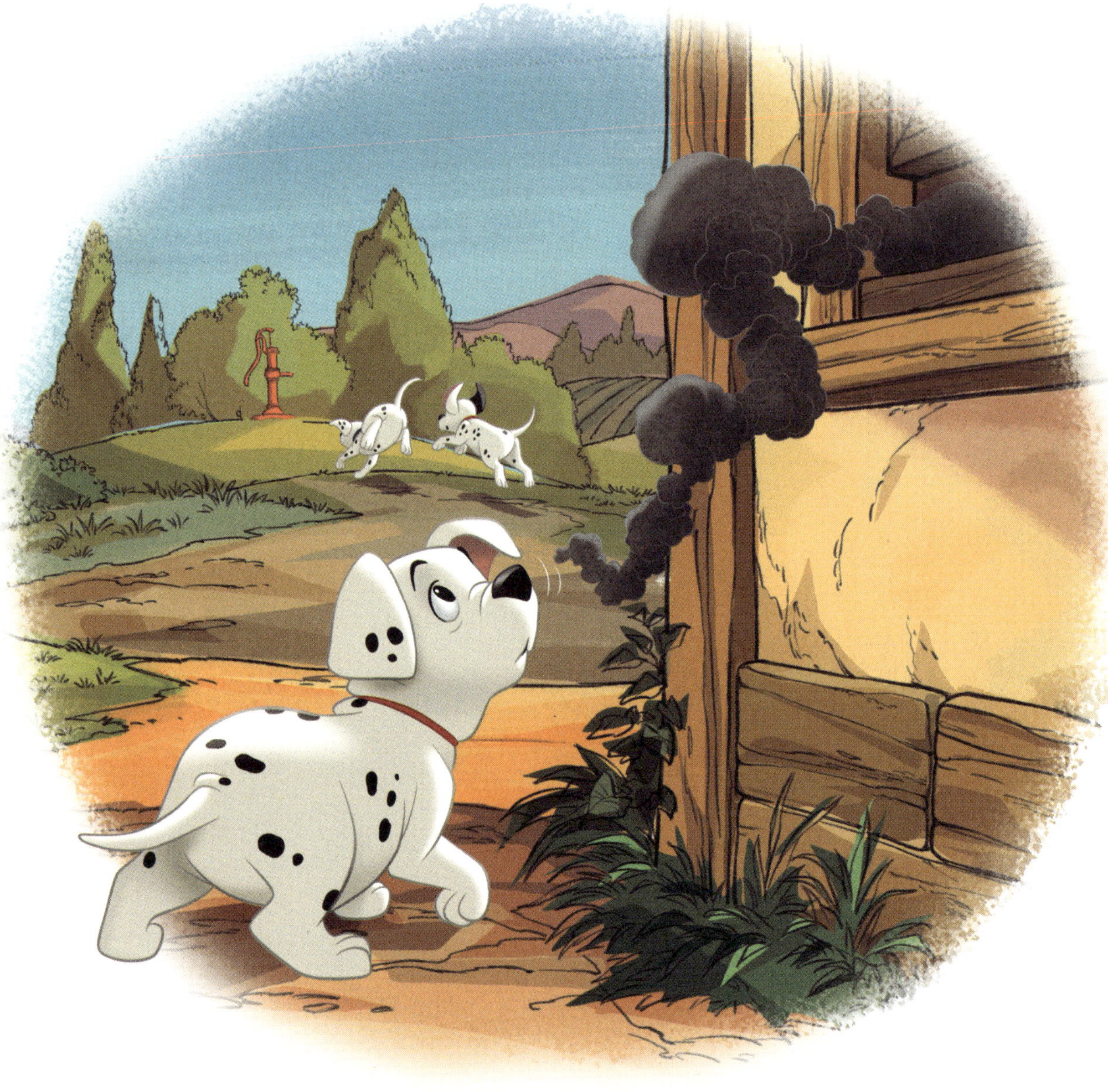

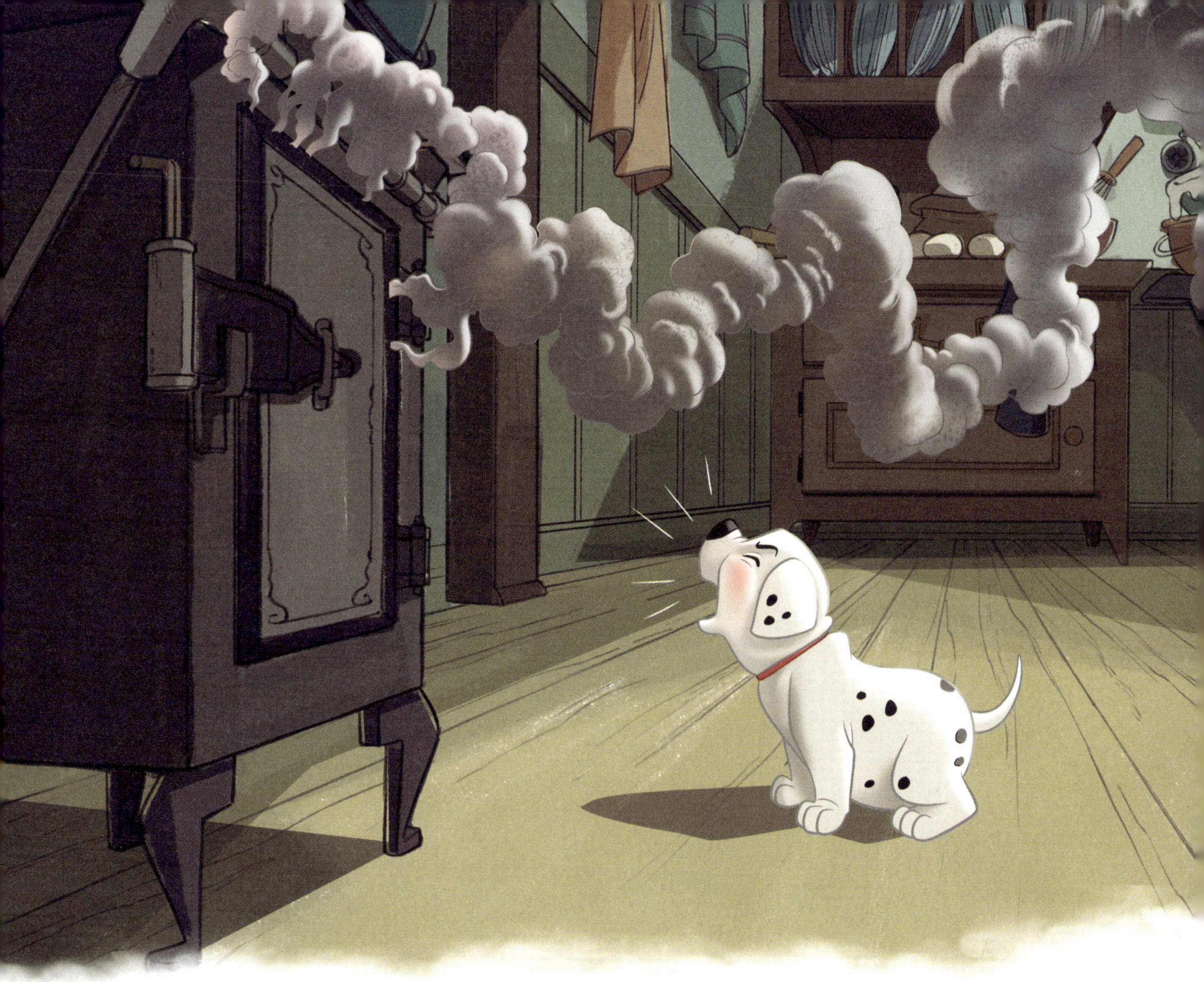

Le jeune dalmatien suit la piste de la fumée. L'odeur le conduit dans la maison. Plus précisément, dans la cuisine. Quelque chose est en train de brûler dans le four !

Rolly sait qu'il ne peut pas rester sans rien faire, alors il se poste devant le four et **aboie de toutes ses forces !**

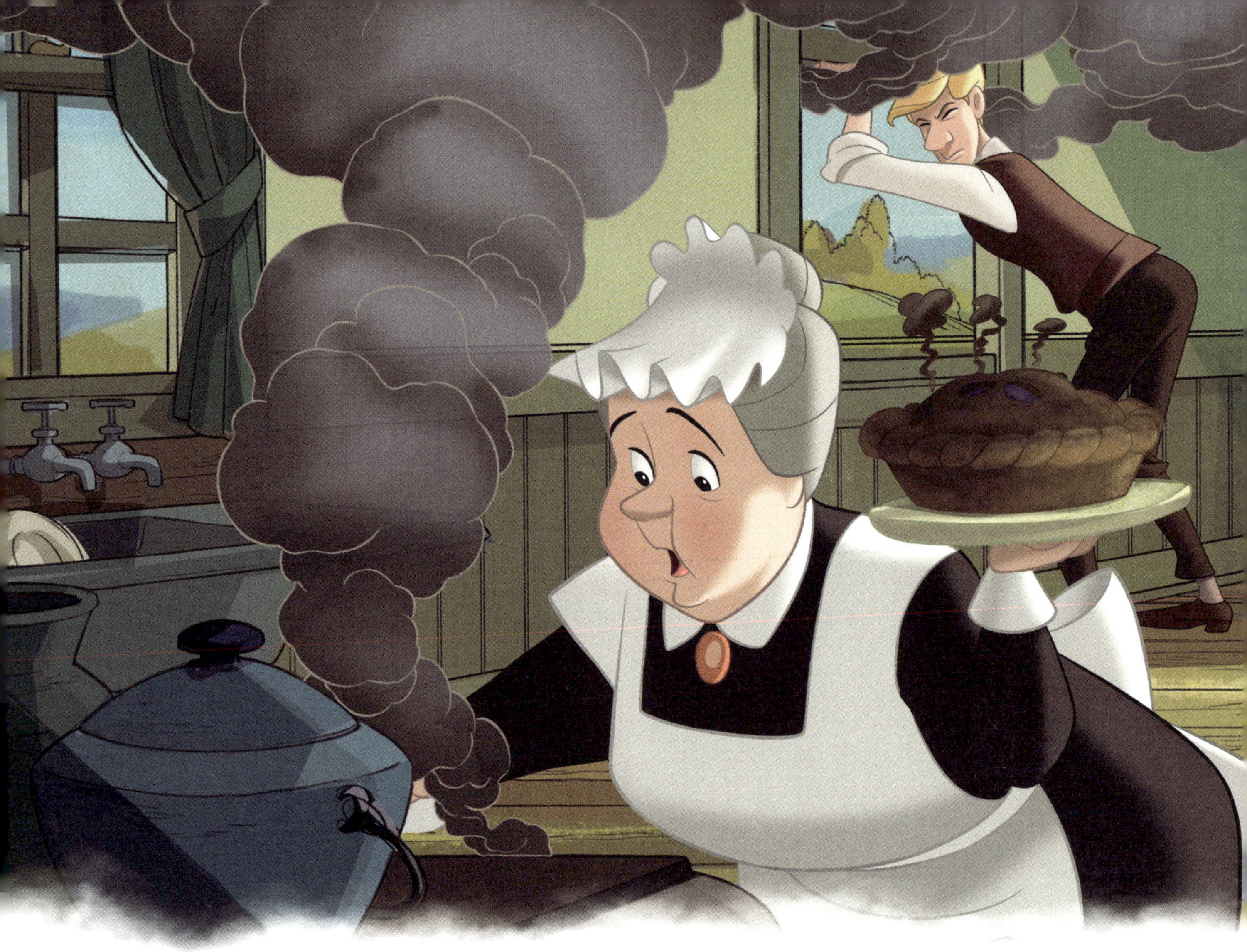

– OUAF ! OUAF !

Ses cris attirent l'attention des humains.

– Ma tarte ! Je l'avais complètement oubliée ! s'exclame Nanny en se précipitant vers le four.

Roger, lui, ouvre vite la fenêtre pendant qu'Anita crée un courant d'air avec la porte afin de chasser la fumée.

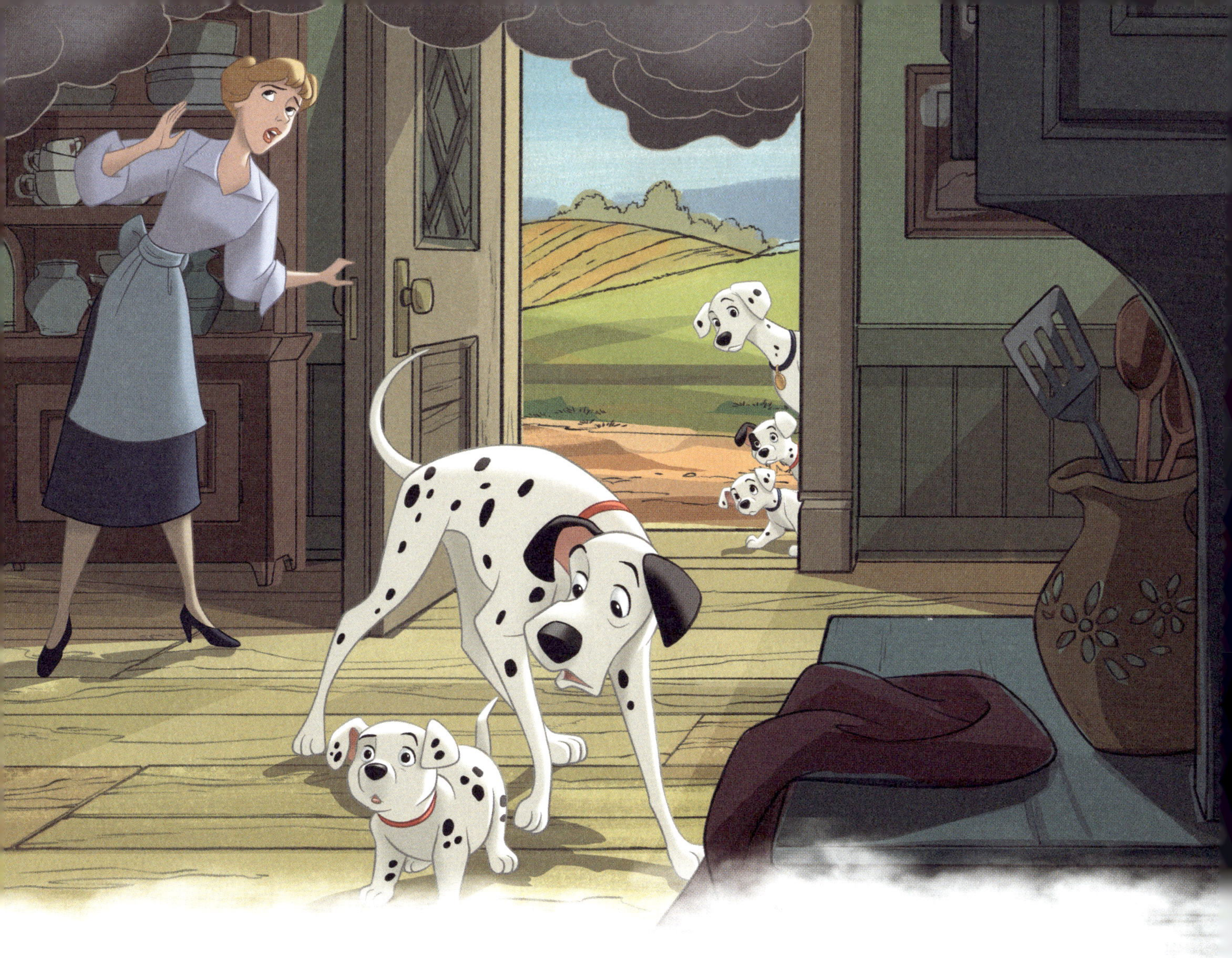

Pongo, Perdita, Patch et Penny ont eux aussi entendu les aboiements de Rolly et viennent aux nouvelles.

– Rolly, mon grand, tu n'as rien ? s'inquiète Pongo.

– Non, papa, le rassure son petit. J'ai juste senti une odeur étrange, et j'ai suivi la piste.

Roger et Anita viennent féliciter le jeune héros tacheté.

– **Un grand merci à toi, Rolly,** lui sourit Roger.

– Oh, oui, ajoute Anita. Sans toi, la ferme entière aurait pu brûler !

Dans leur dos, Nanny intervient soudain :

– Je prépare une bonne récompense pour notre petit pompier.

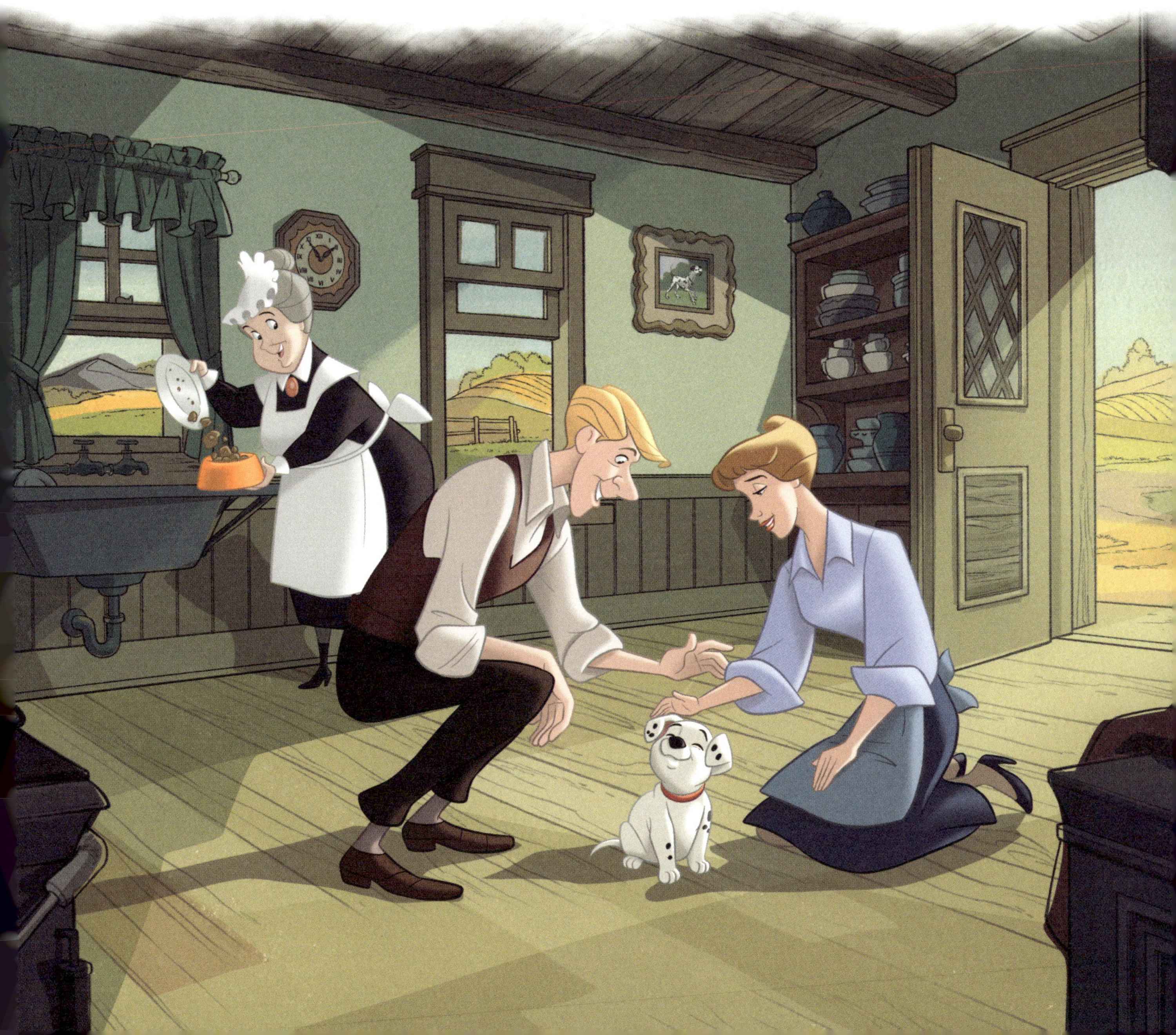

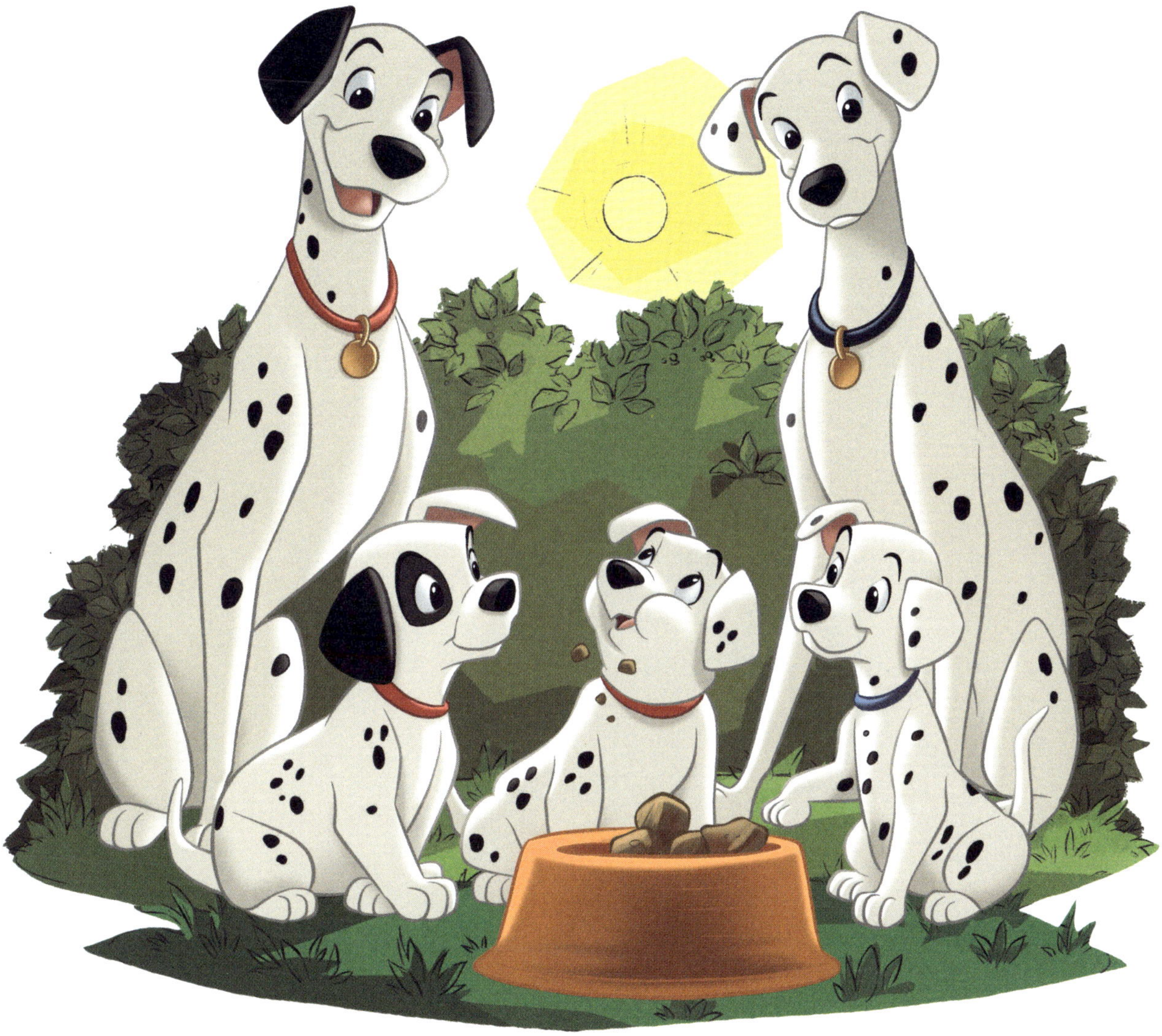

Quelle belle journée pour Rolly ! Le jeune dalmatien a sauvé la ferme, et, en plus, il a reçu un bon goûter en guise de remerciement !

Ce grand gourmand se régale et en fait profiter tout le monde !

– **Je suis fier de toi, mon fils,** lui dit Pongo. Aujourd'hui, tu as fait de ton mieux, et tu as été incroyable, bravo !

Disney

PANPAN

Une journée AVEC PAPA

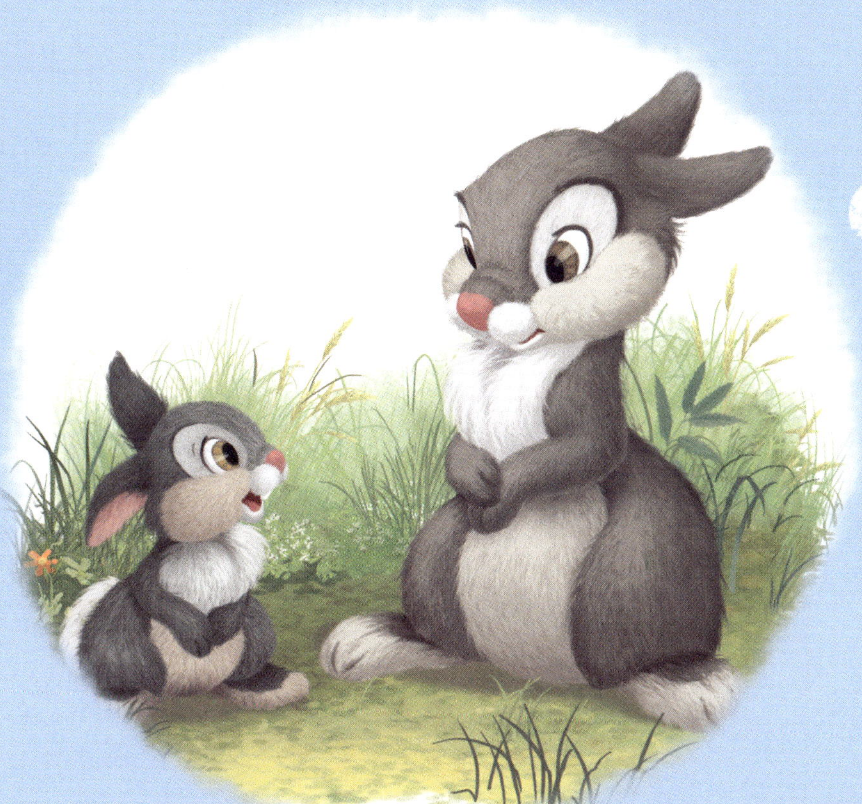

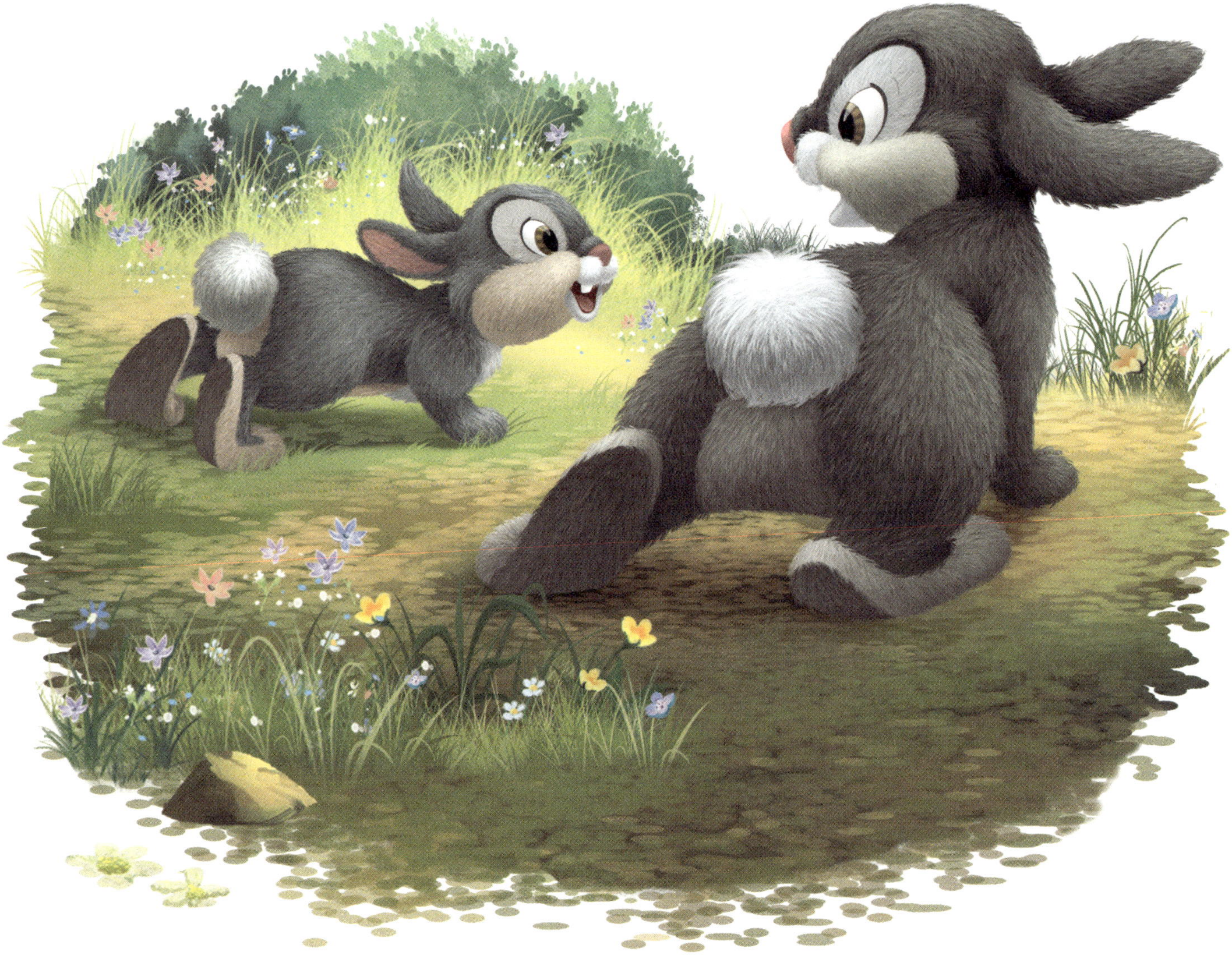

Panpan est fou de joie : aujourd'hui, **il va passer la journée seul avec son papa !** Et le jeune lapin imagine déjà les aventures qu'ils vont pouvoir vivre ensemble.

– Que va-t-on faire, papa ? demande-t-il. On pourrait gravir une montagne enneigée ? Ou explorer une grotte mystérieuse ?

Mais son papa a d'autres idées en tête.

– Nous allons plutôt cueillir des feuilles pour le repas de ce soir.

Panpan est déçu, mais il n'en dit rien. Il se met au travail de bon cœur.

Au bout d'un moment, le petit lapin a soif.

– Tu peux aller boire à la rivière, lui dit son papa. Mais reviens vite !

– **C'est promis, papa,** assure Panpan en s'éloignant.

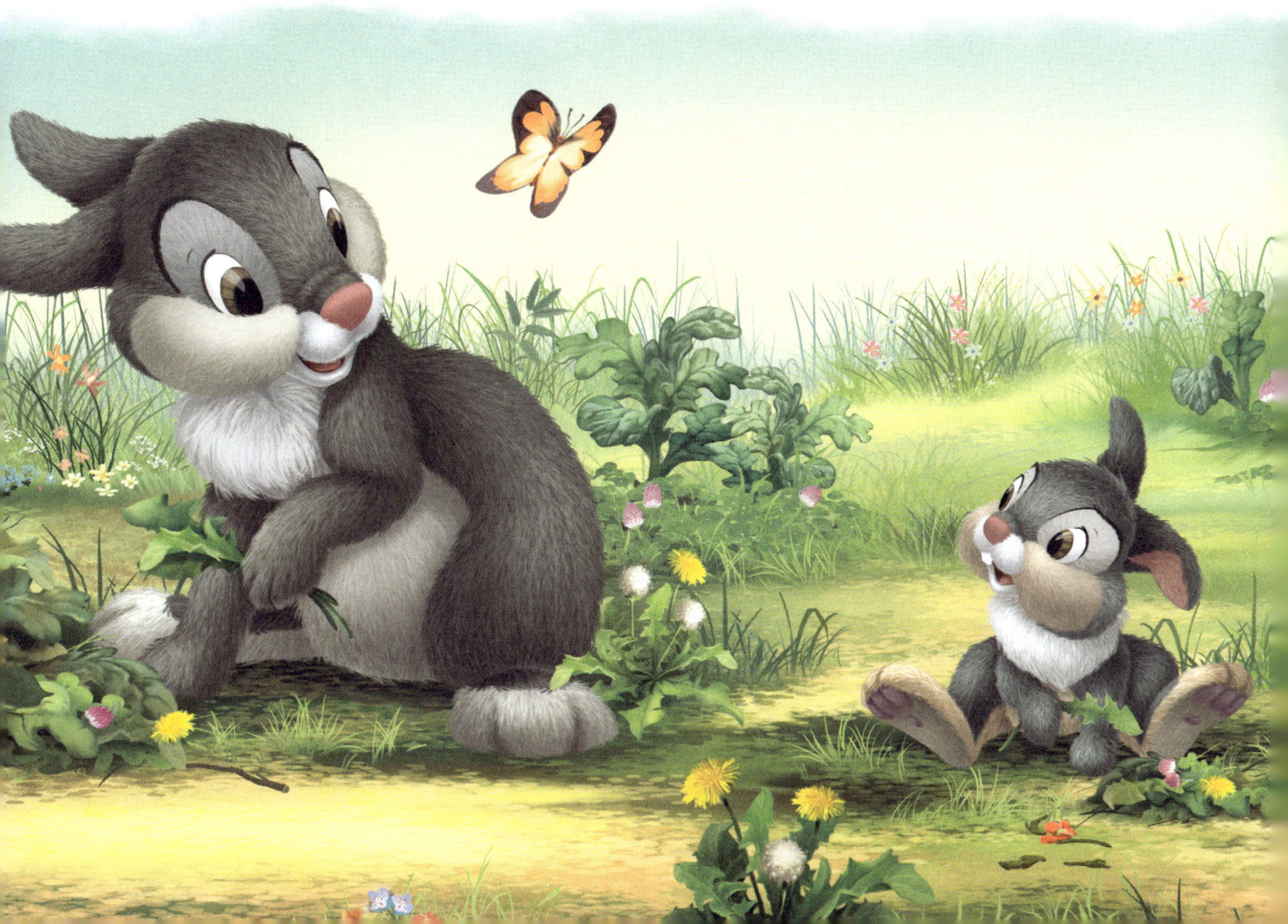

À la rivière, Panpan rencontre une famille de canetons en train de jouer dans les flots.

Ils ont l'air de bien s'amuser !

« Moi aussi, j'aimerais jouer avec eux, songe Panpan. Mais **papa a besoin de moi,** je ne dois pas le faire attendre. »

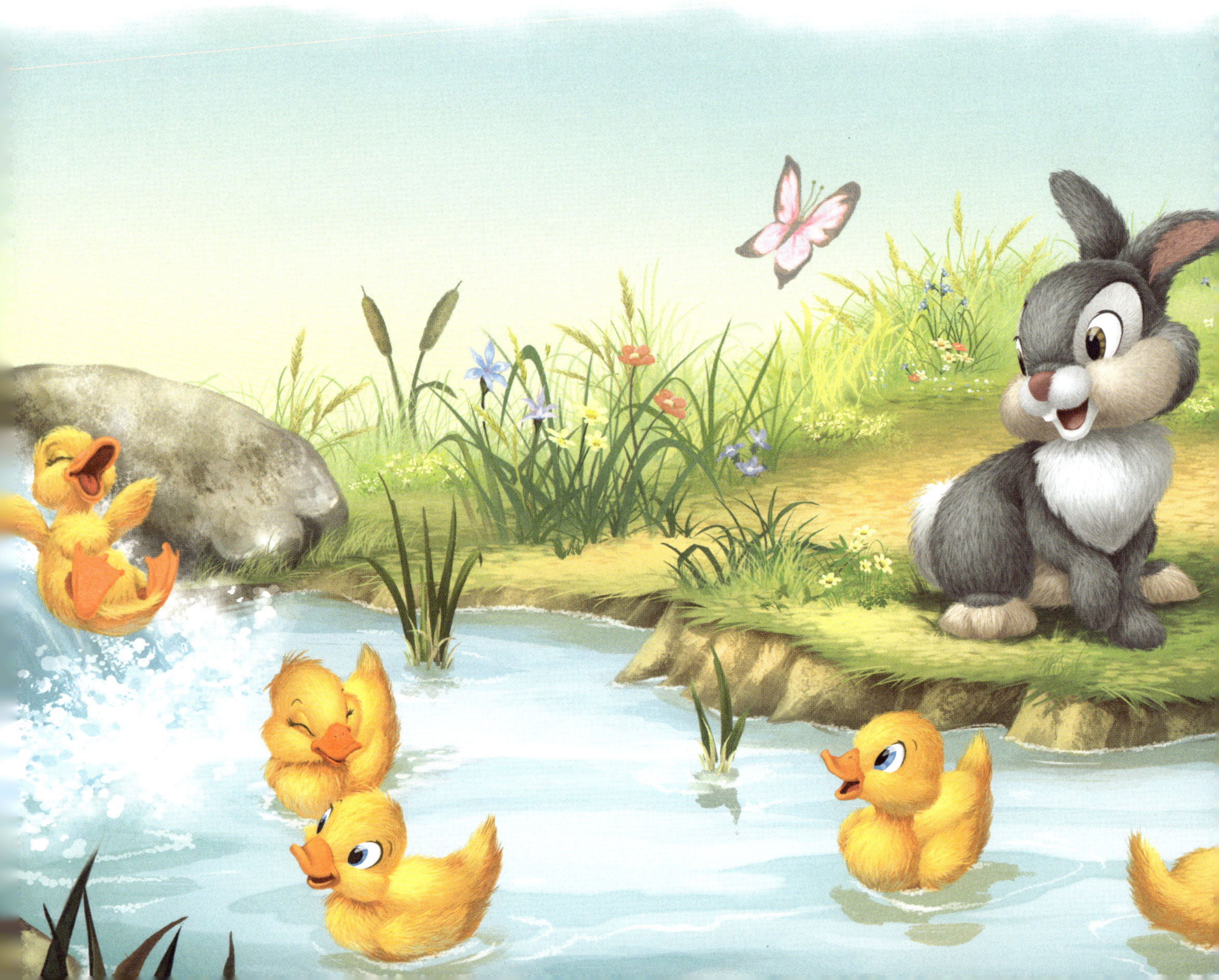

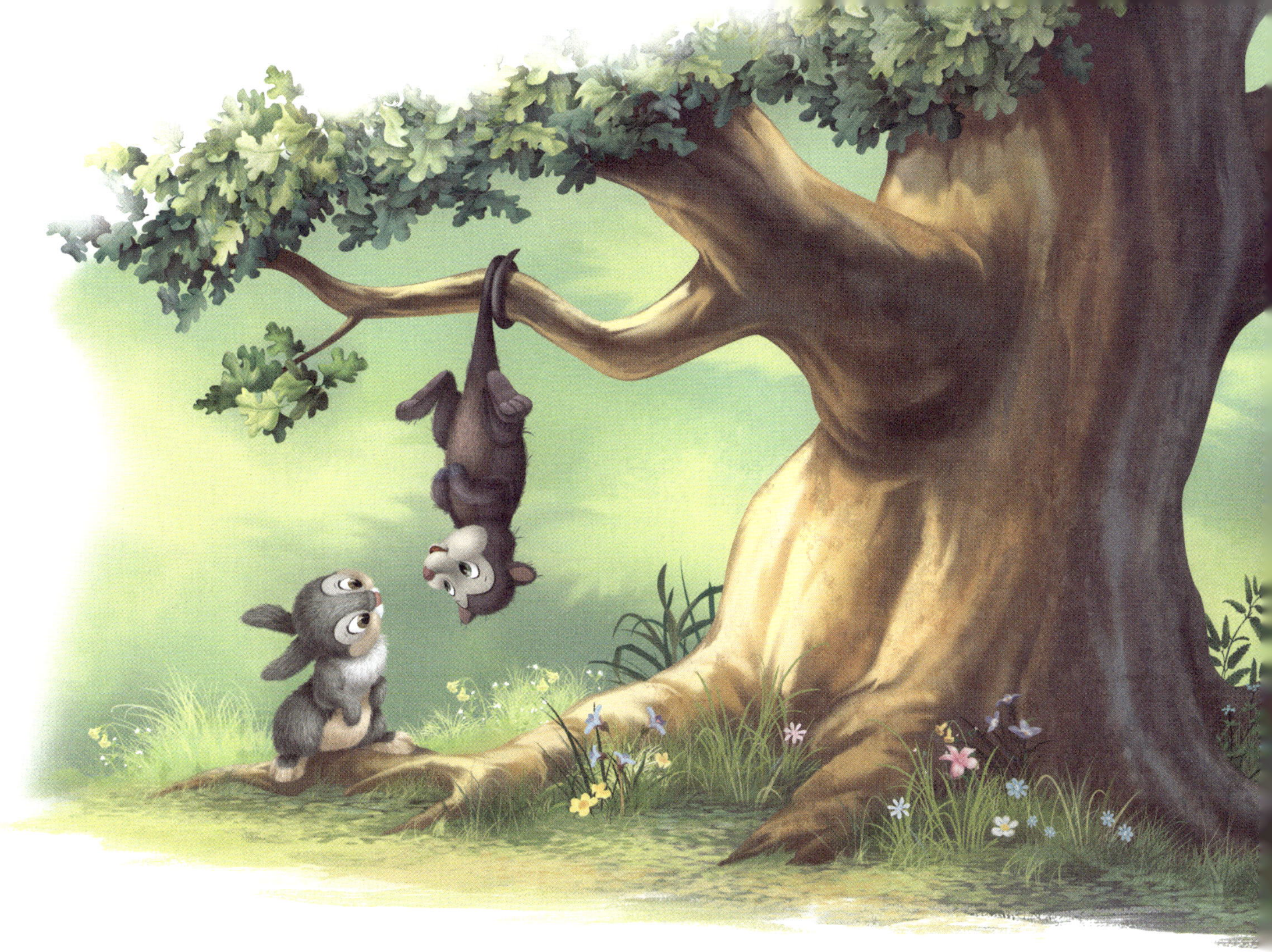

Panpan part retrouver son père quand tout à coup, **il croise son ami l'opossum.**

– Viens avec moi, lui propose celui-ci, on va grimper dans cet arbre.

Panpan hésite un peu, puis accepte :

– D'accord, mais pas longtemps, je dois retourner auprès de mon papa.

Et les voilà partis à l'aventure dans le grand chêne !

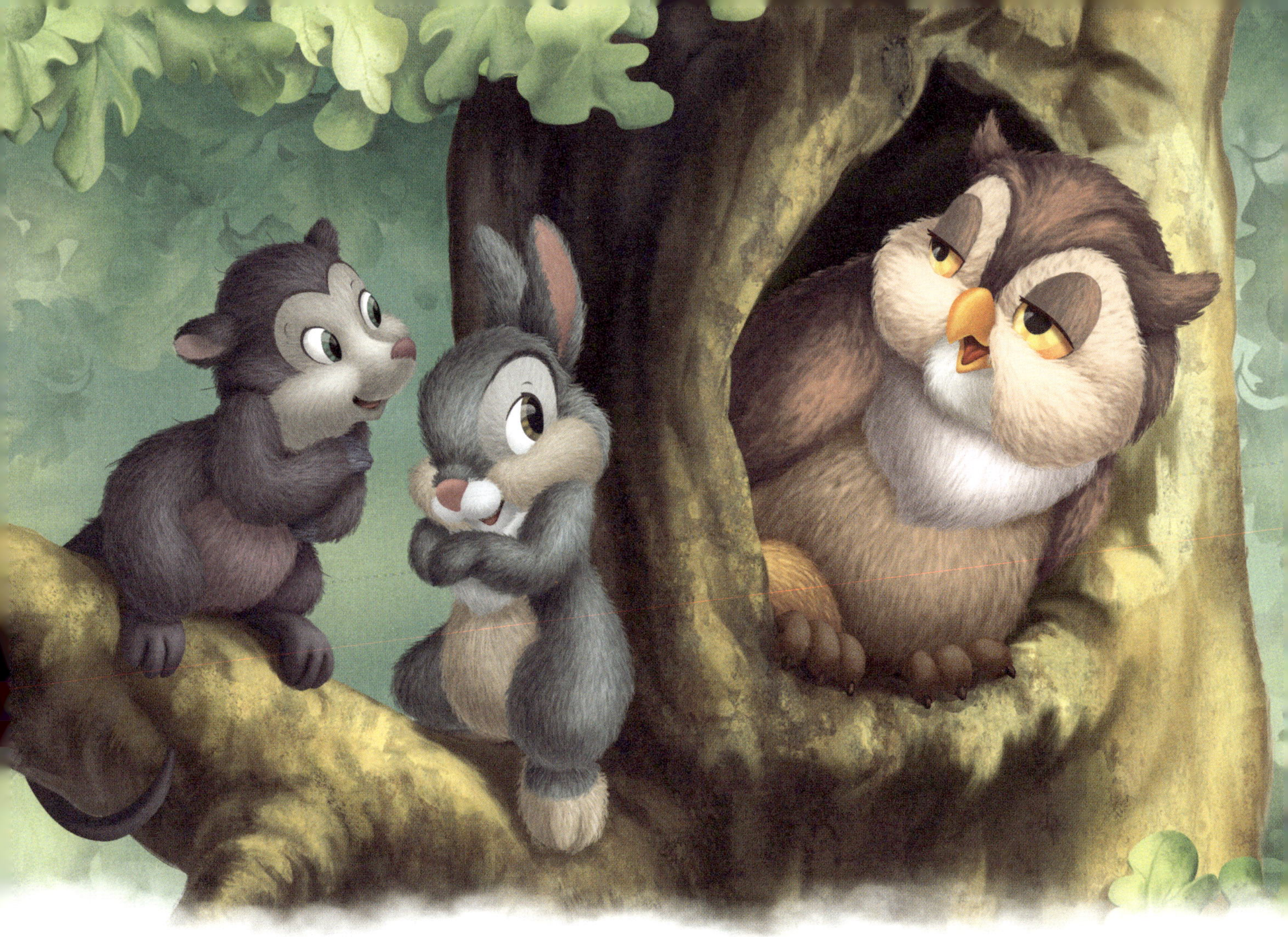

Panpan frappe contre le tronc.

Toc-toc-toc...

– Il y a peut-être quelqu'un à l'intérieur, explique-t-il à son ami.

– Oui, il y a quelqu'un ! lui répond une voix.

C'est Maître Hibou... qui était en train de dormir !

– Bonjour, Maître Hibou, lui dit Panpan. Je suis désolé de t'avoir réveillé...

Les deux amis continuent **leur exploration** d'arbre en arbre. Ils découvrent ainsi des oisillons dans un nid.

– Oh, qu'ils sont mignons ! s'extasie l'opossum.

Ils admirent ensuite une ruche mais... sans oser trop s'approcher.

– J'aime le miel, confie Panpan, mais je n'ai pas envie de me faire piquer !

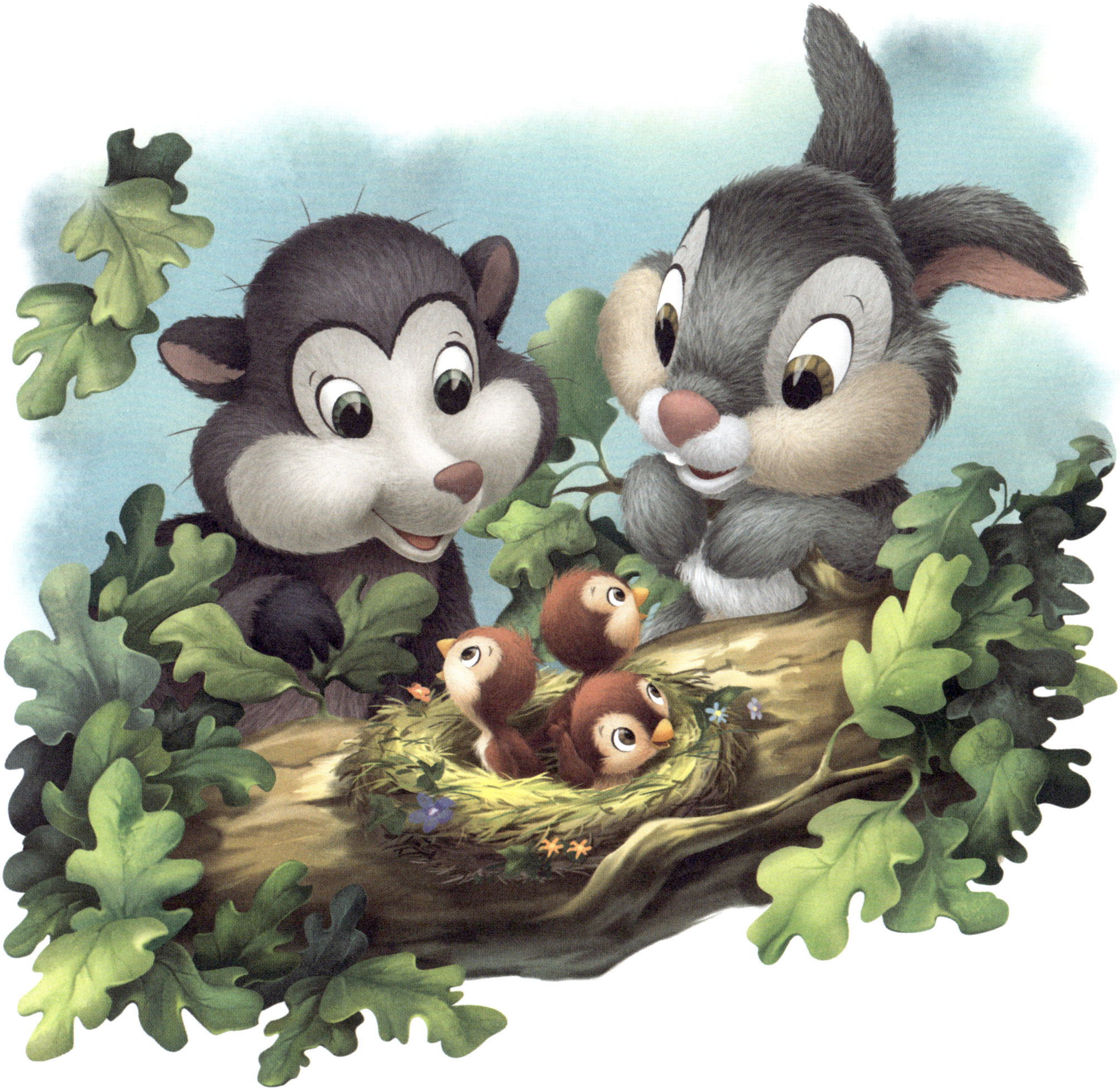

Mais voilà que, tout à coup, l'opossum redescend de l'arbre.

– Il faut que je rentre, Panpan ! s'écrie-t-il. Mon papa m'attend !

Oh ! le petit lapin se rappelle alors que **son père aussi l'attend !**

– Oh, non ! panique Panpan. J'espère qu'il ne se fait pas trop de souci pour moi...

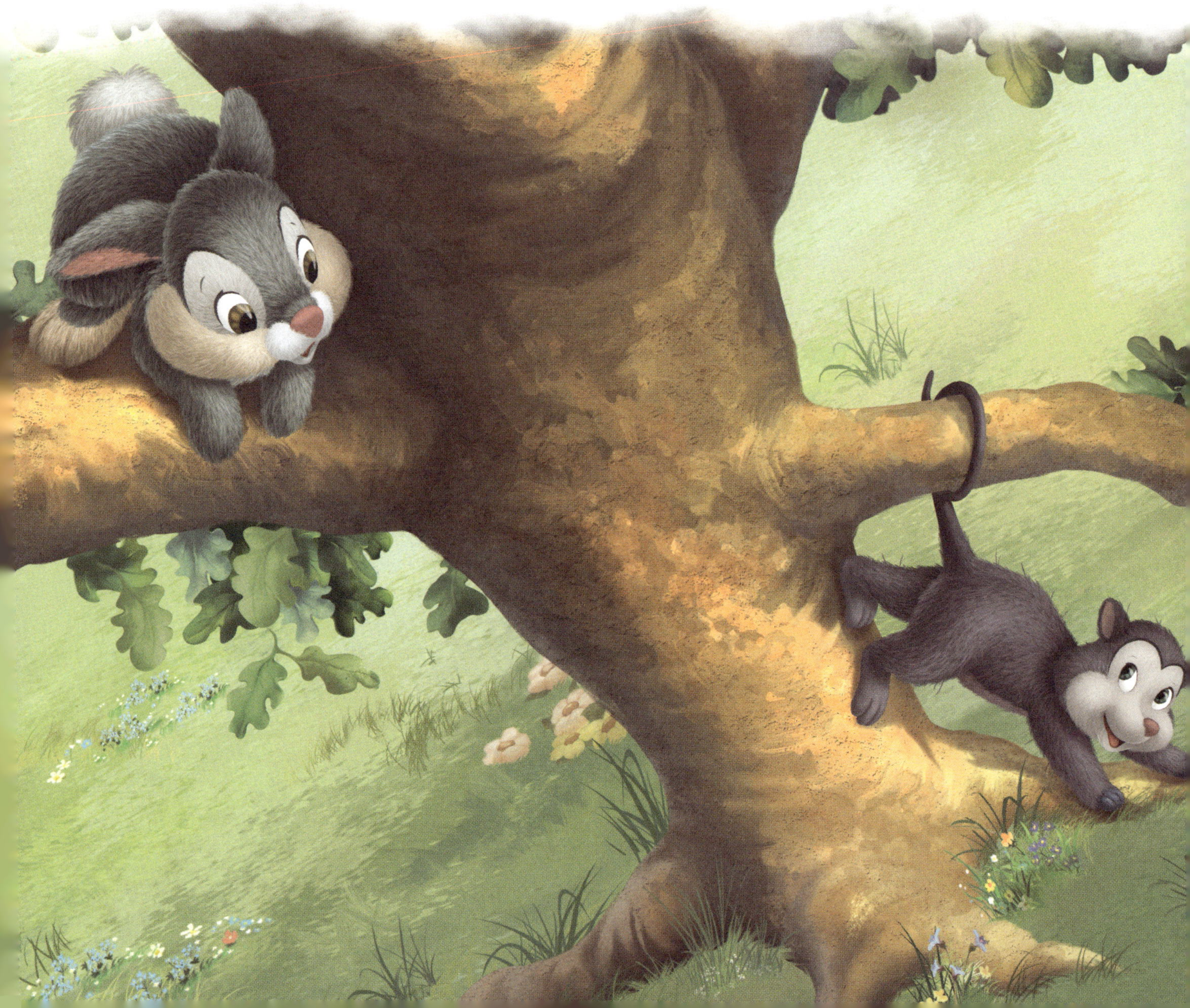

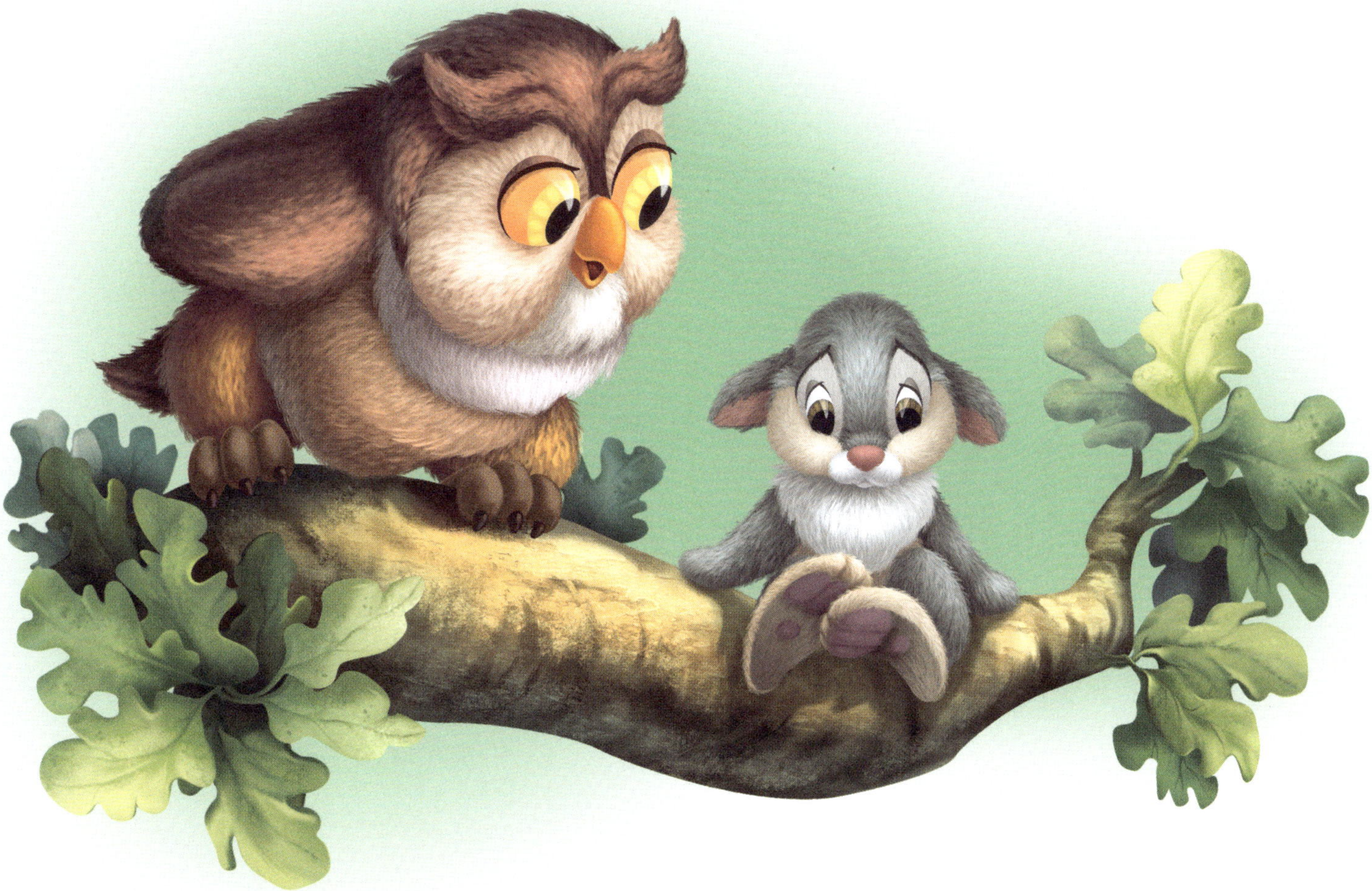

Mais comment faire pour descendre de cet arbre ? Il n'y a pas de branches sur lesquelles il pourrait sauter. Alors, le pauvre petit lapin est obligé d'attendre qu'on vienne l'aider.

– Panpan ? l'interroge Maître Hibou qui passe par là. Que fais-tu tout seul sur cette branche ?

– **J'attends mon papa,** sanglote Panpan. Sans lui, je suis coincé ici...

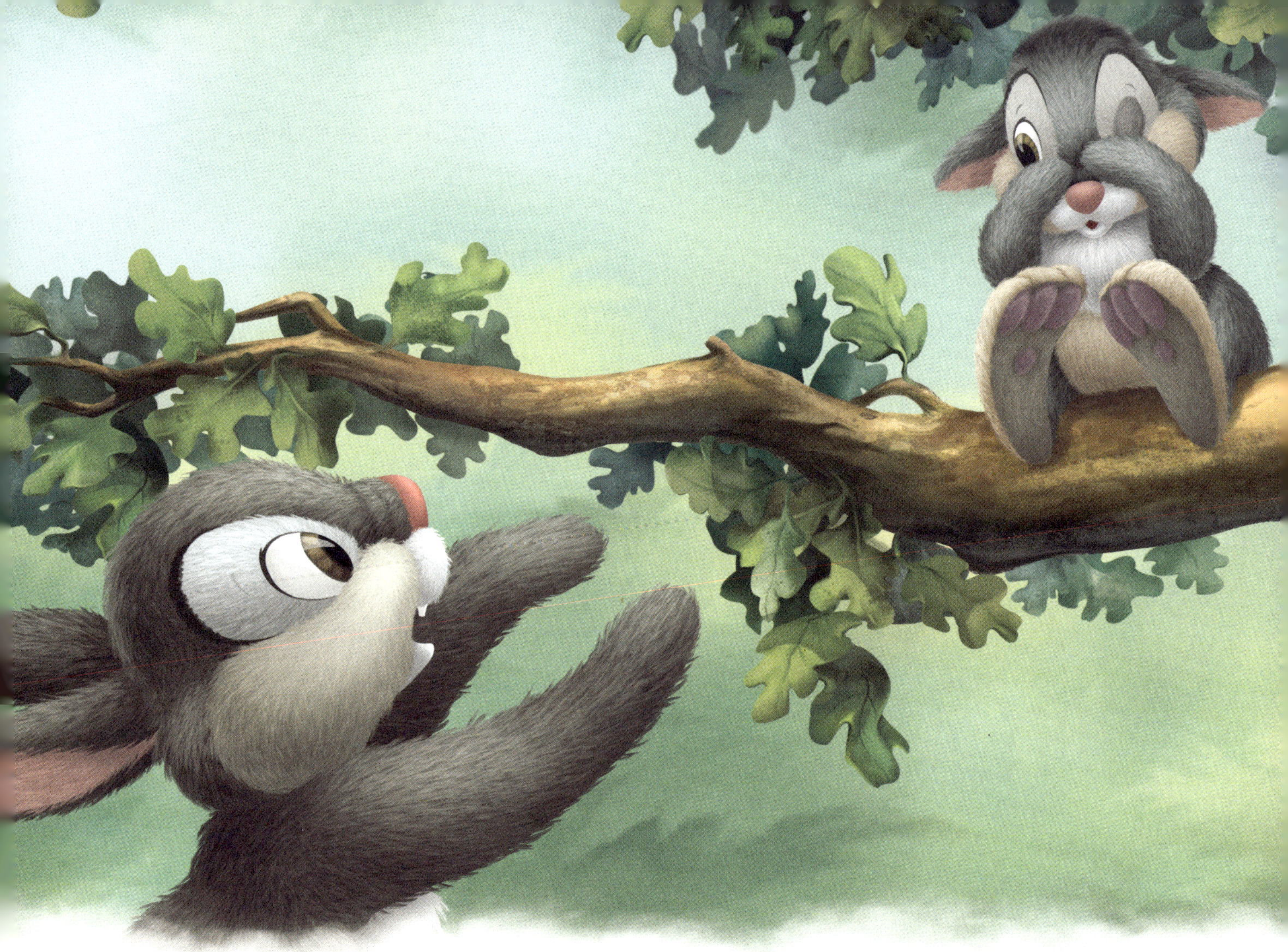

– Panpan ! s'exclame alors une voix au pied de l'arbre. J'ai cru que je ne te retrouverais jamais ! Que fais-tu sur cet arbre ?

– Papa ? répond Panpan d'une voix inquiète. Papa ! J'ai peur… je ne sais pas comment faire pour redescendre.

– **Ne crains rien, mon grand,** le rassure son père. Saute, je vais te rattraper.

Panpan se suspend dans le vide en soulevant l'une de ses pattes, puis l'autre. Là, il lâche prise !

Heureusement, la chute ne dure pas longtemps. Le petit lapin atterrit dans les bras de son papa qui le couvre de bisous.

– Tu ne dois jamais avoir peur de me demander de l'aide, Panpan, lui chuchote son père. **Je serai toujours là pour toi, mon fils.**

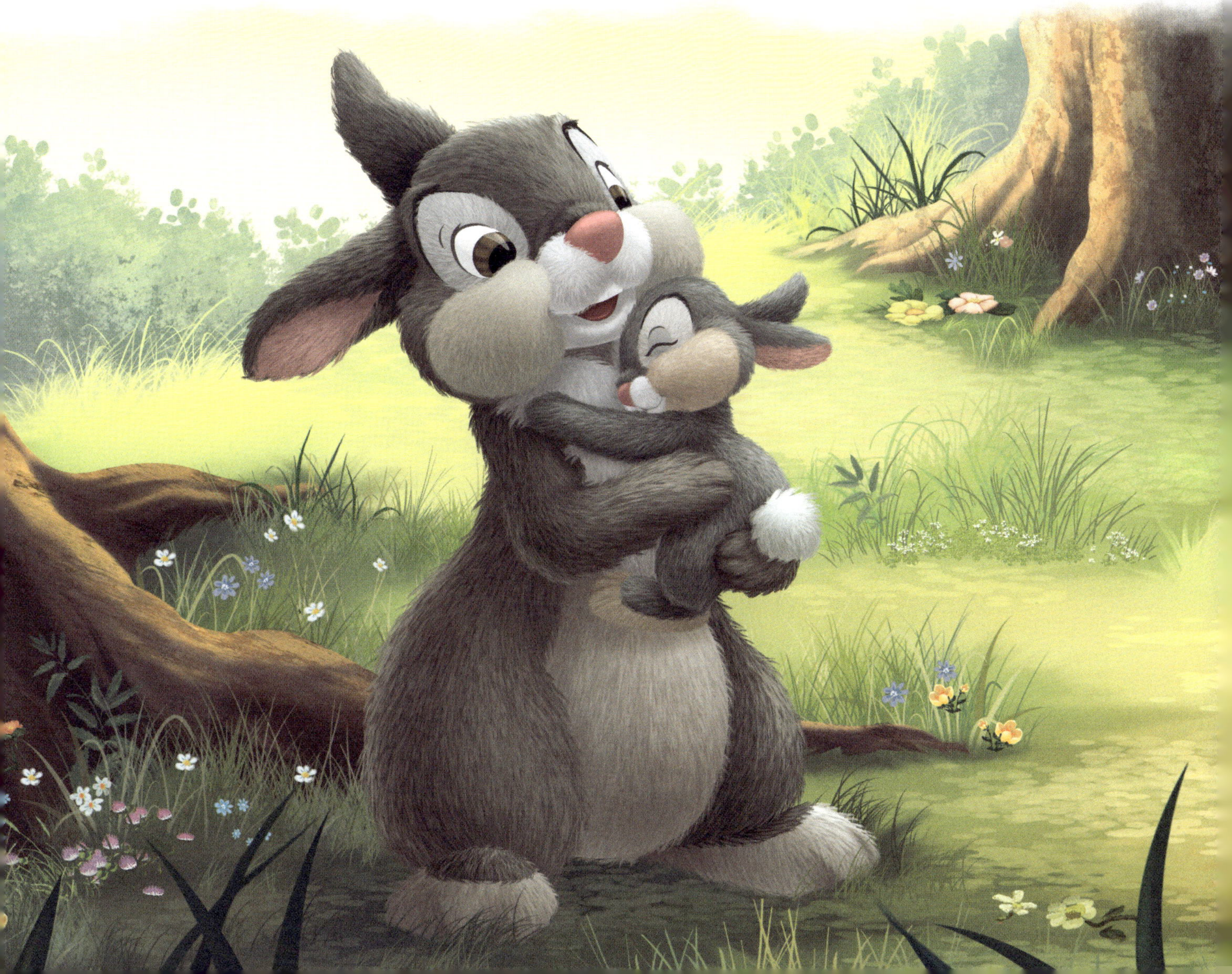